ACADIAN FAMILIES IN EXILE - 1785

and

(Part Two)

EXILED ACADIANS - AN INDEX

Rev. Donald J. Hébert

ACADIAN FAMILIES IN EXILE - 1785

and

(Part Two)

EXILED ACADIANS - AN INDEX

by

Rev. Donald J. Hébert

Hébert Publications

Library of Congress Catalog Card Number: 95-78163

This text may not be reproduced
in its entirety or in part
without the express permission
of the author.

Printed in USA

(Art by Jan Lewis)

CONTENTS

Preface   vi

Introduction   vii

"Twenty-Five Years" of Genealogical Research and Publishing   x

Author's Ancestral Chart   xi

List of Occupations and Abbreviations   xii

View of the ship *L'Amitié*   xiv

Dates of Embarkation and Debarkation of the Seven Ships   1

1. Le Bon Papa - departed France on 10 May 1785   2

2. La Bergère - departed France on 14 May 1785   12

3. Le Beaumont - departed France on 11 June 1785   30

4. Le Saint-Rémi - departed France on 27 June 1785   42

5. L'Amitié - departed France on 20 August 1785   66

6. La Ville d'Archangel - departed France on 12 August 1785   86

7. La Caroline - departed France on 19 October 1785   106

Documents from the Ship Lists   112

The Agreement Concerning Rations and Food Supply
     on the ship *Le Bon Papa*   118

Bibliography and Special Acknowledgments   120

Index of "Acadian Families in Exile"   121

PART TWO: "Exiled Acadians - A General Index"   132

PREFACE

In his excellent work, *Acadian Odyssey*, Oscar Winzerling captures the anguish and trials of so many Acadian families as they traveled in exile from their homeland in Nova Scotia to their motherland, France, to their final resettlement in their new home in Louisiana. Quoting Martìn Navarro's welcoming words to the newly arrived exiles aboard *La Ville d'Archangel*: "I went on board to check the number of passengers. I gave them a speech of welcome in which I reminded them of His Majesty's plan in removing them from France to Louisiana. I stressed their obligation to him, and I did my best to impress on them the humanity of the Spanish nation. Personally I treated them with the utmost kindness...." Then Navarro explained to them his majesty's plan of Acadian colonization in Louisiana. The king had graciously sent instructions to his ministers in Louisiana to help the Acadians in all things until they could support themselves.

The leaders of the group of Acadians aboard *La Ville d'Arcangel* thanked Navarro graciously for his welcome and instructions. They told him that the group was unanimous in its belief that "at long last" it had found "its day of peace and prosperity." They assured him that everyone was eager to begin the work of colonization as soon as he would permit possession of the land their surveyors had chosen.

Navarro expected much from the Acadians as colonists. Many times he expressed to José de Gálvez his faith in these Acadians. "I can assure you that after four years these Acadians will be America's most prosperous and sturdiest colonists, because they love their new home, and are determined to give Louisiana in 1786 its best harvest." As Winzerling observes, "Spain and Louisiana share the unique distinction of having staged the world's largest trans-Atlantic colonization project on the North American continent...to the Acadians of the seven expeditions, France could offer only 'the most sterile lands' in gratitude for unique patriotism."

One may wonder as to what these Acadians had on their minds as they crossed the seas during that three month voyage to a land yet unknown to them. This collection of lists and rolls have been preserved in archives sometimes not readily accessible to the researcher. It is this author's intention to provide another publication of resource material about our Acadian forebears.

Through the humanity of the Spanish nation, the Acadians at last found a home, arable lands, and a new Acadia in South Louisiana.

Rev. Donald J. Hébert
4 July 1995

INTRODUCTION

Winzerling states in *Acadian Odyssey* that "he relied on the records of the Archives of Seville, Spain. These lists are the debarkation list of those Acadians arriving in New Orleans on the ships *Le Bon Papa, Le Beaumont*, and the list of tools and implements given the arrivals from the *L'Amitié, La Caroline, La Ville d'Archangel*, and *Le Beaumont*.
The marriages from passengers on *Le Saint-Rémi* are the only names of the passengers."

Milton and Norma Rieder, on the other hand, "chose to publish registration lists of the seven Acadian expeditions [lists of embarkation] from the French records that include the names of the members of each family registered for the voyage, their ages, relationships and occupations. The original list of *La Ville d'Archangel* is located in the Archives de la Maritime at Brest, France. The other six lists are taken from the Archives Departementales de la Loire Atlantique in Nantes, France."

On 8 February 1786, Martin Navarro had successfully supervised and completed his part in the project of establishing 1,587 Acadian exiles in villages of their own choice.

With the group aboard *La Caroline*, Count de Aranda brought to a close his work of removing 1,596 Acadian exiles from France to Louisiana. Because of withdrawals and failure of others to appear reduced this number of official registration to 1,574 colonists, representing 375 families. The number was further reduced by a loss of 85 through death and 12 through desertions. However, the number gained with 39 births and 15 immigrants. There were also the 28 stowaways -- or 1,624 Acadian colonists which Spain transported from France to Louisiana. Aranda closed his books on the removal of 1,624 colonists at the cost of $61,424.12. Peyrous had realized his dream -- "the removal of the Acadians from France to Louisiana at the expense of the King of Spain."

The dates of embarkation and debarkation differ from various sources, namely because of the fact that ships sometimes lingered at the mouth of the Mississippi due to size, and therefore arrived in New Orleans sometime later. The *Ville d'Archangel*, for example, arrived at Balize (mouth of the River) on 4 November 1785, entered the Mississippi on 11 November, then plowed upstream for 110 miles until she reached New Orleans on 3 December 1785. The *Caroline*, on the other hand, left Nantes to cross the Atlantic in 64 days, reaching Balize on 12 December 1785 and New Orleans five days later, or the 17th. Research in French Archives also reveals that ships did not always leave on the appointed dates, usually due to wind factors and the weather. The dates used in this work are taken from Gérard-Marc Braud's "De Nantes à La Louisiane."

This work includes both the French listing of the Acadians embarking from France as well as the Spanish listing of the Acadians disembarking in New Orleans. The comparison of both these passenger lists enables the researcher to identify some of the individuals that would be otherwise difficult to connect with their families. An example of this is found among the passengers listed on "*Le Bon Papa.*" The French Listing includes with Family #5 an Ester Cordné, identified as "belle-mère" [here translated as "step-mother" and not as "mother-in-law"]. This is the same person as indicated on the Spanish Listing in Family #1 as Esther, "su suegra y viuda." Apparently she embarked for Louisiana along with with her step-son Amable HÉBERT's family, but disembarked at New Orleans with her step-daughter Anne HÉBERT's family. She was Esther Courtney. This comparison of Listings can make it possible to better indentify more persons.

The section entitled "Other References" is an attempt to identify the various families. Exerpts have been indicated from various sources that may enable the researcher to identify these families. The list of marriage and birth/baptism records is neither complete nor exhaustive. The listed references serve as a means of identifying the various families listed. The marriages and baptisms indicated are not meant to be a complete family ancestry, but merely an indication or identification of enough members of that family which enables a more accurate identification of those disembarking at New Orleans. The reader would do well to consult the works quoted in order to obtain a more complete ancestry.

The column heading entitled "Complete Listing" is an english translation of both the French Listing of embarkation in France and the Spanish Listing of debarkation in New Orleans.

The volume's index provides a listing of the names found in both the "Complete Listing" and "Other References" columns. Names indexed from the "Other References" and "Complete Listing" columns are spelled with uniformity. This consistency of spelling facilitates the search for individuals named in the various lists.

About the "General Index" which constitutes the second part of this work

SOMETHING ABOUT THE GENERAL INDEX

A General Index of five (5) separate publications written by Albert J. Robichaux, Jr. and Rev. Donald J. Hébert formd the second part of this volume. It was decided to include this General Index here rather than publish a separate volume. These five publications include the records of Acadians in France found in the various french archives as described in each book. A single General Index of the names found in these five works can prove very useful in doing research on the Acadians in France. This General Index listing includes 25,025 entries.

Additional information about the use of this <u>General Index</u> is found with the Index itself.

Index Sources are listed on the top of each page of the General Index - appearing as:
C =Chatellerault; E =Acadians in Exile; F =Acadian Families; N =Nantes; and S =St-Malo

Each name listed in the Index indicates a reference to one of the five works included. The books included in this general listing are:

> C =<u>The Acadian Exiles in Chatellerault 1773-1785</u>
> by Albert J. Robichaux, Jr. - published in 1983
>
> E =<u>Acadians in Exile 1700-1825</u>
> by Rev. Donald J. Hébert - published in 1980
>
> F =<u>Acadian Families in Exile 1785</u>
> by Rev. Donald J. Hébert - published in 1995
>
> N =<u>The Acadian Exiles in Nantes 1775-1785</u>
> by Albert J. Robichaux, Jr. - published in 1978
>
> S =<u>The Acadian Exiles in Saint-Malo 1758-1785</u>
> by Albert J. Robichaux, Jr. - published in three volumes in 1981

Rev. Donald J. Hébert

8 April 1942 - Born in Lafayette, LA
Son of Louis Hébert and Marie L. Mire

1948 - 1955	Attended Mire Elementary School (grades 1 - 7)
Sept. 1955	Attended 8th grade at Rayne High School
1956-1962	Attended Immaculata Seminary in Lafayette, LA
1962-1967	Seminary studies - St. John's Seminary; Little Rock, Ark.
1967-1968	Studied at Notre Dame Seminary; New Orleans, LA
1 June 1968	Ordained a priest at St. John's Cathedral; Lafayette, LA
2 June 1968	Celebrated First Mass at Assumption Church; Mire, LA
20 June 1970	Began research and collection of church records
April 1974	Published first volume of "Southwest Louisiana Records"
1970-1995	Published a total of 96 genealogy and/or history titles

APPOINTMENTS

15 June 1968	Associate Pastor of St. Francis in Arnaudville, LA
18 June 1970	Associate Pastor of St. Anthony in Eunice, LA
28 October 1975	Pastor of St. Joseph in Cecilia, LA
1 July 1980	Pastor of St. Anthony in Eunice, LA
4 February 1984	Administrator of Annunciation in Duralde, LA
16 August 1985	Pastor of Queen of All Saints in Ville Platte, LA
5 September 1989	Administrator of Assumption Church in Mire, LA

Ancestor Chart

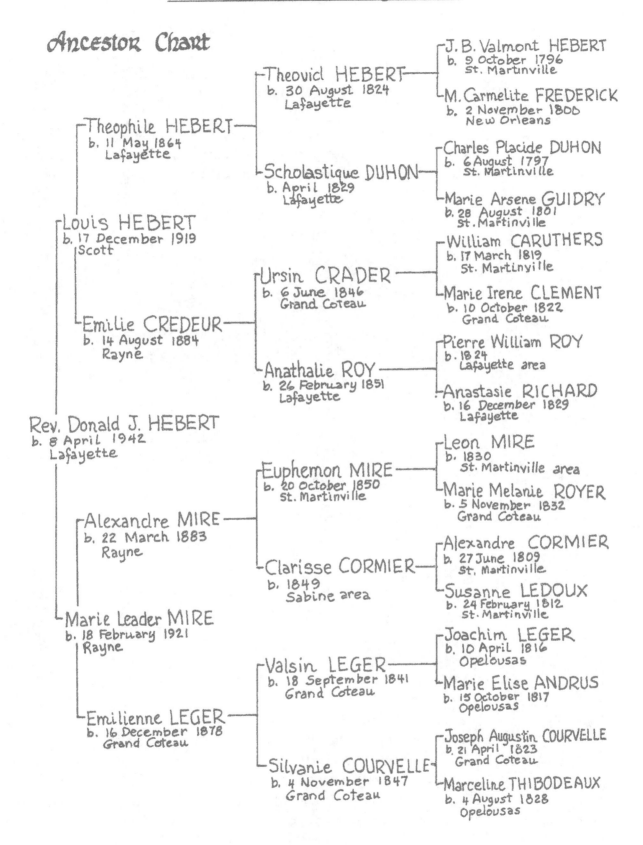

Theovid HEBERT
b. 30 August 1824
Lafayette

— J. B. Valmont HEBERT
b. 9 October 1796
St. Martinville

— M. Carmelite FREDERICK
b. 2 November 1800
New Orleans

Theophile HEBERT
b. 11 May 1864
Lafayette

Scholastique DUHON
b. April 1829
Lafayette

— Charles Placide DUHON
b. 6 August 1797
St. Martinville

— Marie Arsene GUIDRY
b. 28 August 1801
St. Martinville

Louis HEBERT
b. 17 December 1919
Scott

Ursin CRADER
b. 6 June 1846
Grand Coteau

— William CARUTHERS
b. 17 March 1819
St. Martinville

— Marie Irene CLEMENT
b. 10 October 1822
Grand Coteau

Emilie CREDEUR
b. 14 August 1884
Rayne

Anathalie ROY
b. 26 February 1851
Lafayette

— Pierre William ROY
b. 1824
Lafayette area

— Anastasie RICHARD
b. 16 December 1829
Lafayette

Rev. Donald J. HEBERT
b. 8 April 1942
Lafayette

Euphemon MIRE
b. 20 October 1850
St. Martinville

— Leon MIRE
b. 1830
St. Martinville area

— Marie Melanie ROYER
b. 5 November 1832
Grand Coteau

Alexandre MIRE
b. 22 March 1883
Rayne

Clarisse CORMIER
b. 1849
Sabine area

— Alexandre CORMIER
b. 27 June 1809
St. Martinville

— Susanne LEDOUX
b. 24 February 1812
St. Martinville

Marie Leader MIRE
b. 18 February 1921
Rayne

Valsin LEGER
b. 18 September 1841
Grand Coteau

— Joachim LEGER
b. 10 April 1816
Opelousas

— Marie Elise ANDRUS
b. 15 October 1817
Opelousas

Emilienne LEGER
b. 16 December 1878
Grand Coteau

Silvanie COURVELLE
b. 4 November 1847
Grand Coteau

— Joseph Augustin COURVELLE
b. 21 April 1823
Grand Coteau

— Marceline THIBODEAUX
b. 4 August 1828
Opelousas

argueburier	matchlock, gunsmith [usually "armurier"]; The "arquebuses" were the former guns of the Middle Ages, very heavy and supported by a pole. (Source: Maurice Caillebeau; Poitiers, France and Rev. Robert A. Parent; Scranton, Pennsylvania)
à la mamelle	nursling, a suckling
BR	Baton Rouge (refers to family records in the series "Diocese of Baton Rouge Catholic Church Records" published by the Diocesan Archives)
Bona	Bona Arsenault (refers to the reference work "Histoire et Généalogie des Acadiens")
Braud	Gérard-Marc Braud (refers to material found in his work entitled: "De Nantes à La Louisiane")
b.	born
bt.	baptized
ca.	circa; Latin for "about, around"
calfat	calker
Census	"Louisiana Census and Militia Lists, 1770-1789" (refers to the General Census of the Inhabitants of Lafourche of 1 January 1789 in this work by Albert Robichaux)
charpentier	carpenter
charpentier marin	ship carpenter, shipwright
Chat	Chatellerault (refers to family groups found in "The Acadian Exiles in Chatellerault, 1773-1784" by Albert Robichaux, Jr.)
cieur de long	see rather: scieur de long
commerçant	tradesman
coloriste	colorist, painter of toys or postcards
commis	clerk, shop assistant
contre-maître	foreman
cordier	ropemaker
cordonnier	shoemaker
d.	died, deceased
d/o	daughter of
domestique	a servant
elève	student, apprentice, charge - as being responsible for someone
employé	employee,
étranger	stranger, foreigner
Exile	Exile (refers to the family records in "Acadians in Exile" by Rev. Donald J. Hébert)
graveur	stone cutter, also an engraver
idem	Latin expression for "same, identical"
imprimeur	printer

jardinier	gardener
journalier	day laborer
laboureur	plowman
m.	married
manoeuvre	manual laborer, unskilled worker
manouvrier	expert seaman
marchant	merchant, shopkeeper
marin	seaman, sailor
menuisier	woodworker, joiner, house carpenter
mineur	minor, not yet attained majority
Nantes	Nantes (refers to the family groups in "The Acadian Exiles in Nantes, 1775-1785" by Albert Robichaux, Jr.)
NO	New Orleans (refers to family records in the series "Archdiocese of New Orleans Sacramental Records" published by the Archdiocese of New Orleans)
ouvrier	workman, also a carpenter
perceur	driller, borer
perelleur	probably a variant spelling of the next word, "perreyeur"
perreyeur	a quarryman or stone cutter; also spelled "pèréieur." See: Emile Littré's Dictionnaire de la langue française, v.5, p.1744]. Source: Rev. Robert A. Parent; Scranton, Pennsylvania.
poulican	block or pulley maker; Note: "ouvrier qui fabrique des poulies; marchand qui en vend" [French for "laborer who works with pulleys; merchant who sells these]." Block-maker is a good definition; was often times an Acadian profession in the ports of Brittany during the years 1763-1785 (Source: Maurice Caillebeau; Poitiers, France and Rev. Robert A. Parent; Scranton, Pennsylvania).
pulieur	another word for "poulican"
s/o	son of
scieur de long	pit sawyer, to saw planks from larger blocks or trees
SM	St. Malo (refers to the family groups in "The Acadian Exiles in Saint-Malo, 1758-1785" a three volume work by Albert Robichaux, Jr.)
SWLR	Southwest Louisiana Records (refers to the family records in the series "Southwest Louisiana Records" by Rev. Donald J. Hébert)
tailleur	a tailor; but also a cutter of stone, gems or trees
tanneur	tanner of hides
tonnelier	cooper, wet cooper, barrel maker
wid. or widr.	widow or widower
#	Number (refers to the family number)

L'AMITIE – Parti de NANTES pour la LOUISIANE en 1785
(L'AMITIÉ ~ Left NANTES for LOUISIANA in 1785)

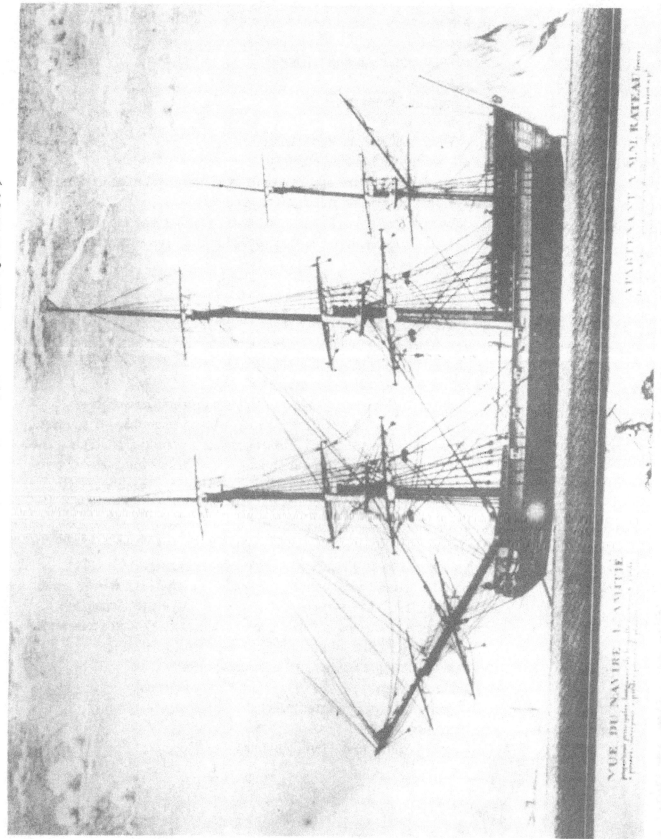

Dates of Embarkation and Debarkation

of the Seven Ships

Bringing the Acadians to Louisiana

1785

1. *Le Bon Papa* - departed France on Tuesday, 10 May 1785
and arrived on 29 July 1785, 80 days at sea; 280 tons

2. *La Bergère* - departed France on Saturday, 14 May 1785
and arrived on 15 August 1785, 93 days at sea; 300 tons

3. *Le Beaumont* - departed France on 11 June 1785
and arrived on 19 August 1785, 69 days at sea; 180 tons

4. *Le Saint-Rémi* - departed France on Thursday, 27 June 1785
and arrived on 10 September 1785, 75 days at sea; 400 tons

5. *L'Amitié* - departed France on 20 August 1785
and arrived on 8 November 1785, 80 days at sea; 400 tons

6. *La Ville d'Archangel* - departed France on 12 August 1785
and arrived on 3 December 1785, 113 days at sea; 600 tons

7. *La Caroline* - departed France on 19 October 1785
and arrived on 17 December 1785, 54 days at sea; 200 tons

1st family (6 persons)	[Number indicates age]			1st family (7 persons)
Joseph LEBLANC	charpentier	54		Josef LEBLANC
Anne HEBERT, sa femme		49		Ana HÉBERT, su muger
Joseph, son fils		15		Josef, su hijo
Simon, idem		13		Simon, ydem
Blanche, sa fille		19		Blanca, ydem
Marie, idem		17		Maria, ydem
				Esther, su suegra y viuda

2nd family (10 persons)				2nd family (10 persons)
André TRAMPLÉ	Marin	59		Andres TRAMPLE
Margueritte LEBLANC, sa femme		48		Margarita LEBLANC, su muger
Jean, son fils	idem	24		Juan, su hijo
Charles, idem	idem	22		Carlos, idem
Jacques, idem	idem	20		Santiago, idem
Servant, idem	idem	15		Servando, idem
Olivier, idem		11		Olivier, idem
André, idem		7		Andres, idem
Isabelle, sa fille		25		Isabel, idem
Marie Magdelaine, idem		17		Maria Magdalena, idem

3rd family (8 persons)				3rd family (8 persons)
Joseph HENRRY	charpentier	40		Josef HENRIQUE
Cécille BRAUD, sa femme		38		Cecilia BREAU, su muger
Jean Laurent, son fils	idem	19		Juan Lorenzo, su hijo
Joseph, idem		14		Josef, idem
Pierre, idem		5		Pedro, ydem
Marie Josèphe, idem		7		Maria Josefa, idem
Anne Françoise, idem		3		Ana Fernanda, ydem
Magdelene Apoline	à la mamelle			Magdalena Polonia, idem

4th family (9 persons)				4th family (9 persons)
Charles LANDRY	charpentier	50		Carlos LANDRY
Margucritte BOUDREAU, sa fcmmc		48		Margarita BOUDEAUT, su muger
Fermin, son fils	marin	22		Fermin, su hijo
Sebastien, idem	idem	18		Sebastian, idem
Louis, idem		14		Luis, idem
Jean, idem		11		Juan, idem
Charles, idem		8		Carlos, idem
François, idem		6		Francisco, idem
Margueritte, sa fille		18		Margarita, idem

5th family (6 persons)				5th family (5 persons)
Amable HÉBERT	charpentier	43		Amable HEBERT
André, son fils		9		Andrés, su hijo
Marie, sa fille		24		Maria, ydem
Geneviève, idem		17		Genoveva, ydem
Isabelle, idem		14		Isabel, idem
Ester CORDNÉ, belle-mère du dit		60		

6th family (2 persons)				6th family (2 persons)
Jean Charles LEBLANC	marin	23		Juan Carlos LEBLANC
Brigide HÉBERT, sa femme		19		Brigida EBERT, su muger

<table>
<tr><td colspan="3">

1st family (7 persons)
</td></tr>
</table>

Joseph LEBLANC	carpenter	54
Anne HÉBERT, his wife		49
Joseph LEBLANC, his son		15
Simon LEBLANC, his son		13
Blanche LEBLANC, his daughter		19
Marie LEBLANC, his daughter		17
Esther [COURTNEY], step-mother; widow		

Chat - #137: Joseph LEBLANC widr. Marguerite TRAHAN s/o René & Jeanne LANDRY m. 1758 Anne HÉBERT d/o Jean & Marguerite TRAHAN

Exile - p.287-289 & Nantes - #214: other records

Exile - p.565: Esther COURTENAY apparently embarked with her step-son, Amable HÉBERT & disembarked with her step-daughter, Anne HÉBERT. See also: Bona - v.4, p.1393 & SM - #511: additional family information

2nd family (10 persons)

André TEMPLÉ	sailor	59
Marguerite LEBLANC, his wife		48
Jean TEMPLÉ, his son	sailor	24
Charles TREPLÉ, his son	sailor	22
Jacques TEMPLÉ, his son	sailor	20
Servant TEMPLÉ, his son	sailor	15
Olivier TEMPLÉ, his son		11
André TEMPLÉ, his son		7
Isabelle TEMPLÉ, his daughter		25
Marie Magdelaine TEMPLÉ, his daughter		17

Chat - #183: André TEMPLÉ widr. Marie DEVAUX m. 1759 Marguerite LEBLANC wid. Charles BRAUD

Nantes - #279: André TEMPLÉ s/o André & Marguerite LEBLANC bt. 1777

3rd family (8 persons)

Joseph HENRY	carpenter	40
Cécile BRAUD, his wife		38
Jean Laurent HENRY, son	carpenter	19
Joseph HENRY, his son		14
Pierre HENRY, his son		5
Marie Josèphe HENRY, his daughter		7
Anne Françoise HENRY, his daughter		3
Magdelaine Appoline HENRY, nursling		

Chat - #116: Joseph HENRY s/o François & Marie DUGAT m. 1764 Cécile BRAUD d/o Antoine & Cécile BOURG. Children: Jean-Laurent b. 1765, Anne Françoise bt. 1781

SM - #555: additional family information
Nantes - #178: additional family information

4th family (9 persons)

Charles LANDRY	carpenter	50
Marguerite BOUDROT, his wife		48
Firmin LANDRY, his son	sailor	22
Sebastien LANDRY, his son	sailor	18
Louis LANDRY, his son		14
Jean LANDRY, his son		11
Charles LANDRY, his son		8
François LANDRY, his son		6
Marguerite LANDRY, his daughter		18

Chat - #123: Charles LANDRY s/o Charles & Marie LEBLANC m. 1759 Marguerite BOUDROT d/o Paul & Marie-Josèphe DOIRON

Nantes - #189: additional family information
SM - #592: additional family information

5th family (6 persons)

Amable HÉBERT	carpenter	43
André HÉBERT, his son		9
Marie HÉBERT, his daughter		24
Geneviève HÉBERT, his daughter		17
Isabelle HÉBERT, his daughter		14
Ester COURTNEY, step-mother of above		60

Nantes - #158: Amable HÉBERT b. ca. 1746 s/o Jean & Marguerite TRAHAN m. ca. 1761 Marie-Anne RICHARD who d. 1780 in Nantes

Exile - p.564-565: Jean HÉBERT m. ca. 1722 Marguerite TRAHAN; a child Amable b. ca. 1746; Jean HÉBERT again m. 8 Oct. 1763 Esther COURTENAY; Amable HÉBERT is her step-son

6th family (2 persons)

Jean Charles LEBLANC	sailor	23
Brigide HÉBERT, his wife		19

BR - v.2, p.459, p.464: Children of Jean Charles LEBLANC & Brigide HÉBERT: Scholastique b. 7 March 1792, Amable André b. 7 Feb. 1794

<u>7th family (5 persons)</u>

Simon LEBLANC	laboureur	62
Marie TRAHAN, sa femme		51
Joseph, son fils	marin	20
Jacques, idem		13
Anne, sa fille		15

<u>8th family (3 persons</u>

Jean LEBLANC	calfac	36
Thérèse HÉBERT, sa femme		35
Marie, sa fille	à la mamelle	

<u>9th family (8 persons)</u>

Alexandre DOUASON	journalier	47
Ursule HÉBERT, sa femme		43
Isaac, son fils		16
Mathurin, idem		12
Joseph, idem		7
Jean B^{te}, idem		2
Marie Rose, sa fille		21
Magdeleine, idem		19

<u>10th family (1 person)</u>

François HÉBERT	charpentier	72

<u>11th family (3 persons)</u>

Anne BOUDREAU, veuve HACHÉ		40
Marie, sa fille		15
Margueritte, idem		11

<u>12th family (6 persons)</u>

Cécille BOURG, veuve HISÉ		48
P^{re}, son fils	journalier	24
Charles, idem	idem	22
Jean B^{te}, idem	idem	17
Grégoire, idem		9
Anne Marie, sa fille		20

<u>13th family (5 persons)</u>

Pierre QUINTIN	charpentier	65
Marie Magdeleine DUGAST, sa femme		50
Anne, sa fille		24
Marie, idem		23
Victoire Françoise, idem		14

<u>14th family (3 persons)</u>

Paul D^{que} BOUDREAUX	marin	24
Marie Olivier LANDRY, sa femme		18
Paul Marie, son fils	à la mamelle	

<u>7th family (5 persons)</u>

Simon LEBLANC
   Maria TRAHAN, su muger
   Josef, su hijo
   Santiago, idem
   Ana, idem

<u>8th family (3 persons)</u>

Juan LEBLANC
   Teresa EBERT, su muger
   Maria, su hijo de 15 Meses

<u>9th family (8 persons)</u>

Alexandro DOUAISON
   Ursula EBERT, su muger
   Isaac, su hijo
   Maturino, idem
   Juan, idem
   Juan Baptista, idem
   Maria Rosa, idem
   Magdalena, idem

<u>10th family (1 person)</u>

Francisco EBERT

<u>11th family (3 persons)</u>

Ana BODREAU, viuda HACHÉ
   Maria HACHÉ, su hija
   Margarita, ydem

<u>12th family (2 persons)</u>

Pedro USÉ
   Maria KIMIN, su muger

<u>13th family (5 persons)</u>

Cecilia BOURG, viuda USÉ
   Carlos USÉ, su hijo
   Juan Bautista, idem
   Gregorio, idem
   Ana Maria, idem

<u>14th family (5 persons)</u>

Pedro KIMIN
   Maria Magdalena, su muger
   Ana, su hija
   Maria, ydem
   Victoria Francisca, idem

<u>15th family (3 persons)</u>

Pablo Domingo BOUDREAUD
   Maria Oliva LANDRY, su muger
   Pablo Marin, su hijo de teta

Nantes - #223: Simon LEBLANC s/o Jacques & Catherine LANDRY m. 1757 Marie TRAHAN d/o Joseph & Élizabeth THERIOT

Nantes - #210: Jean LEBLANC m. 1782 Tarsille HÉBERT; a child Marie Rose was bt. 1784

Chat - #69: Alexandre DOIRON s/o Thomas & Anne GIROIRE m. 1763 Ursule HÉBERT d/o François & Isabelle BOURG

SM - #328 additional family information
Nantes - #102: additional family information

Chat - #100: Jacques HACHÉ s/o Joseph & Marie GAUDET m. 1763 Anne BOUDROT d/o Paul & Marie DOIRON

Nantes - #150: additional family information
Nantes - #184: Pierre Ignace HEUZE m. 1785 Marie-Perrine KIMINE

Chat - #117: Ignace HEUZE widr. Marie-Josèphe RENAUD m. 1759 Cécile BOURG wid. Joseph LONGUESPÉE

SM - #569: additional family information
Nantes - #182: additional family information

Nantes - #185: Pierre KIMINE s/o Jacques & Marie CHIASSON m. 1770 Marie-Madeleine DUGAT d/o Charles & Marie BENOIT; a child Victoire-Francoise b. 1771
SM - #579: additional family information

Nantes - #46: Paul-Dominique BOUDROT m. 1783 Marie-Olive LANDRY; a child Paul-Marie BOUDROT bt. 1784

7th family (5 persons)

Simon LEBLANC	plowman	62
Marie TRAHAN, his wife		51
Joseph LEBLANC, his son	sailor	20
Jacques LEBLANC, his son		13
Anne LEBLANC, his daughter		15

8th family (3 persons)

Jean LEBLANC	calker	36
Thérèse HÉBERT, his wife		35
Marie LEBLANC, his dgtr.; nursling-15 mos.		

9th family (8 persons)

Alexandre DOIRON	day laborer	47
Ursule HÉBERT, his wife		43
Isaac DOIRON		16
Mathurin DOIRON, his son		12
Joseph DOIRON, his son		7
Jean Baptiste DOIRON, his son		2
Marie Rose DOIRON, his daughter		21
Magdelaine DOIRON, his daughter		19

10th family (1 person)

François HÉBERT	carpenter	72

11th family (3 persons)

Anne BOUDREAUX, widow HACHÉ		40
Marie HACHÉ, her daughter		15
Marguerite HACHÉ, her daughter		11

11-A family (2 persons)

Pierre HEUZÉ		
Marie KIMINE, his wife		

12th family (6 persons)

Cécile BOURG, widow HEUZÉ		48
Pierre HEUZÉ, her son	day laborer	24
Charles HEUZÉ, her son	day laborer	22
Jean Baptiste HEUZÉ, son	day laborer	17
Grégoire HEUZÉ, her son		9
Anne Marie HEUZÉ, her daughter		20

13th family (5 persons)

Pierre KIMINE	carpenter	65
Marie Magdelaine DUGAT, his wife		50
Anne KIMINE, his daughter		24
Marie KIMINE, his daughter		23
Victoire Françoise KIMINE, his daughter		14

14th family (3 persons)

Paul Dominique BOUDROT	sailor	24
Marie Olivier LANDRY, his wife		18
Paul Marin BOUDROT, his son; nursling		

15th family (4 persons)		
Jean B^te DUGAT	journalier	49
Marie CLAUSINET, sa femme		43
Marie DUGAT, sa fille		11
Marie HACHÉ, sa mineur		18

16th family (4 persons)
Juan Baptista DUGATS
Maria CLOSINET, su muger
Maria, su hija
Maria HACHÉ, huerfana

16th family (4 persons)		
Jean B^te DUGAST	charpentier	66
Anne BOURG, sa femme		64
Anne, sa fille		21
Marie BOUDREAU, petite fille au dit		5

17th family (4 persons)
Juan Bautista DUGATS
Ana BOURG, su muger
Ana, su hija
Maria BOUDREAUD, su nieta

17th family (7 persons)		
J^h AU COING	marin	36
Élisabeth HENRRY, sa femme		35
Joseph Jean, son fils		8
François Toussaint, idem		6
Isabelle Jeanne, sa fille		11
Marie Modeste, idem		4
Victoire Claire, idem		2

18th family (7 persons)
Josef AUCOIN
Ysabel HENRIQUE, su muger
Juan Josef, si hijo
Francisco Santos, idem
Isabel Juana, ydem
Maria Modesta, ydem
Victoria Clara, idem

18th family (7 persons)		
Eustache LEJEUNE	charpentier	52
Jeanne CHIQUET, sa femme		42
Servand, son fils		15
François, idem		13
Marie Magdeleine, sa fille		23
Marie Rose, idem		2
Pélagie GAUTREAU, sa nièce		15

19th family (6 persons)
Eustachio EL JOVEN
Juana CLIQUET, su muger
Servando, su hijo
Francisco, ydem
Maria Magdalena, idem
Pelagia GOTREAU, su sobrina

19th family (2 persons)		
Jean B^te LEJEUNE	marin	25
Genneviève DOUAISON, sa femme		19

20th family (6 persons)		
Grégoire LEJEUNE	marin	45
Elènne DUMON, sa femme		36
Grégoire, son fils		4
Julien, idem		2
Marie, sa fille		14
Marie Geneviève GOTREAU, sa nièce		19

20th family (6 persons)
Juan Bautista EL JOVEN
Helena DUMONT, su muger
Gregorio, su hijo
Julian, idem
Maria, idem
Maria Genoveva GOTREAU, sobrina

21st family (2 persons)		
Anselme LANDRY	marin	50
Agatte BARIAU, sa femme		50

21st family (2 people)
Anselmo LANDRY
Agata VACIOU, su muger

22nd family (5 persons)		
Jean B^te BOUDREAU	marin	29
Marie Modeste TRAHAN, sa femme		36
Jean Constant, son fils		6
Marie Félicité, sa fille		8
Margueritte, idem		2

22nd family (5 persons)
Juan Bautista BAUDREAU
Maria Modesta TRAHAM, su muger
Juan Constante, su hijo
Maria Felicidad, ydem
Margarita, ydem

15th family (4 persons)		
Jean Baptiste DUGAT	day laborer	49
Marie CLOSSINET, his wife		43
Marie DUGAT, his daughter		11
Marie HACHÉ, a minor child; orphan		18

Nantes - #112: Jean-Baptiste DUGAST m. 1760 Anne BOURG

SM - #359: additional family information

16th family (4 persons)		
Jean Baptiste DUGAT	carpenter	66
Anne BOURG, his wife		64
Anne DUGAT, his daughter		21
Marie BOUDROT, his granddaughter		5

Nantes - #12: Joseph AUCOIN s/o Paul & Marie LEBLANC m. 1770 Élizabeth HENRY d/o François & Marie DUGAST; a child Isabelle-Jeanne bt. 1773

SM - #28: additional family information

17th family (7 persons)		
Joseph AUCOIN	sailor	36
Élizabeth HENRY, his wife		35
Joseph Jean AUCOIN, his son		8
François Toussaint AUCOIN, his son		6
Isabelle Jeanne AUCOIN, his daughter		11
Marie Modeste AUCOIN, his daughter		4
Victoire Claire AUCOIN, his daughter		2

Nantes - #228: Eustache LEJEUNE s/o Jean & Françoise GUÉDRY m. 1773 Jeanne CHIQUET; children: Servan-Mathurin b. 1769, Marie-Jeanne-Perinne-Madeleine b. 1762
Braud - Annex: gives the name Jeanne GICQUEL

18th family (7 persons)		
Eustache LEJEUNE	carpenter	52
Jeanne GICQUEL, his wife		42
Servand LEJEUNE, his son		15
François LEJEUNE, his son		13
Marie Magdelaine LEJEUNE, his daughter		23
Marie Rose LEJEUNE, his daughter		2
Pélagie GAUTROT, his niece		15

BR - v.2, p.495: Children of Jean Baptiste LEJEUNE & Geneviève DUARON: Eusebe bt. 25 Dec. 1801 at age 10 mths. Grandparents of child: Eusebe LEJEUNE & Marie LEJEUNE, Zeno b. 19 June 1794

19th family (2 persons)		
Jean Baptiste LEJEUNE	sailor	25
Geneviève DOIRON, his wife		19

Chat - #141: Grégoire LEJEUNE widr. Charlotte DES CROUTES, s/o Jean & Françoise GUÉDRY m. 1767 Hélène DUMONT d/o Joseph & Madeleine VECO
Nantes - #229: additional family information
SM - #661: additional family information

20th family (6 persons)		
Grégoire LEJEUNE	sailor	45
Hélène DUMONT, his wife		36
Grégoire LEJEUNE, his son		4
Julien LEJEUNE, his son		2
Marie LEJEUNE, his daughter		14
Marie Geneviève GAUTROT, his niece		19

Nantes - #188: Anselme LANDRY m. ca. 1765 Agathe BARRILLOT
SM - #587: additional family information

21st family (2 persons)		
Anselme LANDRY	sailor	50
Agathe BARRILLOT, his wife		50

Chat - #32: Jean-Baptiste BOUDREAUX s/o Alexandre & Marie-Magdeleine VINCENT m. 1774 Marie-Modeste TRAHAN d/o Joseph & Anne THERIOT

Nantes - #41: additional family information

22nd family (5 persons)		
Jean Baptiste BOUDROT	sailor	29
Marie Modeste TRAHAN, his wife		36
Jean Constant BOUDROT, his son		6
Marie Félicité BOUDROT, his daughter		8
Marguerite BOUDROT, his daughter		2

23rd family (3 persons)			23rd family (3 persons)	
Agelique(sic) PINEL veuve LÉGER		44	Angela PINEL viuda LÉGERE	
Louis, son fils	marin	19	Luis LÉGERE, su hijo	
Jean, idem	idem	15	Juan, idem	

24th family (7 persons)			24th family (7 persons)	
Charles BROUSSARD	charpentier	42	Carlos BROUSARD	
Eufroisine MARIOT, sa femme		37	Eufrasia MARIOT, su muger	
Jean Charles, son fils	marin	20	Juan Carlos, su hijo	
François, idem	idem	18	Francisco, ydem	
Pierre, idem		14	Pedro, Ydem	
Dominique, idem		12	Domingo, Ydem	
Paul BOUDREAU, beau fils		13	Pablo BAUDREAUD, hijastro	

25th family (1 person)			25th family (1 person)	
Jean TRAHAN	marin	35	Juan TRAHAM	

26th family (3 persons)			26th family (3 persons)	
Daniel BENOIT	journalier	36	Daniel BÉNOIT	
Henriette LEGENDRE, sa femme		32	Henriqueta LEGENDRE, su muger	
Henrriette, sa fille		7	Henriqueta, su hija	

27th family (6 persons)			27th family (6 persons)	
Pre LEBLANC	menuisier	40	Pedro LEBLANC	
Anne Josèphe LEBERT, sa femme		38	Ana Josef LEBERT, su muger	
Joseph, son fils		17	Josef, su hijo	
Pierre, idem		15	Pedro, idem	
Jean, idem		13	Juan, idem	
Victor, idem		10	Vittorio, idem	

28th family (6 persons)			28th family (6 persons)	
Jean Bte GUÉDRY	charpentier	36	Juan Bautista GUÉDRY	
Margueritte HÉBERT, sa femme		33	Margarita HÉBERT, su muger	
Pierre, son fils		8	Pedro, su hijo	
François, idem		4	Francisco, idem	
Margueritte Félicité, fille;	à la mamelle		Margarita Felicidad, de pecho	
Margueritte, mineur du dit		14	Margarita, hija de GUÉDRY	

29th family (5 persons)			29th family (5 persons)	
Louis STIVIN	marin	36	Luis STIVRIN	
Marie BABIN, sa femme		18	Maria BABIN, su muger	
Louis, son fils		3	Luis, su hijo	
Marie, sa fille		2	Maria, su hija	
François BABIN, frère de la femme; marin		16	Un hijo sin Bautizar	

			30th family (1 person)	
			Francisco BABIN	

30th family (3 persons)			31st family (3 persons)	
Elènne HACHÉ, fille		21	Helena HACHÉ, soltera	
Marie Josèphe, sa soeur		16	Maria Josefa, su hermana	
Élisabeth, idem		8	Isabel, idem	

23rd family (3 persons)		
Angélique PINET widow LÉGER		44
Louis LÉGER, her son	sailor	19
Jean LÉGER, her son	sailor	15

Nantes - #73: Charles BROUSSARD s/o Joseph & Ursule LEBLANC m. 1784 Euphrosine BARRIL-LOT d/o Pierre & Véronique GIROIRE

24th family (7 persons)		
Charles BROUSSARD	carpenter	42
Euphroisine BARRILLOT, his wife		37
Jean Charles BROUSSARD, son; sailor		20
François BROUSSARD, his son; sailor		18
Pierre BROUSSARD, his son		14
Dominique BROUSSARD, his son		12
Paul BOUDROT, stepson		13

25th family (1 person)		
Jean TRAHAN	sailor	35

Chat - #14: Daniel BENOIT s/o Claude & Isabelle THERIOT m. 1768 Henriette LEGENDRE d/o François & Marguerite LABAUVE
Nantes - #20 & SM - #64: additional information
Exile - p.295: additional family information
Nantes - #221: Pierre LEBLANC m. 1767 Anne-Josèphe LEBERT; a child Victor-Charles bt. 1776

26th family (3 persons)		
Daniel BENOIT	day laborer	36
Henriette LEGENDRE, his wife		32
Henriette BENOIT, his daughter		7

27th family (6 persons)		
Pierre LEBLANC	woodworker	40
Anne Josèphe LEBERT, his wife		38
Joseph LEBLANC, his son		17
Pierre LEBLANC, his son		15
Jean LEBLANC, his son		13
Victor LEBLANC, his son		10

Nantes - #140: Jean-Baptiste GUÉDRY m. 1774 Marguerite LEBERT; children: Pierre-Jean-Marie bt. 1776, Marguerite-Félicité bt. 1785

SM - #465: additional family information

28th family (6 persons)		
Jean Baptiste GUÉDRY	carpenter	36
Marguerite LEBERT, his wife		33
Pierre GUÉDRY, his son		8
François GUÉDRY, his son		4
Marguerite Félicité GUÉDRY, dgtr.; nursling		
Marguerite GUÉDRY, dgtr. of GUÉDRY		14

Nantes - #278: Louis-William STEBENS s/o Stanislas & Anne COLCEIN m. 1783 Marie BABIN d/o Simon & Anastasie THERIOT; a child Marie bt. 1783

29th family (5 persons)		
Louis STEBENS	sailor	36
Marie BABIN, his wife		18
Louis STEBENS, his son		3
Marie STEBENS, his daughter		2
A son STEBENS - not baptized		
François BABIN, brother of the wife; sailor		16

29bth family (1 person)		
Francois BABIN [same person listed previously]		

30th family (3 persons)		
Hélène HACHÉ, single woman		21
Marie Josèphe HACHÉ, her sister		16
Élisabeth HACHÉ, her sister		8

31st family (2 persons)
Charles D'AIGRE   poulican   54
    Anne Marie VINCENT, sa femme   55

32nd family (2 persons)
Françoise BOUDREAU, veuve DUGAST   45
    Pierre, son fils   11

33rd family (3 persons)
Margueritte LA BEAUVE, veuve LEGENDRE   55
    Louis, son fils   charpentier   22
    Yves, idem   idem   17

34th family (3 persons)
Jean B^te LEGENDRE   charpentier   25
    Marie Rose TULLIER, sa femme   20
    Rose, sa fille   à la mamelle

"Liste des passagers Acadiens nommés pour s'embarquer dans le Navire Le Bon papa allant à la Nouvelle Orleans dans la Louisiane."

"Nous, Consul d'Espagne en Bretagne chargé de l'expedition des Acadiens pour la Nouvelle-Orleans dans la Louisiane; Certifions que les cent-cinquante six personnes dont est composé la presente Liste, ont été nommés par nous
pour être embarqués dans le Navire Le Bon-Papa, armateur Mr. Peltier Dudoyer allant audit port de la nouvelle-Orleans. A Nantes. Ce 29 Avril 1785. d'Aspres. Archives Departementales: Loire -Inferieure, Marine 458.

Lista o registro de familias Acadianos en la orden en que bajaron del buque nombrado Le Bon Papa. Lista hecha por Anselmo Blanchard con fecha de 29 de julio de 1785 en Nueva Orleans. (Archivo General de Indias, Seville: "Cuba, legajo)

"Lista de Revista pasada á las familias Acadianas arribadas á este Puerto de la Nueva Orleans el Veinte y nueve de Julio del corriente año en la Fragata particular nombrada el Buen Padre su Capitan Mons. Pelletier, y salida de Nantes el ocho de Mayo del mismo." A. Saver

"Nueva Orleans, 29 de Julio de 1785
Nota- Que Maria Rosa el Joven [family #19] hija de Eustaquio el Joven y de Juana Chiquet, que falta [not there] en esta Lista de revista de desembarco..."

32nd family (2 persons)
Carlos DAIGRE
    Ana Maria VINCENT, su muger

33rd family (2 persons)
Francisca BOUDREAUD, viuda DUGATS
    Pedro DUGATS, su hijo

34th family (3 persons)
Margarita LAVEAUX, viuda LEGENDRE
    Luis LEGENDRE, su hijo
    Ydes, idem

35th family (3 persons)
Juan Bautista LEGENDRE
    Maria Rosa TULLIER, su muger
    Rosa, su hija de pecho

36th family (2 persons)
Juan Bautista EL JOVEN
    Elena DOWISON, su muger

Translation:
List of Acadian passengers designated to embark on the ship Le Bon Papa going to New Orleans in Louisiana.

We, Consul of Spain in Brittany charged with the expedition (or transporting) of the Acadians to New Orleans in Louisiana; Certifying that the 156 persons [or 34 families], comprising the present list, have been listed by ourselves to be transported in the ship Le Bon Papa [280 tons], ship owner being Mr. Peltier Dudoyer, going to the said Port of New Orleans. Given at Nantes - 29 April 1785

List of registration of the Acadian families in the order which they embarked the ship named the Le Bon Papa. The attached list by Anselm Blanchard dated 29 July 1785 in New Orleans.

List of Acadian families arriving in this Port of New Orleans on 29 July 1785 in the Frigate named "El Buen Padre" [Le Bon Papa] whose captain was Mr. Pelletier, and left from Nantes on 8 May 1785.

New Orleans, 29 July 1785
Note - That Marie Rose LEJEUNE [family #19] daughter of Eustache LEJEUNE and Jeanne CHIQUET is not on this list of debarkation...

SM - #288: Charles DAIGLE m. ca. 1758 Anne-Marie VINCENT

Chat - #78: Marin DUGAST s/o Jean-Baptiste & Marguerite BENOIT m. 1766 Françoise BOU-DREAUX d/o Paul & Marie-Josèphe DOIRON; SM - #366: additional information
Nantes - #115: additional family information

Nantes - #225: François LEGENDRE m. ca. 1750 Marguerite LABAUVE
SM - #657: additional family information
Exile - p.295: François LEGENDRE s/o Mathurin LEGENDRE & Marie MOREL marriage contract 6 April 1750 Marguerite LABAUVE d/o Antoine & Catherine LAJEUNE; Children: Jean François b. 1 Aug. 1754, Anastasie Angélique b. 25 Feb. 1757

Nantes - #226: Jean-Baptiste LEGENDRE s/o Francois & Marguerite LABAUVE m. 1783 Marie-Rose LETULLIER d/o René & Collet RENAUD; a child Rose bt. 1784

<table>
<tr><td colspan="3">31st family (2 persons)</td></tr>
<tr><td>Charles DAIGLE</td><td>pulley maker</td><td>54</td></tr>
<tr><td>Anne Marie VINCENT, his wife</td><td></td><td>55</td></tr>
<tr><td colspan="3">32nd family (2 persons)</td></tr>
<tr><td>Françoise BOUDROT, widow DUGAT</td><td></td><td>45</td></tr>
<tr><td>Pierre DUGAT, her son</td><td></td><td>11</td></tr>
<tr><td colspan="3">33rd family (3 persons)</td></tr>
<tr><td>Marguerite LABAUVE, widow LEGENDRE</td><td></td><td>55</td></tr>
<tr><td>Louis LEGENDRE, her son</td><td>carpenter</td><td>22</td></tr>
<tr><td>Yves LEGENDRE, her son</td><td>carpenter</td><td>17</td></tr>
<tr><td colspan="3">34th family (3 persons)</td></tr>
<tr><td>Jean Baptiste LEGENDRE</td><td>carpenter</td><td>25</td></tr>
<tr><td>Marie Rose LETULLIER, his wife</td><td></td><td>20</td></tr>
<tr><td>Rose LEGENDRE, daughter; nursling</td><td></td><td></td></tr>
<tr><td colspan="3">35th (36th) family (2 persons)</td></tr>
<tr><td>Jean Baptiste LEJEUNE</td><td></td><td></td></tr>
<tr><td>Hélène DOIRON, his wife</td><td></td><td></td></tr>
</table>

Paimboeuf is a neighboring commune of Nantes. Assigned 39 families of 165 members. Three families (#37, #38, #39) failed to report at departure. Captain Pelletier made the voyage in 81 days. The voyage was a success in its freedom from storms, and from epidemics and sickness of any kind, and the first expedition of 36 Acadian families, comprising 156 persons, arrived in a healthy condition. Only one death, that of a child. [Winzerling, p.130-131]

These people remained about a month recuperating in New Orleans. The expedition picked up 12 new members, 3 thru births, 9 thru new adherents (among which were Michel Léger, Simon Babin). It lost 12 members, 10 thru death and 3 thru desertions. Of 38 families now forming the expedition of Le Bon Papa, 37 voted to settle in Manchac (area around St. Gabriel) on the banks of the Mississippi, and 1 family chose La Fourche (area of Plattenville south of Donaldsonville). [Winzerling p.133]

1st family (5 persons)

Olivier THERRIOT	cordonnier	32
Marie AU COING, sa femme		32
Olivier Marie son fils		7
Jean, idem		2
Jean Charles TERRIOT, son frère; journalier		22

1st family

Olivier TERIOT   Received: 1 each of axe, shovel and meat cleaver; 3 hatchets, and 2 hoes

Jean Charles TERIOT   Received: 1 each of axe, hatchet, hoe, shovel and meat cleaver

2nd family (5 persons)

Olivier AU COING	charpentier	59
Cécille RICHARD, sa femme		48
Natalie, sa fille		17
Margueritte, idem		16
Cécille, idem		14

2nd family

Olivier AUCOING   Received: 1 each of shovel and mcat cleaver; 2 each of axe and hatchet; 3 hoes

3rd family (2 persons)

Charles AU COING	marin	36
Félicité AU COING, soeur		35

3rd family

Charles AUCOING   Received: 1 each of axe, hatchet, shovel and meat cleaver; 2 hoes

4th family (3 persons)

Marie AU COING, femme de Michel LEBLANC, absent		48
Marie Josèphe LEBLANC, sa fille		25
Apoline Eulalie		13

4th family

Marie Josefa LEBLANC   Received: 1 each of axe, hatchet, hoe, shovel and meat cleaver

5th family (2 persons)

Margueritte NOEL, veuve ROQUEMONT		21
Marie, sa soeur		28

5th family

Marguerite NOEL   Received: 1 each of axe, hatchet, hoe, shovel and meat cleaver

6th family (6 persons)

Simon MIEROLLE	cordier	40
Margueritte TRAHAN, sa femme		38
Étienne, son fils		8
Marie, sa fille		18
Isabelle, idem		16
Anne, idem		14

6th family

Simon MASEROLE   Received: 1 each of axe, shovel and meat cleaver; 2 hatchets and 3 hoes

7th family (3 persons)

Jacques TERRIOT	jardinier	25
Françoise GUÉRIN, sa femme		22
Françoise Élisabeth,	à la mamelle	

7th family

Jaques TERIOT   Received: 1 each of axe, hatchet, shovel and meat cleaver; 2 hoes

8th family (3 persons)

Dominique GUÉRIN	journalier	63
Iabelle [Isabelle], sa fille		22
Brigide, idem		15

8th family

Elisabet GUÉRIN   Received: 1 each of axe, hatchet, hoe, shovel and meat cleaver

9th family (3 persons)

Joseph GUÉRIN	journalier	40
Agnés PITRE, sa femme		36
Françoise, sa fille	à la mamelle	

9th family

Joseph GUÉRIN   Received: 1 each of axe, hatchet, shovel, meat cleaver; 2 hoes

10th family

[Apparently not listed as such]

10th family (1 person)

Françoise GUILLOT, fille		19

	1st family (5 persons)	
Nantes - #284: Olivier THERIOT s/o Étienne & Hélène LANDRY m. 1777 Marie AUCOIN d/o Olivier & Marguerite VINCENT; a child Olivier-Marie bt. 1778	Olivier THERIOT shoemaker	32
	Marie AUCOIN, his wife	32
	Olivier Marie THERIOT, his son	7
	Jean THERIOT, his son	2
	Jean Charles THERIOT, brother; laborer	22

	2nd family (5 persons)	
Chat - #7 Olivier AUCOIN widr. Marguerite VIN-CENT s/o Charles & Anne-Marie DUPUIS m. 1765 Cécile RICHARD d/o Pierre & Cécile GRANGER	Olivier AUCOIN carpenter	59
	Cécile RICHARD, his wife	48
Nantes - #14: additional family information	Natalie AUCOIN, his daughter	17
	Marguerite AUCOIN, his daughter	16
	Cécile AUCOIN, his daughter	14

	3rd family (2 persons)	
Census - p.118: Both listed on 1789 Census. Ages given: Charles is 40; Margritte is 25	Charles AUCOIN sailor	36
	Félicité AUCOIN, sister	35

	4th family (3 persons)	
Chat - #138: Michel LEBLANC m. ca. 1758 Marie AUCOIN d/o Charles & Anne-Marie DUPUIS	Marie AUCOIN, wife of Michel LEBLANC, he is absent	48
Nantes - #215: additional family information	Marie Josèphe LEBLANC, her daughter	25
SM - #645: additional family information	Appoline Eulalie LEBLANC	13

	5th family (2 persons)	
Nantes - #273: Guillaume-Jean ROQUEMONT m. 1784 Marie-Marguerite NOEL	Marguerite NOEL, widow ROQUEMONT	21
	Marie NOEL, her sister	28

	6th family (6 persons)	
SM - #706 Simon MAZEROLLE s/o Joseph & Marie-Josèphe DOIRON m. 1763 Marguerite TRAHAN d/o Claude & Hélène AUCOIN; a child Élizabeth-Marie b. 1769	Simon MAZEROLLE ropemaker	40
	Marguerite TRAHAN, his wife	38
	Étienne MAZEROLLE, his son	8
	Marie MAZEROLLE, his daughter	18
Census - p.124: Owned 6 arpents of land	Isabelle MAZEROLLE, his daughter	16
	Anne MAZEROLLE, his daughter	14

	7th family (3 persons)	
Nantes - #282 Jacques THERIOT m. 1784 Françoise GUÉRIN; a child Françoise-Élizabeth bt. 1785	Jacques THERIOT gardener	25
	Françoise GUÉRIN, his wife	22
	Françoise Élizabeth GUÉRIN; nursling	

	8th family (3 persons)	
Nantes - #145: Dominique GUÉRIN m. ca. 1746 Anne LEBLANC; children: Isabelle b. 1760, Brigide b. 1769	Dominique GUÉRIN day laborer	63
	Isabelle GUÉRIN, his daughter	22
SM - #469: additional family information	Brigide GUÉRIN, his daughter	15

	9th family (3 persons)	
Nantes - #146 Joseph GUÉRIN m. 1776 Agnès PITRE; a child Françoise bt. 1784	Joseph GUÉRIN day laborer	40
	Agnès PITRE, his wife	36
	Françoise GUÉRIN, his daughter; nursling	

	10th family (1 person)	
	Françoise GUILLOT, single woman	19

11th family (3 persons)
Margueritte HÉBERT, veuve BOURG   55
    Margueritte, sa fille - veuve AU COING   34
    Fermin, fils de cette dernière veuve   6

11th family
Marguerite EBERT   Received: 1 each of axe, shovel, and meat cleaver; 2 each of hatchet and hoe.

12th family (3 persons)
Antoine AU COING   laboureur   65
    Pierre, son fils   charpentier   20
    Louis, idem   15

12th family
Antoine AUCOING   Received: 1 each of shovel and meat cleaver; 2 each of axe, hatchet and hoe.

13th family (5 persons)
Laure BOURG, veuve HÉBERT   40
    Jean, son fils   15
    Félicité, sa fille   13
    Marie, sa fille   17
    Françoise, idem   11

13th family
Laura BOURG   Received: 1 each of axe, shovel and meat cleaver; 2 hatchets and 3 hoes.

14th family (3 persons)
Charles HÉBERT   laboureur   62
    Marie Y^{te}, sa fille, veuve HENRY   33
    Pierre, fils de cette veuve   14

14th family
Charles HEBERT   Received: 1 each of hatchet, shovel and meat cleaver; 2 each of axe and hoe.

15th family (3 persons)
Claude LEBLANC   laboureur   62
    Dorothée RICHARD, sa femme   50
    Claire LANDRY, belle-mère à la femme   75

15th family
Claude LEBLANC   Received: 1 each of axe, hatchet, shovel and meat cleaver; 2 hoes.

16th family (2 persons)
Marie Magdelaine LANDRY, femme de Jean
    Baptiste COMMEAU, absent   22
    Jean Baptiste COMMEAU, son fils   2

16th family
Marie Magdeleine LANDRY   Received: 1 each of axe, hatchet, hoe, shovel and meat cleaver.

17th family (3 persons)
Jean AUCOING   laboureur   73
    Jeanne TERRIOT, sa femme   62
    Anne Félicité, sa fille   19

17th family
Jean AUCOING   Received: 1 each of axe, shovel and meat cleaver; 2 each of hatchet and hoe.

18th family (1 person)
Marie Anastasie AU COING, femme de J^h
    TERRIOT, absent   26

18th family
Marie Anastasie AUCOING   Received 1 each of axe, hatchet, hoe, shovel and meat cleaver.

19th family (5 persons)
Pierre RICHARD   laboureur   48
    Blanche LEBLANC, sa femme   46
    Marie, sa fille   19
    Pierre, son fils   16
    Rose RICHARD, cousine au dit   30

19th family
Pierre RICHARD   Received 1 each of shovel and meat cleaver; 2 each of axe, hatchet and hoe.

20th family (4 persons)
Tranquille PITRE   tonellier   36
    Élizabeth AU COING, sa femme   46
    Jean Baptiste, son fils   3
    Jean Vincent, idem   1

20th family
Tranquile PITRE   Received 1 each of axe, shovel and meat cleaver; 2 each of hatchet and hoe.

Nantes - #52: Alexandre BOURG m. ca. 1747 Marguerite-Josèphe HÉBERT; a child Marguerite BOURG b. 1750	**11th family (3 persons)** Marguerite HÉBERT, widow BOURG 　　55 　Marguerite BOURG, dgtr.; widow AUCOIN 　34 　Firmin AUCOIN, son of this last widow 　6
SM - #156: additional family information	**12th family (3 persons)** Antoine AUCOIN 　　plowman 　**55** 　Pierre AUCOIN, his son 　carpenter 　20 　Louis AUCOIN, his son 　15
Nantes - #169: Jean-Baptiste HÉBERT s/o Pierre & Marguerite BOURG m. 1766 Luce BOURG d/o Jean & Françoise BENOIT; children: Félicité b. 1771, Françoise b. 1774	**13th family (5 persons)** Laure BOURG, widow HÉBERT 　40 　Jean HÉBERT, her son 　15 　Félicité HÉBERT, her daughter 　13 　Marie HÉBERT, her daughter 　17 　Françoise HÉBERT, her daughter 　11
SM - #517: additional family information	**14th family (3 persons)** Charles HÉBERT 　　plowman 　62 　Marie Y^{te} HÉBERT, widow HENRY 　33 　Pierre HENRY, son of this widow 　14
SM - #632: Claude LEBLANC s/o Jean & Jeanne BOURGEOIS m. 1768 Dorothée RICHARD d/o François & Marie MARTIN	**15th family (3 persons)** Claude LEBLANC 　　plowman 　62 　Dorothée RICHARD, his wife 　50 　Claire LANDRY, mother-in-law of the wife 　75
Nantes - #82 Jean-Baptiste COMMAU s/o Alexis & Dorothée RICHARD m. 1783 Marie-Madeleine LANDRY; a child Jean Baptiste bt. 1783	**16th family (2 persons)** Marie Magdelaine LANDRY, wife 　of Jean Baptiste COMEAUX, absent 　22 　Jean Baptiste COMEAUX, her son 　2
Nantes - #11: Jean AUCOIN m. ca. 1747 Jeanne THERIOT; a child Anne Félicité b. 1765 SM - #21: additional family information	**17th family (3 persons)** Jean AUCOIN 　　plowman 　73 　Jeanne THERIOT, his wife 　62 　Anne Félicité AUCOIN, his daughter 　19
Nantes - #283: Joseph THERIOT m. ca. 1783 Marie-Anastasie AUCOIN	**18th family (1 person)** Marie Anastasie AUCOIN, 　wife of Joseph THERIOT, absent 　26
Nantes - #267: Pierre RICHARD m. ca. 1762 Blanche LEBLANC SM - #822: additional family information	**19th family (5 persons)** Pierre RICHARD 　　plowman 　48 　Blanche LEBLANC, his wife 　46 　Marie RICHARD, his daughter 　19 　Pierre RICHARD, his son 　16 　Rose RICHARD, cousin of the above 　30
Nantes - #262: Tranquille PITRE s/o Amand & Geneviève ARSEMENT m. 1779 Élizabeth AUCOIN d/o Jean-Baptiste & Jeanne THERIOT	**20th family (4 persons)** Tranquille PITRE 　　wet cooper 　36 　Élizabeth AUCOIN, his wife 　46 　Jean Baptiste PITRE, his son 　3 　Jean Vincent PITRE, his son 　1

21st family (3 persons)

Jean RICHARD	laboureur	49
Margueritte LANDRY, sa femme		48
Jean Pierre, son fils		14

21st family

Jean RICHARD   Received 1 each of shovel and meat cleaver; 2 each of axe, hatchet and hoe.

22nd family (3 persons)

Marie Jᵉ RICHARD, veuve LANDRY	46
Marie Magdelaine, sa fille	16
Rose, idem	10

22nd family

Marie Josef RICHARD, veuve LANDRY   Received: 1 each of axe, shovel, meat cleaver; 2 each of hatchet and hoe.

23rd family (4 persons)

Marin POTREAU [Gotreaux]	charpentier	38
Gertrude BOURG, sa femme		38
Jean, son fils		14
Marie, sa fille		9

23rd family

Marin GOTREAU   Received: 1 each of shovel and meat cleaver; 2 each of axe, hatchet and hoe.

24th family (5 persons)

CHELLON, veuve BOURG	56
Jean Baptiste, son fils	16
André, idem	14
Charles, idem	11
Marie, sa fille	18

24th family

Jeanne CHELLON   Received: 1 each of axe, shovel and meat cleaver; 2 each of hatchel and hoe.

25th family (7 persons)

Anne HÉBERT, veuve BLANCHARD		47
Laurent, son fils	menuisier	19
Pierre, idem	imprimeur	15
Moise, idem	idem	13
Elie, idem	idem	11
Marie, sa fille		17
Anne, idem		7

25th family

Ana HEBERT   Received: 1 meat cleaver; 2 shovels; 3 each of axe, hatchet and 4 hoes.

26th family (3 persons)

Ursule BROD, veuve LEBLANC		65
Simon, son fils	journalier	23
Magdeleine LEBLANC, sa petite fille		11

26th family

Ursule BRAUD   Received: 1 each of axe, hatchet, shovel and meat cleaver; 2 hoes.

27th family (4 persons)

Gabriel MOREAU	journallier	61
Marie TRAHAN, sa femme		54
Maximin, son fils	imprimeur	24
Anne, sa fille		18

27th family

Gabriel MOREAU   Received: 1 each of shovel and meat cleaver; 2 each of axe, hatchet and hoe.

28th family (6 persons)

Pierre LANDRY	coloriste	48
Marthe LEBLANC, sa femme		49
Joseph, son fils	graveur	19
Jean Raphael, idem	imprimeur	17
Marie Margueritte, sa fille		15
Anne Susanne, idem		9

28th family

Pierre LANDRY   Received: 1 meat cleaver; 2 each of shovel and hatchet; 3 axe and 4 hoes.

17

BR - v.2, p.623: Jean Pierre RICHARD s/o Jean & Marguerite LANDRY m. 18 Sept. 1798 Isabelle AUCOIN d/o Joseph & Élizabeth HENRY

Chat - #125: Hilaire LANDRY s/o Jean-Baptiste & Marguerite COMMAUX m. 1763 Marie-Josèphe RICHARD d/o Pierre & Cécile GRANGER; a child Marie-Rose LANDRY b. 1774
SM - #594 & Nantes - #192: additional material

SM - #423: Marin GAUTROT s/o Honoré & Marguerite ROBICHAUX m. 1768 Gertrude BOURG d/o Jean & Françoise BENOIST
Census - p.123: Owned 6 arpents of land

Chat - #44: Jean BOURG m. ca. 1762 Jeanne CHAILLOU; a child Charles BOURG b. 1775
BR - v.2, p.120: Charles BOURG s/o Jean Baptiste & Jeanne CHAILOU m. 14 Feb. 1797 Isabelle DUPUIS d/o Joseph & Marie LANDRY

Nantes - #29: Joseph BLANCHARD d. 1783; m. ca. 1760 Anne-Symphore HÉBERT
SM - #89: additional family information
BR - v.2, p.91: Anne BLANCHARD of Nantes d/o Joseph & Anne HÉBERT m. 23 April 1798 Pierre BOURQUE of St. Malo s/o Marin & Osite DAIGLE
Census - p.123: Owned 6 arpents of land

Nantes- #211: Jean-Baptiste LEBLANC d. 1784; m. ca. 1738 Ursule BRAUD; a child Simon b. 1761
SM - #638: additional family information

Exile - p.331: children of Gabriel MOREAU & Marie TRAHAN: François-Marie b. 31 July 1769, Germain-Marie b. 1767, Marie-Anne b. 1765, Pierre Vincent b. 1764

Nantes - #200: Pierre LANDRY s/o Pierre & Anne THERIOT m. ca. 1764 Marthe LEBLANC; children: Anne-Suzanne bt. 1776, Jean Raphael b. 1768

SM - #607: additional family information

21st family (3 persons)
Jean RICHARD   plowman   49
  Marguerite LANDRY, his wife   48
  Jean Pierre RICHARD, his son   14

22nd family (3 persons)
Marie Josèphe RICHARD, widow LANDRY   46
  Marie Magdelaine LANDRY, her daughter   16
  Rose LANDRY, idem   10

23rd family (4 persons)
Marin GAUTROT   carpenter   38
  Gertrude BOURG, his wife   38
  Jean GAUTROT, his son   14
  Marie GAUTROT, his daughter   9

24th family (5 persons)
Jeanne CHELLON, widow BOURG   56
Jean Baptiste BOURG, her son   16
  André BOURG, her son   14
  Charles BOURG, her son   11
  Marie BOURG, her daughter   18

25th family (7 persons)
Anne HÉBERT, widow BLANCHARD   47
  Laurent BLANCHARD, son   woodworker   19
  Pierre BLANCHARD, son   printer   15
  Moise BLANCHARD, son   printer   13
  Elie BLANCHARD, her son   printer   11
  Marie BLANCHARD, her daughter   17
  Anne BLANCHARD, her daughter   7

26th family (3 persons)
Ursule BRAUD, widow LEBLANC   65
  Simon LEBLANC, her son   day laborer   23
  Magdelaine LEBLANC, her granddaughter   11

27th family (4 persons)
Gabriel MOREAU   day laborer   61
  Marie TRAHAN, his wife   54
  Maximin MOREAU, his son   printer   24
  Anne MOREAU, his daughter   18

28th family (6 persons)
Pierre LANDRY   colorist   48
  Marthe LEBLANC, his wife   49
  Joseph LANDRY, his son   engraver   19
  Jean Raphael LANDRY, his son; printer   17
  Marie Marguerite LANDRY, his daughter   15
  Anne Susanne LANDRY, his daughter   9

29th family (3 persons)

Marie LEPRINCE, veuve TRAHAN		43
Antoine Joseph, son fils	journallier	19
Julie, sa soeur		22

29th family

Marie LEPRINCE   Received: 1 each of axe, hatchet, shovel and meat cleaver; 2 hoes.

30th family (9 persons)

Pierre BERTHRAND	manoeuvre	54
Catherine BOURG, sa femme		36
Amb[r]oise Belonny, fils	journalier	18
Jean Augustin, idem	idem	15
Louis, idem		2
Catherine, sa fille		13
Marie, sa idem		11
Adélaïde, idem		7
Anne Magdelene	à la mamelle	

30th family

Pierre BERTRAND   Received: 1 meat cleaver; 2 each of hatchet, hoe; 3 axe; 4 hoes.

31st family (3 persons)

Anne SAVARY, veuve POTTIER	38
Olivier, son fils	10
Jacques Silvin	7

31st family

Anne SAVARY   Received: 1 each of axe, hatchet, shovel and meat cleaver; 2 hoes.

32nd family (2 persons)

Pierre GOTREAU, garçon	charpentier	22
Agnès, sa soeur		26

32nd family

Pierre GOTRAU   Received 1 each of axe, hatchet, shovel, meat cleaver; 2 hoes.

33rd family (3 persons)

Pierre GOTREAU	laboureur	53
Marie DUPLESSIS, sa femme		47
Adélaïde, sa fille		9

33rd family

Pierre GOTRAU   Received: 1 each of axe, hatchet, shovel and meat cleaver; 2 hoes.

34th family (6 persons)

Jean Baptiste BARILLAUD	journalier	50
Marie DAIGLE, sa femme		45
Jacques, son fils	idem	19
Jean, idem	idem	15
Françoise, idem [probably François]		8
Perrine, sa fille		10

34th family

Jean Baptiste BARRILLOU   Received: 1 each of shovel and meat cleaver; 2 hatchets, 3 each of axe and hoe.

35th family (2 persons)

Veuve HÉBERT		57
Pierre Joseph, son fils	journalier	17

35th family

Anne Marie ROBICHAU   Received: 1 each of axe, hatchet, shovel, meat cleaver; 2 hoes.

36th family (8 persons)

Honoré PRAUD	charpentier	52
Elisabette LEBLANC, sa femme		45
Pierre, son fils		5
Charles, idem		3
Olive Élisabeth, sa fille		16
Marie Madeleine, idem		14
Jeanne, idem		8
Rose Marie, idem		3

36th family

Honoré BRAUD   Received: 1 meat cleaver; 2 each of axe, hatchet and shovel; 4 hoes.

Other References	Complete Listing	
Exile - p.303: the marriage of Joseph TRAHAN s/o Joseph & Anne THERIOT m. 1762 Marie LEPRINCE d/o Antoine & Judith BOUDROT	**29th family (3 persons)**	
	Marie LEPRINCE, widow TRAHAN	43
SM - #902: additional family information	Antoine Joseph TRAHAN, son; day laborer	19
	Julie LEPRINCE, her sister	22
Chat - #20: Pierre-Jacques BERTRAND s/o Pierre & Marie-Josèphe MOULAISON m. 1764 Catherine BOURG d/o Charles & Marguerite LANDRY; child Marie BERTRAND b. 1774	**30th family (9 persons)**	
	Pierre BERTRAND manual labor	54
	Catherine BOURG, his wife	36
	Ambroise Belony BERTRAND, son; laborer	18
	Jean Augustin BERTRAND, son; laborer	15
Nantes - #24: additional family information	Louis BERTRAND, his son	2
Exile - p.31: Pierre-Jacques BERTRAND m. 28 Feb. 1764 Catherine BOURG in Cherbourg, France	Catherine BERTRAND, his daughter	13
	Marie BERTRAND, his daughter	11
	Adélaïde BERTRAND, his daughter	7
	Anne Magdelaine BERTRAND, nursling	
	31st family (3 persons)	
SM - #790: Pierre POITIER m. 1771 Anne-Madeleine SAVARY; child Olivier POITIER b. 1772	Anne SAVARY, widow POITIER	38
	Olivier POITIER, her son	10
BR - v.2, p.600: Baptiste Olivier POITIER s/o Pierre & Anne Magdalen SAVARIS m. 30 April 1798 Isabelle NAQUIN d/o Michel & Isabelle HÉBERT	Jacques Silvin POITIER	7
	32nd family (2 persons)	
	Pierre GAUTROT, young man; carpenter	22
	Agnès GAUTROT, his sister	26
Chat - #86: Pierre GAUTROT m. ca. 1758 Marie-Louise DUPLESSIS d/o Claude-Antoine & Catherine LEJEUNE; a child Adélaïde GAUTROT b. 1774	**33rd family (3 persons)**	
	Pierre GAUTROT plowman	53
SM - #426: additional family information	Marie DUPLESSIS, his wife	47
Nantes - #131: additional family information	Adélaïde GAUTROT, his daughter	9
	34th family (6 persons)	
Chat - #9: Jean-Baptiste BARRILLOT s/o Pierre & Véronique GIROIRE m. 1764 Marie DAIGLE d/o Jean & Marie BRAUD; child François b. 1775	Jean Baptiste BARRILLOT day laborer	50
	Marie DAIGLE, his wife	45
	Jacques BARRILLOT, son day laborer	19
	Jean BARRILLOT, his son day laborer	15
Nantes - #16: additional family information	François BARRILLOT, his son	8
SM - #47: additional family information	Perrine BARRILLOT, his daughter	10
	35th family (2 persons)	
	Widow HÉBERT	57
	Pierre Joseph HÉBERT day laborer	17
	36th family (8 persons)	
Chat - #50: Honoré BRAUD s/o Pierre & Marguerite GAUTROT m. 1766 Élizabeth LEBLANC d/o Victor & Marie AUCOIN; a child Olive-Élizabeth BRAUD b. 1769	Honoré BRAUD carpenter	52
	Élizabeth LEBLANC, his wife	45
	Pierre BRAUD, his son	5
	Charles BRAUD, his son	3
	Olive Élizabeth BRAUD, his daughter	16
Nantes - #65: additional family information	Marie Magdelaine BRAUD, his daughter	14
SM - #199: additional family information	Jeanne BRAUD, his daughter	8
	Rose Marie BRAUD, his daughter	3

37th family (4 persons)

Prosper LANDRY	charpentier	60
Élisabeth PITRE, sa femme		55
Jean Pierre, son fils	idem	22
Simon, idem	idem	19

38th family (3 persons)

Marie Joseph LANDRY	32
François Jullien, son elève	3
Geneviève LANDRY, soeur	34

39th family (3 persons)

Jean Pierre BOURG	contremaître	42
Françoise, sa soeur		49
Isabelle, cousine au dit		33

40th family (4 persons)

Olivier LEBLANC	menuisier	38
Marie LEBERT, sa femme		23
Pierre, son fils	à la mamelle	
Marie, sa fille		3

41st family (4 persons)

Louis LE TOLLIERET	menuisier	41
Elisabette LEBLANC, sa femme		29
Henry Aimable, son fils		1
Marie Adélaïde, sa fille		4

42nd family (1 person)

Étienne LEBLANC	laboureur	36

43rd family (6 persons)

Jean OZELÉ	cieur de long	43
Margueritte LANDRY, sa femme		43
Jean Charles, son fils	imprimeur	18
Mathurin, idem	idem	13
Marie Charlotte, sa fille		10
Jullien, son fils		4

44th family (5 persons)

Jacques DOUAIZON	marin	40
Anne BROD, sa femme		38
Jean, son fils	marin	17
Joseph, idem		14
Ursule, sa fille		13

45th family (4 persons)

Isaac HéBERT	imprimeur	32
Marie DAIGLE, sa femme		32
Rémi, son fils		3
plus un enfant	à la mamelle	

37th family

Prosper LANDRY — Received: 1 each of axe, shovel, meat cleaver; 2 hatchet and hoe

Jean Pierre LANDRY — Received: 1 each of axe, hatchet, hoe, shovel and meat cleaver.

Geneviève LANDRY received: 1 each of axe, hatchet, shovel, meat cleaver; 2 hoes.

39th family

Jean Pierre BOURG — Received: 1 each of shovel and meat cleaver; 2 each of axe and hatchet; 3 hoes.

40th family

Olivier LEBLANC — Received: 1 each of axe, hatchet, shovel and meat cleaver; 2 hoes.

41st family

Louis LETULLIER — Received: 1 each of axe, hatchet, shovel and meat cleaver; 2 hoes.

42nd family

Étienne LEBLANC — Received: 1 each of axe, hatchet, shovel, meat cleaver; 2 hoes.

43rd family

Jean Baptiste OZELÉ — Received: 1 each of shovel and meat cleaver; 2 hatchets; 3 each of axe and hoe.

44th family

Jaques DOUESON — Received: 1 each of shovel and meat cleaver; 2 hatchets; 3 each of axe and hoe.

45th family

Isaac EBERT — Received: 1 each of axe, hatchet, shovel and meat cleaver; 2 hoes.

Nantes - #201: Prosper LANDRY s/o Jean-Baptiste & Marguerite COMMAUX m. 1761 Élizabeth PITRE d/o Jean & Marguerite THERIOT; a child Simon LANDRY b. 1765

SM - #610 & BR - v.2, p.426: additional material

SM - #591: Charles LANDRY s/o René & Anne THERIOT m. 7 Nov. 1740 Cécile LEBLANC d/o François & Jeanne HÉBERT; Their children:
Marie Joseph b. ca. 1750 [actually 1753 from age given on embarkation list]
Geneviève b. ca. 1748 [actually 1751 from age given]; m. 10 Nov. 1794 Francisco ROMAGOSA

Nantes - #217: Olivier LEBLANC s/o Victor & Marie AUCOIN m. 1781 Marie-Madeleine LEBERT d/o Charles & Anne ROBICHAUX; a child Pierre-Olivier bt. 1784

Chat - #145 Louis-François LE TOLLIERET s/o Julien & Madeleine LA HAYE m. 1772 Élizabeth LEBLANC d/o Felix & Marie-Josèphe THERIOT; a child Marie Adélaïde b. 1774
SM - #679: additional family information

Chat - #159 Jean-Baptiste OSELET s/o Jean & Jeanne MOYSE m. 1766 Marguerite LANDRY s/o Charles & Cécile LEBLANC; a child Mathurin b. 1772
Nantes - #254: additional family information
SM - #744: additional family information

Chat - #70: Jacques DOIRON s/o Thomas & Anne GIROIRE m. 1765 Anne-Josèphe BRAUD d/o Joseph & Ursule BOURG; a child Ursule DOIRON b. 1771
Census - p.124: Owned 6 arpents of land
Nantes - #104 & SM - #333: additional information

Nantes - #167: Isaac HÉBERT s/o Ambroise & Marie Madeleine BOURG m. 1780 Marie DAIGLE d/o Eustache & Madeleine DUPUIS; a child Rémi bt. 1782
Census - p.121: Owned 6 arpents of land

37th family (4 persons)

Prosper LANDRY	carpenter	60
Élizabeth PITRE, his wife		55
Jean Pierre LANDRY, son	carpenter	22
Simon LANDRY, his son	carpenter	19

38th family (3 persons)

Marie Joseph LANDRY	32
François Jullien, her charge	3
Geneviève LANDRY, sister	34

39th family (3 persons)

Jean Pierre BOURG	foreman	42
Françoise BOURG, his sister		49
Isabelle, cousin of the above		33

40th family (4 persons)

Olivier LEBLANC	woodworker	38
Marie LEBERT, his wife		23
Pierre LEBLANC, his son	a nursling	
Marie LEBLANC, his daughter		3

41st family (4 persons)

Louis LETULLIER	woodworker	41
Élizabeth LEBLANC, his wife		29
Henry Aimable LETULLIER, his son		1
Marie Adélaïde LETULLIER, his daughter		4

42nd family (1 person)

Étienne LEBLANC	plowman	36

43rd family (6 persons)

Jean OSELET	pit sawyer	43
Marguerite LANDRY, his wife		43
Jean Charles OSELET, son	printer	18
Mathurin OSELET, his son	printer	13
Marie Charlotte OSELET, his daughter		10
Julien OSELET, his son		4

44th family (5 persons)

Jacques DOIRON	sailor	40
Anne BRAUD, his wife		38
Jean DOIRON, his son	sailor	17
Joseph DOIRON, his son		14
Ursule DOIRON, his daughter		13

45th family (4 persons)

Isaac HÉBERT	printer	32
Marie DAIGLE, his wife		22
Rémi HÉBERT, his son		3
another child	nursling	

46th family (3 persons)

Natalie PITRE, veuve LEBLANC		50
Jean Baptiste, son fils	marin	17
Marie Geneviève, sa fille		15

46th family

Natalie PITRE — Received: 1 each of axe, hatchet, shovel and meat cleaver; 2 hoes.

47th family (3 persons)

Cécille BOUDREAU, veuve RICHARD		38
Marie Roze, sa fille		14
Jean BOUDREAU, frère de la ditte; marin		18

47th family

Cécile BODRAU — Received: 1 each of axe, hatchet, shovel and meat cleaver; 2 hoes.

48th family (2 persons)

Amand PITRE	laboureur	60
Margueritte, sa fille		24

48th family

Aman PITRE — Received: 1 each of axe, hatchet, shovel and meat cleaver; 2 hoes.

49th family (5 persons)

Amboise [Ambroise] DUGAST	marin	32
Marie Victoire PITRE, sa femme		31
Louis Ambroise, son fils		5
Anne Marie, sa fille		10
Céleste		1

49th family

Ambroise DUGATS — Received: 2 each of axe, hatchet, hoe; 1 each of shovel and meat cleaver.

50th family (3 persons)

Olivier TRAHAN	marin	54
Grégoire, son fils	cordonnier	18
Anne, sa fille		22

50th family

Olivier TRAHAN — Received: 1 each of shovel and meat cleaver; 2 each of axe, hatchet; 3 hoes.

51st family (2 persons)

Marie BRASSEUR, fille		35
Ozite, sa soeur		24

51st family

Marie BRASSEUR — Received: 1 each of axe, hatchet, shovel, meat cleaver; 2 hoes.

52nd family (5 persons)

Joseph TRAHAN	journalier	59
Marie BOUDREAU, sa femme		57
Ancelme, son fils	journalier	19
Marie, sa fille		18
Marguerite, idem		11

52nd family

Joseph TRAHAN — Received: 1 each of hatchet, shovel and meat cleaver; 3 hoes.

53rd family (2 persons)

Mathurin TRAHAN	imprimeur	24
Margueritte ORY, sa femme		19

53rd family

Maturin TRAHAN — Received: 1 each of axe, hatchet, shovel, meat cleaver; 2 hoes.

54th family (1 person)

Alexis DAIGLE	graveur	22

54th family

Alexis DAIGLE — Received: 1 each of axe, shovel, meat cleaver; 2 of hoe & hatchet.

55th family (6 persons)

Charles DUGAST	cieur de long	46
Jean Charles, son fils	marin	20
Pierre OLIVIER, idem	idem	18
Joseph, idem	idem	16
Marie Josèphe, sa fille		22
Margueritte, idem		4

55th family

Charles DUGAST — Received: 1 meat cleaver; 2 each of hatchet and shovel; 3 axes and 4 hoes.

Nantes - #213: Jean-Jacques LEBLANC s/o Jacques & Cécile DUPUIS m. 1766 Nathalie PITRE	**46th family (3 persons)**		
SM - #641b: additional family information	Natalie PITRE, widow LEBLANC		50
	Jean Baptiste LEBLANC, son; sailor		17
	Marie Geneviève LEBLANC, her daughter		15

46th family (3 persons)

Natalie PITRE, widow LEBLANC — 50
Jean Baptiste LEBLANC, son; sailor — 17
Marie Geneviève LEBLANC, her daughter — 15

Nantes - #213: Jean-Jacques LEBLANC s/o Jacques & Cécile DUPUIS m. 1766 Nathalie PITRE
SM - #641b: additional family information

47th family (3 persons)

Cécille BOUDROT, widow RICHARD — 38
Marie Roze RICHARD, her daughter — 14
Jean BOUDROT, brother of the above
    a sailor — 18

SM - #811: Charles RICHARD m. 1763 Cécile BOUDROT; a child Marie Rose RICHARD b. 1771

48th family (2 persons)

Amand PITRE   plowman — 60
Marguerite PITRE, his daughter — 24

49th family (5 persons)

Ambroise DUGAT   sailor — 32
Marie Victoire PITRE, his wife — 31
Louis Ambroise DUGAT, his son — 5
Anne Marie DUGAT, his daughter — 10
Céleste DUGAT — 1

Chat - #75: Ambroise DUGAST s/o Ambroise & Marguerite HENRY m. 1773 Marie PITRE d/o Amand & Geneviève ARSEMAN; a child Anne-Marie DUGAST b. 1774
Nantes - #109: additional family information

54th family (3 persons)

Olivier TRAHAN   sailor — 54
Grégoire TRAHAN, his son   shoemaker — 18
Anne TRAHAN, his daughter — 22

Nantes - #304: Olivier TRAHAN m. ca. 1759 Élizabeth LEJEUNE

51st family (2 persons)

Marie BRASSEUR, single woman — 35
Ozite BRASSEUR, her sister — 24

52nd family (5 persons)

Joseph TRAHAN   day laborer — 59
Marie BOUDROT, his wife — 57
Anselme TRAHAN, his son   day laborer — 19
Marie TRAHAN, his daughter — 18
Marguerite TRAHAN, his daughter — 11

Chat - #189: Joseph TRAHAN m. ca. 1754 Marie BOUDROT; a child Anselme TRAHAN b. 1766

Nantes - #299: additional family information
SM - #900: additional family information

53rd family (2 persons)

Mathurin TRAHAN   printer — 24
Marguerite ORY, his wife — 19

Nantes - #302: Mathúrin TRAHAN s/o Joseph & Marie BOUDROT m. 1784 Perrine-Marguerite ORRY d/o Charles & Perrine HERVE

54th family (1 person)

Alexis DAIGLE   engraver — 22

55th family (6 persons)

Charles DUGAT   pit sawyer — 46
Jean Charles DUGAT, son   sailor — 20
Pierre Olivier DUGAT, son   sailor — 18
Joseph DUGAT, his son   sailor — 16
Marie Josèphe DUGAT, his daughter — 22
Marguerite DUGAT, his daughter — 4

Chat - #76: Charles DUGAST s/o Claude & Marguerite COSTE m. Marguerite DAIGLE; children leaving Chatellerault for Nantes: Jean-Charles, Rene-Olivier, Joseph-Simon, Marie-Josèphe
Nantes - #110: additional family information

56th family (4 persons)

Pierre DUGAST	charpentier	57
Margueritte DAIGLE, sa femme		60
Anne, sa fille		23
Marie, idem		20

56th family

Pierre DUGATS Received: 1 each of axe, shovel and meat cleaver; 2 hatchets; 3 hoes.

57th family (4 persons)

Anne Ozite DUGAST, veuve HÉBERT	30
Charles, son fils	5
Anne, sa fille	4
Margueritte, idem	2

57th family

Anne Ozic DUGATS Received: 1 each of axe, shovel and meat cleaver; 2 each of hatchet and hoe.

58th family (8 persons)

Joseph BOURG	cieur de long	52
Marie Magdelene GRANGER, sa femme		54
Sebastien Joseph, son fils		19
Jean Baptiste, idem		17
Marie Josèphe, sa fille		21
Élisabeth, idem		14
Luce DAIGLE, nièce au dit		24
Margueritte DAIGLE, idem		17

58th family

Joseph BOURG Received: 1 meat cleaver; 2 each of hatchet and shovel; 3 each of axe and hoe.

59th family (2 persons)

| Pierre BOURG | commis | 24 |
| Margueritte DUGAST, sa femme | | 31 |

59th family

Pierre BOURG Received: 1 each of axe, hatchet, shovel and meat cleaver; 2 hoes.

60th family (6 persons)

Jean Baptiste LANDRY	laboureur	64
Isabelle DUGAST, sa femme		44
Jean Baptiste, son fils	tonellier	22
Isabelle, sa fille		24
Margueritte, idem		19
Anne, idem		9

60th family

Jean Baptiste LANDRY Received: 1 each of shovel and meat cleaver; 2 each of axe and hatchet; 3 hoes.

61st family (3 persons)

Marie DAIGRE, veuve BOUDREAU	44
Jean, son fils	11
Marie Roze, sa fille	21

61st family

Marie DAIGRE Received: 1 each of axe, hatchet, shovel and meat cleaver; 2 hoes.

62nd family (3 persons)

Paul DUGAST	charpentier	75
Simon, son fils	idem	37
Anne, sa fille		19

62nd family

Paul DUGATS Received: 1 each of axe, hatchet, shovel and meat cleaver.

Simon DUGATS Received 1 each of axe, hatchet, hoe, shovel and meat cleaver.

63rd family (2 persons)

| Joseph DUPUY | marin | 39 |
| Isabelle, sa fille | | 10 |

63rd family

Joseph DUPUY Received: 1 each of axe, hatchet, shovel and meat cleaver; 2 hoes.

Nantes - #119: Pierre DUGAST s/o Claude & Marguerite COSTE m. ca. 1751 Marguerite DAIGLE
SM - #369: additional family information
	56th family (4 persons)
	Pierre DUGAT carpenter 57
	  Marguerite DAIGLE, his wife 60
	  Anne DUGAT, his daughter 23
	  Marie DUGAT, his daughter 20

56th family (4 persons)

Pierre DUGAT — carpenter — 57
Marguerite DAIGLE, his wife — 60
Anne DUGAT, his daughter — 23
Marie DUGAT, his daughter — 20

Nantes - #163: Charles HÉBERT s/o Charles & Marguerite-Josèphe BOURG m. 1778 Anne-Osite DUGAST d/o Pierre & Marguerite DAIGLE

57th family (4 persons)

Anne Osite DUGAT, widow HÉBERT — 30
Charles HÉBERT, her son — 5
Anne HÉBERT, her daughter — 4
Marguerite HÉBERT, her daughter — 2

Nantes - #58: Joseph BOURG s/o Abraham & Marie THERIOT m. 1760 Marie-Madeleine GRANGER d/o Joseph & Angélique RICHARD; children: Jean Baptiste b. 1767, Élizabeth b. 1770

BR - v.2, p.123: Jean BOURG s/o Joseph & Marie Magdalen GRANGER of St. Malo m. 29 June 1789 Marie HÉBERT d/o Jean Baptiste & Marie Magdalen DUGAS

58th family (8 persons)

Joseph BOURG — pit sawyer — 52
Marie Magdelene GRANGER, his wife — 54
Sebastien Joseph BOURG, his son — 19
Jean Baptiste BOURG, his son — 17
Marie Josèphe BOURG, his daughter — 21
Élizabeth BOURG, his daughter — 14
Luce DAIGLE, niece of the above — 24
Marguerite DAIGLE, niece of the above — 17

Nantes - #61: Pierre BOURG m. 1784 Marguerite-Blanche DUGAST

59th family (2 persons)

Pierre BOURG — clerk — 24
Marguerite DUGAT, his wife — 31

Chat - #64: Jean-Baptiste LANDRY s/o Antoine & Marie LEBLANC m. ca. 1758 Élizabeth DUGAST; a child: Marie-Anne b. 1775, Isabelle b. 1760

60th family (6 persons)

Jean Baptiste LANDRY — plowman — 64
Isabelle DUGAT, his wife — 44
Jean Baptiste LANDRY, son; wet cooper — 22
Isabelle LANDRY, his daughter — 24
Marguerite LANDRY, his daughter — 19
Anne LANDRY, his daughter — 9

61st family (3 persons)

Marie DAIGLE, widow BOUDROT — 44
Jean BOUDROT, her son — 11
Marie Rose BOUDROT, her daughter — 21

Nantes - #39: Jean-Baptiste BOUDROT m. 1764 Marie DAIGLE; child Marie Rose b. 1764

62nd family (3 persons)

Paul DUGAT, — carpenter — 75
Simon DUGAT, his son — carpenter — 37
Anne DUGAT, his daughter — 19

63rd family (2 persons)

Joseph DUPUIS — sailor — 39
Isabelle DUPUIS, his daughter — 10

64th family (8 persons)			64th family
Prosper GIROIR	journalier	41	Prosper CHERVER Received: 1 meat cleaver; 2 shovels; 3 each of axe, hatchet; 4 hoes.
Marie DUGAST, sa femme		39	
Jean Baptiste, son fils	idem	15	
François, idem		11	
Pierre, idem		7	
Marie Paul, sa fille		20	
Anne, idem		18	
Jeanne, idem		13	

65th family (8 persons)			65th family
Magdeleine DUGAST, veuve HÉBERT		43	Magdeleine DUGATS Received: 1 meat cleaver; 2 shovels, 3 each of hoe, axe, hatchet.
Pierre, son fils	manoeuvre	18	
Joseph, idem	idem	15	
François, idem		5	
Étienne, idem	à la mamelle		
Anne, sa fille		20	
Marie, idem		17	
Isabelle, idem		13	

| 66th family (1 person) | | | 66th family |
| Margueritte SEGOILLOT, fille | | 19 | [apparently not listed] |

67th family (5 persons)			67th family
Eustache DAIGRE	charpentier	56	Eustache DAIGLE Received: 1 each of meat cleaver and shovel; 2 each of axe and hatchet; 3 hoes.
Magdeleine DUPUY, sa femme		44	
Jean, son fils		15	
Charles, idem		13	
Étienne, idem	à la mamelle		

68th family (2 persons)			68th family
Étienne DUPUY	marin	36	Étienne DUPUY Received: 1 each of axe, hatchet, shovel, meat cleaver; 2 hoes.
Marie DUGAST, sa femme		20	

69th family (2 persons)			69th family
Fabien AU COIN	charpentier	38	Fabian AUCOING Received: 1 each of axe, hatchet, shovel, meat cleaver; 2 hoes.
Margueritte DUPUY, sa femme		34	

70th family (5 persons)			70th family
Ambroise PITRE	marin	35	Ambroise PITRE Received: 1 meat cleaver; 2 each of axe and hatchet; 3 hoes
Elisabette DUGAST, sa femme		32	
Paul Ambroise, son fils		7	
Marie, sa fille		6	
Jean Marie, son fils		1	

| 71st family (1 persons) | | | 71st family |
| Joseph Benoît GOUDREAU | laboureur | 17 | [apparently not listed] |

| 72nd family (1 person) | | | 72nd family |
| Marie Roze LIVOIRE, fille | | 18 | [apparently not listed] |

Chat - #83: Prosper-Honoré GIROIRE s/o Honoré & Marie-Josèphe THERIOT m. 1764 Marie DUGAST d/o Paul & Marie BOUDROT; a child Jeanne b. 1771		

64th family (8 persons)

Prosper GIROIRE	day laborer	41
Marie DUGAT, his wife		39
Jean Baptiste GIROIRE, son	day laborer	15
François GIROIRE, his son		11
Pierre GIROIRE, his son		7
Marie Paul GIROIRE, his daughter		20
Anne GIROIRE, his daughter		18
Jeanne GIROIRE, his daughter		13

Chat - #83: Prosper-Honoré GIROIRE s/o Honoré & Marie-Josèphe THERIOT m. 1764 Marie DUGAST d/o Paul & Marie BOUDROT; a child Jeanne b. 1771
Census - p.122: owned 6 arpents of land

SM - #442: additional family information
Nantes - #133: additional family information

65th family (8 persons)

Magdeleine DUGAT, widow HÉBERT		43
Pierre HÉBERT, her son	manual labor	18
Joseph HÉBERT, her son	manual labor	15
François HÉBERT, her son		5
Étienne HÉBERT, her son	a nursling	
Anne HÉBERT, her daughter		20
Marie HÉBERT, her daughter		17
Isabelle HÉBERT, her daughter		13

Chat - #110 Jean-Baptiste HÉBERT d. 1784; m. ca. 1758 Marie-Madeleine DUGAST d/o Paul & Marguerite-Marie BOUDROT; child Isabelle b. 1772
Census - p.122: owned 6 arpents of land

Nantes - #168: additional family information
SM - #516: additional family information

66th family (1 person)

Marguerite SEGOILLOT, single girl	19

67the family (5 persons)

Eustache DAIGLE	carpenter	56
Magdelaine DUPUIS, his wife		44
Jean DAIGLE, his son		15
Charles DAIGLE, his son		13
Étienne DAIGLE, his son	nursling	

Nantes - #85 Eustache DAIGLE s/o Bernard & Angélique RICHARD m. 1759 Madeleine DUPUIS d/o Charles & Madeleine TRAHAN
Census - p.122: Owned 6 arpents of land
SM - #290: additional family information

68th family (2 persons)

Étienne DUPUIS	sailor	36
Marie DUGAT, his wife		20

Nantes - #122: Étienne DUPUIS m. 1784 Marie-Osite DUGAST
SM - #379: additional family information
Census - p.122: Owned 6 arpents of land

Census - p.122: Owned 6 arpents of land

69th family (2 persons)

Fabien AUCOIN	carpenter	38
Marguerite DUPUIS, his wife		34

70th family (5 persons)

Ambroise PITRE	sailor	35
Élizabeth DUGAT, his wife		32
Paul Ambroise PITRE, his son		9
Marie PITRE, his daughter		6
Jean Marie PITRE, his son		1

Chat - #162: Ambroise PITRE s/o Amant & Geneviève ARSEMAN m. 1774 Élizabeth DUGAST d/o Paul & Marie BOUDROT; child Paul-Ambroise b. 1775

SM - #767: additional family information

71st family (1 person)

Joseph Benoît GAUTROT	plowman	17

72nd family (1 person)

Marie Rose LIVOIS, single girl	18

<u>Individuals listed - having received the following</u>:

François FRIOU   Received: 1 each of
    axe, hatchet, shovel and meat cleaver; 2 hoes

Antoine MOLLARD   Received 1 each of
    axe, hatchet, shovel and meat cleaver; 2 hoes

Pierre AUCOING   Received: 1 each of
    axe, hatchet, shovel and meat cleaver; 2 hoes

"Liste des passagers Acadiens nommés pour s'embarquer dans le Navire <u>La Bergère</u> allant à La Nouvelle Orleans dans la Louisiane."

"Nous, Consul d'Espagne en Bretagne chargé de l'expedition des Acadiens pour la Louisiane certifions que les deux cent soixante sept personnes mentionnées dans la presente Liste ont été nommée par nous pour s'embarquer dans le Navire <u>La Bergère</u> Armateur Mr. Th. Nonneron Dupin pour passer à la Louisiane. A Nantes ce sept avril 1785. d'Asprer   Marine 458

"Relacion de los Utiles que deben entregarse a los familias Acadianas venidas de Nantes en la Fragata <u>La Bergère</u>, y so las siguientes."

<u>Translation</u>:
List of Acadian passengers designated to embark on the ship <u>La Bergère</u> [300 tons] going to New Orleans in Louisiana.

"We, consul for Spain in Brittany charged with the transporting of the Acadians to Louisiana certifying that the 267 persons mentioned in the present list have been named to embark on the ship <u>La Bergère</u>...at Nantes 7 April 1785

Tools given the Acadian families arriving from Nantes on the frigate <u>La Bergère</u>.

On 7 May, just prior to the departure of Le Bon Papa, 273 passengers representing 73 families were booked for La Bergère. They chose 5 leaders among themselves to preserve peace aboard ship: Oliver Terrio, Charles Dugas, Charles Aucoin, Simon Dugas and Étienne Dupuy. Besides the Acadian Exiles, La Bergère carried 5 French passengers. Arrived in New Orleans without any mishap. Dr. Étienne Fouginet reported 7 births, 6 deaths. The group remained encamped until 4 October at new Orleans, during which the group increased by 12 additional births (including the 7 aboard ship), 5 new adherents and 4 marriages; also 15 deaths (including 6 during the voyage) and 1 desertion. [Winzerling p.134-136]

The group chose La Fourche (area around Plattenville south of Donaldsonville) in the district of Valenzuela. The expedition now numbered 74 families of 268 persons. Six families of 23 persons had chosen Atacapas (area of St. Martinville), 1 family of 3 persons went to Manchac (area around St. Gabriel). [Winzerling p.136]

Juan Prieto, on orders of Martin Navarro, equiped each able worker in the 74 families of La Bergère expedition with farming tools of axes, medium and small hatchets, shovels, hoes and meat cleavers. Cuba legajo 576. Relating the tools distributed to Acadian families: Azados-hoe, Hachas-axe, Chiras-hatchet, cuchillos- meat cleaver or large knife, palas-shovel.

Individuals listed -
François FRIOU

Antoine MOLLARD

Pierre AUCOIN

1st family (9 persons)

Simon DAIGRE	charpentier	49
Anne MICHEL, sa femme		58
Edouard, son fils	idem	21
Simon Pierre, idem	idem	18
Joseph Michel, idem		9
Marie Marguerite, sa fille		24
Anne Geneviève, idem		22
Elisabette, idem		13
Marie Magdelaine, idem		11

2nd family (9 persons)

Olivier DAIGRE	charpentier	53
Victor, son fils	idem	23
François, idem	idem	19
Simon, idem	tonellier	18
Jean Baptiste, idem	journallier	15
Honoré, idem		3
Marie, sa fille		11
Pélagie, idem		9
Eulalie, idem		8

3rd family (6 persons)

Charles HENRY	charpentier	51
Marie LEBLANC, sa femme		45
Marie Magdelaine, sa fille		21
Rose Anastasie, idem		14
Ursule, idem		10
Charles ROBICHAUD, fils de la femme		
	charpentier	17

4th family (6 persons)

Pierre RICHARD	charpentier	74
Françoise DAIGLE, sa femme		55
Anselme, son fils	marin	20
Joseph, idem	charpentier	18
Auguste, idem		11
Marie, sa fille		14

5th family (4 persons)

Pierre LAVERGNE	charpentier	54
Pierre, son fils		12
Victoire, sa fille		22
Marie Magdelaine, idem		12

6th family (5 persons)

Marie Josèphe GRANGER, veuve TRAHAN		46
Jean Baptiste, son fils	charpentier	25
Paul Raymond, idem	idem	19
Marie Renée, sa fille		13
Marie Margueritte, idem		8

1st family (9 persons)

Simon D'AIGLE
   Ana MICHEL, su muger
   Eduardo, su hijo
   Simon, ydem
   Josef, ydem
   Maria Margarita, ydem
   Ana Genoveva, ydem
   Ysabel, ydem
   Maria, idem

2nd family (9 persons)

Olivier D'AIGLE
   Victorio, su hijo
   Fran^{co}, ydem
   Simon, ydem
   Juan Bautista, ydem
   Onorato, ydem
   Maria, Ydem
   Pelagia, idem
   Eulalia, ydem

3rd family (6 persons)

Carlos HENRIQUE
   Maria LEBLANC, su muger
   Marie Magdalena, su hija
   Rosa-Anastasia, idem
   Ursula, idem
   Carlos ROBICHEAU, hija de Maria
* NOTE- Esta familias hu pasado a los
   Atacapaz con tha de 18 de Oct. 1785

4th family (6 persons)

Pedro RICHARD
   Francisca D'AIGLE, su muger
   Anselmo, su hijo
   Josef, ydem
   Augusto, ydem
   Maria, ydem

5th family (3 persons)

Pedro LA VERGNE
   Pedro, su hijo
   Maria Magdalena, ydem

6th family (4 persons)

Juan Bautista TRAHAM, hijo de
   Maria Josefa GRANCHER
   Pablo Raymundo, ydem
   Maria Reyna, ydem
   Maria Margarita, ydem

Nantes - #94: Simon-Pierre DAIGLE s/o Olivier & Françoise GRANGER m. 1785 Anne MICHEL d/o Louis & Marguerite FOREST

1st family (9 persons)

Simon DAIGLE	carpenter	49
Anne MICHEL, his wife		58
Edouard DAIGLE, his son	carpenter	21
Simon Pierre DAIGLE, son	carpenter	18
Joseph Michel DAIGLE, his son		9
Marie Marguerite DAIGLE, his daughter		24
Anne Geneviève DAIGLE, his daughter		22
Élizabeth DAIGLE, his daughter		13
Marie Magdelaine DAIGLE, his daughter		11

Nantes - #92: Olivier DAIGLE s/o Olivier & Françoise GRANGER m. 1758 Marie-Blanche LEBLANC d/o Charles & Élizabeth THIBODEAUX

BR - v.2, p.219: Simon DAIGLE s/o Olivier & Marie Blanche LEBLANC of Belle Isle-en-Mer m. 4 Nov. 1794 Anne Marie LANDRY d/o Grineo & Marguerite BALA

2nd family (9 persons)

Olivier DAIGLE	carpenter	53
Victor DAIGLE, his son	carpenter	23
François DAIGLE, his son	carpenter	19
Simon DAIGLE, his son	wet cooper	18
Jean Baptiste DAIGLE, son	day laborer	15
Honoré DAIGLE, his son		3
Marie DAIGLE, his daughter		11
Pélagie DAIGLE, his daughter		9
Eulalie DAIGLE, his daughter		8

Nantes - #176: Charles HENRY s/o Joseph & Christine PITRE m. Marie LEBLANC; a child Jean Baptiste b. 28 October 1785

3rd family (6 persons)

Charles HENRY	carpenter	51
Marie LEBLANC, his wife		45
Marie Magdelaine HENRY, his daughter		21
Rose Anastasie HENRY, his daughter		14
Ursule HENRY, his daughter		10
Charles ROBICHAUX, wife's son; carpenter		17

* NOTE- This family went on to Attakapas on 18 October 1785.

Exile - p.383: Children of Pierre RICHARD & Françoise DAIGLE:
Pierre-Auguste b. 11 Jan. 1774
Anselme b. 3 Feb. 1765
Julien-Marie b. 17 Nov. 1768

BR - v.2, p.621: Anselme RICHARD s/o Pierre & Françoise DEGLET [DAIGLE] bur. 26 Jan. 1786 at age 21 years

4th family (6 persons)

Pierre RICHARD	carpenter	74
Françoise DAIGLE, his wife		55
Anselme RICHARD, his son	sailor	20
Joseph RICHARD, his son	carpenter	18
Auguste RICHARD, his son		11
Marie RICHARD, his daughter		14

5th family (4 persons)

Pierre LAVERGNE	carpenter	54
Pierre LAVERGNE, his son		12
Victoire LAVERGNE, his daughter		22
Marie Magdelaine LAVERGNE, daughter		12

Nantes - #307 Pierre-Simon TRAHAN s/o Joseph & Marie BLANCHARD m. 1758 Marie-Josèphe GRANGER; a child Marguerite bt. 1777

BR - v.2, p.705: Jean Baptiste TRAHAN s/o Pierre Simon & Josèphe GRANGET m. 22 May 1786 Anne Geneviève DAIGLE d/o Simon Pierre & Magdalen TERIOT

6th family (5 persons)

Marie Josèphe GRANGER, widow TRAHAN		46
Jean Baptiste TRAHAN, son	carpenter	25
Paul Raymond TRAHAN, son; carpenter		19
Marie Renée TRAHAN, her daughter		13
Marie Marguerite TRAHAN, her daughter		8

7th family (6 persons)
Anne GRANGER, veuve TRAHAN		49
Joseph, son fils	journallier	21
François Marie, idem	idem	12
Margueritte, sa fille		24
Marie Anne, idem		16
Julie, idem		14

7th family (4 persons)
Josef TRAHAM, hijo de Anan GRANCHER
  Fran^co, ydem
  Mariana, ydem
  Julia, idem

8th family (6 persons)
Joseph GUÉDRY	calfat	36
Magdelaine COMMEAU, sa femme		34
Joseph, son fils		2
Marie, sa fille		9
Margueritte, idem		7
Reine Elisabette, idem	à la mamelle	

8th family (6 persons)
Josef GUÉDRY
  Magdalena CAUMMEAU, su muger
  Josef, su hijo
  Maria, ydem
  Reyna Ysabel, de pecho
  Margarita, idem

9th family (2 persons)
Charles COMMEAU	charpentier	37
Marie CLAUSINET		

9th family (2 persons)
Carlos COUMMEAU
  Margarita Josef, su muger

10th family (3 persons)
Jean Baptiste HÉBERT	laboureur	32
Anne Dorothée, sa femme		34
Anne Margueritte, sa fille	à la mamelle	

10th family (3 persons)
Juan Bautista EBERT
  Ana Dorotea, su muger
  Ana Margarita, hija de pecho

11th family (3 persons)
Jean DOUAIRON	laboureur	57
Margueritte Josèphe, sa fille		20
Paul DAIGLE, mineur	idem	18

11th family (2 persons)
Juan DOUARON
  Margarita Josefa, su hija

12th family (1 person)
Pablo D'AIGLE, huerfano

12th family (2 persons)
Anne BENOIT, veuve HÉBERT	48
Jean Charles, son fils	13

14th family (2 persons)
Ana VENOI, viuda EBERT
Juan Carlos, su hijo

13th family (5 persons)
Marie MARTIN, veuve COURTIN		47
Jacques Marie, son fils	journallier	16
Françoise, sa fille		22
Mathurine Olive, idem		20
Charlotte Louise, idem		11

46th family (3 persons)
Maria MARTINA, viuda COURTIN
  Santiago Maria, su hijo
  Juana Luisa, ydem

14th family (7 persons)
Pierre POTIER	charpentier	45
Agnès BROUSSARD, sa femme		31
Charles Victor, son fils		16
Pierre Laurent, idem		10
François Constant, idem	à la mamelle	
Constance, sa fille		14
Anne Pauline, idem		12

13th family (7 persons)
Pedro POTIEU
  Ynes BRAUZARD, su muger
  Carlos, su hijo
  Pedro Laurenzo, idem
  Fran^co, ydem
  Constanza, ydem
  Ana, ydem
* NOTE- Paso a los Atacapas

Nantes - #298: Joseph TRAHAN s/o Joseph & Marie BLANCHARD m. 1757 Anne GRANGER d/o François & Anne LANDRY	**7th family (6 persons)**	
	Anne GRANGER, widow TRAHAN	49
	Joseph TRAHAN, her son day laborer	21
	François Marie TRAHAN, son; day laborer	12
	Marguerite TRAHAN, her daughter	24
	Marie Anne TRAHAN, her daughter	16
	Julie TRAHAN, her daughter	14
Chat - #91: Joseph GUÉDRY s/o Claude & Anne LEJEUNE m. 1772 Magdeleine COMMAUX d/o Joseph & Marguerite HÉBERT	**8th family (6 persons)**	
	Joseph GUÉDRY calker	36
Census - p.122: Owned 6 arpents of land	Magdelaine COMEAUX, his wife	34
	Joseph GUÉDRY, his son	2
SM - #466: additional family information	Marie GUÉDRY, his daughter	9
Nantes - #141: additional family information	Marguerite GUÉDRY, his daughter	7
	Reine Élizabeth GUÉDRY, daughter; nursling	
	9th family (2 persons)	
	Charles COMEAUX carpenter	37
	Marie CLOSSINET	
Nantes - #171: Jean-Pierre HÉBERT s/o Pierre & Anne BENOIST m. 1784 Anne-Dorothée DOIRON d/o Jean & Anne THIBODAUX; a child Anne-Marguerite HÉBERT bt. 1785	**10th family (3 persons)**	
	Jean Baptiste HÉBERT plowman	32
	Anne Dorothée [DOIRON], his wife	34
	Anne Marguerite HÉBERT, daughter; nursling	
	11th family (3 persons)	
	Jean DOIRON plowman	57
	Marguerite Josèphe DOIRON, daughter	20
	Paul DAIGLE, a minor and an orphan;	
	#12 on the debarkation list laborer	18
Exile - p.185 & SM - #515: Jean Baptiste HÉBERT s/o Jean & Marguerite TRAHAN m. 6 Feb. 1770 Anne BENOIST d/o Pierre & Élizabeth LEJUGE; a child: Jean Charles HÉBERT b. 6 Jan. 1772	**12th family (2 persons)**	
	Anne BENOIT, widow HÉBERT	48
	Jean Charles HÉBERT, her son	13
	13th family (5 persons)	
BR - v.2, p.205: Mathurine Olive COURTIN d/o Louis & Marie MARTIN m. 3 July 1786 Jean RAMIREZ of Spain s/o François & Bernarde CORRALES	Marie MARTIN, widow COURTIN	47
	Jacques Marie COURTIN, son; day laborer	16
	Françoise COURTIN, her daughter	22
	Mathurine Olive COURTIN, her daughter	20
	Charlotte Louise COURTIN, her daughter	11
	14th family (7 persons)	
Nantes - #263: Pierre POITIER s/o Pierre & Marie DOUCET m. 1783 Agnès BROUSSARD d/o Joseph & Ursule LEBLANC; a child François-Constant POITIER bt. 1784	Pierre POITIER carpenter	45
	Agnès BROUSSARD, his wife	31
	Charles Victor POITIER, his son	16
	Pierre Laurent POITIER, his son	10
	François Constant POITIER, son; a nursling	
	Constance POITIER, his daughter	14
	Anne Pauline POITIER, his daughter	12
	*NOTE- This family went to Attakapas	

15th family (7 persons)			15th family (7 persons)
Jean DOUAISON	charpentier	45	Juan Bautista LOUARON
Marie Blanche BERNARD, sa femme		43	Maria Blanca RAINARD, su muger
Louis Toussaint, son fils		3	Luis Santos, su hijo
Jean Charles, idem		2	Juan Carlos, idem
Marie, sa fille		17	Maria, su hija
Rose, idem		13	Rosa, idem
Ursule, idem		6	Yrsula, idem
			* NOTE- Paso a los Atacapas

16th family (6 persons)			16th family (6 persons)
François DAIGLE	laboureur	40	Franco D'AIGLE
Jeanne AULAI, sa femme		47	Juana AULAI, su muger
Louis, son fils	calfat	18	Luis, su hijo
Jeanne, sa fille		16	Juana, ydem
Adélaïde, idem		15	Adelaida, ydem
Louise, idem		10	Luisa, idem

17th family (5 persons)			17th family (5 persons)
François ARBOURG	calfat	45	Franco ARBOURG
Marie HERVORY, sa femme		40	Maria HENRIQUE, su muger
François Henry, son fils	marin	18	Francisco, su hijo
Jean Louis Fermin, idem		15	Juan Luis, idem
Frédéric Edouard, idem		13	Federico, idem

18th family (4 persons)			18th family (4 persons)
Joseph TRAHAN		44	Josef TRAHAM
Margueritte LAVERGNE, sa femme		30	Margarita LAVERGNE, su muger
Joseph Rémi, son fils		4	Josef Remigio, su hijo
Antoinette, sa fille		2	Antonia, ydem

19th family (3 persons)			19th family (3 persons)
Pélagie DOUAISON veuve LALANDE		31	Pelagia DOUARON, viuda LA LENDE
Jean Edouard, son fils		8	Juan Eduardo LALENDE, su hijo
Emelie, sa fille		11	Emilia, ydem

20th family (2 persons)			20th family (2 persons)
Jean Baptiste LAGARENNE	laboureur	55	Juan Bautista LAGARINE
Anne DOUAISON, sa femme		46	Ana DOUARON, su muger

21st family (1 person)			21st family (1 person)
Margueritte Josèphe DOUAISON veuve DUGAST		50	Margarita DOUARON viuda DUGATS

22nd family (5 persons)			22nd family (4 persons)
Pierre HÉBERT	journallier	45	Pedro EBERT
Charlotte POTIER, sa femme		41	Carlotta POTIEU, su muger
Anne, sa fille		11	Ana, su hija
Jean HÉBERT, frère du dit	idem	40	Pedro, ydem niño depecho
Pierre Joseph, son fils	à la mamelle		

			23rd family (1 person)
			Juan Bautista EBERT, paso a los Atacapas

Chat - #71: Jean-Baptiste DOIRON m. ca. 1765 Marie-Blanche
    BERNARD

Exile - p.113: The children of Jean-Baptiste DOIRON &
    Marie-Blanche BERNARD:
    Emelie b. 26 October 1766
    Marie-Hypolithe Honoré b. 13 July 1768

Nantes - #106: additional family information

15th family (7 persons)		
Jean Baptiste DOIRON	carpenter	45
Marie Blanche BERNARD, his wife		43
Louis Toussaint DOIRON, his son		3
Jean Charles DOIRON, his son		2
Marie DOIRON, his daughter		17
Rose DOIRON, his daughter		13
Ursule DOIRON, his daughter		6

* NOTE- this family went on to Attakapas

Exile - p.94: François DAIGLE s/o Abraham & Anne
    BOUDROT m. 1761 Jeanne HOLLEY d/o Thomas
    & Scolastique LE GENTILHOMME; a child Louis
    b. 1766

16th family (6 persons)		
François DAIGLE	plowman	40
Jeanne HOLLEY, his wife		47
Louis DAIGLE, his son	calker	18
Jeanne DAIGLE, his daughter		16
Adélaïde DAIGLE, his daughter		15
Louise DAIGLE, his daughter		10

Chat - #104: François HAMBOURG s/o François &
    Thérèse DESCOUTEAUX m. 1765 Marie HENRY
    d/o Joseph & Christine PITRE

BR - v.2, p.20: François HAMBOURG m. 27 Sept.
    1790 Marie Jeanne DAIGLE

17th family (5 persons)		
François HARBOURG	calker	45
Marie HENRY, his wife		40
François Henry HARBOURG, his son; sailor		18
Jean Louis Firmin HARBOURG, his son		15
Frédéric Edouard HARBOURG, his son		13

Nantes - #300 Joseph TRAHAN s/o Claude & Anne
    LEBLANC m. 1778 Marguerite LAVERGNE d/o
    Pierre & Anne LORD; a child: Antoinette bt. 1782

18th family (4 persons)	
Joseph TRAHAN	44
Marguerite LAVERGNE, his wife	30
Joseph Rémi TRAHAN, his son	4
Antoinette TRAHAN, his daughter	2

Chat - #119: Joseph LALANDE m. ca. 1772 Marie-
    Pélagie DOIRON; a child Emilie LALANDE b.
    1774

19th family (3 persons)	
Pélagie DOIRON widow LALANDE	31
Jean Edouard LALANDE, her son	8
Emelie LALANDE, her daughter	11

20th family (2 persons)		
Jean Baptiste LAGARENNE	plowman	**55**
Anne DOIRON, his wife		46

Exile - p.123-124: Jean Baptiste DUGAT m. Marguerite
    Josèphe DOIRON; Children: Jean Baptiste b. 22 Jan.
    1770, Jean Pierre b. 4 July 1764, Pierre b. 26 Sept.
    1766, Jean Marie Alexis b. 7 June 1763

21st family (1 person)	
Marguerite Josèphe DOIRON	
widow DUGAT	50

Nantes - #174: Pierre HÉBERT s/o Pierre & Marie
    BERNARD m. 1783 Charlotte POITIER d/o Chris-
    topher & Anne BOUDROT; child Pierre-Joseph bt.
    1785

22nd family (5 persons)		
Pierre HÉBERT	day laborer	45
Charlotte POITIER, his wife		41
Anne HÉBERT, his daughter		11
Jean HÉBERT, brother of the above;		
	a day laborer	40
Pierre Joseph HÉBERT, his son; a nursling		

* NOTE- Jean Baptiste HÉBERT went
    to Attakapas

23rd family (4 persons)

François Alexandre DAIGLE	laboureur	22
Rose Adélaïde BOURG, sa femme		19
Emelie Adélaïde, sa fille		1
François Joseph, son fils	à la mamelle	

24th family (4 persons)

Fran^co Alexandro D'AIGLE
   Rosa Adelaida BOURG, su muger
   Emilia Adelaida, su hija
   Juan Josef, ydem   depecho

24th family (5 persons)

Moïse LEBLANC	calfat	24
Angélique DE LA FORESTERIE, sa femme		24
Jean Martin, son fils		1
Marie Josèphe, sa fille		3
Marie Josèphe BELMER, cousine au dit		16

25th family (1 person)

Rosa DOUARON, tiene su Marido ausente

25th family (4 persons)

Jean GUÉDRY	calfat	50
Marie LEBLANC, sa femme		50
Jean, son fils	charpentier	27
Jacques, idem	idem	17

26th family (5 persons)

Juan GUÉDRY
   Maria LEBLANC, su muger
   Juan, su hijo
   Santiago, idem
   Maria Josef BELLEME, su prima

26th family (5 persons)

Joseph LEBLANC	calfat	17
Jacques, son frère	charpentier	14
François, idem	cordier	13
Magdelaine, sa soeur		11
Geneviève, idem		9

27th family (4 persons)

Josef LEBLANC
   Santiago, su hermano
   Fran^co, idem
   Magdalena, ydem

27th family (5 persons)

Charles GUÉDRY	cieur de long	57
Joseph, son fils	charpentier	18
Jean, idem	journallier	17
Jacques, idem	idem	15
Anne Laurence, sa fille		26

28th family (4 persons)

Carlos GUÉDRY
   Josef, su hijo
   Juan, idem
   Ana Lorenza, ydem

28th family (2 persons)

Pierre GUÉDRY	charpentier	23
Louise BLANDIN, sa femme		27

29th family (2 persons)

Pedro GUÉDRY
   Luisa BLANDIN, su muger

29th family (2 persons)

Joseph BROD	marin	23
Marie TRAHAN, sa femme		19

30th family (2 persons)

Josef BREAUD
   Maria TRAHAM, su muger

30th family (2 persons)

François Xavier BOUDREAU	charpentier	25
Margueritte DUGAST, sa femme		24

31st family (2 persons)

Fran^co Xavier BAUDREAUD
   Margarita DUGATS, su muger

Nantes - #86: François-Alexandre DAIGLE s/o François & Jeanne AULAY m. ca. 1782 RoseAdélaïde BOURG d/o Joseph & Rose DOIRON

Exile - p.94: François Alexandre DAIGLE s/o François & Jeanne HOLLEZ b. 3 Feb. 1763

Nantes - #216: Moyse LEBLANC s/o Jean-Baptiste & Marguerite BELLEMERE m. 1780 Angélique DE LA FORESTRIE d/o Jean & Marie BONNIERE

BR - v.2, p.340: Jean GUÉDRY s/o Jean & Marie LEBLANC m. 8 March 1786 Céleste BUDRO d/o Pierre & Magdalen BURQUE
Jacques GUÉDRY s/o Jean & Marie LEBLANC m. Marie BONVILIN buried 15 Oct. 1801 at age 34 years.

Nantes - #68: Joseph BRAUD s/o Joseph & Marie-Madeleine VINCENT m. 1785 Marie-Blanche TRAHAN d/o Louis-Athanase & Marguerite LEBLANC

Nantes - #36: François-Xavier BOUDROT s/o Antoine & Brigitte PART m. 1785 Marguerite DUGAST d/o Claude & Marguerite CYR

23rd family (4 persons)

François Alexandre DAIGLE	plowman	22
Rose Adélaïde BOURG, his wife		19
Emelie Adélaïde DAIGLE, his daughter		1
François Joseph DAIGLE, his son; nursling		

24th family (5 persons)

Moise LEBLANC	calker	24
Angélique DE LA FORESTERIE, his wife		24
Jean Martin LEBLANC, his son 1		
Marie Josèphe LEBLANC, his daughter		3
Marie Josèphe BELMER, cousin of the above		16

24-A family (1 person)

Rosa DOIRON, her husband is absent

25th family (4 persons)

Jean GUÉDRY	calker	50
Marie LEBLANC, his wife		50
Jean GUÉDRY, his son	carpenter	27
Jacques GUÉDRY, his son	carpenter	17

26th family (5 persons)

Joseph LEBLANC	calker	17
Jacques LEBLANC, his brother; carpenter		14
François LEBLANC, his brother; ropemaker		13
Magdelaine LEBLANC, his sister		11
Geneviève LEBLANC, his sister		9

27th family (5 persons)

Charles GUÉDRY	pit sawyer	57
Joseph GUÉDRY, his son	carpenter	18
Jean GUÉDRY, his son	day laborer	17
Jacques GUÉDRY, his son	day laborer	15
Anne Laurence GUÉDRY, his daughter		26

28th family (2 persons)

Pierre GUÉDRY	carpenter	23
Louise BLANDIN, his wife		27

29th family (2 persons)

Joseph BRAUD	sailor	23
Marie TRAHAN, his wife		19

30th family (2 persons)

François Xavier BOUDROT	carpenter	25
Marguerite DUGAT, his wife		24

31st family (5 persons)				32nd family (5 persons)	
Jacques MOULAISON	charpentier	38		Santiago MOULAISON	
Marie DOUAISON, sa femme		41		Maria DOUAIRON, su muger	
Jacques, son fils		6		Santiago, su hijo	
Rose, sa fille		10		Rosa, ydem	
Sophie, idem		9		Sofia, ydem	

32nd family (7 persons)				33rd family (7 persons)	
Pierre GUÉDRY	ouvrier	31		Pedro GUÉDRY	
Marie Josèphe LEBERT, sa femme		29		Maria Josef LEBERT, su muger	
Pierre Joseph, son fils		10		Pedro Josef, su hijo	
Jean Pierre, idem		4		Juan Pedro, idem	
Joseph Fermin, idem	à la mamelle			Josef Fermin, ydem	de pecho
Marie Rose, sa fille		6		Maria Rosa, ydem	
Pierre LEBERT, neveu de la dite		13		Pedro LEBERT, su subrino	

33rd family (5 persons)				34th family (5 persons)	
Paul LEBLANC,	charpentier	38		Pablo LEBLANC	
Anne BOUDREAU, sa femme		36		Ana BAUDREAUD, su muger	
Adélaïde, sa fille		3		Adélaïde, su hija	
Rosalie, idem	à la mamelle			Rosalia, idem	de pecho
Rose TRAHAN, sa nièce		23		Rosa TRAHAM, su sobrina	

34th family (2 persons)			35th family (1 person)	
Margueritte Ange DUBOIS,			Juan Luis D'AIGRE, hija de Margarita	
veuve Jⁿ DAIGRE	29		Angela DUBOI que queda en el Hosp ¹	
Jean Louis, son fils	10			

35th family (5 persons)				38th family (4 persons)	
Allain BOURG	journallier	43		Alein BOURG	
Marie COMMEAU, sa femme		40		Maria COUMMEAU, su muger	
François, son fils		11		Franᶜᵒ, su hijo	
Alexis, idem		1		Genoveva, ydem	
Geneviève, sa fille		20			

36th family (1 person)		
Pierre FOREST, garçon	marin	25

37th family (2 persons)				37th family (2 persons)	
Charles GRANGER	marin	33		Carlos GRANCHER	
Joseph DAIGRE, son neveu	marin	14		Josef D'AIGRE, su sobrino	

38th family (3 persons)				37th family (2 persons)	
Jean Baptiste DAIGRE	laboureur	45		Juan Bautista D'AIGRE	
Marie Claudine VALET, sa femme		31		Maria Claudia VALET, su muger	
Jean René, son fils		1			

39th family (3 persons)				39th family (3 persons)	
Joseph CAILLOUET	charpentier	31		Josef CALLOIT	
Élisabeth LEBLANC, sa femme		32		Ysabel LEBLANC, su muger	
Jacques, son fils	à la mamelle			Santiago, hijo	de pecho

Chat - #156: Jacques MOULAISON s/o Jacques & Cécile MÉLANÇON m. 1774 Marie-Blanche DOIRON d/o Paul & Marguerite MICHEL; a child Rose MOULAISON b. 1775

Nantes - #244: additional family information

Chat - #92: Pierre GUÉDRY s/o Claude & Anne LEJEUNE m. 1773 Marie-Josèphe LEBERT d/o Paul & Marie LA PIERRE; child Pierre b. 1774

Nantes - #142: additional family information
SM - #467: additional family information

Chat - #139: Paul LEBLANC s/o Claude & Madeleine BOUDROT m. 1770 Anne BOUDROT d/o François & Anne-Marie THIBODAUX
Nantes - #218: additional family information
SM - #646: additional family information

Nantes - #87: Jean DAIGLE s/o Pierre & Madeleine GAUTROT m. 1770 Marguerite-Ange DUBOIS d/o Joseph-Ange & Anne MICHEL
SM - #295: additional family information

Chat - #39: Alain BOURG s/o François & Madeleine HÉBERT m. 1764 Anne-Marie COMMAUX d/o Joseph & Marguerite HÉBERT
Census - p.121: Owned 6 arpents of land

Nantes - #51: additional family information
SM - #154: additional family information

Nantes - #91: Jean-Baptiste DAIGLE m. ca. 1783 Marie-Claudine VALET; a child Jean-René bt. 1784

Nantes - #76: Joseph CAILLOUET s/o Joseph & Marie METOT m. 1784 Élizabeth LEBLANC d/o Pierre & Marguerite GAUTROT

31st family (5 persons)		
Jacques MOULAISON	carpenter	38
Marie DOIRON, his wife		41
Jacques MOULAISON, his son		6
Rose MOULAISON, his daughter		10
Sophie MOULAISON, his daughter		9
32nd family (7 persons)		
Pierre GUÉDRY	workman	31
Marie Josèphe LEBERT, his wife		29
Pierre Joseph GUÉDRY, his son		10
Jean Pierre GUÉDRY, his son		4
Joseph Firmin GUÉDRY, son; a nursling		
Marie Rose GUÉDRY, his daughter		6
Pierre LEBERT, nephew of the above		13
33rd family (5 persons)		
Paul LEBLANC	carpenter	38
Anne BOUDROT, his wife		36
Adélaïde LEBLANC, his daughter		3
Rosalie LEBLANC, daughter; a nursling		
Rose TRAHAN, his niece		23
34th family (2 persons)		
Marguerite Ange DUBOIS, widow of		
Jean DAIGLE		29
Jean Louis DAIGLE, her son		10
35th family (5 persons)		
Allain BOURG	day laborer	43
Marie COMEAUX, his wife		40
François BOURG, his son		11
Alexis BOURG, his son		1
Geneviève BOURG, his daughter		20
36th family (1 person)		
Pierre FOREST, young man	sailor	25
37th family (2 persons)		
Charles GRANGER	sailor	33
Joseph DAIGLE, his nephew; sailor		14
38th family (3 persons)		
Jean Baptiste DAIGLE	plowman	45
Marie Claudine VALET, his wife		31
Jean René DAIGLE, his son		1
39th family (3 persons)		
Joseph CAILLOUET	carpenter	31
Élizabeth LEBLANC, his wife		32
Jacques CAILLOUET, his son; a nursling		

40th family (2 persons)
Jean Pierre DUGAST   charpentier   20
   Jeanne CABON, sa femme   34

41st family (1 person)
Pierre VINCENT, garçon   tonellier   36

42nd family (1 person)
Jean Baptiste DUHON, garçon   laboureur   25

43rd family (1 person)
Jean Charles RICHARD, garçon laboureur   19

44th family (1 person)
Jean Marie GRANGER, garçon   charpentier   19

45th family (3 persons)
Pierre HENRY   laboureur   61
   Margueritte TRAHAN, sa femme   54
   Civil François, son fils   marin   18

46th family (1 person)
Louis François MONT RÉAL, domestique
   de Mr Peyroux

"Liste des Acadiens qui doivent s'embarquer dans le Navire Le Beaumont Capitaine Mr. Olivier Daniel, pour La Nouvelle Orleans dans la Louisiane. [List of Acadians who are to embark on Le Beaumont Captain is Mr. Olivier Daniel, for New Orleans in Louisiana.]

"Nous, Consul d'Espagne en Bretagne chargé de l'expedition des Acadiens pour la louisiane. Certifions que les cent soixante dix-huit personnes denommé ci-dessus sont celles que nous avons nommés pour s'embarquer sur le Navire Le Beaumont allant au Port de la Nouvelle-Orleans dans la Louisiane. Nantes 25 May 1785. d'Asperer"

Translation:
We, Consul of Spain in Brittany charged with the transporting of the Acadians for Louisiana. Certify that the 178 persons listed above are those named to embark on the ship *Le Beaumont* going to the Port of New Orleans in Louisiana. At Nantes on 25 May 1785.

"Lista de Acadianos que llegaron a bordo del buque Le Beaumont. Lista hecha por Pedro Aragon y Villegas el 6 de septiembre de 1785, Nueva Orleans. Legajo 626A from Archivo General de Indias, Seville."

40th family (2 persons)
Juan Pedro DUGATS
   Juana CABON, su muger

41st family (1 person)
Pedro VINCENT

42nd family (1 person)
Juan Bautista DOUHONE

43rd family (1 person)
Juan Carlos RICHARD

44th family (1 person)
Juan Maria GRANCHER

45th family (3 persons)
Pedro HENRIQUE
   Margarita TRAHAM, su muger
   Cecilio Fran^{co}, su hijo

47th family (2 persons)
Juan GARCIA
   Fran^{ca} COURTIN, su muger

48th family (6 persons)
Magdalena LEBLANC, viuda TRAHAM
   Pablo TRAHAM, su hijo
   Simon, ydem
   Alexo, ydem
   Maria, ydem
   Rosalia, ydem

49th family (2 persons)
Josef COSTA
   Margarita TRAHAM, su muger

50th family (2 persons)
Fran^{co} Miguel BETANCOURT
   Victoria LA VERGNE, su muger

51st family (5 persons) * NOTE- del Bon Papa
Juan Bautista GUÉDRY
   Pedro, su hijo
   Fran^{co}, idem
   Margarita Felicidad   de pecho
   Margarita, huerfana e hija del ocho

A medium-sized frigate the Le Beaumont [180 tons] of late construction and speedy. Captian Daniel crossed the Atlantic in record time, 70 days. Though there were no births, there was some sickness and 2 deaths aboard ship. The group of 41 families chose Baton Rouge, 5 families went to Atacapas (St. Martinville) and 3 families to La Fourche (area around Plattenville). The group lost 6 more members: 4 by death and 2 by desertion, but acquired 7 new additions: 1 birth, 3 new adherents and 3 marriages. [Winzerling pp.137-138]

This group arrived in New Orleans on 19 August 1785, arriving four days after the arrival of La Bergère which had left France a month earlier.[Braud - p. 99]

45th family (3 persons)
Nantes - #180: Pierre HENRY m. ca. 1758 Marguerite TRAHAN
SM - #562: Their child: Cyrille François b. 1767

47th family (2 persons)
BR - v.2, p.304: Joseph Louis GARCIA s/o Juan & Marie Francisca CARTEN [COURTIN] b. 10 Sept. 1792

48th family (6 persons)
Chat - #187: Isidore TRAHAN m. ca. 1752 Marie-Madeleine LEBLANC; a child Alexis-Romain TRAHAN b. 1774
Exile - p.422: children of Isidore TRAHAN & Marie-Madeleine LEBLANC:
Jean Baptiste TRAHAN b. 8 Feb. 1766
Magdalen TRAHAN d. 7 July 1764
Paul-Isidore TRAHAN b. 31 March 1764

40th family (2 persons)		
Jean Pierre DUGAT	carpenter	20
Jeanne CABON, his wife		34

41st family (1 person)		
Pierre VINCENT, young man	wet cooper	36

42nd family (1 person)		
Jean Baptiste DUHON, young man; plowman		25

43rd family (1 person)		
Jean Charles RICHARD, young man; plowman		19

44th family (1 person)		
Jean Marie GRANGER, young man; carpenter		19

45th family (3 persons)		
Pierre HENRY	plowman	61
Marguerite TRAHAN, his wife		54
Civil François HENRY, his son; sailor		18

46th family (1 person)
Louis François MONTRÉAL, servant
   to Mr. PEYROUX

47th family (2 persons)
Juan GARCIA
   Françoise COURTIN, his wife

48th family (6 persons)
Magdelaine LEBLANC, widow TRAHAN
   Paul TRAHAN, her son
   Simon TRAHAN, her son
   Alexis TRAHAN, her son
   Marie TRAHAN, her daughter
   Rosalie TRAHAN, her daughter

49th family (2 persons)
Joseph COSTA
   Marguerite TRAHAN, his wife

50th family (2 persons)
François Michel BETANCOURT
   Victoire LAVERGNE, his wife

51st family (5 persons) * NOTE- from ship the Bon Papa
Jean Baptiste GUÉDRY
   Pierre GUÉDRY, his son
   François GUÉDRY, his son
   Marguerite Félicité GUÉDRY, his daughter
                  a nursling
   Marguerite GUÉDRY, an orphan; girl at age   8

1st family (6 persons)

Joseph Ignace HÉBERT	contre-maitre	37
Anne DUGAT, sa femme		36
Pierre, son fils		15
Olivier, idem		11
Ambroise, idem		2
Ysabelle, sa fille		9

2nd family (4 persons)

Pierre DUGAT	charpentier	51
Rose LEBLANC, sa femme		40
Rose, sa fille		3
Anne Perinne	à la mamelle	

3rd family (5 persons)

Anne HÉBERT, veuve ROBICHAUD		45
Joseph, son fils		12
Jean Pierre, idem		2
Marie, sa fille		17
Anne, idem		15

4th family (6 persons)

Jean B^{te} HÉBERT	cordonier	35
Anne Josèphe DUGAT, sa femme		36
Jean Joseph, son fils		14
Ambroise Mathurin, idem		12
Simon, idem		7
Alexis Thomas, idem		2

5th family (2 persons)

Alexis DUGAT	charpentier	58
Marie Rose, sa fille		20

6th family (11 persons)

Joseph DUGAT	cieur de long	43
Anastasie BARILLOT, sa femme		43
Joseph, son fils	charpentier	23
François, idem		14
Jean Pierre, idem		10
Marie, sa fille		21
Cécille, idem		19
Elisabet, idem		17
Anastasie		12
Anne, idem		6
Marguerite, idem		2

7th family (6 persons)

Pierre Olivier PITRE	journalier	46
Rosalie HÉBERT, sa femme		40
Marie, sa fille		18
Magdelaine, idem		4
Enriete, idem		3
Pierre, son fils		1

Other References	Complete Listing		
Nantes - #173: Joseph-Ignace HÉBERT s/o Jean & Madeleine DOIRON m. 1768 Anne DUGAST d/o Joseph & Marie HÉBERT	**1st family (6 persons)**		
	Joseph Ignace HÉBERT	foreman	37
	Anne DUGAT, his wife		36
	Pierre HÉBERT, his son		15
	Olivier HÉBERT, his son		11
	Ambroise HÉBERT, his son		2
	Isabelle HÉBERT, his daughter		9
Nantes - #118: Pierre DUGAST m. 1779 Rose LEBLANC d/o Jacques & Marguerite LABAUVE	**2nd family (4 persons)**		
	Pierre DUGAT	carpenter	51
	Rose LEBLANC, his wife		40
	Rose DUGAT, his daughter		3
	Anne Perinne DUGAT, dgtr.; a nursling		
Chat - #176: Pierre ROBICHAUX widr. Anne-Marie BLANCHARD m. 1761 Anne HÉBERT d/o Jean & Madeleine DOIRON	**3rd family (5 persons)**		
	Anne HÉBERT, widow ROBICHAUX		45
Nantes - #272: additonal family information	Joseph ROBICHAUX, her son		12
SM - #838: additional family information	Jean Pierre ROBICHAUX, her son		2
	Marie ROBICHAUX, her daughter		17
	Anne ROBICHAUX, her daughter		15
Chat - #111: Jean-Baptiste HÉBERT s/o Jean & Marie Madeleine DOIRON m. 1768 Anne-Josèphe DUGAST d/o Alexis & Anne BOURG; a child Ambroise Mathurin HÉBERT b. 1772	**4th family (6 persons)**		
	Jean Baptiste HÉBERT	shoemaker	35
	Anne Josèphe DUGAT, his wife		36
	Jean Joseph HÉBERT, his son		14
	Ambroise Mathurin HÉBERT, his son		12
Nantes - #170: additional family information	Simon HÉBERT, his son		7
SM - #518: additional family information	Alexis Thomas HÉBERT, his son		2
	5th family (2 persons)		
	Alexis DUGAT	carpenter	58
	Marie Rose DUGAT, his daughter		20
	6th family (11 persons)		
Chat - #77: Joseph DUGAST widr. Anastasie HENRY s/o Joseph & Marie HÉBERT m. 1770 Anastasie BARRILLOT d/o Pierre & Véronique GIROIRE; children: Jean-Pierre b. 1775, Cécille b. 1765, Anastasie b. 1773	Joseph DUGAT	pit sawyer	43
	Anastasie BARRILLOT, his wife		43
	Joseph DUGAT, his son	carpenter	23
	François DUGAT, his son		14
	Jean Pierre DUGAT, his son		10
	Marie DUGAT, his daughter		21
	Cécille DUGAT, his daughter		19
Nantes - #114: additional family information	Elisabet DUGAT, his daughter		17
SM - #364: additional family information	Anastasie DUGAT, his daughter		12
	Anne DUGAT, his daughter		6
	Marguerite DUGAT, his daughter		2
	7th family (6 persons)		
Chat - #165: Pierre Olivier PITRE s/o Germain & Marguerite GIROIRE m. 1765 Rosalie HÉBERT d/o Jean & Madeleine DOIRON	Pierre Olivier PITRE	day laborer	46
	Rosalie HÉBERT, his wife		40
	Marie PITRE, his daughter		18
	Magdelaine PITRE, his daughter		4
SM - #783: additional family information	Henriette PITRE, his daughter		3
Nantes - #261: additional family information	Pierre PITRE, his son		1

8th family (4 persons)

Pierre MICHEL	journalier	46
Joseph, son fils	marin	25
Gertrudis, sa fille		19
Marie, idem		5

9th family (2 persons)

Pierre GAUTRAU	charpentier	25
Magdelaine MICHEL, sa f^e		21

10th family (4 persons)

Marguerite HÉBERT, veuve GAUTRAU		59
Jean, son fils	marin	21
Charles, idem		18
Victoire, sa fille		16

11th family (8 persons)

Joseph GAUTRAU	journalier	63
Anne PITRE, sa femme		45
Joseph, son fils		15
Pierre, idem		13
Charles, idem		10
Jean, idem		8
François, idem		8
Rose, sa fille		22

12th family (5 persons)

Théodore BOURG	charpentier	39
Anne GRANGER, sa femme		54
Théodore, son fils		14
Anne, sa fille		19
Magdeleine, idem		17

13th family (1 person)

Jean B^{te} DAIGRE	marin	20

14th family (5 persons)

Anselme PITRE	journalier	45
Jean Pierre, son fils	idem	21
Marie Françoise, sa fille		18
Marguerite, idem		14
Isabelle Olive, idem		12

15th family (7 persons)

Anastasie LEVRON, veuve LEJEUNE		45
Joseph, son fils	marin	22
Alexis, idem		13
Marie Rose, sa fille		18
Marguerite, idem		16
Magdeleine, idem		6
Rosalie, idem		2

8th family (4 persons)		
Pierre MICHEL	day laborer	46
Joseph MICHEL, his son	sailor	25
Gertrude MICHEL, his daughter		19
Marie MICHEL, his daughter		5

BR - v.2, p.316: Children of Pierre Grégoire GAU-
TROT & Magdelaine MICHEL: Étienne b. 1 Sept.
1788, Marguerite Rosalie b. 10 Sept. 1794, Marie
Magdalen b. 2 Feb. 1793

9th family (2 persons)		
Pierre GAUTROT	carpenter	25
Magdelaine MICHEL, his wife		21

SM - #409: Alexandre GAUTROT s/o Henry-François
m. ca. 1744 Marguerite HÉBERT; a child Victoire
b. 1766

10th family (4 persons)		
Marguerite HÉBERT, widow GAUTROT		59
Jean GAUTROT, his son; sailor		21
Charles GAUTROT, his son		18
Victoire GAUTROT, his daughter		16

Chat - #85: Joseph GAUTROT widr. Marie-Josèphe
HÉBERT m. 1764 Anne PITRE d/o Germain; children: Charles GAUTROT b. 1774, Rose GAUTROT
b. 1763

SM - #421: additional family information

11th family (8 persons)		
Joseph GAUTROT	day laborer	63
Anne PITRE, his wife		45
Joseph GAUTROT, his son		15
Pierre GAUTROT, his son		13
Charles GAUTROT, his son		10
Jean GAUTROT, his son		8
François GAUTROT, his son		8
Rose GAUTROT, his daughter		22

SM - #185: Théodore BOURG s/o Jean & Élizabeth
HÉBERT m. 1764 Anne GRANGER; a child Théodore BOURG b. 1770

BR - v.2, p.120: Anne BOURG d/o Théodore & Anne
GRANGER m. 25 Oct. 1791 Mathurin D'AUNIS

12th family (5 persons)		
Théodore BOURG	carpenter	39
Anne GRANGER, his wife		54
Théodore BOURG, his son		14
Anne BOURG, his daughter		19
Magdelaine BOURG, his daughter		17

13th family (1 person)		
Jean Baptiste DAIGLE	sailor	20

SM - #768: Anselme PITRE s/o Jean & Marguerite
THERIOT m. 1763 Isabelle DUGAST d/o Pierre &
Élizabeth BOURG; children: Jean Pierre b. 1763,
Marguerite b. 1771, Isabelle-Olive b. 1773

14th family (5 persons)		
Anselme PITRE	day laborer	45
Jean Pierre PITRE, his son	day laborer	21
Marie Françoise PITRE, his daughter		18
Marguerite PITRE, his daughter		14
Isabelle Olive PITRE, his daughter		12

Nantes - #227: Amand LEJEUNE d. 1784; m. ca. 1755
Anastasie LEVRON; a child Rosalie bt. 1783

BR - v.2, p.493: Alexis LEJEUNE s/o Aman & Anasta-
sie LEVRON of Acadia m. 8 Jan. 1794 Françoise
Marie Barbara TRAHAN d/o Marin & Marie
Magdelaine LEBLANC

15th family (7 persons)		
Anastasie LEVRON, widow LEJEUNE		45
Joseph LEJEUNE, his son	sailor	22
Alexis LEJEUNE, his son		13
Marie Rose LEJEUNE, his daughter		18
Marguerite LEJEUNE, his daughter		16
Magdelaine LEJEUNE, his daughter		6
Rosalie LEJEUNE, his daughter		2

16th family (2 persons)

Jean LEJEUNE	marin	29
Félicité BOUDRAU, sa femme		31

17th family (3 persons)

Jean B^te DURAMBOURG	journalier	50
Magdeleine HENRRY, sa femme		45
Marie Jeanne, sa fille		18

18th family (6 persons)

Jean Charles BOUDRAU	perelleur	51
Marguerite GUÉDRY, sa femme		34
Pierre David, son fils		2
Enrriette, sa fille		13
Marguerite, idem		3
[unnamed child]	à la mamelle	

19th family (2 persons)

Felix BOUDRAU	charpentier	54
Magdeleine HÉBERT, sa fem^e		56

20th family (3 persons)

Augustin TRAHAN	charpentier	50
Bibianne LEBLANC, sa fem^e		40
Marie Modeste, sa fille		12

21st family (3 persons)

Gerome GUÉRIN	journalier	32
Marie PITTRE, sa femme		36
Jean Pierre, son fils	à la mamelle	

22nd family (5 persons)

Joseph ROBICHAUD	journalier	56
Jean B^te, son fils	domestique	21
François Xavier, idem		16
Marie, sa fille		14
Renée, idem		9

23rd family (3 persons)

Marie HÉBERT, veuve MOISE		43
Joseph, son fils		12
Marie, sa fille		6

24th family (4 persons)

Ambroise NAQUIN	laboureur	60
Elizabet BOURG, sa femme		58
Joseph, son fils	charpentier	19
Pierre, idem	idem	19

Nantes - #231: Jean LEJEUNE s/o Amand & Anastasie LEVRON m. 1782 Félicité BOUDROT d/o Felix & Marie-Josèphe LEBLANC		

16th family (2 persons)

Jean LEJEUNE	sailor	29
Félicité BOUDROT, his wife		31

Nantes - #124: Jean-Baptiste DURAMBOURG m. ca. 1759 Madeleine HENRY

17th family (3 persons)

Jean Baptiste DARAMBOURG	day laborer	50
Magdelaine HENRY, his wife		45
Marie Jeanne DURAMBOURG, his dgtr.		18

Nantes - #42 Jean-Charles BOUDROT s/o François & Angélique DOIRON m. 1780 Marguerite-Victoire GUÉDRY d/o Charles & Madeleine HÉBERT; a child Henriette b. 1772

SM - #133: additional family information

18th family (6 persons)

Jean Charles BOUDROT	wood polisher	51
Marguerite GUÉDRY, his wife		34
Pierre David GUÉDRY, his son		2
Henriette GUÉDRY, his daughter		13
Marguerite GUÉDRY, his daughter		3
child GUÉDRY	a nursling	

BR - v.2, p.111: Felix BOUDREAUX widr. Magdelaine HÉBERT m. 30 Aug. 1787 La Luce BOURG wid. Pierre HÉBERT

19th family (2 persons)

Felix BOUDROT	carpenter	54
Magdelaine HÉBERT, his wife		56

Exile - p.420: Augustin TRAHAN s/o Claude & Marie THIARD m. 3 July 1764 Bibienne LEBLANC d/o Pierre & Marguerite GAUTREAU

20th family (3 persons)

Augustin TRAHAN	carpenter	50
Vivianne LEBLANC, his wife		40
Marie Modeste TRAHAN, his daughter		12

21st family (3 persons)

Jérôme GUÉRIN	day laborer	32
Marie PITRE, his wife		36
Jean Pierre GUÉRIN, his son	a nursling	

SM - #835 Joseph ROBICHAUX m. ca. 1754 Anne-Osite HÉBERT; children Jean Baptiste b. 1763, François Xavier b. 1768, Marie b. 1770

22nd family (5 persons)

Joseph ROBICHAUX	day laborer	56
Jean Baptiste ROBICHAUX, son; servant		21
François Xavier ROBICHAUX, his son		16
Marie ROBICHAUX, his daughter		14
Renée ROBICHAUX, his daughter		9

Nantes - #250: Joseph MOYSE d. 1779 m. ca. 1770 Marie HÉBERT; children: Marie-Josephine bt. 1779, Joseph b. 1773

23rd family (3 persons)

Marie HÉBERT, widow MOYSE		43
Joseph MOYSE, his son		12
Marie MOYSE, his daughter		6

Nantes - #251 Ambroise NAQUIN s/o Jacques & Jeanne MÉLANÇON m. ca. 1749 Élizabeth BOURG; children: twins Joseph and Pierre b. 1766

SM - #734: additional family information

24th family (4 persons)

Ambroise NAQUIN	plowman	60
Élizabeth BOURG, his wife		58
Joseph NAQUIN, his son	carpenter	19
Pierre NAQUIN, his son	carpenter	19

25th family (5 persons)

Pierre BOURG	journalier	56
Marie NAQUIN, sa fem^e		46
Pierre, son fils		18
Jeanne, sa fille		20
Victoire, idem		11

26th family (5 persons)

Charles Olivier GUILLOT	charpentier	38
Magdeleine BOUDRAU, sa fem^e^e		40
Jean Michel, son fils		14
Simon François, idem		12
Isabel, sa fille		10

27th family (4 persons)

Michel AU COING	menuisier	30
Marie Rosalie DE LA FORESTRIE		29
Marie Françoise, sa fille		5
Rosa Adélaïde, idem	à la mamelle	

28th family (7 persons)

Joseph HÉBERT	marin	32
Jeanne DE LA FORESTRIE, sa fem^e		30
Joseph, son fils		11
Charles, idem		10
Louis Jean, idem		5
Marie, sa fille		8
Anne Marguerite, idem	à la mamelle	

29th family (4 persons)

Jean GARNIER	charpentier	34
Ozite Perpétue THERIOT, sa fem^e		30
Jeanne Marie, sa fille		1
Marie Françoise, idem	à la mamelle	

30th family (7 persons)

Charles NAQUIN	laboureur	48
Jean, son fils		14
Paul, idem		3
Anne, sa fille		18
Ives, idem		16
Ludovinne, idem		10
Renne, idem		8

31st family (4 persons)

Charles DUGAT	laboureur	60
Anne NAQUIN, sa fem^e		50
Rose GAUTRAU, fille à la fem^e		20
Anne LEBERT, sa mineur		9

Nantes - #60: Pierre BOURG s/o François & Madeleine HÉBERT m. 1761 Anne-Marie NAQUIN d/o Jacques & Jeanne MÉLANÇON; a child Jeanne BOURG b. 1765		

SM - #184: additional family information

25th family (5 persons)

Pierre BOURG	day laborer	56
Marie NAQUIN, his wife		46
Pierre BOURG, his son		18
Jeanne BOURG, his daughter		20
Victoire BOURG, his daughter		11

SM - #478: Charles-Olivier GUILLOT s/o Jean-Baptiste & Marie-Madeleine ARCEMENT m. 1766 Madeleine-Josèphe BOUDROT; Children: Jean Michel b. 1769, Simon François b. 1772

26th family (5 persons)

Charles Olivier GUILLOT	carpenter	38
Magdelaine BOUDROT, his wife		40
Jean Michel GUILLOT, his son		14
Simon François GUILLOT, his son		12
Isabelle GUILLOT, his daughter		10

Nantes - #13: Michel AUCOIN s/o Pierre & Marguerite DUPUIS m. 1779 Marie-Rosalie DE LA FORESTERIE d/o Jean & Marie-Madeleine BONNIERE; a child Rosalie bt. 1784

27th family (4 persons)

Michel AUCOIN	woodworker	30
Marie Rosalie DE LA FORESTRIE		29
Marie Françoise AUCOIN, his daughter		5
Rosa Adélaïde AUCOIN, dgtr.; a nursling		

Chat - #113: Joseph HÉBERT s/o Charles & Marguerite LEBLANC m. 1772 Jeanne DE LA FORESTERIE d/o Jean & Marie-Madeleine BONNIERE; a child Charles b. 1775

SM - #522: additional family information
Nantes - #172: additional family information

28th family (7 persons)

Joseph HÉBERT	sailor	32
Jeanne DE LA FORESTERIE, his wife		30
Joseph HÉBERT, his son		11
Charles HÉBERT, his son		10
Louis Jean HÉBERT, his son		5
Marie HÉBERT, his daughter		8
Anne Marguerite HÉBERT, dgtr., nursling		

Nantes - #277: Christian SPIGER [Jean GARNIER] m. Osite-Perpétue THERIOT d/o Charles & Marie BOUDROT; a child Marie Françoise GARNIER bt. 1785

29th family (4 persons)

Jean GARNIER	carpenter	34
Ozite Perpétue THERIOT, his wife		20
Jeanne Marie GARNIER, his daughter		1
Marie Françoise GARNIER, dgtr.; nursling		

Chat - #158: Charles NAQUIN s/o François & Angélique BLANCHARD m. 1765 Anne DOIRON d/o Thomas & Anne GIROIRE who d. 18 July 1782; Children: Marguerite-Ludivine b. 1775, Renée b. 1777, Paul b. 1780

30th family (7 persons)

Charles NAQUIN	day laborer	48
Jean NAQUIN, his son		14
Paul NAQUIN, his son		3
Anne NAQUIN, his daughter		18
Ives NAQUIN, his daughter		16
Ludovinne NAQUIN, his daughter		10
Renné NAQUIN, his daughter		8

SM - #357 Charles DUGAST s/o Joseph m. 1765 Anne NAQUIN; a child Rose b. 1762

31st family (4 persons)

Charles DUGAT	plowman	60
Anne NAQUIN, his wife		50
Rose GAUTROT, wife's daughter		20
Anne LEBERT, his minor child		9

32nd family (5 persons)
Jean Grégoire BLANCHARD   perelleur   37
   Marie Magdeleine LIVOIR   31
   Jean B^te, son fils   8
   Marie, sa fille   9
   Pierre Charles, son fils   à la mamelle

33rd family (3 persons)
Hilaire CLIMENT   charpentier   39
   Jean, son fils   8
   Marie, sa fille   10

34th family (7 persons)
Joachin TRAHAN   laboureur   50
   Augustin TRAHAN, son fils   18
   Jean Marie, idem   10
   Anne, sa fille   21
   Félicité, idem   14
   Catherine, idem   12
   Marie Vincent   1

35th family (8 persons)
Pierre TRAHAN   laboureur   48
   Marguerite DUHON, sa fem^e   44
   Joseph, son fils   8
   Geneviève, sa fille   23
   Paulinne, idem   18
   Marguerite, idem   16
   Anne, idem   12
   Marie Françoise, idem   10

36th family (6 persons)
Blais THIBODAU   charpentier   62
   Catherine DEGLE, sa femme   60
   François, son fils   journalier   18
   Joseph, idem   idem   17
   Isabelle, sa fille   10
   Joseph Nicolas HÉBERT, neveu du dit
                     menuissier   31

37th family (3 persons)
Fermin THIBODAU   marin   25
   Marie Magdeleine THERIOT, sa fem^e   20
   Fermin Blais, son fils   2

38th family (5 persons)
Antoine BOUTARI   charpentier   48
   Marie SOLNIER, sa fem^e   37
   Auguste, son fils   9
   Antoine, idem   7
   Guillaume, idem   à la mamelle

Other References

Chat - #24: Jean-Grégoire BLANCHARD, a wood polisher m. ca. 1774 Marie-Madeleine LIVOIS; a child Marie-Madeleine BLANCHARD b. 1775

Census - p.121: Owned 6 arpents of land.

Chat - #56: Hilaire CLÉMENT s/o Jean & Marie-Josèphe RUDOUZE m. 1774 Tarsille NAQUIN d/o François & Angélique BLANCHARD; a child Marie CLÉMENT b. 1775

SM - #247: additional family information

Exile - p.426: Children of Joachim TRAHAN & Marie Magdalen DUHON:
Marie Victoire b. 9 July 1781, d. 25 Feb. 1782
Catherine b. 24 April 1773
Marie Félicité b. 16 Jan. 1770
Marie Vincente b. 28 April 1784

Nantes - #306: Pierre TRAHAN m. ca. 1762 Marguerite DUHON

Nantes - #286: Blaise THIBODAUX s/o Antoine & Suzanne COMMAUX m. ca. 1752 Catherine DAIGLE

SM - #881: additional family information

Nantes - #287: Firmin THIBODAUX s/o Blaise & Catherine DAIGLE m. 1783 Marie-Madeleine THERIOT d/o Charles & Marie BOUDROT; a child Firmin-Blaise bt. 1783

Chat - #47: Antoine BOUTARY m. ca. 1756 Marie-Marguerite SAULNIER; Children Guillaume BOUTARY bt. 1785, Antoine bt. 1778

Nantes - #62: additional family information

Complete Listing

32nd family (5 persons)

Jean Grégoire BLANCHARD	wood polisher	37
Marie Magdelaine LIVOIS		31
Jean Baptiste BLANCHARD, his son		8
Marie BLANCHARD, his daughter		9
Pierre Charles BLANCHARD, son; nursling		

33rd family (3 persons)

Hilaire CLÉMENT	carpenter	39
Jean CLÉMENT, his son		8
Marie CLÉMENT, his daughter		10

34th family (7 persons)

Joachim TRAHAN	plowman	50
Augustin TRAHAN, his son		18
Jean Marie TRAHAN, his son		10
Anne TRAHAN, his daughter		21
Félicité TRAHAN, his daughter		14
Catherine TRAHAN, his daughter		12
Marie Vincent TRAHAN		1

35th family (8 persons)

Pierre TRAHAN	plowman	48
Marguerite DUHON, his wife		44
Joseph TRAHAN, his son		8
Geneviève TRAHAN, his daughter		23
Pauline TRAHAN, his daughter		18
Marguerite TRAHAN, his daughter		16
Anne TRAHAN, his daughter		12
Marie Françoise TRAHAN, his daughter		10

36th family (6 persons)

Blaise THIBODEAUX	carpenter	62
Catherine DAIGLE, his wife		60
François THIBODEAUX, a son; day laborer		18
Joseph THIBODEAUX, his son; day laborer		17
Isabelle THIBODEAUX, his daughter		10
Joseph Nicolas HÉBERT, nephew of the above said	woodworker	31

37th family (3 persons)

Firmin THIBODEAUX	sailor	25
Marie Magdelaine THERIOT, his wife		20
Firmin Blais THIBODEAUX, his son		2

38th family (5 persons)

Antoine BOUTARY	carpenter	48
Marie SAUNIER, his wife		37
Auguste BOUTARY, his son		9
Antoine BOUTARY, his son		7
Guillaume BOUTARY, his son; a nursling		

39th family (2 persons)
Guillaume HAMON   charpentier   24
   Marguerite SOLNIER, sa fem^e   27

40th family (6 persons)
Etiene DAROIS   tanneur   47
   Magdeleine TRAHAN, sa fem^e   45
   Elizabet, sa fille   24
   Marie, idem   18
   Susanne, idem   16
   Elizabet, idem   8

41st family (2 persons)
Pierre THERIOT   perelleur   42
   Pierre, son fils   15

42nd family (6 persons)
Jean TRAHAN   laboureur   43
   Magdeleine HéBERT, sa fem^e   47
   Michel, son fils   marin   21
   Pierre, idem   charpentier   18
   Marie Louise, sa fille   16
   Félicité, idem   14

43rd family (3 persons)
Pierre LABOVE   charpentier   36
   Anne BONFILS, sa fem^e   32
   Jean DUGAT, fils à la femme   13

44th family (4 persons)
Jean Batiste BOUDRAU   perceur   25
   Marguerite BEDIN   23
   Jean B^te, son fils   2
   Jean Charles, idem   à la mamelle

45th family (4 persons)
Honnoré COMMAU   charpentier   67
   Anastasie BELMER, sa fem^e   45
   Joseph BOUDRAU, fils à la femme; marin   17
   Charles, idem   marin   14

46th family (6 persons)
Joseph HÉBERT   charpentier   51
   Marie BENOIT, sa fem^e   48
   Joseph, son fils   tanneur   24
   Marie, sa fille   22
   Sophie, idem   15
   Sophie BENOIT, nièce au dit   8

Nantes - #155: Guillaume HAMON s/o Joseph & Marie DAMEUE m. 1780 Marguerite SAULNIER d/o Charles & Euphrosine LALANDE

Chat - #61: Étienne DARROIS m. ca. 1759 Madeleine TRAHAN; a child Marie-Élizabeth bt. 1776

Nantes - #97: additional family information

Exile - p.422: Children of Jean-Baptiste TRAHAN & Magdalen HÉBERT:
Jean-Michel b. 21 Aug. 1764
Marie Louise b. 27 Aug. 1768

Nantes - #186: Pierre LABAUVE s/o Jean & Anne SAULNIER m. 1784 Jeanne BONFILS d/o François & Marie SEVIN

Chat - #30: Jean-Baptiste BOUDROT s/o Jean-Baptiste & Anastasie BELLEMERE m. 1778 Marguerite BEDEL called Picard

Nantes - #81: Honoré COMMAUX s/o Jean-Baptiste & Anne-Marie THIBODAUX m. 1784 Anastasie BELLEMER d/o Jacques & Marie LANDRY

SM #519: Joseph HÉBERT s/o Jacques & Marguerite LANDRY m. 1766 Marie BENOIST d/o Charles & Madeleine THERIOT; a child Sophie b. 1769

39th family (2 persons)

Guillaume HAMONT	carpenter	24
Marguerite SAUNIER, his wife		27

40th family (6 persons)

Étienne DARROIS	tanner	47
Magdalaine TRAHAN, his wife		45
Élizabeth DARROIS, his daughter		24
Marie DARROIS, his daughter		18
Susanne DARROIS, his daughter		16
Élizabeth DARROIS, his daughter		8

41st family (2 persons)

Pierre THERIOT	wood polisher	42
Pierre THERIOT, his son		15

42nd family (6 persons)

Jean TRAHAN	plowman	49
Magdelaine HÉBERT, his wife		47
Michel TRAHAN, his son	sailor	21
Pierre TRAHAN, his son	carpenter	18
Marie Louise TRAHAN, his daughter		16
Félicité TRAHAN, his daughter		14

43rd family (3 persons)

Pierre LABAUVE	carpenter	36
Anne BONFILS, his wife		32
Jean DUGAT, son of the wife		13

44th family (4 persons)

Jean Baptiste BOUDROT	borer	25
Marguerite BEDEL		23
Jean Baptiste BOUDROT, his son		2
Jean Charles BOUDROT, a son; nursling		

45th family (4 persons)

Honoré COMEAUX	carpenter	67
Anastasie BELLEMERE, his wife		45
Joseph BOUDROT, wife's son; sailor		17
Charles BOUDROT, wife's son; sailor		14

46th family (6 persons)

Joseph HÉBERT	carpenter	51
Marie BENOIT, his wife		48
Joseph HÉBERT, his son	a tanner	24
Marie HÉBERT, his daughter		22
Sophie HÉBERT, his daughter		15
Sophie BENOIT, niece to the above		8

47th family (5 persons)
Honnoré CARET	journalier	50
Françoise BENOIT, sa fem^e		40
Pierre, son fils	idem	24
Madeleine THERIOT, veuve BENOIT		70
Victoire BENOIT, nièce au dit		14

48th family (3 persons)
Pierre TRAHAN	journalier	66
Marie CLÉMENZAU, sa fem^e		32
Louise Rennee, sa fille		2

49th family (4 persons)
Jean B^te DAIGLE	perelleur	48
Marie BOUDRAU, sa fem^e		50
Joseph, son fils		11
Anne, sa fille		15

50th family (5 persons)
Atanase BOURQUE	marin	45
Luce BRAUD, sa feme		33
Joseph, son fils		13
Charles, idem		10
Marie Rose, sa fille	à la mamelle	

51st family (1 person)
Mathurin COMMAU	marin	25

52nd family (1 person)
Marie TRAHAN, fille		20

53rd family (8 persons)
Charles LEBLANC	journalier	52
Rosalie TRAHAN, sa femme		40
Pierre Honnoré, son fils	charpentier	19
André, idem	journalier	18
Jean B^te, idem	à la mamelle	
Marie Rose, sa fille		21
Marie Françoise, idem		16
Barbe, idem		12

54th family (4 persons)
Joseph Philipe HENRY	marin	22
Marie TIBODAU, sa femme		32
Nicolas METRA, fils à la femme		3
Joseph METRA, idem	à la mamelle	

55th family (5 persons)
Jean THIBODAU	marin	37
Marie DUGAT, sa femme		18
Jacques, son fils	calfat	18
Marie, sa fille		14
Elisabet THIBODAU, veuve BOURBON		40

SM - #227: Honoré CARRET s/o Ignace & Cécile HENRY m. 1759 Françoise BENOIST d/o Charles & Marie-Madeleine THERIOT; a child Pierre b. 1761

SM - p.51: Victoire BENOIT d/o Augustin & Madeleine GAUTROT b. 11 Nov. 1772. Her father Augustin BENOIT is a brother to Charles BENOIST spouse of Madeleine THERIOT

Nantes - #305: Pierre TRAHAN s/o Pierre & Madeleine COMMAUX m. 1783 Marie CLÉMENCEAU d/o Jean & Françoise GAUTROT

Chat - #59: Jean-Baptiste DAIGLE m. ca. 1762 Marie BOUDROT; a child Anne b. 1769

Nantes - #89: additional family information

SM - #297: additional family information

Chat - #41: Athanase BOURG s/o François & Marguerite HÉBERT m. 1768 Luce or Louise BRAUD d/o Joseph & Ursule BOURG; a child Charles b. 1755

Nantes - #53: additional family information

SM - #159: additional family information

Chat - #134: Charles LEBLANC widr. Anne BENOIST s/o Claude & Madeleine BOUDROT m. 1763 Rosalie TRAHAN d/o Claude & Marie TILLARD; Children: Jean-Baptiste bt. 1784, Pierre Honoré b. 1765, Barbe b. 1772

Nantes - #207: additional family information

SM - #629: additional family information

Nantes - #179: Joseph-Philippe HENRY s/o Pierre & Marguerite TRAHAN m. 1785 Marie THIBODAUX d/o Pierre & Hélène GAUTROT wid. Nicolas METRA

Nantes - #288: Jean THIBODAUX s/o Pierre & Hélène GAUTROT m. 1785 Marie DUGAST d/o Michel & Françoise DURAND

SM - #885: additional family information

SM - #153: Jacques BOURBON m. ca. 1763 Élizabeth THIBODAUX

47th family (5 persons)

Honoré CARRET	day laborer	50
Françoise BENOIT, his wife		40
Pierre CARRET, his son	day laborer	24
Madelaine THERIOT, widow BENOIT		70
Victoire BENOIT, niece to the above		14

48th family (3 persons)

Pierre TRAHAN	day laborer	66
Marie CLÉMENCEAU, his wife		32
Louise Renné TRAHAN, his daughter		2

49th family (4 persons)

Jean Baptiste DAIGLE	48
Marie BOUDROT, his wife	50
Joseph DAIGLE, his son	11
Anne DAIGLE, his daughter	15

50th family (5 persons)

Athanase BOURG	sailor	45
Luce BRAUD, his wife		33
Joseph BOURG, his son		13
Charles BOURG, his son		10
Marie Rose BOURG, dgtr.; a nursling		

51st family (1 person)

Mathurin COMEAUX	sailor	25

52nd family (1 person)

Marie TRAHAN, young girl	20

53rd family (8 persons)

Charles LEBLANC	day laborer	52
Rosalie TRAHAN, his wife		40
Pierre Honoré LEBLANC, son; carpenter		19
André LEBLANC, his son	day laborer	18
Jean Baptiste LEBLANC, son; a nursling		
Marie Rose LEBLANC, his daughter		21
Marie Françoise LEBLANC, his daughter		16
Barbe LEBLANC, his daughter		12

54th family (4 persons)

Joseph Philipe HENRY	sailor	22
Marie THIBODEAUX, his wife		32
Nicolas METRA, wife's son		3
Joseph METRA, wife's son	a nursling	

55th family (5 persons)

Jean THIBODEAUX	sailor	37
Marie DUGAT, his wife		18
Jacques THIBODEAUX, son; calker		18
Marie THIBODEAUX, his daughter		14
Élizabeth THIBODEAUX, wid. BOURBON		40

56th family (5 persons)

Ygnace CARET	journalier	36
Magdeleine CLÉMENZAU, sa fem^e		34
Eustache, son fils	à la mamelle	
Jean, idem		14
Marie, sa fille		7

57th family (6 persons)

Pierre LECOQ	marin	40
Ysabelle VINCENT, sa fem^e		28
Marie, sa fille		11
Guillaume, son fils		9
Victoire, idem		1
Françoise, idem	à la mamelle	

Ceux de Morlais arrivés à Paimboeuf pour
  s'embarquer sur le même Navire:

1st family (4 persons)

Michel LEVRON	charpentier	55
Marguerite TRAHAN, sa fem^e		50
Joseph Marie, son fils	idem	17
Marie, sa fille		22

2nd family (2 persons)

Eustache TRAHAN	charpentier	40
Marie LEBLANC, sa femme		58

3rd family (8 persons

Marin TRAHAN	charpentier	40
Marguerite INO, sa fem^e		20
Jean B^{te}, son fils	idem	21
Jean Marie, idem		8
François, idem		7
Madeleine, sa fille		23
Marguerite, idem		15
Barbe, idem		11

4th family (8 persons)

Charles GAUTRAU	charpentier	44
Pélagie TRAHAN, sa femme		39
Charles, son fils	pulieur	19
Jean Marie, idem		7
Pierre, idem		4
Jean B^{te}, idem	à la mamelle	
Madeleine, sa fille		18
Aspasie, idem		2

5th family (2 persons)

Joseph RICHARD	tonnelier	32
Marie Elizabet, sa fille		10

SM - #229: Ignace CARRET s/o Ignace & Cécile HENRY m. 1767 Marie-Madeleine CLÉMENÇEAU d/o Jean & Françoise GAUTROT

Chat - #140: Pierre-François LECOQ s/o Jacques & Madeleine LAURANT m. 1774 Élizabeth VINCENT d/o Charles & Euphrosine DUON; Children: Guillaume bt. 1775, Victoire bt. 1784

Nantes - #224: additional family information

Exile - p.305: Children of Michel LEVRON & Marguerite TRAHAN: Marie-Joseph-Françoise b. 22 Oct. 1762

Exile - #421: Eustache TRAHAN s/o René & Marguerite MÉLANÇON m. 1766 Marie LEBLANC

Exile - p.151: Children of Charles GAUTROT & Pélagie TRAHAN:
Jean-Baptiste-Simon b. 19 June 1784
Jean-Charles-Joseph b. 23 June 1765
Jean-Louis-Laurent b. 10 Aug. 1771

56th family (5 persons)

Ignace CARRET	day laborer	36
Magdelaine CLÉMENÇEAU, his wife		34
Eustache CARRET, his son	a nursling	
Jean CARRET, his son		14
Marie CARRET, his daughter		7

57th family (6 persons)

Pierre LECOQ	sailor	40
Isabelle VINCENT, his wife		28
Marie LECOQ, his daughter		11
Guillaume LECOQ, his son		9
Victoire LECOQ, his daughter		1
Françoise LECOQ, his daughter; a nursling		

Those from Morlaix arriving at Paimboeuf in order to embark on the same ship:

1st family (4 persons)

Michel LEVRON	carpenter	55
Marguerite TRAHAN, his wife		50
Joseph Marie LEVRON, his son; carpenter		17
Marie LEVRON, his daughter		22

2nd family (2 persons)

Eustache TRAHAN	carpenter	40
Marie LEBLANC, his wife		58

3rd family (8 persons)

Marin TRAHAN	carpenter	40
Marguerite INO, his wife		20
Jean Baptiste TRAHAN, his son; carpenter		21
Jean Marie TRAHAN, his son		8
François TRAHAN, his son		7
Magdelaine TRAHAN, his daughter		23
Marguerite TRAHAN, his daughter		15
Barbe TRAHAN, his daughter		11

4th family (8 persons)

Charles GAUTROT	carpenter	44
Pélagie TRAHAN, his wife		39
Charles GAUTROT, son;	block maker	19
Jean Marie GAUTROT, his son		7
Pierre GAUTROT, his son		4
Jean Baptiste GAUTROT, son; nursling		
Magdelaine GAUTROT, his daughter		18
Aspasie GAUTROT, his daughter		2

5th family (2 persons)

Joseph RICHARD	cooper	32
Marie Élizabeth RICHARD, his daughter		10

6th family (4 persons)

Paul TRAHAN	charpentier	42
Marie Josèphe TRAHAN, sa fem^e		44
Paul, son fils		16
Pierre, idem		5

7th family (4 persons)

Tranquille LEPRINCE	charpentier	63
Susanne BOURQUE, sa femme		57
Ysabelle, sa fille		30
Marguerite, idem		24

8th family (2 persons)

Charles RICHARD	talleur [tailleur]	31
Marie Josèphe TRAHAN, sa fem^e		39

9th family (1 person)

Pierre TRAHAN	charpentier	28

10th family (1 person)

Jean B^te TRAHAN	charpentier	34

11th family (1 person)

Thomas LEBLANC	talleur [tailleur]	39

12th family (1 person)

Joseph LEBLANC	employé	37

13th family (2 persons)

Marguerite TRAHAN, veuve		49
Augustine Pélagie, sa fille		12

14th family (3 persons)

Marie RICHARD, fille		44
Marguerite, sa soeur		42
Elizabet, idem		33

15th family (2 persons)

Alexis LEVRON	charpentier	24
Anne TRAHAN, sa femme		24

16th family (5 persons)

Lambert BILLARDIN	employé	40
Marguerite DAIGRE, sa fem^e		37
Marie Jeanne, sa fille		6
Marguerite, idem		3
Étienne, son fils		10

Exile - p.426: Paul TRAHAN s/o Joseph & Élizabeth THERIOT m. 1767 Marie-Josèphe TRAHAN d/o René & Marguerite MELANÇON; Children: Paul b. 1768, Pierre b. 1779

Exile - p.302: Marie Marguerite LEPRINCE d/o Tranquille & Suzanne LEBOURG [BOURG] m. 18 Sept. 1775 Thomas Calegan HOUARDON

Exile - p.380: Charles RICHARD m. 1785 Marie-Jeanne TRAHAN

BR - v.2, pp.620, 626: Children of Charles RICHARD & Marie Josèphe TRAHAN:
Anastasie Marguerite b. 15 March 1801
Marie Félicité b. 26 Nov. 1789

Exile - p.420,425: Joseph TRAHAN m. Marguerite TRAHAN; their children:
Augustine Pélagie b. 28 August 1772 at Morlaix
Pierre Grégoire b. 23 Nov. 1769
Marie Josèphe b. 3 March 1766 at Morlaix
Paul Joseph b. 30 July 1768 at Morlaix

Exile - p.305: Alexis LEVRON s/o Michel & Marguerite TRAHAN m. 7 Feb. 1785 Ann TRAHAN d/o Charles & Françoise THERIOT

BR - v.2, p.720: Marguerite VILLARDIN of Morlaix d/o Albert & Marguerite DAIGLE m. 4 Oct. 1802 Julien OSSELLET of Nantes s/o Jean Baptiste & Marguerite LANDRY

Marie Jeanne VILLARDIN of Morlaix d/o Lambert & Marguerite DAIGRE m. 24 Oct. 1803 Joseph BOUDREAUX of St. Malo s/o Aman & Marie NOX [NOGUES]

6th family (4 persons)

Paul TRAHAN	carpenter	42
Marie Josèphe TRAHAN, his wife		44
Paul TRAHAN, his son		16
Pierre TRAHAN, his son		5

7th family (4 persons)

Tranquille LEPRINCE	carpenter	63
Susanne BOURG, his wife		57
Isabelle LEPRINCE, his daughter		30
Marguerite LEPRINCE, his daughter		24

8th family (2 persons)

Charles RICHARD	tailor	31
Marie Josèphe TRAHAN, his wife		19

9th family (1 persons)

Pierre TRAHAN	carpenter	28

10th family (1 person)

Pierre Baptiste TRAHAN	carpenter	34

11th family (1 person)

Thomas LEBLANC	tailor	39

12th family (1 person)

Joseph LEBLANC	worker	37

13th family (2 persons)

Marguerite TRAHAN, widow		49
Augustine Pélagie TRAHAN, her dgtr.		12

14th family (3 persons)

Marie RICHARD, an unmarried woman		44
Marguerite RICHARD, her sister		42
Élizabeth RICHARD, her sister		33

15th family (2 persons)

Alexis LEVRON	carpenter	24
Anne TRAHAN, his wife		24

16th family (5 persons)

Lambert BILLARDIN	worker	40
Marguerite DAIGLE, his wife		37
Marie Jeanne BILLARDIN, his daughter		6
Marguerite BILLARDIN, his daughter		3
Étienne BILLARDIN, his son		10

Supplément à la liste des Acadiens embarqués dans le
navire Le Saint-Rémi pour la nouvelle- orleans.

1st family (8 persons)
Grégoire BENOIT	journalier	40
Marie Rose CARET, sa femme		32
Jean Marie, son fils		10
Donnatien, idem		8
Raymond	à la mamelle	
Marie Rose, sa fille		9
Françoise, idem		5
Thérèse CARET, soeur de la femme		29

2nd family (2 persons)
Simon LANDRY	marin	50
Margueritte GOTREAU, sa femme		59

3rd family (6 persons)
P^{re} LEBLANC	journalier	49
Françoise TRAHAN, sa femme		47
Simon, son fils		9
Marie, sa fille		22
Geneviève, sa fille		21
Françoise, idem	à la mamelle	

4th family (3 persons)
Charles LEBLANC	journalier	67
Magdeleine GOTREAU, sa femme		68
Margueritte, sa fille		18

5th family (3 persons)
Anne DAIGLE, veuve MICHEL		43
Marie, sa fille		20
Anne, idem		15

6th family (4 persons)
Aimable LANDRY	graveur	19
Ysaac Abraham, son frère		13
Jeanne Margueritte, sa soeur		20
Bonne Louise Marie, idem		17

Additional list of Acadians embarked on the ship Le Saint-Rémi bound for New Orleans.

1st family (8 persons)		
Grégoire BENOIT	day laborer	40
Marie Rose CARRET, his wife		32
Jean Marie BENOIT, his son		10
Donatien BENOIT, his son		8
Raymond BENOIT	a nursling	
Marie Rose BENOIT, his daughter		9
Françoise BENOIT, his daughter		5
Thérèse CARRET, sister of the wife		29

Chat - #15: Grégoire BENOIST s/o Claude & Isabelle THERIOT m. 1770 Marie-Rose CARRET d/o Jean & Rose TRAHAN; Children: Marie-Rose bt. 1775, Remond-Grégoire bt. 1783, Jean-Marie b. 1773

SM - #65: additional family information
Nantes - #21: additional family information

2nd family (2 persons)		
Simon LANDRY	sailor	50
Marguerite GAUTROT, his wife		59

SM #613: Simon LANDRY m. ca. 1761 Marguerite GAUTROT

3rd family (6 persons)		
Pierre LEBLANC	day laborer	49
Françoise TRAHAN, his wife		47
Simon LEBLANC, his son		9
Marie LEBLANC, his daughter		22
Geneviève LEBLANC, his daughter		21
Françoise LEBLANC, his daughter; nursling		

Nantes - #220: Pierre LEBLANC s/o Jean & Françoise BLANCHARD m. 1758 Françoise TRAHAN d/o Joseph & Élizabeth THERIOT

4th family (3 persons)		
Charles LEBLANC	day laborer	67
Magdelaine GAUTROT, his wife		68
Marguerite LEBLANC, his daughter		18

Nantes - #206: Charles LEBLANC s/o René & Jeanne LANDRY m. 1758 Madeleine GAUTROT d/o Pierre & Marie BUJEAUD

5th family (3 persons)		
Anne DAIGLE, widow MICHEL		43
Marie MICHEL, her daughter		20
Anne MICHEL, her daughter		15

SM - #628: additional family information
Chat - #152: François MICHEL m. ca. 1762 Anne DAIGLE; a child Anne MICHEL b. 1770
Nantes - #240: additional family information

6th family (4 persons)		
Aimable LANDRY	engraver	19
Isaac Abraham LANDRY, his brother		13
Jeanne Marguerite LANDRY, his sister		20
Bonne Louise Marie LANDRY, his sister		17

Exile - p.271: Children of Joseph LANDRY & Jeanne VARONQUER:
Aimable-Étienne b. 10 Dec. 1765
Abraham-Isaac b. 1 Feb. 1772
Anne-Adélaïde b. 3 Feb. 1771
Bonne-Marie-Louise b. 14 April 1767
Jean-Baptiste-Leonor b. 31 Jan. 1773
Magdalen-Geneviève b. 18 Oct. 1769

Exile - p.273: Joseph LANDRY widr. Cécile d'ENTREMONT s/o René & Marie-Josèphe Mius d'ENTREMONT m. 26 April 1763 Jeanne-Marie-Magdalen VARANGUE d/o Antoine & Jeanne LETERRIER
Nantes - #198: additional family information

Lista parcial de vientitres casamientos acadianos arrega-
lados por Navarro, 20 noviembre 1785.

Marriages celebrated on 20 November 1785
Joseph ADAM, immigrant

Margarite ----- [19th family on Le Saint-Rémi]
****

Luis Antonio CHARRIE, immigrant

Marie HACHÉ (daughter of Francisca DOUCET,
    widow of HACHÉ) [54th family on Le Saint-Rémi]
****

Santiago DAVOIR [of the ship La Amistad]

****

Agustin DOUAN (son of Honorato DOUAN & Ana
    TRAHAM) [62nd family on Le Saint-Rémi]

Margarita LEBLANC (daughter of Carlos & Magdalena
    GAUTREAUX)   [She died at the hospital; on Le
    Saint-Rémi]
****

Tourchet DE LA GARDE alias Leonor

Francisca CROCHET, sister of Agustin DOUAN
****

Josef LEJEUNE (son of Anastasia LEBRON,
    widow LEJEUNE)

Maria LANDRY [18th family on Le Saint-Rémi]
****

B. Marriages celebrated 2 December 1785
Luis PINEL [5th family on Le Saint-Rémi]

Blanca VINCENT [8th family on Le Saint-Rémi]
****

Vincente NEVEU, immigrant

Cecilia HEBERT (daughter of Estevan EBERT)
[20th family on Le Saint-Rémi]
****

Partial List of 23 marriages Navarro arranged
on 20 November 1785.

A. Marriages celebrated on 20 November 1785

NO - v.4: Josef ADANA of La Rochelle s/o Nicolas &
Maria BLANCHARD m. 24 Nov. 1785 Margarita
CROCHET of St. Malo d/o Yfe [Yves] & Pelagia
BENOIT

Joseph ADAMS, an immigrant

Marguerite [CROCHET] [19th family Le Saint-Rémi]
****

NO - v.4: Luis Antonio CHARRIER of Poitou s/o Luis
& Maria DELORMO m. 1 Dec. 1785 Mariana
HACHÉ of St. Malo d/o Pedro & Ana DUMOND

Louis Antoine CHARRIÉ, immigrant

Marie HACHÉ (daughter of Françoise DOUCET,
widow of HACHÉ) [54th family Le Saint-Rémi]
****

NO - v.4: Jacobo DUBOIS, native of Normandy,
France s/o Olivier & Margarita VALO m. 24 Nov.
1785 Maria MIGUEL of St. Malo d/o Francisco &
Ana DAIGLE

Jacques DAVOIR [from the L'Amitié]

Marie MICHEL [60th family on Le Saint-Rémi]
****

NO - v.4: Agustin DUN [DUHON] of Berilamer [Belle
Ile-en-Mer] s/o Honorato & Ana DUN m. 4 Dec.
1785 Margarita LEBLANC of St. Malo d/o Carlos &
Magdalena GOD [GAUTROT]

Augustin DUHON (son of Honoré DUHON & Anne
TRAHAN) [62nd family on Le Saint-Rémi]

Marguerite LEBLANC (daughter of Charles & Magdeleine GAUTROT) She died at the hospital; of Le
Saint-Rémi.
****

NO - v.4: Leonardo DE LA GARDE of Surget, France
s/o Gartau & Francisca CHARPATAN m. 2 Aug.
1785 Francisca CROCHET of St. Malo d/o Yfe
[Yves] & Pelagia BENOIT

Leonard [Tourchet] DE LA GARDE

Françoise CROCHET, sister of Augustin DUHON
****

NO - v.4: Josef LEGEUNE, native of Liverpool,
England s/o Amand & Anastasia LEBRON m. 24
Nov. 1785 Bonne Maria Adélaïde LANDRY of
Normandy, France d/o Germano & Cecilia
LAGARENNE

Joseph LEJEUNE (Anastasie LEVRON
wid. LEJEUNE)

Marie LANDRY [18th family on Le Saint-Rémi]
****

B. Marriages celebrated 2 December 1785

NO - v.4: Luis PINEL of Cherbourg in Normandy,
France s/o Carlos & Mariana DUREL m. 2 Dec.
1785 Maria VICENTE d/o Juan & Ursula HEBERT

Louis PINET [5th family on Le Saint-Rémi]

Blanche VINCENT [8th family on Le Saint-Rémi]
****

NO - v.4: Vicente NEVEAU of Ludaine in Tarhe(??)
s/o Vicente & Maria BÉNARD m. 2 Dec. 1785
Cecilia HEVERT of Normandy, France d/o Estevan
& Maria LAVERGNE

Vincent NEVEU, immigrant

Cécile HÉBERT (daughter of Étienne HÉBERT) [20th
family on Le Saint-Rémi]
****

A larger frigate than either Le Bon Papa, La Bergère or Le Beaumont. Le Saint-Rémi [400 tons] had 325 passengers plus 16 stowaways or 341 passengers with a great load of baggage, furniture and trunks. The unhealthy congestion and smallpox left 12 children dead. Scurvy caused the death of 3 women. Upon arriving smallpox claimed 16 more victims and much sickness in their camp in New Orleans. After regaining health there were 19 new adherents, celebration of 8 births and 5 marriages. Of the group, 85 families chose La Fourche (area around Plattenville), 2 families chose Atacapas (St. Martinville) and Opelousas while 2 families chose Nueva Galvez (often called Galveztown; at the confluence [coming or flowing together of the two streams] of the Amite River and Bayou Manchac or southeast of Baton Rouge) and Baton Rouge. [Winzerling pp.139, and 143]

C. Marriages celebrated 3 December 1785
Luis JOUDICE, surgeon on Le Saint-Rémi

Ana JAQUES [65th family on the La Amistad]
****

Carlos MACLE

Marie BÉNARD (daughter of Josef BÉNARD and Juana RICHARD) [64th family on Le Saint-Rémi]
****

D. Marriage celebrated 6 December 1785
Silvestre GOMEZ, immigrant

Carlota FOUQUET [65th family on Le Saint-Rémi]
****

E. Marriage celebrated 12 December 1785
Mathurino ALIOT, immigrant

Cecilia BOUDREAU (Estevan BOUDREAU) [35th family on Le Saint-Rémi]
****

F. Marriages celebrated 14 December 1785
Luis MENARD, immigrant

Maria Josefa RICHARD, wid. Baset CAVENZA [21st family on Le Saint-Rémi]
****

Juan CROCHET [19th family on LE Saint-Rémi]

Maria Martha BOUDREAU (daughter of Josef & Margarita RICHARD) [19th family on Le Saint-Rémi]
****

"Liste des Acadiens nommés pour s'embarquer sur le Navire Le Saint-Rémi Capitaine Mr. Baudin allant à la Louisiane."

"Nous, Consul d'Espagne en Bretagne chargé de l'expedition des Acadiens pour la Louisiane. Certifions que les trois cents dix personnes denommés, ci-dessus sont celles que nous avons nommés pour s'embarquer sur le Navire Le Saint-Rémi allant au Port de la Nouvelle Orleans dans la Louisiane. A Nantes, ce 25 Juin 1785. d'Asperer"

Translation:
List of Acadians designated to embark the ship Le Saint-Rémi, Captain Mr. Baudin, going to Louisiana.

We, Consul of Spain in Brittany charged with the transporting of the Acadians to Louisiana. Certifying that the 310 persons listed above are those we have listed to embark on the ship Le Saint-Rémi going to the Port of New Orleans in Louisiana. At nantes, on 25 June 1785.

C. Marriages celebrated 3 December 1785
Louis JUDICE, surgeon on Le Saint-Rémi

Anne JACQUES [65th family on the La Amistad]
****

NO - v.4: Carlos Daniel MACLE of Arle in Franche Comte s/o Basilio & ----- m. 4 Dec. 1785 ----- -------

Charles MACLE

Marie BÉNARD (daughter of Joseph BÉNARD and Jeanne RICHARD) [64th family on Le Saint-Rémi]
****

NO - v.4: Silvestre GOMES, native of Senseca, Castille s/o Silverio & Maria GUTIERRES m. 6 Dec. 1785 Maria Carlota FOUQUET of Puerto Luis, France d/o Juan & Margarita QUIMIN

D. Marriage celebrated 6 December 1785
Silvestre GOMEZ, immigrant

Charlotte FOUQUET [65th family on Le Saint-Rémi]
****

NO - v.4: Maturina AYO of La Rochelle s/o Pedro & Margarita RUSOD m. 11 Dec. 1785 Cecilia BUDREAU of St. Malo d/o Estevan & Margarita BUDREAU

E. Marriage celebrated 12 December 1785
Mathurin AYO, immigrant

Cécile BOUDREAUX (Étienne BOUDREAUX) [35th family on Le Saint-Rémi]
****

NO - v.4: Luis MENARD of Bu--os(??) s/o Pedro & Margarita BOYER m. 14 Dec. 1785 Maria Josefa RICHARD of Acadia, wid. Francisco PACET d/o Juan Bautista & -----

F. Marriages celebrated 14 December 1785
Louis MENARD, immigrant

Marie Josèphe RICHARD, widow Baset CAVENZA [21st family on Le Saint-Rémi]
****

Jean CROCHET [19th family on Le Saint-Rémi]

Marie Marthe BOUDREAUX (daughter of Joseph & Marguerite RICHARD) [19th family on Le Saint-Rémi]
****

1st family (4 persons)
Jean GUSMAN	journalier	50	
Rose BONNERY, sa femme		42	
Jean Thomas, son fils		2	
Rosalie Charlotte, sa fille		21	

1st family
Juan GUZMAN

2nd family (3 persons)
Jean BROUSSARD	charpentier	40	
Margueritte COMMEAU, sa femme		32	
Jean, son fils		11	

2nd family
Juan BAUSARD   Received: 1 each of axe, medium axe, shovel, knife; 2 hoes

3rd family (1 person)
Charles DOUCET, garçon	charpentier	40	

3rd family
Carlos DOUCET   Received: 1 each of axe, shovel, hoe, and knife

4th family (4 persons)
Jean DE LAUNE	charpentier	48	
Marianne PARS, sa femme		34	
Marie Céleste, sa fille	à la mamelle		
P^{re}, son fils		7	

4th family

5th family (3 persons)
Jean B^{te} LEBLANC	cordonier	44	
Élisabeth AU COIN, sa femme		50	
Marie Marguerite SEMER, nièce au dit		19	

5th family
Juan Bautista LEBLANC   Received: 1 each of axe, medium axe, shovel, hatchet, knife; 2 hoes

6th family (4 persons)
Marie MOISE, veuve Olivier PITRE	45	
Louis Constant, son fils	10	
Victoire, sa fille	19	
Françoise, idem	14	

6th family
Maria MOISES, widow Olivier   Received: 1 each of axe, medium axe, shovel, knife; 2 hoes

7th family (2 persons)
J^h AU COIN	journalier	60	
Magdeleine BOUDREAU, sa femme		58	

7th family

8th family (5 persons)
Christophe DELAUNE	charpentier	34	
Marie BOUDREAU, sa femme		30	
Jean B^{te}, son fils		10	
Louis Auguste, idem		1	
Céleste BOUDREAU, fille; soeur à la femme		20	

8th family

9th family (5 persons)
Jean François DE LA MASIERE	charpentier	37	
Véronique RENNEAU, sa femme		37	
Jean B^{te}, son fils		8	
Louise Céleste, sa fille		6	
Rose Jeanne, idem		4	

9th family
Juan Francisco DE LA MASSIERE   Received: 1 each of axe, medium axe, shovel, knife; 3 hoes

10th family (2 persons)
Grégoire SEMÉ	cordier	16	
Françoise SEMÉ, sa soeur		24	

10th family

Chat - #89: Jean GOUSMAN s/o Jean & Marie BARRILLOT m. 1760 Rose BONNEVIE d/o Jacques & Marguerite LORD	**1st family (4 persons)**
Nantes - #134: additional family information	

1st family (4 persons)

Jean GOUSMAN	day laborer	50
Rose BONNEVIE, his wife		42
Jean Thomas GOUSMAN, his son		2
Rosalie Charlotte GOUSMAN, his daughter		21

Chat - #53 Jean BROUSSARD s/o Joseph & Ursule LEBLANC m. 1773 Marguerite COMMAUX; a child Jean-Baptiste b. 1774

Nantes - #74: additional family information

2nd family (3 persons)

Jean BROUSSARD	carpenter	40
Marguerite COMEAUX, his wife		32
Jean BROUSSARD, his son		11

3rd family (1 person)

Charles DOUCET, young man	carpenter	40

Chat - #67: Jean DELAUNE s/o Christopher & Marguerite CAISSY m. 1773 Marie-Anne PART d/o Eustache & Anastasie de BELLEFONTAINE

Nantes - #101: additional family information

4th family (4 persons)

Jean DELAUNE	carpenter	48
Marianne PART, his wife		34
Marie Céleste DELAUNE, dgtr; a nursling		
Pierre DELAUNE, his son		7

5th family (3 persons)

Jean Baptiste LEBLANC	shoemaker	44
Élisabeth AUCOIN, his wife		50
Marie Marguerite SEMER, his niece		19

Nantes - #260: Olivier PITRE s/o Claude & Marguerite DOIRON m. 1763 Marie MOYSE d/o Louis & Marie PETIT

SM - #781: additional family information

6th family (4 persons)

Marie MOYSE, widow Olivier PITRE	45
Louis Constant PITRE, her son	10
Victoire PITRE, her daughter	19
Françoise PITRE, her daughter	14

7th family (2 persons)

Joseph AUCOIN	day laborer	60
Magdelaine BOUDROT, his wife		58

Chat - #66: Christopher DELAUNE s/o Christopher & Marguerite CAISSY m. 1774 Marie BOUDROT d/o Pierre & Cécile VECO; a child Jean-Baptiste DELAUNE b. 1775

Nantes - #100: additional family information

8th family (5 persons)

Christophe DELAUNE	carpenter	34
Marie BOUDROT, his wife		30
Jean Baptiste DELAUNE, his son		10
Louis Auguste DELAUNE, his son		1
Céleste BOUDREAU, girl; sister of the wife		20

Chat - #65: Jean-François DE LA MAZIERE m. ca. 1768 Véronique RENAUD; a child Rose-Jeanne DE LA MAZIERE bt. 1781

9th family (5 persons)

Jean François DE LA MAZIERE	carpenter	37
Véronique RENAUD, his wife		37
Jean Baptiste DE LA MAZIERE; his son		8
Louise Céleste DE LA MAZIERE; his dgtr.		6
Rose Jeanne DE LA MAZIERE, his dgtr.		4

10th family (2 persons)

Grégoire SEMER	ropemaker	16
Françoise SEMER, his sister		24

11th family (4 persons)

Colette RENNEAU, veuve TOUILLIER		45
Jean Charles, son fils	charpentier	19
Ysidore, idem		14
Adélaïde, sa fille		16

11th family

Coleda BAINEAUD   Received: 1 each of axe, medium axe, shovel, knife; 2 hoes

12th family (4 persons)

François LANDRY	charpentier	60
Jean J^{ques}, son petit fils		15
Bonne Marie, sa petite fille		16
Jean Charles LANDRY, neveu au dit; marin		18

12th family

Francisco LANDRY   Received: 1 each of knife; 2 of shovel, hatchet; 3 axe and hoe

13th family (4 persons)

Zacarie BOUDREAU	charpentier	60
Margueritte VALOIS, sa femme		50
Benjamin, son fils	calfat	19
J^{ques} DUBOIS, fils à la femme		14

13th family

Zacariah BOUDREAUX   Received: 1 each of knife and shovel; 2 of axe and hoe

14th family (7 persons)

J^h BOUDREAU	charpentier	40
Margueritte RICHARD, sa femme		40
Jean Charles, son fils	marin	18
Joseph, idem		9
Marie Marthe, sa fille		20
Sophie, sa fille		3
Marie HÉBERT, sa mineure		12

14th family

Josef BOUDREAU   Received: 1 each of shovel, hatchet and knife; 2 axe; 3 hoes

15th family (3 persons)

Charles BOUDREAU	charpentier	21
Marie GOTREAU, sa femme		19
Charles Marie, son fils	à la mamelle	

15th family

Juan Carlos BOUDREAU   Received: 1 each of axe, shovel, hatchet, and knife; 2 medium axe, and hoe

16th family (3 persons)

Joseph SEMER	laboureur	60
Marie, sa fille		25
Anne Françoise, idem		21

16th family

Josef SEMAR   Received: 1 each of axe, shovel, hatchet and knife; 2 hoes

17th family (4 persons)

Jean Charles HACHÉ	marin	22
Marie PINEL, sa femme		20
Frédéric HACHÉ, frère au dit; journalier		15
Marie Bonne, soeur au dit		18

17th family

Juan Carlos HACHE   Received: 1 each of axe, medium axe, shovel, hatchet and knife; 2 hoes

18th family (5 persons)

Ursule HÉBERT, veuve Jean VINCENT		45
Anne Blanche, sa fille		23
Marie Blanche, idem		17
Jeanne Margueritte, idem		12
Flore Adélaïde, idem		11

18th family

Ursula HEBERT   Received: 1 each of axe, shovel, hatchet and knife; 3 hoes

Nantes - #235: René LETULLIER d. 1784; m. ca. 1762 Colette RENAUD d/o Jean & Marie-Magdeleine POITIER

BR - v.2, p.709: Adélaïde TULLIER d/o René & Colette RENAUD m. 13 Feb. 1790 Jean Marie TRAHAN

11th family (4 persons)

Colette RENAUD, widow LETULLIER		45
Jean Charles LETULLIER, son; carpenter		19
Isidore LETULLIER, her son		14
Adélaïde LETULLIER, her daughter		16

Exile - p.271: Germain LANDRY s/o François & d. Marie BABEIN m. 30 July 1767 Cécille LAGARENNE d/o Jean Baptiste & Anne POITIER; children: Bonne Marie Adélaïde b. 27 July 1769, Jean Jacques Frédérique b. 26 July 1770

12th family (4 persons)

François LANDRY	carpenter	60
Jean Jacques LANDRY, grandson		15
Bonne Marie LANDRY, granddaughter		16
Jean Charles LANDRY, his nephew; sailor		18

Nantes - #49: Zacharie BOUDROT s/o Jean-Baptiste & Cécile CORPORON m. 1782 Marguerite VALLOIS

13th family (4 persons)

Zacharie BOUDROT	carpenter	60
Marguerite VALLOIS, his wife		50
Benjamin BOUDROT, his son; calker		19
Jacques DUBOIS, son of the wife		14

Chat - #34: Joseph BOUDROT s/o Michel & Claire COMMAUX m. 1763 Marguerite RICHARD d/o Jean & Cécile GAUTROT; a child Marie Marthe b. 1764

Census - p.124: Owned 6 arpent of land

Nantes - #43: additional family information

14th family (7 persons)

Joseph BOUDROT	carpenter	40
Marguerite RICHARD, his wife		40
Jean Charles BOUDROT, his son; sailor		18
Joseph BOUDROT, his son		9
Marie Marthe BOUDROT, his daughter		20
Sophie BOUDROT, his daughter		3
Marie HÉBERT, his minor child		12

Nantes - #32: Charles BOUDROT s/o Zacharie & Marguerite DAIGLE m. ca. 1784 Marie GAUTROT d/o Joseph & Anne PITRE

15th family (3 persons)

Charles BOUDROT	carpenter	21
Marie GAUTROT, his wife		19
Charles Marie BOUDROT, son; nursling		

SM - #859: Joseph SEMER m. ca. 1754 Anne LANDRY d. 1766; a child Anne Françoise b. 1763

16th family (3 persons)

Joseph SEMER	plowman	60
Marie SEMER, his daughter		25
Anne Françoise SEMER, his daughter		21

17th family (4 persons)

Jean Charles HACHÉ	sailor	22
Marie PINET, his wife		20
Frédéric HACHÉ, his brother; day laborer		15
Marie Bonne HACHÉ, his sister		18

Chat - #192: Jean VINCENT m. ca. 1760 Ursule HÉBERT

BR - v.2, p.721: Marguerite VINCENT d/o Jean & Ursule HÉBERT m. 20 Aug. 1798 Joseph BAYE s/o Joseph & Cecilia GESAN

18th family (5 persons)

Ursule HÉBERT, widow Jean VINCENT		45
Anne Blanche VINCENT, her daughter		23
Marie Blanche VINCENT, her daughter		17
Jeanne Marguerite VINCENT, daughter		12
Flore Adélaïde VINCENT, her daughter		11

19th family (6 persons)

Pélagie BENOIT, veuve d'Yves CROCHET		44
Jean, son fils	marin	24
Yves, son fils	idem	16
Julien, idem		12
Françoise, sa fille		22
Margueritte, idem		19

19th family

Pelagia BENOIT　　Received: 1 each of hatchet; 2 od axe, shovel, hoe and knife

Juan CROCHET　　Received: 1 each of axe, medium axe, and shovel; 2 hoes

20th family (3 persons)

Jean B^te DOUCET	perseur	19
Marie Anne PRÉCIEUX, sa mère		52
François, son fils	journalier	14

20th family

Juan Bautista DOUCET　　Received: 1 each of shovel, and knife; 2 of axe and hoe

21st family (4 persons)

Charles PINEL	laboureur	54
Anne DUREL, sa femme		50
Marie Magdeleine, sa fille		14
Louis, son fils	marin	22

21st family

Carlos PINEL　　Received: 1 each of axe, shovel, hatchet and knife; 2 hoes

Louis PINEL　　Received: 1 each of axe, shovel, hatchet and knife; 2 hoes

22nd family (4 persons)

Louis LAMOUREUX dit ROCHEFORT; marin		44
Marie HÉBERT, sa femme		36
Jean Louis, son fils	marin	20
Adelaïde, sa fille		10

22nd family

23rd family (3 persons)

Marie J^he RICHARD,	
veuve François BANET	50
Marie, sa fille	5
Marie Geneviève, soeur de la dite veuve	32

23rd family

24th family (5 persons)

Louis GAUDET	charpentier	57
Marie HÉBERT, sa femme		54
François Louis, son fils		12
Magdeleine, sa fille		28
Margueritte, idem		20

24th family

25th family (5 persons)

Michel DOUCET	charpentier	45
Marie Blanche COUSINE, sa femme		37
Jean B^te Michel, son fils		12
Eleonnore, sa fille		15
Marguerite, idem		9

25th family

26th family (1 person)

Marguerite BENOIT, veuve PRECIEUSE	32

26th family

27th family (4 persons)

J^h DOUCET	laboureur	53
Ange, son fils		15
Marie Marthe, sa fille		19
Magdeleine, idem		17

27th family

Chat - #57: Yves CROCHET s/o Guillaume & Julienne DURAND m. 1758 Pélagie BENOIST d/o Claude & Élizabeth THERIOT			

SM - #276: additional family information

Chat - #72: Augustin DOUCET widr. Cécile MIUS m. 1752 Marie-Anne PRÉCIEUX d/o Joseph & Anne HACHÉ

Chat - #161: Charles PINET s/o Noël & Rose HENRY m. 1753 Anne DUVAL d/o Charles & Judith CHIASSON

Chat - #120: Louis LAMOUREUX called Rochefort m. 1763 Marie HÉBERT d/o Jean & Marguerite MOUTON; a child Adélaïde b. 1774

Chat - #74: Michel DOUCET m. 1768 Marie-Blanche COUSIN d/o Jean & Judith GUÉDRY

Nantes - #108: additional family information

Chat - #169: Joseph PRÉCIEUX s/o Joseph & Anne HACHÉ m. 1775 Marguerite BENOIST d/o Claude & Élizabeth THERIOT

19th family (6 persons)

Pélagie BENOIT, widow of Yves CROCHET		44
Jean CROCHET, his son	sailor	24
Yves CROCHET, his son	sailor	16
Julien CROCHET, his son		12
Françoise CROCHET, his daughter		22
Marguerite CROCHET, his daughter		19

20th family (3 persons)

Jean Baptiste DOUCET	borer	19
Marie Anne PRÉCIEUX, his mother		52
François DOUCET, his son	day laborer	14

21st family (4 persons)

Charles PINET	plowman	54
Anne DUREL, his wife		50
Marie Magdelaine PINET, his daughter		14
Louis PINET, his son	sailor	22

22nd family (4 persons)

Louis LAMOUREUX dit ROCHEFORT; sailor		44
Marie HÉBERT, his wife		36
Jean Louis LAMOUREUX, his son		20
Adélaïde LAMOUREUX, his daughter		10

23rd family (3 persons)

Marie Josèphe RICHARD,	
widow François BASSET	30
Marie BASSET, her daughter	5
Marie Geneviève RICHARD, widow's sister	32

24th family (5 persons)

Louis GAUDET	carpenter	57
Marie HÉBERT, his wife		54
François Louis GAUDET, his son		12
Magdelaine GAUDET, his daughter		28
Marguerite GAUDET, his daughter		20

25th family (5 persons)

Michel DOUCET	carpenter	45
Marie Blanche COUSIN, his wife		37
Jean Baptiste Michel DOUCET, his son		12
Eleonore DOUCET, his daughter		15
Marguerite DOUCET, his daughter		9

26th family (1 person)

Marguerite BENOIT, widow PRÉCIEUX	32

27th family (4 persons)

Joseph DOUCET	plowman	53
Ange DOUCET, his son		15
Marie Marthe DOUCET, his daughter		19
Magdelaine DOUCET, his daughter		17

28th family (6 persons)

Veuve BOUDREAUX		60
J^h, son fils	charpentier	19
Charles Michel, idem	calfat	24
Etienne, idem	marin	18
Margueritte, sa fille		16
Marie Magdeleine, idem		20

28th family

Brigida PART, widow BOUDREAU
    Received: 1 each of hatchet and knife; 2 of axe, shovel and hoe

29th family (5 persons)

Alexis BROD	journalier	61
Marie GUILLOT, sa femme		62
Margueritte, sa fille		20
Fabien GUILLOT, son neveu au dit; marin		23
Jean GOTREAU, cousin au dit; marin		22

29th family

Alexo BREAUD   Received: 1 each of axe, medium axe, shovel and knife; 2 hoes

Fabian GUILLOT   1 axe, shovel, hoe and knife

Juan GAUTREAU   Rec'd 1 axe, shovel, hoe, knife

30th family (8 persons)

Louis DENTIN	menuisier	38
Eleine AU COIN, sa femme		37
Jeanne DENTIN		16
Marie, idem		12
Anne, idem		9
Julie, idem		7
François(sic) DOUAISON, fille de la femme		17
Marie, idem		12

30th family

Luis DANTIN   Received: 1 each of axe, medium axe, shovel, hatchet and knife; 3 hoes

31st family (7 persons)

Étienne HÉBERT	marin	38
Magdeleine BROD, sa femme		36
Louis, son fils		15
Guillaume, idem		12
Gabriel, idem		10
Cécille, sa fille		18
Marie Magdeleine, idem	à la mamelle	

31st family

Estevan HEBERT   Received: 1 each of medium axe and knife; 2 of axe, shovel and hoe

32nd family (2 persons)

| Ambroise HÉBERT | menuisier | 39 |
| Jean P^{re}, son frère | charpentier | 38 |

32nd family

Ambrosio HEBERT   Received: 1 knife; 2 of axe, shovel and hoe

33rd family (2 persons)

| Margueritte BLANCHARD, veuve BERTHRAND | | 60 |
| J^n, son fils | marin | 20 |

33rd family

Juan BELTRAND   1 axe, shovel, hoe and knife

34th family (8 persons)

Benoît COMMEAU	charpentier	48
Anne BLANCHARD, sa femme		45
Jean, son fils	idem	19
Anne Eleonnore, sa fille		14
Margueritte, idem		12
Marie Anne Victoire, idem		16
Rose, idem		5
Magdeleine BLANCHARD, belle soeur		40

34th family

Benite CAUMMEAU   Received: 1 each of axe, shovel and knife; 3 hatchets; 4 hoes

Nantes - #31: Antoine BOUDROT d. 1776 s/o Jean-Baptiste & Louise SAULNIER m. 1747 Brigitte PART d/o Michel & Élizabeth HÉBERT; their children:

SM - #117: Etienne b. 29 December 1766
    Marguerite Joseph b. 17 April 1768
    Charles Michel b. 23 October 1761

SM - #193: Alexis BRAUD s/o Antoine & Marguerite DUGAST m. ca. 1745 Marie-Josèphe GUILLOT d/o René & Marguerite DOIRON

SM - #477: a child Fabien-Amateur GUILLOT b. 1763

Nantes - #96: Louis DANTIN s/o Louis & Marguerite LA SONDE m. 1784 Hélène AUCOIN d/o Antoine & Élizabeth AMIRAULT

Nantes - #165: Étienne HÉBERT s/o Jean & Marguerite MOUTON m. 1781 Anne-Madeleine BRAUD d/o Alexis & Marie-Josèphe THIBODAUX; a child Marie-Madeleine bt. 1785

Nantes - #23: Jean BERTRAND d. 1781; m. ca. 1762 Marguerite BLANCHARD

Nantes - #80: Benoist COMMAUX s/o Maurice & Marguerite THIBODAUX m. ca. 1764 Anne BLANCHARD; a child Rose-Julie COMMAUX bt. 1779

BR - v.2, p.201: Rose COMEAUX of Nantes d/o Benoît & Anne BLANCHARD m. 1 April 1799 Simon GUILLOT of St. Malo

28th family (6 persons)

Widow BOUDROT [Brigitte PART]		60
Joseph BOUDROT, her son; carpenter		19
Charles Michel BOUDROT, son; calker		24
Étienne BOUDROT, her son; sailor		18
Marguerite BOUDROT, her daughter		16
Marie Magdelaine BOUDROT, daughter		20

29th family (5 persons)

Alexis BRAUD	day laborer	61
Marie GUILLOT, his wife		62
Marguerite BRAUD, his daughter		20
Fabien GUILLOT, his nephew; sailor		23
Jean GAUTROT, his cousin; sailor		22

30th family (8 persons)

Louis DANTIN,	house carpenter	38
Elène AUCOIN, his wife		37
Jeanne DANTIN, his daughter		16
Marie DANTIN, his daughter		12
Anne DANTIN, his daughter		9
Julie DANTIN, his daughter		7
Françoise DOIRON, daughter of the wife		17
Marie DOIRON, daughter of the wife		12

31st family (7 persons)

Étienne HÉBERT	sailor	38
Magdelaine BRAUD, his wife		36
Louis HÉBERT, his son		15
Guillaume HÉBERT, his son		12
Gabriel HÉBERT, his son		10
Cécille HÉBERT, his daughter		18
Marie Magdelaine HÉBERT, dgtr.; nursling		

32nd family (2 persons)

Ambroise HÉBERT	house carpenter	39
Jean Pierre HÉBERT, his brother; carpenter		38

33rd family (2 persons)

Marguerite BLANCHARD, widow BERTRAND		60
Jean BERTRAND, her son	sailor	20

34th family (8 persons)

Benoît COMEAUX	carpenter	48
Anne BLANCHARD, his wife		45
Jean COMEAUX, his son	carpenter	19
Anne Eleonore COMEAUX, his daughter		14
Marguerite COMEAUX, his daughter		12
Marie Anne Victoire COMEAUX, daughter		16
Rose COMEAUX, his daughter		5
Magdelaine BLANCHARD, sister-in-law		40

36th family (6 persons)
Jean Charles BENOIT	marin	36
Marie HACHÉ, sa femme		34
Jean Marie, son fils		14
Paul Frédéric, idem		9
François Renné, idem		7
Sophie Rennée, sa fille		2

36th family (9 persons)
Étienne BOUDREAU	menuisier	42	Esteban BOUDREAU　Received: 1 each of medium axe, hatchet and knife; 2 of axe, shovel; 3 hoes
Margueritte THIBAUDEAU, sa femme		40	
Jʰ, son fils	idem	19	
Blaise, idem		16	
Yves, idem	à la mamelle		Josef BOUDREAU　Received: 1 each of axe, medium axe, shovel and knife; 2 hoes
Étienne, idem		5	
Cécille, sa fille		17	
Anne, idem		14	
Margueritte, idem		3	

37th family (2 persons)
Anne OLIVIER, veuve HACHÉ	56	Ana OLIVIER
Magdeleine Apauline, sa fille		
jedis(sic) nièce	10	

38th family (2 persons)
Jean TIBODEAU	calfat	20	Juan TIBODEAU　Received: 1 each of axe, shovel, hatchet and knife; 2 hoes
Marie Rose DAMOUR, sa femme		24	

39th family (2 persons)
Ysabelle BOUDREAU, veuve TIBODEAU	56
Marie, sa fille	17

40th family (2 persons)
Ursule BROD, veuve PITRE	45	Ursula BREAUD　Received: 1 each of axe, shovel, hatchet and knife; 2 hoes
Ursule, sa fille	22	

41st family (6 persons)
Eustache BERTHRAND	charpentier	49	Eustaguio BELTRAN　Received: 1 each of axe, medium axe, shovel and knife; 3 hoes
Margueritte LANDRY, sa femme		37	
Louis Martin, son fils	à la mamelle		
Magdeleine, sa fille		19	
Marie Geneviève, idem		11	
Marie Josèphe, idem		7	

42nd family (2 persons)
Charles GIROIR	calfat	56	Carlos GIROIR
Michele PÉTRY, sa femme		58

43rd family (4 persons)
Atanase BOURG	marin	45	Athanasio BOURG　Received: 1 each of axe, medium axe and knife; 2 of shovel and hoe
Luce BROD, sa femme		33	
Jʰ, son fils		13	
Charles, idem		10	

Chat - #16: Jean-Charles BENOIST s/o Charles & Madeleine THERIOT m. 1770 Anne-Marie HACHÉ d/o Jean-Baptiste & Anne OLIVIER; a child Paul-Frédéric b. 1775

SM - #67: additional family information

36th family (6 persons)

Jean Charles BENOIT	sailor	36
Marie HACHÉ, his wife		34
Jean Marie BENOIT, his son		14
Paul Frédéric BENOIT, his son		9
François René BENOIT, his son		7
Sophie Renée BENOIT, his daughter		2

Chat - #27: Étienne BOUDROT s/o Étienne & Marie-Claire AUCOIN m. 1764 Marguerite THIBODAUX; Children:
Marguerite BOUDROT bt. 1782
Yves BOUDROT bt. 1785
Jean-Étienne bt. 1779

Nantes #33: additional family information

36th family (9 persons)

Étienne BOUDROT	house carpenter	42
Marguerite THIBODEAUX, his wife		40
Joseph BOUDROT, his son; carpenter		19
Blaise BOUDROT, his son		16
Yves BOUDROT, his son	a nursling	
Étienne BOUDROT, his son		5
Cécille BOUDROT, his daughter		17
Anne BOUDROT, his daughter		14
Marguerite BOUDROT, his daughter		3

Nantes - #151: Jean-Baptiste HACHÉ s/o Jean-Baptiste & Marie-Anne GENTIL m. 1750 Anne OLIVIER d/o Pierre & Françoise BONNEVIE

SM - #486: additional family information

37th family (2 persons)

Anne OLIVIER, widow HACHÉ	56
Magdelaine Apolline HACHÉ, daughter of her niece	10

BR - v.2, p.694: Children of Jean THIBODEAUX & Rose D'AMOUR:
Frédéric Eloi b. 12 March 1794
Joseph b. 24 Dec. 1787

38th family (2 persons)

Jean THIBODEAUX	calker	20
Marie Rose DAMOUR, his wife		24

Nantes - #289: Olivier THIOBODAUX d. 1782; m. 1760 Élizabeth BOUDROT; a child Marie b. 1768

39th family (2 persons)

Isabelle BOUDROT, widow THIBODEAUX	56
Marie THIBODEAUX, her daughter	17

SM - #774: François PITRE m. 1762 Ursule BRAUD; a child Ursule b. 1763

40th family (2 persons)

Ursule BRAUD, widow PITRE	45
Ursule PITRE, her daughter	22

Chat - #18: Eustache BERTRAND s/o Jean & Françoise LÉGER m. 1764 Marguerite LANDRY d/o Benjamin & Marguerite BABIN
Nantes - #22: additional family information
BR v.2, p.88: Marie Magdalen BERTRAND wid. Moyse LEBALNC d/o Eustache & Marguerite Geneviève LANDRY m. 19 Aug. 1792 François DUBOIS of Paris

41st family (6 persons)

Eustache BERTRAND	carpenter	49
Marguerite LANDRY, his wife		37
Louis Martin BERTRAND, his son; nursling		
Magdelaine BERTRAND, his daughter		19
Marie Geneviève BERTRAND, his dgtr.		11
Marie Josèphe BERTRAND, his daughter		7

SM - #439: Charles GIROIRE s/o Jacques & Marie BOISSEAU m. 1761 Michelle PATRU

42nd family (2 persons)

Charles GIROIRE	calker	56
Michele PÉTRY, his wife		58

Chat - #41: Athanase BOURG s/o François & Marguerite HÉBERT m. 1768 Luce or Louise BRAUD d/o Joseph & Ursule BOURG; Children: Charles b. 1775, Joseph b. 1772
Nantes - #53 & SM - #159: additional material

43rd family (4 persons)

Athanase BOURG	sailor	45
Luce BRAUD, his wife		33
Joseph BOURG, his son		13
Charles BOURG, his son		10

44th family (2 persons)
Marie DOUCET, veuve MOULAISON		60
Jh, son fils	marin	45

Maria DOUCET   Received: 1 each of
axe, shovel, hatchet and knife; 2 hoes

45th family (3 persons)
Magdeleine BLANCHARD,	
veuve Charles BOURG	48
Charles, son fils	11
Joseph Florent, idem	7

Magdalena BLANCHARD   Received: 1 each of
axe, medium axe, shovel and knife; 2 hoes

46th family (4 persons)
Ygnace AMOND	perreyeur [perrayeur]	39
Anne Jh BOURG, sa femme		37
Anne Magdeleine, sa fille		12
Marie Modeste, idem		10

Ignacio HAMOND   Received: 1 each of
axe, shovel and knife; 2 of hoe and hatchet

47th family (2 persons)
Lusien BOURG	charpentier	21
Marie TRAHAN, sa femme		25

Luciano BOURQUE   Received: 1 each of
axe, shovel, hatchet and knife; 2 hoes

48th family (3 persons)
Jean BOURG	cordier	25
Catherine VIAUD, sa femme		33
Catherine, sa fille	à la mamelle	

Juan BOURQUE   Received: 1 each of
axe, shovel, hatchet and knife; 2 hoes

49th family (4 persons)
Marin BOUDREAU	cordonnier	53
Pélagie BARIAU, sa femme		39
Étienne, son fils		13
Marie, sa fille	à la mamelle	

Marin BOUDREAU   Received: 1 each of
axe, medium axe and knife; 2 of shovel and hoe

50th family (1 person)
Jh AU COIN	marin	33

51st family (7 persons)
Margueritte BOUDREAU,	
veuve Binjamin PITRE	46
Étienne, son fils	7
Jean, idem	4
Marie, sa fille	23
Magdeleine, idem	21
Cécille, idem	15
Margueritte, idem	14

Margarita BOUDREAU   Received: 1 each of
axe, medium axe and knife; 2 of shovel and hoe

52nd family (5 persons)
Basille CHAISON	tonnelier	36
Monique COMMEAU, sa femme		38
Charles, son fils		3
Louis, idem	à la mamelle	
Adélaïde, sa fille		11

Exile - p.334: Pierre MOULAISON s/o Gabriel &
    Marie AUBOIS d. 1769 at age 60 years m. Marie
    DOUCET

44th family (2 persons)

Marie DOUCET, widow MOULAISON		60
Joseph MOULAISON, her son; sailor		45

Chat - #42: Charles BOURG s/o Louis & Cécile
    MICHEL m. ca. 1759 Madeleine BLANCHARD; a
    child Joseph-Florent bt. 1776
Nantes - #55: additional family information
SM - #161: additional family information

45th family (3 persons)

Magdelaine BLANCHARD,		
widow of Charles BOURG		48
Charles BOURG, her son		11
Joseph Florent BOURG, her son		7

Chat - #103: Ignace HAMON s/o Jean & Marie
    BLANCHARD m. 1770 Anne BOURG d/o Louis &
    Cécile MICHEL
Nantes - #156: additional family information

46th family (4 persons)

Ignace HAMONT	quarryman	39
Anne Joseph BOURG, his wife		37
Anne Magdelaine HAMONT, his daughter		12
Marie Modeste HAMONT, his daughter		10

47th family (2 persons)

Lucien BOURG	carpenter	21
Marie TRAHAN, his wife		25

48th family (3 persons)

Jean BOURG	ropemaker	25
Catherine VIAUD, his wife		33
Catherine BOURG, his daughter; nursling		

Chat - #35: Marin BOUDROT s/o Étienne & Marie-Claire
    AUCOIN m. 1765 Pélagie BARRILLOT d/o Pierre
    & Véronique GIROIRE; a child Étienne b. 1772

49th family (4 persons)

Marin BOUDROT	shoemaker	53
Pélagie BARRILLOT, his wife		39
Étienne BOUDROT, his son		13
Marie BOUDROT, his daughter; nursling		

SM - #141: additional family information
Nantes - #45: additional family information

50th family (1 person)

Joseph AUCOIN	sailor	33

Chat - #164: Benjamin PITRE s/o Claude & Marguerite
    DOIRON m. 1759 Marguerite BOUDROT d/o Jean
    & Catherine BRASSEAU; Children: Étienne bt.
    1778, Jean bt. 1780, Marguerite b. 1770

51st family (7 persons)

Marguerite BOUDROT,		
widow of Benjamin PITRE		46
Étienne PITRE, her son		7
Jean PITRE, her son		4
Marie PITRE, her daughter		23
Magdelaine PITRE, her daughter		21
Cécille PITRE, her daughter		15
Marguerite PITRE, her daughter		14

Nantes - #259: additional family information
SM - #770: additional family information

Chat - #54: Basile CHIASSON m. ca. 1772 Monique
    COMMAUX; child Anne-Adélaïde b. 1774
SWLR - v.1, p.126: Basil CHIASSON widr. Monique
    COMAU s/o Pierre & Catherine BOURGEOIS of
    Beau Sejour, Acadie m. 20 July 1789 Anne-Marie
    THIBAUDOT [State Archives record]
Exile - p.78: Anonime s/o Basile & Monique CAUMOT
    d. 9 April 1773
Nantes - #78: additional family information

52nd family (5 persons)

Basile CHIASSON	cooper	36
Monique COMEAUX, his wife		38
Charles CHIASSON, son fils		3
Louis CHIASSON, his son	a nursling	
Adélaïde CHIASSON, his daughter		11

53rd family (4 persons)

Jean CHAISON	charpentier	56
Anne JOUANNE, sa femme		40
Joseph, son fils	cordier	19
Pierre, idem		15

Juan CHAISON — Received: 1 each of hatchet and knife; 2 of axe, shovel and hoe

54th family (3 persons)

Charles BLANCHARD	cordonnier	51
Souillac, son fils	charpentier	
Charles, idem	marin	16

55th family (4 persons)

Ambroise HÉBERT	charpentier	54
Phelicité LEJEUNE, sa femme		45
Gertrude, sa fille		16
Angélique GOTREAU, nièce au dit		20

Ambrosio HEBERT

56th family (6 persons)

François BLANCHARD	laboureur	54
Elènne GIROIR, sa femme		43
Joseph, son fils		10
Françoise, sa fille		20
Marie, idem		15
Margueritte, idem		5

Francisco BLANCHARD — Received: 1 each of axe, medium axe and knife; 2 shovel; 3 hoes

57th family (5 persons)

Françoise DOUCET, femme de Louis HACHÉ		46
P^re, son fils		10
P^re HACHÉ, son mineur		16
J^h HACHÉ, idem		10
Marie HACHÉ, idem		19

Francisca DOUCET — Received: 1 each of axe, medium axe, hatchet and knife; 2 of shovel and hoe

58th family (3 persons)

P^re LEBLANC	charpentier	49
Marie LANDRY, sa femme		52
Margueritte, sa fille		16

Pedro LEBLANC — Received: 1 each of axe, shovel, hatchet and knife; 2 hoes

59th family (5 persons)

Honnoré DUHON	charpentier	47
Anne TRAHAN, sa femme		48
Augustin, son fils	marin	20
Jacques, idem		17
Jean Charles, idem		13

Honorado DOUAN

60th family (9 persons)

Chrisostome TRAHAN	laboureur	43
Anne GRANGÉ, sa femme		41
Jean Chrisostome, son fils		10
Joseph, idem		7
Renné, idem	à la mamelle	
Anne Julie, sa fille		20
Marie Magdeleine, idem		18
Marthe, idem		14
Margueritte, idem		5

Chrisostome TRAHAN — Received: 1 each of hatchet and knife; 2 of axe and shovel; 3 hoes

Chat - #55: Jean-Baptiste CHIASSON s/o François & Anne DOUCET m. Anne-Perinne JOANNE d/o Jacques & Perinne CHARPENTIER	**53rd family (4 persons)**	
	Jean CHIASSON	carpenter	56
	Anne JOANNE, his wife		40
	Joseph CHIASSON, his son	ropemaker	19
	Pierre CHIASSON, his son		15

54th family (3 persons)

Charles BLANCHARD	shoemaker	51
Souillac BLANCHARD, his son; carpenter		20
Charles BLANCHARD, his son; sailor		16

Chat - #105: Ambroise HÉBERT m. ca. 1754 Félicité LEJEUNE; a child Gertrude b. 1769
Nantes - #160: additional family information
SM - #500: additional family information

55th family (4 persons)

Ambroise HÉBERT	carpenter	54
Félicité LEJEUNE, his wife		45
Gertrude HÉBERT, his daughter		16
Angélique GAUTROT, his niece		20

Chat #23: François BLANCHARD s/o Joseph & Anne DUPUIS m. 1763 Helen-Judith GIROIRE d/o Honoré & Marie-Josèphe THERIOT; Children: Joseph-François b. 1775, Françoise b. 1765
Nantes - #27: additional family information
SM - #82: additional family information
Census - p.122: owned 6 arpents of land

56th family (6 persons)

François BLANCHARD	plowman	54
Hélène GIROIRE, his wife		43
Joseph BLANCHARD, his son		10
Françoise BLANCHARD, his daughter		20
Marie BLANCHARD, his daughter		15
Marguerite BLANCHARD, his daughter		5

Chat - #102: Louis HACHÉ s/o Jean-Baptiste & Anne-Marie GENTIL m. 1770 Françoise DOUCET; a child Pierre-Charles bt. 1774
Nantes - #153: additional family information
SM - #488: additional family information

57th family (5 persons)

Françoise DOUCET, wife of Louis HACHÉ	46
Pierre HACHÉ, her son	10
Pierre HACHÉ, her minor	16
Joseph HACHÉ, her minor	10
Marie HACHÉ, her minor	19

Nantes - #222: Pierre LEBLANC m. ca. 1757 Marie-Blanche LANDRY; a child Marguerite b. 1769

58th family (3 persons)

Pierre LEBLANC	carpenter	49
Marie LANDRY, his wife		52
Marguerite LEBLANC, his daughter		16

Exile - p.125: A child of Honoré & Marie-Anne TRAHAN: Honoré-Jacques-Marie-Louis DUHON b. 25 Aug. 1768

59th family (5 persons)

Honoré DUHON	carpenter	47
Anne TRAHAN, his wife		48
Augustin DUHON, his son	sailor	20
Jacques DUHON, his son		17
Jean Charles DUHON, his son		13

Exile - p.420: Children of Jean Chrisosthome TRAHAN & Anne GRANGER:
Jean Chrisosthome b. 31 Aug. 1774,
Anne-Julie b. 13 July 1765,
Joseph Rose b. 16 April 1777
Marie Marthe b. 2 Oct. 1770
Census - p.118: Owned 6 arpents of land.

60th family (9 persons)

Chrisostome TRAHAN	plowman	43
Anne GRANGER, his wife		41
Jean Chrisostome TRAHAN, his son		10
Joseph TRAHAN, his son		7
René TRAHAN, his son	a nursling	
Anne Julie TRAHAN, his daughter		20
Marie Magdeleine TRAHAN, his daughter		18
Marthe TRAHAN, his daughter		14
Marguerite TRAHAN, his daughter		5

61st family (3 persons)

Jean METRA, aleman	journalier	46
Margueritte BOURG, sa femme		52
Anne Margueritte, sa fille		18

Juan MAITRAI   Received: 1 each of axe, shovel, hatchet and knife; 2 hoes

62nd family (5 persons)

J^h RENARD, russien	tailleur	46
Jeanne RICHARD, sa femme		40
Martin, son fils		7
Marie, sa fille		19
Anne, idem		2

Joseph RENARD

63rd family (8 persons)

Bennoit BLANCHARD	marin	45
Magdeleine FOREST, sa femme		43
Joachim, son fils		16
Moïse, idem		3
Marie Magdeleine, sa fille		18
Marie Bennony, son fils		13
Céleste, idem		8
Anne, sa fille		11

Bellony BLANCHARD   Received: 1 each of medium axe and knife; 2 axe, shovel and hoe

64th family (3 persons)

Marie LEBLANC, femme de Jean DAIGLE		25
Marie, sa fille		1
Margueritte, idem	à la mamelle	

Juan DAIGLE   Received: 1 each of axe, shovel, hatchet and knife; 2 hoes

65th family (4 persons)

Olivier BOUDREAU	laboureur	74
Anne DUGAST, sa femme		56
Jean, son fils	idem	17
Marie, sa fille		18

66th family (3 persons)

Marie J^h THERIOT, veuve GIROIR		65
Eudoze, sa fille		38
Marie Rose, idem		23

Maria Josefa THERIOT   Received: 1 each of axe, shovel, hatchet and knife; 2 hoes

67th family (4 persons)

Joseph BROD	marin	30
Margueritte TEMPLÉ, sa femme		32
Joseph, son fils		9
Eulalie, sa fille	à la mamelle	

Josef BREAUD   Received: 1 each of axe, medium axe and knife; 2 hoes

68th family (4 persons)

Jean FOUQUET	laboureur	52
Margueritte QUIMINE, sa femme		50
Marie Charlotte, sa fille		15
Jeanne Magdeleine, idem		11

Juan FOUGUET   Received: 1 each of axe, medium axe, shovel and knife; 2 hoes

81

SM - #717: Jean METRA s/o Jacques & Jeanne VEUVRE m. 1765 Marguerite BOURG d/o Louis & Cécile MICHEL; a child Marguerite b. 1767

Chat - #21: Bénony BLANCHARD s/o Joseph & Anne DUPUIS m. 1766 Madeleine FOREST d/o Jacques & Claire VINCENT; Children: Céleste bt. 1776, Moyse bt. 1782, Joachim b. 1768

Nantes - #25: additional family information
SM - #79: additional family information

Nantes - #90: Jean-Baptiste DAIGLE s/o Jean & Marie-Judith DUREL m. 1783 Marie LEBLANC d/o Pierre & Marie LANDRY;
a child: Marguerite-Louise DAIGLE bt. 1785

SM - #143: Olivier BOUDROT m. 1762 Anne DUGAST d/o Charles & Marie BENOIST; a child Marie b. 1766

SM - #440: Honoré GIROIRE m. ca. 1741 Marie-Josèphe THERIOT; Children: Eudoxile b. 1747, Marie-Rose b. 1761

Chat - #51: Joseph-Gabriel BRAUD s/o Joseph & Ursule BOURG m. 1777 Marguerite TEMPLE d/o André & Marie DEVAUX; a child Joseph bt. 1778;
Nantes - #69: additional information
Census - p.124: Owned 6 arpents of land

NO - v.4, p.133: Marie Charlotte FOUQUET of Port Louis, France d/o Jean & Marguerite QUIMIN m. 6 Dec. 1785 Silvestre GOMES

61st family (3 persons)

Jean MÉTRA, a German	day laborer	46
Marguerite BOURG, his wife		52
Anne Marguerite MÉTRA, his daughter		18

62nd family (5 persons)

Joseph BENARD, a Russian	tailor	46
Jeanne RICHARD, his wife		40
Martin BENARD, his son		7
Marie BENARD, his daughter		19
Anne BENARD, his daughter		2

63rd family (8 persons)

Benoît BLANCHARD	sailor	45
Magdelaine FOREST, his wife		43
Joachim BLANCHARD, his son		16
Moise BLANCHARD, his son		3
Marie Magdelaine BLANCHARD, dgtr.		18
Marie Bennony BLANCHARD, daughter		13
Céleste BLANCHARD, his daughter		8
Anne BLANCHARD, his daughter		11

64th family (3 persons)

Marie LEBLANC, wife of Jean DAIGLE	25
Marie DAIGLE, her daughter	1
Marguerite DAIGLE, daughter; a nursling	

65th family (4 persons)

Olivier BOUDROT	plowman	74
Anne DUGAT, his wife		56
Jean BOUDROT, his son	plowman	17
Marie BOUDROT, his daughter		18

66th family (3 persons)

Marie Joseph THERIOT, widow GIROIRE	65
Eudoze GIROIRE, her daughter	38
Marie Rose GIROIRE, her daughter	23

67th family (4 persons)

Joseph BRAUD	sailor	30
Marguerite TEMPLÉ, his wife		32
Joseph BRAUD, his son		9
Eulalie BRAUD, his daughter; a nursling		

68th family (4 persons)

Jean FOUQUET	plowman	52
Marguerite KIMINE, his wife		50
Marie Charlotte FOUQUET, his daughter		15
Jeanne Magdelaine FOUQUET, daughter		11

69th family (2 persons)

Marie GOTRAUD, fille		20	Maria GAUTREAU Received: 1 each of
Magdeleine, sa soeur		18	axe, shovel, hatchet and knife; 2 hoes

70th family (4 persons)

Marie Henriette POTIER, veuve ROSICAUD		46	Maria Henriqueta POTIEUX Received: 1 each of
Jean François, son fils	marin	20	axe, shovel, hatchet and knife; 2 hoes
Anne Margueritte, sa fille		17	
Marie Henriette, idem		15	

71st family (8 persons)

Élisabeth DUHON, veuve AU COIN		43	Isabel DOUAN Received: 1 each of
Anne Marie, sa fille		24	axe, medium axe, shovel and knife; 3 hoes
Geneviève, idem		20	
Marie Madeleine, idem		17	
Marie Félicité, idem		15	
lisabeth, idem		13	
Anne Augustine, idem		11	
Marie Reyne, idem		6	

72nd family (7 persons)

Anastasie LEBRUN, veuve LEJEUNE		45	Anastasia LEBRON Received: 1 each of
J^h, son fils	marin	22	hoe, hatchet and knife; 2 of medium axe, shovel; 3
Alexis, idem		13	axe
Marie Rose, sa fille		18	
Margueritte, idem		16	Josef LEJEUNE Received: 1 each of
Adelaïde, idem		6	axe, medium axe, and knife; 2 shovel and hoe
Rosalie, idem	à la mamelle		

73rd family (3 persons)

Ygnace BOUDREAU	charpentier	36
Anne PIERÇON, sa femme		26
Charles, son fils		2

74th family (1 person)

Jean Paul TRAHAN	marin	16	Juan Pablo TRAHAM Received: 1 each of
			axe, shovel, hoe and knife

75th family (3 persons)

Nicolas ALBERT	charpentier	45
Marie Marthe BENOIT, sa femme		40
Gabriel, son fils		12

76th family (3 persons)

Pierre LAURENTY, alleman	argueburier	41	Pedro LORENCY
Marie VIDET, sa femme		42	
P^{re}, son fils	cordonnier	17	

83

Other References	Complete Listing	
	69th family (2 persons)	
	Marie GAUTROT, young woman	20
	Magdelaine GAUTROT, her sister	18
	70th family (4 persons)	
Nantes - #264: Jean-Baptiste RASSICOT s/o René & Marie HACHÉ m. ca. 1760 Marie-Henriette POITIER	Marie Henriette POITIER, widow RASSICOT	46
	Jean François RASSICOT, her son; sailor	20
	Anne Marguerite RASSICOT, her daughter	17
	Marie Henriette RASSICOT, her daughter	15
	71st family (8 persons)	
Nantes - #3: Alexandre AUCOIN d. 1780; m. Élizabeth DUHON; a child Marie-Reine bt. 1778	Élizabeth DUHON, widow AUCOIN	43
	Anne Marie AUCOIN, her daughter	24
	Geneviève AUCOIN, her daughter	20
Exile - p.15: Their children:	Marie Magdelaine AUCOIN, her daughter	17
Anne Augustine b. 16 July 1775	Marie Félicité AUCOIN, her daughter	15
Élizabeth Joseph b. 16 June 1772	Élisabeth AUCOIN, her daughter	13
Marie Félicité b. 4 Feb. 1770	Anne Augustine AUCOIN, her daughter	11
Marie Madeleine b. 8 Jan. 1768	Marie Reine AUCOIN, her daughter	6
	72nd family (7 persons)	
Nantes - #227: Amand LEJEUNE d. 1784; m. ca. 1755 Anastasie LEVRON; Children: Rosalie bt. 1783, Anne-Adélaïde bt. 1779	Anastasie LEBRUN, widow LEJEUNE	45
	Joseph LEJEUNE, her son sailor	22
	Alexis LEJEUNE, her son	13
	Marie Rose LEJEUNE, her daughter	18
	Marguerite LEJEUNE, her daughter	16
	Adélaïde LEJEUNE, her daughter	6
	Rosalie LEJEUNE, her dgtr.; a nursling	
	73rd family (3 persons)	
Nantes - #37: Ignace BOUDROT m. ca. 1780 Anne PIERSON; a child Charles bt. 1783	Ignace BOUDROT carpenter	36
	Anne PIERSON, his wife	26
BR - v.2, p.115:	Charles BOUDROT, his son	2
a child: Louis BOUDREAUX b. 8 Sept. 1789		
	74th family (1 person)	
	Jean Paul TRAHAN sailor	16
	75th family (3 persons)	
Chat - #1: Nicolas Gabriel ALBERT m. ca. 1759 Marie-Marthe BENOIST; a child Nicolas-Gabriel bt. 1774	Nicolas ALBERT carpenter	45
	Marie Marthe BENOIT, his wife	40
	Gabriel ALBERT, his son	12
	76th family (3 persons)	
	Pierre LAURENTY, a German gunsmith	41
	Marie VIDET, his wife	42
	Pierre LAURENTY, his son shoemaker	17

77th family (7 persons)

P^re Joseph JACQUES, alleman; menuisier	45	Pedro Joseph JACQUE
Anne DRAPPEAU, sa femme	41	
Joseph, son fils	15	
Jean, idem	10	
Anne, sa fille	20	
Victoire, idem	17	
Marie	2	

78th family (3 persons)

J^h PITRE	charpentier	22
Marie HÉBERT		17
J^h HÉBERT, son frère		15

"Liste des familles Acadiens qui doivent s'embarquer dans le Navire <u>L'Amitié</u> de La Rochelle Capn. le Sr. Baltremieux pour le nouvelle-orleans dans la Louisiane."
Legajo 576 of Cuba dated 14 April 1786

<u>Translation</u>: List of families embarking on the ship <u>L'Amitié</u> from LaRochelle, Captain Sieur Baltremieux, for New Orleans in Louisiana.

<u>Names with no reference on the Embarkation list:</u>

Josef ADAM - 1 axe, shovel and hatchet; 2 hoes

Mathurina ALLIOT - 1 axe, shovel, hatchet and knife; 2 hoes

Mathurino Juan AU COING - 1 axe, shovel, hoe, hatchet and knife

Juan Fran^co AVARAT - 1 axe, shovel, hatchet and knife; 2 hoes

Simon BABIN

Margarita BENOIT - 1 axe, shovel, hoe, hatchet and knife

Francisco BOUCITE - 1 axe, shovel, hatchet and knife; 2 hoes

Luis Antonio CHARRIE - 1 axe, shovel, hatchet and knife; 2 hoes

Santiago DAVOIR - 1 axe, shovel, hatchet, and knife; 2 hoes

Leneor DE LA GARDE - 1 axe, shovel, hatchet, 2 hoes

Bernardo DUGATS - 1 axe, shovel, hatchet, knife; 2 hoes

Claudio Epifano LE FAIBRE

Carlos FARDY

Estevan GALLETIER - 1 axe, shovel, and hatchet; 2 hoes

Juan HAINEMENT

Miguel LEGERE

Luis MAURICE - 1 axe, medium axe, hoe, hatchet, knife; 2 shovels

Vicente NEVEU - 1 axe, shovel, hatchet and knife; 2 hoes

Juan Bautista SIMON - 1 axe, shovel and hatchet; 2 hoes

NOTE: <u>Distribution of Acadian families from</u> <u>**La Amistad** to be established at La Fourche of Chetimachas</u>. 15 December 1785 - Juan Prieto

85 hachar grander [axe], 28 medias hachar [medium axe or hatchet], 85 palas ciento [shovel], 49 Hazadas [hoes], 46 chuelar [meat cleaver, large knife], 70 cutrer [cutter, knife]

This group aboard the L'Amitié [400 tons] included 270 passengers from 68 families. A few non-Acadians also came. Captain was Joseph Beltremieux. Much sickness aboard; six died. Group finally totalled 93 families. Original of 68 families plus 17 marriages, 10 births, 24 new adherents. Only group that did not lose any member through death while in New Orleans. There were 71 families that settled in La Fourche in Valenzuela (area around Plattenville in upper Assumption Parish, south of Donaldsonville), 3 families at Atacapas (St. Martinville) and 17 families at Nueva Galvez (southeast of Baton Rouge). [Winzerling pp.144-146]

77th family (7 persons)

Pierre Joseph JACQUES, German; carpenter	45
Anne DRAPEAU, his wife	41
Joseph JACQUES, his son	15
Jean JACQUES, his son	10
Anne JACQUES, his daughter	20
Victoire JACQUES, his daughter	17
Marie JACQUES, his daughter	2

78th family (3 persons)

Joseph PITRE	carpenter	22
Marie HÉBERT		17
Joseph HÉBERT, his brother		15

Names with no reference on the Embarkation list:
Joseph ADAM
Mathurina ALLIOT
Mathurin Jean AUCOIN
Jean François AVARAT
Simon BABIN
Marguerite BENOIT
François BOUCITE
Louis Antoine CHARRIE
Jacques DAVOIR
Leneor DE LA GARDE
Bernard DUGATS
Claude Epiphane LE FAIBRE
Carlos FARDY
Étienne GALLETIER
Jean HAINEMENT
Michel LÉGER
Louis MAURICE
Vincent NEVEU
Jean Baptiste SIMON

NOTE: Distribution of Acadian families from La Amistad to be established at La Fourche of Chetimachas. 15 December 1785 - Juan Prieto
85 hachar grander [axe], 28 medias hachar [medium axe or hatchet], 85 palas ciento [shovel], 49 Hazadas [hoes], 46 chuelar [meat cleaver, knife], 70 cutrer [knife or cutter]

1st family (2 persons)

Marie RICHARD, veuve de Claude PITRE	42	Marie RICHARD	Received: 1 each of axe, hatchet, shovel, knife, large knife, 2 hoes
Marie PITRE, sa fille	16		

2nd family (8 persons)

Joseph AUCOIN, père	64	Josef AU COING	Received: 1 each of knife, large knife; 2 hatchets; 3 axe, shovel; 4 hoes
Anne HÉBERT, sa femme	48		
François AUCOIN, son fils	15		
Anne AUCOIN, sa fille	21		
Gabriel, idem, son fils	13		
Marie Magdelaine, sa fille	11		
Françoise, idem, sa fille	8		
Jacinte, garçon, né le 6 Avril 1785			

3rd family (9 persons)

Pierre HÉBERT, père	50	Pedro HEBERT	Received: 1 each of hatchet, knife, large knife; 2 axe; 3 of shovel and hoe
Suzanne PITRE, sa femme	55		
Pierre HÉBERT, leur fils	22		
François HÉBERT, idem	18		
Joseph HÉBERT, idem	15		
Mathurin HÉBERT, idem	13		
Jean B^te HÉBERT, idem	11		
Marie HÉBERT, leur fille	24		
Marguerite HENRY, belle fille	35		

4th family (6 persons)

Joseph AUCOIN, père	41	Josef AU COING	Received: 1 each of knife, large knife; 2 of axe, hatchet, shovel and hoe
Alexis AUCOIN, son fils	20		
Fabien, idem	15		
Mathurin, idem	14	Alexo AU COING	Received: 1 each of axe, hatchet, hoe, knife, large knife; 2 shovels
Joseph, idem	10		
Marie Ozitte BROC	40		

5th family (4 persons)

Luce Perpétue BOURG, veuve [HÉBERT]	43	Lucia Perpetua BOURQUE	Received: 1 each of axe, hatchet, shovel, knife large knife; 2 hoes
Victoire HÉBERT, enfant	18		
Anne HÉBERT, idem	11		
Julienne HÉBERT, idem	4		

6th family (10 persons)

Jean BOURG, père	50	Juan BOURQUE, Padre	Received: 1 each of knife, large knife; 2 of axe, hatchet; 3 of shovel, hoe
Anne DAIGLE, sa femme	40		
Marie BOURG, sa fille	17		
François, idem, son fils	16		
Marguerite, idem, sa fille	15		
Magdelaine, idem, sa fille	12		
Jeanne, idem, sa fille	7		
Jean, idem, son fils	6		
Joseph, idem, son fils	3		
Charlote Françoise, idem, née le 26 May 1785			

1st family (2 persons)	
Marie RICHARD, widow of Claude PITRE	42
Marie PITRE, her daughter	16

SM - #773: Claude PITRE s/o Claude & Marguerite DOIRON m. 1764 Marie-Blanche RICHARD d/o Pierre & Marie BOUDROT; child Marie b. 1769

2nd family (8 persons)	
Joseph AUCOIN, father	64
Anne HÉBERT, his wife	48
François AUCOIN, his son	15
Anne AUCOIN, his daughter	21
Gabriel AUCOIN, his son	13
Marie Magdelaine AUCOIN, his daughter	11
Françoise AUCOIN, his daughter	8
Jacinte AUCOIN, a boy, born 6 April 1785	

SM - #25: Joseph AUCOIN s/o Alexis & Marie BOURG m. 1759 Anne HÉBERT d/o Jean & Claire DUGAST; a child Gabriel b. 1772

3rd family (9 persons)	
Pierre HÉBERT, father	50
Suzanne PITRE, his wife	55
Pierre HÉBERT, their son	22
François HÉBERT, their son	18
Joseph HÉBERT, their son	15
Mathurin HÉBERT, their son	13
Jean Baptiste HÉBERT, their son	11
Marie HÉBERT, their daughter	24
Marguerite HENRY, daughter-in-law	35

SM - #532: Pierre HÉBERT s/o Jean & Claire DUGAST m. 1760 Susanne PITRE d/o Jean & Marguerite THERIOT; a child Mathurin b. 1771

BR - v.2, p.371: Mathurin HÉBERT of St. Malo s/o Pierre & Susanne PITRE m. 18 Sept. 1797 Marie BOURQUE of St. Malo d/o Xavier & Isabelle LEBLANC

BR - v.2, p.373: Pierre John HÉBERT of St. Malo s/o Pierre & Susanne PITRE m. 26 May 1788 Anne AUCOIN d/o Joseph & Anne HÉBERT

4th family (6 persons)	
Joseph AUCOIN, father	41
Alexis AUCOIN, his son	20
Fabien AUCOIN, his son	15
Mathurin AUCOIN, his son	14
Joseph AUCOIN, his son	10
Marie Ozitte BRAUD	40

5th family (4 persons)	
Luce Perpétue BOURG, widow [HÉBERT]	43
Victoire HÉBERT, child	18
Anne HÉBERT, child	11
Julienne HÉBERT, child	4

Nantes - #169: Jean-Baptiste HÉBERT s/o Pierre & Marguerite BOURG d. 1779; m. 1766 Luce BOURG d/o Jean & Françoise BENOIST

SM - #517: additional family information

6th family (10 persons)	
Jean BOURG, Sr.	50
Anne DAIGLE, his wife	40
Marie BOURG, his daughter	17
François BOURG, his son	16
Marguerite BOURG, his daughter	15
Magdelaine BOURG, his daughter	12
Jeanne BOURG, his daughter	7
Jean BOURG, his son	6
Joseph BOURG, his son	3
Charlote Françoise BOURG, his daughter, born on 26 May 1785	

SM - #171: Jean BOURG s/o Jean & Marie PITRE m. 1767 Anne-Josèphe DAIGLE d/o Jean & Marie BRAUD; Children: François b. 1769, Marguerite b. 1770, Magdelaine b. 1772

BR - v.2, p.121,123, 125: Their children:

Jeanne BOURG m. 27 Aug. 1798 Bartholome HENRY

François BOURG m. 20 Feb. 1792 Madeleine COMO

Marguerite Perine BOURG m. 26 May 1800 Michel AUCOIN

7th family (7 persons)

Jean BOURG, père	40	Juan BOURQUE, hijo Received: 1 each of
Marie DUPUY, sa femme	36	axe, hatchet, knife, and large knife; 2 shovels, 3
Yves BOURG, son fils	6	hoes
Jean B^te Simon Louis, idem,		
agé de 9 mois		
Marguerite, idem, leur fille	16	
Isabelle, idem, leur fille	12	
Marie, idem, leur fille	8	

8th family (6 persons)

Marie THERIOT, veuve		Maria THERIOT Received: 1 each of
de Joseph COMO	42	knife, large knife; 2 of axe, hatchet' 3 of shovel and
Elie COMO, fils	19	hoe
Joseph, idem, fils	17	
Simon, idem, fils	15	
Jeanne, idem, fille	11	
Marie, idem, fille	6	

9th family (3 persons)

Louis CLAUSTINET, père	54	Luis CLOUSTINET Received: 1 each of
Marie DAIGLE, sa femme	37	axe, hatchet, shovel, knife, large knife; 2 hoes
Geneviève GIROUERE, du 1er		
mariage de Marie D'AIGLE	16	

10th family (11 persons)

Jean LONGUÉSPÉE, père	45	Juan LANGUEEPEE Received: 1 each of
Marie Françoise BOURG, sa femme	40	knife, large knife; 2 of axe, hatchet; 3 shovels; 4
Marie LONGUESPÉE, leur fille	20	hoes
Anne, idem, leur fille	18	
Marguerite, idem, leur fille	15	
Jean Jacques, idem, leur fils	14	
Pierre, idem, leur fils	12	
Corentine, idem, leur fille	10	
Louis, idem, leur fils	6	
Jean B^te, idem, leur fils	4	
Hélène, idem, leur fille;		
agé de 8 mois		

11th family (5 persons)

Alexandre AUCOIN, père	45	Alexandro AU COING Received: 1 each of
Rozalie TERIAULT, sa femme	45	axe, hatchet, knife, large knife; 2 of shovel and hoe
Mathurin AUCOIN, son fils	4	
Marie, idem, sa fille	20	
Marie Jeanne, idem, sa fille	8	

	7th family (7 persons)
Chat - #45: Jean BOURG s/o François & Marie-Josèphe HÉBERT m. 1768 Marie DUPUIS d/o Ambroise & Anne AUCOIN; Children: Marie bt. 1776, Yves b. 1778	Jean BOURG, Jr. ["hijo"] — 40
	Marie DUPUIS, his wife — 36
	Yves BOURG, his son — 6
	Jean Baptiste Simon Louis BOURG, his son, at 9 months old
SM - #172: additional family information	Marguerite BOURG, their daughter — 16
Nantes - #57: additional family information	Isabelle BOURG, their daughter — 12
	Marie BOURG, their daughter — 8

	8th family (6 persons)
SM - #257: Joseph COMMAUX d. 1784 s/o Jean-Baptiste & Marie AUCOIN m. 1764 Marie THERIOT; a child Elie b. 1765	Marie THERIOT, the widow of Joseph COMEAUX — 42
	Elie COMEAUX, a son — 19
	Joseph COMEAUX, a son — 17
	Simon COMEAUX, a son — 15
	Jeanne COMEAUX, a daughter — 11
	Marie COMEAUX, a daughter — 6

	9th family (3 persons)
SM - #249: Louis CLOSSINET m. 1774 Marguerite DAIGLE d/o Jean & Anne-Marie BRAUD	Louis CLOSSINET, father — 54
	Marie DAIGLE, his wife — 37
	Geneviève GIROIRE, from the first marriage of Marie DAIGLE — 16

	10th family (11 persons)
SM - #685 Jean LONGUESPÉE s/o Louis & Anne BRASSEAU m. 1762 Marie-Françoise BOURG d/o Joseph & Françoise BOURG; children: Laurentine-Urienne b. 1776, Marguerite b. 1769	Jean LONGUESPÉE, father — 45
	Marie Françoise BOURG, his wife — 40
	Marie LONGUESPÉE, their daughter — 20
	Anne LONGUESPÉE, their daughter — 18
	Marguerite LONGUESPÉE, their daughter — 15
	Jean Jacques LONGUESPÉE, their son
	Pierre LONGUESPÉE, their son — 12
	Corentine LONGUESPÉE, their daughter — 10
	Louis LONGUESPÉE, their son — 6
	Jean Baptiste LONGUESPÉE, their son — 4
	Hélène LONGUESPÉE, their daughter; at age 8 months

	11th family (5 persons)
SM - #12: Alexandre AUCOIN s/o Charles & Anne-Marie DUPUIS m. ca. 1761 Rosalie THERIOT	Alexandre AUCOIN, father — 45
	Rosalie THERIOT, his wife — 45
	Mathurin AUCOIN, his son — 4
	Marie AUCOIN, his daughter — 20
	Marie Jeanne AUCOIN, his daughter — 8

12th family (6 persons)

Victor DESFORETS, père	50	Victor DESFOREST Received: 1 each of
Marie Jeanne RICHER, sa femme	16	hatchet, knife, large knife; 2 of axe, shovel; 3 hoes
Joseph Victor DESFORETS, leur fils	24	
Jean, idem, leur fils	11	
Étienne Gilles, idem, leur fils	7	
Anne Perrine, leur fille	20	
Servanne Julienne, idem, leur fille	17	
Marie Adelaïde, idem, leur fille	15	
Jeanne Isabelle, idem, leur fille	12	

13th family (4 persons)

Jacques DESFORETS, père de Victor	75	Santiago DESFOREST Received: 1 each of
Angélique RICHET, sa femme	43	axe, hatchet, shovel, knife, large knife; 2 hoes
Étienne DESFORETS, neveu du di^t	30	
Marie Jeanne BILLERA, veuve de François LE SOMMER	27	

14th family (1 person)

Anne FORET, veuve de Simon LEBLANC	30

15th family (6 persons)

Jean Jacques THERIOT, père	55	Juan Santiago THERIOT Received: 1 each of
Geneviève THERIOT, sa fille	21	axe, knife, large knife; 2 of hatchet, hoe; 3 shovels
Marie, idem, sa fille	19	
Jeanne, idem, sa fille	14	
Rosalie, idem, sa fille	12	
Marguerite, idem, sa fille	6	

16th family (3 persons)

Ambroise DUPUY, père	43	Ambrosio DUPUY Received: 1 each of
Anne THERIOT, sa femme	40	knife, large knife; 2 of axe, hatchet, shovel and hoe
Marguerite DUPUY, leur fille	8	

17th family (4 persons)

Jacques FORET, père	55	Santiago FOREST Received: 1 each of
Marie COMO, sa femme	50	knife, large knife; 2 of axe, shovel and hoe
Pierre FORET, leur fils	15	
Marie de FOREST, fille de Victor	21	

18th family (3 persons)

Jean B^te AUCOIN	25	Juan Bautista AU COING Received: 1 each of
Marie FORET, sa femme	20	axe, hatchet, shovel, knife, large knife; 2 hoes
Marie Jeanne, née le 13 fevrier		

SM - #399: Victor FOREST s/o Jacques & Claire VINCENT m. 1784 Marie-Jeanne-Catherine RICHER d/o André & Madeleine RENOUX; a child Joseph-Victor b. 1760

12th family (6 persons)	
Victor FOREST, father	50
Marie Jeanne RICHER, his wife	46
Joseph Victor FOREST, their son	24
Jean FOREST, their son	11
Étienne Gilles FOREST, their son	7
Anne Perrine FOREST, their dgtr.	20
Servanne Julienne FOREST, their daughter	17
Marie Adelaïde FOREST, daughter	15
Jeanne Isabelle FOREST, daughter	12

13th family (4 persons)	
Jacques FOREST, father of Victor	75
Angélique RICHET, his wife	43
Étienne FOREST, nephew of the above	30
Marie Jeanne BILLEZA, widow of François LE SOMMER	27

SM - #651: Simon LEBLANC m. 1766 Anne-Rosalie FOREST

14th family (1 person)	
Anne FOREST, widow of Simon LEBLANC	30

15th family (6 persons)	
Jean Jacques THERIOT, father	55
Geneviève THERIOT, his daughter	21
Marie THERIOT, his daughter	19
Jeanne THERIOT, his daughter	14
Rosalie THERIOT, his daughter	12
Marguerite THERIOT, his daughter	6

SM - #378: Ambroise DUPUIS m. 1764 Anne THERIOT

16th family (3 persons)	
Ambroise DUPUIS, father	43
Anne THERIOT, his wife	40
Marguerite DUPUIS, their daughter	8

Nantes - #126: Jacques FOREST m. ca. 1760 Marguerite COMMAUX; a child Pierre b. 1769
SM - #395: additional family information

17th family (4 persons)	
Jacques FOREST, father	55
Marie COMEAUX, his wife	50
Pierre FOREST, their son	15
Marie FOREST, daughter of Victor	21

SM - #23: Jean-Baptiste AUCOIN s/o Claude & Marie-Joseph SAUNIER m. 1784 Marie FOREST d/o Jacques & Marguerite COMMAUX

18th family (3 persons)	
Jean Baptiste AUCOIN	27
Marie FOREST, his wife	20
Marie Jeanne AUCOIN, born on 13 February [1785]	

19th family (10 persons)

Victor BOUDRO, père	55
Geneviève RICHARD, sa femme	37
Joseph, enfant de la 1ère femme	27
Marie Rose, idem	31
Cécile, idem	15
François Pre LE LORRE, mari de Marie Rose	30
Sophie, fille du 2e mariage	11
Noël, idem	9
Anne Jeanne, née le 17 janvier dernier	
Marguerite PIERRE, fille de Geneviève et de Simon PIERRE, son premier mari	17

Victor BOUDREAU   Received: 1 each of hatchet, knife, large knife; 2 of axe, hoes; 3 shovels

20th family (6 persons)

Barthelemy HENRY, père	41
Anne BOURG, sa femme	39
François HENRY, leur fils	15
Jacques HENRY, idem	12
Barthelemy HENRY, idem	9
Marie HENRY, idem	3

Bartholome HENRIQUE   Received: 1 each of hatchet, knife, large knife; 2 of axe, hoe; 3 shovels

21st family (12 persons)

Michel AUCOIN, père	53
Isabelle HÉBERT, sa femme	48
Jean AUCOIN, leur fils	23
Michel, idem, leur fils	16
Pierre, idem, leur fils	14
François, idem, leur fils	11
Constant, idem, leur fils	2
Marie, idem, leur fille	21
Anne, idem, leur fille	19
Isabelle, idem, leur fille	13
Floriane, idem, leur fille	4
Grégoire, idem, leur fils	18

Miguel AU COING   Received: 1 each of knife, large knife; 2 hatchets; 3 of axe and hoe, 4 shovels

22nd family (6 persons)

Pierre AUCOIN, père	44
Hélène HÉBERT, sa femme	44
Victoire AUCOIN, leur fille	20
Anne, idem, leur fille	15
Jean, idem, leur fils	13
Françoise, idem, leur fille	11

*Marginal Note - cette famille Embarque pas

23rd family (7 persons)

Claude AUCOIN, père	57
Marie Joseph SAULNIER, sa femme	48
Perpétue AUCOIN, leur fils	22
Anastasie, idem, leur fille	17
Mathurin, idem, leur fils	13
Marie, idem, leur fille	12
Pierre, idem, leur fils	9

Claudio AU COING   Received: 1 each of hatchet, knife, large knife; 2 of axe, hoe; 3 shovels

SM - #150: Victor BOUDROT s/o Antoine & Cécile BRASSAUX m. 1773 Geneviève RICHARD d/o Charles & Catherine GAUTROT

19th family (10 persons)	
Victor BOUDROT, father	55
Geneviève RICHARD, his wife	37
Joseph BOUDROT, child of first wife	27
Marie Rose BOUDROT, 1st wife's child	31
Cécile BOUDROT, child of first wife	15
François Pierre LE LORRE, husband of Marie Rose	30
Sophie BOUDROT, dgtr- 2nd marriage	11
Noël BOUDROT, son- 2nd marriage	9
Anne Jeanne BOUDROT, b. 17 Jan. 1785	
Marguerite PIERRE, dgtr. of Geneviève and Simon PIERRE, her first husband	17

BR - v.2, p.376: Bartholome HENRY s/o Bartholome & Anne BOURQUE m. 27 Aug. 1798 Jeanne BOURQUE

Child of Barthelemy HENRY & Anne BOURG:
Jean Baptiste bt. 24 August 1788 at age 6 mths.

20th family (6 persons)	
Barthelemy HENRY, father	41
Anne BOURG, his wife	39
François HENRY, their son	15
Jacques HENRY, their son	12
Barthelemy HENRY, their son	9
Marie HENRY, their son	3

SM - #31: Michel AUCOIN s/o Antoine & Élizabeth AMIRAULT m. ca. 1758 Élizabeth HÉBERT; children: Constant b. 1782, Marie b. 1764, Grégoire b. 1767

21st family (12 persons)	
Michel AUCOIN, father	53
Isabelle HÉBERT, his wife	48
Jean AUCOIN, their son	23
Michel AUCOIN, their son	16
Pierre AUCOIN, their son	14
François AUCOIN, their son	11
Constant AUCOIN, their son	2
Marie AUCOIN, their daughter	21
Anne AUCOIN, their daughter	19
Isabelle AUCOIN, their daughter	13
Floriane AUCOIN, their daughter	4
Grégoire AUCOIN, their son	18

SM - #37: Pierre AUCOIN s/o Alexis & Hélène BLANCHARD m. 1763 Hélène HÉBERT d/o Jean & Claire DUGAST; children: Victoire b. 1764, Jean b. 1771

22nd family (6 persons)	
Pierre AUCOIN, father	44
Hélène HÉBERT, his wife	44
Victoire AUCOIN, their daughter	20
Anne AUCOIN, their daughter	15
Jean AUCOIN, their son	13
Françoise AUCOIN, their daughter	11
*Marginal Note - this family did not embark	

SM - #20: Claude AUCOIN m. ca. 1757 Marie-Joseph SAUNIER; a child Perpétue b. 1763

23rd family (7 persons)	
Claude AUCOIN, father	57
Marie Joseph SAUNIER, his wife	48
Perpétue AUCOIN, their son	22
Anastasie AUCOIN, their daughter	17
Mathurin AUCOIN, their son	13
Marie AUCOIN, their daughter	12
Pierre AUCOIN, their son	9

24th family (5 persons)

Charles AUCOIN, père	50	Carlos AU COING	Received: 1 each of
Magdelaine TRAHAN	48	axe, hatchet, shovel, hoe, knife and large knife	
Pierre AUCOIN, leur fils	28		
Marie D'AIGLE, fille de Charles D'AIGLE			
et de Marie Blanche AUCOIN	17		
Françoise TRAHAN, veuve Pasq^al HÉBERT	38		

25th family (6 persons)

Simon AUCOIN, père	53	Simon AU COING	Received: 1 each of
Marie Gen^ve THERIOT, sa femme	50	hatchet, knife, large knife; 2 hoes	
Perpétue AUCOIN, leur fils	24		
Marg^te Gen^ve, idem, leur fille	16		
Anne Olive, idem, leur fille	12		
Rose Félicité, idem, leur fille	11		

26th family (11 persons)

Marin BOURG, père	45	Marin BOURQUE	Received: 3 axe, 2
Marie Osithe D'AIGLE	40	hatchets; 4 shovels	
Jean Pierre BOURG, leur fils	20		
Marie Luce, leur fille	22		
Marguerite Joseph, idem, leur fille	17		
Marin Joseph, idem, leur fille	16		
Rose Magdelaine, idem, leur fille	13		
P^re Jean B^te, idem, leur fille	12		
M^ie Françoise Magd^e Joseph, idem-leur fille	10		
Fran^s George, idem, leur fils	7		
Guillaume Jean, idem, leur fils	4		

27th family (4 persons)

Joseph HÉBERT, père	45	Josef HEBERT	Received: 1 each of
M^ie Magd^e AUCOIN, sa femme	44	axe, hatchet, knife, large knife; 2 of shovel and hoe	
Marie HÉBERT, leur fille	17		
Victoire, idem, leur fille	14		

28th family (8 persons)

Claude GUÉDRY, père	60	Claudo GUÉDRY	Received: 1 each of
Anne MOYZE, sa femme	54	knife, large knife; 2 hatchets; 3 axe, shovel and hoe	
Marie GUÉDRY, leur fille	21		
Fran^s GUÉDRY, leur fils	19		
Suliac, idem, leur fils	17		
Malo, idem, leur fils	15		
Pierre, idem, leur fils	12		
Ollivier, idem, leur fils	8		

29th family (7 persons)

Aman BOUDRO, père	52	Amano BOUDREAU	Received: 1 each of
Marie Vogue, sa femme	35	hatchet, knife, large knife; 2 of axe, hoe; 3 shovels	
Jean B^te, leur fils	15		
Fran^s, idem, leur fils	14		
Marie, idem, leur fille	6		
Joseph, idem, leur fils	4		
Hélène, idem, 8 mois			

	25th family (5 persons)
SM - #18: Charles AUCOIN m. ca. 1754 Madeleine TRAHAN	Charles AUCOIN, father 50
	Magdelaine TRAHAN 48
	Pierre AUCOIN, their son 28
	Marie DAIGLE, dgtr. of Charles DAIGLE and of Marie Blanche AUCOIN 17
	Françoise TRAHAN, wid. Pascal HÉBERT 38
	25th family (6 persons)
SM - #38: Simon AUCOIN m. ca. 1758 Marie-Geneviève THERIOT	Simon AUCOIN, father 53
	Marie Geneviève THERIOT, his wife 50
	Perpétue AUCOIN, their son 24
	Marguerite Geneviève AUCOIN, dgtr 16
	Anne Olive AUCOIN, their daughter 12
	Rose Félicité AUCOIN, their daughter 11
	26th family (11 persons)
SM - #180: Marin BOURG s/o Jean & Françoise BENOIST m. 1763 Marie-Ozite DAIGLE d/o Olivier & Angélique DOIRON	Marin BOURG, father 45
	Marie Osithe DAIGLE 40
	Jean Pierre BOURG, their son 20
	Marie Luce BOURG, their daughter 22
	Marguerite Joseph BOURG, their daughter 17
	Marin Joseph BOURG, their son 16
	Rose Magdelaine BOURG, their daughter 13
	Pierre Jean Baptiste BOURG, their son 12
	Marie Françoise Magd. Joseph BOURG-dgtr 10
	François George BOURG, their son 7
	Guillaume Jean BOURG, their son 4
	27th family (4 persons)
SM - #521: Joseph HÉBERT s/o François & Élizabeth BOURG m. 1764 Marie-Madeleine AUCOIN d/o Joseph & Anne TRAHAN	Joseph HÉBERT, father 45
	Marie Magdelaine AUCOIN, his wife 44
	Marie HÉBERT, their daughter 17
	Victoire HÉBERT, their daughter 14
	28th family (8 persons)
SM - #464: Claude GUÉDRY m. 1762 Anne MOYSE	Claude GUÉDRY, father 60
	Anne MOYSE, his wife 54
BR - v.2, p.341: Their children:	Marie GUÉDRY, their daughter 21
Malo at age 26 years m. 4 July 1797 Marguerite DUPUIS	François GUÉDRY, their son 19
Marie m. 24 October 1788 Pierre AUCOIN	Suliac GUÉDRY, their son 17
Souillac m. 27 Dec. 1789 Rose Anastasie AUCOIN	Malo GUÉDRY, their son 15
	Pierre GUÉDRY, their son 12
	Olivier GUÉDRY, their son 8
	29th family (7 persons)
SM #111: Amant BOUDROT s/o François & Angélique DOIRON m. 1777 Marie-Perinne NOGUES d/o Charles & Françoise RAIMOND	Amant BOUDROT, father 52
	Marie NOGUES, his wife 35
	Jean Baptiste BOUDROT, their son 15
SM - vol. 3, #903: marriage record	François BOUDROT, their son 14
BR - v.2, p.116: Marie BOUDREAUX d/o Aman & Marie NOGUE m. 18 Feb. 1800 François AUCOIN	Marie BOUDROT, their daughter 6
	Joseph BOUDROT, their son 4
	Hélene BOUDROT, 8 month old

30th family (3 persons)

Magdelaine AUCOIN, veuve		Magdalena AU COING Received: 1 each of
de Ch^es TRAHAN	69	axe, hatchet, hoe, knife; 2 shovels
Marie TRAHAN, sa fille	47	
Marguerite TRAHAN, idem	40	

31st family (7 persons)

Jean B^te AUCOIN, père	66	Juan Bautista AU COING Received: 1 each of
Marguerite THERIO, sa femme	57	knife, large knife; 2 of axe, hatchet; 3 of shovel and
Marie AUCOIN, leur fille	27	hoe
Jean Baptiste, idem, leur fils	21	
Rose Magdelaine, idem, leur fille	19	
Rose Anastasie, idem, leur fille	16	
Pierre, idem, leur fils	11	

32nd family (8 persons)

Jean PITRE, père	58	Juan PITRE Received: 1 each of
Félicité D'AIGLE, sa femme	55	hatchet, knife, large knife; 3 of axe, shovel and hoe
Charlotte M^ie PITRE, leur fille	20	
Pierre, idem, leur fils	19	
Jacques, idem, leur fils	18	
Fran^s, idem, leur fils	17	
Félicité, idem, leur fille	16	
Marguerite, idem, leur fille	14	

33rd family (7 persons)

Joseph HÉBERT, fils Joseph	50	Josef HEBERT Received; 1 each of
Marguerite D'AIGLE, sa femme	45	axe, hatchet, knife, large knife; 2 hoes, 3 shovels
Pierre Jean HÉBERT, leur fils	17	
Marie Joseph, idem, leur fille	18	
Thérèse Anne HÉBERT, leur fille	12	
Marguerite RICHARD, fille de Marguerite		
D'AIGLE, veuve d'Honoré RICHARD	15	
Jean Pierre, née le 21 fevrier dernier		

34th family (3 persons)

Pierre HENRY, père	51	Pedro ENRYQUE Received: 1 each of
Marie Joseph BOURG, sa femme	50	knife, large knife; 2 axe, shovel and hoe
Jean HENRY, leur fils	21	

35th family (6 persons)

Jean HENRY, père	53	Juan ENRIQUE Received: 1 each of
Marie PITRE, sa femme	53	hatchet, knife, large knife; 2 of axe, hoe; 3 shovels
Maximilien HENRY, leur fils	24	
Isabelle, idem, leur fille	21	
Marguerite Rose, idem, leur fille	16	
Marie HENRY, soeur de Jean	55	

SM - #891: Charles TRAHAN m. ca. 1735 Madeleine
AUCOIN; a child Marie b. 1736

30th family (3 persons)

Magdelaine AUCOIN, widow	
of Charles TRAHAN	69
Marie TRAHAN, her daughter	47
Marguerite TRAHAN, her daughter	40

SM - #22: Jean AUCOIN m. ca. 1757 Marguerite
THERIOT; a child Jean Baptiste b. 1766

31st family (7 persons)

Jean Baptiste AUCOIN, father	66
Marguerite THERIOT, his wife	57
Marie AUCOIN, their daughter	27
Jean Baptiste AUCOIN, their son	21
Rose Magdelaine AUCOIN, their daughter	19
Rose Anastasie AUCOIN, their daughter	16
Pierre AUCOIN, their son	11

SM - #777: Jean-Baptiste PITRE m. ca. 1757 Félicité
DAIGLE

BR - v.2, p.593: Félicité PITRE d/o Jean & Félicité
DAIGLE m. 12 April 1789 Jean FARINE
Marguerite PITRE d/o Jean & Félicité DAIGLE m.
31 October 1791 Jean MORANGE

32nd family (8 persons)

Jean PITRE, father	58
Félicité DAIGLE, his wife	55
Charlotte Marie PITRE, their daughter	20
Pierre PITRE, their son	19
Jacques PITRE, their son	18
François PITRE, their son	17
Félicité PITRE, their dgtr.	16
Marguerite PITRE, their daughter	14

33rd family (7 persons)

Joseph HÉBERT, son of Joseph HÉBERT	50
Marguerite DAIGLE, his wife	45
Pierre Jean HÉBERT, their son	17
Marie Joseph HÉBERT, their daughter	18
Thérèse Anne HÉBERT, their daughter	12
Marguerite RICHARD, dgtr. of Marguerite	
D'AIGLE, widow of Honoré RICHARD	15
Jean Pierre HÉBERT, born 21 Feb. [1785]	

SM - #561: Pierre HENRY s/o Jean & Madeleine
THERIOT m. 1756 Marguerite-Josèphe BOURG d/o
Charles & Cécile MÉLANÇON

34th family (3 persons)

Pierre HENRY, father	51
Marie Joseph BOURG, his wife	50
Jean HENRY, their son	21

SM - #551: Jean HENRY s/o Jean & Madeleine
THERIOT m. 1752 Marie PITRE d/o Joseph &
Isabelle BOUDROT

35th family (6 persons)

Jean HENRY, father	53
Marie PITRE, his wife	53
Maximilien HENRY, their son	24
Isabelle HENRY, their daughter	21
Marguerite Rose HENRY, their daughter	16
Marie HENRY, sister of Jean HENRY	55

36th family (11 persons)

Ambroise BOURG, père	53
M^{ie} Modeste MOULAISON, sa femme	40
M^{ie} Victoire BOURG, leur fille	20
Modeste Aimée, idem, leur fille	18
Magdelaine BOURG, leur fille	16
Julie Thérèse, idem, leur fille	14
Isabelle, idem, leur fille	12
Joseph, idem, leur fils	8
Pélagie, idem, leur fille	5
Modeste, idem, leur fille	3
Ambroise, idem, leur fille	1

Ambrosio BOURQUE   Received: 1 each of hatchet, knife, large knife; 2 of axe, hoe; 4 shovels

37th family (5 persons)

Charles HENRY, père	49
Françoise HÉBERT, sa femme	47
Charles HENRY, leur fils	9
Françoise Victoire, idem, leur fille	15
Marguerite Toussainte, idem, leur fille	13

Carlos HENRIQUE   Received: 1 each of axe, hatchet, knife, large knife; 2 of shovel, hoe

38th family (3 persons)

Pierre HENRY, fils Pierre	28
Fran^{se}, idem, soeur de Pierre HENRY	23
Angélique, idem, soeur idem	21

Pedro HENRIQUE   Received: 1 each of axe, hatchet, hoe, knife, large knife; 2 shovels

39th family (10 persons)

Simon COMO, père	44
Marguerite AUCOIN, sa femme	45
Marie COMO, leur fille	21
Isabelle, idem, leur fille	19
Magdelaine, idem, leur fille	18
Félicité, idem, leur fille	16
Jean B^{te}, idem, leur fils	14
Alexandre, idem, leur fils	11
Pierre, idem, leur fils	9
Joseph Marie, née le 7 mars 1785	

Simon CAUMEAU   Received: 1 each of knife, large knife; 2 of axe, hatchet; 3 hoes; 4 shovels

40th family (3 persons)

Ambroise LONGUESPÉE, père	52
Marguerite HENRY, sa femme	40
Janvier LONGUESPÉE, leur fils	20

Ambrosio LONGUESPÉE   Received: 1 each of knife, large knife; 2 of axe, shovel, hoe

41st family (7 persons)

Anne THERIOT, veuve de Joseph GRANGER	36
Anna LANDRY, fille du 1er mari	17
Joseph GRANGER	20
Jeanne	8
Ignace GRANGER, enfant	15
Françoise Eulalie, idem, enfant	7
P^{re} Marie, idem, enfant	3

Ana THERIOT   Received: 1 each of hatchet, knife, large knife; 2 of axe, hoe; 3 shovels

42nd family (1 person)

Joseph Ignace GODET	38

Josef Ignacio GAUDET   Received: 1 each of axe, hatchet, shovel, hoe, knife, large knife

SM - #157: Ambroise BOURG s/o Charles & Cécile MÉLANÇON m. 1763 Marie-Modeste MOLAISON d/o Jacques & Cécile MÉLANÇON	**36th family (11 persons)**	
	Ambroise BOURG, father	53
	Marie Modeste MOULAISON, his wife	40
	Marie Victoire BOURG, their daughter	20
	Modeste Aimée BOURG, their daughter	18
	Magdelaine BOURG, their daughter	16
	Julie Thérèse BOURG, their daughter	14
	Isabelle BOURG, their daughter	12
	Joseph BOURG, their son	8
	Pélagie BOURG, their daughter	5
	Modeste BOURG, their daughter	3
	Ambroise BOURG, their son	1

SM - #541: Charles HENRY s/o Jean & Madeleine THERIOT m. 1756 Françoise HÉBERT d/o Joseph & Isabelle BENOIST	**37th family (5 persons)**	
	Charles HENRY, father	49
	Françoise HÉBERT, his wife	47
	Charles HENRY, their son	9
	Françoise Victoire HENRY, their daughter	15
	Marguerite Toussainte HENRY, their dgtr.	13

	38th family (3 persons)	
	Pierre HENRY, son of Pierre HENRY	28
	Françoise HENRY, sister of Pierre HENRY	23
	Angélique HENRY, sister of Pierre HENRY	21

SM - #261: Simon COMMAUX s/o Jean-Baptiste & Marie AUCOIN m. ca. 1763 Marguerite AUCOIN	**39th family (10 persons)**	
	Simon COMEAUX, father	44
	Marguerite AUCOIN, his wife	45
	Marie COMEAUX, their daughter	21
	Isabelle COMEAUX, their daughter	19
	Magdelaine COMEAUX, their daughter	18
	Félicité COMEAUX, their daughter	16
	Jean Baptiste COMEAUX, their son	14
	Alexandre COMEAUX, their son	11
	Pierre COMEAUX, their son	9
	Joseph Marie COMEAUX, b. 7 March 1785	

SM - #684: Ambroise LONGUESPÉE s/o Louis & Anne BRASSEAU m. 1763 Marguerite HENRY d/o François & Marie DUGAST	**40th family (3 persons)**	
	Ambroise LONGUESPÉE, father	52
	Marguerite HENRY, his wife	40
	Janvier LONGUESPÉE, their son	20

SM - #453: Joseph GRANGER s/o Joseph & Marguerite THERIOT m. 1776 Anne THERIOT	**41st family (7 persons)**	
	Anne THERIOT, wid. of Joseph GRANGER	36
	Anna LANDRY, dgtr. of 1st marriage	17
	Joseph GRANGER	20
	Jeanne GRANGER	8
	Ignace GRANGER, child	15
	Françoise Eulalie GRANGER, child	7
	Pierre Marie GRANGER, child	3

	42nd family (1 person)	
	Joseph Ignace GAUDET	38

43rd family (7 persons)

Charles HENRY, père	49	Carlos HENRIQUE Received: 1 each of
Marguerite THERIOT, sa femme	50	hatchet, knife, large knife; 2 of axe, hoe; 3 shovels
Jean B^te HENRY, leur fils	18	
Marie Joseph, idem	22	
Jeanne Françoise, idem, leur fille	17	
Françoise GUÉRIN, veuve		
de François THERIOT	79	
Marie THERIOT, sa fille	52	

44th family (10 persons)

René LANDRY, père	53	Renato LANDRY Received: 1 each of
Marie LANDRY, sa fille	22	knife, large knife; 2 of axe, hatchet, hoe; 4 shovels
Servanne, idem, sa fille	20	
Jean Raphael, idem, son fils	18	
Marguerite LANDRY, sa fille	16	
Anne, idem, sa fille	11	
Pierre, idem, son fils	9	
Joseph, idem, son fils	6	
Jeanne, idem, sa fille	5	
Paul BABIN, beau-frère de René LANDRY	52	

45th family (3 persons)

Victoire DUGAST, veuve de Thomas AYÉ	38	Victoria DUGATS, viuda HENRY Received: 1 each
Thomas HAYÉ, enfant, son fils	10	of axe, hoe, knife; 2 of hatchet and shovel; 5 large
Louis HAYÉ, son fils	6	knives

46th family (2 persons)

Anne Joseph HENRY, veuve		Ana THERIOT Received: 1 each of
de Théodore THERIOT	33	axe, hatchet, hoe, knife, large knife; 2 shovels
Angélique THERIOT, son enfant	4	

47th family (5 persons)

Charles PITRE, père	56	Carlos PITRE Received: 1 each of
Anne HENRY, sa femme	52	knife, large knife; 2 of axe, hoe; 3 shovels
Joseph PITRE, leur enfant	19	
Marguerite, idem, leur fille	15	
Isabelle, idem, leur fille	11	

48th family (8 persons)

Pierre ARCEMENT, père	52	Pedro ARSEMENT Received: 1 each of
Marie HÉBERT, sa femme	50	axe, hatchet, knife, large knife; 2 hoes; 4 shovels
Marguerite ARCEMENT, leur fille	24	
*Marginal Note - embarque pas		
Marie, idem, leur fille	22	
Victoire, idem, leur fille	18	
Perine, idem, leur fille	16	
Guillaume, idem, leur fils	13	
Julie, idem, leur fille	12	
Françoise, idem, leur fille	9	

SM - #542: Charles HENRY s/o Jean & Marie HÉBERT m. 1761 Marguerite-Josèphe THERIOT d/o François & Françoise GUÉRIN	

43rd family (7 persons)

Charles HENRY, father	49
Marguerite THERIOT, his wife	50
Jean Baptiste HENRY, their son	18
Marie Joseph HENRY	22
Jeanne Françoise HENRY, their dgtr.	17
Françoise GUÉRIN, widow of François THERIOT	79
Marie THERIOT, her daughter	52

SM - #611: René LANDRY m. ca. 1761 Marguerite BABIN; children: Servanne b. 1764, Jean Raphael b. 1767

44th family (10 persons)

René LANDRY, father	53
Marie LANDRY, his daughter	22
Servanne LANDRY, his daughter	20
Jean Raphael LANDRY, his son	18
Marguerite LANDRY, his daughter	16
Anne LANDRY, his daughter	11
Pierre LANDRY, his son	9
Joseph LANDRY, his son	6
Jeanne LANDRY, his daughter	5
Paul BABIN, broth.-in-law of René LANDRY	52

45th family (3 persons)

Victoire DUGAT, widow of Thomas AILLET [widow HENRY in the Spanish listing]	38
Thomas AILLET, a child, her son	10
Louis AILLET, her son	6

SM - #877: Théodore THERIOT s/o François & Françoise GUÉRIN m. 1777 Anne-Josèphe HENRY d/o Pierre & Marie-Madeleine PITRE

46th family (2 persons)

Anne Joseph HENRY, widow of Théodore THERIOT	33
Angélique THERIOT, her child	4

SM - #711: Charles PITRE s/o Joseph & Isabelle BOUDROT m. 1752 Anne HENRY d/o Jean & Marie HÉBERT

47th family (5 persons)

Charles PITRE, father	56
Anne HENRY, his wife	52
Joseph PITRE, their child	19
Marguerite PITRE, their daughter	15
Isabelle PITRE, their daughter	11

SM - #9: Pierre ARCEMENT m. ca. 1757 Marie HÉBERT d/o Jean & Madeleine DOIRON

BR - v.2, p.31: Guillaume ARCEMENT s/o Pierre & Marie HÉBERT m. 14 Feb. 1803 Marianne AYSSENE

Perrine ARCEMENT d/o Pierre & Marie HÉBERT m. 7 Sept. 1789 Jean Charles RICHARD

48th family (8 persons)

Pierre ARCEMENT, father	52
Marie HÉBERT, his wife	50
Marguerite ARCEMENT, their daughter	24
*Marginal Note - she did not embark	
Marie ARCEMENT, their daughter	22
Victoire ARCEMENT, their daughter	18
Perine ARCEMENT, their daughter	16
Guillaume ARCEMENT, their son	13
Julie ARCEMENT, their daughter	12
Françoise ARCEMENT, their daughter	9

49th family (7 persons)

Jacques Mieus D'ENTREMONT, père	29
Marie HERVÉ, sa femme	30
Jacques Ferdinand, leur fils	1
Jean Louis LANGLINÉ, du 1er mariage de Marie HERVÉ et de Jean Louis LANGLINÉ	11
Marie Jeanne LANGLINÉ, du 1er mariage de Marie HERVÉ et de Jean Louis LANGLINÉ	9
Angélique LANGLINÉ, du 1er mariage de Marie HERVÉ et de Jean Louis LANGLINÉ	7
Marguerite LANDRY, veuve de Jacques Mieus D'entremont, Père	56

*Marginal Note - "Cette famille n'embarque pas à St. M°"

*Another Marginal Note - "Emb^{ué} à Nantes"

50th family (2 persons)

Joseph MÉLANÇON	68	Josef MÉLANÇON Received: 1 each of
Ursule HÉBERT, sa femme	72	axe, hatchet, shovel, hoe, knife, large knife

51st family (7 persons)

Charles THIBODEAU, père	63	Carlos TIBODEAU Received: 1 each of
Magdelaine HENRY, sa femme	58	knife, large knife; 2 of axe, hoe; 4 shovels
Pierre Charles THIBODEAU, leur fils jumeaux	20	
Jeanne Tarsile, idem, leur fille jumeaux	20	
Marguerite, idem, leur fille	22	
Hélène, idem, leur fille	18	
Marie Victoire, idem, leur fille	15	

52nd family (11 persons)

Fran^s Xavier BOURG, père	44	Fran^{co} Xavier BOURQUE Received: 1 each of
Marguerite Pélagie HENRY, sa femme	34	knife, large knife; 2 of axe, hatchet; 3 hoes; 4 shov-
Felix Xavier BOURG, leur fils	15	els
Joseph Faustin, idem, leur fils	11	
Marie Isabelle, idem, leur fille	8	
Maximilien, idem, leur fils	6	
Isabelle, idem, leur fille	4	
Pierre, idem, leur fils	1	
Anne Victoire, née le 14 May 1785		
Charles BOURG, mary(sic) de Marg^{te} LEBLANC	46	
Marguerite LEBLANC	40	

53rd family (6 persons)

Fran^s GALIEN, père	45
Henriette GROSSIN, sa femme	36
Marie Jeanne GALIEN, leur fille	9
Fran^s Julien, idem, leur fils	6
Bon, idem, leur fils	4
Julien François, idem, leur fils	2

*Note - "la famille GALLIEN n'embarque pas"

49th family (7 persons)	
Jacques MIUS d'ENTREMONT, father	29
Marie HERVÉ, his wife	30
Jacques Ferdinand d'ENTREMONT, son	1
Jean Louis LANGLINÉ, from 1st marriage	
of Marie HERVÉ & Jean Louis LANGLINÉ	11
Marie Jeanne LANGLINÉ, of 1st marriage	
of Marie HERVÉ & Jean Louis LANGLINÉ	9
Angélique LANGLINÉ, from 1st marriage	
of Marie HERVÉ & Jean Louis LANGLINÉ	7
Marguerite LANDRY, widow of Jacques	
Mius D'entremont, Sr.	56

*Marginal Note - "This family did not embark
at St. Malo"

*Another Marginal Note - "Embarked at Nantes"

SM - #710: Joseph MÉLANÇON m. ca. 1761 Ursule HÉBERT d/o Jacques & Marguerite LANDRY

50th family (2 persons)	
Joseph MÉLANÇON	68
Ursule HÉBERT, his wife	72

SM - #882: Charles THIBODAUX s/o Philippe & Élizabeth VINCENT m. 1751 Madeleine HENRY d/o Jean & Marie HÉBERT

51st family (7 persons)	
Charles THIBODEAUX, father	63
Magdelaine HENRY, his wife	58
Pierre Charles THIBODEAUX,	
their son, a twin	20
Jeanne Tarsile THIBODEAUX,	
their daughter, a twin	20
Marguerite THIBODEAUX, their daughter	22
Hélène THIBODEAUX, their daughter	18
Marie Victoire THIBODEAUX, their dgtr.	15

SM - #168: François-Xavier BOURG s/o Charles & Cécile MÉLANÇON m. 1781 Marguerite-Pélagie HENRY d/o Pierre & Marie-Madeleine PITRE

52nd family (11 persons)	
François Xavier BOURG, father	44
Marguerite Pélagie HENRY, his wife	34
Felix Xavier BOURG, their son	15
Joseph Faustin BOURG, their son	11
Marie Isabelle BOURG, their daughter	8
Maximilien BOURG, their son	6
Isabelle BOURG, their daughter	4
Pierre BOURG, their son	1
Anne Victoire BOURG, born 14 May 1785	
Charles BOURG, husband	
of Marguerite LEBLANC	46
Marguerite LEBLANC	40

53rd family (6 persons)	
François GALIEN, father	45
Henriette GROSSIN, his wife	36
Marie Jeanne GALIEN, their daughter	9
François Julien GALIEN, their son	6
Bon GALIEN, their son	4
Julien François GALIEN, their son	2

*Note - The GALLIEN family did not embark

54th family (3 persons)

Jean B^te TERRIAU	en 1785	39
Anne Angélique BRIAND		42
Jean Baptiste TERRIAU, leur enfant		8

Embarqais(sic) en ce Port le 5 Juillet 1785
sur le Navire <u>La Ville d'Archangel</u>...
pour la Nouvelle Orleans

Additional persons embarking)

Pierre Jean EON, Prêtre Dumonier [Aumônier]		
De Dinan embarqué sur le N^re <u>La Ville</u>		
<u>D'Arcangel</u> avec permission de l'Eveque de		
St. Malo en date du 14 Juillet 1785		36

Juan Bautista THERIOT　　　Received: 1 each of
axe, hatchet, hoe, knife, large knife; 2 shovels

<u>Names with no reference on the embarkation list</u>:

Gurdon Thomas CALIGAN　　Received: 1 each of
axe, hatchet, shovel, hoe, knife, large knife

Maria Juana VILLERE　　　Received; 1 each of
axe, hatchet, shovel, hoe, knife, large knife

Maria Isabel DESFOREST　　Received: 1 each of
axe, hatchet, shovel, hoe, knife, large knife

Fran^co Pedro LE LOREC　　Received: 1 each of
axe, hatchet, hoe, knife, large knife; 2 shovel

Fran^ca GUÉRIN, viuda THERIOT　Received: 1 each of
axe, hatchet, hoe, knife, large knife; 2 shovels

Carlos BOURQUE　　　　　Received: 1 each of
axe, hatchet, hoe, knife, large knife; 2 shovels

Carlos AU COING　　　　　Received: 1 each of
axe, hatceht, hoe, knife, large knife; 2 shovel

Alexo AU COING　　　　　Recieved: 1 each of
axe, hatchet, hoe, knife, large knife; 2 shovels

Fran^co HEBERT　　　　　Received: 1 each of
axe, hatchet, hoe, knife, large knife; 2 shovels

Nicolas COURTUA　　　　　Received: 1 each of
axe, hatchet, hoe, knife, large knife; 2 shovels

Santiago BLANCHARD　　　Received: 1 each of
axe, hatchet, hoe, knife, large knife; 3 shovels

Juan BIAFRE??　　　　　　Received: 1 each of
axe, hatchet, hoe, knife, large knife; 2 shovels

Signed: Juan Prieto
Nueva Orleans 17 Enero de 1786 [New Orleans, 17
January 1786]

The "Rôle d'équipage" [Crew List] for La Ville d'Archangel [600 tons] indicates that the ship left St. Malo on 12 August 1785 in mid-August and arrived at Balize (a fortified outpost at the mouth of the Mississippi River with a crude lighthouse consisting of building a fire on high ground in order to signal in ships entering at the mouth of the Mississippi) on 4 November 1785, but went aground. They had been out of provisions for some days and had 38 very sick passengers. [Winzerling p.147]

This group rose from 50 to 60 families representing 299 members. It lost 15 members to death and 2 by desertion, yet gained 2 births, 11 new adherents and 7 marriages. [Winzerling p.149]

Established 53 families of 271 members at Bayou des Ecores (Thompson Creek; area between Baton Rouge and St. Francisville), 6 families of 21 members at La Fourche (area around Plattenville) and 1 family of 7 at New Orleans. [Winzerling p.149]

54th family (3 persons)

Jean Baptiste THERIOT	in 1785	39
Anne Angélique BRIAND		42
Jean Baptiste TERRIOT, their child		8

Embarked in this Port on 5 July 1785
on the ship La Ville d'Archangel...
bound for New Orleans

Additional persons embarking)

Pierre Jean EON, priest chaplain from	36

  Dinan embarked...on La Ville D'Arcangel
with the permission of the Bishop of St. Malo
dated 14 July 1785

1st family (4 persons)

Jean DE LAUNE	charpentier marin	48
Marie PARS, sa femme		34
Pierre, son fils		1
Marie Céleste, sa fille	à la mamelle	

Juan de LAUNE   Received: 1 each of axe, hatchet, shovel, knife and meat cleaver; 2 hoes

2nd family (5 persons)

Christophe DE LAUNE	charpentier marin	34
Marie BOUDREAU, sa femme		30
Jean Baptiste, son fils		10
Louis Auguste, idem		2
Céleste BOUDREAU, soeur de la femme		20

Xstoval de LAUNE   Received: 1 each of hatchet, knife, meat cleaver; 2 each of axe, and shovel; 3 hoes

3rd family (4 persons)

Louis L'AMOUREUX DIT rochefort	marin	44
Marie HÉBERT, sa femme		36
Jean Louis, son fils	idem	20
Adélaïde, sa fille		10

Luis AMOUREUX   Received: 1 each of hatchet, knife and meat cleaver; 2 each of axe and shovel; 3 hoes

4th family (5 persons)

Louis GODET	charpentier	57
Marie HÉBERT, sa femme		54
François Louis, son fils		12
Magdeleine, sa fille		28
Margueritte, idem		20

Luis GAUDET   Received 1 each of hatchet, knife and meat cleaver; 2 each of axe and shovel; 3 hoes

5th family (5 persons)

Michel DOUCET	charpentier	45
Marie Blanche COUSIN, sa femme		37
Jean Bte, son fils		12
Eleonnore, sa fille		15
Margueritte, idem		9

Miguel DOUCET   Received: 1 each of hatchet, knife and meat cleaver; 2 each of axe and shovel; 3 hoes

6th family (4 persons)

Jh DOUCET	laboureur	53
Ange, son fils		15
Marie Margueritte, sa fille		19
Magdeleine, idem		17

Josef DOUCET   Received: 1 each of axe, hatchet, knife and meat cleaver; 2 each of hoe and shovel

7th family (4 persons)

Olivier BOUDREAU	laboureur	74
Anne DUGAST, sa femme		52
Jean, son fils	idem	17
Marie, sa fille		18

Olivier BOUDREAU   Received: 1 each of axe, hatchet, shovel, knife and meat cleaver; 2 hoes

8th family (4 persons)

Ambroise HÉBERT	contre-maitre	56
Félicité LEJEUNE, sa femme		45
Gertrude, sa fille		16
Angélique GOTREAU, sa nièce		20

Ambrosio HEBERT   Received: 1 each of hatchet, knife and meat cleaver; 2 each of axe and shovel; 3 hoes

Chat - #67: Jean DELAUNE s/o Christopher & Marguerite CAISSY m. 1773 Marie-Anne PART d/o Eustache & Anastasie de BELLEFONTAINE

Nantes - #101: additional family information

Chat - #66: Christopher DELAUNE s/o Christopher & Marguerite CAISSY m. 1774 Marie BOUDROT d/o Pierre & Cécile VECO; a child Jean-Baptiste b. 1775

Nantes - #100: additional family information

Chat - #120: Louis LAMOUREUX called Rochefort m. 1763 Marie HÉBERT d/o Jean & Marguerite MOUTON

BR - v.2, p.307-308: François GAUDET s/o Louis & Marie HÉBERT of La Rochelle m. 11 July 1796 Marie ROGER d/o Joseph & Anastasie DUGAS Marguerite GAUDET d/o Louis & Marie HÉBERT m. 5 March 1786 Guiyon ARSENAULT

Chat - #74: Michel DOUCET m. 1768 Marie-Blanche COUSIN d/o Jean & Judith GUÉDRY; a child Marguerite-Bénony DOUCET bt. 1775

Nantes - #108: additional family information

SM - #143: Olivier BOUDROT m. 1762 Anne DUGAST

BR - v.2, p.113: Jean BOUDREAUX of St. Malo s/o Olivier & Anne DUGAT m. 26 Dec. 1802 Françoise PITRE d/o Olivier & Marie MOYSE

Chat - #105: Ambroise HÉBERT m. ca. 1754 Félicité LEJEUNE

SM - #500: additional family information

Nantes - #160: additional family information

1st family (4 persons)

Jean DELAUNE	ship's carpenter	48
Marie PART, his wife		34
Pierre DELAUNE, his son		1
Marie Céleste DELAUNE, his daughter; a nursling		

2nd family (5 persons)

Christophe DELAUNE	ship's carpenter	34
Marie BOUDROT, his wife		30
Jean Baptiste DELAUNE, his son		10
Louis Auguste DELAUNE, his son		2
Céleste BOUDROT, wife's sister		20

3rd family (4 persons)

Louis LAMOUREUX dit ROCHEFORT; sailor		44
Marie HÉBERT, his wife		36
Jean Louis LAMOUREUX, his son; sailor		20
Adélaïde LAMOUREUX, his daughter		10

4th family (5 persons)

Louis GAUDET	carpenter	57
Marie HÉBERT, his wife		54
François Louis GAUDET, his son		12
Magdelaine GAUDET, his daughter		28
Marguerite GAUDET, his daughter		20

5th family (5 persons)

Michel DOUCET	carpenter	45
Marie Blanche COUSIN, his wife		37
Jean Baptiste DOUCET, his son		12
Eleonore DOUCET, his daughter		15
Marguerite DOUCET, his daughter		9

6th family (4 persons)

Joseph DOUCET	plowman	53
Ange DOUCET, his son		15
Marie Marguerite DOUCET, his daughter		19
Magdelaine DOUCET, his daughter		17

7th family (4 persons)

Olivier BOUDROT	plowman	74
Anne DUGAT, his wife		52
Jean BOUDROT, his son	plowman	17
Marie BOUDROT, his daughter		18

8th family (4 persons)

Ambroise HÉBERT	foreman	54
Félicité LEJEUNE, his wife		45
Gertrude HÉBERT, his daughter		16
Angélique GAUTROT, his niece		20

9th family (3 persons)

Charles BLANCHARD	cordonnier	51	Carlos BLANCHARD	Received: 1 each of hatchet, knife and meat cleaver; 2 each of axe, hoe and shovel
Souillac, son fils	charpentier	20		
Charles, idem	marin	16		

10th family (4 persons)

Basile CHAISON	tonnelier	36	Basilio CHAISON	Received: 1 each of axe, hatchet, shovel, knife and meat cleaver; 2 hoes
Monique COMMEAU		38		
Charles, son fils		3		
Adélaïde, sa fille		11		

11th family (3 persons)

Nicolas ALBERT	charpentier	45	Nicolas ALBERT	Received: 1 each of axe, hatchet, shovel, knife and meat cleaver; 2 hoes
Marie Marthe BENOIT, sa femme		40		
Gabriel, son fils		12		

12th family (3 persons)

Ygnace BOUDREAU	charpentier	36	Ignacio BOUDREAU	Received: 1 each of axe, hatchet, shovel, knife and meat cleaver; 2 hoes
Anne PIERÇON, sa femme		26		
Charles, son fils		2		

13th family (3 persons)

Martin PITRE	charpentier	22	Martin PITRE	Received: 1 each of hatchet, knife and meat cleaver; 2 each of axe, hoe and shovel
Josef HÉBERT, son frère		15		
Marie HÉBERT, sa soeur		17		

14th family (2 persons)

| Claude Louis LEGAIGNEUR | journalier | 50 | Claudio LE GAGNEUR | Received: 1 each of axe, hatchet, shovel, knife and meat cleaver; 2 hoes |
| Marie Josèphe HALLIERE, sa femme | | 50 | | |

15th family (1 person)

| Joseph TERRIOT | marin | 27 | Josef THERIOT | Received: 1 axe, hatchet, shovel, knife, meat cleaver; 2 hoes |

16th family (1 person)

| Jean Bᵗᵉ DOIRON | marin | 25 | Juan Bautista DOUERON | Received 1 axe, hatchet, shovel, hoe, knife and meat cleaver |

17th family (2 persons)

| Joseph BOUDREAU | marin | 22 | Jososef(sic) BOUDREAU | Received: 1 each of axe, hatchet, shovel, knife, meat cleaver; 2 hoes |
| Juliene BROSIENE, sa femme | | 20 | | |

18th family (4 persons)

Charles GOTREAU	laboureur	49	Carlos GAUTREAU	Received 1 each of hatchet, knife and meat cleaver; 2 each of axe, shovel and hoe
Marie Magdeleine MÉLANÇON, sa femme		49		
François Marie, son fils		14		
Rosalie GOTREAU, sa fille		5		

19th family (6 persons)

Pʳᵉ MONTAIN	laboureur	22	Pedro MAINTOY	Received: 1 each of hatchet, knife and meat cleaver; 3 each of axe, shovel and hoe
Joseph, son frère	idem	16		
Jean-Baptiste, idem	idem	13		
Pʳᵉ Paul, idem		7		
Françoise, sa soeur		19		
Margueritte		10		

BR - v.2, p.100: Suliac BLANCHARD s/o Charles & Marguerite DUGAS of St. Malo m. 30(sic) Feb. 1786 Celest BUDRO

Chat - #54: Basile CHIASSON m. ca. 1772 Monique COMMAU; a child Anne-Adélaïde bt. 1774

SWLR - v.1, p.126: Basil CHIASSON widr. Monique COMAU s/o Pierre & Catherine BOURGEOIS m. 20 July 1789 Anne-Marie THIBAUDOT [LA. State Archives record]

Chat - #1: Nicolas-Gabriel ALBERT m. ca. 1759 Marie-Marthe BENOIST; a child Nicolas-Gabriel bt. 1774

Nantes - #37: Ignace BOUDROT m. ca. 1780 Anne PIERSON; a child Charles bt. 1783

BR - v.2, p.115: Louis BOUDROT s/o Ignace & Anne PIERSON b. 8 Sept. 1789

BR - v.2, p.116: Marie Lucie BOUDREAUX d/o Joseph & Julia BROSSIE b. 24 March 1790
Braud- Annex: Name of wife appears as Julienne MOINE]

SM - #412: Charles GAUTROT s/o Pierre & Agnès LEBLANC m. 1763 Madeleine MÉLANÇON d/o Jean & Cécile AUCOIN
Census - p.125: Owned 6 arpents of land
Exile - p.571 & BR - v.2, p.553: Pierre MONTET b. 23 Jan. 1764 s/o Guillaume & Marie VINCENT m. 23 March 1788 Félicité AUCOIN; Celestine, a child b. 25 March 1797 has these grandparents: Pats. Guillaume MONTET & Marie VINCENT, Mats. Jean AUCOIN & Jeanne THERIOT.
Braud - Annex: lists this family name as MONTET

9th family (3 persons)

Charles BLANCHARD	shoemaker	51
Souillac BLANCHARD, his son; carpenter		20
Charles BLANCHARD, his son; sailor		16

10th family (4 persons)

Basile CHIASSON	cooper	36
Monique COMEAUX		38
Charles CHIASSON, his son		3
Adélaïde CHIASSON, his daughter		11

11th family (3 persons)

Nicolas ALBERT	carpenter	45
Marie Marthe BENOIT, his wife		40
Gabriel ALBERT, his son		12

12th family (3 persons)

Ignace BOUDROT	carpenter	36
Anne PIERSON, his wife		26
Charles BOUDROT, his son		2

13th family (3 persons)

Martin PITRE	carpenter	22
Joseph HÉBERT, his brother		15
Marie HÉBERT, his sister		17

14th family (2 persons)

Claude Louis LEGAGNEUR	day laborer	50
Marie Josèphe HALLIER, his wife		50

15th family (1 person)

Joseph THERIOT	sailor	27

16th family (1 person)

Jean Baptiste DOIRON	sailor	25

17th family (2 persons)

Joseph BOUDROT	sailor	22
Juliene MOINE, his wife		20

18th family (4 persons)

Charles GAUTROT	plowman	49
Marie Magdelaine MÉLANÇON, his wife		49
François Marie GAUTROT, his son		14
Rosalie GAUTROT, his daughter		5

19th family (6 persons)

Pierre MONTET	plowman	22
Joseph MONTET, his brother; plowman		16
Jean-Baptiste MONTET, brother; plowman		13
Pierre Paul MONTET, his brother		7
Françoise MONTET, his sister		19
Marguerite MONTET		10

20th family (1 person)
Joseph DUHON   laboureur   19   Josef DOUAN   Received: 1   axe, hatchet, shovel, hoe, knife and meat cleaver

21st family (1 person)
Claude Marie LEBLANC   laboureur   20   Claudio Maria LEBLANC   Received: 1   axe, hatchet, shovel, hoe, knife and meat cleaver

22nd family (1 person)
Basile Marie RICHARD   laboureur   Basilio RICHARD   Received: 1   axe, hatchet, shovel, hoe, knife and meat cleaver

23rd family (1 person)
Marie BOUDREAU, veuve   Maria BOUDREAU   Received: 1   axe,
   Charles TERRIOT   laboureur   40   hatchet, shovel, hoe, knife and meat cleaver

24th family (1 person)
Jean Charles BENOIT   marin   36

25th family (Plus la famille de
Étienne François ANGILBERT, étranger   32   Estevan Francisco ANGILBERT   Received: 1 each of axe, hatchet, shovel, knife and meat cleaver; 2 hoes
   imprimeur en Lauze
   Félicité HÉBERT, sa femme; acadiene   28
   Marie Adélaïde, sa fille   à la mamelle

Pedro Montagne CATALAN   Received: 1 each of axe, hatchet, shovel, knife, meat cleaver and hoe

Guido QUERIVEN   Received: 1 each of axe, hatchet, shovel, knife and meat cleaver; 2 hoes

Renato ARMEAU   Received: 1 each of axe, hatchet, shovel, knife and meat cleaver; 2 hoes

"Liste des familles Acadiens qui doivent s'embarquer pour la nouvelle-Orleans dans la Louisiane dans le Navire La Caroline. Capt. Baud.

"Nous, Consul d'Espagne en Bretagne chargé de l'expedition des Acadiens pour la nouvelle orleans dans la Louisiane. Certifions que les individus mentionés dans la presente Liste, sont ceux qui doivent s'embarquer dans le Navire La Caroline Capitain le Sr. Baudin. A Nantes ce 22 Septembre 1785. d'Asperer
Legajo 576 of Cuba dated 17 Jan. 1786

Translation:
List of Acadian families which should be embarking for New Orleans in Louisiana on the ship La Caroline. Captain Baud

We, Consul of Spain in Brittany in charge of the transporting of the Acadians for New Orleans in Louisiana. Certifying that the individuals given in the present list, are those who will be embarking on the ship La Caroline, Captain Sieur Baud. At nantes on 22 September 1785.

111

Joseph DUHON   plowman   19

21st family (1 person)
Claude Marie LEBLANC   plowman   20

22nd family (1 person)
Basile Marie RICHARD   plowman

Nantes - #280: Charles THERIOT m. ca. 1757 Marie BOUDROT

23rd family (1 person)
Marie BOUDROT, widow Charles THERIOT   40

24th family (1 person)
Jean Charles BENOIT   sailor   36

25th family (Add the following family)
Étienne François ANGILBERT, stranger   32
    printer in Lauze

Nantes - #1: Étienne-François ANGILBERT m. ca. 1784 Félicité HÉBERT; a child Marie-Adélaïde bt. 1785

    Félicité HÉBERT, his wife; an acadian   28
    Marie Adélaïde ANGILBERT; daughter;
    a nursling

La Caroline Sailed under Captain Nicolas Baudin and crossed the Atlantic in 64 days. Arriving at Balize on 17 December 1785, she took on a pilot, sailed up the Mississippi in five days (presumably arriving on 17 Dec. 1785), discharged her cargo of trunks and 28 families of 80 persons and immediatley started back to Nantes with a cargo of wood. [Winzering p.150]

During the month spent in New Orleans, the expedition had an increment of 3 births, 5 new adherents and 2 marriages. Its losses were 1 death, 1 desertion. Six families went to Nueva Galvez (area southeast of Baton Rouge), 18 families of 54 persons went to La Fourche (area around Plattenville). [Winzerling p.151

17...... { Juan Bautista Dugats.
Ana Boura su muger.
Ana su hija.
Maria Boudreaud su Nieta. } 4.

18..... { Josef Aucoin.
Ysabel Henrique su muger
Juan Josef su hijo.
Francisco Santos Ydem.
Isabel Juana Ydem
Maria Modesta Ydem.
Victoria Clara Ydem. } 7.

19...... { Eustachio el Joven.
Juana Cliquet su muger.
Servando su hijo.
Francisco Ydem.
Maria Magdalena Ydem.
Delugia Gotreau su sobrina. } 6.

20...... { Juan Bautista el Joven.
Helena Dumont su muger.
Gregorio su hijo.
Julian Ydem.
Maria Ydem.
Maria Genoveva Gotreau Sobrina. } 6.

21..... { Anselmo Landry.
Agata Vaciou su Muger. } 2.

22..... { Juan Bautista Baudreau.
Maria Modesta traham su muger.
Juan Constante su hijo.
Maria Felicidad Ydem.
Maraarita Ydem. } 5.

Document of debarkation list [families 17-22 of Le Bon Papa] - transcribed on page 6

Relacion de los Utiles que deben entregarse á las Familias Acadianas venidas de Nantes en la Fragata la Bergere, y se las Siguientes. A Saver.

Nombres de las familias.	Hachas g.ˢ	Idem chicas.	Azadas.	Palas.	Cuchillos.	(
Olivier Teriot	1	3	2	1	1	
Jean Charles Teriot	1	1	1	1	1	
Olivier Aucoing	2	2	3	1	1	
Charles Aucoing	1	1	2	1	1	
Marie Josefe Leblanc	1	1	1	1	1	
Marguerite Nöel	1	1	1	1	1	
Simon Maserole	1	2	3	1	1	
Jaques Teriot	1	1	2	1	1	
Elisabet Guérin	1	1	1	1	1	
Joseph Guérin	1	1	2	1	1	
Pierre Guillot	1	1	2	1	1	
Marguerite Ebrat	1	2	2	1	1	
Antoine Aucoing	2	2	2	1	1	
Laurent Bourg	1	2	3	1	1	
Charles Hebert	2	1	2	1	1	
Claude Leblanc	1	1	2	1	1	
Marie Magdeleine Landry	1	1	1	1	1	
Jean Aucoing	1	2	2	1	1	
Marie Anastasie Aucoing	1	1	1	1	1	
Pierre Richard	2	2	2	1	1	
Franquile Pitre	1	2	2	1	1	
Jean Richard	2	2	2	1	1	
Marie Josef Richard Veuve Landry	1	2	2	1	1	
Marin Gotreau	2	2	2	1	1	
Jeanne Chelion	1	2	2	1	1	
Ana Hebert	3	3	4	2	1	
	34	42	54	27	26	2

Document of families from <u>La Bergère</u> receiving tools from the Spanish - transcribed on page 12-28

...rs qu^e doivent s'embarquer dans le Navire Le Beaumont, Capitaine ─

...es Famille)	metiers	ages		leurs noms	metiers	ag...
	Charpentier	49		**onzieme Famille**		
...emme	idem	58		Jean Douairon	Laboureur	5.
	idem	21	3.	marguritte Josephe Safille		2.
	idem	18		Paul daigle, mineur	idem	1½
		9		**12.e Famille**		
...e Safille		24	2.	anne Benoit veuve hubert		4½
		22		jean Charles Son fils		1.
		13		**13.e Famille**		
...e idem		11		Marie Martin veuve Courtin		4.
...mille				Jacques marie Sonfils	Journallier	1.
	Charpentier	53.	5.	françoise Safille		2.
	idem	23.		Mathurine olive idem		2.
	idem	19.		Charlotte Louise idem		1
	Tonellier	68.		**14.e Famille**		
...eus	Journallier	15		Pierre Potier	Charpentier	4.
		9.		agnes Broussard Safemme		6
		11.		Charles Victor Son fils		1.
		9.	7.	Pierre Laurent idem		1.
		8.		françois Constant idem	a la mamelle	
...mille.				Constance Safille		1.
	Charpentier	51.		anne Pauline idem		1.
...Safemme		45		**15.e Famille**		
...Safille		21		Jean Douaison	Charpentier	
idem		14		marie Blanche Bernard Safemme		9.
		10.		Louis toussaint Son fils		
...fils de la femme	Charpentier	17.	7.	Jean Charles idem		
...amille				marie Safille		
	Charpentier	74		Rose idem		
...Safemme		55		Ursule idem		
...s	marin	20		**16.e Famille**		
	Charpentier	18.		françois daigle	Laboureur	
		11.		Jeanne aulai Safemme		
		14.		Louis Sonfils	Calfat	
...Famille			6.	Jeanne Safille		
	Charpentier	54.		adelaide idem		
		12.		Louise idem		
...e idem		22.		**17.e Famille**		
		12.		françois arbourg	Calfat	
...famille				marie hervory Safemme		
...rançois St trahan		46.	5.	françois henry Sonfils	marin	
...Son fils	Charpentier	25.		Jean Louis ... idem		
...idem	idem	19.				
...Safille		13.				
...idem		8.				

Document of embarkation list of Le Beaumont [families 11-17] - transcribed on pages 32 and 34

114

10	———————	Juan Douazon
11.	2	Margarita Josefa su hija
12.	1.	Pablo D'aigle huerfano

Passó a los
Atacapares —

13   7
{
Pedro Poticu
Ynès Brauzard su muger
Carlos su hijo
Pedro Lorenzo idem
Fran.co Ydem
Constanza ydem.
Ana ydem
}

| 14 | 2. | Ana venoi viuda ebert |
| | | Juan Carlos su hijo |

Passó a los
Atacapas —

15   7
{
Juan Bautista Douazon
Maria Blanca Rainard su muger.
Luis Santos su hijo
Juan Carlos idem
}

15.
Maria su hija
Rosa idem
Ursula idem

Document of debarkation list of <u>Le Beaumont</u> [families 11-15] - transcribed on pages 32 and 34

115

Dates des Changemens	NOMS, SURNOMS, DEMEURES ET QUALITE'S.	Avances.
	De l'autre part ... 65	147. Personne
	Marin Bourg, Père .... 45.	
	Marie Ositte D'aigle, ... 40.	
	Jean Pierre Bourg, leur fils .... 20.	
	Marie Luce, Idem leur fille ...... 22.	
	Marguerite Joseph, Idem leur fille ... 17.	
	Marin Joseph, Idem leur fille ... 16.	11. Idem
	Rose Magdelaine, Idem leur fille ... 13.	
	Pre Jean Bte Idem leur fille ... 12.	
	Mie Françoise Magd. Josephe Idem leur fille ... 10.	
	Fran. George, Idem leur fils ... 7.	
	Guillaume Jean, Idem leur fils ... 4.	
	Joseph hebert, Père .... 45.	
	Mie Magd. Aucoin, sa femme ... 44.	4. Idem
	Marie hebert, leur fille ... 17.	
	Victoire, Idem leur fille ... 11.	
	Claude Guedry, Père .... 60.	
	Anne Moyse, sa femme ... 54.	
	Marie Guedry, leur fille ... 21.	162 Personnes

Document of embarkation list of <u>La Ville d'Archangel</u> [families 26-28] - transcribed on page 94

116

Dates des Changemens	NOMS, SURNOMS, DEMEURES ET QUALITÉS.	Avances.
	Cy Contre	162 Personnes
	Suite de la famille Guedry 3	
	Jean Guedry, leur fils 19	
	Juliac, Idem leur fils 17	
	Malo, Idem leur fils 15	8. Idem
	Pierre, Idem leur fils 12	
	Ollivier Idem leur fils 8	
	Aman Boudro, Pere 52	
	Marie Vogue, sa femme 35	
	Jean Bte leur fils 15	
	Fran. Idem leur fils 11	7. Idem
	Marie, Idem leur fille 6	
	Joseph Idem leur fils 1	
	Helene, Idem Enoire	
	Magdelaine Aucoin, veuve de Ch. Trahan . . . 69	
	Marie Trahan, Enfans de ville 1	3. Idem
	Marguerite Trahan, Idem 10	
	Jean Bte Aucoin, Pere 66	
	Marguerite Theriot, sa femme 5	180 Personnes

Document of embarkation list of <u>La Ville d'Archangel</u> [families 28-31] - transcribed on pages 94 & 96

117

Conditions of Contract - Chartering the *BON PAPA* - dated: 6 May 1785

These conditions of the contracts entered by the Spanish Government and the ships transporting the Acadian families; "la Convention" [the Agreement] between the Courts of France and Spain." Contract done 8 May 1785 at Nantes.

1. The ships should carry the passengers up to the port of New Orleans in Louisiana where the general debarkation of the Acadians ought to take place and not elsewhere from the River under no circumstances; but if it is impossible for the ships to enter the Mississippi and debarkation must take place other than the [Mississippi] River, the cost of transporting all passengers and their baggage [belongings] to reach New Orleans will be borne by the ship.

2. Each vessel of 300 tons will not depart with over 225 passengers with their belongings.

3. The "armateurs" [ship's owners] are to care for the passenger's food - for simple ration - from their embarkation up until their debarkation at New Orleans. The ship's owners will carry the necessary foods for at least a three (3) month voyage, the kind and distribution ought to be as follows:

4. The ship's owners are also responsible for the passenger's comfort and accomodations, such as cabins, water, pots, all utensils for the distribution of food and "le coffre de Chirurgie" [the surgeons equipment].

5. The ships will be prepared to receive the passengers on the appointed date of this Agreement - the failure to do so will oblige the ship's owners to pay the "solde" [daily wages] being paid by His Catholic Majesty to each passenger until the moment of embarkation.

6. The vessels being prepared to set sail on the date appointed, if delay in embarkation is caused by other than contrary winds, the ship's owners shall be paid two "Louis" [french coin; a twenty-franc piece] per day for damages.

7. The embarkation and debarkation will be done at the king's expenses with the assistance of the ship's crew.

8. The embarkation of passengers will not be done until the day when the ship is able to set sail.

9. The embarkation done, the captian will be obliged to set sail without delay to travel directly to their destination and if the ship is delayed for other than contrary winds, the people will be fed on board at the expense of the ship.

10. Infants at the breast and even those born aboard ship during the passage will pay nothing for their passage and will not be part of the count of passengers aboard ship.

11. Passengers are allowed 10 days during which to disembark in New Orleans.

12. Ships are exempt of all "droits" [possibly "droits de port" or harbor dues].

13. Embarkation will take place at Paimboeuf or a more accessible place.

14. Contract costs are borne by ship's owners.

15. There are to be named two "chefs" [heads or leaders] for each 100 persons, who are to be given preferential treatment, or as that of the secondary officers.

16. Excess provisions for the passengers after debarkation will remain with the ship.

118

17. At the moment of embarkation an exact count will be kept of all passengers.

18. Concerns the equiping of each ship.

19. All the sick as well as the "femmes en couche" [women in confinement during pregnancy] will be cared for and fed with fresh supplies which ought to be brought aboard for such use; their quantity will be fixed among ourselves, in proportion to the number of passengers, on the day of the Agreement.

   The "chefs" [heads or leaders] will be responsible for the distribution of rations according to what is required.

20. In any port of His Majesty's - food for passengers will be furnished by the Government of that place as long as they stay...

21. Captains will not permit passengers to disembark in any port except for cases of contagious sickness.

22. Before engaging any ship, visits will be conducted to ascertain the ship's accomodations for the passengers and the location of foods.

23. Payment will be made when news of the ship's actual departure has been verified.

NOTE - The belongings of the Acadians will consist of a bed and a trunk per person. On the "entrepont" [between deck] there will be the beds and one trunk only for each family and the rest in the "calle" ["cale" or ship's hold].
Quantity and distribution of rations of food the ship should supply for the Acadians on the voyage from Nantes to New Orleans in Louisiana:

"Pain - biscuit" [bread - biscuit] - 18 ounces a day; [6 for breakfast, 6 at dinner, 6 at supper].

Drink: Wine- 3/4 of a pint [0.23 litres] per day; ¼ at breakfast, ¼ at dinner, ¼ at supper
Drink: Eau-de-Vie [brandy or spirits]: 3 boujarrons [a tin cup used to distribute drink to the sailors] a day
Note - For 40 days - red wine; for 40 other days - white wine; then for 10 days - eau de vie

Dinner: Lard, salé [salted fish], salted beef, morue [cod fish], cheese, beans, fayols [white beans], rice.
Supper: beans, fayols, rice
Seasoning: olive oil and vinegar for cod, vegetables and rice.

Rations for the sick
Fresh bread - 20 ounces a day.
Drink - Vin de Bordeaux - 3/4 cup a day
Dinner: fresh lamb - 12 ounces a day [all ships had live chicken aboard, all except *La Caroline* which carried six sheep.
Supper: Rice, prunes

NOTE - Nine cords of wood to burn per 100 persons.
Vinegar for sprinkling the vessel.
One barrel of water, at least, for each person.

BIBLIOGRAPHY

Arsenault, Bona. Histoire et Généalogie des Acadiens. Carleton, Quebec, Canada: Lemeac, 1988.

Brasseaux, Carl. The Founding of New Acadia.

Braud, Gérard-Marc. De Nantes à La Louisiane - en 1785, 1600 Acadiens quittent le vieux Continent, à Destination de la Nouvelle-Orléans. Nantes, France: Ouest Éditions, 1994.

Centre d'études Acadiennes. Inventaire Général des Sources Documentaires Sur les Acadiens. Volume 1. Moncton, N.B., Canada: Éditions d'Acadie, 1975.

Hébert, Rev. Donald. Acadians in Exile. Cecilia, Louisiana: Hebert Publications, 1980.

Rieder, Milton and Norma. The Crew and Passenger Registration Lists of the Seven Acadian Expeditions of 1785. Metairie, Louisiana: privately published, 1965.

Robichaux, Jr., Albert J. The Acadian Exiles in Nantes, 1775-1785 Harvey, Louisiana: privately published, 1978.

Robichaux, Jr., Albert J. The Acadian Exiles in St-Malo, 1758-1785 3 volumes, Eunice, Louisiana: Hebert Publications, 1981.

Robichaux, Jr., Albert J. The Acadian Exiles in Chatellerault, 1773-1785. Eunice, Louisiana: Hebert Publications, 1983.

Robichaux, Jr., Albert J. Colonial Settlers Along Bayou Lafourche. Hebert Publications.

Winzerling, Rev. Oscar W. Acadian Odyssey" first printed in 1955. Eunice, Louisiana: Hebert Publication, 1981- second printing.

SPECIAL ACKNOWLEDGMENTS

Braud, Gérard-Marc - provided some important details and notes on this Acadian Odyssey. The view of the ship L'Amitié was made possible by Mr. Braud.

Brasseaux, Carl - Center for Louisiana Studies; Lafayette, LA - who shared so much of his own research and knowledge with me for this work.

Caillebeau, Maurice - Poitiers, France - who provided me with much new material which has been included in my work "Acadians in Exile." This has been useful in further identifying these Acadian families as they resettled in South Louisiana.

Conrad, Glenn - Center for Louisiana Studies; Lafayette, LA - whose expertise and knowledge has enabled me to more acccurately understand the Acadian Exile experience.

Lemieux, Donald - State Archivist and Director of the Louisiana Archives; Baton Rouge, LA - for making available certain ship lists for this work.

Parent. Rev. Robert A. - for furnishing some valuable word definitions of the period.

Rieder, Jr., Milton and Norma - whose work "The Crew and Passenger Registration Lists of the Seven Acadian Expeditions of 1785" was very useful in many instances in my correct reading and interpretation of the original documents.

Robichaux, Jr., Albert J. - Terrytown, LA - for providing documentation as well as other references useful to identifying the Acadian families as they resettled in South Louisiana.

Vincent, Clyde - Beaumont, Texas - for providing material important for this work.

Winzerling, Rev. Oscar W. - whose work "Acadian Odyssey" has been most useful in ascertaining many dates and facts about this particular Acadian Odyssey to Louisiana.

INDEX

"A"

-----, François Jullien, 21
-----, Isabelle, 21
Adam, Joseph, 85
Adams, Joseph, 63
Adams, Nicolas, 63
Aillet, Louis, 101
Aillet, Mathurin, 65
Aillet, Pierre, 65
Aillet, Thomas, 101
Albert, Gabriel, 83, 109
Albert, Nicolas, 83, 109
Alliot, Mathurina, 85
Amirault, Élizabeth, 73, 93
Angilbert, Étienne François, 111
Angilbert, Marie Adélaïde, 111
Arcement, Françoise, 101
Arcement, Genevieve, 15, 23, 27
Arcement, Guillaume, 101
Arcement, Julie, 101
Arcement, Marguerite, 101
Arcement, Marie, 101
Arcement, Marie Magdelaine, 49
Arcement, Perine, 101
Arcement, Pierre, 101
Arcement, Victoire, 101
Arsenault, Guiyon, 107
Aubois, Marie, 77
Aucoin, Alexandre, 83, 89
Aucoin, Alexis, 87, 93, 104
Aucoin, Anastasie, 93
Aucoin, Anne, 87, 89, 93
Aucoin, Anne Augustine, 83
Aucoin, Anne Félicité, 15
Aucoin, Anne Marie, 83
Aucoin, Anne Olive, 95
Aucoin, Antoine, 15, 73, 93
Aucoin, Cécile, 13, 109
Aucoin, Charles, 13, 29, 89, 95, 104
Aucoin Claude 91, 93
Aucoin, Constant, 93
Aucoin, Elene, 73
Aucoin, Élizabeth, 15, 67, 83
Aucoin, Fabien, 27, 87
Aucoin, Félicité, 13
Aucoin, Firmin, 15
Aucoin, Floriane, 93
Aucoin, François 87, 93, 95
Aucoin, François Toussaint, 7
Aucoin, Françoise, 87, 93
Aucoin, Gabriel, 87
Aucoin, Genevieve, 83
Aucoin, Grégoire, 93

Aucoin, Helene, 13
Aucoin, Isabelle, 17, 93
Aucoin, Isabelle Jeanne, 7
Aucoin, Jacinte, 87
Aucoin, Jean, 15, 93
Aucoin, Jean Baptiste, 15, 91, 97
Aucoin, Joseph, 7, 17, 67, 77, 87, 95
Aucoin, Joseph Jean, 7
Aucoin, Louis, 15
Aucoin, Magdelaine, 97
Aucoin, Marguerite, 13, 99
Aucoin, Marguerite Genevieve, 95
Aucoin, Marie, 13, 19, 21, 89, 93, 97, 99
Aucoin, Marie Anastasie, 15
Aucoin, Marie Blanche, 95
Aucoin, Marie Claire, 75, 77
Aucoin, Marie Félicité, 83
Aucoin, Marie Françoise, 49
Aucoin, Marie Jeanne, 89, 91
Aucoin, Marie Magdelaine, 83, 87, 95
Aucoin, Marie Modeste, 7
Aucoin, Marie Reine, 83
Aucoin, Mathurin, 87, 89, 93
Aucoin, Mathurin Jean, 85
Aucoin, Michel, 49, 87, 93
Aucoin, Natalie, 13
Aucoin, Olivier, 13
Aucoin, Paul, 7
Aucoin, Perpétue, 93, 95
Aucoin, Pierre, 15, 29, 49, 93, 95, 97
Aucoin, Rosa Adélaïde, 49
Aucoin, Rose Anastasie, 95, 97
Aucoin, Rose Félicité, 95
Aucoin, Rose Magdelaine, 97
Aucoin, Simon, 95
Aucoin, Victoire, 93
Aucoin, Victoire Claire, 7
Aucoin, widow, 15
Avarat, Jean François, 85
Ayssene, Marianne, 101

"B"

Babin, François, 9
Babin, Marguerite, 75
Babin, Marie, 9, 69
Babin, Paul, 101
Babin, Simon, 85
Bala, Marguerite, 31
Barrillot, Agathe, 7
Barrillot, Anastasie, 43

Barrillot, Euphroisine, 9
Barrillot, François, 19
Barrillot, Jacques, 19
Barrillot, Jean, 19
Barrillot, Jean Baptiste, 19
Barrillot, Marie, 67
Barrillot, Pélagie, 77
Barrillot, Perrine, 19
Barrillot, Pierre, 9, 19, 43, 77
Basset, François, 71
Basset, Marie, 71
Baye, Joseph, 69
Bedel, Marguerite, 53
Bellemère, Anastasie, 53
Bellemère, Jacques, 53
Bellemère, Marguerite, 37
Bellemère, Marie Josèphe, 37
Benard, Anne, 81
Benard, Joseph, 65, 81
Benard, Marie, 63, 65, 81
Benard, Martin, 81
Benoît, Anne, 33, 55
Benoît, Augustin, 55
Benoît, Charles, 53, 55, 75
Benoît, Claude, 9, 61, 71
Benoît, Daniel, 9
Benoît, Donatien, 61
Benoît, François René, 75
Benoît, Françoise, 15, 17, 55, 61, 87, 95
Benoît, Grégoire, 61
Benoît, Henriette, 9
Benoît, Isabelle, 99
Benoît, Jean Charles, 75, 111
Benoît, Jean Marie, 61, 75
Benoît, Marguerite, 11, 71, 85
Benoît, Marie, 5, 53, 81
Benoît, Marie Marthe, 83, 109
Benoît, Marie Rose, 61
Benoît, Maurice, 73
Benoît, Paul Frédéric, 75
Benoît, Pélagie, 63, 71
Benoît, Pierre, 33
Benoît, Raymond, 61
Benoît, Sophie, 53
Benoît, Sophie Renee, 75
Benoît, Victoire, 55
Bernard, Marie, 35
Bernard, Marie Blanche, 35
Bertrand, Adélaïde, 19
Bertrand, Ambroise Belony, 19
Bertrand, Anne Magdelaine, 19
Bertrand, Catherine, 19
Bertrand, Eustache, 75
Bertrand, Jean, 73, 75

Bertrand, Jean Augustin, 19
Bertrand, Louis, 19
Bertrand, Louis Martin ,75
Bertrand, Magdelaine, 75
Bertrand, Marie, 19,
Bertrand, Marie Genevieve, 75
Bertrand, Marie Josèphe, 75
Bertrand, Pierre, 19
Betancourt, François Michel, 41
Biafre, Jean, 104
Billardin Étienne 59
Billardin Lambert 59
Billardin Marguerite 59
Billardin Marie Jeanne 59
Billeza, Marie Jeanne, 91
Blanchard, Angélique, 49, 51
Blanchard, Anne, 17, 73, 81
Blanchard, Anne Marie, 43
Blanchard, Benoît, 81
Blanchard, Celeste, 81
Blanchard, Charles, 79, 109
Blanchard, Elie, 17
Blanchard, François, 79
Blanchard, Françoise, 61, 79
Blanchard, Helene, 93
Blanchard, Jacques, 105
Blanchard, Jean Baptiste, 51
Blanchard, Jean Grégoire, 51
Blanchard, Joachim, 81
Blanchard, Joseph, 17, 79, 81
Blanchard, Laurent, 17
Blanchard, Magdelaine, 73, 77
Blanchard, Marguerite, 73, 79
Blanchard, Marie, 17, 31, 33, 51,
  63, 77, 79
Blanchard, Marie Bennony, 81
Blanchard, Marie Magdelaine, 81
Blanchard, Moise, 17, 81
Blanchard, Pierre, 17
Blanchard, Pierre Charles, 51
Blanchard, Souillac, 79, 109
Blandin, Louise, 37
Boisseau, Marie, 75
Bonfils, Anne, 53
Bonfils, François, 53
Bonnevie, Françoise, 75
Bonnevie, Jacques, 67
Bonnevie, Rose, 67
Bonniere, Marie, 37
Bonniere, Marie Madeleine, 49
Bonvilin, Marie, 37
Boucite, François, 85
Boudrot, Alexandre 7
Boudrot, Aman, 59, 95
Boudrot, Anne, 5, 35, 39, 75

Boudrot, Anne Jeanne, 93
Boudrot, Antoine, 37, 73, 93
Boudrot, Benjamin, 69
Boudrot, Blaise, 75
Boudrot, Cécile, 23, 65, 75, 93
Boudrot, Celeste, 37, 67, 107, 109
Boudrot, Charles, 53, 69, 83, 109
Boudrot, Charles Marie, 69
Boudrot, Charles Michel, 73
Boudrot, Étienne, 65, 73, 75, 77
Boudrot, Félicité, 47
Boudrot, Felix, 47
Boudrot, François, 39, 47, 95
Boudrot, François Xavier, 37
Boudrot, Françoise, 11
Boudrot, Helene, 95
Boudrot, Ignace, 83, 109
Boudrot, Isabelle, 75, 97, 101
Boudrot, Jean, 23, 25, 77, 81, 107
Boudrot, Jean Baptiste, 7, 25, 53,
  69, 73, 95
Boudrot, Jean Charles, 47, 53, 69
Boudrot, Jean Constant, 7
Boudrot, Joseph, 53, 59, 65, 69,
  73, 75, 93, 95, 109
Boudrot, Judith, 19
Boudrot, Louis, 83, 109
Boudrot, Magdelaine, 39, 49, 55,
  67
Boudrot, Marguerite, 3, 7, 65, 73,
  75, 77
Boudrot, Marie, 7, 23, 27, 49, 51,
  55, 67, 77, 81, 87, 95, 107, 111
Boudrot, Marie Félicité, 7
Boudrot, Marie Lucie, 109
Boudrot, Marie Magdelaine, 73
Boudrot, Marie Marthe, 65, 69
Boudrot, Marie Rose, 25, 93
Boudrot, Marin, 77
Boudrot, Michel, 69
Boudrot, Noel, 93
Boudrot, Olivier, 81, 107
Boudrot, Paul, 3, 5, 9, 11
Boudrot, Paul Dominique, 5
Boudrot, Paul Marin, 5
Boudrot, Pierre, 37, 67, 107
Boudrot, Sophie, 69, 93
Boudrot, Victor, 93
Boudrot, Yves, 75
Boudrot, Zacharie, 69
Bourbon, Jacques, 55
Bourg, Abraham, 25
Bourg, Alexandre, 15
Bourg, Alexis, 39
Bourg, Allain, 39

Bourg, Ambroise, 99
Bourg, Andre, 17
Bourg, Anne, 7, 43, 45, 93
Bourg, Anne Joseph, 77
Bourg, Anne Victoire, 103
Bourg, Athanase, 55, 75
Bourg, Catherine, 19, 77
Bourg, Cécile, 3, 5
Bourg, Charles, 17, 19, 55, 75,
  77, 97, 99, 103, 104
Bourg, Charlote Françoise, 87
Bourg, Élizabeth, 25, 45, 47, 95
Bourg, Felix Xavier, 103
Bourg, François, 39, 49, 55, 75,
  87, 89
Bourg, François George, 95
Bourg, François Xavier, 103
Bourg, Françoise, 21
Bourg, Françoise, 89
Bourg, Genevieve, 39
Bourg, Gertrude, 17
Bourg, Guillaume Jean, 95
Bourg, Isabelle, 5, 89, 99, 103
Bourg, Jean, 15, 17, 25, 45, 77,
  87, 89, 95
Bourg, Jean Baptiste, 17, 25
Bourg, Jean Baptiste Simon Louis,
  89
Bourg, Jean Pierre, 21, 95
Bourg, Jeanne, 49, 87, 93
Bourg, Joseph 25, 37, 55, 75, 87,
  89-99
Bourg, Joseph Faustin, 103
Bourg, Joseph Florent, 77
Bourg, Julie Thérèse, 99
Bourg, La Luce, 47
Bourg, Laure, 15
Bourg, Louis, 77, 81
Bourg, Luce Perpétue, 87
Bourg, Lucien, 77
Bourg, Magdelaine, 37, 45, 87, 99
Bourg, Marguerite, 15, 81, 87, 89
Bourg, Marguerite Joseph, 25, 95
Bourg, Marie, 17, 87, 89
Bourg, Marie Françoise, 89
Bourg, Marie Françoise Magde-
  laine Joseph, 95
Bourg, Marie Isabelle, 103
Bourg, Marie Josèphe, 25, 97
Bourg, Marie Luce, 95
Bourg, Marie Madeleine, 21
Bourg, Marie Rose, 55
Bourg, Marie Victoire, 99
Bourg, Marin, 17, 95
Bourg, Marin Joseph, 95

Bourg, Maximilien, 103
Bourg, Modeste, 99
Bourg, Modeste Aimee, 99
Bourg, Pélagie, 99
Bourg, Pierre, 17, 25, 49, 103
Bourg, Pierre Jean Baptiste, 95
Bourg, Rose Adélaïde, 37
Bourg, Rose Magdelaine, 95
Bourg, Sebastien Joseph, 25
Bourg, Susanne, 59
Bourg, Théodore, 45
Bourg, Ursule, 21, 55, 75, 81
Bourg, Victoire, 49
Bourg, Xavier, 87
Bourg, Yves, 89
Bourgeois, Catherine, 77, 109
Bourgeois, Jeanne, 15
Boutary, Antoine, 51
Boutary, Auguste, 51
Boutary, Guillaume, 51
Boyer, Marguerite, 65
Brasseur, Anne 89, 99
Brasseur, Catherine, 77
Brasseur, Cécile, 93
Brasseur, Marie, 23
Brasseur, Ozite, 23
Braud, Alexis, 73
Braud, Anne, 21
Braud, Anne Marie, 89
Braud, Antoine, 3
Braud, Antoine, 73
Braud, Cécile, 3
Braud, Charles, 3
Braud, Eulalie, 81
Braud, Honore, 19
Braud, Jeanne, 19
Braud, Joseph, 21, 37, 55, 75, 81
Braud, Luce, 55, 75
Braud, Magdelaine, 73
Braud, Marguerite, 73
Braud, Marie, 19, 87
Braud, Marie Magdelaine, 19
Braud, Marie Ozitte, 87
Braud, Olive Élizabeth, 19
Braud, Pierre, 19
Braud, Rose Marie, 19
Braud, Ursule, 17, 75
Briand, Anne Angélique, 105
Broussard, Agnès, 33
Broussard, Charles, 9
Broussard, Dominique, 9
Broussard, François, 9
Broussard, Jean, 67
Broussard, Jean Baptiste, 67
Broussard, Jean Charles, 9

Broussard, Joseph, 9, 33, 67
Broussard, Pierre, 9
Bujeaud, Marie, 61

"C"

Cabon, Jeanne, 41
Caillouet, Jacques, 39
Caillouet, Joseph, 39
Caissy, Marguerite, 67, 107
Caligan, Gurdon Thomas, 104
Carret, Eustache, 57
Carret, Honore, 55
Carret, Ignace, 55, 57
Carret, Jean, 57, 61
Carret, Marie, 57
Carret, Marie Rose, 61
Carret, Pierre, 55
Carret, Thérèse, 61
Cavenza, Baset, 65
Charpatan, Françoise, 63
Charpentier, Perinne, 79
Charrié, Louis Antoine, 63, 85
Charrier, Louis, 63
Chellon, Jeanne, 17
Chiasson, Adélaïde, 77, 109
Chiasson, Anonime, 77
Chiasson, Basile, 77, 109
Chiasson, Charles, 77, 109
Chiasson, François, 79
Chiasson, Jean, 79
Chiasson, Joseph, 79
Chiasson, Judith, 71
Chiasson, Louis, 77
Chiasson, Marie, 5
Chiasson, Pierre, 77, 79, 109
Clemenceau, Jean, 55, 57
Clemenceau, Magdelaine, 57
Clemenceau, Marie, 55
Clement, Hilaire, 51
Clement, Jean, 51
Clement, Marie, 51
Clossinet, Louis, 89
Clossinet, Marie, 7
Clossinet, Marie, 33
Colcein, Anne, 9
Comeaux, Alexandre, 99
Comeaux, Alexis, 15
Comeaux, Anne Eleonore, 73
Comeaux, Benoît, 73
Comeaux, Charles, 33
Comeaux, Claire, 69
Comeaux, Elie, 89
Comeaux, Félicité, 99
Comeaux, Honore, 53

Comeaux, Isabelle, 99
Comeaux, Jean, 73
Comeaux, Jean Baptiste, 15, 53, 89, 99
Comeaux, Jeanne, 89
Comeaux, Joseph, 33, 39, 89
Comeaux, Joseph Marie, 99
Comeaux, Magdelaine, 33, 55, 99
Comeaux, Marguerite, 17, 21, 67, 73, 91
Comeaux, Marie, 39, 89, 91, 99
Comeaux, Marie Anne Victoire, 73
Comeaux, Mathurin, 55
Comeaux, Monique, 77, 109
Comeaux, Pierre, 99
Comeaux, Rose, 73
Comeaux, Simon, 89, 99
Comeaux, Suzanne, 51
Corporon, Cécile, 69
Corrales, Bernarde, 33
Costa, Joseph, 41
Coste, Marguerite, 23, 25
Courtin, Charlotte Louise, 33
Courtin, Françoise, 33, 41
Courtin, Jacques Marie, 33
Courtin, Louis, 33
Courtin, Mathurine Olive, 33
Courtois, Nicholas, 104
Courtney, Esther, 3
Cousin, Jean, 71, 107
Cousin, Marie Blanche, 71, 107
Crochet, Françoise, 63, 71
Crochet, Guillaume, 71
Crochet, Jean, 65, 71
Crochet, Julien, 71
Crochet, Marguerite, 63, 71
Crochet, Yves 63, 71
Cyr, Marguerite, 37

"D"

D'Aunis, Mathurin, 45
Daigle, Abraham, 35
Daigle, Adélaïde, 35
Daigle, Alexis, 23
Daigle, Anne, 55, 61, 63, 87
Daigle, Anne Genevieve, 31
Daigle, Anne Josèphe, 87
Daigle, Bernard, 27
Daigle, Catherine, 51
Daigle, Charles, 11, 27, 95
Daigle, Edouard, 31
Daigle, Élizabeth, 31
Daigle, Emelie Adélaïde, 37

Daigle, Étienne, 27
Daigle, Eulalie, 31
Daigle, Eustache, 21, 27
Daigle, Felicité, 97
Daigle, François, 31, 35, 37
Daigle, François Alexandre, 37
Daigle, François Josèphe, 37
Daigle, Françoise, 31
Daigle, Honoré, 31
Daigle, Jean, 19, 27, 39, 81, 87, 89
Daigle, Jean Baptiste, 31, 39, 45, 55
Daigle, Jean Louis, 39
Daigle, Jean René, 39
Daigle, Jeanne, 35
Daigle, Joseph, 39, 55
Daigle, Joseph Michel, 31
Daigle, Louis, 35
Daigle, Louise, 35
Daigle, Luce, 25
Daigle, Marguerite, 23, 25, 59, 69, 81, 97
Daigle, Marie, 19, 21, 25, 31, 81, 89, 95
Daigle, Marie Jeanne, 35
Daigle, Marie Magdelaine, 31
Daigle, Marie Marguerite, 31
Daigle, Marie Osithe, 95
Daigle, Olivier, 31, 95
Daigle, Osite, 17
Daigle, Paul, 33
Daigle, Pélagie, 31
Daigle, Pierre, 39
Daigle, Simon, 31
Daigle, Simon Pierre, 31
Daigle, Victor, 31
Dameue, Marie, 53
Damour, Marie Rose, 75
Dantin, Anne, 73
Dantin, Jeanne, 73
Dantin, Julie, 73
Dantin, Louis, 73
Dantin, Marie, 73
Darambourg, Jean Baptiste, 47
Darambourg, Marie Jeanne, 47
Darrois, Élizabeth, 53
Darrois, Étienne, 53
Darrois, Marie, 53
Darrois, Susanne, 53
Davoir, Jacques, 63, 85
De Bellefontaine, Anastasie, 67, 107
De La Foresterie, Angélique, 37
De La Foresterie, Jean, 37, 49

De La Foresterie, Jeanne, 49
De La Foresterie, Marie Rosalie, 49
De La Garde, Gartau, 63
De La Garde, Leonard, 63, 85
De La Masière, Jean Baptiste, 67
De La Masière, Jean François 67
De La Masière, Louise Celeste, 67
De La Masière, Rose Jeanne, 67
Delaune, Christophe, 67, 107
Delaune, Jean, 67, 107
Delaune, Jean Baptiste, 67, 107
Delaune, Louis Auguste, 67, 107
Delaune, Marie Celeste, 67, 107
Delaune, Pierre, 67, 107
Delormo, Marie, 63
Descouteaux, Thérèse, 35
Descroutes, Charlotte, 7
Devaux, Marie, 3, 81
Doiron, Alexandre, 5
Doiron, Angélique, 47, 95
Doiron, Anne, 35, 49
Doiron. Anne Dorothée, 33
Doiron, Emelie, 35
Doiron, Françoise, 73
Doiron, Geneviève, 7
Doiron, Hélène, 11
Doiron, Isaac, 5
Doiron, Jacques, 21
Doiron, Jean, 21, 33
Doiron, Jean Baptiste, 5, 35, 109
Doiron, Jean Charles, 35
Doiron, Joseph, 5, 21
Doiron, Louis Toussaint, 35
Doiron, Magdelaine, 5, 43, 101
Doiron, Marguerite, 67, 73, 77, 87
Doiron, Marguerite Josèphe, 33, 35
Doiron, Marie, 5, 35, 39, 73
Doiron, Marie Hypolithe Honoré, 35
Doiron, Marie Josèphe, 3, 11, 13
Doiron, Marie Rose, 5
Doiron, Marie-Pélagie, 35
Doiron, Mathurin, 5
Doiron, Paul, 39
Doiron, Rose, 35
Doiron, Rose, 37
Doiron, Thomas, 5, 21, 49
Doiron, Ursule, 21, 35
Doucet, Ange, 71, 107
Doucet, Anne, 79
Doucet, Augustin, 71
Doucet, Charles, 67

Doucet, Eleonore, 71, 107
Doucet, François, 71
Doucet, Françoise, 63, 79
Doucet, Jean Baptiste, 71, 107
Doucet, Jean Baptiste Michel, 71
Doucet, Joseph, 71, 107
Doucet, Magdelaine, 71, 107
Doucet, Marguerite, 71, 107
Doucet, Marie, 33, 77
Doucet, Marie Marguerite, 107
Doucet, Marie Marthe, 71
Doucet, Michel, 71, 107
Drapeau, Anne, 85
Dubois, François, 75
Dubois, Jacques, 69
Dubois, Joseph Ange, 39
Dubois, Marguerite Ange, 39
Dubois, Olivier, 63
Dugat, Alexis, 43
Dugat, Ambroise, 23
Dugat, Anastasie, 43, 107
Dugat, Anne, 7, 25, 43, 81, 107
Dugat, Anne Josèphe, 43
Dugat, Anne Marie, 23
Dugat, Anne Osite, 25
Dugat, Anne Perinne, 43
Dugat, Bernard, 85
Dugat, Cécille, 43
Dugat, Celeste, 23
Dugat, Charles, 5, 23, 29, 49, 81
Dugat, Claire, 87, 93
Dugat, Claude, 23, 25, 37
Dugat, Élizabeth, 27, 43
Dugat, François, 43
Dugat, Isabelle, 25, 45
Dugat, Jean, 53
Dugat, Jean Baptiste, 7, 11, 35
Dugat, Jean Charles, 23
Dugat, Jean Marie Alexis, 35
Dugat, Jean Pierre, 35, 41, 43
Dugat, Joseph, 23, 43, 49
Dugat, Louis Ambroise, 23
Dugat, Magdeleine, 27
Dugat, Marguerite, 23, 25, 37, 43, 73, 109
Dugat, Marie, 7, 25, 27, 43, 55, 99
Dugat, Marie Josèphe, 23
Dugat, Marie Magdelaine, 5, 25
Dugat, Marie Rose, 43
Dugat, Marin, 11
Dugat, Michel, 55
Dugat, Paul, 25, 27
Dugat, Paul Joseph, 59
Dugat, Pierre 11, 25, 35, 43, 45

Dugat, Pierre Olivier, 23
Dugat, Rose, 43
Dugat, Simon, 25, 29
Dugat, Victoire, 101
Duhon, Augustin, 63, 79
Duhon, Élizabeth, 83
Duhon, Euphrosine, 57
Duhon, Honoré, 63, 79
Duhon, Jacques, 79
Duhon, Jean Baptiste, 41
Duhon, Jean Charles, 79
Duhon, Joseph, 111
Duhon, Marguerite, 51
Duhon, Marie Magdalen, 51
Dumont, Anne, 63
Dumont, Hélène, 7
Dumont, Joseph, 7
Duplessis, Claude Antoine, 19
Duplessis, Marie, 19
Dupuis, Ambroise, 89, 91
Dupuis, Anne, 79, 81
Dupuis, Anne Marie, 13, 89
Dupuis, Cécile, 23
Dupuis, Charles, 27
Dupuis, Étienne, 27, 29
Dupuis, Isabelle, 17, 25
Dupuis, Joseph, 17, 25
Dupuis, Magdelaine, 21, 27
Dupuis, Marguerite, 27, 49, 91, 95
Dupuis, Marie, 89
Durand, Françoise, 55
Durand, Julienne, 71
Durel, Marianne, 63
Durel, Marie Judith, 81
Duval, Anne, 71
Duval, Charles, 71

"E"

Eon, Pierre Jean (Rev.), 105

"F"

Fardy, Carlos, 85
Farine, Jean, 97
Forest, Anne, 91
Forest, Anne Perrine, 91
Forest, Étienne, 91
Forest, Étienne Gilles, 91
Forest, Jacques, 81, 91
Forest, Jean, 91
Forest, Jeanne Isabelle, 91
Forest, Joseph Victor, 91
Forest, Magdelaine, 81

Forest, Marguerite, 31
Forest, Marie, 91
Forest, Marie Adélaïde, 91
Forest, Marie Isabelle, 104
Forest, Pierre, 39, 91
Forest, Servanne Julienne, 91
Forest, Victor, 91
Fouginet, Étienne, 29
Fouquet, Charlotte, 65
Fouquet, Jean, 65, 81
Fouquet, Jeanne Magdelaine, 81
Fouquet, Marie Charlotte, 81
Friou, François, 29

"G"

Galien, Bon, 103
Galien, François, 103
Galien, François Julien, 103
Galien, Julien François, 103
Galien, Marie Jeanne, 103
Galletier, Étienne, 85
Garcia, Joseph Louis, 41
Garcia, Juan, 41
Garnier, Jean, 49
Garnier, Jeanne Marie, 49
Garnier, Marie Françoise, 49
Gaudet, François Louis, 71, 107
Gaudet, Joseph Ignace, 99
Gaudet, Louis, 71, 107
Gaudet, Magdelaine, 71, 107
Gaudet, Marguerite, 71, 107
Gaudet, Marie, 5
Gautrot, Adélaïde, 19
Gautrot, Agnès, 19
Gautrot, Alexandre, 45
Gautrot, Angélique, 79, 107
Gautrot, Aspasie, 57
Gautrot, Catherine, 93
Gautrot, Cécile, 69
Gautrot, Charles, 45, 57, 109
Gautrot, Étienne, 45
Gautrot, François, 45
Gautrot, François Marie, 109
Gautrot, Françoise, 55, 57
Gautrot, Hélène, 55
Gautrot, Henry François, 45
Gautrot, Honoré, 17
Gautrot, Jean, 17, 45, 73
Gautrot, Jean Baptiste, 57
Gautrot, Jean Louis Laurent, 57
Gautrot, Jean Marie, 57
Gautrot, Joseph, 45, 69
Gautrot, Joseph Benoît, 27

Gautrot, Magdelaine, 39, 55, 57, 61, 63, 83
Gautrot, Marguerite, 19, 39, 47, 61
Gautrot, Marguerite Rosalie, 45
Gautrot, Marie, 17, 69, 83
Gautrot, Marie Geneviève, 7
Gautrot, Marie Magdalen, 45
Gautrot, Marin, 17
Gautrot, Pélagie, 7
Gautrot, Pierre, 19, 45, 57, 61, 109
Gautrot, Rosalie, 109
Gautrot, Rose, 45, 49
Gautrot, Victoire, 45
Gentil, Anne Marie, 79
Gentil, Marie Anne, 75
Gesan, Cécile, 69
Gicquel, Jeanne, 7
Giroire, Anne, 5, 21, 27, 49
Giroire, Charles, 75
Giroire, Elenne, 79
Giroire, Eudoze, 81
Giroire, François, 27
Giroire, Geneviève, 89
Giroire, Honoré, 27, 79, 81
Giroire, Jacques, 75
Giroire, Jean Baptiste, 27
Giroire, Jeanne, 27
Giroire, Marguerite, 43
Giroire, Marie Paul, 27
Giroire, Marie Rose, 81
Giroire, Pierre, 27
Giroire, Prosper, 27
Giroire, Véronique, 9, 19, 43, 77
Gomez, Silverio, 65
Gomez, Silvestre, 65, 81
Gousman, Jean, 67
Gousman, Jean Thomas, 67
Gousman, Rosalie Charlotte, 67
Granger, Anne, 33, 45, 79
Granger, Cécile, 13, 17
Granger, Charles, 39
Granger, François, 33
Granger, Françoise, 31
Granger, Françoise Eulalie, 99
Granger, Ignace, 99
Granger, Jean Marie, 41
Granger, Jeanne, 99
Granger, Joseph, 25, 99
Granger, Marie Josèphe, 31
Granger, Marie Magdelene, 25
Granger, Pierre Marie, 99
Grossin, Henriette, 103
Guedry, Anne Laurence, 37

Guedry, Charles, 37, 47
Guedry, child, 47
Guedry, Claude, 33, 39, 95
Guedry, François, 9, 41, 95
Guedry, Françoise, 7
Guedry, Henriette, 47
Guedry, Jacques, 37
Guedry, Jean, 37
Guedry, Jean Baptiste, 9, 41
Guedry, Jean Pierre, 39
Guedry, Joseph, 33, 37
Guedry, Joseph Firmin, 39
Guedry, Judith, 71, 107
Guedry, Malo, 95
Guedry, Marguerite, 9, 33, 41, 47
Guedry, Marguerite Felicité, 9, 41
Guedry, Marie, 33, 95
Guedry, Marie Rose, 39
Guedry, Olivier, 95
Guedry, Pierre, 9, 37, 39, 41, 95
Guedry, Pierre David, 47
Guedry, Pierre Joseph, 39
Guedry, Reine Élizabeth, 33
Guedry, Suliac, 95
Guérin, Brigide, 13
Guérin, Dominique, 13
Guérin, Françoise, 13, 101, 104
Guérin, Françoise Élizabeth, 13
Guérin, Isabelle, 13
Guérin, Jean Pierre, 47
Guérin, Jérôme, 47
Guérin, Joseph, 13
Guillot, Charles Olivier, 49
Guillot, Fabien, 73
Guillot, Françoise, 13
Guillot, Isabelle, 49
Guillot, Jean Baptiste, 49
Guillot, Jean Michel, 49
Guillot, Marie, 73
Guillot, René, 73
Guillot, Simon, 73
Guillot, Simon François, 49
Gutierres, Maria, 65

"H"

Haché, Anne, 71
Haché, Elisabeth, 9
Haché, Frédéric, 69
Haché, Hélène, 9
Haché, Jacques, 5
Haché, Jean Baptiste, 75, 79
Haché, Jean Charles, 69
Haché, Joseph, 5, 79
Haché, Louis, 79

Haché, Magdelaine Apolline, 75
Haché, Marguerite, 5
Haché, Marie, 5, 7, 63, 75, 79, 83
Haché, Marie Bonne, 69
Haché, Marie Josèphe, 9
Haché, Pierre, 63, 79
Hainement, Jean, 85
Hallier, Marie Josèphe, 109
Hamont, Anne Magdaleine, 77
Hamont, Guillaume, 53
Hamont, Ignace, 77
Hamont, Jean, 77
Hamont, Joseph, 53
Hamont, Marie Modeste, 77
Harbourg, François, 35
Harbourg, François Henry, 35
Harbourg, Frédéric Edouard, 35
Harbourg, Jean Louis Firmin, 35
Hébert, Alexis Thomas, 43
Hébert, Amable, 3
Hébert, Ambroise, 21, 43, 73, 79, 107
Hébert, Ambroise Mathurin, 43
Hébert, André, 3
Hébert, Anne, 3, 17, 25, 27, 35, 43, 87
Hébert, Anne Marguerite, 33, 49
Hébert, Anne Osite, 47
Hébert, Brigide, 3
Hébert, Cécile, 63, 73
Hébert, Charles, 15, 25, 49
Hébert, child, 21
Hébert, Élizabeth, 45, 73
Hébert, Étienne, 27, 63, 73
Hébert, Felicité, 15, 111
Hébert, François, 5, 27, 87, 95, 104
Hébert, Françoise, 15, 99
Hébert, Gabriel, 73
Hébert, Geneviève, 3
Hébert, Gertrude, 79, 107
Hébert, Guillaume, 73
Hébert, Hélène, 93
Hébert, Isaac, 21
Hébert, Isabelle, 3, 19, 27, 43, 93
Hébert, Jacques, 53, 103
Hébert, Jean, 3, 15, 33, 35, 43, 71, 73, 87, 93, 101, 107
Hébert, Jean Baptiste, 15, 25, 27, 33, 35, 43, 87
Hébert, Jean Charles, 33
Hébert, Jean Joseph, 43
Hébert, Jean Pierre, 33, 73, 97
Hébert, Joseph, 27, 49, 53, 85, 87, 95, 97, 99, 109

Hébert, Joseph Ignace, 43
Hébert, Joseph Nicolas, 51
Hébert, Julienne, 87
Hébert, Louis, 73
Hébert, Louis Jean, 49
Hébert, Magdelaine, 39, 47, 49, 53
Hébert, Marguerite, 15, 25, 33, 39, 45, 55, 75
Hébert, Marie, 3, 15, 25, 27, 43, 47, 49, 53, 69, 71, 85, 87, 95, 101, 103, 107, 109
Hébert, Marie Josèphe, 45, 89, 97
Hébert, Marie Magdelaine, 73
Hébert, Marie Yvette, 15
Hébert, Mathurin, 87
Hébert, Olivier, 43
Hébert, Pascal, 95
Hébert, Pierre, 15, 27, 33, 35, 43, 47, 87
Hébert, Pierre Jean, 97
Hébert, Pierre Joseph, 19, 35
Hébert, Rémi, 21
Hébert, Rosalie, 43
Hébert, Simon, 43
Hébert, Sophie, 53
Hébert, Thérèse, 5
Hébert, Thérèse Anne, 97
Hébert, Ursule, 5, 63, 69, 103
Hébert, Victoire, 87, 95
Henry, Anastasie, 43
Henry, Angélique, 99
Henry, Anne, 101
Henry, Anne Françoise, 3
Henry, Anne Joseph, 101
Henry, Barthélémy, 87, 93
Henry, Cécile, 55, 57
Henry, Charles, 31, 99, 101
Henry, Cirille François, 41
Henry, Élizabeth, 7, 17
Henry, François, 3, 7, 93, 99
Henry, Françoise, 99
Henry, Françoise Victoire, 99
Henry, Isabelle, 97
Henry, Jacques, 93
Henry, Jean, 97, 99, 101, 103
Henry, Jean Baptiste, 31, 101
Henry, Jean Laurent, 3
Henry, Jeanne Françoise, 101
Henry, Joseph, 3, 31, 35
Henry, Joseph Pillipe, 55
Henry, Magdelaine, 47, 103
Henry, Magdelaine Appoline, 3
Henry, Marguerite, 23, 87, 99
Henry, Marguerite Pélagie, 103

Henry, Marguerite Rose, 97
Henry, Marguerite Toussainte, 99
Henry, Marie, 35, 93, 97
Henry, Marie Josèphe, 3, 101
Henry, Marie Magdelaine, 31
Henry, Maximilien, 97
Henry, Pierre, 3, 15, 41, 55, 97, 99, 101, 103
Henry, Rose, 71
Henry, Rose Anastasie, 31
Henry, Ursule, 31
Hervé, Marie, 103
Hervé, Perrine, 23
Heuzé, Anne Marie, 5
Heuzé, Charles, 5
Heuzé, Grégoire, 5
Heuzé, Ignace, 5
Heuzé, Jean Baptiste, 5
Heuzé, Pierre, 5
Holley, Jeanne, 35, 37
Holley, Thomas, 35
Houardon, Thomas Calegan, 59

"I"

Ino, Marguerite, 57

"J"

Jacques, Anne, 65, 85
Jacques, Jean, 85
Jacques, Joseph, 85
Jacques, Marie, 85
Jacques, Pierre Joseph, 85
Jacques, Victoire, 85
Joanne, Anne, 79
Joanne, Jacques, 79
Judice, Louis, 65

"K"

Kimine, Anne, 5
Kimine, Jacques, 5
Kimine, Marguerite, 65, 81
Kimine, Marie, 5
Kimine, Pierre, 5
Kimine, Victoire Françoise, 5

"L"

La Haye, Madeleine, 21
La Pierre, Marie, 39
La Sonde, Marguerite, 73
Labauve, Antoine, 11
Labauve, Jean, 53

Labauve, Marguerite, 9, 11, 43
Labauve, Pierre, 53
Lagarelle, Cécile, 63, 69
Lagarenne, Jean Baptiste, 35
LaHaye, Madeleine, 21
Lalande, Emelie, 35
Lalande, Euphrosie, 53
Lalande, Jean Edouard, 35
Lalande, Joseph, 35
Lamoureux, Adélaïde, 71
Lamoureux, Adélaïde, 107
Lamoureux, Jean Louis, 71, 107
Lamoureux, Louis, 71, 107
Landry, Aimable, 61
Landry, Anna, 99
Landry, Anne, 25, 33, 69, 101
Landry, Anne Adélaïde, 61
Landry, Anne Marie, 31
Landry, Anne Susanne, 17
Landry, Anselme, 7
Landry, Antoine, 25
Landry, Benjamin, 75
Landry, Bonne Marie, 69
Landry, Bonnie Louise Marie, 61
Landry, Catherine, 5
Landry, Charles, 3, 21
Landry, Claire, 15
Landry, Firmin, 3
Landry, François, 3, 69
Landry, Geneviève, 21
Landry, Germain, 63, 69
Landry, Grineo, 31
Landry, Hélène, 13
Landry, Hilaire, 17
Landry, Isaac Abraham, 61
Landry, Isabelle, 25
Landry, Jean, 3
Landry, Jean Baptiste, 17, 21, 25
Landry, Jean Baptiste Leonor, 61
Landry, Jean Charles, 69
Landry, Jean Jacques, 69
Landry, Jean Pierre, 21
Landry, Jean Raphael, 17, 107
Landry, Jeanne, 3, 61, 101
Landry, Jeanne Marguerite, 61
Landry, Joseph, 17, 61, 101
Landry, Louis, 3
Landry, Magdalen Geneviève, 61
Landry, Marguerite, 3, 17, 19, 21, 25, 53, 59, 75, 101, 103
Landry, Marie, 17, 53, 63, 79, 81, 101
Landry, Marie Joseph, 21
Landry, Marie Magdelaine, 15, 17
Landry, Marie Marguerite, 17

Landry, Marie Olive, 5
Landry, Pierre, 17, 101
Landry, Prosper, 21
Landry, René, 61, 101
Landry, Rose, 17
Landry, Sebastien, 3
Landry, Servanne, 101
Landry, Simon, 21, 61
Langliné, Angélique, 103
Langliné, Jean Louis, 103
Langliné, Marie Jeanne, 103
Laurant, Madeleine, 57
Laurenty, Pierre, 83
Lavergne, Marguerite, 35
Lavergne, Marie, 63
Lavergne, Marie Magdelaine, 31
Lavergne, Pierre, 31, 35
Lavergne, Victoire, 31, 41
Le Faibre, Claude Epiphane, 85
Le Gentilhomme, Scolastique, 35
Le Lorre, François Pierre, 93
Le Sommer, François, 91
Lebert, Anne, 49
Lebert, Anne Josèphe, 9
Lebert, Charles, 21
Lebert, Marguerite, 9
Lebert, Marie, 21
Lebert, Marie Josèphe, 39
Lebert, Paul, 39
Lebert, Pierre, 39
Leblanc, Adélaïde, 39
Leblanc, Agnès, 109
Leblanc, Amable Andre, 3
Leblanc, Andre, 55
Leblanc, Anne, 5, 13, 35
Leblanc, Appoline Eulalie, 13
Leblanc, Barbe, 55
Leblanc, Blanche, 3, 15
Leblanc, Cécile, 21
Leblanc, Charles, 31, 55, 61, 63
Leblanc, Claude, 15, 39, 55
Leblanc, Claude Marie, 111
Leblanc, Élizabeth, 19, 21, 39
Leblanc, Étienne, 21
Leblanc, Felix, 21
Leblanc, François, 37
Leblanc, Françoise, 61
Leblanc, Geneviève, 37, 61
Leblanc, Isabelle, 87
Leblanc, Jacques, 5, 23, 37, 43
Leblanc, Jean, 5, 9, 15, 61
Leblanc, Jean Baptiste, 17, 23, 37, 55, 67
Leblanc, Jean Charles, 3
Leblanc, Jean Jacques, 23

INDEX

Leblanc, Jean Martin, 37
Leblanc, Joseph, 3, 5, 9, 37, 59
Leblanc, Magdelaine, 17, 37, 41
Leblanc, Marguerite, 3, 37, 49, 61, 63, 79, 103
Leblanc, Marie, 3, 5, 7, 21, 25, 31, 37, 57, 61, 81
Leblanc, Marie Blanche, 31
Leblanc, Marie Françoise, 55
Leblanc, Marie Geneviève, 23
Leblanc, Marie Josèphe, 13, 37, 47
Leblanc, Marie Magdelaine, 45
Leblanc, Marie Rose, 55
Leblanc, Marthe, 17
Leblanc, Michel, 13
Leblanc, Moise, 37
Leblanc, Moyse, 75
Leblanc, Olivier, 21
Leblanc, Paul, 39
Leblanc, Pierre, 9, 21, 39, 47, 61, 79, 81
Leblanc, Pierre Honoré, 55
Leblanc, René, 3, 61
Leblanc, Rosalie, 39
Leblanc, Rose, 43
Leblanc, Scholastique, 3
Leblanc, Simon, 3, 5, 17, 61, 91
Leblanc, Thomas, 59
Leblanc, Ursule, 9, 33, 67
Leblanc, Victor, 9, 19, 21
Leblanc, Viviane, 47
LeCoq, Françoise, 57
LeCoq, Guillaume, 57
LeCoq, Jacques, 57
LeCoq, Marie, 57
LeCoq, Pierre, 57
LeCoq, Victoire, 57
Legagneur, Claude Louis, 109
Legendre, Anastasie Angélique, 11
Legendre, François, 9, 11
Legendre, Henriette, 9
Legendre, Jean Baptiste, 11
Legendre, Jean François, 11
Legendre, Louis, 11
Legendre, Mathurin, 11
Legendre, Rose, 11
Legendre, Yves, 11
Léger, Françoise, 75
Léger, Jean, 9
Léger, Louis, 9
Léger, Michel, 85
Lejeune, Adélaïde, 83
Lejeune, Alexis, 45, 83
Lejeune, Amand, 45, 47, 63, 83

Lejeune, Anne, 33, 39
Lejeune, Catherine, 11, 19
Lejeune, Élizabeth, 23
Lejeune, Eusebe, 7
Lejeune, Eustache, 7
Lejeune, Felicité, 79, 107
Lejeune, François, 7
Lejeune, Grégoire, 7
Lejeune, Jean, 7, 47
Lejeune, Jean Baptiste, 7, 11
Lejeune, Joseph, 45, 63, 83
Lejeune, Julien, 7
Lejeune, Magdelaine, 45
Lejeune, Marguerite, 45, 83
Lejeune, Marie, 7
Lejeune, Marie Magdelaine, 7
Lejeune, Marie Rose, 7, 45, 83
Lejeune, Rosalie, 45, 83
Lejeune, Servan Mathurin, 7
Lejeune, Zeno, 7
Lejuge, Élizabeth, 33
LeLorec, François Pierre, 104
Leprince, Antoine, 19
Leprince, Isabelle, 59
Leprince, Julie, 19
Leprince, Marguerite, 59
Leprince, Marie, 19
Leprince, Tranquille, 59
Leterrier, Jeanne, 61
Letullier, Adélaïde, 69
Letullier, Henry Aimable, 21
Letullier, Isidore, 69
Letullier, Jean Charles, 69
Letullier, Julien, 21
Letullier, Louis, 21
Letullier, Marie Adélaïde, 21
Letullier, Marie Rose, 11
Letullier, René, 11, 69
Levron, Alexis, 59
Levron, Anastasie, 45, 47, 63, 83
Levron, Joseph Marie, 57
Levron, Marie, 57
Levron, Michel, 57, 59
Livois, Marie Magdelaine, 51
Livois, Marie Rose, 27
Longuespee, Ambroise, 99
Longuespee, Anne, 89
Longuespee, Corentine, 89
Longuespee, Hélène, 89
Longuespee, Janvier, 99
Longuespee, Jean, 89
Longuespee, Jean Baptiste, 89
Longuespee, Jean Jacques, 89
Longuespee, Joseph, 5
Longuespee, Louis, 89, 99

Longuespee, Marguerite, 89
Longuespee, Marie, 89
Longuespee, Pierre, 89
Lord, Anne, 35
Lord, Marguerite, 67

"M"

Macle, Basile, 65
Macle, Charles, 65
Macle, Charles Daniel, 65
Martin, Marie, 15, 33
Maurice, Louis, 85
Mazerolle, Anne, 13
Mazerolle, Étienne, 13
Mazerolle, Isabelle, 13
Mazerolle, Joseph, 13
Mazerolle, Marie, 13
Mazerolle, Simon, 13
Melançon, Cécile, 39, 97, 99, 103
Melançon, Jean, 109
Melançon, Jeanne, 47, 49
Melançon, Joseph, 103
Melançon, Marguerite, 57, 59
Melançon, Marie Magdelaine, 109
Menard, Louis, 65
Menard, Pierre, 65
Metot, Marie, 39
Métra, Anne Marguerite, 81
Métra, Jacques, 81
Métra, Jean, 81
Métra, Joseph, 55
Métra, Nicolas, 55
Michel, Anne, 31, 39, 61
Michel, Cécile, 77, 81
Michel, François, 61, 63
Michel, Gertrude, 45
Michel, Joseph, 45
Michel, Louis, 31
Michel, Magdelaine, 45
Michel, Marguerite, 39
Michel, Marie, 45, 61, 63
Michel, Pierre, 45
Mius d'Entremont, Cécile, 61, 71
Mius d'Entremont, Jacques Ferdinand, 103
Mius d'Entremont, Jacques, 103
Mius d'Entremont, Marie Josèphe, 61
Moine, Juliene, 109
Mollard, Antoine, 29
Montet, Françoise, 109
Montet, Jean Baptiste, 109
Montet, Joseph, 109
Montet, Marguerite, 109

Montet, Pierre, 109
Montet, Pierre Paul, 109
Montreal, Louis François, 41
Morange, Jean, 97
Moreau, Anne, 17
Moreau, François Marie, 17
Moreau, Gabriel, 17
Moreau, Germain Marie, 17
Moreau, Maximin, 17
Moreau, Pierre Vincent, 17
Morel, Marie, 11
Moulaison, Gabriel, 77
Moulaison, Jacques, 39, 99
Moulaison, Joseph, 77
Moulaison, Marie Josèphe, 19
Moulaison, Marie Modeste, 99
Moulaison, Pierre, 77
Moulaison, Rose, 39
Moulaison, Sophie, 39
Mouton, Marguerite, 71, 73, 107
Moyse, Anne, 95
Moyse, Jeanne, 21
Moyse, Joseph, 47
Moyse, Louis, 67
Moyse, Marie, 47, 67, 107

"N"

Naquin, Ambroise, 47
Naquin, Anne, 49
Naquin, Charles, 49
Naquin, François, 49, 51
Naquin, Isabelle, 19
Naquin, Ives, 49
Naquin, Jacques, 47, 49
Naquin, Jean, 49
Naquin, Joseph, 47
Naquin, Ludovinne, 49
Naquin, Marie, 49
Naquin, Michel, 19
Naquin, Paul, 49
Naquin, Pierre, 47
Naquin, Renée, 49
Naquin, Tarsille, 51
Neveu, Vincent, 63, 85
Noel, Marguerite, 13
Noel, Marie, 13
Nogues, Charles, 95
Nogues, Marie, 59, 95

"O"

Olivier, Anne, 75
Olivier, Pierre, 75
Ory, Charles, 23

Ory, Marguerite, 23
Ory, Perrine Marguerite, 23
Oselet, Jean, 21
Oselet, Jean Baptiste, 59
Oselet, Jean Charles, 21
Oselet, Julien, 21, 59
Oselet, Marie Charlotte, 21
Oselet, Mathurin, 21

"P"

Pacet, François, 65
Part, Brigitte, 37, 73
Part, Eustache, 67, 107
Part, Marianne, 67
Part, Marie, 107
Part, Michel, 73
Petit, Marie, 67
Pétry, Michele, 75
Peyroux, Mr., 41
Pierre, Marguerite, 93
Pierre, Simon, 93
Pierson, Anne, 83, 109
Pinet, Angélique, 9
Pinet, Charles, 63, 71
Pinet, Louis, 63, 71
Pinet, Marie, 69
Pinet, Marie Magdelaine, 71
Pinet, Noel, 71
Pitre, Agnès, 13
Pitre, Amand, 15, 23, 27
Pitre, Ambroise, 27
Pitre, Anne, 45, 69
Pitre, Anselme, 45
Pitre, Benjamin, 77
Pitre, Cécille, 77
Pitre, Charles, 101
Pitre, Charlotte Marie, 97
Pitre, Christine, 31, 35
Pitre, Claude, 67, 77, 87
Pitre, Élizabeth, 21
Pitre, Étienne, 77
Pitre, Felicité, 97
Pitre, François, 75, 97
Pitre, Françoise, 67, 107
Pitre, Germain, 43, 45
Pitre, Henriette, 43
Pitre, Isabelle, 101
Pitre, Isabelle Olive, 45
Pitre, Jacques, 97
Pitre, Jean, 21, 45, 77, 87, 97
Pitre, Jean Baptiste, 15
Pitre, Jean Marie, 27
Pitre, Jean Pierre, 45
Pitre, Jean Vincent, 15

Pitre, Joseph, 85, 97, 101
Pitre, Louis Constant, 67
Pitre, Magdelaine, 43, 77
Pitre, Marguerite, 23, 45, 77, 97, 101
Pitre, Marie, 27, 43, 47, 77, 87, 97
Pitre, Marie Françoise, 45
Pitre, Marie Madeleine, 101, 103
Pitre, Marie Victoire, 23
Pitre, Martin, 109
Pitre, Natalie, 23
Pitre, Olivier, 67, 107
Pitre, Paul Ambroise, 27
Pitre, Pierre, 43, 97
Pitre, Pierre Olivier, 43
Pitre, Suzanne, 87
Pitre, Tranquille, 15
Pitre, Ursule, 75
Pitre, Victoire, 67
Poitier, Anne Pauline, 33
Poitier, Baptiste Olivier, 19
Poitier, Cécile, 69
Poitier, Charles Victor, 33
Poitier, Charlotte, 35
Poitier, Christopher, 35
Poitier, Constance, 33
Poitier, François Constant, 33
Poitier, Jacques Silvin, 19
Poitier, Magdeleine, 69
Poitier, Marie Henriette, 83
Poitier, Olivier, 19
Poitier, Pierre, 19, 33
Poitier, Pierre Laurent, 33
Précieux, Joseph, 71
Précieux, Marie Anne, 71

"R"

Raimond, Françoise, 95
Ramirez, François, 33
Ramirez, Jean, 33
Rassicot, Anne Marguerite, 83
Rassicot, Jean Baptiste, 83
Rassicot, Jean François, 83
Rassicot, Marie Henriette, 83
Rassicot, René, 83
Renaud, Colette, 11, 69
Renaud, Jean, 69
Renaud, Marie Josèphe, 5
Renaud, Véronique, 67
Renoux, Madeleine, 91
Richard, Anastasie Marguerite, 59
Richard, Angélique, 25, 27
Richard, Anselme, 31

Richard, Auguste, 31
Richard, Basile Marie, 111
Richard, Cécile, 13
Richard, Charles, 23, 59, 93
Richard, Dorothée, 15
Richard, Élizabeth, 59
Richard, François, 15
Richard, Geneviève, 93
Richard, Honoré, 97
Richard, Jean, 17, 69
Richard, Jean Charles, 41, 101
Richard, Jean Pierre, 17
Richard, Jeanne, 65, 81
Richard, Joseph, 31, 57
Richard, Julien Marie, 31
Richard, Marguerite, 59, 65, 69, 97
Richard, Marie, 15, 31, 59, 87
Richard, Marie Anne, 3
Richard, Marie Élizabeth, 57
Richard, Marie Felicité, 59
Richard, Marie Geneviève, 71
Richard, Marie Josèphe, 17, 65, 71
Richard, Marie Roze, 23
Richard, Pierre, 13, 15, 17, 31, 87
Richard, Rose, 15
Richer, André, 91
Richer, Marie Jeanne, 91
Richet, Angélique, 91
Robichaux, Anne, 21, 43
Robichaux, Charles, 31
Robichaux, François Xavier, 47
Robichaux, Jean Baptiste, 47
Robichaux, Jean Pierre, 43
Robichaux, Joseph, 43, 47
Robichaux, Marguerite, 17
Robichaux, Marie, 43, 47
Robichaux, Pierre, 43
Robichaux, Renée, 47
Roger, Joseph, 107
Roger, Marie, 107
Romagosa, Francisco, 21
Roquemont, Guillaume Noel, 13
Rudouze, Marie Josèphe, 51
Rusod, Marguerite, 65

"S"

Saunier, Anne, 53
Saunier, Charles, 53
Saunier, Louise, 73
Saunier, Marguerite, 53
Saunier, Marie, 51
Saunier, Marie Joseph, 91, 93

Savary, Anne, 19
Segoillot, Marguerite, 27
Semer, Anne Françoise, 69
Semer, Françoise, 67
Semer, Grégoire, 67
Semer, Joseph, 69
Semer, Marie, 69
Semer, Marie Marguerite, 67
Sevin, Marie, 53
Simon, Jean Baptiste, 85
Spiger, Christian, 49
Stebens, boy, 9
Stebens, Louis, 9
Stebens, Marie, 9
Stebens, Stanislas, 9

"T"

Templé, André, 3, 81
Templé, Charles, 3
Templé, Isabelle, 3
Templé, Jacques, 3
Templé, Jean, 3
Templé, Marguerite, 81
Templé, Marie Magdelaine, 3
Templé, Olivier, 3
Templé, Servant, 3
Theriot, Angélique, 101
Theriot, Anne, 7, 17, 19, 91, 99
Theriot, Charles, 49, 51, 111
Theriot, Élizabeth, 5, 59, 61, 71
Theriot, Étienne, 13
Theriot, François, 101
Theriot, Françoise, 59
Theriot, Geneviève, 91
Theriot, Isabelle, 61
Theriot, Jacques, 13
Theriot, Jean, 13
Theriot, Jean Baptiste, 105
Theriot, Jean Charles, 13
Theriot, Jean Jacques, 91
Theriot, Jeanne, 15, 91
Theriot, Joseph, 15, 109
Theriot, Magdelaine, 31, 53, 55, 75, 97, 99
Theriot, Marguerite, 21, 45, 87, 91, 97, 99, 101
Theriot, Marie, 25, 89, 91, 101
Theriot, Marie Geneviève, 95
Theriot, Marie Joseph, 81
Theriot, Marie Josèphe, 21, 27, 79
Theriot, Marie Magdelaine, 51, 55
Theriot, Olivier, 13, 29
Theriot, Olivier Marie, 13
Theriot, Ozite Perpétue, 49

Theriot, Pierre, 53
Theriot, Rosalie, 89, 91
Theriot Théodore, 101
Thiard, Marie, 47
Thibodeaux, Anne, 33
Thibodeaux, Anne Marie, 39, 53, 77, 109
Thibodeaux, Antoine, 51
Thibodeaux, Blaise, 51
Thibodeaux, Charles, 103
Thibodeaux, Élizabeth, 31, 55
Thibodeaux, Firmin, 51
Thibodeaux, Firmin Blais, 51
Thibodeaux, François, 51
Thibodeaux, Frédéric Eloi, 75
Thibodeaux, Hélène, 103
Thibodeaux, Isabelle, 51
Thibodeaux, Jacques, 55
Thibodeaux, Jean, 55, 75
Thibodeaux, Jeanne Tarsile, 103
Thibodeaux, Joseph, 51, 75
Thibodeaux, Marguerite, 73, 75, 103
Thibodeaux, Marie, 55, 75
Thibodeaux, Marie Josèphe, 73
Thibodeaux, Marie Victoire, 103
Thibodeaux, Olivier, 75
Thibodeaux, Philippe, 103
Thibodeaux, Pierre, 55
Thibodeaux, Pierre Charles, 103
Tillard, Marie, 55
Trahan, Alexis, 41
Trahan, Anne, 23, 51, 59, 63, 79, 95
Trahan, Anne Julie, 79
Trahan, Anselme, 23
Trahan, Antoine Joseph, 19
Trahan, Antoinette, 35
Trahan, Augustin, 47, 51
Trahan, Augustine Pélagie, 59
Trahan, Barbe, 57
Trahan, Catherine, 51
Trahan, Charles, 59, 97
Trahan, Chrisosthome, 79
Trahan, Claude, 13, 35, 47, 55
Trahan, Eustache, 57
Trahan, Felicité, 51, 53
Trahan, François, 57
Trahan, François Marie, 33
Trahan, Françoise, 61, 95
Trahan, Françoise Marie Barbara, 45
Trahan, Geneviève, 51
Trahan, Grégoire, 23
Trahan, Isidore, 41

Trahan, Jean, 9, 53
Trahan, Jean Baptiste, 31, 41, 57
Trahan, Jean Chrisosthome, 79
Trahan, Jean Marie, 51, 57, 69
Trahan, Jean Paul, 83
Trahan, Joachim, 51
Trahan, Joseph, 5, 7, 19, 23, 31, 33, 35, 51, 59, 61, 79
Trahan, Joseph Remi, 35
Trahan, Julie, 33
Trahan, Louis Athanase, 37
Trahan, Louise Renné, 55
Trahan, Magdelaine, 27, 41, 53, 57, 95
Trahan, Marguerite, 3, 13, 23, 33, 41, 51, 55, 57, 59, 79, 97
Trahan, Marie, 5, 17, 23, 37, 41, 55, 77, 97
Trahan, Marie Anne, 33
Trahan, Marie Blanche, 37
Trahan, Marie Françoise, 51
Trahan, Marie Josèphe, 59
Trahan, Marie Louise, 53
Trahan, Marie Magdeleine, 79
Trahan, Marie Marguerite, 31
Trahan, Marie Modeste, 7, 47
Trahan, Marie Reneé, 31
Trahan, Marie Victoire, 51
Trahan, Marie Vincent, 51
Trahan, Marin, 45, 57
Trahan, Marthe, 79
Trahan, Mathurin, 23
Trahan, Michel, 53
Trahan, Olivier, 23
Trahan, Paul, 41, 59
Trahan, Paul Raymond, 31
Trahan, Pauline, 51
Trahan, Pélagie, 57
Trahan, Pierre, 51, 53, 55, 59
Trahan, Pierre Baptiste, 59
Trahan, Pierre Grégoire, 59
Trahan, Pierre Simon, 31
Trahan, René, 57, 59, 79
Trahan, Rosalie, 41, 55
Trahan, Rose, 39, 61
Trahan, Simon, 41

"V"

Valet, Marie Claudine, 39
Valo, Marguerite, 63
Valois, Marguerite, 69
Varongue, Antoine, 61
Varongue, Jeanne, 61
Veco, Cécile, 67, 107

Veco, Madeleine, 7
Veuvre, Jeanne, 81
Viaud, Catherine, 77
Videt, Marie, 83
Villeré, Marie Jeanne, 104
Vincent, Anne Blanche, 69
Vincent, Anne Marie, 11
Vincent, Blanche, 63
Vincent, Charles, 57
Vincent, Claire, 81, 91
Vincent, Élizabeth, 103
Vincent, Flore Adélaïde, 69
Vincent, Isabelle, 57
Vincent, Jean, 63, 69
Vincent, Jeanne Marguerite, 69
Vincent, Marguerite, 13
Vincent, Marie Blanche, 69
Vincent, Marie Magdeleine 7, 37
Vincent, Pierre, 41

PART TWO

"Exiled Acadians - General Index"

GENERAL INDEX

ABOUT THIS GENERAL INDEX

This is a General Index of five (5) separate publications written by Albert J. Robichaux, Jr. and Rev. Donald J. Hébert. These publications include the records of Acadians in France found in the various french archives described in each book. A single General Index of the names found in these five works can prove quite helpful in doing research. This General Index listing includes 25,025 entries.

Index Sources are listed on the top of each page of the General Index - appearing as:
C =Chatellerault; E =Acadians in Exile; F =Acadian Families; N =Nantes; and S =St-Malo

Each name listed in the Index indicates a reference to one of the five works included. The books included in this general listing are:

> C =The Acadian Exiles in Chatellerault 1773-1785
> > by Albert J. Robichaux, Jr. - published in 1983
> > 1,562 index entries are included in this General Index

> E =Acadians in Exile 1700-1825
> > by Rev. Donald J. Hébert - published in 1980
> > 12,035 index entries are included in this General Index

> F =Acadian Families in Exile 1785
> > by Rev. Donald J. Hébert - published in 1995
> > 1,586 index entries are included in this General Index

> N =The Acadian Exiles in Nantes 1775-1785
> > by Albert J. Robichaux, Jr. - published in 1978
> > 1,867 index entries are included in this General Index

> S =The Acadian Exiles in Saint-Malo 1758-1785
> > by Albert J. Robichaux, Jr. - published in three volumes in 1981
> > S1 =3,147 index entries are included in this General Index
> > S2 =3,005 index entries are included in this General Index
> > S3 =1,823 index entries are included in this General Index

Example of entry arrangement - (see page 240 of the General Index)

Hebert, Ambroise, C-54, 65, 133	(refers to "Exiles in Chatellerault")
Hebert, Ambroise, E-184, 188-189, 191	(refers to "Acadians in Exile")
Hebert, Ambroise, F-21, 43, 73, 79, 107	(refers to "Acadian Families in Exile")
Hebert, Ambroise, N-84-85, 89, 94, 136, 175, 233-234	(refers to "Acadian Exiles in Nantes")
Hebert, Ambroise, S1-16	(refers to vol. 1 of "Exiles of St. Malo")
Hebert, Ambroise, S2-445-448, 466, 474, 612, 629, 762	(refers to vol. 2 of "Exiles of St. Malo")
Hebert, Ambroise, S3-826, 884	(refers to vol. 3 of "Exiles of St. Malo")

HINTS for the use of this General Index

- Most names are listed under a single spelling in order to easier locate entries.
> Daigle, Daigre and Daigue are all listed as Daigle.
> Giroir, Girouard and Giroire are listed as Giroire

- Some names appear under several spellings.
> Prince, Prieur, etc. also appear as LePrince and LePrieur.
> Quemine and Kimine are listed separately, etc.

A

Abadie, Marie, C-71
Abadie, Marie, E-103
Abel, Theotiste, S2-603
Ablin, Jean, E-1, 17
Abram, widow, E-522
Abuset, Julien, S2-557
Acadian Families at Belle-Ile-
  en-Mer in 1765, E-455, 554
Acadians and Canadians from
  St-Pierre et Miquelon at Le
  Havre in 1801, E-455, 637
Acadians and Canadians having
  the right to Aid in 1803, E-
  455, 644
Acadians and Canadians refu-
  gees from St-Pierre et Mique-
  lon to leave Le Havre for
  Lorient in 1802, E-455, 641
Acadians at Belle-Ile-en-Mer in
  1765, E-455, 580
Acadians at Champflore, Marti-
  nique in 1766, E-455, 598
Acadians at Cherbourg in 1775,
  E-455, 603
Acadians Exiles from St-Pierre
  et Miquelon at Le Havre in
  1797, E-455, 630
Acadians in France around St-
  Malo in 1793, E-455, 616
Acadians in France during the
  French Revolution in 1789-
  1812, E-455, 606
Acadians in French Colonies
  during the French Revolution
  in 1791-1804, E-455, 607
Acadians in Morlaix in 1791, E-
  455, 608, 610
Acadians in Morlaix in 1972, E-
  455, 613
Acadians listed at Poitou in
  1797, E-455, 635
Achalet, Noel, N-217
Achi, Marie, E-42, 126
Achinel, Barthelemy, E-10-11
Achinel, Jacques, E-10
Achinel, Jean Baptiste, E-11
Achinel, Jean Barthelemy, E-11

Achinel, Marie Adelaide, E-11
Achinel, Marie Louise, E-11
Acinolo, Barthelemy, E-85
Adam, Antoine, E-296, 417
Adam, Jean, E-276
Adam, Jean, S3-866
Adam, Joseph, F-85
Adam, Laurent, E-617
Adam, Louis Noel, E-344, 392
Adam, Marie, E-620
Adams, Joseph, F-63
Adams, Nicolas, F-63
Adan, Jean, S2-584
Adieu, Francois, E-357
Adrien, Jeanne, E-292
Agasse, Jeanne, S1-58
Agnes, Francois, E-11
Agnes, indian, E-316
Agnes, Joseph, E-11, 262
Aguilar, Jean Emanuel, E-11
Aguilar, Jean Sebastien, E-11
Aigret, Jacques, E-89, 168, 337
Aillebout, Charles Joseph, E-11
Aillebout, Marie Charlotte, E-11
Aillet, Louis, F-101
Aillet, Mathurin, F-65
Aillet, Pierre, F-65
Aillet, Thomas, F-101
Aimard, Jacques, E-376
Ainse, Jacques, E-11
Alaire, Angelique, E-617
Alary, Francois, E-22
Albert, Anne, C-79
Albert, Anne Perine, E-584, 596
Albert, Anne Perrine, C-1, 3,
  127
Albert, Claude, E-11
Albert, Charles, E-584, 596
Albert, Claude Francois, E-11
Albert, Gabriel, F-83, 109
Albert, Jacques Albert, E-11
Albert, Jacques Firmin, E-11
Albert, Jean, E-11, 174
Albert, Jean Baptiste, E-11
Albert, Jean Jacques, E-11
Albert, Jean Pierre, C-1
Albert, Louis Francois, C-2
Albert, Louis Francois, E-11
Albert, Marie, E-11, 174
Albert, Marie Adelaide, E-11

Albert, Marie Madeleine, C-1
Albert, Nicholas Gabriel, C-1
Albert, Nicolas, C-78, 109, 119,
  124, 127-128
Albert, Nicolas, E-333, 584, 596
Albert, Nicolas, F-83, 109
Albert, Perrine, C-77
Albert, Pierre, E-11
Albert, Rosalie, E-11
Albert, Suzanne, C-1, 78, 119
Albert, Suzanne, E-584, 596
Albert, Urbain, E-11
Aleu, Antoine, E-349
Alev, Marie, E-68
Alin, Julienne, E-14
Alix, Rene, S1-255
Allain, Aimee, E-57
Allain, Angelique, E-617
Allain, Francois, E-584, 596
Allain, Gillette, S2-590
Allain, Jacquemine, S1-363
Allain, Jacquemine, S3-1011
Allain, Jean, S1-1
Allain, Jean, S3-1074
Allain, Jean Paul Rene, E-196
Allain, Julie, E-11
Allain, Julienne, E-14
Allain, Julles Philippe, E-11
Allain, Louis, E-522
Allain, Madeleine, S2-449
Allain, Marie, E-128, 149-150,
  267
Allain, Rene, N-192
Allaire, Angelique, S2-689
Allaire, Jerome, E-369
Alland, Jean Francois, E-370
Allard, Elisabeth, E-11, 137
Allard, Jacques, E-337
Allard, Jean, E-11, 137
Allard, Louis, E-25, 409
Allard, Marie Anne, E-122, 139
Allary, Francois, E-12, 109
Allary, Jean, E-109
Allary, Marie Anne, E-12, 109
Allegre, Marie Anne Michelle,
  E-155, 281, 281, 370
Allemand, Genevieve, E-90, 379
Allen River named after Louis
  Allen, E-210
Allenet, Mr., E-128

Allier, Jean Baptiste, E-12
Alliot, Mathurina, F-85
Alson, -----, S1-1
Alson, Cecile, S1-1
Alson, Francois, S1-1
Alson, Pierre, S1-1
Amand, Marie, E-284
Amar, Laurent, E-257
Ambert, Marie Antoinette, E-29, 172
Amelin, Nicolas, E-355, 388
Amelin, Nicolas, S1-44
Amelin, Rene, S3-866
Ameline, Charlotte, S2-668
Ameline, Jean, S1-360
Ameline, Joseph, S1-177
Ameline, Marie, S2-757
Ameline, Marie, S3-837
Ameline, Marie Madeleine, E-146
Amelinne, Joseph, S3-896
Amelot, Marie, E-360, 405
Amet, Michelle, E-11
Amias, Jean Baptiste, E-371
Amien, Genevieve, E-282-283
Amiens, Jeanne Genevieve, E-285-286
Amillet, Elisabeth, E-279
Amillet, Marie, E-255
Amiot, Louise Victoire, E-343
Amiot, Madeleine, E-12, 270
Amiot, Marguerite, E-12, 433, 435-437
Amiot, Noel, E-12, 435
Amiot DeVincelotte, Louis Victoire, E-384
Amiras, Catherine, E-15
Amirault, C., C-154
Amirault, Catherine, E-16
Amirault, Elizabeth, C-34
Amirault, Elizabeth, F-2, 93
Amirault, Elizabeth, N-49, 55, 229
Amirault, Elizabeth, S1-8-9, 22, 255, 268
Amirault, Marie, C-64
Amirault, Marie, N-107
Amirault, Pierre, C-25, 63, 71, 84, 91, 121
Amirault, Vincent, C-46
Amont, Jacqueline, E-293

Amus, Jean Baptiste, E-12
Amus, Marie, E-12, 27
Anclot, Jean, S3-904
Andille, Marguerite, E-307
Andre, Alexis, S1-352
Andre, Francois, S1-1
Andre, Jacques, E-108, 256
Andre, Philippe, E-185
Angard, Marie Madeleine, E-315
Angaux, Charles, S1-1
Angaux, Jacques, S1-1
Angaux, Jeanne-Marie, S1-2
Angaux, Louis, S1-2
Angaux, Marie-Louise, S1-2
Angaux, Marie-Rose, S1-2
Angaux, Marie-Rose-Guillemette, S1-2
Angaux, Nicolas, S1-1-2.
Angaux, Rose, S1-2
Angaux, Simon, S1-2
Angaux, Vincent, S1-2
Angebert, Anne Catherine, E-12, 86
Angebert, Joseph, E-12, 86
Angers, Pierre, E-43, 119, 176, 311
Angers, Pierre, S1-281, 320
Angibeaud, Marie, E-80
Angilbert, Etienne Francois, F-111
Angilbert, Etienne Francois, N-2
Angilbert, Marie Adelaide, F-111
Angilbert, Marie Adelaide, N-2
Angot, Etienne, E-620
Angot, Guillaume, E-616
Angot, Jeanne, E-616
Angot, Judith, E-616
Angot, Julien, E-616
Angot, Louis, E-616
Angot, Marie Louise, E-12
Angot, Nicolas, E-12
Angot, Nicolas, S3-932
Angot, Rose, E-620
Angot, Simon, E-616
Angot, Simon, S3-932
Angot, Therese Angelique, E-360, 405
Angot, Vincent, E-616
Angot, Vincent, S3-932

Anguetil, Jean Baptise, E-361
Anjot, Guillaume, S1-263
Anne, indian, E-142, 353
Anne Marie, indian, E-316
Anquetil, Guillaume, S1-3
Anquetil, Jean-Francois, S1-3
Anquetil, Louis, S1-3
Anquetil, Louis-George, S1-3
Anquetil, Thomas, S1-3
Anquetit, Jan Francois, S3-968
Anquetit, Thomas, S3-968
Anselme dit Laliberte, Antoine, E-12, 168
Anselme dit Laliberte, Joseph Antoine, E-12, 168
Ansoine, Gabriel Joseph Suzanne, E-12
Ansoine, Jeanne Joseph, E-12
Ansoine, Joseph, E-12, 86
Ansoine, Mr., E-386
Antchepy, Marie, E-101, 391
Anthoinne, Laurence Francoisse, S3-1053
Anthon, Angele, E-615
Anthon, Isabelle, E-615
Anthon, Jean, E-615
Anthon, Jean Nicolas, E-415
Anthon, Roze, E-615
Anthon, Toussaint, E-615
Antoine, Catherine, S1-228
Antoine, Catherine, S3-1053
Anton, Elisabeth Terio, E-610
Apart, Brigitte, S1-90-91, 383
Apart, Michel, S1-90
Aqurnault, Pol, S3-985
Arbonne, Joseph, E-12
Arbonne, Pierre, E-12
Arbour, Francois, E-12, 193
Arbour, Guillaume, E-12
Arbour, Pierre, E-12
Arbour, Susanne, E-12
Arbourg, Chrisosthome, E-12
Arcement, Cecile, E-302
Arcement, Charles-Suliac, S1-4
Arcement, Francoise, F-101
Arcement, Genevieve, C-37, 82
Arcement, Genevieve, F-15, 23, 27
Arcement, Genevieve, N-140, 145, 237
Arcement, Genevieve, S1-288

INDEX SOURCES C=Chatellerault; E=Acadians in Exile; F=Acadian Families; N=Nantes; S=St-Malo

Arcement, Genevieve, S2-655-656
Arcement, Genevieve, S3-1143
Arcement, Guillaume, F-101
Arcement, Guillaume-Romain, S1-4
Arcement, Jenevieve, S3-933
Arcement, Julie, F-101
Arcement, Marguerite, F-101
Arcement, Marguerite, S2-716
Arcement, Marguerite-Ludi-vinne, S1-3-4
Arcement, Marie, F-101
Arcement, Marie Magdelaine, F-49
Arcement, Marie-Josephe, S1-3
Arcement, Marie-Madeleine, S1-389-391
Arcement, Perine, F-101
Arcement, Perinne-Madeleine, S1-4
Arcement, Pierre, F-2
Arcement, Pierre, S1-3-4
Arcement, Pierre, S2-457
Arcement, Pierre, S2-673
Arcement, Tranquille-Francoise, S1-4
Arcement, Victoire, F-101
Arcement, Victoire-Helene, S1-4
Arceneaux, Abraham, E-13-14, 33, 108, 368, 488, 522
Arceneaux, Abraham, S1-297
Arceneaux, Ambroise, E-13
Arceneaux, Andre, E-13
Arceneaux, Anne, E-184, 550-551
Arceneaux, Anne Marie, E-13, 431
Arceneaux, Anne-Marie, S2-776-777
Arceneaux, Antoine, E-108, 299
Arceneaux, Basil, E-13
Arceneaux, Catherine, E-9, 435
Arceneaux, Charles, E-13, 365, 522, 550, 553
Arceneaux, Charles, S1-214
Arceneaux, Claude, E-13, 14
Arceneaux, Elie, E-13
Arceneaux, Francois, E-97, 550
Arceneaux, Francoise, E-44

Arceneaux, Francoise, E-551
Arceneaux, Guiyon, F-107
Arceneaux, Jacque, E-13
Arceneaux, Jacques Francois, E-107
Arceneaux, Jean, E-13, 92, 270, 402
Arceneaux, Jean Baptiste, E-551
Arceneaux, Jean Francois, E-13
Arceneaux, Jean Jacques, E-550
Arceneaux, Jeanne, E-551
Arceneaux, Jeanne, S2-451
Arceneaux, Joseph, E-13-14, 47, 104, 107
Arceneaux, Judith, E-13
Arceneaux, Julie, E-13
Arceneaux, Louis, E-13
Arceneaux, Louise, S1-297-298
Arceneaux, Magdelaine, E-551
Arceneaux, Marguerite, E-107-108, 550-551, 625
Arceneaux, Marie, E-13, 104, 107, 184, 431, 551
Arceneaux, Marie Anne, E-13
Arceneaux, Marie Magdelaine, E-13, 78, 104, 112, 189
Arceneaux, Marie Rosalie, E-13, 42
Arceneaux, Marie Therese, E-36, 377
Arceneaux, Marie-Madeleine, S1-4, 198
Arceneaux, Paul, E-551
Arceneaux, Pierre, E-13-14, 82, 92, 104, 431, 472, 488, 522, 550-551
Arceneaux, Pierre, S1-4, 226
Arceneaux, Pierre, S2-776
Arceneaux, Rosalie, E-13-14
Arceneaux, Theraize, E-14
Archambaud, Joseph, E-72
Archambeau, Louis, E-13, 418
Arches, Joseph, E-14
Archier, Antoine Joseph, N-2
Archier, Antoine Julien, N-2, 166, 252
Archier, Francois, N-2, 252
Ardoin, Antoine, E-14
Ardoin, Francois, E-14
Ardoin, Guillaume, E-14
Ardoin, Izabelle, E-429

Ardoin, Joseph, E-14
Ardoin, Louis, E-14
Ardoin, Louis Marie, E-14
Ardoin, Marie Ange, E-14
Ardoin, Marie Anne, E-14
Ardoin, Marie Francoise, E-14
Ardoin, Marie Louise, E-14
Ardoin, Perrine, E-14
Ardoin, Rosalie, E-14
Ardoin, Rose, E-14
Areau, Dominique, E-368
Arisinedis, Bernard, E-439
Armand, Jean Michel, E-322
Armand, Louis, E-14
Arnaud, Charles, E-381
Arnaud, Francois, C-2
Arnaud, Gabriel, C-2
Arnaud, Henriette Julie, C-2
Arnaud, Jacque, C-2, 36, 127-128
Arnaud, Jean, C-2
Arnaud, Jean, E-337
Arnaud, Marguerite , C-14
Arnaud, Marianne Josephe, C-2
Arnaud, Martial, C-2, 6, 31, 125
Arnaud, Pierre, C-2-3 127-128
Arnaud, Rene, C-1, 3, 127
Arnauld, Francois, C-104
Arnauld, Jeanne, E-166, 386
Arnauld, Marguerite Rose, E-13, 343
Arnauld, Martial, C-104
Arnauld, Rosalie, E-368
Arnault, Deportes, E-10
Arnault, Jean, C-102, 104
Arnault, Martial, C-109
Arnault, Pierre, S3-1011
Arnault, Rene, C-79
Arnaux, Pierre, S2-510
Arnoux, Blaise-Andre, S1-356
Arondel, Anne, E-14, 20
Arondel, Charles, E-14
Arondel, Francoise, E-14, 112
Arondel, Jacques, E-14, 258
Arondel, Marie, E-4-5
Aroqui, Jeanne, E-434
Arost, Marie, E-352
Arrichoury Le Blanc, Jeanne, E-14
Arrichoury Le Blanc, Pierre, E-14, 315

Arrichovry Leblanc, Jeanne, E-315

Arroguy, Bernard, E-9

Arroguy, Ignace, E-9

Arroguy, Jeanne, E-9, 361

Arrot, Claude, E-14, 69, 351, 370

Arrot, Claude, S2-680

Arrot, Magdeleine, E-351

Arrot, Marie, E-14

Arsemane, Cecile, E-14

Arsemane, Marie Madeleine, S3-908

Arsemanne, Marie Magdelaine, C-2, 104

Artel De Rouville, Louis Antoine, E-15, 150

Artel De Rouville , Jean Baptiste, E-15, 150

Asbourgs, Francois, C-124

Assard, Mathieu, E-123

Assemont, Jean-Baptiste, S1-5

Aubert, Jacques, E-125

Aubert, Marie, E-22, 328

Aubert, Marie Francoise, E-358

Aubert, Marie Jeanne, E-348

Aubert de la Chesnay, Angelique, E-102, 356

Aubert de la Chesnay, Mathieu, E-356

Auberte, Jacques, E-269

Auberte, Jeanne, E-269

Aubertin, Henri, E-131

Aubertin, Pierre, E-131

Aubin, Louis, E-169, 373

Aubin, Louis, S1-375

Aubin, Therese, E-89

Aubois, Jeanne, E-15

Aubois, Marie, C-36

Aubois, Marie, E-15, 334

Aubois, Marie, F-77

Aubois, Marie, N-134

Aubois, Michel, E-15

Aubonne, Joseph, E-279

Aubonne, Pierre, E-279

Aubouin, Jean, E-15, 321, 359

Aubourg, Clothilde Desire, E-180

Aubourg, Desire, E-180

Aubourg, Desire Clotilde, E-15, 25, 55

Aubourg, Desire Edmond, E-15

Aubourg, Pierre, E-15, 55

Aubourg, Victoire Desiree, E-15

Aubriere, Marie, E-350

Aubry, Marguerite, E-411

Aubry, Marguerite, S2-729

Aucan, Marguerite, E-15

Aucan, Nicolas, E-15

Aucher, Estienne, E-478

Aucoin, Agnesse, E-509

Aucoin, Alexander, S1-5-6, 10, 27, 209, 211

Aucoin, Alexandre, E-15-16, 162, 189, 425, 554

Aucoin, Alexandre, F-83, 89

Aucoin, Alexandre, N-2-3

Aucoin, Alexandre, S2-572, 743

Aucoin, Alexis, E-47

Aucoin, Alexis, E-509, 522

Aucoin, Alexis, F-87, 93

Aucoin, Alexis, N-2-5, 63, 221

Aucoin, Alexis, S1-7, 15, 18-20, 28, 74, 165, 301

Aucoin, Alexis, S3-870-871, 873-874

Aucoin, Alexis-Joseph, S1-19

Aucoin, Amand, N-3-4

Aucoin, Amant, C-3

Aucoin, Anastasie, F-93

Aucoin, Anastasie, S1-12, 14

Aucoin, Angelique, S1-273, 309

Aucoin, Angelique, S2-615

Aucoin, Anne, E-554

Aucoin, Anne, F-87, 89, 93

Aucoin, Anne, N-230, 243

Aucoin, Anne, S1-9, 15, 17-18, 20, 24, 98, 135, 137, 142, 145, 174, 195, 196, 208, 242, 250, 298, 313-314

Aucoin, Anne, S2-475, 481, 498-500, 738, 766

Aucoin, Anne, S3-864, 869, 885-886, 895, 949, 1109, 1152-1153

Aucoin, Anne Augustine, E-15

Aucoin, Anne Augustine, F-83

Aucoin, Anne Augustine, N-3

Aucoin, Anne Elizabeth, C-4,

Aucoin, Anne Felicite, E-15

Aucoin, Anne Felicite, F-15

Aucoin, Anne Felicite, N-6

Aucoin, Anne Francoise, C-3

Aucoin, Anne Marie, F-83

Aucoin, Anne Marie, N-3

Aucoin, Anne Olive, F-95

Aucoin, Anne-Anastasie, S1-11

Aucoin, Anne-Angelique, S1-29

Aucoin, Anne-Felicite, S1-13

Aucoin, Anne-Julienne, S1-14

Aucoin, Anne-Marguerite, S1-20

Aucoin, Anne-Marie, S1-16

Aucoin, Anne-Olive, S1-30

Aucoin, Anne-Theodose, S1-23

Aucoin, Annette, N-4

Aucoin, Anselme, S1-27-28

Aucoin, Antoine, C-3-4, 20, 34

Aucoin, Antoine, E-522

Aucoin, Antoine, F-15, 73, 93

Aucoin, Antoine, N-49, 55, 229

Aucoin, Antoine, S1-8-10, 22, 72, 255, 268

Aucoin, Antoine, S3-947, 1102, 1112

Aucoin, Augustine, E-7

Aucoin, Cecile, E-15, 144, 323, 509

Aucoin, Cecile, F-13, 109

Aucoin, Cecile, N-8

Aucoin, Cecile, S1-341

Aucoin, Cecile, S2-615-616

Aucoin, Charles, C-4, 68, 81

Aucoin, Charles, E-276

Aucoin, Charles, F-13, 29, 89, 95

Aucoin, Charles, N-4-5, 7, 111, 130, 199, 241

Aucoin, Charles, S1-5, 10-12, 25, 30, 105, 233

Aucoin, Charles, S2-571, 764

Aucoin, Charles, S3-838, 881, 886, 1016, 1020, 1100-1101

Aucoin, Charles-Etienne, S1-19

Aucoin, Charles-Joseph, S1-11

Aucoin, Chrisostome, S1-8-9, 22, 148

Aucoin, Claude, E-15

Aucoin, Claude, F-91, 93

Aucoin, Claude, S1-11-12, 14, 310

Aucoin, Claude, S2-465, 552

Aucoin, Claude, S3-926, 1100

Aucoin, Coecile, S3-1118

Aucoin, Constance-Jean-Baptiste, S1-24

Aucoin, Constant, F-93

Aucoin, Constant, S1-24

Aucoin, Elene, F-73

Aucoin, Elisabeth, S3-846, 898

Aucoin, Elizabeth, C-4, 39, 64

Aucoin, Elizabeth, F-15, 67, 83

Aucoin, Elizabeth, N-3, 6, 77, 145, 237

Aucoin, Elizabeth, S1-12-13, 22, 26, 69, 316, 382

Aucoin, Elizabeth, S2-531-532, 564, 612

Aucoin, Elizabeth Jeanne, N-7

Aucoin, Elizabeth Joseph, E-16

Aucoin, Elizabeth-Anne, S1-25

Aucoin, Fabien, F-27, 87

Aucoin, Fabien, N-3-4, 209, 221

Aucoin, Fabien, S1-7, 19-20, 147, 158, 362

Aucoin, Fabien-Isaac, S1-19

Aucoin, Felicite, F-13

Aucoin, Felicite, S1-5, 10, 25, 209, 211, 377

Aucoin, Felicite, S2-571, 745

Aucoin, Firmin, E-7

Aucoin, Firmin, F-15

Aucoin, Firmin, N-4, 8, 29, 196, 236, 241

Aucoin, Firmin, S1-25-26

Aucoin, Firmin, S2-572

Aucoin, Firmin, S3-894, 1014, 1020

Aucoin, Firmin Louis, N-5

Aucoin, Floriane, F-93

Aucoin, Florianne, S1-24

Aucoin, Florianne-Marguerite, S1-24

Aucoin, Francois, C-96, 118, 166

Aucoin, Francois, E-123, 285, 302, 403

Aucoin, Francois, F-87, 93, 95

Aucoin, Francois, N-4-5, 130, 195, 241

Aucoin, Francois, S1-17-18, 24, 212

Aucoin, Francois, S3-947

Aucoin, Francois Charles, C-4

Aucoin, Francois Rene, C-3

Aucoin, Francois Toussaint, F-7

Aucoin, Francois Toussaint, N-6-7

Aucoin, Francois-Alexis, S1-29

Aucoin, Francois-Augustin, S1-12

Aucoin, Francois-Charles, S1-9

Aucoin, Francois-David, S1-23

Aucoin, Francois-Etienne, S1-24

Aucoin, Francois-Malo, S1-17

Aucoin, Francoise, E-616

Aucoin, Francoise, F-87, 93

Aucoin, Francoise, N-108, 122

Aucoin, Francoise, S1-9, 18, 22, 148, 268, 271

Aucoin, Francoise, S2-541

Aucoin, Francoise Victoire, N-3

Aucoin, Francoise-Marie, S1-16

Aucoin, Francoise-Theotiste, S1-5

Aucoin, Francoise-Victoire, S1-17

Aucoin, Gabriel, F-87

Aucoin, Gabriel, S1-18

Aucoin, Gabriel-Guillaume, S1-17

Aucoin, Genevieve, C-155

Aucoin, Genevieve, E-554

Aucoin, Genevieve, F-83

Aucoin, Genevieve, N-3

Aucoin, Genevieve, S1-15, 22, 67, 242, 250, 360

Aucoin, Genevieve, S2-523

Aucoin, Genevieve, S3-832, 869

Aucoin, Gregoire, F-93

Aucoin, Gregoire, S1-24

Aucoin, Gregoire-Alexis, S1-23

Aucoin, Guillaume, S3-922, 926, 928-929, 931, 933-934

Aucoin, Helene, C-34, 53-54, 166

Aucoin, Helene, E-2

Aucoin, Helene, F-13

Aucoin, Helene, N-49-50, 55, 84-85, 229

Aucoin, Helene, S1-7-9, 19, 23, 136, 148, 159, 242, 255, 268, 274, 303, 362

Aucoin, Helene, S2-445, 612, 762

Aucoin, Hyacinthe, E-6-7, 324

Aucoin, Hyacinthe-Laurent, S1-17

Aucoin, Isabelle, E-16, 177, 509

Aucoin, Isabelle, F-17. 93

Aucoin, Isabelle, S1-23-24, 68, 174, 242, 250, 381

Aucoin, Isabelle, S2-435, 467

Aucoin, Isabelle Jeanne, F-7

Aucoin, Isabelle-Jeanne, S1-21

Aucoin, Jacinte, F-87

Aucoin, Jacinthe, S1-18

Aucoin, Jean, E-7, 15-16

Aucoin, Jean, F-15, 93

Aucoin, Jean, N-6, 237, 248

Aucoin, Jean, S1-8, 12-14, 17, 24, 167

Aucoin, Jean, S2-481

Aucoin, Jean Baptiste, F-15, 91, 97

Aucoin, Jean Baptiste, N-145

Aucoin, Jean Baptiste, S3-903, 1100

Aucoin, Jean Charles, E-16

Aucoin, Jean Marie, E-16

Aucoin, Jean-Baptiste, S1-11-14, 109, 325

Aucoin, Jean-Baptiste, S2-467

Aucoin, Jean-Baptiste-Fabien, S1-5

Aucoin, Jean-Charles, S1-16, 22, 26, 28

Aucoin, Jean-Joseph, S1-29

Aucoin, Jean-Victor, S1-27

Aucoin, Jeanne, E-457, 474

Aucoin, Jeanne, S1-24

Aucoin, Joachim, E-16

Aucoin, Joseph, C-155

Aucoin, Joseph, F-7, 17, 67, 77, 87, 95

Aucoin, Joseph, N-6-7, 195, 214, 222

Aucoin, Joseph, S1-7, 12-21, 24, 26, 27-28, 69, 151, 174, 211, 309

Aucoin, Joseph, S2-458-459, 467, 477, 487, 497, 578, 605, 755

Aucoin, Joseph, S3-836, 853, 870-874, 880, 882, 886, 890-891, 900, 930, 1024, 1141

Aucoin, Joseph Jean, F-7
Aucoin, Joseph Jean, N-6-7
Aucoin, Joseph Marie, N-4
Aucoin, Joseph-Marie, S1-19
Aucoin, Joseph-Michel, S1-22
Aucoin, Joseph-Yves, S1-16
Aucoin, Julie-Marie-Francoise, S1-17
Aucoin, Lexy, E-16
Aucoin, Louis, E-509
Aucoin, Louis, F-15
Aucoin, Louis Paul, E-16
Aucoin, Louis-Jean, S1-9
Aucoin, Louise, S1-342-343
Aucoin, Louise Adelaide, N-7
Aucoin, Madeleine, N-160
Aucoin, Madeleine, S1-5, 10, 21-22, 25, 50, 211, 315
Aucoin, Madeleine, S2-571, 578, 759-761
Aucoin, Magdelaine, C-154
Aucoin, Magdelaine, F-97
Aucoin, Malo-Dieutonne, S1-20
Aucoin, Malo-Jean, S1-20
Aucoin, Marguerite, E-620
Aucoin, Marguerite, F-13, 99
Aucoin, Marguerite, N-8
Aucoin, Marguerite, S1-7, 10, 13, 15, 20-23, 69, 136, 142, 148-149, 211-212, 244, 309-310
Aucoin, Marguerite, S2-467, 523, 612
Aucoin, Marguerite, S3-1024
Aucoin, Marguerite Genevieve, F-95
Aucoin, Marguerite Susanne, E-124
Aucoin, Marguerite-Francoise, S1-9
Aucoin, Marguerite-Genevieve, S1-25, 30
Aucoin, Marguerite-Josephe, S1-6
Aucoin, Marguerite-Suzanne, S1-26-27
Aucoin, Marie, C-3-4, 22, 24, 38, 68, 155
Aucoin, Marie, E-274, 425, 509
Aucoin, Marie, F-13, 19, 21, 89, 93, 97, 99

Aucoin, Marie, N-8, 35, 117-118, 157-158, 176, 248
Aucoin, Marie, S1-6-7, 10, 12-16, 18, 24-27, 30, 70, 79, 96, 131, 141-142, 144, 154, 165, 207-210, 251
Aucoin, Marie, S2-465, 529, 571-572, 574, 578-579, 605, 607, 670, 707, 744, 767
Aucoin, Marie, S3-823, 847, 867, 875-876, 880, 887, 889, 893
Aucoin, Marie Anastasie, F-15
Aucoin, Marie Anastasie, N-157
Aucoin, Marie Anne, E-125, 424
Aucoin, Marie Barbe, E-6, 16
Aucoin, Marie Blanche, F-95
Aucoin, Marie Claire, C-14, 17
Aucoin, Marie Claire, F-75, 77
Aucoin, Marie Claire, S3-838, 845
Aucoin, Marie Felicite, E-16
Aucoin, Marie Felicite, F-83
Aucoin, Marie Felicite, N-3
Aucoin, Marie Francoise, E-16
Aucoin, Marie Francoise, F-49
Aucoin, Marie Francoise, N-7
Aucoin, Marie Jeanne, E-7
Aucoin, Marie Jeanne, F-89, 91
Aucoin, Marie Josephe, E-123
Aucoin, Marie Josephe, E-16, 124, 271-272, 554
Aucoin, Marie Josephe, N-5, 6, 60, 130, 195
Aucoin, Marie Josephine, N-3
Aucoin, Marie Lucie, N-5
Aucoin, Marie Madeleine, E-16, 173, 324
Aucoin, Marie Madeleine, N-3
Aucoin, Marie Magdelaine, F-83, 87, 95
Aucoin, Marie Magdelaine, S3-882
Aucoin, Marie Magdeleine, C-75
Aucoin, Marie Modeste, F-7
Aucoin, Marie Modeste, N-6-7
Aucoin, Marie Reine, F-83
Aucoin, Marie Reine, N-3
Aucoin, Marie-Anastasie, S1-13
Aucoin, Marie-Anne, S1-12, 18

Aucoin, Marie-Blanche, S1-18, 39, 232-233
Aucoin, Marie-Cecile, S1-25
Aucoin, Marie-Claire, S1-96-97, 110
Aucoin, Marie-Elizabeth, S1-5, 29
Aucoin, Marie-Felicite, S1-28
Aucoin, Marie-Francoise, S1-13
Aucoin, Marie-Genevieve, S1-6
Aucoin, Marie-Gertrude, S1-12
Aucoin, Marie-Jeanne, S1-6, 14
Aucoin, Marie-Josephe, S1-20-23, 26-27, 66-67
Aucoin, Marie-Josephe, S2-522, 524
Aucoin, Marie-Madeleine, S1-5, 15, 17-18, 27, 29, 131, 265
Aucoin, Marie-Madeleine, S2-467-468, 523
Aucoin, Marie-Madeleine-Julienne, S1-19
Aucoin, Martin, E-472, 509, 522
Aucoin, Martin, S1-8, 10, 309
Aucoin, Martin, S2-615
Aucoin, Mathurin, F-87, 89, 93
Aucoin, Mathurin, N-195
Aucoin, Mathurin, S1-12, 20
Aucoin, Mathurin Jean, F-85
Aucoin, Mathurin-Amand, S1-26
Aucoin, Mathurin-Casimir, S1-12
Aucoin, Mathurin-Jean, S1-19
Aucoin, Michel, E-509, 522
Aucoin, Michel, F-49, 87, 93
Aucoin, Michel, N-7, 51, 60, 181, 243
Aucoin, Michel, S1-8, 13, 21-22, 24, 26, 66, 69, 148, 250
Aucoin, Michel, S2-706, 713, 758
Aucoin, Michel, S3-823, 832, 846, 940, 947, 1152-1153
Aucoin, Michel-Pierre, S1-23
Aucoin, Michelle, E-456, 472
Aucoin, Natalie, F-13
Aucoin, Natalie, N-8
Aucoin, Natalie-Marie, S1-25
Aucoin, Noel, E-7
Aucoin, Noel-Alexandre, S1-6

Aucoin, Olivier, C-4
Aucoin, Olivier, F-13
Aucoin, Olivier, N-4, 7-8, 157, 176, 189, 207, 236
Aucoin, Olivier, S1-5, 8, 10, 25-26
Aucoin, Olivier, S2-528, 571, 701, 703, 733
Aucoin, Olivier, S3-1020, 1153
Aucoin, Olivier Louis, N-8
Aucoin, Ozite, S1-15, 22
Aucoin, Ozite-Perpetue, S1-30
Aucoin, Paul, E-16
Aucoin, Paul, F-7
Aucoin, Paul, N-6
Aucoin, Paul, S1-20, 26-27
Aucoin, Paul, S2-499, 522
Aucoin, Paul, S3-1141
Aucoin, Perinne-Marie, S1-6
Aucoin, Perpetue, F-93, 95
Aucoin, Perpetue, S1-11-12, 29-30, 315
Aucoin, Perpetue, S2-466
Aucoin, Pierre, E-16
Aucoin, Pierre, F-15, 29, 49, 93, 95, 97
Aucoin, Pierre, N-7, 243
Aucoin, Pierre, S1-6-7, 11-12, 16-17, 19-21, 24, 27-29, 96, 195, 211, 232, 303
Aucoin, Pierre, S2-445, 459, 465, 606, 612, 678
Aucoin, Pierre, S3-873, 880, 884, 1100, 1152
Aucoin, Pierre Charles, C-4
Aucoin, Pierre-Alexis, S1-16
Aucoin, Pierre-Fiacre, S1-27
Aucoin, Pierre-Firmin, S1-14
Aucoin, Pierre-Jean, S1-12, 19
Aucoin, Pierre-Joseph-Antoine, S1-9
Aucoin, Pierre-Josephe, S1-28
Aucoin, Pierre-Paul, S1-23, 26
Aucoin, Pierre-Simon, S1-27
Aucoin, Radegonde, S1-16, 18
Aucoin, Rene, C-64
Aucoin, Rene, E-522
Aucoin, Rene, S1-11
Aucoin, Rene, S2-531
Aucoin, Rosa Adelaide, F-49
Aucoin, Rosalie, N-7

Aucoin, Rose Anastasie, F-95, 97
Aucoin, Rose Felicite, F-95
Aucoin, Rose Magdelaine, F-97
Aucoin, Rose-Anastasie, S1-13
Aucoin, Rose-Felicite, S1-30
Aucoin, Rose-Madeleine, S1-13
Aucoin, Silvain, E-15-16, 47, 113, 193
Aucoin, Simon, F-95
Aucoin, Simon, S1-13-14, 29-30, 100, 314-315
Aucoin, Simon, S2-612, 742
Aucoin, Simon, S3-1100
Aucoin, Sylvain, C-79, 142
Aucoin, Sylvain, N-134
Aucoin, Tarsile, S1-21, 27, 69
Aucoin, Tarsille, S2-499, 524
Aucoin, Theodore, S1-7
Aucoin, Ursule, N-115
Aucoin, Ursule, S1-9
Aucoin, Ursule, S2-567-569
Aucoin, Ursule, S3-1025
Aucoin, Victoire, F-93
Aucoin, Victoire, S1-17, 29
Aucoin, Victoire Claire, F-7
Aucoin, Victoire Claire, N-6, 7
Aucoin, Victoire-Helene, S1-28
Aucoin, Vincent, E-7
Aucoin, widow, F-15
Aucoin, Yves, S1-16
Aucun, Jean Baptiste, E-114
Audaire, Jeanne, E-25, 141, 265, 404
Audaire, Louis, E-262, 265
Audaire, Magdelaine, E-16, 66
Auday, Antoine, E-180
Audebeau, Marie, E-28, 332
Audebert, Jean, E-346
Audet, Louise, E-257-258
Audi, Joseph, E-356
Audille, Marguerite, E-385
Audinet, Catherine, E-439
Audinet, Jean Charles, E-16, 137
Audinet, Jean Joseph, E-16, 137
Audinet, Marie Anne, E-16, 256
Audinot, Guillaume, S3-899
Audouart, Antoine, E-30
Audouin, Marie, E-121
Audy, Marguerite, E-23

Auffroy, Jeanne, S2-780
Auger, Alexandre Guillaume, E-17, 159
Auger, Catherine Agathe, E-17, 159
Auger, Francois Marguerite, E-17
Auger, Francoise, E-73, 294
Auger, Francoise Marguerite, E-152
Auger, Marie, E-17, 61, 105, 340, 357, 406
Auger, Marie Anne, E-357
Auger, Olive, S1-3
Augier De Charente, Anne Domitille, E-17
Augier De Charente, Daniel, E-17
Augier De Charente, Henriette Hyppolyte, E-17
Auguetil, Marie, E-353
Augusain, Fabien, C-133
Augustin, Claudine, S2-686
Augustin, Claudine, S3-983
Aulay, Jeanne, N-44
Aunay, Jean Baptiste, E-29
Aunay, Michel, E-17, 152
Aunay, Suzanne, E-17, 152
Aunel, Magdelaine, E-17
Aunel, Pierre, E-17
Aunel, Victoire, E-17
Aunels, Pierre, E-84, 360
Auniere, Pierre, E-17, 90
Aunis, Charles, E-17
Aunix, Marguerite, E-307
Aupinel, Joseph, E-298, 331
Aurray, Michel, E-17
Aurray, Pierre, E-17
Aury, Guillaume, E-353
Ausericq, Francoise, E-160, 268
Ausquichoury, Jean, E-17, 153
Ausquichoury, Joachim, E-17, 153
Aussan, Marie, E-135, 318
Autand, Francois, E-378
Autant, Jean, E-17, 393
Autexier, Marie Anne, C-94
Auxtexier, Jean, C-112
Auzelet, Jeanne, E-12, 168
Auzelet, Magdalen, E-17, 35, 43
Avarat, Jean Francois, F-85

Averty, Jeanne, C-160
Avnaut, Madeleine, E-102, 395
Avoqui, Jeanne, E-362
Avril, Louise, E-1, 17
Aynas, Marie, E-107
Ayssene, Marianne, F-101

B

Babel, Marie, E-390
Babin, Alain, S1-31
Babin, Amand, S1-31
Babin, Anastasie, S1-35
Babin, Anastasie-Victoire, S1-37
Babin, Anne, E-118, 152, 499, 560, 565
Babin, Anne, S1-33, 35-37, 173-176, 353
Babin, Anne, S2-542, 553, 689
Babin, Anne, S3-886, 1069
Babin, Anne Margueritte, E-18
Babin, Anne Marie, E-363
Babin, Anne-Adelaide, S1-35
Babin, Anne-Marguerite, S1-34
Babin, Anne-Marie, S1-31
Babin, Anne-Marie, S2-553
Babin, Antoine, E-456, 472, 499
Babin, Basile, S1-31
Babin, Bonaventure, E-554
Babin, Bonnaventure, S1-33-34
Babin, Catherine, E-499
Babin, Catherine, N-105, 106
Babin, Catherine, S1-107, 207
Babin, Catherine, S2-530
Babin, Charles, E-18, 164, 472, 522, 560
Babin, Charles, S1-30-32
Babin, Claude, E-554, 560, 565
Babin, Claude, S1-30-31, 33
Babin, Claude, S2-553, 569
Babin, Claudine, C-91, 114
Babin, Elizabeth, N-141, 254
Babin, Elizabeth, S1-32
Babin, Elizabeth, S2-657
Babin, Francois, C-5
Babin, Francois, E-18
Babin, Francois, F-9
Babin, Francois, N-9, 153
Babin, Francois-Laurent, S1-33
Babin, Francois-Marie, S1-37

Babin, Francoise, E-499
Babin, Francoise, S1-32
Babin, Francoise Bertrandele, E-18
Babin, Francoise-Marie, S1-34
Babin, girl, E-18
Babin, Guillaume, S3-1108
Babin, Jacques, S1-31
Babin, Jan, S3-1069
Babin, Jean, E-499, 522
Babin, Jean, N-8
Babin, Jean, S1-32-34, 36
Babin, Jean, S2-689
Babin, Jean Baptiste Auguste, E-18
Babin, Jean Charles, E-18
Babin, Jean Charles, S3-1021
Babin, Jean-Charles, S1-31, 34
Babin, Jeanne, E-476
Babin, Jeanne Francoise, E-18
Babin, Joseph, E-18, 18-19, 180, 554, 560
Babin, Joseph, S1-31-36, 218, 300
Babin, Joseph, S2-740
Babin, Joseph, S3-1098
Babin, Joseph Moise, E-18
Babin, Joseph Nicaise, E-554
Babin, Joseph-Nicaise, S1-33
Babin, Josephe, S3-1090, 1098
Babin, Laurent, E-18-19, 66, 560
Babin, Laurent, S1-31
Babin, Laurent Alexandre, E-18
Babin, Laurent Francois, E-18
Babin, Louis Joseph, E-18
Babin, Magdelaine, E-18, 90, 499
Babin, Magloire, C-5
Babin, Magloire, N-9
Babin, Magloire, S1-36-37
Babin, Marguerite, C-10
Babin, Marguerite, E-273, 499
Babin, Marguerite, F-75
Babin, Marguerite, N-153, 177
Babin, Marguerite, S1-6, 30, 32, 35-36
Babin, Marguerite, S2-542-543, 557, 569
Babin, Marguerite-Francoise, S1-35

Babin, Marie, C-5, 63
Babin, Marie, E-18, 181, 186, 189, 272, 347, 476, 554
Babin, Marie, F-9, 69
Babin, Marie, N-8-9, 153, 194
Babin, Marie, S1-32, 34, 36-37
Babin, Marie, S2-543, 565, 567, 569
Babin, Marie Anne, E-18
Babin, Marie Josephe, E-18
Babin, Marie-Anne, S1-32
Babin, Marie-Josephe, S1-31
Babin, Marie-Josephe-Vincent, S2-698
Babin, Marie-Theotiste, S1-33
Babin, Marie-Victoire, S1-33-34
Babin, Mathurin Louis, E-18
Babin, Mathurin-Louis, S1-34
Babin, Nanette, E-20, 388
Babin, Paul, F-101
Babin, Paul, S1-32-33, 36
Babin, Paul, S2-690
Babin, Paul, S3-970
Babin, Pierre, C-67
Babin, Pierre, S1-36
Babin, Pierre, S2-558, 561
Babin, Pierre Moyse, E-18
Babin, Pierre-Joseph, S1-37
Babin, Pierre-Moise, S1-33
Babin, Rene, E-18, 180
Babin, Rene, S2-558
Babin, Simon, C-5, 139
Babin, Simon, F-85
Babin, Simon, N-8-9, 153, 194, 254
Babin, Simon, S1-32, 35-37, 366
Babin, Simon, S2-542
Babin, Simon, S3-1069
Babin, Victoire, E-554
Babin, Victoire, S1-34
Babin, Victoire Rosalie, E-19
Babin, Victoire-Marguerite, S1-35
Babin, Victor-Angelique, S1-34
Babin, Vincent, E-499, 522
Babin , Jean, C-5, 17
Babineaux, Anne, E-19, 185, 190
Babineaux, Anne Marie, E-19, 320, 353-354

INDEX SOURCES C=Chatellerault; E=Acadians in Exile; F=Acadian Families; N=Nantes; S=St-Malo

Babineaux, Charles, E-19
Babineaux, Francois, E-19
Babineaux, Joseph, E-19, 82, 190
Babineaux, Marguerite, E-82-83
Babineaux, Marie, E-83
Babineaux, Mathurin, E-19
Babineaux, Mr., E-124
Babineaux, Pierre, E-19
Babineaux Hill named after Jean Babineau, E-210
Babut, Marie Francoise Elizabeth, N-43, 242
Babut, Pierre, N-43, 242
Bachelier, Elisabeth, E-108
Bachelier, Jean, E-11, 174
Bacq, Andre, N-192
Badec, Jeanne, E-108
Badon, Marie, E-257
Bagau, Jean, E-19
Bagau, Victoire, E-19
Bahiey, Jean, S1-205
Bahnaud, Francois, E-345
Bahnaud, Mathurin, E-345
Bahuaud, Pierre, E-584, 596
Baillaird, Marguerite, E-37
Baillarge, Antoinette, C-90, 129
Baillarge, Pierre, C-129
Baillarget, Marie, E-19, 172, 262
Baillarjaud, Marie, E-256
Baille, Francois, S2-640
Baille, Marie, S1-173
Baillehache, M., E-334
Baillet, Charles, E-144
Baillet, Martin, E-411
Baillif, Louis, E-19
Baillif, Marie Louise, E-19, 361-364, 367
Bailly, Marie, E-59, 350
Bailly, Marie Marthe, E-70, 77
Baioles, Barbe, E-456
Bairc, Charles, S2-489
Baire, Francois, S1-23
Baisse, Jean, E-19
Baja, Marie, E-313
Bajolet, Nicolas, E-19
Bajolet, Nicolas Joseph, E-19, 178
Bala, Marguerite, F-31
Balaire, Marie, E-264

Balanger, Marie, E-19
Balin, Catherine, C-40, 113
Ballet, Jeanne, S1-56, 85
Ballet, Jeanne, S2-607
Ballet, Pierre, S1-56
Ballet, Pierre, S2-607
Ballois, Jean, E-23, 82
Balon, Antoine, E-19, 22
Balon, Francois, E-19
Balsac, Marthe, E-125, 280
Banastre, Adrien, S1-278
Banet, Julien, E-19-20, 355
Banet, Marie, E-19, 355
Banet, Marie Gabriel, E-354-355
Banet, Pierre Joseph, E-14, 20
Banier, Olive, E-38, 159
Baradeau, Jacques, E-20, 325, 339
Baranger, Magdeleine, E-379
Baranton, Jacques, E-123, 312, 377
Baratarache, Jeanne, E-314
Barault, Marie, E-476
Barbanson, Jacques, S2-624
Barbatteau, Philippe, E-20, 388
Barbatteau, Therese, E-20, 388
Barbe, Marie Madeleine, N-138, 151
Barbe, Marie Madeleine, S1-104
Barbe, Marie-Madeleine, S2-640
Barbeauson, Pierre, E-21, 159
Barbereau, Jean, E-20, 346
Barbereau, Pierre, E-20, 346
Barbier, Anne, E-601
Barbier, Francois, E-20, 151
Barbier, Jacques, E-20, 138
Barbier, Marguerite, E-20, 175, 419
Barbier, Marguerite, S1-321
Barbier, Marguerite, S3-991
Barbier, Martin, E-20
Barbier, Modeste, S1-357
Barbier, Nicolas, E-20
Barbier, Pierre, E-20
Barbot, Pierre (Father), C-78, 119
Barbudau, Gabriel, E-20, 345
Barbudau, Jean, E-20, 345
Barbudeau, Marie Anne, C-109

Barbudeau, Pierre Gabriel, C-109
Bard, Francois, S1-42, 375
Bard, Francois Jean, S3-1060
Bard, Francois-Jean, S1-37-38
Bard, Francoise-Louise, S1-38
Bard, Jean Baptiste, S3-1060
Bard, Jean-Baptiste, S1-37
Bardacet, Andre, E-20
Bardacet, Marie Elisabeth, E-20
Bardesire, Elizabeth, E-38
Bardet, Fransoisse, N-241
Bardin, Catherine, E-72
Bardin, Jean, E-161
Bardin, Pierre, N-192
Bardon, Antoine, E-585, 596
Bardon, Jean, E-20, 412
Bardon, Louis, E-20
Bardon, Marguerite, E-585, 596,
Bardot, Anne Susanne, E-40
Bareau, Francois, C-74, 117
Barillac, Francois, E-21, 157
Barillac, Joseph, E-21
Barillac, Marguerite, E-21
Barille, Jacques, E-21
Barille, Pierre, E-21, 272
Barillon, Suzanne, E-26, 378
Barillot, Agathe, F-7
Barillot, Agathe, N-25, 102, 197
Barillot, Agathe, S1-39, 92, 95, 110
Barillot, Agathe, S2-522
Barillot, Agathe, S3-844
Barillot, Anastasie, C-38
Barillot, Anastasie, F-43
Barillot, Anastasie, N-61-62
Barillot, Anastasie, S1-110, 298-299, 360
Barillot, Anastasie, S2-527
Barillot, Anastasie, S3-852
Barillot, Anne, S1-39-40
Barillot, Anne, S2-759
Barillot, Anne-Jeanne, S1-39
Barillot, Anne-Marie-Josephe, S1-40
Barillot, Charles-Olivier, S1-40
Barillot, Charles-Pierre, S1-39
Barillot, Euphroisine, F-9
Barillot, Euphrosine, C-15, 29, 69

Barillot, Euphrosine, N-19, 38, 202

Barillot, Euphrosine, S1-39-40, 98-99

Barillot, Euphrosine, S2-526, 544, 573

Barillot, Euphrosine, S3-843, 851

Barillot, Francois, C-5

Barillot, Francois, F-19

Barillot, Franocis, N-9

Barillot, Jacques, C-5

Barillot, Jacques, F-19

Barillot, Jacques, N-9

Barillot, Jacques-Alain, S1-38

Barillot, Jean, C-5

Barillot, Jean, E-20

Barillot, Jean, F-19

Barillot, Jean, N-9

Barillot, Jean Baptiste, C-5, 18

Barillot, Jean Baptiste, F-19

Barillot, Jean Baptiste, N-9

Barillot, Jean Baptiste, S3-840, 1047

Barillot, Jean-Baptiste, S1-38-40, 110, 239

Barillot, Jean-Baptiste, S2-667, 670

Barillot, Jean-Marie, S1-38

Barillot, Jean-Pierre, S1-38

Barillot, Jeanne, E-525

Barillot, Joseph Marie, N-9

Barillot, Joseph-Marie, S1-40

Barillot, Louis Constant, N-9

Barillot, Marguerite, N-56

Barillot, Marguerite, S1-266, 271

Barillot, Marie, C-18, 45

Barillot, Marie, E-497

Barillot, Marie, F-67

Barillot, Marie, N-71

Barillot, Marie, S1-38, 110, 125, 134, 251, 299

Barillot, Marie, S2-522

Barillot, Marie-Blanche, S1-233-234

Barillot, Marie-Blanche, S2-667

Barillot, Marie-Rose, S1-38

Barillot, Martaise, S2-522

Barillot, Nicolas, E-472, 522

Barillot, Olivee, S3-847-848, 850

Barillot, Olivier, S1-39-40, 99, 270

Barillot, Olivier, S2-522, 538-539, 754

Barillot, Olivier, S3-834-835, 839-840, 846, 851, 1047, 1127

Barillot, Pelagie, C-17-18

Barillot, Pelagie, F-77

Barillot, Pelagie, N-24-25

Barillot, Pelagie, S1-110, 299, 359

Barillot, Pelagie, S3-845

Barillot, Perinne, S1-39

Barillot, Perrine, F-19

Barillot, Perrine, N-9

Barillot, Perrinne, C-5

Barillot, Pierre, C-5, 15, 17, 38

Barillot, Pierre, F-9, 19, 43, 77

Barillot, Pierre, N-38, 202

Barillot, Pierre, S1-38-39, 98, 110, 233, 298

Barillot, Pierre, S2-544

Barillot, Pierre, S3-835, 840, 843, 845, 851-852, 1047

Barillot, Praxede, E-340

Barillot, Praxede, S1-358

Barillot, Therese, S1-39

Barisson, Jean, E-279, 412

Baritau, Jean Baptiste, E-21, 156

Bariteau, Michel, E-20, 325

Barlataye, Maurice, E-314

Barnabe, Ambroise, E-21

Barnabe, Marie, E-286

Barnabe, Marie Jeanne, E-21

Barnabe Village named after Barnabe Martin, E-213

Barnaud, Andre, E-418

Barodeau, Francois, E-20

Barois, Marie Marguerite Genevieve, E-432

Baron, Andre, E-155, 157

Baron, Angelique, E-21, 411

Baron, Catherine, E-81, 353

Baron, Jeanne, E-160, 413

Baron, Marie, E-21, 418

Baron, Nicolas, E-21, 353

Baron, Pierre, E-13, 21, 52, 319, 411, 430

Baron , Catherine, E-21

Barousse, Jean, E-22, 330

Barquet, Mr., E-282

Barraud, Antoinette, E-21

Barraud, Jean, E-21

Barrayte, Francois, E-635

Barre, Francois Jean, E-584, 593

Barre, Jean, S1-41, 75

Barre, Rene, E-21, 36, 430

Barre, Thomas, S1-41

Barreau, Andre, E-21

Barreau, Francois, E-21

Barreau, Jean, E-21, 259, 354, 409

Barreau, Marianne, E-21, 159

Barreau, Marie, E-159, 377

Barreau, Marie Marguerite, E-21

Barreau, Monique, C-vii-viii, xi

Barreau, Pierre, E-21

Barreau, Suzanne, E-155

Barret, Jeanne, E-120, 384

Barriere, Marie, E-275, 294, 380

Barriere, Sieur, E-160

Barron, Catherine Charlotte, E-21

Barron, Jean, E-21

Barron, Julline-Marie-Solain, S1-323

Barry, Jeanne, N-37, 204

Bartellier, Marie, E-195

Barto, Anne, E-195

Bartran or Bertrand, Francois, E-22

Bartran or Bertrand, Renee, E-22

Baschamps, -----, S3-915

Basere, Anne, E-338, 344

Basillon, Jeanne, E-584, 593

Basire, Marie, E-145

Basle, Jeanne, S3-996

Basle, Pierre, S3-996

Basmeuil, Rene, S1-41

Basse, Francois, C-6, 87, 134-135

Basse, Jacques Philipe, C-6, 134

Basse, Jeanne, C-6

Basse, Rose Sophie, C-6

Basset, Charles, E-22

Basset, Francois, C-72

Basset, Francois, F-71

Basset, Francois, N-9-10

Basset, Jacques, E-294

INDEX SOURCES C=Chatellerault; E=Acadians in Exile; F=Acadian Families; N=Nantes; S=St-Malo

Basset, Marie, F-71
Basset, Marie, N-10
Basset, Perinne, S2-429, 436
Basset, Perinne, S3-1043
Basset, Perrine, N-79
Basset, Perrinne, C-51
Basset, Pierre, C-51
Basset, Pierre, E-13, 22
Basset, Pierre, S2-429
Basset, Pierre, S3-1043
Basset, Pierre-Joseph, S1-312
Basset, Rose, N-10
Bassicot, Francoise, E-309
Bastarache, Francois, E-214
Bastarache, Jean, E-472, 601
Bastarache, Jeanne, E-181, 601
Bastarache - village named for
  Jean Bastarache, E-214
Baste, Etiennette, S2-780
Baste, Jan Barthelemi, S3-1014
Baste, Janne, S3-1014
Baste, Jean Baptiste, N-173
Baste, Jean-Barthelemi, S2-780
Baste, Jeanne, N-173
Baste, Jeanne, S2-780
Bastra, Marguerite, E-142, 148
Batazar, Joseph, E-133
Bateau, Marie, E-349
Batenioux, Antoine, E-22
Batiny, Jeanne, E-345
Batonnet, Joseph, E-22, 294
Baucher, Jeanne, E-22, 349
Baucher, Marie Madeleine, E-
  125, 390
Baucher, Marie Marguerite, E-
  275
Baucher, Marie Reine, E-20,
  71332, 346
Baucher, Parnelle Reyne, E-72,
  344
Baucher, Renee, E-287
Baudard, Marie, E-412
Baude, Anselme, C-112
Baudeau, Adelaide, C-7
Baudeau, Adelaide, E-635
Baudeau, Francois, E-635
Baudeau, Francois-Marie, C-6
Baudeau, Gabriel, C-6, 106
Baudeau, Marie, C-7
Baudeau, Marie, E-635
Baudeau, Marie Thereze, C-7

Baudeau, Rene, C-6, 106
Baudelle, Marie Anne, E-148
Baudeloche, Francois, N-213
Baudeloche, Francois, S3-1151
Baudereau, Marie Madeleine, E-
  136
Baudes, Jean, E-64
Baudet, Ancelme, C-95
Baudet, Andre, E-22
Baudet, Jean, E-22, 349, 433
Baudet, Louis, S3-1150
Baudet, Marie, E-22, 433
Baudin, Jean, E-302
Baudin, Marguerite, E-11
Baudon, Marie Therese, E-334
Baudouard, Jean, S3-881, 884,
  886-888, 890, 892, 897, 901
Baudouard, Pierre, S3-875-877
Baudouin, Guy, E-22, 150
Baudouin, Helene, E-432
Baudouin, Marie Anne, E-15,
  150
Baudouin, Marie Jeanne, E-22,
  150
Baudouin, Mr., E-138
Baudouin, Pierre, E-145, 276
Baudouin, Rose, E-138
Baudro, Alexandre, E-147
Baudro, Pierre, E-147
Baudry, Anne, E-97, 295
Baudry, Elisabeth, E-57-58, 290
Baudry, Etienne, S2-548
Baudry, Francois, E-333
Baudry, Francoise, E-290, 390
Baudry, Genevieve, E-22, 328
Baudry, Guillaume Prosper, E-
  22
Baudry, Isabelle, E-1, 630
Baudry, Isabelle Marguerite, E-
  55
Baudry, Jean, E-91
Baudry, Jean Baptiste, E-22
Baudry, Jean Marie, E-191
Baudry, Jeanne, S1-186
Baudry, Jeanne, S2-770
Baudry, Joseph, E-307
Baudry, Marguerite, E-301, 385
Baudry, Marie, E-90, 149, 637
Baudry, Pierre, E-22, 328
Baudry, Toussain, E-142

Baujoin, Marie Marguerite, E-
  314, 386
Baule, Catherine, E-21
Baulien, Helene, E-22
Baulien, Louis, E-22
Baulu, Gabriel Louis, E-635
Baulu, Jean, E-635
Baulu, Louis, C-102
Baulu, Marie, E-635
Baulu, Martin, E-635
Baulu, Pierre, E-635
Baulu, Rosalie, E-635
Baure, Anne, S1-42
Baure, Anne, S3-914
Bautodier, Elisabeth, E-78, 376
Baye, Augustin, E-69
Baye, Joseph, F-69
Bayeau, Marie, E-394
Bayeau, Raymond, E-394
Bayneau, Elisabeth Eleonore, E-
  432
Bayou, Rose, E-456
Bazert, Louis, E-81, 259
Bazert, Louis, S2-516
Bazile, Guillemette, S2-731
Bazile, Louise, S2-597
Bazile, Michel, E-644
Bazile, Perinne-Marie-Felicite,
  S1-183
Bazille, Jeanne, E-254, 441
Bazin, Jacques Christophe, E-
  22, 279
Bazin, Mathurine, S2-474
Beau, Elizabeth, E-350
Beau, Felix, E-628
Beau, Jeanne, E-25, 409
Beau, Joseph, E-22
Beau-Pied, Maurille, S3-904
Beaubassin, Philippe, E-120
Beaubassin, Philippe, S1-281
Beaubois, Helene, E-158
Beauchamp, -----, E-37
Beauchamp, Louis, E-22
Beauchamps, Francois, E-1, 22,
  330
Beauchamps, Jeanne, E-328,
  392
Beauchamps, Louis, E-330
Beauche, Genevieve, E-306, 346
Beauche, Jeanne, E-22, 152,
  174, 358

144

INDEX SOURCES C=Chatellerault; E=Acadians in Exile; F=Acadian Families; N=Nantes; S=St-Malo

Beaudon, Andre, E-168
Beaudry, Jacques, E-72
Beaugendre, Pierre, S2-645
Beaugendre, Pierre, S3-1054
Beaulac, Mr., E-387
Beaulien, Pierre, E-117
Beaulieu, Anastasie, E-23
Beaulieu, Anne, E-23
Beaulieu, Francois, E-22
Beaulieu, Froisine, E-23
Beaulieu, Helene, E-23
Beaulieu, Jean Louis, E-23
Beaulieu, Louis, E-23, 342
Beaulieu, Louis Fontaine
  surnamed Beaulieu, E-214
Beaulieu, Marie, E-23
Beaulieu, Marie Anne, E-23
Beaulieu, Pierre, E-23
Beaulieu, Susanne Marguerite,
  E-23
Beaulieu-Collet, Marie, S1-205-
206
Beaumanoir, Jan, S3-929
Beaumanoir, Jean, S2-777
Beaumont, Amand-Henry, S1-
42
Beaumont, Cecile, E-617
Beaumont, Francois, E-620
Beaumont, Henriette, E-620
Beaumont, Jean, E-23
Beaumont, Marguerite, E-23, 82
Beaumont, Marie Adelaide, E-
621
Beaumont, Marie-Adelaide, S1-
42
Beaumont, Michel, E-620, 621
Beaumont, Michel, S1-41-42,
184
Beaumont, Michel, S2-505
Beaumont, Michel, S3-1068
Beaumont, Michel Simon, E-
621
Beaumont, Michel-Simon, S1-
42, 184
Beaumont, Rosalie, S1-41-42
Beaumont, Rosalie, S2-505, 557
Beaunne, Maricheau (Father),
C-127-128
Beaupied, Maurille, C-29
Beaupied, Maurille, S1-255

Beaupre - founded by Rene
  Richard, E-214
Beaurin, Elisabeth, E-120, 384
Beauromain, Marie, S2-515
Beauromain, Marie, S3-984
Beaury, John, S1-42
Beaury, Louis-Joseph, S1-43
Beaury, Louise-Pelagie, S1-43
Beaury, Marie Rose, E-617
Beaury, Marie-Modeste, S1-42
Beaury, Marie-Rose, S1-42
Beaury, Pierre, S1-37, 42, 43
Beaussett, Marie Anne, E-90,
375
Beautier, Louis, E-342
Beautier, Pierre, E-342
Beauvais, Jeanne-Francoise, S1-
50
Becet, Francoise, S2-607
Becet, Francoise, S3-996
Bechet, Georges Louis, E-281
Bechevalur, Jeanne, E-37
Beciere, Raymon, E-426
Becognie, Rene, C-103
Becque Dit Belleamour, Pierre,
E-23
Bedeau, Louis, E-295, 344
Bedefer, Julien, S3-872
Bedel, Antoine, S3-1073, 1079
Bedel, Eustache, S1-43, 325
Bedel, Eustache, S3-1101
Bedel, Marguerite, C-16, 154
Bedel, Marguerite, F-53
Bedel, Marguerite, N-21
Bedel, Suzanne, S2-674
Bedex, Marie Josephe, E-138,
415
Bedouin, Etienne, S1-44
Beduneau, Anne Francoise, E-
24, 329
Beduneau, Louis, E-24
Beduseau, Marie, E-12, 109
Begaud, Francoise-Victoire, S1-
44
Begaud, Jacques, S1-44
Begaud, Louise-Marie, S1-44
Begaud, Pierre, S1-44
Begue, Anne, E-366
Beii, Rene, E-156
Beillard, Madeleine, E-12, 168
Belair, Antoine, E-24

Belair, Pierre, E-24, 38, 301,
442
Belanger, Marguerite, E-304
Belanger, Marie, E-432
Belee, Francois, S1-44-45
Belee, Nicolas, S1-44-45
Belet, Jean, E-143
Beliard, Jean, N-219
Beliard, Joseph, N-10, 109, 219,
222, 229
Beliard, Mathurin, N-10, 219
Belile, Jeanne, C-72
Belin, Marie, E-24, 348, 418
Belin, Pierre, N-193
Belineau, Jean, E-522
Belino, Judith, E-43
Beliot, Yves, S3-1128, 1133,
1137-1138
Belisle, E-213
Belisle, Anne, E-25, 409
Beliveau, Anne, E-24, 162, 165-
166, 381
Beliveau, Antoine, E-456, 472,
496
Beliveau, Athanaze, E-24
Beliveau, Catherine, E-24
Beliveau, Charles, E-496
Beliveau, Jean, E-472, 496
Beliveau, Jean Baptiste, E-24
Beliveau, Joseph, E-24
Beliveau, Judith, S1-115
Beliveau, Judith, S2-430
Beliveau, Judithe, E-43-44
Beliveau, Louis, E-24, 47, 178
Beliveau, Louis, E-79
Beliveau, Louis, S1-199
Beliveau, Louise, E-116, 118
Beliveau, Magdelaine, E-164,
344-346, 496
Beliveau, Marie, E-61, 272, 271,
273
Beliveau, Marie, S1-336
Beliveau, Rose, E-24, 294
Bellaire, Pierre, E-23, 268
Bellec, Pierre, E-25
Bellefontaine, Anastasie, C-33,
81
Bellefontaine, Anastasie, E-323,
346
Bellefontaine, Joseph de, E-603

Bellefontaine, Michel, E-121, 439
Bellefontaine, Michel, S1-283
Bellemere, Anastasie, C-15-17, 72
Bellemere, Anastasie, F-53
Bellemere, Anastasie, N-21, 42, 205
Bellemere, Anastasie, S1-45, 104
Bellemere, Anne-Marie, S1-47
Bellemere, Bruno, C-7
Bellemere, Bruno, S1-45-47, 341, 350
Bellemere, Felicite, E-621
Bellemere, Felicite, S1-46
Bellemere, Jacques, F-53
Bellemere, Jacques, N-42, 115, 205
Bellemere, Jean, S1-47
Bellemere, Jean-Baptiste, S1-47
Bellemere, Jean-Jacques, S1-46
Bellemere, Jean-Pierre, S1-45
Bellemere, Jeanne, N-34
Bellemere, Jeanne, S1-161
Bellemere, Jeanne, S2-675
Bellemere, Joseph, S1-45-47, 107
Bellemere, Josephe-Marie, S1-45
Bellemere, Marguerite, E-282-283, 285, 288, 567
Bellemere, Marguerite, F-37
Bellemere, Marguerite, N-115, 117, 181
Bellemere, Marguerite, S2-565-566
Bellemere, Marie, C-15
Bellemere, Marie, S1-47, 58, 324
Bellemere, Marie Josephe, F-37
Bellemere, Marie Marguerite, C-7
Bellemere, Marie-Marguerite, S1-45-47
Bellemere, Michelle-Francoise, S1-45
Bellemere, Perinne-Victoire, S1-46
Bellemere, Pierre, E-25
Bellemere, Pierre, S1-45-46

Bellemere, Rosalie-Genevieve, S1-45
Beller, Antoine, E-309
Bellet, Jean, E-153
Bellette, Mathieu, E-25
Bellette, Pierre, E-25
Belliard, Michel, E-17
Bellier, Marie, E-112
Bellino, Judith, E-41, 44
Bellion, Anne Gene dite, E-35
Bellot, Francois, E-25, 34, 318
Bellotte, Marie, S1-279
Bellotte, Perinne, S1-279
Bellotte, Perinne, S3-1084
Belly, Anne, E-409
Belly, Elizabeth, N-152, 193
Belmer, Josef, S3-1021
Belmere, Joseph, S2-622
Beloin, Susanne, E-86, 266, 123, 283, 291, 378
Beloin, Suzanne, S1-215
Belon, Elisabeth, E-584, 593
Belou, Jacque, E-456
Belvin, Susanne, E-127, 259, 315
Belvin, Susanne, S2-516
Belvin, Suzanne, S1-308
Benard, Ambroise Constantin, E-25, 56
Benard, Anne, F-81
Benard, Anne, S1-363
Benard, Anne, S2-510
Benard, Anne, S3-1007
Benard, Augustin, E-108
Benard, Jean, E-359
Benard, Jean Joseph, E-108
Benard, Joseph, F-65, 81
Benard, Joseph, S1-195
Benard, Julien Jacques, E-25, 56
Benard, Marguerite, N-224
Benard, Marie, F-63, 65, 81
Benard, Martin, F-81
Benard, Pierre, S1-363
Benard, Pierre, S3-1007
Benard, Pierre Duguen, E-389
Benard, Rene, N-219
Benatre, Adrien, S2-436
Benatre, Francois, S3-1093
Benet, Catherine, E-25, 265
Beneteau, Pierre, E-275
Benicour, Felicite, E-45

Benin, Pierre, N-193
Benoist, Abraham, S1-55
Benoist, Adelaide, S1-50
Benoist, Anastasie, C-16
Benoist, Anne, C-1, 52, 57, 66, 74, 124
Benoist, Anne, E-25, 185, 313
Benoist, Anne, F-33, 55
Benoist, Anne, N-81, 92, 112, 250
Benoist, Anne, S1-48, 50-51, 53-55, 222
Benoist, Anne, S2-437, 460, 475-476, 556-557, 768
Benoist, Anne, S3-963, 988, 1012, 1062, 1065
Benoist, Anne Marie, E-25, 119, 433, 435-437, 637
Benoist, Anne-Marie, S1-50, 288-289, 293
Benoist, Augustin, C-7-8
Benoist, Augustin, E-25, 436
Benoist, Augustin, F-55
Benoist, Augustin, N-10
Benoist, Augustin, S1-47-50, 52, 55, 346
Benoist, Augustin, S2-505, 587, 751
Benoist, Augustin, S3-974, 1000, 1022, 1046, 1063
Benoist, Ausite Blanche, E-26, 352
Benoist, Baptiste, S1-53-54
Benoist, Catherine, E-26, 97, 153, 349, 412, 415-416
Benoist, Catherine, S2-647
Benoist, Charles, C-9
Benoist, Charles, E-27
Benoist, Charles, F-53, 55, 75
Benoist, Charles, S1-50-52, 54-55, 187
Benoist, Charles, S2-463, 526, 688
Benoist, Charles, S3-833, 963, 1022, 1059, 1071
Benoist, Claire, E-286
Benoist, Claude, C-8, 28, 52, 86
Benoist, Claude, E-522
Benoist, Claude, F-9, 61, 71
Benoist, Claude, N-11, 81
Benoist, Claude, S1-49, 52, 222

Benoist, Claude, S2-437
Benoist, Claude, S3-974, 1012, 1046, 1063
Benoist, Clement, E-26-27, 492, **522**
Benoist, Daniel, C-8, 16, 138
Benoist, Daniel, F-9
Benoist, Daniel, N-11, 198, 245
Benoist, Daniel, S1-48, 52, 222
Benoist, Daniel, S2-581
Benoist, Daniel, S3-948, 1022, 1046, 1063
Benoist, Daniel Henry, C-8
Benoist, Daniel-Henry, S1-52
Benoist, Desiree, E-136
Benoist, Desiree Elisabeth, E-26
Benoist, Donatien, N-11
Benoist, Donnatien, F-61
Benoist, Elisabeth, E-26-27
Benoist, Elisabeth, S3-1013
Benoist, Elizabeth, S1-48
Benoist, Elizabeth, S2-709
Benoist, Etienne, E-26-27, 349
Benoist, Francois, C-8
Benoist, Francois, E-255
Benoist, Francois, N-11
Benoist, Francois, S1-50
Benoist, Francois Rene, F-75
Benoist, Francois-Jean-Baptiste, S1-48
Benoist, Francoise, F-15, 17, 55, 61, 87, 95
Benoist, Francoise, N-11, 31, 56, 88, 91, 233
Benoist, Francoise, S1-51, 53, 140-141, 153, 187, 266, 271, 350
Benoist, Francoise, S2-462, 464, 556, 585
Benoist, Francoise, S3-879, 963, 1133, 1137
Benoist, Francoise-Apollonie, S1-49
Benoist, Genevieve, E-26, 127
Benoist, Gregoire, C-8-9, 28
Benoist, Gregoire, F-61
Benoist, Gregoire, N-11, 245-246
Benoist, Gregoire, S1-52-53, 189, 233
Benoist, Gregoire, S2-437

Benoist, Gregoire, S3-988, 1012, 1022, 1062-1063
Benoist, Guillaume, N-188
Benoist, Henriette, F-9
Benoist, Henriette Reine, N-11
Benoist, Isabelle, F-99
Benoist, Isabelle, S1-53-54, 328
Benoist, Isabelle, S2-459, 464, 484
Benoist, Izabelle, S3-926
Benoist, Jacques, E-26-27, 34, 136-140, 383, 405
Benoist, Jacquette, E-492
Benoist, Jaqueline, E-473
Benoist, Jean, C-131
Benoist, Jean, E-25-26, 313, 352, 383, 492, 522
Benoist, Jean, S1-51, 53-54
Benoist, Jean Charles, C-9
Benoist, Jean Charles, F-75, 111
Benoist, Jean Charles, N-250
Benoist, Jean Louis, E-26
Benoist, Jean Marie, C-9
Benoist, Jean Marie, F-61, 75
Benoist, Jean Marie, N-11
Benoist, Jean Marie Augustin, N-10
Benoist, Jean-Charles, S1-51, 54
Benoist, Jean-Charles, S2-434
Benoist, Jean-Louis, S1-53-54
Benoist, Jean-Marie, S1-53-54
Benoist, Jean-Marie-Augustin, S1-48
Benoist, Jeanne-Eleonore-Anastasie, S1-52
Benoist, Joseph, E-26
Benoist, Joseph, S1-53-54
Benoist, Joseph, S3-975
Benoist, Joseph Marc, E-26
Benoist, Joseph Marie, C-8
Benoist, Joseph-Francois, S1-53
Benoist, Josephe Marie, N-11
Benoist, Judith, S1-51, 55
Benoist, Julien, S2-729
Benoist, Jullien, S3-975
Benoist, Lazare, S1-54
Benoist, Louis-Marie, S1-50
Benoist, Madeleine, S2-609-610
Benoist, Magdelaine, S3-1089
Benoist, Marguerite, C-26, 28, 39, 73, 86, 138

Benoist, Marguerite, F-11, 71, 85
Benoist, Marguerite, N-24, 62, 98, 217, 223
Benoist, Marguerite, S1-48, 200, 223, 291-292, 295, 300
Benoist, Marguerite, S2-432, 437, 440-441, 596
Benoist, Marguerite, S3-961, 1031, 1081, 1121
Benoist, Marie, E-26, 36, 296-297, 333, 378, 584, 592
Benoist, Marie, F-5, 53, 81
Benoist, Marie, N-61
Benoist, Marie, S1-51, 54, 111, 187
Benoist, Marie, S2-463-464, 518, 556, 688-689, 731
Benoist, Marie, S3-940, 948, 950, 1022, 1045
Benoist, Marie Anne, E-26
Benoist, Marie Catherine, E-27
Benoist, Marie Claire, E-282-283
Benoist, Marie Jullienne, S3-975
Benoist, Marie Louise, E-26
Benoist, Marie Madeleine, E-27
Benoist, Marie Marthe, C-1, 3, 78, 119, 127
Benoist, Marie Marthe, E-27, 153, 584, 596
Benoist, Marie Marthe, F-83, 109
Benoist, Marie Rose, C-8-9
Benoist, Marie Rose, F-61
Benoist, Marie Rose, N-11
Benoist, Marie Therese, E-27
Benoist, Marie-Jeanne, S1-49
Benoist, Marie-Julienne, S2-729
Benoist, Martin, E-27, 349, 472, 522
Benoist, Mathurin, C-8
Benoist, Mathurin, N-11
Benoist, Mathurin, S1-48
Benoist, Maurice, F-73
Benoist, Michel, E-584, 593
Benoist, Nicolas-Jean-Sebastien, S1-50
Benoist, Ozite, S1-53-54
Benoist, Paul, S1-54-55
Benoist, Paul Frederic, C-9

Benoist, Paul Frederic, F-75
Benoist, Pelagie, C-8, 28, 86
Benoist, Pelagie, F-63, 71
Benoist, Pelagie, S1-222-223
Benoist, Perinne-Jeanne, S1-48
Benoist, Pierre, C-7, 56
Benoist, Pierre, E-26-27, 127,
  255, 385, 492
Benoist, Pierre, F-33
Benoist, Pierre, N-10
Benoist, Pierre, S1-47, 50-51, 55
Benoist, Pierre, S2-460, 475
Benoist, Pierre, S3-1000, 1062
Benoist, Raymond, F-61
Benoist, Remond Gregoire, N-
  11
Benoist, Simon, S1-48
Benoist, Sophie, F-53
Benoist, Sophie Renee, F-75
Benoist, Valentine, E-136
Benoist, Victoire, F-55
Benoist, Victoire Marie, C-8
Benoist, Victoire Marie, N-11
Benoist, Victoire-Marie, S1-49
Benon, Jean, E-584, 593
Benon, Marie, E-584, 593
Benvit, Desire, E-136
Bera, Rene, E-29
Beranger, Alexis, E-27, 319
Beranger, Alice, E-27
Beranger, Jean, E-27, 320
Beranger, Joseph, E-27
Beranger, Pierre, E-27
Beranne, Pierre, C-122
Beraud, Pierre, E-356
Beraud, Therese, E-344, 392
Berbadeau, Marie, E-73
Berbudeau, Jean, C-9
Berbudeau, Jean Gabriel, C-9,
  95
Berbudeau, Magdelaine, E-419
Berbudeau, Marie Anne, C-75
Berbudeau, Marie Reine, C-6, 9,
  24, 75-76, 95
Berbudeau, Marie Reine, E-635
Berbudeau, Paris, C-119
Berelihouine, Suzanne Marie, E-
  369
Beret, Ambroise, E-12, 27
Beret, Nicolas, E-27
Bergaud, Francoise, E-317

Berge, Pierre, E-38
Bergeau, Isabelle, S2-737
Bergeau, Isabelle, S3-973
Berger, Marie Anne Chuffel, E-
  120
Bergeron, Jean, E-406
Bergeron, Marie Anne, E-603
Bergle, Stiagia, N-152, 226
Bergon, Francoise, E-27
Berloin, Susanne, E-104, 169,
  255, 341, 376
Berloin, Suzanne, S1-375
Berloin, Suzanne, S2-513, 688
Berluquet, Jean Baptiste, E-27,
  139
Berluquet, Pierre, E-27, 139
Bernaiche, Gratienne, S1-264
Bernard, -----, E-27
Bernard, Anne Marie, C-84
Bernard, Anne Marie, E-193,
  367
Bernard, Anne Marie, N-70, 146
Bernard, Arnaud, E-28, 304
Bernard, Dominique, E-27
Bernard, Elisabeth, E-59, 72,
  134, 155, 348, 368, 412
Bernard, Etienne, E-28, 369
Bernard, Eutrope, E-28
Bernard, Francois, E-28, 332
Bernard, Francoise, S1-71
Bernard, Helene, E-28
Bernard, Henriette, S2-544-545
Bernard, indian, E-142
Bernard, Jacques, E-28, 30, 134
Bernard, Jean, E-28, 126
Bernard, Jean Baptiste, E-192
Bernard, Jeanne, E-28, 73, 189,
  369, 385, 584, 594
Bernard, Joseph, S3-1102
Bernard, Laurent, E-28
Bernard, Louis, E-27-28, 70,
  321, 342, 406
Bernard, Madelaine, E-584, 594
Bernard, Marianne, E-132
Bernard, Marie, E-28, 84, 192-
  194, 255-256, 584, 594
Bernard, Marie, F-35
Bernard, Marie, N-94-95, 200,
  207
Bernard, Marie, S2-698

Bernard, Marie Anne, E-28,
  134, 379
Bernard, Marie Blanche, C-35
Bernard, Marie Blanche, E-113-
  114, 192
Bernard, Marie Blanche, F-35
Bernard, Marie Blanche, N-57
Bernard, Marie Charlotte, E-28
Bernard, Marie Elizabeth, E-30
Bernard, Marie Magdalen, E-
  192, 194
Bernard, Marie Magdeleine, C-
  58-59
Bernard, Mr., E-369
Bernard, Pierre, C-84
Bernard, Pierre, E-28, 137, 156,
  256, 304
Bernard, Pierre, S2-544
Bernard, Radegonde, E-28
Bernard, Rene, C-58
Bernard, Rene, E-28, 522
Bernard, Rene, S1-94
Bernard, Servanne, E-295, 417
Bernard, Simon, E-28
Bernard, Therese, E-134
Bernard, Ursule, E-28, 584, 594
Bernardeau, Jeanne, N-83, 228
Bernardeau, Joseph, C-65
Bernardo, Guillaume, E-14
Berni, Jaques, E-584, 597
Bernier, Charles, E-379
Berrurier, Pierre, E-120
Berry, Jacques, C-152
Berry, Marie Rose, E-617
Berry, Pierre, C-152
Bersonine, Marie Felix, E-28,
  357
Bersonine, Pierre, E-28, 357
Bersouine, Felicite, E-295
Bersouine, Marie, E-120, 384
Bertau, Josephe, S2-560
Bertaud, Francoise, N-247
Bertaud, Marie-Josephe, S2-602,
  604
Berteau, Agathe, E-166
Berteau, Anne, E-18, 29, 289,
  328
Berteau, Anne, S2-627
Berteau, Antoine, E-29
Berteau, Antoinette Francoise,
  E-29

Berteau, Fancion, E-29
Berteau, Francois, E-26, 107
Berteau, Francoise, E-29, 145, 318, 351
Berteau, Gabriel, E-5
Berteau, Gabrielle, E-3
Berteau, Gregoire, E-29
Berteau, Guillaume, E-326, 436
Berteau, Jacob, E-373
Berteau, Jacques, E-29, 145
Berteau, Jean Baptiste, E-29
Berteau, Joseph Antoine, E-329
Berteau, Marguerite, E-29, 145, 586, 591
Berteau, Marguerite Antoinette, E-29
Berteau, Marie, E-140, 153, 383, 391, 584, 595
Berteau, Marie Anne, E-29
Berteau, Marie Gabriel, E-29
Berteau, Marie Rose, E-29
Berteau, Marie Suray, E-3, 5
Berteau, Marie-Rose, S2-627
Berteau, Pierre, E-29, 145, 351
Berteau, Pierre Thomas, E-29
Berteau, Therese, E-29, 420
Bertelay, Jacques, E-114
Bertelet, Pierre, E-389
Bertet, Marguerite, E-29, 174
Berthe, Marie, E-195
Berthelot, Dubois, E-102
Berthelot, Jean, E-29, 172, 254
Berthelot, Marie, E-29, 254
Berthelot, Pierre, E-265
Berthelot, Pierre, S2-595
Berthelot, Pierre, S3-990
Berthelot, Susanne Olive, S3-990, 1029
Berthelot, Susanne-Olive, S2-595
Berthemin, Joseph, E-405
Berthome, Pierre, E-36
Berthult, Antoine, E-158
Bertin, Andre, E-30
Bertin, Louis, E-30-31, 268
Bertin, Marie, E-26
Berton, Jean, C-xiii
Bertrand, Adelaide, F-19
Bertrand, Adelaide, N-13
Bertrand, Alexandre, E-30

Bertrand, Ambroise Belony, F-19
Bertrand, Ambroise Belony, N-13
Bertrand, Ambroise Benony, E-30
Bertrand, Angelique, C-13
Bertrand, Angelique, E-33
Bertrand, Anne, E-328
Bertrand, Anne Madeleine, N-13
Bertrand, Anne Magdelaine, F-19
Bertrand, Antoine, E-31-32
Bertrand, Benony, C-11
Bertrand, Benony, N-13
Bertrand, Catherine, E-17
Bertrand, Catherine, F-19
Bertrand, Catherine, N-13
Bertrand, Charles, E-274
Bertrand, Charles, N-12
Bertrand, Claude, E-472
Bertrand, Clement, E-456
Bertrand, Cosme, E-30
Bertrand, Eustache, C-10
Bertrand, Eustache, E-30-31, 273
Bertrand, Eustache, F-75
Bertrand, Eustache, N-11-12, 177
Bertrand, Francois, E-30-31, 97
Bertrand, Francois, N-13
Bertrand, Genevieve Adelaide Francoise, E-30
Bertrand, Gregoire, E-30-31
Bertrand, Guillaume Eustache, N-12
Bertrand, Jacques, C-10
Bertrand, Jean, C-10
Bertrand, Jean, E-30-31, 119, 139, 153, 313, 356
Bertrand, Jean, F-73, 75
Bertrand, Jean, N-12
Bertrand, Jean Augustin, C-11
Bertrand, Jean Augustin, E-30
Bertrand, Jean Augustin, F-19
Bertrand, Jean Augustin, N-13
Bertrand, Jean Baptiste, E-30
Bertrand, Jean Baptiste Leonor, E-30
Bertrand, Jean Francois, E-90
Bertrand, Jean Nicolas, N-12

Bertrand, Jean Pierre, C-91
Bertrand, Joseph, N-12
Bertrand, Josephe, E-125
Bertrand, Josephe, E-392
Bertrand, Leonor Jean Baptiste, E-31
Bertrand, Louis, F-19
Bertrand, Louis, N-13
Bertrand, Louis Martin, F-75
Bertrand, Louis Martin, N-12
Bertrand, Madeleine Marguerite, C-10
Bertrand, Madeleine Marguerite, N-12
Bertrand, Magdelaine, F-75
Bertrand, Magdeleine, E-150, 356
Bertrand, Marguerite, E-72, 97, 295, 344
Bertrand, Marguerite Lucie, N-12
Bertrand, Marguerite Lucile, C-10
Bertrand, Marianne, E-30
Bertrand, Marie, C-11
Bertrand, Marie, E-31-31, 55, 65, 121, 167, 270, 291, 292, 604
Bertrand, Marie, F-19
Bertrand, Marie, N-13
Bertrand, Marie, S1-283
Bertrand, Marie Anne, E-30-31
Bertrand, Marie Blanche, E-114
Bertrand, Marie Catherine, C-11
Bertrand, Marie Catherine, E-31
Bertrand, Marie Catherine, N-13
Bertrand, Marie Francoise, E-31, 301
Bertrand, Marie Genevieve, C-10
Bertrand, Marie Genevieve, E-31
Bertrand, Marie Genevieve, F-75
Bertrand, Marie Genevieve, N-12
Bertrand, Marie Jeanne, E-31
Bertrand, Marie Josephe, E-1, 17, 31, 97, 101, 109, 118, 300, 392
Bertrand, Marie Josephe, F-75

Bertrand, Marie Louise, E-17
Bertrand, Marie Louise, N-12
Bertrand, Marie Marguerite, E-31
Bertrand, Marie Modeste, E-31
Bertrand, Marie Modeste, N-12
Bertrand, Marie Renee, E-306
Bertrand, Marie Rose, E-313
Bertrand, Marie-Anne, C-10
Bertrand, Michel, E-31, 109
Bertrand, Philippe, E-31, 115, 317
Bertrand, Pierre, C-10, 153
Bertrand, Pierre, E-30-31, 47, 109, 153, 358
Bertrand, Pierre, F-19
Bertrand, Pierre, N-13
Bertrand, Pierre Antoine, E-32
Bertrand, Pierre Etienne, E-31, 301
Bertrand, Pierre Jacques, C-10-11
Bertrand, Pierre Jacques, E-30
Bertrand, Pierre Joseph, C-11
Bertrand, Pierre Joseph, N-13
Bertrand, Renee, E-19, 105, 300, 392
Bertrand, Renote, E-92, 392
Bertrand, Ursule, E-30
Bertre, Marie, S1-6
Berty, Anne, C-164
Bery, Alexis, N-234
Bery, Magdeleine, C-30, 152
Bescan, Pierre, E-169, 172
Besiaud, Francois, E-386
Beslievre, Catherine, S1-55
Beslievre, Jeanne, S1-55-56
Beslievre, Louis, S1-55
Beslievre, Marie-Madeleine, S1-56
Beslievre, Pierre, S1-55-56
Beslievre, Renee, S1-56
Besrest, Jeanne, S2-432
Besseliere, Pierre, S1-85
Besselievre, Jacques, E-35, 278
Bessier, Arnaud, E-280
Bessin, Janne, S3-1094
Bessin, Jeanne, S1-197
Besson, -----, E-5
Besson, Francois Marie, E-5
Besson, Honore, E-5

Besson, Jean, E-108
Besson, Marie, E-349, 394
Besson, Pierre, E-172, 262
Betancourt, Francois Michel, F-41
Betre, Pierre, S1-314
Bette, Jean Josse, E-32
Bette, Josse, E-32, 403
Beugnon, Mathurin, S1-166
Beurier, Jean, E-621
Beurier, Nicolas, E-621
Beurier, Pierre, E-621, 623
Beuron, Louis, E-621
Beuron, Madeleine Jeanne, E-621
Bezieau, Jacques (Mrs.), E-32
Bezieaux, Jacques, E-294, 348
Bezier, Francois, S1-335
Biayo, -----, S3-923
Biche, Jean, S1-222
Bichot, Claude Robert, E-436
Bidaut, Pierre, E-32, 357
Bidaut, Pierre Francois, E-32
Bidel, Francoise, E-91, 295
Bidou, Pierre, E-257
Bidoux, Jacques, E-177
Bie, Jean, E-32, 339
Bie, Jean Baptiste, E-32, 339
Bienvenue, -----, S3-958
Bienvenue, Francois Hyacinthe Cajetan, S3-957
Bieron, Rene, C-150
Biffaut, Jean, S1-56
Biffaut, Jean, S2-607
Biffaut, Jean, S3-996
Bige, Marie, S2-583, 587
Bigot, Marguerite, E-122, 441
Bigot, Mathieu, E-354
Bilaud, Michel Simon, E-183, 190
Bileraes, Joseph, S3-993
Billanon, Marie Jeanne, E-32
Billard, Anne, S1-57-58
Billard, Francoise, E-32
Billard, Francoise, S1-57-58
Billard, Jean Baptiste, E-584-585, 593
Billard, Jean-Baptiste-Marie, S1-57
Billard, Joachim-Jean, S1-58
Billard, Louis Charpentier, E-32

Billard, Louise, E-584-585, 593
Billard, Louise, S1-57-58
Billard, Marie, S1-192
Billard, Marie Rose, E-584-485, 593
Billard, Marie-Rose, S1-57-58
Billard, Pierre, E-32
Billard, Pierre, S1-57
Billard, Simon, E-28, 32, 70, 120, 255, 584-585, 593
Billard, Simon, S1-57-58, 190-191
Billard, Simon, S2-513
Billard, Simon, S3-979
Billardin, Etienne, F-59
Billardin, Lambert, F-59
Billardin, Marguerite, F-59
Billardin, Marie Jeanne, F-59, 91
Billau, Jacques, E-13
Billaud, Jeanne, E-405
Bille, Mr., E-375
Billeray, Anne Brigitte, E-554
Billeray, Anne-Brigitte, S1-58
Billeray, Charles, S1-58
Billeray, Claude-Joseph, S1-58-59
Billeray, Jean Joseph, E-554
Billeray, Jean-Claude, S1-58
Billeray, Jeanne, S1-58-59
Billeray, Joseph, E-331, 554
Billeray, Joseph-Jean, S1-58
Billeray, Marie Jeanne, E-554
Billeray, Mrie-Jeanne, S1-58
Billerey, Joseph, S3-871, 923, 993
Billie, J., E-375
Billon, Jean, E-172, 418
Bilz, Jeanne Marguerite, E-288-289
Bin, Madeleine, E-46
Bincur, Firmin, S3-927
Binet, Jean Jacques, E-361, 363
Binjamin, Francois, C-120
Biraud, Robert, E-441
Biron, Francois, E-32, 403
Biron Dit Lagelee, Gabriel, E-32, 403
Birot, Daniel, E-32, 73, 309
Birot, Marie Anne, E-90, 196
Biscondeguy, Catherine, E-32

INDEX SOURCES   C=Chatellerault;   E=Acadians in Exile;   F=Acadian Families;   N=Nantes;   S=St-Malo

Biscondeguy, Pierre, E-32
Biscuilet, Celestin, E-365
Biseuil, Jean Celestin, E-637
Bisson, Jacques-Sebastien, S1-59
Bisson, Jean, E-621
Bisson, Jean, S1-59
Bisson, Jean Baptiste, E-616
Bisson, Jeanne, S1-59
Bisson, Louis, E-616
Bisson, Louise, S1-59
Bisson, Marguerite, E-616
Bisson, Marie, E-621
Bisson, Marie, S1-59
Bisson, Simon, E-616
Bisson, Thomas, E-621
Bisson, Thomas, S1-59
Bisson, Victor, E-616
Bissonnau, Denys, S2-676
Biton, Angelique, E-72, 348
Bivier, Basile, E-286
Bizot, Jeanne, E-107
Black Cove now known as
  Karsdale, E-209
Black Point, E-209
Blain, Angelique, S1-60
Blain, Augustin, S1-60
Blain, Bertrand, S1-60
Blain, Francoise, E-31
Blain, Francoise, S1-60-61
Blain, Genevieve, S1-61
Blain, Guillemette, S1-62
Blain, Guilmette, E-366
Blain, Jacques, S1-60-61
Blain, Jean, S1-62
Blain, Jean-Francois, S1-61-62
Blain, Jean-Francois, S2-750
Blain, Jean-Francoise, S1-60
Blain, Joseph, S1-62
Blain, Joseph-Ignace, S1-61
Blain, Louis, S1-61
Blain, Madeleine, S1-61-62
Blain, Madeleine, S2-741
Blain, Marguerite, E-360, 366
Blain, Marguerite, S1-61-62
Blain, Marie, S1-62
Blain, Marie-Francoise, S1-61
Blais, Louis, E-333
Blanc, Marie Blanche, E-96
Blanchard, Agathe, E-359, 363,
  366

Blanchard, Agnes, E-598
Blanchard, Alexandre Joseph,
  N-17
Blanchard, Alexis, S1-62-63, 70
Blanchard, Alexis, S2-665
Blanchard, Ambroise, S1-66, 68,
  75
Blanchard, Angelique, C-132
Blanchard, Angelique, C-27, 80
Blanchard, Angelique, F-49, 51
Blanchard, Angelique, S2-636,
  638
Blanchard, Angelique, S3-1130
Blanchard, Angelique Michel,
  N-14
Blanchard, Anne, E-82-83, 474,
  490, 523, 525, 598
Blanchard, Anne, F-17, 73, 81
Blanchard, Anne, N-14, 16, 41-
  42
Blanchard, Anne, S1-15-16
Blanchard, Anne, S3-870, 1111
Blanchard, Anne Catherine, E-
  11
Blanchard, Anne Marie, C-89
Blanchard, Anne Marie, F-43
Blanchard, Anne Marie, N-151
Blanchard, Anne-Josephe, S1-68
Blanchard, Anne-Marie, S2-
  714-716
Blanchard, Anselme, E-32, 115
Blanchard, Anselme, S1-73
Blanchard, Anselme, S3-1026,
  1075
Blanchard, Antoine, E-490, 522
Blanchard, Bellarmin, S2-632
Blanchard, Belonnie, S3-888
Blanchard, Belony, N-13-14
Blanchard, Bennon, S3-1120
Blanchard, Benoit, F-81
Blanchard, Benony, C-11
Blanchard, Benony, S1-63-66,
  70, 304, 324
Blanchard, Benony-Jacques, S1-
  64
Blanchard, boy, S1-63
Blanchard, Celeste, F-81
Blanchard, Celeste, N-14
Blanchard, Charles, C-11-12
Blanchard, Charles, F-79, 109
Blanchard, Charles, N-14

Blanchard, Charles, S1-64-66,
  68, 70, 72, 74, 304
Blanchard, Charles, S3-1112
Blanchard, Charles-Pierre-Marc,
  S1-64
Blanchard, Charlotte, S1-222
Blanchard, Cirile-Henry, S1-73
Blanchard, Clotilde, E-32
Blanchard, Delle, E-383
Blanchard, Elenne, S3-874
Blanchard, Elie, F-17
Blanchard, Elisabeth, E-136,
  318, 382, 598
Blanchard, Elisabeth Felicite, E-
  32
Blanchard, Elizabeth, N-4-5,
  130, 241
Blanchard, Enselme, S3-1035
Blanchard, Etienne, N-13, 16
Blanchard, Etienne, S1-65
Blanchard, Etienne Charles
  Larie, C-11
Blanchard, Eudoxe-Marie-Gil-
  lette, S1-65
Blanchard, Felicite, E-598
Blanchard, Francis, C-12
Blanchard, Francois, E-33, 341
Blanchard, Francois, F-79
Blanchard, Francois, N-15, 237
Blanchard, Francois, S1-64-66,
  70, 72, 265, 357, 360
Blanchard, Francois, S2-624,
  715
Blanchard, Francois, S3-823,
  827-828, 1111-1112, 1127,
  1130
Blanchard, Francois Xavier, C-
  89
Blanchard, Francois Xavier, N-
  225
Blanchard, Francois Xavier, S3-
  899
Blanchard, Francois-Jean, S1-69
Blanchard, Francois-Xavier, S1-
  65, 71
Blanchard, Francois-Xavier, S2-
  542, 658, 715
Blanchard, Francoise, C-12, 35
Blanchard, Francoise, E-22, 33,
  279, 484, 567
Blanchard, Francoise, F-61, 79

Blanchard, Francoise, N-15, 120

Blanchard, Francoise, S1-257, 276

Blanchard, Francoise-Helene, S1-65

Blanchard, Germain, S1-21, 66-70

Blanchard, Germain, S3-823, 827, 846, 1107

Blanchard, girl, S1-73

Blanchard, Gregoire, S1-293

Blanchard, Guillaume, E-33, 96, 213, 255, 472, 522

Blanchard, Guillaume, S1-71

Blanchard, Heleine, C-21

Blanchard, Helene, F-93

Blanchard, Helene, N-3-4, 63, 66, 209, 221

Blanchard, Helene, S1-7-18, 28, 74, 266-267, 301, 303, 339

Blanchard, Helene, S3-871, 873

Blanchard, Isabelle, E-33

Blanchard, Isabelle, N-195

Blanchard, Isabelle, S1-176

Blanchard, Isabelle, S2-526, 535

Blanchard, Isabelle, S3-833

Blanchard, Isabelle-Genevieve, S1-62

Blanchard, J. Gregoire, S1-301

Blanchard, Jacques, F-105

Blanchard, Jacques-Joseph, S1-69

Blanchard, Jean, E-417, 472, 598

Blanchard, Jean, N-15

Blanchard, Jean, S1-15, 22, 66-70, 251, 295

Blanchard, Jean, S2-458, 523

Blanchard, Jean, S3-846, 870

Blanchard, Jean Baptiste, F-51

Blanchard, Jean Baptiste, N-16, 60

Blanchard, Jean Baptiste, S3-1105

Blanchard, Jean Frederic, C-13

Blanchard, Jean Frederic, E-33, 74

Blanchard, Jean Gregoire, C-12

Blanchard, Jean Gregoire, F-51

Blanchard, Jean Gregoire, N-15-16

Blanchard, Jean-Antoine, S1-68

Blanchard, Jean-Baptiste, S1-74, 292

Blanchard, Jean-Gregoire, S1-68

Blanchard, Jean-Marie, S1-69

Blanchard, Jean-Pierre, S1-75

Blanchard, Jeanne, E-33, 96, 490

Blanchard, Jeanne-Francois, S1-67

Blanchard, Jehan, E-456

Blanchard, Joachim, F-81

Blanchard, Joachim, N-14

Blanchard, Joachim-Jacques, S1-64

Blanchard, Joseph, C-11-13, 20, 159

Blanchard, Joseph, E-1, 33, 74, 165, 407, 598

Blanchard, Joseph, F-17, 79, 81

Blanchard, Joseph, N-14-17, 103, 175, 241

Blanchard, Joseph, S1-9-10, 62-66, 70-74

Blanchard, Joseph, S2-462, 493, 563, 715, 736

Blanchard, Joseph, S3-823, 827, 888, 1026, 1035-1036, 1075, 1112, 1120, 1137

Blanchard, Joseph Francois, C-12

Blanchard, Joseph Jean Francois, N-16

Blanchard, Joseph Nicolas, N-16

Blanchard, Joseph-Jean-Francois, S1-71

Blanchard, Joseph-Mathurin, S1-71

Blanchard, Julien, S1-14

Blanchard, Julienne, S2-778

Blanchard, Julienne-Francoise, S1-67

Blanchard, Laurence, S2-466

Blanchard, Laurent, F-17

Blanchard, Laurent, N-16

Blanchard, Laurent-Olivier, S1-72

Blanchard, Louis, C-104

Blanchard, Louis Augustin, C-13

Blanchard, Louis Augustin, N-17

Blanchard, Louis-Francois, S1-122

Blanchard, Louis-Sulia, S1-72

Blanchard, Madeleine, C-20-21, 41

Blanchard, Madeleine, N-30

Blanchard, Madeleine, S1-130-131, 340

Blanchard, Madeleine, S2-442, 476, 478

Blanchard, Magdelaine, F-73, 77

Blanchard, Magdeleine, E-33, 114, 150, 181, 255, 326, 379, 382-384, 399, 458, 598

Blanchard, Magdeleine, S3-922

Blanchard, Marc, E-32

Blanchard, Marguerite, E-31, 33, 341-342, 598

Blanchard, Marguerite, F-73, 79

Blanchard, Marguerite, N-12

Blanchard, Marguerite, S1-66

Blanchard, Marguerite Anne, N-15

Blanchard, Marguerite-Francoise, S1-69

Blanchard, Marguerite-Marie, S1-74

Blanchard, Marguerite-Modeste, S1-71

Blanchard, Marie, C-19, 53, 80, 137

Blanchard, Marie, E-33, 126, 157, 286, 341-342, 474, 485, 490, 523, 598-599

Blanchard, Marie, F-17, 31, 33, 51, 63, 77, 79

Blanchard, Marie, N-14-16, 137, 162, 165, 170

Blanchard, Marie, S1-67-68, 115, 185

Blanchard, Marie, S2-442, 628, 715

Blanchard, Marie, S3-853-854, 1001, 1127

Blanchard, Marie Anne, C-12

Blanchard, Marie Bennony, F-81

Blanchard, Marie Benony, N-14

Blanchard, Marie Josephe, N-26

Blanchard, Marie Madeleine, N-14

Blanchard, Marie Magdalen, E-33, 150

Blanchard, Marie Magdelaine, F-81

Blanchard, Marie Sophie, E-33

Blanchard, Marie-Anne, S1-63, 71

Blanchard, Marie-Francoise, S1-65

Blanchard, Marie-Jeanne, S1-67

Blanchard, Marie-Josephe, S1-72

Blanchard, Marie-Josephe, S2-631-632

Blanchard, Marie-Madeleine, S1-63, 72, 74

Blanchard, Marin, S2-443

Blanchard, Martin, E-456, 472, 522

Blanchard, Martin, N-5

Blanchard, Martin, S1-70-71

Blanchard, Michel, E-82, 598

Blanchard, Michel, S1-71

Blanchard, Moise, F-17, 81

Blanchard, Moyse, N-14, 16

Blanchard, Nicole, S1-63

Blanchard, Perinne, S1-67-68

Blanchard, Pierre, E-598

Blanchard, Pierre, F-17

Blanchard, Pierre, N-3, 16, 63

Blanchard, Pierre, S1-7, 74-75, 301

Blanchard, Pierre, S2-458

Blanchard, Pierre Charles, F-51

Blanchard, Pierre Charles, N-16

Blanchard, Pierre Sebastien, N-15

Blanchard, Pierre, Jr. , S1-75

Blanchard, Pierre, Sr., S1-74

Blanchard, Pierre-Joseph, S1-72

Blanchard, Rene, E-485, 490, 522

Blanchard, Rene, S2-563

Blanchard, Rosalie, N-14

Blanchard, Rosalie Adelaide, N-15

Blanchard, Rose Anne, S1-64-65

Blanchard, Simon, S1-62

Blanchard, Souillac, F-79, 109

Blanchard, Souillac, N-14

Blanchard, Suliac-Francois, S1-64

Blanchard, Toussaint, C-13

Blanchard, Toussaint, E-33

Blanchard, Xavier, N-175

Blanchard, Ysabelle, S3-849

Blanchard, Zacharie, E-33

Blanchet, Elie, E-33, 149

Blanchet, Etienne, S3-1017

Blanchet, Francois, E-33, 372

Blanchet, Jean, E-33-34, 307, 372

Blanchet, Jeanne, E-175

Blanchet, Louis, E-34, 157, 307

Blanchet, Marie, E-73

Blanchet, Michel, E-33, 149

Blandin, Louise, F-37

Blangere, Elisabeth, E-34, 152

Blangy, Therese, E-284

Blanson, Cecile, C-142

Blaquaire, Louis, E-34, 107, 281, 316

Blaquaire, Louis Joseph, E-34

Blaquaire, Pierre, E-34

Blaquere, Barbe, S1-76

Blaquere, Louis, S1-75

Blaquere, Louis, S2-520

Blaquere, Louis, Jr., S1-75

Blaquere, Marie-Anne, S1-75

Blaquere, Pierre, S1-75

Blay, Angelique, E-26, 405

Blay, Louis, E-26, 34, 355

Bleau, Francois, E-34, 318

Blein, Julien, E-10

Blereau, Pierre, C-129

Blesine, Apoline, E-584, 592

Bleu, Marie Therese, E-122, 196

Blin, -----, E-34

Blin, Angelique, E-154, 290

Blin, Anne, E-587, 594

Blin, Antoinette, S1-256

Blin, Esther, E-34

Blin, Francoise, E-29-30

Blin, Guillemette, E-637

Blin, Helene, S1-347

Blin, Henriette Theodora, E-34

Blin, Jean, E-34, 362

Blin, Jean Sr., E-638

Blin, Joseph Ignace, E-34

Blin, Madeleine, E-34, 428, 638

Blin, Marguerite, E-34, 359, 361-365, 642

Blondeau, Jacques, S2-668

Blondeau, Jacques, S3-829

Blondeau, Jean, E-34

Blondeau, Marie-Vincent, S2-668

Blondeaux, Elisabeth, E-109

Blondel, Francois, E-146, 371

Blondel, Jeanne, E-403, 441

Blondel, Jeanne, S2-772

Blondin, Jean, E-35

Blondin, Joseph, E-35, 278

Blondin, Marie, E-35, 278

Blondin, Marie Josephe, E-35

Bloody Creek, E-214

Blor, Louis, C-118

Blou, Anne, E-522

Blou, Cecile, E-341, 528

Blou, Francoise, E-518

Blou, Jacques, E-472

Blou, Jeanne, E-518

Blou, Magdelaine, E-526

Blou, Margueritte, E-525

Blou, Marie, E-517, 527

Blou, Marie Joseph, E-526

Bloudin, Jean, E-156

Blouin, Francoise, C-125

Blouin, Jeanne, C-48, 125

Boal, Catherine, E-10

Bocage, Anne, E-35, 278

Bocage, Jean, E-278

Bodard, Joseph, E-413

Bodard, Marguerite, E-331, 580

Bodard, Marie, E-35, 196, 257, 413

Bodart, Francois, E-522

Bodeneuf, Julien, S2-783

Bodeneuf, Julien, S3-928

Bodeneuf, Perinne, S2-778, 783

Bodeneuf, Perinne, S3-928

Bodenu, Joseph, S3-928

Bodenue, Guillaume, S3-928

Bodin, Gilles, S1-327

Bodin, Jean, E-135

Bodin, Marguerite, E-262

Bodin, Mr., E-197

Bodin, Rene, S3-888

Bodin, Simon, E-197

Bodiou, Marie, E-25
Bodo, Marie, E-167
Bodron, Pierre, E-393
Bodros, Claude, E-35
Bodros, Joseph, E-35
Boetvin, Guillemette, N-77, 186
Bogard, Catherine, E-458
Bogard, Jean, E-36
Boideau, Elisabeth, E-296
Boidron, Catherine, E-17
Boilay, Claude, E-95
Boileau, Jean, E-35, 73, 100, 404
Boileau, Marie, E-157
Boileau, Pierre, E-35, 404
Boiniere, Marie Magdeleine, E-35, 102
Boiniere, Pierre, E-35, 102
Boinniere, Francois, E-295
Boinot, Jean, E-259, 352
Bois, Francois, E-35
Bois, Francoise, E-35
Bois, Genevieve, E-35
Bois, Jean Francois, E-35
Bois, Marie, E-35
Bois, Pierre, E-35, 88
Boisdon, Jean, E-35
Boisdon, Marguerite, E-35
Boisfier, Francois, E-35
Boisfier, Gabrielle, E-35, 144
Boisgards, Marie, E-35, 156
Boisgards, Pierre, E-35, 156
Boisie, Marie, E-275
Boislais, Claude, E-36
Boislais, Marie Francoise, E-36
Boismary, Claude Chenu, E-61
Boismoreau, Jacques, E-36, 259
Boismorel, Jean Petit, S1-173
Boismory, Mr., E-197
Boisrame, Marguerite Francoise, E-36
Boisrame, Pierre, E-36, 58
Boissard, Marie, E-391
Boissard, Pierre, E-36, 332
Boissard, Simon, E-36, 332
Boisseau, Andre, E-146
Boisseau, Claire, S2-455, 469-470
Boisseau, Francois, E-522
Boisseau, Louis, E-36, 102
Boisseau, Marguerite, E-36, 63

Boisseau, Marguerite, S1-269
Boisseau, Marie, E-157, 383
Boisseau, Marie, F-75
Boisseau, Marie, S1-359-360
Boisseau, Marie, S3-839, 980
Boisseau, Nomme, E-157
Boisseau, Pierre, E-414, 438
Boissette, Jeanne, E-158
Boisson, -----, E-36
Boisson, Antoine, E-36, 377
Boisson, Barthelemy, E-36
Boisson, Nicolas, E-36
Boitre, Josephine, E-184
Boix, Marguerite, E-12, 435
Bokman, Carl Anton, E-36, 369
Bokman, Laurent, E-36, 369
Bolque, Francois, S3-869
Bolu, Angelique, C-13
Bolu, Gabriel Louis, C-13, 24, 93, 102-103
Bolu, Louis, C-14
Bolu, Marguerite, C-14
Bolu, Marin, C-13, 103
Bolu, Martin, C-14
Bon, Marie, E-32, 73
Bonamour, Jean, E-112
Bonamour, Marie, E-22, 330
Bonar, Jean, E-423
Bonche, Marie, E-255
Bonche, Marie, S2-513
Boncorse, Francoise, E-286
Bonet, Joseph, S3-1150
Boneteau, Pierre, E-102
Boneturier, Pierre, E-34
Boney, Marguerite, E-348, 362
Bonfante, Marie, E-358, 378
Bonfils, Anne, F-53
Bonfils, Francois, F-53
Bonfils, Francois, N-101, 206
Bonfils, Jeanne, N-100, 206
Bonin, Joseph, E-349
Bonin, Magdeleine, E-390
Bonin, Marguerite, E-369
Bonin, Marie Catherine, E-60
Bonin, Marie Francoise, E-36, 430
Bonin, Pierre, E-349
Bonnain de la Chausse, Pierre, E-175
Bonnal, Michel, E-36
Bonnard, Elisabeth, E-27

Bonnaudet, Felix, E-354
Bonne, Augustin, E-430
Bonneau, Henriette, C-22
Bonneau, Jeanne, E-36, 105
Bonneau, Pierre, E-99
Bonnefon, Barthelemy, E-37
Bonnefon, Joseph, E-37, 156
Bonnefon, Madeleine Josephine, E-37
Bonnefon, Pierre, E-37, 133
Bonnefous, Jean, E-111
Bonnejean, Elizabeth, E-335
Bonnejean, Elizabeth, S2-591
Bonnelle, Andre, E-195
Bonneres, Marie Madeleine, E-267
Bonnerie, Charles, E-418
Bonnet, Andre, E-172
Bonnet, Francois, E-409
Bonnet, Jean, E-155, 315
Bonnetis, Marie Jacquette, E-37, 324
Bonnevie, Aimee Victoire, E-638, 641
Bonnevie, Amand, E-1, 37, 55, 117, 630, 632, 638, 641
Bonnevie, Amand, S1-76-77
Bonnevie, Amand dit Beaumont, S1-76
Bonnevie, Benjamin Adolphe, E-37, 641
Bonnevie, Francois Auguste, E-37, 638, 641
Bonnevie, Francoise, E-359, 630, 638
Bonnevie, Francoise, F-75
Bonnevie, Francoise, N-80
Bonnevie, Francoise, S2-434
Bonnevie, Gratien, E-638
Bonnevie, Jacques, C-45
Bonnevie, Jacques, F-67
Bonnevie, Jacques, N-71
Bonnevie, Jacques, S1-76
Bonnevie, Jean, S1-77
Bonnevie, Jean Hyppolite, E-37
Bonnevie, Joseph Antoine, N-71
Bonnevie, Joseph Hippolite, E-37
Bonnevie, Marie, E-638
Bonnevie, Marie, S1-77

Bonnevie, Marie Francoise, E-641

Bonnevie, Marie Luce, E-37

Bonnevie, Marie Modeste, E-38, 117, 119, 642

Bonnevie, Marie-Madeleine, S1-76

Bonnevie, Marie-Modeste, S1-76-77

Bonnevie, Michel, E-37, 630

Bonnevie, Modeste, E-632

Bonnevie, Modeste, S1-77

Bonnevie, Mr., E-58

Bonnevie, Pierre, E-1, 37-38, 58, 117, 186, 362, 436, 630, 638, 641

Bonnevie, Pierre, S1-76-77

Bonnevie, Pierre Gratient, E-56, 641

Bonnevie, Remi, E-37, 181, 638, 641

Bonnevie, Rosalie, S1-76-77

Bonnevie, Rosalie Charlotte, N-71

Bonnevie, Rose, C-9, 45-46

Bonnevie, Rose, E-290

Bonnevie, Rose, F-67

Bonnevie, Rose, N-71

Bonnevie, Sophie, E-630, 638, 641

Bonnevie, Victoire, E-38

Bonnevie, widow, E-1

Bonneville, -----, E-37

Bonneville, Pierre, E-37

Bonnie, Francois, S1-354

Bonniere, Anne, E-267

Bonniere, Anne, E-38

Bonniere, Anne, S1-80, 263

Bonniere, Anne, S2-719

Bonniere, Anne Marie, E-38

Bonniere, Anne-Marie, S1-81

Bonniere, Bernard, S1-78

Bonniere, Bertrand, E-159

Bonniere, Bertrand, E-38

Bonniere, Charles, S1-80

Bonniere, Charlotte, E-38

Bonniere, Charlotte, S1-80

Bonniere, Felicite, S1-78

Bonniere, Francois, S1-77-78, 281

Bonniere, Francois, S2-581, 721

Bonniere, Francois, S3-964

Bonniere, Francois Michel, E-61

Bonniere, Francois Michel Joseph, E-38

Bonniere, Francois-Marie, S1-78

Bonniere, Francois-Michel, S1-77, 79

Bonniere, Francois-Michel, S2-772

Bonniere, Francoise, S1-78

Bonniere, Jacques, S3-875

Bonniere, Jean Pierre, N-243

Bonniere, Jean-Jacques, S1-79-80

Bonniere, Jean-Jacques, S2-578, 707

Bonniere, Jean-Pierre, S1-81

Bonniere, Jeanne, E-159

Bonniere, Jeanne, E-38

Bonniere, Jeanne, S1-78

Bonniere, Joseph, S1-78

Bonniere, Julien, S1-78

Bonniere, Julien, S2-466, 468

Bonniere, Marie, C-155

Bonniere, Marie, E-38

Bonniere, Marie, F-37

Bonniere, Marie, N-117, 181

Bonniere, Marie, S1-78, 80-81, 158

Bonniere, Marie Madeleine, C-57

Bonniere, Marie Madeleine, E-267

Bonniere, Marie Madeleine, F-49

Bonniere, Marie Madeleine, N-7, 51-52, 93, 243

Bonniere, Marie Magdeleine, S3-899, 901

Bonniere, Marie-Jacquemine Rose, S1-81

Bonniere, Marie-Madeleine, S1-77, 79-80, 259-261

Bonniere, Marie-Madeleine, S2-468

Bonniere, Michel-Joseph, S1-80

Bonniere, Pierre, C-155

Bonniere, Pierre, E-314, 580

Bonniere, Pierre, N-51

Bonniere, Pierre, S1-77, 79-80, 158, 259, 263

Bonniere, Pierre, S2-704, 719

Bonniere, Pierre, S3-936, 964, 1004

Bonniere, Pierre, Jr., S1-81

Bonniere, Rosalie, E-183, 267

Bonniere, Rosalie, E-38, 356, 558, 580

Bonniere, Rosalie, S1-79, 81, 263

Bonniere, Rosalie, S2-452, 704-705

Bonniere, Rosalie, S3-1004

Bonniere, Rose, C-155

Bonniere, Rose, S1-80

Bonniere, Servanne, E-32, 403

Bonnieu, Francoise Perrine, E-617

Bonnieu, Pierre, E-617

Bonniex, Jean, S2-552

Bonnin, Marie, E-21

Bonor, Perrine, E-423

Bonouvrier, Elie, E-38, 395

Bonouvrier, Jean, E-38, 395

Bontiere, Jean Francois Anque, S3-968

Bonvilin, Marie, F-37

Bonville, Philippe, S3-975

Borbudeau, Jean Gabriel, C-112

Borbudeau, Marie Reine, C-112

Borchet, Philippe, S3-904

Borcour, Joseph, E-10

Bordage, Jean, E-262

Bordas, Catherine, S1-81

Bordas, Etienne, S1-81

Bordas, Jean-Baptiste, S1-81

Bordas, Marie, S1-81

Bordassy, Andre, E-38, 365

Bordassy, Francois, E-38

Borde, Antoine, E-38, 86

Borde, Catherine, E-38

Borde, Etienne Valentin, E-38, 51

Borde, Jean, E-38, 86

Borde, Rose Eugenie Claude Victoire, E-38, 51

Bordier, Francois, E-40, 100

Bordier, Jean, E-40, 61, 100

Bordier, Rene, S1-250

Bordos, Etienne, E-40

Bordos, Jean Baptiste, E-40
Bordot, Catherine Antoinette, E-40
Bordot, Francois, E-40
Borel, Louis, E-266
Borie, Marguerite, E-432
Boriend, Julien, S2-475
Borine, Gabriel, S1-82
Borine, Jacques, S1-82
Borine, Jean, S1-82
Borique, Nicolas, E-406
Borisis, Marie Rose, E-584, 594
Borisis, Pierre, E-584, 594
Borloh, Perrine, E-429
Borne, Jean, E-35, 418
Borni, Bazile, E-197, 442
Bornicq, Laurent, E-40, 166
Borny, Agnes, S2-593
Borny, Francois, S1-83
Borny, Francoise-Felicite, S1-82
Borny, Jacques, S1-82-83
Borny, Jean, S1-82-83
Borny, Joseph-Alexandre, S1-82
Borny, Louis, S1-83
Borny, Marie-Jeanne, S1-82
Borny, Michelle, S2-650-651
Boron, Marie, E-379
Bory, Marie, E-621
Boschier, Rene, S2-598
Bosens, Pierre, E-45
Bossard, Louise, E-337
Bosset, Anne Thereze, E-110, 346
Bosset, Pierre, E-418
Boteral, Reine, S2-668
Botier, Magdeleine, E-64, 101, 262, 308
Botrel, Francoise, S1-222
Botrel, Jeanne, S2-754
Botrel, Louis, E-266
Bottereau, Marie Jeanne Josephe, E-3
Bottereau, Marie Joseph, E-5
Bottereau, Yves Anne, E-3, 5
Bottier, Magdelaine, E-40
Bottier, Nicolas, E-40, 308, 416
Bouairon, Marie Joseph, E-336
Boubarne, Louis, S2-731
Boucard, Jean, E-174
Bouchard, Charles, E-584, 594
Bouchard, Etienne, E-168

Bouchard, Guione, S2-669
Bouchard, Helene, S1-83-84
Bouchard, Jean, E-40, 108, 318, 325
Bouchard, Marguerite, S2-733
Bouchard, Marie, E-584, 594
Bouchard, Marie, S1-83-84, 376
Bouchard, Nicolas, S1-83-84, 373-374, 376
Bouchard, Nicolas, S2-512
Bouchard, Nicolas, S3-919, 961, 1009
Bouchard, Perinne, S1-6
Bouchard, Pierre, S2-695
Bouchat, Catherine, E-62, 197
Boucher, Angelique, E-105, 193
Boucher, Anne, E-78, 376
Boucher, Bernard, E-584, 596
Boucher, Bernard, S1-84-85
Boucher, Bernard, S2-515
Boucher, Bernard, S3-953-954, 996
Boucher, Bernardine, S1-85
Boucher, Denis, E-60
Boucher, Etienne, E-41, 53, 91
Boucher, Felicite, E-41, 53, 146
Boucher, Francois, E-30, 32, 36, 69, 77, 99, 109, 114, 139, 156, 259, 264, 309, 316, 338, 346, 367, 370, 376, 386, 406
Boucher, Honore, E-256, 382
Boucher, Jean, E-41, 53
Boucher, Jean Eugene, E-41, 53
Boucher, Jean-Baptiste, S1-84
Boucher, Jean-Pierre, S1-84
Boucher, Jeanne, E-157, 174, 315
Boucher, Louise, E-584, 596
Boucher, Madeleine, E-27-28, 41, 53
Boucher, Madeleine Simon, E-28
Boucher, Marguerite, E-296
Boucher, Marie, C-9
Boucher, Marie, E-41, 91, 432
Boucher, Marie Helene, E-41, 53
Boucher, Marie Henriette, E-109
Boucher, Marie Reine, E-19, 345

Boucher, Marie-Louise, S1-84-85
Boucher, Michel, S1-84
Boucher, Nicolas, E-584, 596
Boucher, Nicolas, S1-85
Boucher, Pierre, E-41, 522
Boucher, Reine, E-338
Boucher, Reine Marie, E-392
Boucher, Therese, S1-84-85
Bouchereau, Etienne, E-121
Bouchereau, Pierre, E-121
Bouchet, Marie-Louise, S2-515
Boucite, Francois, F-85
Boudeau, Jean, E-44
Boudeau, Marguerite, E-621
Boudeau, Pierre, E-44, 270, 441
Boudet, Elisabeth, E-41
Boudet, Jean, E-41, 299
Boudet, Jeanne Marie, E-147
Boudet, Philipe, E-41, 299
Boudier, Jacquette Therese, E-91, 295, 389
Boudieux, Catherine, E-174
Boudinal, Julien, S2-705
Boudouard, Jean, S3-898-899
Boudreaux, Abraham, E-472
Boudreaux, Agathe-Charlotte, S1-92
Boudreaux, Agnes, S1-89-90
Boudreaux, Alexandre, C-16, 148
Boudreaux, Alexandre, F-7
Boudreaux, Alexandre, S1-85, 170
Boudreaux, Alexis, C-157
Boudreaux, Alexis, E-41
Boudreaux, Alexis, N-247
Boudreaux, Alexis, S1-94-95
Boudreaux, Alexis, S2-527
Boudreaux, Aman, F-59, 95
Boudreaux, Amand, S1-94-95
Boudreaux, Amand, S2-766
Boudreaux, Amand, S3-850, 896, 903
Boudreaux, Amant, S1-86-87, 97, 108, 116
Boudreaux, Anastasie, E-41, 435, 438
Boudreaux, Anastasie, S1-39-40, 87, 102
Boudreaux, Anastasie, S2-535

Boudreaux, Anastasie-Marie-
Celeste, S1-110
Boudreaux, Anasthasie, S3-835
Boudreaux, Andre, C-157
Boudreaux, Andre, E-41
Boudreaux, Andre, N-26
Boudreaux, Andre Claude, E-41
Boudreaux, Angelique, E-635
Boudreaux, Anne, C-51, 68-69,
156
Boudreaux, Anne, E-13, 41, 43,
47, 94, 104, 129, 160, 169,
178, 307, 352, 365-369, 403,
423, 493, 522, 555, 590, 596
Boudreaux, Anne, F-5, 35, 39,
75
Boudreaux, Anne, N-4, 18, 26,
72, 79, 80, 94, 112, 118-119,
130, 139, 182, 200, 241
Boudreaux, Anne, S1-4, 47, 89-
90, 97, 99, 104, 113-115, 118,
203, 238
Boudreaux, Anne, S2-430-431,
436, 502, 525, 554, 557, 572,
597, 599, 646, 676, 770
Boudreaux, Anne, S3-938, 941-
943, 1057, 1067
Boudreaux, Anne Francoise, E-
41
Boudreaux, Anne Henriette, C-
14
Boudreaux, Anne Henriette, N-
18
Boudreaux, Anne Jeanne, F-93
Boudreaux, Anne Josette, N-108
Boudreaux, Anne Marie, E-95
Boudreaux, Anne Marie
Michelle, E-41
Boudreaux, Anne Pelagie, C-17
Boudreaux, Anne Pelagie, N-24
Boudreaux, Anne-Henriette, S1-
98
Boudreaux, Anne-Jeanne, S1-
93, 119-120
Boudreaux, Anne-Josephe, S1-
87
Boudreaux, Anne-Josette, S1-
101
Boudreaux, Anne-Josette, S2-
541-542

Boudreaux, Anne-Marie, S1-88,
104, 111-112
Boudreaux, Anonime, E-41
Boudreaux, Anselme, E-546
Boudreaux, Anselme, S1-87-89,
99, 108, 239
Boudreaux, Anselme, S3-834,
1000
Boudreaux, Antoine, F-37, 73,
93
Boudreaux, Antoine, N-17, 19,
215
Boudreaux, Antoine, S1-89-91,
101, 114, 116-117, 246
Boudreaux, Antoine, S3-905,
914, 1002, 1078
Boudreaux, Antoine-Charles,
S1-119
Boudreaux, Augustin, S1-91-93,
107, 175, 251
Boudreaux, Augustin, S2-759
Boudreaux, Augustin, S3-830
Boudreaux, Basile, N-26, 247
Boudreaux, Basile, S1-106
Boudreaux, Basile, S2-628
Boudreaux, Basile, S3-854, 863,
1127
Boudreaux, Bazile, C-19, 80,
156-157
Boudreaux, Bazile, E-41, 106,
167, 194, 334
Boudreaux, Bazile, S1-94-95,
111-115
Boudreaux, Bazile-Pierre, S1-
116
Boudreaux, Benjamin, C-19
Boudreaux, Benjamin, F-69
Boudreaux, Benjamin, N-197
Boudreaux, Benjamin, S1-120
Boudreaux, Benjamin Hilaire,
N-27
Boudreaux, Benjamin-Hilaire,
S1-121
Boudreaux, Blaise, F-75
Boudreaux, Blaise Julian, C-14
Boudreaux, Blaise Julien, N-18
Boudreaux, Blaise-Julien, S1-98
Boudreaux, Brigide-Anne, S1-
91
Boudreaux, Cecile, E-42, 107,
130, 380

Boudreaux, Cecile, F-23, 65, 75,
93
Boudreaux, Cecile, S1-96, 118,
120
Boudreaux, Cecile, S2-694
Boudreaux, Cecile Marguerite,
C-14
Boudreaux, Cecile Marguerite,
N-18
Boudreaux, Cecile-Marguerite,
S1-98
Boudreaux, Celeste, C-99
Boudreaux, Celeste, F-37, 67,
107, 109
Boudreaux, Celeste, S1-94-95
Boudreaux, Celestine Sibilas, N-
27
Boudreaux, Charles, E-42, 414,
472, 493, 522-523, 585, 593
Boudreaux, Charles, F-53, 69,
83, 109
Boudreaux, Charles, N-17-18,
20, 27, 42
Boudreaux, Charles, S1-87, 95-
98, 104, 108, 110, 112-114,
120-121, 203
Boudreaux, Charles, S2-734
Boudreaux, Charles, S3-835,
838, 840-845, 943, 967
Boudreaux, Charles Marie, F-69
Boudreaux, Charles Marie, N-18
Boudreaux, Charles Michel, F-
73
Boudreaux, Charles Michel, N-
17
Boudreaux, Charles-Michel, S1-
90
Boudreaux, Charles-Olivier, S1-
95-96, 112
Boudreaux, child, S1-109
Boudreaux, Claude, E-17, 41,
43-44, 472, 493, 523, 549
Boudreaux, Claude, N-111
Boudreaux, Claude, S1-107,
115, 235
Boudreaux, Claude, S2-430, 554
Boudreaux, Cyprien, C-19
Boudreaux, Cyprien, S1-94
Boudreaux, David Valentin, C-
14

Boudreaux, David Valentin, N-18

Boudreaux, Denis, E-42, 523

Boudreaux, Denis, S1-95

Boudreaux, Denis, S2-597

Boudreaux, Elisabeth, E-42

Boudreaux, Elisabeth, S3-831

Boudreaux, Elizabeth, N-160

Boudreaux, Elizabeth, S1-100

Boudreaux, Elizabeth, S2-758-760

Boudreaux, Etienne, C-14, 17-18, 21

Boudreaux, Etienne, F-65, 73, 75, 77

Boudreaux, Etienne, N-17-18, 25, 226-227, 229, 244

Boudreaux, Etienne, S1-91, 96-98, 102, 110

Boudreaux, Etienne, S2-754, 766

Boudreaux, Etienne, S3-836, 838, 840-842, 844-845, 847-848, 850, 855, 857, 858-859, 886, 1141, 1151

Boudreaux, Euphrosine, S1-94-95

Boudreaux, Felicite, E-286, 423-424, 555

Boudreaux, Felicite, F-47

Boudreaux, Felicite, N-19, 127, 235

Boudreaux, Felix, E-9, 42, 44, 287, 289, 413, 555

Boudreaux, Felix, F-47

Boudreaux, Felix, N-18, 127, 208, 235

Boudreaux, Felix Marie, N-23

Boudreaux, Francois, C-5, 14-15, 29, 68

Boudreaux, Francois, E-42-43, 472, 478, 523

Boudreaux, Francois, F-39, 47, 95

Boudreaux, Francois, N-18-19, 22, 38, 118, 202, 225

Boudreaux, Francois, S1-85-86, 88-89, 95-96, 98-99, 103, 105, 108

Boudreaux, Francois, S2-534, 572, 622

Boudreaux, Francois, S3-834-835, 851, 883, 896, 998, 1021, 1067

Boudreaux, Francois Marie, N-21-22

Boudreaux, Francois Xavier, C-15

Boudreaux, Francois Xavier, F-37

Boudreaux, Francois Xavier, N-17, 19-20, 60, 215

Boudreaux, Francois-Joseph, S1-86

Boudreaux, Francois-Xavier, S1-90-91

Boudreaux, Francoise, C-39, 80

Boudreaux, Francoise, E-144

Boudreaux, Francoise, F-11

Boudreaux, Francoise, N-62

Boudreaux, Francoise, S1-113-114, 202-203, 278, 300

Boudreaux, Francoise, S2-431, 526

Boudreaux, Francoise, S3-1031

Boudreaux, Francoise-Anne-Renee, S1-94

Boudreaux, Francoise-Mathur-ine, S1-115

Boudreaux, Genevieve, S1-101

Boudreaux, Genevieve-Sophie, S1-119

Boudreaux, Germain, S1-86, 99-100, 105, 167

Boudreaux, Germain, S3-930

Boudreaux, girl, S1-109

Boudreaux, Helene, F-95

Boudreaux, Helene-Marie-Rose, S1-117, 120

Boudreaux, Henriette Charlotte, N-23

Boudreaux, Henriette Josephe, N-24

Boudreaux, Henriette-Charlotte, S1-106

Boudreaux, Honore, S1-100-102

Boudreaux, Ignace, F-83, 109

Boudreaux, Ignace, N-20

Boudreaux, Ignace, S1-101, 119

Boudreaux, Isaac, C-19, 114

Boudreaux, Isaac, E-635

Boudreaux, Isaac, S1-114

Boudreaux, Isabelle, E-42

Boudreaux, Isabelle, F-75, 97, 101

Boudreaux, Isabelle, S1-92, 102

Boudreaux, Isabelle, S2-493, 661

Boudreaux, Isabelle-Jeanne, S1-116

Boudreaux, Isabelle-Josephe, S1-93

Boudreaux, Isabelle-Rose, S1-92

Boudreaux, Jacques-Francois, S1-88

Boudreaux, Jacques-Joseph, S1-87

Boudreaux, Jan Charle, S3-942

Boudreaux, Jean, C-16, 83, 156

Boudreaux, Jean, E-24, 42, 44, 65, 407, 423, 435, 523, 630

Boudreaux, Jean, F-23, 25, 77, 81, 107

Boudreaux, Jean, N-20-21, 26-27, 72, 142, 205, 253

Boudreaux, Jean, S1-39, 87, 97, 108, 251

Boudreaux, Jean, S2-660

Boudreaux, Jean, S3-835, 912

Boudreaux, Jean Baptiste, C-15-17, 19, 148, 154

Boudreaux, Jean Baptiste, E-43-44, 347, 354, 493

Boudreaux, Jean Baptiste, F-7, 25, 53, 69, 73, 95

Boudreaux, Jean Baptiste, N-17, 20-22, 27, 42, 108

Boudreaux, Jean Baptiste, S3-834, 880, 883, 1002, 1024

Boudreaux, Jean Basile, C-18

Boudreaux, Jean Charles, C-14, 17, 148

Boudreaux, Jean Charles, E-42, 126

Boudreaux, Jean Charles, F-47, 53, 69

Boudreaux, Jean Charles, N-21-24, 74, 83, 225, 227-228

Boudreaux, Jean Constant, F-7

Boudreaux, Jean Constant, N-22

Boudreaux, Jean Cyprien, S3-863

Boudreaux, Jean Etienne, N-18
Boudreaux, Jean Joseph, N-23
Boudreaux, Jean Louis, C-15
Boudreaux, Jean Louis, N-19
Boudreaux, Jean Marie, E-42
Boudreaux, Jean Marie Magdeleine, E-42
Boudreaux, Jean Pierre, C-18
Boudreaux, Jean Pierre, N-25
Boudreaux, Jean-Baptiste, S1-85-86, 90-91, 99, 101-102, 104, 107, 112, 117-119, 121, 170, 234
Boudreaux, Jean-Baptiste, S2-541, 783
Boudreaux, Jean-Basile, S1-110
Boudreaux, Jean-Charles, S1-87, 96, 105-106, 109, 227, 376
Boudreaux, Jean-Charles, S2-534, 770
Boudreaux, Jean-Cyprien, S1-94, 106-107
Boudreaux, Jean-Cyprien, S2-537, 617
Boudreaux, Jean-Francois, S1-103
Boudreaux, Jean-Louis, S1-99
Boudreaux, Jean-Pierre, S1-91
Boudreaux, Jean-Zacharie, S1-47, 107
Boudreaux, Jeanne, E-458, 476
Boudreaux, Jeanne, S2-514
Boudreaux, Jeanne Adelaide, E-42
Boudreaux, Joseph, C-15-17, 87
Boudreaux, Joseph, E-13, 42-43, 177, 367, 523, 555
Boudreaux, Joseph, F-53, 59, 65, 69, 73, 75, 93, 95, 109
Boudreaux, Joseph, N-17, 21, 23-25, 42, 216-218, 244
Boudreaux, Joseph, S1-40, 87, 89, 90, 96-97, 102-104, 107-110, 113-115, 117, 120
Boudreaux, Joseph, S2-530, 574, 679, 710
Boudreaux, Joseph, S3-845, 883, 900, 902, 941, 998, 1010, 1025, 1039-1040, 1052
Boudreaux, Joseph Ian, E-555

Boudreaux, Joseph Larie, C-14-15, 18
Boudreaux, Joseph Marie, N-18, 21, 23-24
Boudreaux, Joseph Simon, E-43
Boudreaux, Joseph-Francois, S1-98
Boudreaux, Joseph-Jacques, S1-86
Boudreaux, Joseph-Marie, S1-89, 97, 100, 104-105, 108, 110
Boudreaux, Josephe, E-24, 177
Boudreaux, Josephe, S2-470
Boudreaux, Judith, E-24, 43, 47, 150, 177, 302
Boudreaux, Judith, F-19
Boudreaux, Judith, S2-767
Boudreaux, Louis, C-99, 156-157
Boudreaux, Louis, F-83, 109
Boudreaux, Louis, N-24, 27, 221, 223
Boudreaux, Louis Jean Joseph, N-21
Boudreaux, Louise, C-17
Boudreaux, Louise, E-43, 186-187, 407-408, 429, 632
Boudreaux, Louise Felicite, E-43
Boudreaux, Madeleine, E-13, 43, 80, 177, 282, 524
Boudreaux, Madeleine, F-39, 49, 55, 67
Boudreaux, Madeleine, N-112, 118, 161
Boudreaux, Madeleine, S1-88, 102, 117, 120, 179
Boudreaux, Madeleine, S2-556, 572, 762
Boudreaux, Madeleine Cecile, N-26
Boudreaux, Madeleine-Josephe, S1-111-112, 389
Boudreaux, Madeleine-Marguerite, S1-93
Boudreaux, Magdelaine, C-66, 68, 88, 146, 156-157
Boudreaux, Magdeleine, S3-908, 988, 1067

Boudreaux, Marain, S3-834, 836, 838, 840-844, 851-852, 882, 886, 891, 1047, 1127
Boudreaux, Marain fils, S3-835
Boudreaux, Marguerite, C-17, 46, 62-63, 83-84, 158, 166
Boudreaux, Marguerite, E-13, 43, 100, 108, 128, 130, 276, 365, 456, 493, 528-529, 621, 635
Boudreaux, Marguerite, F-3, 7, 65, 73, 75, 77
Boudreaux, Marguerite, N-68, 102-103, 111, 142-143
Boudreaux, Marguerite, S1-11, 26, 46-47, 92, 94-95, 100, 108-109, 113-114, 116, 119, 120-121, 249, 251, 315
Boudreaux, Marguerite, S2-465
Boudreaux, Marguerite, S2-525, 527-528, 530, 552, 555, 574, 622, 628, 660-661, 664, 710, 718
Boudreaux, Marguerite, S3-897, 912-913, 967, 1052
Boudreaux, Marguerite Genevieve, C-18
Boudreaux, Marguerite Jeanne, E-34
Boudreaux, Marguerite Josephe, N-17, 135-136
Boudreaux, Marguerite Josephe, S3-924
Boudreaux, Marguerite Marie, C-56, 58
Boudreaux, Marguerite Marie, N-22, 63, 90, 94
Boudreaux, Marguerite Reine, N-23
Boudreaux, Marguerite Suzanne, N-18
Boudreaux, Marguerite-Jeanne, S1-115, 118
Boudreaux, Marguerite-Joseph, S1-91
Boudreaux, Marguerite-Josephe, S1-103, 111-112
Boudreaux, Marguerite-Marie, S1-103, 301-303
Boudreaux, Marguerite-Marie, S2-460, 482

Boudreaux, Marie, C-15, 18-19, 29, 33, 42, 45, 49, 82, 97, 99, 162

Boudreaux, Marie, E-43, 81, 95, 116, 147-148, 195, 276, 336, 366, 386, 407, 434, 476, 493, 528-529

Boudreaux, Marie, F-7, 23, 27, 49, 51, 55, 67, 77, 81, 87, 95, 107, 111

Boudreaux, Marie, N-18, 23, 46, 53, 61, 70, 83, 153, 155, 159, 166-167, 171, 219, 222, 226, 227-228, 240

Boudreaux, Marie, S1-46, 92-93, 95, 100, 105-106, 109, 112, 114, 116, 120-121, 235-236, 243-245, 344, 361, 387, 391

Boudreaux, Marie, S2-456, 527, 656, 663-664, 672, 702, 743, 766-767

Boudreaux, Marie, S3-828, 841, 871, 906-907, 933, 935

Boudreaux, Marie Adelaide, N-24

Boudreaux, Marie Anne, E-96, 635

Boudreaux, Marie Anne, N-25

Boudreaux, Marie Blanche, N-10, 109

Boudreaux, Marie Felicite, F-7

Boudreaux, Marie Felicite, N-22

Boudreaux, Marie Francoise, E-43

Boudreaux, Marie Jeanne, E-9

Boudreaux, Marie Jeanne Josephe, E-43

Boudreaux, Marie Joseph, E-43, 147, 306

Boudreaux, Marie Joseph, S3-854, 892

Boudreaux, Marie Josephe, C-80

Boudreaux, Marie Lucie, F-109

Boudreaux, Marie Madeleine, N-17

Boudreaux, Marie Magdelaine, E-42-44, 134, 347, 354

Boudreaux, Marie Magdelaine, F-73

Boudreaux, Marie Marguerite, C-16

Boudreaux, Marie Marthe, C-17

Boudreaux, Marie Marthe, F-65, 69

Boudreaux, Marie Marthe, N-24

Boudreaux, Marie Pelagie, N-25

Boudreaux, Marie Perrine, E-44

Boudreaux, Marie Rose, F-25, 93

Boudreaux, Marie Rose, N-21

Boudreaux, Marie Vincente, E-9, 44

Boudreaux, Marie-Belony, S1-116

Boudreaux, Marie-Blanche, S1-109

Boudreaux, Marie-Celeste, S1-95

Boudreaux, Marie-Henriette, S1-88

Boudreaux, Marie-Josephe, S1-94-95, 104, 106, 114

Boudreaux, Marie-Josephe, S2-628, 694, 701-702

Boudreaux, Marie-Madeleine, S1-90, 102

Boudreaux, Marie-Marthe, S1-108

Boudreaux, Marie-Rose, S1-103, 118, 120

Boudreaux, Marie-Rose, S2-694

Boudreaux, Marie-Sophie, S1-93

Boudreaux, Marin, C-15, 17-18

Boudreaux, Marin, F-77

Boudreaux, Marin, N-24, 25

Boudreaux, Marin, S1-39, 98, 110

Boudreaux, Marin, S3-845, 1047, 1127

Boudreaux, Mathurin, N-24

Boudreaux, Mathurin, S1-111-113

Boudreaux, Mathurin, S3-856

Boudreaux, Michel, E-41-44, 165, 167, 367, 456, 472, 478, 523

Boudreaux, Michel, F-69

Boudreaux, Michel, S1-108-110

Boudreaux, Michel, S2-552

Boudreaux, Michel, S3-892, 897, 998

Boudreaux, Mr., E-291

Boudreaux, Noel, F-93

Boudreaux, Noel, S1-120

Boudreaux, Noel-Victor, S1-119

Boudreaux, Olivier, E-472

Boudreaux, Olivier, F-81, 107

Boudreaux, Olivier, S1-111-112, 289, 389

Boudreaux, Olivier, S3-908, 940

Boudreaux, Paul, C-15, 39, 51, 62

Boudreaux, Paul, E-42, 126, 547

Boudreaux, Paul, F-3, 5, 9, 11

Boudreaux, Paul, N-19, 38, 62, 102, 116, 202, 226, 234

Boudreaux, Paul, S1-88, 97, 113-114, 120-121, 202, 300

Boudreaux, Paul, S2-431, 525, 659

Boudreaux, Paul, S2-568

Boudreaux, Paul, S3-942-943, 967, 1025, 1031

Boudreaux, Paul Dominique, F-5

Boudreaux, Paul Dominique, N-25-27, 102, 197

Boudreaux, Paul Marie, N-25-26

Boudreaux, Paul Marin, F-5

Boudreaux, Paul-Dominique, S1-121

Boudreaux, Paul-Joseph, S1-92

Boudreaux, Paul-Marie, S1-99

Boudreaux, Pierre, C-15, 18, 33, 36, 99, 156

Boudreaux, Pierre, E-41-44, 111, 441, 555, 635

Boudreaux, Pierre, F-37, 67, 107

Boudreaux, Pierre, N-10, 19-20, 22, 24, 26, 27, 109, 219, 223, 253

Boudreaux, Pierre, S1-18, 87-88, 90, 95, 99, 101, 103, 105, 107, 112, 114-115, 118, 236, 277, 383, 392

Boudreaux, Pierre, S2-430-431, 568, 570, 631, 745, 758

Boudreaux, Pierre, S3-831, 906-908, 941, 1067, 1127

Boudreaux, Pierre Anne, N-25

Boudreaux, Pierre David, N-23

Boudreaux, Pierre Jean, N-26

Boudreaux, Pierre Jean Joseph, C-17

Boudreaux, Pierre Jean Joseph, N-24

Boudreaux, Pierre Paul, C-19

Boudreaux, Pierre-Charles, S1-106

Boudreaux, Pierre-Hilaire, S1-89

Boudreaux, Pierre-Jean, S1-99, 103

Boudreaux, Pierre-Jean-Joseph-Marie, S1-109

Boudreaux, Pierre-Mathurin, S1-86

Boudreaux, Pierre-Olivier, S1-104

Boudreaux, Pierre-Paul, S1-94-95, 115-116

Boudreaux, Prudent, S1-89-90, 116-117

Boudreaux, Prudent, S3-1002, 1049, 1078

Boudreaux, Prudent-Olivier, S1-118

Boudreaux, Raphael Benjamin, E-635

Boudreaux, Reine, N-22

Boudreaux, Rene, E-493, 523

Boudreaux, Rene-Antoine, S1-119

Boudreaux, Rosalie, E-44, 189, 272, 406-407, 414-416

Boudreaux, Rosalie, S2-533

Boudreaux, Rose, E-635

Boudreaux, Rose-Genevieve, S1-106

Boudreaux, Rose-Theotiste, S1-115

Boudreaux, Simon, S1-88

Boudreaux, Simon, S2-605

Boudreaux, Simon, S3-890

Boudreaux, Simon Bruno, E-44, 555

Boudreaux, Sophie, F-69, 93

Boudreaux, Sophie, N-24

Boudreaux, Sophie, S1-120

Boudreaux, Theodore, S1-89-90

Boudreaux, Theodose, S1-116, 118, 272

Boudreaux, Victor, F-93

Boudreaux, Victor, S1-89, 117-120

Boudreaux, Victor, S2-456, 661, 674, 693

Boudreaux, Victor, S3-1002, 1078, 1119

Boudreaux, Xavier, S1-91

Boudreaux, Yves, E-9, 44

Boudreaux, Yves, F-75

Boudreaux, Yves, N-18

Boudreaux, Zacharie, F-69

Boudreaux, Zacharie, N-17, 25, 27, 156, 191, 197, 215

Boudreaux, Zacharie, S1-90, 109, 120-121

Boudreaux, Zacharie, S2-734

Boudreaux, Zacharie, S3-906, 940, 987

Boudron, Henriette, E-363

Boudry, Genevieve, E-300, 337

Bouellonne, Angelique, S1-151

Boueman, Barthelemy, E-26, 296

Bouenel, Jean, S2-503

Bouenel, Nicolas, S2-757

Bouessiere, Jean, E-621

Bouessiere, Jeanne, E-621

Bouet, Andre, E-44, 139, 152, 172, 348

Bouet, Jean, E-125, 280

Bouet, Pierre, E-348

Bouex de Villemort, Marie Sophie de, C-73

Bouge, Marguerite, E-80, 137

Bougniot, Jean, E-40, 100

Bougrat, Francois, E-345

Bouhier, Francois, E-159, 621

Bouilie, Marie, E-621

Bouillie, Francois Sr., E-617

Bouillie, Francoise, E-621

Bouillie, Jean Jr., E-617

Bouillie, Jeanne, E-621

Bouin, Joseph, E-393

Bouinier, Anne, S3-993

Bouinier, Francois, S3-975, 978, 993, 997

Bouinier, Pierre, S3-978, 993

Bouja, Denys, E-409

Boujat, Catherine, E-38

Boujou, Rene, E-393, 409

Boulanger, Elisabeth, E-121, 584, 595

Boulanger, Elizabeth, S1-284

Boulanger, Elizabeth, S2-512, 514

Boulanger, Isabelle, E-44, 135, 145

Boulanger, Jean Baptiste, E-44, 145

Boulanger, Jean Robert, E-44, 145

Boulanger, Marianne Isabelle, E-121

Boulanger, Marianne-Isabelle, S1-284

Boulanger, Noel, E-44, 255

Boulanger, Noel, S2-512

Boulangere, Isabelle, E-255

Boulard, Joseph, E-191

Boulau, Perrine, E-429

Boulay, Francoise, S2-480

Bouleau, Francois, E-45, 439

Bouleau, Louis, E-45, 439

Boulet, M., S2-680

Boulet, Marie, S2-727

Boulier, Charlotte, S1-319

Boulier, Charlotte, S2-592

Boulier, Charlotte, S3-986

Boulineau, Andre, E-45, 159, 316

Boulineau, Gabriel, E-45

Boulineau, Jean, E-45, 316

Boulineau, Pierre, E-45, 90

Boullier, Jacques, N-208

Boullot, -----, S3-978, 1087

Boullot, Ainee, S3-1087, 1092

Boullot, Anne, E-621

Boullot, Anne, S1-122-123

Boullot, Anne, S3-1087

Boullot, Anne Louise, E-621

Boullot, Bertrand, S1-122-123

Boullot, Bnd., S3-1087

Boullot, Chalres, S1-122-123, 193, 204

Boullot, Charles, E-45, 381

Boullot, Charles-Pierre, S1-122

Boullot, Clement, E-617, 621

Boullot, Francois, E-621

Boullot, Isabelle, S3-989

Boullot, Jacques, E-45

Boullot, Jean Pierre, E-621

Boullot, Jean-Clement, S1-178
Boullot, Jean-Pierre, S1-122-123
Boullot, Jeanne, S3-1087
Boullot, Jeanne Perrine, E-621
Boullot, Jeanne-Perinne, S1-122
Boullot, Jn. Pre., S3-1096
Boullot, Joseph, E-621
Boullot, Josephine, E-621
Boullot, Louis Francois, E-616
Boullot, Marguerite, S1-122
Boullot, Olive, E-621
Boullot, Olive Louise, S3-1086-1087
Boullot, Olive-Louise, S1-122, 355
Boullot, Perinne, E-45, 314, 419, 429
Boullot, Perinne, S1-122
Boullot, Pierre, E-45, 381
Boullot, Pierre, S1-122, 355
Boullot, Pierre, S3-978, 1086
Boulogne-Sur-Mer, E-45-46
Boulon, Charles Nicolas, E-87
Boulon, Charles Rene, E-46, 88
Boulon, Francoise Catherine, E-46, 87, 89
Boulon, Gabriel, E-88
Boulon, Rose Adelaide, E-87
Boulot, Clement, C-157
Boulque, Heleine, S3-869
Boulque, Jean, S3-867
Boulque, Rose, S3-867-868
Boulu, Gabriel, C-108
Boulu, Louis, C-108
Bounieux, Francoise, E-621
Bouquet, Jean, E-141
Bouquinet, Jean, E-34
Bour, Bernard, E-456
Bour, Francois, E-456
Bour, Jehan, E-456
Bourbon, -----, S3-1077
Bourbon, Jacque, S3-891, 1077
Bourbon, Jacques, C-34
Bourbon, Jacques, F-55
Bourbon, Jacques, N-27-28
Bourbon, Jacques, S1-123
Bourbon, Jacques, S2-707, 752
Bourbon, Jacques, Sr., S2-546
Bourbon, Robert, S1-330
Bourbonne, Catherine, E-46

Bourbonne, Simon, E-46
Bourdageau, Pierre, E-140
Bourdailleau, Catherine, E-46, 357
Bourdain, Pierre, E-358
Bourdajeau, Pierre, E-376
Bourde, Adelaide, E-622
Bourde, Claire, E-622
Bourde, Francoise, E-622
Bourde, Marie Catherine, E-622
Bourde, Nobelmen Joseph, S1-343
Bourde, Perrine, E-622
Bourdel, Guillaume, E-46
Bourdel, Louis Jean, E-46, 188
Bourdelais, -----, S3-1125
Bourdon, Pierre, E-584, 596
Bourdonnaye, Jean, E-625
Boure, Cecile, S2-733
Bouree, Francois Ee., S3-852
Bouret, Francoise-Jeanne, S2-668
Bourg, Abraham, E-47, 472, 484, 501, 523
Bourg, Abraham, F-25
Bourg, Abraham, N-31
Bourg, Abraham, S1-146
Bourg, Abraham, S3-921
Bourg, Adelaide, C-74
Bourg, Adelaide Rose, E-47
Bourg, Agnes, N-74
Bourg, Agnes, S1-376-377
Bourg, Agnes, S2-600
Bourg, Agnes, S3-1106
Bourg, Agnes-Blanche, S1-134
Bourg, Aimee Modeste, E-47
Bourg, Alain, C-19
Bourg, Alain, N-28
Bourg, Alain, S1-4, 123-124, 157, 384
Bourg, Alain, S2-635
Bourg, Alain, S3-1107, 1119
Bourg, Alexandre, C-20
Bourg, Alexandre, E-523, 547
Bourg, Alexandre, F-15
Bourg, Alexandre, N-5, 29, 236
Bourg, Alexandre, S1-125-126, 129, 148, 273, 348
Bourg, Alexandre, S2-455, 481, 616, 630

Bourg, Alexandre, S3-921, 939, 949, 949, 1106, 1110, 1112, 1137
Bourg, Alexis, C-21
Bourg, Alexis, E-47
Bourg, Alexis, F-39
Bourg, Alexis, N-28, 30
Bourg, Allain, F-39
Bourg, Amand, E-47
Bourg, Ambroise, E-30, 47, 334, 357, 523
Bourg, Ambroise, F-99
Bourg, Ambroise, N-28
Bourg, Ambroise, S1-126-129, 156-157
Bourg, Ambroise David, N-32
Bourg, Ambroise-David, S1-158
Bourg, Amy-Modeste, S1-127
Bourg, Anastasie, S1-299-300
Bourg, Andre, E-47, 262
Bourg, Andre, F-17
Bourg, Angelique, E-186
Bourg, Anne, C-12, 53, 57
Bourg, Anne, E-24, 44, 82, 358, 484, 493, 504, 547, 622
Bourg, Anne, F-7, 43, 45, 93
Bourg, Anne, N-60-61, 91
Bourg, Anne, S1-23, 125-126, 148-150, 285-287, 292-293, 300
Bourg, Anne, S2-442, 462, 481, 559, 569, 616-617, 621, 713
Bourg, Anne, S3-853, 939, 945, 949, 1103, 1105, 1136
Bourg, Anne Joseph, C-21
Bourg, Anne Joseph, F-77
Bourg, Anne Josephe, N-83
Bourg, Anne Madeleine, C-22
Bourg, Anne Marie, E-47
Bourg, Anne Marie, N-2-3, 5
Bourg, Anne Modeste, C-21
Bourg, Anne Victoire, F-103
Bourg, Anne-Charlotte, S1-142
Bourg, Anne-Dorate, S1-126
Bourg, Anne-Francoise, S1-131, 148
Bourg, Anne-Gregoire, S1-136
Bourg, Anne-Jeanne, S1-143
Bourg, Anne-Josephe, S1-144, 152

Bourg, Anne-Marguerite, S1-126

Bourg, Anne-Marie, S1-140-141, 150, 165

Bourg, Anne-Modeste, S1-132

Bourg, Anne-Perinne, S1-158

Bourg, Anne-Radegonde, S1-126

Bourg, Anne-Theodose, S1-158

Bourg, Anselme, S1-124, 129

Bourg, Antoine, E-456, 472, 504

Bourg, Antoine, S1-135

Bourg, Antoine-Yves, S1-146

Bourg, Athanase, C-20

Bourg, Athanase, F-55

Bourg, Athanase, F-75

Bourg, Athanase, N-29-30

Bourg, Athanase, S1-129, 133-134, 169, 268

Bourg, Athanase, S3-1134

Bourg, Athanaze, S2-706

Bourg, Augustin-Xavier, S1-138

Bourg, Benony, S1-129-130

Bourg, Bernard, E-472, 523

Bourg, Blanche, S1-125

Bourg, Boniface, S1-133

Bourg, boy, S1-130

Bourg, Catherine, C-10-11

Bourg, Catherine, E-30, 31, 47, 493

Bourg, Catherine, F-19, 77

Bourg, Catherine, N-13

Bourg, Cecile, C-59-60

Bourg, Cecile, E-47

Bourg, Cecile, F-3, 5

Bourg, Cecile, N-96, 98-99, 214

Bourg, Cecile, S1-163-164

Bourg, Cecile, S2-496, 509-511, 599-602

Bourg, Cecile, S3-1108, 1123

Bourg, Cecile Jean, S3-1151

Bourg, Cecile-Jean, S1-130

Bourg, Charles, C-10, 20-22

Bourg, Charles, E-47-48, 303, 431, 616

Bourg, Charles, F-17, 19, 75, 77, 97, 99, 103

Bourg, Charles, F-55

Bourg, Charles, N-30, 152, 244

Bourg, Charles, S1-24, 104, 126, 130-132, 134-139, 142, 145, 148-150, 152, 155, 163, 242, 273

Bourg, Charles, S2-482, 498, 502, 621

Bourg, Charles, S3-837, 846, 850, 853, 855, 858, 927, 930, 946, 949, 1070

Bourg, Charles Joseph, E-47

Bourg, Charles-Alain, S1-243

Bourg, Charles-Simon, S1-149

Bourg, Charlote Francoise, F-87

Bourg, Charlotte-Francoise, S1-144

Bourg, Claire, E-484

Bourg, Claire, N-60

Bourg, Constance, S1-149

Bourg, Elisabelle, S3-1112

Bourg, Elisabeth, S1-64

Bourg, Elisabeth-Celeste, S1-127

Bourg, Elizabeth, C-12, 83

Bourg, Elizabeth, E-337, 547

Bourg, Elizabeth, F-25, 45, 47, 95

Bourg, Elizabeth, N-14, 31-32, 63, 88, 114, 138, 141

Bourg, Elizabeth, S1-152, 303-305

Bourg, Elizabeth, S2-466, 634-635, 657

Bourg, Elizabeth-Blanche, S1-147

Bourg, Elizabeth-Felicite, S1-138

Bourg, Elizabeth-Helene, S1-158

Bourg, Elysabeth, S3-882

Bourg, Eustache, E-95, 280

Bourg, Eustache, S1-132-133, 151-152

Bourg, Fabien-Joseph, S1-147

Bourg, Felix Xavier, F-103

Bourg, Felix-Xavier, S1-138

Bourg, Francois, C-19-20, 22

Bourg, Francois, S1-123, 129, 131-135, 137, 139, 141-142, 144, 149, 157, 241-242, 250-251, 266, 336

Bourg, Francois, E-47, 504, 547

Bourg, Francois, F-39, 49, 55, 75, 87, 89

Bourg, Francois, N-28-30, 32

Bourg, Francois, S2-473, 481, 488, 498, 523, 668, 749, 755

Bourg, Francois, S3-864, 895, 905, 930, 945-946, 1107, 1119, 1134

Bourg, Francois George, F-95

Bourg, Francois Simon, N-29

Bourg, Francois Xavier, F-103

Bourg, Francois Xavier, S3-926-927, 930

Bourg, Francois-Jeanne, S1-136

Bourg, Francois-Marie, S1-142

Bourg, Francois-Xavier, S1-128, 137-139

Bourg, Francois-Xavier, S2-494, 501-502, 669

Bourg, Francoise, C-18, 47-50, 125-126

Bourg, Francoise, E-47, 323, 484, 616

Bourg, Francoise, F-21, 89

Bourg, Francoise, S1-69, 90-91, 134-135, 145, 266, 273, 345, 350, 388, 391-393

Bourg, Francoise, S2-488, 615, 639

Bourg, Francoise, S3-946, 1104

Bourg, Francoise-Charlotte, S1-148

Bourg, Francoise-Genevieve, S1-145

Bourg, Francoise-Josephe, S1-156-157

Bourg, Francoise-Marie, S1-145

Bourg, Genevieve, C-22

Bourg, Genevieve, F-39

Bourg, Genevieve, N-28

Bourg, Gertrude, F-17

Bourg, Gertrude, S1-134, 140-141, 349-350

Bourg, Gertrude, S2-462, 716

Bourg, Gertrude, S3-1137

Bourg, Gregoire, S1-125-126

Bourg, Guillaume Jean, F-95

Bourg, Helene, S1-136, 143, 149, 242

Bourg, Helene-Germaine, S1-148

Bourg, Huguette, E-473
Bourg, Huguette, S2-628
Bourg, Isabelle, C-11, 22, 34
Bourg, Isabelle, E-47, 493, 505, 523, 622
Bourg, Isabelle, F-5, 89, 99, 103
Bourg, Isabelle, N-189
Bourg, Isabelle, S1-63, 129, 146, 265, 384
Bourg, Isabelle, S2-454-455, 470
Bourg, Isabelle, S3-826, 1003, 1116, 1120
Bourg, Isabelle-Charlotte, S1-150
Bourg, Isabelle-Germaine, S1-145
Bourg, Isabelle-Laurence, S1-149
Bourg, Jacques, E-115
Bourg, Jacques Alain, N-28
Bourg, Jacques Charles, N-30
Bourg, Janvier, S1-133
Bourg, Jean, C-21-22, 53, 89
Bourg, Jean, E-47, 262, 472, 501, 523
Bourg, Jean, F-15, 17, 25, 45, 77, 87, 89, 95
Bourg, Jean, N-31, 88, 91, 108, 122, 233
Bourg, Jean, S1-68, 125, 131, 134-136, 139-144, 146, 149, 151, 153, 158, 159, 240, 313, 350, 360
Bourg, Jean, S2-462, 488, 499, 541, 670, 755
Bourg, Jean, S3-847, 850, 895, 936, 946, 1133, 1137
Bourg, Jean, S3-879
Bourg, Jean Baptiste, E-493, 547
Bourg, Jean Baptiste, F-17, 25
Bourg, Jean Baptiste, N-32
Bourg, Jean Baptiste Simon Louis, F-89
Bourg, Jean Baptiste Simon Louis, N-31
Bourg, Jean Francois, E-47
Bourg, Jean Marie, N-28, 32
Bourg, Jean Pierre, C-20, 57, 88, 133

Bourg, Jean Pierre, F-21, 95
Bourg, Jean Pierre, N-234, 248
Bourg, Jean-Baptiste, S1-140-141, 147, 350
Bourg, Jean-Baptiste, S2-462
Bourg, Jean-Baptiste-Simon-Louis, S1-146
Bourg, Jean-Charles, S1-131, 134
Bourg, Jean-Christophe, S1-148
Bourg, Jean-Joseph-Marie, S1-138
Bourg, Jean-Louis, S1-131
Bourg, Jean-Marie, S1-143
Bourg, Jean-Mathurin, S1-145
Bourg, Jean-Perinne, S1-150
Bourg, Jean-Pierre, S1-150, 153, 156-157, 159, 339
Bourg, Jean-Pierre, S2-447
Bourg, Jeanne, E-83, 473, 484, 501, 504, 622
Bourg, Jeanne, F-49, 87, 93
Bourg, Jeanne, N-33, 60, 63
Bourg, Jeanne, S1-26, 144, 303
Bourg, Jeanne, S3-1003
Bourg, Jeanne-Anne, S1-143
Bourg, Jeanne-Madeleine-Francoise, S1-157
Bourg, Joseph, C-74, 153
Bourg, Joseph, E-47-48, 114, 547, 616, 620
Bourg, Joseph, F-25, 37, 75, 87, 89, 99
Bourg, Joseph, F-55
Bourg, Joseph, N-30-33, 44, 74, 136, 210
Bourg, Joseph, S1-22-24, 125-126, 129-130, 133, 140-141, 144, 146-151, 158, 179, 376
Bourg, Joseph, S2-461, 481, 600, 614, 616, 629, 706, 713
Bourg, Joseph, S3-916, 921, 936, 944-945, 948-949, 1035, 1106, 1110, 1137
Bourg, Joseph Andre, N-28
Bourg, Joseph Faustin, F-103
Bourg, Joseph Florent, C-21
Bourg, Joseph Florent, F-77
Bourg, Joseph Florent, N-30
Bourg, Joseph-Alain, S1-123

Bourg, Joseph-Barthelemy, S1-153
Bourg, Joseph-Faustin, S1-128
Bourg, Joseph-Firmin, S1-141
Bourg, Joseph-Marguerite, S1-150
Bourg, Joseph-Marie, S1-144
Bourg, Joseph-Marin, S1-129
Bourg, Joseph-Pierre, S1-151, 153
Bourg, Josephe, E-161
Bourg, Julie Therese, F-99
Bourg, Julie-Therese, S1-129
Bourg, La Luce, F-47
Bourg, Laure, F-15
Bourg, Louis, C-20, 43, 53
Bourg, Louis, F-77, 81
Bourg, Louis, N-32
Bourg, Louis, S1-130, 132, 151-153, 348
Bourg, Louis, S2-442, 621, 670
Bourg, Louis, S3-842, 853, 1126
Bourg, Louis Alexis, N-28
Bourg, Louise, S1-127
Bourg, Luce, C-48-49
Bourg, Luce, N-91
Bourg, Luce, S1-72, 153, 350, 392
Bourg, Luce, S2-461, 474
Bourg, Luce, S3-905, 1133
Bourg, Luce Perpetue, F-87
Bourg, Luce-Perpetue, S1-124, 140-141
Bourg, Luce-Perpetue, S2-473
Bourg, Lucien, F-77
Bourg, Lucien, S1-130
Bourg, Madeleine, E-47, 416, 493
Bourg, Madeleine, N-20, 24, 26-27, 72, 223, 253
Bourg, Madeleine, S1-11, 126, 128-129, 144, 153, 155
Bourg, Madeleine, S2-531, 561, 615
Bourg, Madeleine-Adelaide, S1-127-128
Bourg, Madeleine-Jeanne, S1-142
Bourg, Madeleine-Josephe, S1-266-268

Bourg, Madeleine-Josephe, S2-706

Bourg, Madeleine-Julienne, S1-158

Bourg, Madeleine-Marie, S1-136

Bourg, Madeleine-Perinne, S1-143

Bourg, Magdalene Josephe, E-43, 113-114, 559

Bourg, Magdelaine, F-37, 45, 87, 99

Bourg, Magdeleine, C-33, 64, 67, 99

Bourg, Marain, S3-879

Bourg, Marguerite, C-22, 43

Bourg, Marguerite, E-60, 148, 361-362, 365, 371, 484, 493, 501, 504, 529-530, 616

Bourg, Marguerite, F-15, 81, 87, 89

Bourg, Marguerite, N-4, 28-29, 31, 33, 91, 114, 122, 189, 224, 236

Bourg, Marguerite, S1-4, 9-10, 24, 34, 66-69, 72, 125-126, 131, 135, 139, 144, 146, 149, 150-152, 266-267, 273, 347, 349, 390-391

Bourg, Marguerite, S2-447, 461-462, 481, 489, 537, 621, 633, 676, 697, 713

Bourg, Marguerite, S3-1151

Bourg, Marguerite, S3-823, 842, 846, 944, 1131, 1133

Bourg, Marguerite Joseph, F-25, 95

Bourg, Marguerite Josephe, C-87

Bourg, Marguerite Josephe, E-191, 276

Bourg, Marguerite Josephe, N-86, 149

Bourg, Marguerite-Charlotte, S1-136

Bourg, Marguerite-Josephe, S1-23, 133, 138, 148, 154, 157

Bourg, Marguerite-Josephe, S2-450-451, 502, 504, 662, 705, 707, 712

Bourg, Marguerite-Marie, S1-145

Bourg, Marguerite-Perinne, S1-142

Bourg, Marguerite-Suzanne, S1-133

Bourg, Marguerite-Tarsille, S1-124

Bourg, Marguerite-Theodose, S1-150

Bourg, Marguerite-Victoire, S1-157

Bourg, Marie, E-157, 188, 197, 282, 386, 456, 472, 484, 493, 501, 504, 525, 622

Bourg, Marie, F-17, 87, 89

Bourg, Marie, N-31, 87, 188, 233

Bourg, Marie, S1-15, 69, 93, 125, 130, 132, 135-137, 139, 142, 144, 146, 155-156, 159, 228, 235, 238, 250, 336, 350

Bourg, Marie, S2-462, 481, 498, 510, 699, 711

Bourg, Marie, S3-829, 864-865, 870, 1070, 1117

Bourg, Marie Francoise, F-89

Bourg, Marie Francoise, S3-916

Bourg, Marie Francoise Magde-laine Joseph, F-95

Bourg, Marie Genevieve, C-90

Bourg, Marie Isabelle, F-103

Bourg, Marie Joseph, E-185, 283, 286, 371

Bourg, Marie Joseph, F-97

Bourg, Marie Josephe, F-25

Bourg, Marie Josephe, N-32, 108

Bourg, Marie Luce, F-95

Bourg, Marie Madeleine, E-188, 329

Bourg, Marie Madeleine, F-21

Bourg, Marie Madeleine, N-32, 84, 89, 136, 234

Bourg, Marie Magdelaine, S3-884

Bourg, Marie Rose, F-55

Bourg, Marie Rose, N-29

Bourg, Marie Victoire, F-99

Bourg, Marie-Elizabeth, S1-137-138

Bourg, Marie-Francoise, S1-131, 149, 377

Bourg, Marie-Francoise, S2-600-601

Bourg, Marie-Genevieve, S1-123

Bourg, Marie-Jacquemine, S1-136, 250

Bourg, Marie-Josephe, S1-142, 147, 153

Bourg, Marie-Josephe, S2-541-542

Bourg, Marie-Luce, S1-153

Bourg, Marie-Madeleine, S1-124, 126, 131, 152, 157, 369, 384

Bourg, Marie-Madeleine, S2-445-446, 629, 635

Bourg, Marie-Marguerite-Constance, S1-127-128

Bourg, Marie-Modeste, S1-128

Bourg, Marie-Rose, S1-126, 349

Bourg, Marie-Sebastienne, S1-134

Bourg, Marie-Suline, S1-157

Bourg, Marie-Victoire, S1-127-128, 138

Bourg, Marin, F-17

Bourg, Marin, F-95

Bourg, Marin, S1-12, 140, 153-154, 247

Bourg, Marin, S2-462, 550, 694

Bourg, Marin Joseph, F-95

Bourg, Marin-Joseph, S1-154

Bourg, Martin, E-472, 523

Bourg, Martin, S1-141

Bourg, Mary, E-16

Bourg, Mathieu Athanase, N-29

Bourg, Mathurin, S1-154-155, 369

Bourg, Mathurin, S3-882, 887, 1117-1118, 1120, 1122-1123, 1126, 1132-1133

Bourg, Maximilien, F-103

Bourg, Maximiline-Ambroise, S1-128

Bourg, Michel, E-47, 523

Bourg, Michel, N-64

Bourg, Michel, S1-154-156, 170-171, 306, 369

Bourg, Michel, S2-699-700

Bourg, Michel, S3-1070, 1117, 1124-1125, 1138
Bourg, Modeste, F-99
Bourg, Modeste, S1-128-129
Bourg, Modeste Aimee, F-99
Bourg, Modeste-Aimee, S1-128
Bourg, Modeste-Emee, S1-128
Bourg, Ozite, S1-135
Bourg, Paul, S1-135
Bourg, Paul, S2-569
Bourg, Pelagie, F-99
Bourg, Pelagie, S1-128-129
Bourg, Perine, E-457, 472
Bourg, Perpetue, E-303
Bourg, Perpetue, S1-156
Bourg, Pierre, C-4, 19
Bourg, Pierre, E-278, 501, 504, 523, 547
Bourg, Pierre, F-17
Bourg, Pierre, F-25, 49, 103
Bourg, Pierre, N-32-33, 65, 203, 210, 237
Bourg, Pierre, S1-123, 129, 147, 155-158, 299, 325, 345
Bourg, Pierre, S2-483, 635
Bourg, Pierre, S3-1104-1105, 1107, 1119
Bourg, Pierre Jean, C-21
Bourg, Pierre Jean, N-30
Bourg, Pierre Jean Baptiste, F-95
Bourg, Pierre-Alain, S1-124
Bourg, Pierre-Jean, S1-132
Bourg, Pierre-Jean-Baptiste, S1-154
Bourg, Pierre-Jean-Francois, S1-138
Bourg, Pierre-Marguerite, S1-137
Bourg, Pierre-Olivier, S1-157
Bourg, Raymond, S1-125-126
Bourg, Rene, E-484, 505
Bourg, Rosalie, E-344
Bourg, Rosalie-Josephe, S1-124
Bourg, Rose, S1-39, 72, 143, 252
Bourg, Rose Adelaide, F-37
Bourg, Rose Adelaide, N-44-45
Bourg, Rose Magdelaine, F-95
Bourg, Rose-Madeleine, S1-154

Bourg, Rose-Perinne, S1-141, 151
Bourg, Rose-Perinne, S2-670
Bourg, Sebastien Joseph, F-25
Bourg, Sebastien Joseph, N-32
Bourg, Simon, S1-156
Bourg, Sulienne, S1-158
Bourg, Susanne, F-59
Bourg, Tarsile, S1-125
Bourg, Theodore, F-45
Bourg, Theodore, N-182, 210
Bourg, Theodore, S1-80, 140-141, 147, 153, 158-159
Bourg, Theodore, S3-873, 936
Bourg, Theodore-Prosper-Etienne, S1-159
Bourg, Theodose, S1-159
Bourg, Therese-Julie, S1-127-128
Bourg, Thomas-Francois-Joseph, S1-129
Bourg, Ursule, C-13, 20, 24, 35, 85, 93, 101, 103, 107, 157
Bourg, Ursule, F-21, 55, 75, 81
Bourg, Ursule, N-29, 35, 136
Bourg, Ursule, S1-129, 168-169, 270
Bourg, Ursule, S2-506, 537, 629-631, 665
Bourg, Ursule, S3-925, 1110, 1131, 1134
Bourg, Victoire, F-49
Bourg, Victoire, N-33
Bourg, Victoire, S1-155, 159, 325
Bourg, Victoire, S2-700
Bourg, Victor, S3-936
Bourg, Xavier, F-87
Bourg, Xavier, S1-377
Bourg, Xavier, S2-756
Bourg, Yves, F-89
Bourg, Yves, N-31
Bourg, Yves, S1-146
Bourg, Yves-Jean, S1-145
Bourg Village named after Antoine Bourg, E-209
Bourgarel, Marie Anne, E-168
Bourgeois, Anne, E-13, 406, 435-436, 475, 515, 552
Bourgeois, Anne, N-19, 169, 180

Bourgeois, Anne, S1-226
Bourgeois, Anne Esther, E-600
Bourgeois, Apolonie, E-336
Bourgeois, Catherine, F-77, 109
Bourgeois, Charles, E-456, 515, 523, 552
Bourgeois, Claude, E-515, 523, 552
Bourgeois, Claude, N-156
Bourgeois, Claude, S1-95
Bourgeois, Claude, S2-734
Bourgeois, Claude, S3-1064
Bourgeois, Estiennette, E-513
Bourgeois, Francois, E-513
Bourgeois, Francoise, E-473
Bourgeois, Germain, E-472
Bourgeois, Guillaume, E-472, 492, 516, 523
Bourgeois, Henriette, E-360, 362-363
Bourgeois, Honnore, E-552
Bourgeois, Jacob, E-456, 472
Bourgeois, Jacques, E-293, 552
Bourgeois, Jacques Augustin, C-22
Bourgeois, Jean, E-99, 126
Bourgeois, Jean Baptiste, E-552
Bourgeois, Jean Claude, E-126
Bourgeois, Jeanne, E-307, 365, 514, 552
Bourgeois, Jeanne, F-15
Bourgeois, Jeanne, N-113, 119
Bourgeois, Jeanne, S2-559, 597
Bourgeois, Jeanne, S3-989, 1049
Bourgeois, Joseph, E-513, 552, 600
Bourgeois, Joseph, S1-300
Bourgeois, Madeleine, S1-214
Bourgeois, Madeleine, S2-623
Bourgeois, Magdelaine, E-91, 167, 315, 330, 435, 517, 529, 552
Bourgeois, Magdeleine, S3-1064
Bourgeois, Marguerite, E-11, 35, 63, 176, 185, 360, 362-365, 407-408, 475, 632, 642
Bourgeois, Marie, E-54, 84, 86, 437, 458, 474-475, 513, 516, 528, 552

Bourgeois, Marie, N-114
Bourgeois, Marie, S1-8
Bourgeois, Marie, S2-752, 758
Bourgeois, Marie, S3-831
Bourgeois, Marie Angelique, E-53-54
Bourgeois, Marie Madeleine, N-156
Bourgeois, Marie Magdalen, E-42
Bourgeois, Marie-Josephe, S2-756-758, 760
Bourgeois, Marie-Madeleine, S1-95-96
Bourgeois, Marie-Madeleine, S2-734
Bourgeois, Michel, E-517, 552
Bourgeois, Nicolas, E-72
Bourgeois, Paul, E-552
Bourgeois, Pierre, E-552
Bourgeois, Rosalie, E-278-279, 414
Bourgeois, Theotiste, E-13
Bourgeois, Victoire, E-68
Bourgeon, Marie, E-440
Bourges, Louise, S2-783
Bourges, Louise, S3-928
Bourgneuf, Sophie, S1-56
Bourgois, Jean Baptiste, C-22
Bourgon, Marie Henriette, E-360
Bourgonne, Antoinette, E-379, 399
Bourgot, Rene, S1-220
Bourgot, Renee, S3-861
Bourgouin, Antoine, E-117
Bourgouin, Louis, E-117
Bourgue, Charle, C-153
Bourguignolle, Louis Emmanuel, E-88
Bourguignon, Jean, E-195, 276
Bourguignon, Marie, E-195, 333
Bourguignon, Marie Madeleine, E-195
Bourguigon, Jean, E-440
Bourguigon, Pierre, E-440
Bouri, Jean, S3-914
Bouri, Pierre, S3-914, 994
Bourier, -----, N-246
Bourier, Francois, N-245
Bourillon, Marie Anne, E-337

Bourit, Pierre, E-410
Bourle, Marie Marguerite, E-61
Bourlieau, Jean, E-403
Bourlier, Marie Charlotte, E-64, 349
Bourneuf, Anne, S1-159-160
Bourneuf, Anne, S2-620
Bourneuf, Celine, S1-364
Bourneuf, Francois, S1-160
Bourneuf, Francoise, S1-160
Bourneuf, Jeanne, S1-159-160
Bourneuf, Jeanne, S2-620
Bourneuf, Julien, S1-160-161
Bourneuf, Julienne, S1-160
Bourneuf, Sebastien, S1-160-161
Bourneuf, Sophie, S1-160
Bouron, Jeanne, E-359, 409
Bourosa, Marie, E-34, 152
Bourre, Jeanne, E-472
Bourre, Marguerite, E-147
Bourreau, Etienne, E-51
Bourreau, Jacques, E-51
Bourreau, Jean, E-51, 409
Bourreau, Marianne, E-51, 140
Bourreau, Marie, E-51
Bourreau, Marthe, E-51
Boursicot, Jean, E-410
Boursicot, Louis, E-410
Boursicot, Suzanne, E-51, 410
Bourtinel, Alexis, S2-780
Bousan, Andre, E-51
Bousan, Marguerite, E-51, 377
Bousaus, Marguerite, E-378
Boussot, Marie Anne, E-66, 375
Boutan, Idabelle, E-23
Boutary, Anne Marie Claudine, N-33
Boutary, Antoine, C-23, 97, 134, 155
Boutary, Antoine, F-51
Boutary, Antoine, N-33-34, 183, 206
Boutary, Antoine Hipolite, C-156
Boutary, Auguste, F-51
Boutary, Auguste, N-34
Boutary, Augustin, C-156
Boutary, Guillaume, F-51
Boutary, Guillaume, N-33-34
Boutary, Marie Claude, C-23

Boutary, Marie Claude, N-34
Boutary, Marie Josephe, C-23
Bouteau, Jean Charles Louis, E-357
Bouteillee, Servanne, S2-439
Bouteiller, Elie, E-51, 319
Bouteiller, Marie Anne, E-51
Bouteiller, Marie Henriette, E-51
Bouteiller, Vincent, E-51, 319
Bouteillier, Elie, E-119
Boutet, Marie Anne, C-75
Boutet, Michel Louis, C-23, 137
Boutet, Pierre, C-23, 136
Boutin, Alexandre, E-51
Boutin, Eustache, S2-583, 587
Boutin, Francois, E-38, 51
Boutin, Jean Baptiste, E-35, 51, 404
Boutin, Jean Francois, E-38, 51, 328
Boutin, Jeanne, E-35
Boutin, Joseph, E-277, 328, 523
Boutin, Louis, E-34, 51, 59, 114
Boutin, Marie, E-51
Boutin, Pierre, E-325, 392
Boutin, Sieur Joseph, E-51
Boutineau, Louis, E-376, 394
Boutinet, Elisabeth, E-83, 406
Boutiron, Eugenie, E-196
Bouton, Henry, E-51-52, 185, 189, 300, 337, 439-440
Bouton, Jean Baptiste Henry, E-52, 337
Bouton, Nicolas, E-51, E-52
Bouton, Prosper Joseph, E-52
Boutreau, Madeleine, E-134
Boutterel, Cecille, E-66, 131
Bouvard, Pierre (Fr.), E-33, 255
Bouvet, Francoise-Jeanne, S2-759
Bouvet, Madeleine, S2-498
Bouvier, Jeanne, E-148, 195
Bouviere, Marie, E-52
Boux, Ee. Francois, S3-832
Bouyer, Herbert, E-295
Bouyer, Jean, E-157, 338, 350
Bouyer, Marie, E-28, 304
Bouzin, Francois, S2-648
Bovy, Pierre, S3-1060
Boy, Antoine, E-176, 411

Boy, Joseph, E-53, 411
Boyer, Marguerite, F-65
Boyer, Marie, E-69, 325
Boyer, Marie-Jeanne, S2-771
Boyer, Pierre, E-156
Boyer, Robert, E-379
Boynard, Marguerite, E-21, 52
Boyse, Benoni, C-162
Braget, Marie Madeleine, E-27
Branchard, Jean Hypolite, E-52
Branet, Besnard, E-52
Branet, Louis Marie, E-52
Branger, Francoise, E-301
Brar, Julien, S3-1072, 1085
Brard, Antoine, E-36
Brasode, Susanne, E-267, 386
Brassard, Anne, E-117
Brassaude, Anne, S3-1114
Brasseur, Anne, F-89, 99
Brasseur, Anne, N-113
Brasseur, Anne, S2-559, 599-
600, 602
Brasseur, Anne, S3-916
Brasseur, Brigitte, E-52, 392
Brasseur, Catherine, C-83
Brasseur, Catherine, F-77
Brasseur, Catherine, N-142
Brasseur, Catherine, S2-660
Brasseur, Catherinne, S3-912
Brasseur, Cecile, F-93
Brasseur, Cecile, S3-1002, 1078
Brasseur, Isabelle, S2-675
Brasseur, Joseph, N-34
Brasseur, Marguerite, N-74
Brasseur, Marie, C-8
Brasseur, Marie, F-23
Brasseur, Mathieu, E-52, 523
Brasseur, Mathieu, N-34
Brasseur, Mathieu, S2-675
Brasseur, Ozite, F-23
Brasseur, Pierre, E-523
Brasseur, Pierre, S2-602
Brasseur, Rosalie, C-157
Braud, Agnes, E-53, 302, 585,
592
Braud, Alexis, F-73
Braud, Alexis, N-77, 88, 186,
188
Braud, Alexis, S2-447
Braud, Alexis, S3-826, 905-906,
908

Braud, Ambroise, E-53
Braud, Angelique, C-20, 24, 55,
59, 85, 101, 108
Braud, Angelique, N-36
Braud, Angelique, S2-507
Braud, Anne, C-3, 7, 23
Braud, Anne, E-47, 53, 409, 488
Braud, Anne, F-21
Braud, Anne, N-169
Braud, Anne, S2-441, 448, 533-
534, 684
Braud, Anne, S3-947, 1015,
1102
Braud, Anne Josephe, C-34-35
Braud, Anne Josephe, N-56
Braud, Anne Madeleine, N-88,
188
Braud, Anne Marie, F-89
Braud, Anne-Josephe, S2-506
Braud, Antoine, E-488, 523
Braud, Antoine, F-3, 73
Braud, Antoine, N-35, 37, 96
Braud, Antoine, S2-483, 487,
496
Braud, Antoine, S3-823, 1103-
1104, 1106, 1108-1110, 1113-
1114, 1116, 1123, 1127, 1134
Braud, Antoine , C-59, 101
Braud, Antoinette, E-140
Braud, Augustin, S3-965
Braud, Cecile, C-59
Braud, Cecile, E-13, 107, 299
Braud, Cecile, F-3
Braud, Cecile, N-96-97
Braud, Cecile, S2-482, 496
Braud, Cecile, S3-1123
Braud, Charle, S3-966
Braud, Charles, C-94
Braud, Charles, E-53-54
Braud, Charles, F-3
Braud, Charles, N-35, 154
Braud, Charles, S2-731
Braud, Elie, C-24
Braud, Elie, N-35
Braud, Elisabeth, E-53
Braud, Etienne, E-20, 53
Braud, Eulalie, F-81
Braud, Eulalie, N-37
Braud, Felicite, E-41, 53
Braud, Felix, N-34-35
Braud, Felix, S2-505

Braud, Felix, S3-966, 971, 1051
Braud, Francois, C-101
Braud, Francois, E-53, 325, 428,
432, 488, 523
Braud, Francois Xavier, C-34,
59
Braud, Francoise, C-14
Braud, Francoise, E-140, 413
Braud, Francoise, N-3, 63
Braud, Francoise Perrine, N-34
Braud, Gabriel, C-24
Braud, Gabriel, E-53
Braud, Hesse, S2-665
Braud, Honore, C-24, 100
Braud, Honore, F-19
Braud, Honore, N-35
Braud, Honore, S2-575, 578
Braud, Honore, S3-843, 880,
885, 887, 889, 898
Braud, Isabelle Francoise, C-93,
102
Braud, Isabelle Francoise, S3-
1131-1132
Braud, Isabelle-Francoise, S2-
506, 537
Braud, Jan Baptiste, S3-971
Braud, Jean, E-38, 350, 395,
489, 523
Braud, Jean, S3-1003, 1117-
1118, 1120, 1122-1123, 1126,
1133
Braud, Jean Baptiste, E-53, 155
Braud, Jean Baptiste, N-34
Braud, Jean Charles, C-24, 157
Braud, Jean Charles, N-35
Braud, Jeanne, E-53, 327, 335,
350, 417, 489
Braud, Jeanne, F-19
Braud, Jeanne, N-35
Braud, Jeanne, S1-345
Braud, Jeanne, S3-878
Braud, Jeanne-Francoise, S1-
164
Braud, Joseph, C-102, 108
Braud, Joseph, C-13, 20, 24, 35,
85, 93, 101, 103, 107-108
Braud, Joseph, F-21, 37, 55, 75,
81
Braud, Joseph, N-29, 35-37, 63,
167, 218
Braud, Joseph, S2-506, 537, 665

Braud, Joseph, S1-85, 129, 168-170, 270, 303

Braud, Joseph, S3-823, 924-925, 1003, 1131-1132, 1134

Braud, Joseph Gabriel, C-24, 94

Braud, Joseph Gabriel, N-36

Braud, Joseph-Gabriel, S2-506

Braud, Joseph-Pierre, S1-166

Braud, Jullien, S3-1079

Braud, Louise, C-20

Braud, Luce, C-20

Braud, Luce, F-55, 75

Braud, Luce, N-29-30

Braud, Luce, S1-129, 169

Braud, Luce, S3-1134

Braud, Lucie, S2-483

Braud, Madeleine, S1-121, 162-163, 192, 237, 295

Braud, Magdelaine, F-73

Braud, Marguerite, E-53, 488

Braud, Marguerite, F-73

Braud, Marguerite, S1-170, 237, 389

Braud, Marguerite, S2-732

Braud, Marguerite Pelagie, N-128

Braud, Marguerite-Blanche, S1-162

Braud, Marguerite-Josephe, S1-168-169

Braud, Marguerite-Josephe, S2-506, 663

Braud, Marie, C-5, 24

Braud, Marie, E-53, 98-99, 330, 489

Braud, Marie, F-19, 87

Braud, Marie, N-35

Braud, Marie, S1-38, 141, 162-163, 171, 293, 295

Braud, Marie, S3-840, 847, 1121-1122

Braud, Marie Angelique Gene-vieve, E-53

Braud, Marie Genevieve, E-54

Braud, Marie Henriette, N-34

Braud, Marie Madeleine, E-54

Braud, Marie Madeleine, N-35

Braud, Marie Magdelaine, F-19

Braud, Marie Modeste, E-54, 322, 330

Braud, Marie Ozitte, F-87

Braud, Marie Victoire, N-77, 186

Braud, Marie-Anne, S1-238-240

Braud, Marie-Jeanne, S1-169

Braud, Marie-Josephe, S1-168-169

Braud, Marie-Madeleine, S1-167-168, 171, 378

Braud, Marie-Ozite, S1-165

Braud, Marie-Therese, S1-166

Braud, Mathurin, N-35

Braud, Mathurin-Marin, S1-166

Braud, Michel, E-53

Braud, Modeste, S1-164

Braud, Olive, C-24

Braud, Olive, N-35

Braud, Olive Elizabeth, F-19

Braud, Olive Elizabeth, N-35

Braud, Olive-Elizabeth, S1-167

Braud, Ollivier, S3-863

Braud, Perinne-Julienne, S1-166

Braud, Perpetue, S1-165, 168-169

Braud, Pierre, C-24

Braud, Pierre, E-53, 54, 69, 98-99, 111, 173, 302, 411, 417, 488, 523, 585, 592

Braud, Pierre, F-19

Braud, Pierre, N-35, 37, 179

Braud, Pierre, S1-8, 162, 167

Braud, Pierre, S3-889

Braud, Pierre Firmin, E-302

Braud, Pierre Paul, N-35

Braud, Pierre-Paul, S1-167

Braud, Reine Elizabeth, N-36

Braud, Rene, E-489

Braud, Renee, E-456

Braud, Rosalie, C-13, 25, 93, 103

Braud, Rosalie, E-635

Braud, Rosalie, S1-169-270

Braud, Rose, C-103

Braud, Rose Marie, F-19

Braud, Rose Marie, N-35

Braud, Seraphin, S1-154, 170-171, 295

Braud, Seraphin, S3-1121, 1124-1125

Braud, Simon, S1-165

Braud, Simon-Jospeh, S1-169

Braud, Susanne, E-489

Braud, Suzanne, S1-163-164

Braud, Ursule, F-17, 75

Braud, Ursule, N-115

Braud, Ursule, S1-129, 168-169, 211, 270

Braud, Ursule, S2-436, 465, 497, 540, 564-565, 665

Braud, Ursulle, S3-925

Braud, Victoire, S1-162-163, 392

Braud, Victoire Perpetue, E-54

Braud, Vincent, E-456, 472

Braud, Vital, E-54, 431

Braun, Vinceslas, E-161

Breard, Antoine, E-36

Breard, Francois, E-33

Bregeat, Joseph, E-54

Breginal, Francois, S2-774

Breguera, Pierre, E-156

Brehaut, Etienne, S2-485

Brehier, Francois, E-54, 101

Brehier, Noel, E-54, 101

Bremont, Claire, E-100

Bresdou, Marie Francoise, E-54, 303

Brest and the Acadians, E-54

Breston, Antoine, E-54

Breston, Joseph, E-54

Bretaud, Gregoire, E-54

Bretaud, Jacques, E-54, 78

Bretaud, Jacques Aubin, E-54

Bretaud, Jacques dit Montaury, E-55

Bretaud, Joseph, E-55

Bretaud, Louis, E-55

Bretocq, Francoise, E-110

Breton, Bonaventure, E-55

Breton, Francois, E-55, 345

Breton, Jean, E-55

Breton, Marguerite, E-104

Breton, Marie Magdelaine, E-55, 308

Breton, Roch Francois, E-55

Bretonniere, Nicolas Francois, E-622

Brety, Gilbert Bon, N-37, 162, 204, 206

Brety, Jean, N-37, 204

Breuil, Jacques, E-350

Brevaut, Guillaume, S2-429

Breyer, Francois, E-626

Briand, Adelaide Zoe Sophie, E-641

Briand, Alexis, E-55

Briand, Anne, E-55, 84-85, 77, 335-336

Briand, Anne Angelique, F-105

Briand, Anne Genevieve, E-55

Briand, Anne Victoire, E-15, 55, 641

Briand, Annc-Marguerite, S1-172

Briand, Anne-Marguerite-Francoise-Xavier-Therese, S1-171

Briand, Antoine Auguste, E-55

Briand, Bernard, E-58

Briand, Catherine, E-55, 300

Briand, Catherine Francoise Desiree, E-55, 300

Briand, Celeste Aimee, E-55

Briand, Celeste Eugenie, E-56

Briand, Celestin, E-55 57-58, 290

Briand, Domitille, E-25, 56, 641

Briand, Emelie Francoise, E-56

Briand, Etienne, E-37, 58, 633

Briand, Etienne Benjamin, E-56, 190, 643

Briand, Euphrosine, E-180

Briand, Euphrosine Marie, E-56, 641

Briand, Felix Theophile, E-56

Briand, Francois, E-15, 25, 37, 55, 59, 182, 190, 404, 434-436, 633, 641, 643

Briand, Francois, S1-171

Briand, Francois, S3-950

Briand, Francois Jules, E-56-57

Briand, Francois Napoleon, E-15, 56-57

Briand, Francois Nicolas, E-58-59, 180

Briand, Francois-Victoire, S1-171

Briand, Francoise, E-37-38, 117, 186, 332, 630, 641

Briand, Francoise, S1-172

Briand, Francoise Eugenie, E-57, 641

Briand, Genevieve, E-57, 181-182, 184-186, 189-190, 642

Briand, Genevieve Melanie, E-56-57, 181

Briand, Gennevieve Luce, E-57

Briand, Genny, E-57

Briand, George, S1-172

Briand, George-Cyprien, S1-171

Briand, George-Fabien, S1-172

Briand, Georges, E-58, 429

Briand, Georgine, E-56

Briand, Guillaume, S3-922

Briand, Helene, E-57

Briand, Henriette Eulalie, E-57

Briand, Jean, E-55-58, 110, 362, 434, 631

Briand, Jean Baptiste, E-56-57, 59, 83

Briand, Jean Baptiste Francois Xavier, E-59

Briand, Jean Pierre, E-57

Briand, Jean-Baptiste, S1-172

Briand, Jeanne, S1-150

Briand, Joseph, E-36, 55, 57-59, 83, 631

Briand, Joseph, S1-172

Briand, Joseph Benony, E-57

Briand, Josephine Rosalie, E-58

Briand, Julie, E-631

Briand, Julien, S1-19, 172

Briand, Julien, S2-459

Briand, Julien, S3-872

Briand, Jullien, S2-474

Briand, Laurent, E-58, 429, 641

Briand, Laurent, S1-172

Briand, Laurent, S3-872

Briand, Laurent-Rene, S1-172

Briand, Laurente, E-434

Briand, Louis, E-58, 631

Briand, Louise (or Lisette), S1-172

Briand, Louise Felicite, E-58

Briand, Magdelene, E-58

Briand, Marguerite, E-36, 58

Briand, Marguerite Francoise, E-36

Briand, Marie, E-37, 55, 423, 633

Briand, Marie Elizabeth, E-58, 290

Briand, Marie Francoise, E-58

Briand, Marie Magdeleine, E-56, 58, 59, 119, 180, 364, 643

Briand, Martin, E-15, 25, 37-38, 56-59, 110, 180, 189, 363, 434, 436, 641

Briand, Melanie Genevieve, E-641

Briand, Mr., E-436

Briand, Nicolas, E-56

Briand, Pierre, E-59

Briand, Pierre Francois, E-57, 435

Briand, Rose Emelie, E-59

Briand, Thomas, E-56

Briand, Vital Hyppolite, E-59

Briand de la Villeroux, Francois Nicolas, E-110

Briand de la Villeroux, Marie Madeleine, E-109

Briant, -----, E-6

Briant, Francois, E-1, 631

Briant, Francois, S1-221

Briant, Martin, E-1, 631

Briant, widow, E-1

Briar, Anne, E-262, 299

Briard, Michel, E-405

Briare, Elime, E-592

Briaud, Marguerite, E-55, 345

Bricault, Guillaume, C-158

Bricaut, Francois, C-166

Bricet, Jean Anne, E-103

Bricette, Gervais, S2-725

Bricette, Marie-Josephe, S2-725

Bridier, Jean, E-59, 412

Bridier, Pierre, E-59, 412

Brie, Jacqueline, S2-512

Brie, Jaqueline, E-255

Brien, -----, E-5

Briere, Jean, S2-595

Briere, Jean, S3-992

Briere, Jeanne, S2-595

Briere, Jeanne, S3-992

Brieux, Jacquemine, S2-598

Brik, Joseph, E-180

Brillan, Celestin, E-630

Brillan, Marie, E-630

Brilland, Domitille, E-631

Brilland, Francois, E-185, 631

Brilland, Genevieve, E-631, 633

Brilland, Jeanne, E-631

Brilland, Luce, E-638

Brilland, Melania, E-631

Brillant, Anne Victoire, E-638

Brillant, Demilitte, E-638
Brillant, Francois, E-638
Brillant, Genevieve, E-638
Brillant, Jean, E-638
Brillant, Jean Jr., E-638
Brillant, Louis, E-592
Brillant, Louise, E-585
Brillant, Marguerite Francoise, E-585, 592
Brillant, Marie, E-638
Brillant, Melania, E-638
Brilloit, Jacques, E-347
Brillou, Francois, E-378
Brillou, Marie Anne, E-354, 368
Brillouette, Pierre, E-257
Brin, Magdalaine, E-474
Brindo, Jacques, E-272
Brio, Gertrude, S2-486
Briomaut, Marie Anne, E-79
Brionne, Alexandre Dominique, C-91
Briou, Gilles, S1-370
Briquesin, Annie Desiree, E-59
Briquesin, Pierre, E-59
Briquet, Francois, S1-172
Briquet, Jean-Henri-Louis, S1-172
Briquet, Louis, S1-172
Briquet, Louis, S2-649
Briquet, Marie-Therese, S1-173
Brisard, Louis, E-60
Brisard, Marguerite, E-60, 386
Brisard, Pierre, E-60, 386
Brisard, Rene, E-386
Briscard, Francois, E-60
Briscard, Marie Francoise, E-60
Brisset, Charlotte, E-90
Brisson, Joseph, E-59, 155, 350
Brisson, Joseph, S1-173
Brisson, Louise, S1-173
Brisson, Marie Clothilde, E-59, 155
Brisson, Rene, E-59, 155, 350
Brisson, Rene, S1-173
Brizard, Louis, E-348
Broca, Francois, E-379
Brochard, Jacques, E-45
Brochet, Jeanne, E-60, 344
Brode, Anne, S3-834
Brode, Anne Marie, S3-832, 839

Bronse, Marie Elisabeth Sophie, E-60
Bronse, Marie Philippe, E-60
Bronse, Pierre, E-60
Broque, Barbe, E-350
Brosard, Joseph, E-289
Brosset, Leonarde, E-117
Brosset, Suzanne, E-585, 591
Brouard, Louis, E-139, 325
Brouillier, Marie Charlotte, E-40, 308, 416
Brounart, Jacques, S3-833
Broune, Elisabeth, E-60
Broune, Guillaume, E-60
Broune, Joseph, E-60
Broune, Pierre, E-60
Broussard, Agnes, C-25, 45, 100
Broussard, Agnes, E-60
Broussard, Agnes, F-33
Broussard, Agnes, N-70, 146, 201
Broussard, Bonne Marguerite, E-60
Broussard, Catherine, E-60, 271
Broussard, Catherine, N-103, 175
Broussard, Charles, C-25, 100, 115
Broussard, Charles, E-60
Broussard, Charles, F-9
Broussard, Charles, N-19, 38, 201-202
Broussard, Charles, S1-15, 92, 106, 143, 173-174, 177, 310
Broussard, Charles, S2-522-523, 617-618, 664, 749
Broussard, Charles, S3-886
Broussard, Charles-Jean, S1-177
Broussard, Claude, S1-173-175
Broussard, Claude, S3-886
Broussard, Dominique, C-25
Broussard, Dominique, F-9
Broussard, Dominique, N-38
Broussard, Elisabeth, S3-856, 863
Broussard, Elizabeth, S1-106, 176-177
Broussard, Elizabeth, S2-617, 755
Broussard, Firmin, S1-174, 176

Broussard, Florence Adelaide, N-38
Broussard, Francois, C-25
Broussard, Francois, E-60, 472
Broussard, Francois, F-9
Broussard, Francois, N-38
Broussard, Francois, S1-174, 176
Broussard, Gregoire, S1-175
Broussard, Guillaume Medard, N-38
Broussard, Isabelle, S1-93, 116, 177
Broussard, Isabelle, S2-527, 536, 749
Broussard, J. Jan, S3-861
Broussard, Jacques, C-25
Broussard, Jacques, N-38
Broussard, Jan, S3-862, 863
Broussard, Jean, C-25, 100
Broussard, Jean, E-60, 83, 177, 271, 214, 618, 622
Broussard, Jean, F-67
Broussard, Jean, N-38-39, 201-202, 205, 211, 248
Broussard, Jean, S1-93
Broussard, Jean, S2-748
Broussard, Jean, S3-848, 862
Broussard, Jean Baptiste, C-25
Broussard, Jean Baptiste, F-67
Broussard, Jean Baptiste, N-38-39
Broussard, Jean Charles, F-9
Broussard, Jean Charles Joseph, C-25
Broussard, Jean Charles Joseph, N-38
Broussard, Jean-Baptiste, S1-91, 175-177
Broussard, Jean-Baptiste-Paul, S1-175-176
Broussard, Jean-Baptiste-Paul, S2-614
Broussard, Jean-Joseph, S1-177
Broussard, Joseph, C-25, 45, 100
Broussard, Joseph, E-60
Broussard, Joseph, F-9, 33, 67
Broussard, Joseph, N-38, 70, 146, 201-202
Broussard, Joseph, S1-175

Broussard, Joseph Dominique, E-60

Broussard, Joseph-Charles, S1-174

Broussard, Joseph-Osithe, S1-177

Broussard, Louis, C-25

Broussard, Louis, N-38

Broussard, Madeleine, S1-175, 241

Broussard, Madeleine, S2-739, 748, 766

Broussard, Madeleine-Josephe, S1-174

Broussard, Magdelaine, E-482

Broussard, Magdelaine, S3-848, 859

Broussard, Magdelene, S3-952

Broussard, Mare, E-51

Broussard, Marguerite, S1-175

Broussard, Marguerite, S2-682-683

Broussard, Marie, E-618

Broussard, Marie, S1-106

Broussard, Marie, S2-681, 774

Broussard, Marie Anne, E-71, 330

Broussard, Marie-Isabelle, S1-174

Broussard, Marie-Josephe, S1-177

Broussard, Marie-Marguerite, S1-177

Broussard, Monique, E-60

Broussard, Pierre, C-25

Broussard, Pierre, E-60, 482, 523, 618

Broussard, Pierre, F-9

Broussard, Pierre, N-38-39

Broussard, Pierre, S1-106, 132, 174, 176-178

Broussard, Pierre, S2-527, 535, 617, 738

Broussard, Pierre, S3-856, 863

Broussard, Pierre-Jean, S1-176

Broussard, Pierre-Paul, S1-176-177

Broussard, Rosalie, E-622

Broussard, Rosalie, S1-175

Broussard, Suzanne, E-283

Brousse, Jean-Louise, S1-178

Brousse, Jeanne, S1-178

Brousse, Julien, E-61

Brousse, Louis, S1-178

Brousse, Louis-Julien, S1-178, 334

Brousse, Marie, E-61

Brousse, Marie, S1-178

Brousse, Marie-Francoise, S1-178

Brousse, Thomas, E-585, 595

Brousseau, Pierre Michel, E-391

Broussier, Marie, C-40, 105

Broussier, Pierre, C-105

Broutin, Louis Adrien, E-61, 275

Broutin, Pierre Francois, E-61, 275

Brulard, Charles Alexis, E-154

Brulin, Angelique Rose, E-184

Brument, Mr., E-276

Brun, Abraham, E-487

Brun, Andree, E-474

Brun, Antoine, E-523, 487

Brun, Bastien, E-473

Brun, Charles, E-61

Brun, Claude, E-487, 523

Brun, Denis, E-345, 376

Brun, Francois Pierre, E-16, 66

Brun, Francoise, E-456

Brun, Jean, E-213, 487, 523

Brun, Jeanne, E-487

Brun, Magdelaine, E-473, 458

Brun, Marie, E-188, 283-284, 287, 329, 472, 613-614

Brun, Marie, S1-285

Brun, Marie, S2-628-629, 631-632

Brun, Marie, S3-1103

Brun, Marie Magdalen, E-61, 262

Brun, Pierre, E-69

Brun, Sebastien, E-523

Brun, Sebastien, S2-628

Brun, Theresa, E-348

Brun, Vincent, E-456, 473, 487

Brun Village named after Vincent Brun, E-213

Brunau, Elizabeth, E-371

Brunet, Alexandre, E-191

Brunet, Catherine, E-61, 317

Brunet, Francoise Catherine, E-183

Brunet, Isabelle, E-132

Brunet, Jacques, E-61, 317

Brunet, Jacques Marie Blaize, E-61, 127, 387

Brunet, Jeanne Marie de la Soceliere, E-61

Brunet, Marie, E-33, 269, 372, 393

Brunet, Marie, S2-623

Brunet de la Soceliere, Jeanne Marie, E-387

Brunneteau, Elisabeth, E-41, 144, 182, 194

Bruon, Marie, E-121, 265

Brute, Marie Angelique Jeanne, E-116

Bruyard, Jacques, E-19

Bryant, Marguerite, E-74, 304

Buard, Jean-Baptiste, S1-179

Buard, Jean-Baptiste, S2-760

Buart, Jean Baptiste, E-585, 591

Buaut, Marguerite, E-110-111, 411

Buaut, Marie Madeleine, E-411

Buche, Francois Xavier, N-184

Bucourt, Antoine, N-184

Bugaret, Catherine, E-476

Bugeard, Amand, E-38

Bugeau, Alain, S3-921

Bugeaud, Alain, S1-146, 179-180

Bugeaud, Jean, S1-180, 280

Bugeaud, Joseph, S1-180

Bugeaud, Louis-Amand, S2-515

Bugeaud, Madeleine, E-315

Bugeaud, Madeleine, S2-516

Bugeaud, Marie, S1-252

Bugeaud, Marie Madeleine, E-79, 258-259, 342, 429

Bugeaud, Marie-Louise, S1-179

Bugeaud, Marie-Madeleine, S1-200

Bugeaud, Marie-Rose, S1-180

Bugeaud, Simon, S1-179

Bugeaud, Xavier, S1-180

Buhaut, Marguerite, E-112

Buhaut, Marie, E-110, 411

Buisson, Francois, E-44

Buisson, Valentin, E-38, 357, 390, 406
Bujeau, Alain, N-31
Bujeau, Marie, N-47, 111
Bujeaud, Marie, F-61
Bujold, Paul, S2-515
Bujould, Marie-Madeleine, S2-515
Bul, Jeanne, E-99, 126
Bulin, Angelique Rose, E-185
Buot, Anne, E-22
Buot, Francois, E-61
Buot, Jean, E-61
Buot, Joseph, E-61
Buot, Marguerite, E-53, 61, 110
Buot, Marie, E-53, 61
Buot, Marie Julie, E-61
Buot, Pierre Athanase, E-61
Buret, Berisier, S1-323
Buret, Pierre-Jean, S2-478
Burgos, Jeanne, E-18
Burjon, Pierre, E-17, 61
Bursel, Marie, E-358
Burton, Antoine, E-62
Busie, Marie Barbe, E-44, 145
Busnel, Bernard, S2-530
Busnel, Francois, S1-180-181
Busnel, Francois-Jean, S1-181
Busnel, Francoise, E-635
Busnel, Francoise, S1-180-181
Busnel, Francoise-Marie, S1-181
Busnel, Guillaume, S1-262
Busnel, Jacque, C-37, 123-124
Busnel, Jacques, E-61, 117
Busnel, Jacques, S1-181
Busnel, Jean Victor, E-635
Busnel, Marguerite, E-635
Busnel, Marie, E-622
Busnel, Marie, S1-181
Busnel, Marie, S3-1066
Busnel, Marie Cecile, S3-1066
Busnel, Marie Joseph, C-90
Busnel, Marie Joseph, E-635
Busnel, Marie-Cecile, S1-181, 317
Busnel, Nicolas, E-61
Busnel, Perinne-Francoise, S1-181
Busnel, Pierre, S1-181
Busnel, Yves, S1-181, 317

Busnel, Yves, S3-1066
Busquet, Antoine, E-62, 197
Busquet, Jeanne, E-61, 197
Busquet, Louis Charles, E-62
Busquet, Louise Charles, E-196-197
Busquet, Louise Charlotte, E-196-197
Busquet, Marie, E-62
Bussiere, Anne Gabriel de la, C-31
Bussiere du Chilloux, Louis de la, C-31
Butel, Angelique-Therese, S2-590
Butel, Louis, E-292
Butter de Bleque, Elisabeth Rose, E-313
Buyant, Marie, E-54, 111

C

Cabane, Guillaume, E-394
Cabanne, Edouard, S3-824
Cabel, Antoine, E-63
Cabofy, -----, S3-1048
Cabofy, Jeanne Therese, S3-1048
Cabofy, Joseph, S3-1048
Cabofy, Veve., S3-1048
Cabon, Jeanne, F-41
Cabouffy, Jeanne, S1-182
Cabouffy, Jeanne Therese, S1-182, 333
Cabouffy, Joseph, S1-182, 204, 333
Cabouffy, Louise, S1-182
Caboussy, Jeanne, E-624
Caboussy, Louise, E-618, 622-623
Cabresbine, Antoine, E-63, 105
Cabresbine, Jean Joseph, E-63, 105
Cadet, Charles, E-523
Cadet, Mr., E-123, 345
Cadet, Pierre, E-440
Cadieux, Francois, S1-185
Cadieux, Francois, S3-1001
Cadieux, Francoise, S1-185
Cadieux, Francoise, S3-1001
Cadieux, Jean, S3-1001

Cadot, Etienne, E-133
Cadran, Pierre, E-621-622
Cadran, Pierre Olivier, E-622
Cahurel, Marguerite, E-622
Cai----, Pierre, E-322
Caillau, Andre, E-412
Caillaud, Marie, C-164
Caille, Pierrette, E-83, 89
Cailleau, Andre, E-36, 63
Cailleau, Jean, E-140
Caillebeau, Maurice, E-8
Caillitte, Marie Josephe, E-333, 418
Caillo, Germain, N-39, 165, 230
Caillo, Guillaume, N-39, 230
Caillo, Julien, N-230
Caillou, Julien, N-186
Caillouet, Jacques, F-39
Caillouet, Jacques, N-39
Caillouet, Joseph, F-39
Caillouet, Joseph, N-39, 119, 208
Caissier, Claude, E-1, 74
Caissier, Marguerite, E-1, 74, 104
Caissy, Agnes, S1-214
Caissy, Amand-Louis, S1-184
Caissy, Cecile, S1-37, 83, 370, 372-374, 376
Caissy, Cecile, S2-512, 687
Caissy, Cecile, S3-919, 951
Caissy, Francoise-Theodose, S1-183
Caissy, Genevieve-Sophie-Ulalie, S1-184
Caissy, girl, S1-185
Caissy, Henriette-Victoire, S1-183
Caissy, Jean, S1-83, 183-184, 319, 371, 374
Caissy, Jean, S2-449, 512, 591
Caissy, Jean, S3-917, 919, 956, 1001
Caissy, Jean-Baptiste, S1-183
Caissy, Jean-Baptiste, S2-480
Caissy, Jeanne, S1-372
Caissy, Joseph, S2-511
Caissy, Madeleine, S1-319, 321, 374
Caissy, Madeleine, S2-591
Caissy, Magdeleine, E-335

Caissy, Marguerite, C-33
Caissy, Marguerite, F-67, 107
Caissy, Marguerite, N-53-54
Caissy, Marguerite, S1-320, 371
Caissy, Marie, C-94
Caissy, Marie, N-61, 100
Caissy, Marie, S1-183-184, 294,
   371-373
Caissy, Marie, S2-449, 518, 731
Caissy, Marie, S3-956
Caissy, Marie-Genevieve, S1-
   184-185
Caissy, Marie-Gervaise, S1-182
Caissy, Marie-Madeleine, S1-
   261
Caissy, Marie-Marguerite, S1-
   183
Caissy, Michel, S1-42, 182, 184
Caissy, Michel, S2-461, 505
Caissy, Michel, S3-918, 1001
Caissy, Michel-Claude, S1-183
Caissy, Ozite, S1-182, 184
Caissy, Paul, S1-183-185, 192,
   199
Caissy, Paul, S2-460
Caissy, Paul, S3-917-918, 1001
Caissy, Paul, Jr., S1-185
Caissy, Pierre, S1-183
Caissy, Pierre, S2-480
Caissy, Pierre-Paul, S1-183
Calais and Dunkerque and the
   the Acadians, E-63, E-64
Calande, Genevieve, E-585, 593
Calegan, Jean Thomas, E-63,
   302
Calegan, Thomas, E-63, 302
Calinon dit Laloy, Claude
   Francois, E-64, 134
Calisan, Elizabeth, S1-324
Calisan, Elizabeth, S3-1088
Calivue, M., C-244
Callebeau, Maurice, E-7
Callipet, Francoise-Perinne, S2-
   769
Calvados, E-64
Calve, Catherine, S1-37
Came, Amable Jean Joseph, E-
   308
Came, Francois, E-308
Came Sieur de Saint Ague,
   Amable Jean Joseph, E-64

Came Sieur de Saint Ague,
   Francois, E-64
Camet, Marie, E-153, 416
Campagna, Michel, E-64, 149
Campion, Jean Baptiste, E-64,
   349
Campion, Marie Madeleine, E-
   64, 349
Campistron, Etienne, E-64-64,
   269
Campistron, Jean, E-64-65
Campistron, Jean Francois, E-64
Campistron, Jeanne Francoise,
   E-64
Campistron, Mr., E-65, 140
Campon, Barthelemy, E-329
Campun, Marie, E-425
Camus, Gervaise, E-64
Camus, Jean, S1-185-186
Camus, Jean-Baptiste, S1-186
Camus, Jean-Francois, S1-185
Camus, Jean-Rene, S1-186
Camus, Jeanne, S1-186
Camus, Nicolas, E-64
Camus, Pierre, E-64, 109, 174
Candelain, Nicolas, E-303, 327
Canderats, Marguerite, E-32
Canea, Michel, E-65
Canea, Pierre, E-65
Canet, Pelagie, C-91
Caniche, Mr., E-70
Canier, Pierre, E-275
Canol, Marianne, E-473
Cantin, Michel, E-138
Cantineau, Francoise, E-168
Capare, Jeanne Jean, E-115
Capelan, Marie, S2-623
Capelle, Francoise, E-188-189
Capitanei, Francois Marie, E-65
Capitanei, Marie Sophie, E-65
Capitanei, Nathalie, E-65
Capitanei, Vincent, E-65
Caplan, Mathurin, E-407
Capplain, Louis Robert, E-160
Cara, Jean Martin, E-161
Carat, Pierre, E-168
Carbon, Anne, E-65
Carbon, Joseph, E-65
Cardinal, Jean Baptiste, E-64
Cardinal, Jeanne, E-65, 269
Cardinal, Joseph, E-64-65

Cardinal, Marie, E-64-65, 140,
   269
Cardinal, veuve, E-64
Cardonis, Anne, E-427
Care, Anne, N-76, 211
Care, Marguerite, E-33
Caret, Honore, S2-556
Caret, Honore, S3-963, 1000,
   1059, 1063, 1081
Caret, Ignace, S3-963, 1040
Caret, Jean, S3-1063
Caret, Marie, S3-987, 1065,
   1075, 1077
Caret, Marie Rose, S3-1063
Caret, Marie-Rose, S2-556
Careton, Anne, E-65, 69
Careton, Pierre, E-65, 69
Cari, Magdalen, E-356
Carica, Dominique, E-65
Carica, Margueritte Hybour, E-
   65
Carica, Mr., E-292
Carica, Pierre, E-65
Caricat, Elizabeth, E-254, 419
Carier, Francoise, E-18-19
Carier, Marie, E-289
Carier, Marie Anne, E-18
Carier, Marie Francine, E-18
Carier, Michelle, E-19
Cariere, Francoise, E-18
Carne, Jacques, E-523
Carodee, Alain, E-11
Caron, Chaterine Angelique, E-
   41, 299
Carosse, Marie, E-626
Carot, Jeanne, E-65
Carot, Marie, E-326, 376
Carot, Pierre, E-65, 355, 394
Carouar, Francois, S3-990
Carre, Angelique, E-84-85
Carre, Anne, E-551
Carre, Anne Marie, E-66, 298
Carre, Augustine, E-85
Carre, Bernard, E-65
Carre, Charles, E-298
Carre, Elisabeth, E-319
Carre, Francoise, E-118
Carre, Ignace, E-66, 298
Carre, Isabelle, E-116-118
Carre, Jacques, E-551

Carre, Magdeleine, E-317-318, 320, 551
Carre, Marguerite, E-33, 341, 551
Carre, Marie, E-65, 80, 117, 298, 551
Carre, Pierre, E-65, 523, 551
Carre, Sergent, E-10
Carre, Therese, E-65, 174
Carrerot, Barbe Blanche, E-65, 128
Carrerot, Francoise Ovide, E-105, 300
Carrerot, Jean Baptiste, E-15, 150
Carrerot, Josephe, E-66, 104
Carrerot, Philipe, E-15, 150
Carrerot, Pierre Andre, E-65-66, 104, 128
Carret, Anne, S1-188
Carret, Charles, S1-186, 188
Carret, Eustache, F-57
Carret, Eustache-Ignace, S1-189
Carret, Francois, S1-188
Carret, Francoise, S1-318
Carret, Henriette, S2-623
Carret, Honore, C-60
Carret, Honore, F-55
Carret, Honore, N-245-246
Carret, Honore, S1-51, 186-188
Carret, Ignace, F-55, 57
Carret, Ignace, S1-186-189
Carret, Ignace, S2-583-584
Carret, Jean, C-8
Carret, Jean, F-57, 61
Carret, Jean, N-11
Carret, Jean, S1-53, 187, 189
Carret, Jean-Marie, S1-187
Carret, Joseph, S1-187-188
Carret, Madeleine, N-103, 175
Carret, Marie, C-52
Carret, Marie, F-57
Carret, Marie, N-81, 125
Carret, Marie, S1-73, 187-189, 236
Carret, Marie, S2-437, 492-493, 583-585
Carret, Marie Rose, F-61
Carret, Marie Rose, N-11
Carret, Marie Rose , C-8-9, 28

Carret, Marie-Madeleine, S1-189
Carret, Marie-Rose, S1-53, 189
Carret, Pierre, F-55
Carret, Pierre, S1-186
Carret, Pierre, S2-492
Carret, Pierre-Marin, S1-187
Carret, Rosalie, S1-186
Carret, Suzanne, S1-186
Carret, Therese, F-61
Carret, Therese, S1-189
Carret, Zenon, S1-188
Carrie, Marie, C-42-43
Carriere, Fancione, E-66
Carriere, Francoise, E-66
Carriere, Jean Pierre, E-312
Carriere, Jeanne, E-18
Carriere, Marie Francoise, E-18
Carriere, Martin, E-66
Carriere, Therese, E-288
Cartet, Marguerite, E-44, 441
Cartier, Marguerite, E-441
Carton, Louis Joseph, E-318
Casaux, Marie Victoire, E-20
Cascabel, Jean, E-66, 133
Cascabel, Marie, E-66, 133
Cascabel, Maurice, E-133
Caset, Anne, E-138
Casette, Marie, E-591
Casmane, Jean, E-585, 592
Cassagne, Susanne, E-101
Cassagnoles, Bernard, E-32, 403
Cassaignolles, Antoinette, E-66, 329
Cassaignolles, Nicolas, E-66
Casselin, Joseph, E-172
Cassier, Pierre, E-275
Cassin, Louis, S3-1153
Cassin, Susanne, E-101, 326
Castagne, Cecile, E-66, 353
Castaign, Antoine, S1-190
Castaign, Jean-Baptiste, S1-190
Castaign, Olive, S1-190
Castaing, Antoine, E-66, 77, 131, 261
Castaing, Jean, E-66, 131
Castaing, Mr., E-26
Castaing, Rose, E-126, 128, 389
Castan, Claire, E-24, 348
Castel, Bonne Jacqueline Francoise, N-19, 38, 202

Castel, Bonne, E-60
Castille, Simon Joseph, E-66, 157
Castin, Mr., E-131
Caston, Susanne, E-276
Catel, Bonne Jacqueline Francoise, C-25
Catelie, Anne, S1-122
Catherine, indian, E-353
Cathou, Jean fils, S3-1024
Catier, Harme, E-66, 375
Catier, Jean Baptiste, E-66, 375
Catignon, Jacques Farcy, E-196-197
Catignon, Marie Anne, E-197
Catineau, Jean, E-90
Catiole, Dame Anne Josephe, C-135
Catron, Jacques, E-26, 378
Catrou, Jean, E-418
Caty, Marie Jeanne, E-179, 295
Cauchon, Adrien, E-182
Caudan, Gillette, N-110, 251
Caudan, Marc, N-110, 251
Cauge, Marie Barbe, E-51
Caumont, Louise, E-56, 59
Caumout, Margueritte, S3-1100
Cauquilles, Charles, E-87
Cauquilles, Marie Catherine, E-87
Caurion, Marthe, E-80
Cauten, Louis, E-384
Cavalier, Pierre, E-16, 585, 595
Cavalier, Rene, E-585, 595
Caveleau, Pierre, E-66
Cavelier, Jacques, E-97
Cavenza, Baset, F-65
Cavivel, Pierre, E-104, 335
Cayenne, E-68
Cayenne and the Acadians, E-67, E-68
Cayenne, South America, E-67
Caylan, Jean, E-68
Caylan, Marie, E-68
Caylan, Marie Modeste, E-68
Cayra, Joseph, E-68, 117
Caza, Guillaume, S2-545
Caza, Guillaume, S3-995
Caza, Marguerite, S2-545
Caza, Marguerite, S3-995
Cazeaux, Jean, E-174

INDEX SOURCES C=Chatellerault; E=Acadians in Exile; F=Acadian Families; N=Nantes; S=St-Malo

Cazenave, Bernard, E-68, 80
Cazenave, Jean, E-68
Cazette, Marie, E-585
Ceig, Marguerite, E-256
Ceineray, Jean Baptiste, N-242
Celar, Jeanne, E-587, 595
Celestin, Marguerite, S2-565
Celestin dit Bellemere, Jacques, N-115
Celestin dit Bellemere, Marguerite, N-115
Census of Acadia in 1671, E-455-456
Census of Acadia in 1686, E-455, 472
Census of Acadia in 1714, E-455, 522
Census of Sinnamary, Cayenne in French Guyane in 1765, E-455, 583
Centanni, Rosario, C-viii
Ceriaud, Marie, E-271
Certain, Pierre, S1-223
Chaban, Marie Francoise, E-195, 391
Chabot, Jean, E-68, 327
Chabot, Jeanne, E-68
Chabot, Pierre, E-22, 585, 592
Chabourit, Jacques, E-406
Chagneau, Francois, E-257
Chagneau, Pierre, E-270
Chagnoleau, Alexis, E-73
Chagnoleau, Jean, E-140, 169
Chaigne, Francois, E-68, 130
Chaigne, Jacques, E-155
Chaigne, L., E-68
Chaigne, Louis, E-68, 130
Chaigne, Louis Felix, E-68
Chaigneau, Armand, E-196
Chaigneau, Guy Mathurin, E-68
Chaigneau, Jean Laurent, E-68
Chaigneau, Louise Felicite, E-68
Chaillot, Marie Jeanne, E-59, 412
Chaillou, Gabrielle, E-68
Chaillou, Jeanne, C-21-22
Chaillou, Marie, E-69, 71
Chaillou, Mathieu, E-69
Chaillou, Pierre, E-100
Chaillou, Rene, E-68
Chaillou, Simon, E-68-69, 258

Chainay, Mr., E-131, 317, 346
Chainee, Genevieve, E-111
Chaisson, Anne, E-74
Chaland, Jacques, E-69
Chalelet, Jean, E-69
Chalelet, Louis, E-69
Chalet, Rene, E-181
Chalmet d'Elino, Marie Anne, E-616
Chalot, Anne, S2-715
Chalot, Marie, E-72
Chambaud, Jean, E-69, 325
Chambaud, Joseph, E-69, 325
Chambond, Jean Pierre, E-65, 69
Chambond, Pierre, E-69
Chambout, Martial, E-302
Champagne, Madeleine Aimee, E-184-186, 390
Champagnon, Julien, E-69
Champagnon, Marie Rose, E-69
Champion, Madeleine, E-69
Chanceauline, Martin, E-278
Chancerel, Jean, E-69, 370
Chancerel, Julienne, E-14, 69, 351, 370
Chancerel, Julienne, S2-648
Chanceul, Francois, E-70, 328
Chanceul, Guillaume, E-70, 328
Chantelaille, Anne, E-440
Chapeau, Anne Henriette, E-292-293
Chapeau, Henriette, E-292
Chapel, L., S3-925
Chapel, Pierre, S2-778
Chapel, Pierre, S3-928
Chapelard, Gregoire, E-28, 357
Chapelerie, Jacques, E-337
Chapelle, Adelaide, E-618
Chapelle, Jeanne, E-618
Chapelle, Pierre, E-618
Chapelle, Pierre-Ferrard, S2-668
Chaperon, Claude Gabriel, E-69, 173
Chaperon, Jean, E-69
Chaperon, Marie, E-69
Chaperon, Marie Catherine, E-69
Chaperon, Pierre, E-69
Chapet, -----, S3-929, 931

Chaplon, Gabriel, E-34, 45, 65, 70, 302, 333, 345, 358
Chaplon, Gabriel, S2-644
Chaplon, Joseph, E-376
Chaplon, Pierre, E-70
Chappeau, Helene, E-98
Chappeau, Henriette, E-291
Chappeau, Marianne, E-291
Chapperon, Pierre, E-38, 174
Charandeau, Francois, E-635
Charandeau, Marie Louise, E-635
Charandeau, Therese, E-635
Chardevel, -----, S3-1146
Chardevel, Guillemette, S1-194
Chardevel, Guillemette, S3-1146-1147
Chardevel, Joseph, S3-1146
Chardevel, M., S3-1146
Chardevel, Marie-Anne, S1-195
Chardevel, Mathurin, S3-1146-1147
Chardin, Perrine, C-159
Chardon, Andre, E-393
Chardon, Jeanne, C-94
Charente-Maritime, E-70
Charie, Etienne, N-192
Charier, Anne Henriette, E-122
Charier, Louis Jacques, E-122
Charier, Marie, E-376
Charlan, Amable, E-197
Charlan, Archange, E-197
Charlant, Marie, S2-442
Charlemagne, Anne, E-70, 80, 391
Charlemagne, Jean, E-70, 391
Charlier, Marie, E-307, 401
Charpatan, Francoise, F-63
Charpenteau, Antoine, E-393
Charpentier, Alexandre, S1-192
Charpentier, Anne Marie Josephe, E-28
Charpentier, Anne-Marie, S1-191
Charpentier, Charles, E-28, 32, 44, 70, 268, 316, 332
Charpentier, Charles, S1-57, 190-192, 209
Charpentier, Claire, S1-192
Charpentier, Dumozier, S3-1048
Charpentier, Genevieve, S1-249

Charpentier, Genevieve-Marguerite, S1-192
Charpentier, George, E-32, 70
Charpentier, George, S11-191, 225
Charpentier, Georges, S1-191-192
Charpentier, Georges, S3-999, 1072
Charpentier, Jacques, E-21, 32, 70, 77
Charpentier, Jean, E-21, 32, 70, 403
Charpentier, Joseph, E-70
Charpentier, Joseph, S1-191-192
Charpentier, Josephe, E-120
Charpentier, Josephe, S1-281
Charpentier, Louis, E-12, 70, 170, 585, 593
Charpentier, Louis, S1-191-193, 375
Charpentier, Louis, S2-517, 519
Charpentier, Louis, S3-979
Charpentier, Louis-Charles, S1-193
Charpentier, Louis-Jacques-Laurent, S1-193
Charpentier, Madeleine-Felix, S1-192
Charpentier, Marie, E-585, 593
Charpentier, Marie Josephe, E-32, 70, 141, 255, 268
Charpentier, Marie-Josephe, S1-57-58, 190, 332
Charpentier, Marie-Josephe, S2-514
Charpentier, Mr., E-79
Charpentier, Mr., S1-198
Charpentier, Nicolas, E-326
Charpentier, Perinne, C-27
Charpentier, Perinne, F-79
Charpentier, Perinne, S1-201
Charpentier, Perinne, S3-1050
Charpentier, Suzanne, S1-191
Charpentier, Theotiste-Simone, S1-192
Charpentier, Thomas, S1-193
Charpy, J., C-vii
Charretier, Antoine, E-19
Charretier, Joseph, E-19, 345
Charrie, Louis Antoine, F-63, 85

Charrier, Claude, E-69, 71
Charrier, Jean, E-71
Charrier, Louis, F-63
Charrier, Marie, E-257, 394
Charron, Augustin, E-168
Charron, Paul, E-326
Charron, Simon, E-69, 71
Chartier, Joseph, E-71, 345
Chartier, Pierre, E-71, 345
Chartier, Thomasse, E-438
Charvet, Antoine Joseph, E-71
Charvet, Joseph Maximilien, E-71
Chasegros, Marie, E-472
Chassin, Francois, E-330
Chassin, Francois Nicolas, E-392
Chassin, Marie Charlotte, E-330
Chassin, Nicolas, E-392
Chassin de Thierry, Francois, E-71
Chassin de Thierry, Francois Nicolas, E-71
Chassin de Thierry, Marie Charlotte, E-71
Chassin de Thierry, Marie Josephe, E-71-72
Chassin de Thierry, Mr., E-72
Chassin de Thierry, Nicolas, E-71
Chasson, Louis, E-292
Chataignier, Jean, S1-193-194
Chataignier, Pierre, S1-193-194
Chate, Julien, E-119
Chate, Julien, S1-280
Chateau, Pierre, E-350, 405
Chateignier, Jean, E-622, 625
Chateignier, Pierre, E-622
Chatel, Claude, E-28, 169-170, 268, 306, 373
Chatel, Claude, S1-372, 375
Chatel, Claude, S2-597
Chatelier, Antoine, E-71
Chatelier, Henriette Francois, E-71
Chatelier, Jean, E-71
Chatelier, Marie, E-315, 376
Chatelier, Marie Francoise, E-71
Chatelier, Marie Madeleine, E-71
Chatelier, Martel, E-71

Chaterine, indian, E-71
Chatillon, Jeanne, E-320
Chaullepied, Anne, C-78
Chaulseberger, Marie Anne, E-120
Chaumerin, Jean, E-35
Chaumerin, Sauveur, E-35, 278
Chaumette, Jean Baptiste, E-72, 197
Chaumier, Louis, E-72
Chaumiere, Jean Gabriel, E-72, 137
Chaumiere, Louis, E-137
Chaury, Marie, E-173, 349
Chauserel, Jean, S2-680
Chauserel, Julienne, S2-680
Chaussepied, Anne, C-119
Chautrel, Perinne, S1-318
Chauveau, Jean, E-18, 90
Chauveau, Marie Magdelaine, E-16, 137
Chauveau, Martin, E-256
Chauvelin de Beauregard, Francois Marie, E-71-72
Chauvelin de Beauregard, Francois Silvain, E-71-72
Chauvenet, Anne, E-72, 90
Chauvenet, Francois, E-72, 90
Chauvet, Charles, E-524
Chauvet, Elie, E-159
Chauvet, Jacques, E-72
Chauvet, Marie, E-35, 72, 144
Chauvet, Marie Charlotte, E-71-72, 120, 303
Chauvet, Marie Joseph, E-358
Chauvet, Nicolas, E-412
Chauvignon, Pierre, E-72, 344
Chauvignon de la Prune, Claude, E-72, 344
Chauvin, Jacques, E-72
Chauvin, Jean, E-72, 299
Chauvin, Jeanne, E-72, 123, 348
Chauvin, Jeanne Marie, E-72, 299
Chauvin, Louise, E-187, 429
Chauvin, Magdelaine, E-100
Chauvin, Pierre, E-72, 153, 406
Chauvine, Francoise, E-32, 403
Chaux, Julienne, S2-643
Chaux, Jullienne, S3-1042
Chavelon, Gabriel, E-585, 591

Chaveneau, Marie Catherine, C-11

Chavigney de la Chevrotiere, Elisabet, E-77, 264

Chazal, Jean, E-585, 591

Chazanier, Anne, E-100, 141

Cheboule, Mathurin, E-72

Cheboule, Pierre, E-72, 83

Chebrat, Jeanne, E-457

Chehu, Pierre, S3-904

Chellon, Jeanne, F-17

Chelmies, Denis, E-65, 174

Chemin, Francois, E-72

Chemin, Jacques, E-73, 294

Chemin, Jean, E-73, 131

Chemin, Jean Nicolas, E-73

Chemin, Jeanne, E-73

Chemin, Louis, E-73

Chemin, Marguerite, E-73, 97, 168, 419

Chemin, Marie, E-73, 385

Chemin, Nicolas, E-73, 97, 385

Chemin, Pierre, E-72-73, 131

Cheminant, Rene, E-95

Chemine, Pierre, C-26

Chemineau, Jeanne, E-32, 73

Chemineau, Nicolas, E-32, 73

Chenais, Genevieve, E-73

Chenais, Jean Baptiste, E-73

Chenais, Marie, S3-979

Chenard, Jeanne, S1-367

Chenay, Francois, E-74

Chenay, Joseph Felix, E-74, 293

Chenay, Marie Josephe, E-65, 431

Chene, Antoine, S1-146

Chenebaud, Marie, C-120

Chenel, Jean Baptiste, E-146

Chenel, Marie Josephe, E-146

Chenet, Jean, S1-194

Chenet, Jeanne-Jacquemine, S1-194

Chenet, Joseph, E-335

Chenet, Marie, S3-972

Chenet, Marie-Josephe, S1-57, 190-192

Chenie, Elisabeth, S3-1087

Cheniere, Martin, E-270

Chenouille, Catherine, E-74, 106

Chenouille, Jean Baptiste, E-74

Cheparet, Cecile, E-74

Cheparet, Jacques Martin, E-23, 341

Cheparet, Jean Baptiste, E-74

Cheparet, Martin, E-74

Cheramy, Anne, S1-195

Cheramy, Anne-Marie, S1-194

Cheramy, Francois, S3-1146

Cheramy, Jean, S1-195

Cheramy, Joseph, S1-194-196

Cheramy, Joseph, S3-1146-1147, 1152-1153

Cheramy, Marguerite-Angelique, S1-195

Cheramy, Marie-Anne, S1-195

Cheramy, Mathurinne, S1-195

Cherbourg Acadians in 1774, E-74

Cherbourg and the Acadians in 1758, E-75

Cherbourg in France, E-75

Cherbourg: Ste-Trinite Church Annals, E-75-77

Cheron, Marie Josephe, E-65-66, 105, 128

Cherot, Madeleine, S2-647

Cherveteau, Julie, C-42

Chery, Hubert, E-120

Chesnard, Pierre, E-119

Chesne, Jean Baptiste, E-47, 184

Chesneau, Anne, E-77, 291

Chesneau, Mr., E-291

Chesnel, Anne, E-78, 123

Chevalier, Adrien, S1-197

Chevalier, Augustin, E-77

Chevalier, Charles, S1-197

Chevalier, Charlotte, E-66, 77

Chevalier, Francois, E-66, 77, 264

Chevalier, Francois, N-40, 127, 245

Chevalier, Francois Benjamin, N-40, 245

Chevalier, Francois Henry, E-77, 391

Chevalier, Genevieve, E-168, 355

Chevalier, Jacob, E-77, 257

Chevalier, Jacquemine, S2-566

Chevalier, Jacquemine, S3-1082

Chevalier, Jacques, E-377, 405

Chevalier, Jean, E-77

Chevalier, Jean, N-40, 245

Chevalier, Jean, S1-197

Chevalier, Jeanne, E-77, 152

Chevalier, Joseph, N-40

Chevalier, Josephine Magdeleine, E-77, 336

Chevalier, Louis-Francois-Marie, S1-197

Chevalier, Louise, E-77, 299, 622, 626

Chevalier, Louise, S1-196-197

Chevalier, Madeleine, E-105

Chevalier, Marguerite, C-164

Chevalier, Marguerite, E-77, 139

Chevalier, Marguerite, S1-44

Chevalier, Marie, E-138, 141, 404, 441

Chevalier, Marie, N-40

Chevalier, Marie Anne, E-54

Chevalier, Marie Genevieve, E-77, 264

Chevalier, Marie Madeleine Julie, E-182

Chevalier, Pierre, E-350

Chevalier, Pierre Marie Symon, N-242

Chevalier, Suzanne, E-70, 77, 257

Chevalier, Therese, E-426

Chevalier, Vital, E-78, 101

Chevalier, Vital, S1-196-197, 258

Chevalier, Vital Henry, E-77

Chevallier, Escuyer, E-262

Chevallier, Therese, C-98

Chevallier, Therese, E-269

Chevalon, Marguerite, E-275

Chevary, Abraham, E-78

Chevary, Anne Marie, E-78

Chevary, Antoine, E-78

Chevary, Francoise, E-78

Chevary, Marguerite, E-78

Chevary, Marie, E-78

Chevary, Marie Modeste, E-78

Cheveland, Catherine, E-78

Chevery, Denis, E-78

Chevet, Francois, E-625

Chevet, Francois, S1-181, 198

Chevet, Francois Mathurin, S3-1094

Chevet, Francois-Mathurin, S1-197

Chevet, Jeanne-Perinne, S1-197

Chevet, Julien, S1-197

Chevet, Julien, S3-1094

Chevet, Mathurine, S3-1094

Chevette, Mathurine, S1-197

Chevilleau, Francois, E-78, 376

Chevilleau, Louis, E-78

Chevilleau, Marie, E-78

Chevilleau, Pierre, E-78, 376

Chevillon, Jeanne, E-157, 338

Chevraux, Marie, S1-205

Chevreuil, Ludivine, C-161

Chevreux, Francoise, E-373

Chevri, Charles, S1-198

Chevros, Marie Anne, E-22

Chezanne, Elisabeth, E-585, 596

Chiasson, Abraham, E-549

Chiasson, Adelaide, F-77, 109

Chiasson, Adelaide, N-41

Chiasson, Agnes, E-525

Chiasson, Agnes, S1-335

Chiasson, Angelique, E-523

Chiasson, Angelique, S2-492

Chiasson, Anne, C-26

Chiasson, Anne, E-1, 78, 123, 178, 368, 549

Chiasson, Anne, S1-198-199, 201

Chiasson, Anne Adelaide, C-26

Chiasson, Anne Adelaide, N-41

Chiasson, Anne Marie Marthe, N-41

Chiasson, Anne Rosalie, C-27

Chiasson, Anne-Marie Marthe, C-26

Chiasson, Anonime, E-78

Chiasson, Anonime, F-77

Chiasson, Basile, E-78

Chiasson, Basile, F-77, 109

Chiasson, Basile, N-40

Chiasson, Catherine, E-78, 376

Chiasson, Charles, F-77, 109

Chiasson, Charles, N-41

Chiasson, Chrisostome, S1-199

Chiasson, Chrisostome, S2-598

Chiasson, Chrisostome, S3-1057

Chiasson, Etienne Isidore, E-78

Chiasson, Etienne Pierre, E-78

Chiasson, Francois, C-26

Chiasson, Francois, E-43, 78-79, 104, 170, 176, 178, 549

Chiasson, Francois, F-79

Chiasson, Francois, S1-184, 198-200, 373

Chiasson, Francois, S3-917, 961, 1050

Chiasson, Francoise, E-78, 86, 145-146, 274-275, 346

Chiasson, Francoise, N-139

Chiasson, Francoise, S1-2, 214

Chiasson, Francoise, S2-644-645

Chiasson, Francoise, S3-915, 1054, 1057

Chiasson, Gabriel, E-78-79, 123, 132, 346, 524

Chiasson, Gabriel, S1-198

Chiasson, Gabriel, S2-516, 644

Chiasson, Genevieve, E-79

Chiasson, Jean, C-27

Chiasson, Jean, F-79

Chiasson, Jean, S1-199, 201-202

Chiasson, Jean, S2-646

Chiasson, Jean, S3-919, 961, 1031, 1050, 1054

Chiasson, Jean Baptiste, C-26-27

Chiasson, Jean Baptiste, E-79, 104, 358, 524

Chiasson, Jean Francois, E-79

Chiasson, Jean Guillaume, C-27

Chiasson, Jean Joseph, E-79

Chiasson, Jean-Baptiste, S1-198-201, 292

Chiasson, Jean-Baptiste, S2-681

Chiasson, Jean-Francois, S1-200

Chiasson, Joseph, C-27

Chiasson, Joseph, E-78-79

Chiasson, Joseph, F-79

Chiasson, Joseph, S1-198-200

Chiasson, Joseph-Francois, S1-201

Chiasson, Josephe, S3-951

Chiasson, Judic, E-132

Chiasson, Judith, C-82

Chiasson, Judith, E-79, 131-133, 355, 371-372, 549

Chiasson, Judith, F-71

Chiasson, Louis, F-77

Chiasson, Louis, N-41

Chiasson, Louis, S1-199

Chiasson, Louis Basile, N-40

Chiasson, Louis Joseph, N-40

Chiasson, Louise, E-79

Chiasson, Louise, S1-201

Chiasson, Louise Felicite, E-79

Chiasson, Louise-Felicite, S1-199

Chiasson, Magdalen, E-79

Chiasson, Marguerite, E-93, 132, 549

Chiasson, Marie, C-51, 61

Chiasson, Marie, E-23, 47, 79, 101-102, 104, 111, 117, 126, 132, 170, 176-177, 184, 255, 262, 267-268, 270, 301, 311, 341, 363, 367-368, 371, 374, 377-378, 431-432, 529-530

Chiasson, Marie, F-5

Chiasson, Marie, N-42, 51, 100

Chiasson, Marie, S1-83-84, 193, 199, 259, 261, 307, 320

Chiasson, Marie, S2-429, 433, 513-514, 518, 626, 776

Chiasson, Marie, S3-901, 915, 919, 972

Chiasson, Marie Genevieve, E-79

Chiasson, Marie Joseph, E-79, 111, 170, 373

Chiasson, Marie Josephe, E-549

Chiasson, Marie Judith, E-274-275, 355

Chiasson, Marie Magdalaine, E-79, 268, 367

Chiasson, Marie-Genevieve, S1-200

Chiasson, Marie-Josephe, S1-199, 282, 372-373

Chiasson, Marie-Josephe, S2-516-518, 580

Chiasson, Marie-Madeleine, S1-200

Chiasson, Nicolas Joseph, E-79

Chiasson, Pierre, E-79

Chiasson, Pierre, F-77, 79, 109

Chiasson, Pierre Louis, C-27

Chiasson, Pierre-Louis, S1-201

Chiffell, Pierre, E-325
Chinaille, Catherine, E-304
Chinaille, Jean Baptiste, E-304
Chiquet, Jeanne, N-125
Chiron, George, E-15
Chivretteau, Pol, C-131
Cholet, Jacques, E-79, 96, 284, 287
Cholet, Jean, E-318
Cholet, Marie, E-262, 318
Chollou, Francois, S3-931
Chollou, Joseph, S3-875, 878, 931
Cholus, Enogat, S1-288
Cholus, Veronique, S1-288
Chopin, Jean Baptiste, E-139
Chopin, Jeanne Marguerite, E-139
Chopin, Marguerite, E-139
Chopin, Marie, E-139
Choris, Gabriel, S3-1066
Chotard, Jeanne, N-170, 222
Chotard, Mr., E-139
Choumarin, Anne Francoise, E-623
Choume, Joseph, E-60, 348
Chouques, Laurent, E-79
Choutan, Pierre, E-80, 277
Christ, Estelle, E-80
Christ, Louis, E-80
Christophle, Jean, E-80, 264
Christophle, Marie, E-80, 146, 264-265
Christy, Agathe-Anne-Calixte-Pallieue, S2-577
Chuprat, Jean, E-418
Ciardin, Pierre, S2-504
Cibot, Pierre, E-86
Cireaud, Francois, E-80
Cireaud, Leonard, E-43, 80-81
Cirou, Andre, E-166, 386
Clachet, Magdelaine, E-256
Clairambeau, Rene, E-394
Claparede, Jacques, E-80, 137, 405
Claparede, Jean, E-80, 405
Claparede, Louis Joseph, E-80, 137
Claparede, Mathurin, E-80
Clarambeau, Anne Catherine, E-80, 391

Clarambeau, Jean, E-391
Clarambeau, Louis, E-70, 80, 391
Clarie, Jean Etienne, E-272
Clastinet, Louis, S1-340
Clastinet, Louis, S3-860
Claude, Claude, E-601
Claude, Henry, E-601
Claude, Jehan, E-458
Clave, Anne, C-164
Clave, Magdelaine, E-92, 268
Claveau, Charles, E-80
Claveau, Jean, E-270, 327
Claveau, Marie, E-80
Claveau, Pierre, E-80
Claveau, Renee Marie, E-68, 80
Clavel, Francoise, E-333
Clavery, Jean, E-80
Clavery, Marie, E-80
Clemence, Marie, E-31, 317
Clemenceau, Jean, F-55, 57
Clemenceau, Jean, N-169, 246
Clemenceau, Jean, S1-189, 202
Clemenceau, Madeleine, S2-696
Clemenceau, Magdelaine, F-57
Clemenceau, Marie, C-53
Clemenceau, Marie, E-115, 262, 318-319
Clemenceau, Marie, F-55
Clemenceau, Marie, N-78, 169, 246
Clemenceau, Marie, S1-189, 202
Clemenceau, Marie, S2-428-429, 432
Clemenceau, Marie-Anne, S2-549
Clemenceau, Marie-Madeleine, S1-189
Clemens, Marie, S3-937
Clemenso, Jan, S3-1040
Clemenso, Marie, S3-1040
Clement, Catherine, E-81
Clement, Francois, N-41
Clement, Helaire, C-27, 80, 132-133
Clement, Hilaire, F-51
Clement, Hilaire, N-41
Clement, Hilaire, S1-121-202
Clement, Jean, C-27, 132
Clement, Jean, E-27, 153

Clement, Jean, F-51
Clement, Jean, N-41
Clement, Jean, S1-202
Clement, Jean Baptiste, E-80
Clement, Jean Hilaire, N-41
Clement, Louise, E-80
Clement, Madeleine, N-41
Clement, Marie, C-27
Clement, Marie, F-51
Clement, Marie, N-41
Clement, Michel, E-80
Clenet, Louis, E-81, 340
Clerambeau, Louis, E-63
Clerc, Jeanne, C-40, 48, 113, 125
Clerc, Mathurin, E-66
Clerc, Silvain, C-48, 125
Clere, Louis, E-81
Clere, Raphael, E-81
Clermont, Catherine, E-300, 311
Clermont, Francois, E-81, 622
Clermont, Francois, S1-186
Clermont, Francois, S2-770
Clermont, Jeanne, E-428, 622
Clermont, Jeanne, S1-185-186
Clermont, Jeanne, S2-770-771
Clermont, Mademoiselle, C-37
Clermont, Marie Louise, E-81
Clerouin, Jean, E-385
Clerqua, Jean, C-71, 131
Clerque, Mrs., C-69
Clerte, Jeanne, C-6, 106
Clerton, Pierre, E-73
Cloate, Marie Joseph, E-187
Cloccinel, Joseph, S3-1031
Cloccinet, Aimable, E-81
Cloccinet, Anne, N-62
Cloccinet, Gregoire, N-62
Cloccinet, Joseph, N-62
Cloccinet, Louis, E-81
Cloccinette, Marguerite, E-117, 430
Cloccynet, Louis, E-317
Clochet, Jean, E-413
Clochet, Magdelaine, E-406
Cloistre, Pierre, S2-563
Clolus, Enogat, S3-950
Clolus, Veronique, S3-950
Clopeau, Marie, E-359, 378
Cloquesinal, Marie, E-586
Cloquesinel, Louise, E-586

Closhieur, -----, S2-603
Closier, Francois, S1-86
Clossinet, Anne, C-39
Clossinet, Gregoire, C-39
Clossinet, Gregoire, S1-202-203
Clossinet, Jeanne, S1-301
Clossinet, Jeanne-Marguerite, S1-203
Clossinet, Joseph, S1-113, 202-203, 300
Clossinet, Joseph , C-38
Clossinet, Louis, F-89
Clossinet, Louis, S1-203, 240, 356
Clossinet, Louis, S2-519, 526, 603, 761
Clossinet, Louis, S3-911
Clossinet, Louise, S2-726-727
Clossinet, Marguerite, S2-773
Clossinet, Marie, F-7, 33
Clossinet, Marie, S1-43, 356-357
Clossinet, Marie, S2-513, 761
Clossinet, Marie Louise, S3-911
Clossinet, Marie-Louise, S2-761
Clossinet, Marie-Marguerite, S1-203
Clossinet, Pierre, S1-203
Clossiunet, Marie, E-255
Clostinet, Louis, C-41
Clouet, N., S3-931
Cloutier, Pierre, S2-524
Cloxtinel, Louis, S3-1031
Cochard, Jean, E-257
Cochard, Marie Anne, E-386
Coche, Mathurin, S2-691
Cocher, Etienne, E-29
Cocherel, Catherine Sertanne Jeanne, E-622
Cocherel, Charlotte, E-629
Cocherel, Francois, E-81, 149
Cocherel, Jeanne, E-262, 319
Cocherel, Mathurin, E-81, 149, 622
Cocherel, Pierre Jean, E-622
Cocherelle, Charlotte, E-618
Cocheret, Catherine-Servanne-Jeanne, S1-205
Cocheret, Charlotte, S1-204
Cocheret, Charlotte-Josephe, S1-204

Cocheret, Francois, S1-204
Cocheret, Francois-Eloy, S1-204
Cocheret, Francoise-Jeanne, S1-205
Cocheret, Gabriel-Charles-Pierre, S1-205
Cocheret, Jean, S1-205
Cocheret, Jean-Mathurin, S1-204-205
Cocheret, Mathurin, S1-204-205, 337
Cocheret, Mathurin, S2-585, 640
Cocheret, Mathurin-Gilles, S1-204
Cocheret, Mathurin-Guillaume, S1-204
Cocheret, Mathurin-Servan-Marie, S1-205
Cocheret, Pierre-Jean, S1-205
Cochu, Jacques, E-473
Cochu, Pierre, E-515
Codet, Dominique, E-81
Codet, Francois, E-585, 595
Codet, Marie, E-585, 595
Codet, Marie Suzanne, E-585, 595
Codet, Marie Victoire, E-81
Coeffe, Margueritte, E-112
Coeffe, Marie Jeanne, E-275, 294
Coetit, Pierre, S3-935
Coeur, Marie, E-622
Coeure, Lausrant, S3-935
Coeuret, Claude, E-81, 405
Coeuret, Francois Audet, E-81, 405
Coeuru, Joseph, S1-279
Coeuru, Marie, S2-724
Coffain, Anne, E-196
Cognac, Marguerite, E-22, 358
Coiffe, Marie Jeanne, E-61, 275
Coin, Baptiste, E-81
Coin, Francois, E-150
Coin, Simon, E-81
Colcein, Anne, F-9
Colcein, Anne, N-153, 177
Colchmith, Josue, E-28, 376
Colet, Laurent, E-309
Colet, Marie Madeleine, E-111
Colette, Bonne, E-60

Colin, Jean, E-73
Colin, Jean Baptiste, E-585, 592
Colin, Therese, E-585, 592
Colin dit Lafleur, Hubert, E-172
Collar, Pierre, S1-363
Colleson, Nicolle, E-457
Collet, Fanchon, E-622
Collet, Jeanne Marie, E-623
Collet, Louise, E-623
Collet, Marie Francoise, E-95
Collet, Marie Josephe, E-623
Collet, Marie-Beaulieu, S1-205
Collet, Pierre Francois Baulieu, E-20, 138
Collette, Francois, E-191
Collier, Francois Louis, E-63
Collin, Felicite, E-8
Collin, Felicite Nationale, E-81
Collin, Francois, E-8, 81
Collin, Hubert dit Lafleur, E-81
Collin, Jean Baptiste, E-8, 81
Collin, Jean Pierre, E-81
Collin, Jean Pierre Joseph, E-8
Collin, Nicaise, E-81
Collin La Buissiere, M., E-330
Collino, Jean Francois, E-10
Collongne, Dominique, E-81, 138
Collongne, Jean, E-138
Collongne, Pierre, E-81
Colly, Jean Louis, E-281, 384
Colombe, Pierre, S3-847
Colombel, Pierre, S2-737
Colonge, Jean, E-81, 385
Colonge, Jean Baptiste, E-81
Colonge, Marie, E-82
Colson, Nicole, E-473
Com, Andre, E-72
Combes, Barthelemy, E-23, 82
Combes, Jean Baptiste, E-23, 82
Combes, Marie, E-131
Come, Anne, E-179
Comeaux, Abraham, E-500, 524
Comeaux, Agne, E-179
Comeaux, Alexandre, E-19, 82, 500, 524
Comeaux, Alexandre, F-99
Comeaux, Alexandre, S1-212

Comeaux, Alexandre-Simon, S1-211

Comeaux, Alexis, F-15
Comeaux, Alexis, N-42, 238
Comeaux, Alexis, S1-206-207, 210
Comeaux, Alexis, S2-560
Comeaux, Alexis, S3-998, 1003, 1049
Comeaux, Amilienne, E-21
Comeaux, Anne, E-24, 82, 105, 151, 160, 176-178, 294, 492, 500, 598, 600
Comeaux, Anne, N-42, 116
Comeaux, Anne, S1-49, 238, 336
Comeaux, Anne, S2-568, 674, 690, 693
Comeaux, Anne, S3-1025, 1033
Comeaux, Anne Eleonore, F-73
Comeaux, Anne Eleonore, N-42
Comeaux, Anne La Feubine, E-473
Comeaux, Anne Leonor, E-82
Comeaux, Anne Marie, C-20
Comeaux, Anne Marie, N-28
Comeaux, Anne Marie, S3-1119
Comeaux, Anne-Marie, S1-123
Comeaux, Antoine, E-484
Comeaux, Augustin, E-524
Comeaux, Bazile-Toussaint, S1-209
Comeaux, Benois, E-31, 82-83
Comeaux, Benoist, C-13
Comeaux, Benoist, N-41-42
Comeaux, Benoit, F-73
Comeaux, Catherine, E-500
Comeaux, Catherine, S1-232
Comeaux, Catherine, S2-445
Comeaux, Catherine, S3-880, 884
Comeaux, Charles, E-19, 82-83, 598
Comeaux, Charles, F-33
Comeaux, Charles, S1-206-207, 311
Comeaux, Charles-Marin, S1-209
Comeaux, Charles-Simon, S1-212
Comeaux, Charlotte, N-22
Comeaux, Charlotte, S1-99, 105
Comeaux, Charlotte, S2-770

Comeaux, Claire, C-17
Comeaux, Claire, F-69
Comeaux, Claire, S1-108, 110
Comeaux, Claire, S2-552
Comeaux, Claire, S3-897, 998
Comeaux, Claire-Sophie, S1-211
Comeaux, Claude, S1-206-207
Comeaux, Colette, E-118
Comeaux, David, S1-208, 311
Comeaux, Elie, F-89
Comeaux, Elie, S1-209-210, 315
Comeaux, Elie-Marie, S1-208
Comeaux, Elisabeth, S3-1024
Comeaux, Elizabeth, E-82, 303
Comeaux, Elizabeth, S1-209, 212, 244, 325
Comeaux, Elizabeth, S2-572-573, 620, 700
Comeaux, Elizabeth-Madeleine, S1-211
Comeaux, Estienne, E-456, 492, 524
Comeaux, Etienne, S1-116, 210
Comeaux, Etienne, S2-464
Comeaux, Etienne, S3-926, 1002
Comeaux, Eustache, S1-207, 210
Comeaux, Felicite, E-32, 82, 601
Comeaux, Felicite, F-99
Comeaux, Felicite, S1-212
Comeaux, Felicite-Augustine, S1-211
Comeaux, Francois, E-83, 89, 598
Comeaux, Francoise, C-15
Comeaux, Francoise, E-598
Comeaux, Francoise, S1-11, 102-103, 107
Comeaux, Francoise, S2-464
Comeaux, Francoise, S3-883, 926
Comeaux, Hely, S1-212
Comeaux, Honore, C-25-26
Comeaux, Honore, E-82-83
Comeaux, Honore, F-53

Comeaux, Honore, N-42, 184, 205

Comeaux, Isabelle, C-20
Comeaux, Isabelle, F-99
Comeaux, Isabelle, S1-103, 212
Comeaux, Isabelle, S2-753
Comeaux, Jean, E-82, 473, 484, 492, 524, 598
Comeaux, Jean, F-73
Comeaux, Jean, N-42, 105-106, 205
Comeaux, Jean, S1-107, 206-208, 237, 311
Comeaux, Jean, S2-530
Comeaux, Jean, S3-893, 895, 1016, 1021, 1049
Comeaux, Jean Baptiste, E-82
Comeaux, Jean Baptiste, F-15, 53, 89, 99
Comeaux, Jean Baptiste, N-42-43, 105, 238
Comeaux, Jean Baptiste, S3-887, 1024, 1049
Comeaux, Jean-Baptiste, S1-104, 206-208, 210-212
Comeaux, Jean-Baptiste, S2-750
Comeaux, Jean-Baptiste-Elie, S1-209
Comeaux, Jeanne, E-72, 83, 474, 500
Comeaux, Jeanne, F-89
Comeaux, Jeanne, S1-209-210
Comeaux, Jeanne-Marie, S1-209
Comeaux, Joseph, C-20, 26, 46
Comeaux, Joseph, E-21, 82-83, 298, 500, 524, 598
Comeaux, Joseph, F-33, 39, 89
Comeaux, Joseph, N-28, 42
Comeaux, Joseph, S1-6, 123, 207-212, 381
Comeaux, Joseph, S2-571
Comeaux, Joseph, S3-836, 883, 887, 895, 1119
Comeaux, Joseph Anne, E-83
Comeaux, Joseph Marie, F-99
Comeaux, Joseph-Marie, S1-212
Comeaux, Joseph-Mathurin, S1-208
Comeaux, Louise, E-56, 83
Comeaux, Ludivise, E-598
Comeaux, Madeleine, E-275, 403

INDEX SOURCES C=Chatellerault; E=Acadians in Exile; F=Acadian Families; N=Nantes; S=St-Malo

Comeaux, Madeleine, N-116, 165, 169
Comeaux, Madeleine, S1-92, 123, 209-210, 212, 381
Comeaux, Madeleine, S2-464, 544, 716
Comeaux, Magdelaine, C-46-47, 68
Comeaux, Magdelaine, F-33, 55, 99
Comeaux, Marguerite, C-25, 63
Comeaux, Marguerite, E-42, 60, 65, 83, 156, 500, 601
Comeaux, Marguerite, F-17, 21, 67, 73, 91
Comeaux, Marguerite, N-38-39, 42, 68, 75, 104-106, 108, 134
Comeaux, Marguerite, S1-14, 43, 206-208, 210, 311, 325-326, 357
Comeaux, Marguerite, S2-527-528, 530-531, 540, 573-574
Comeaux, Marguerite Anastasie, E-83
Comeaux, Marguerite-Francois, S1-212
Comeaux, Margueritte, S3-924, 1101
Comeaux, Marie, C-15
Comeaux, Marie, E-83, 89, 195, 322, 327, 428, 492, 500, 598, 601
Comeaux, Marie, F-39, 89, 92, 99
Comeaux, Marie, S1-93, 98, 114, 119, 165, 170, 198, 210-212, 238
Comeaux, Marie, S2-537, 659, 677-679
Comeaux, Marie, S3-855, 1002, 1021
Comeaux, Marie Anne, N-42
Comeaux, Marie Anne Victoire, F-73
Comeaux, Marie Anne Victoire, N-42
Comeaux, Marie Joseph, S3-1037
Comeaux, Marie Josephe, N-106
Comeaux, Marie Josephine, E-598

Comeaux, Marie-Anne, S2-659
Comeaux, Marie-Elizabeth, S1-209
Comeaux, Marie-Josephe, S1-116, 210
Comeaux, Marie-Josephe, S2-534, 540
Comeaux, Marie-Luce, S1-211
Comeaux, Marie-Madeleine, S1-211-212
Comeaux, Mathurin, F-55
Comeaux, Mathurin, S1-213
Comeaux, Maurice, N-41
Comeaux, Monique, C-26
Comeaux, Monique, E-78, 178
Comeaux, Monique, F-77, 109
Comeaux, Monique, N-40
Comeaux, Pierre, E-82-83, 456, 473, 484, 492, 524
Comeaux, Pierre, F-99
Comeaux, Pierre, S1-212, 244
Comeaux, Pierre, S3-1024
Comeaux, Pierre-Paul, S1-211
Comeaux, Rosalie, E-598
Comeaux, Rose, E-33
Comeaux, Rose, F-73
Comeaux, Rose, N-42
Comeaux, Rose Julie, N-42
Comeaux, Simon, E-83
Comeaux, Simon, F-89, 99
Comeaux, Simon, S1-6, 27, 207-210, 212-213
Comeaux, Simon, S2-749
Comeaux, Simon, S3-1016
Comeaux, Simon-Pierre, S1-208
Comeaux, Susanne, S3-850
Comeaux, Suzanne, C-14, 21
Comeaux, Suzanne, E-418
Comeaux, Suzanne, F-51
Comeaux, Suzanne, N-30, 152, 244
Comeaux, Suzanne, S1-97, 131
Comeaux, Suzanne, S2-753
Comeaux, widr., E-82
Commalleau, Magdeleine, E-328, 392
Commere, Charlotte, E-20, 138
Commere, Louis, E-83
Commere, Marie, E-83
Commereu, Olivier, S1-213
Commereu, Olivier, S2-777

Commiere, Pierre, E-368
Commode, Anne, S3-974
Commode, Susanne, S3-838
Comode, Anne, E-26
Compagnac, Jeanne, E-83, 406
Compagnac, Pierre, E-83
Compagnion, Julien, E-83
Compagnion, Marie Jeanne, E-83
Compagnon, Aimee, E-603
Compagnon, Francois, E-603
Compagnon, Jacques, E-603
Compagnon, Joseph, E-603
Compagnon, Julien, E-378, 603
Compere, Jean, E-73
Compere, Marie, E-73, 97, 385
Comte, Joseph, E-333, 369
Comte, Magdeleine, E-83, 140
Comte, Marie, E-44
Comte, Pierre, E-348
Conamda, Francoise, E-150
Conard, Xavier Francois, E-623
Confalens, Jean, E-126
Conge, Marie Barbe, E-52
Coniam, Therese, N-133
Conian, Antoine, C-79
Conian, Therese, C-79
Conivette, Francoise, C-3
Conivette, Francoise, N-3-4
Consican, Anne, E-84
Consican, Jean, E-84
Constan, Marie Catherine, E-42, 383
Constant, Hypolithe, E-84
Constant, Jacques, E-84
Constantin, Jean, E-107
Conte, Jean, E-325
Conte, Marie Anne, E-126, 157
Contin, Pierre, E-84
Contineau, Francoise, E-84
Convenance, Jacques, S2-480, 683
Convenance, Jacques, S3-969, 1068
Convenance, Marie, C-44
Convenance, Marie, S1-184, 352
Convenance, Marie, S2-505, 582, 587
Convenance, Marie Jeanne, S3-1068

Convenance, Marie-Jeanne, S1-42

Convenance, Marie-Jeanne, S2-480

Coperon, Cicille, E-503

Coperon, Isabelle, E-503

Coperon, Jean, E-473, 503

Coperon, Jeanne, E-503

Coperon, Magdelaine, E-503

Coperon, Marguerite, E-503

Coperon, Marie, E-503

Copin, Marie, C-155

Coquesinel, Louise, E-593

Coquesinel, Marie, E-593

Coquetiere, Anne, E-22, 433

Cor, -----, S3-958

Cor, Joseph, S3-957

Corabasse, Courneuve, E-283

Corbin, Charle, S3-1040

Corbin, Marie, S1-317

Corbin, Marie, S3-1066

Corbin De Bazonge, Rene, S2-519

Corbineau, Jean, E-122, 370

Cordie, Marie, E-169, 172

Cordier, Francoise, E-61, 317

Cordon, Jeanne, S1-358

Cordreu, Jean Gilbert, E-262

Core-Marecue, Alexandre, S2-623

Coret, Toussaint, S3-950

Corlieu, Anne, E-84

Corlieu, Francoise, E-13

Corlieu, Marie, E-84, 255

Corlieu, Marie Anne, E-317

Cormier, Agnes, E-529, 548

Cormier, Alexandre, E-84

Cormier, Alexis, E-84, 518, 524

Cormier, Amman, E-84

Cormier, Anastasie, E-86

Cormier, Angelique, E-85, 518

Cormier, Anne, E-288, 526, 547-548

Cormier, Anne, S2-432, 680

Cormier, Barthelemy, E-84

Cormier, Catherine, E-546-547

Cormier, Cecile, E-547

Cormier, Charles, E-84-85

Cormier, Claire, E-530

Cormier, Claude, E-85

Cormier, Daniel, E-84

Cormier, Elizabeth, E-84, 168

Cormier, Felicite, E-84

Cormier, Francois, E-84, 86, 518, 524, 547

Cormier, Francois Alexis, E-84

Cormier, Germain, E-84, 518, 524, 547

Cormier, Gratien, E-84

Cormier, Hyppolite, E-68

Cormier, Jacques, E-85

Cormier, Jacques, S1-213, 277

Cormier, Jacques, S2-717

Cormier, Jean, E-84-85, 332, 360, 364, 437

Cormier, Jean, S2-653, 671

Cormier, Jean Baptiste, E-84-85, 546, 548

Cormier, Jean Charles, E-85

Cormier, Jeanne, E-518

Cormier, Joseph, E-84-85, 434, 547,

Cormier, Laurent, E-84-85, 282

Cormier, Laurent, S2-692

Cormier, Lemand, E-84

Cormier, Lisette, S1-300

Cormier, M., E-85

Cormier, Magdelaine, E-85, 286-287, 353, 434-435, 518, 546, 548

Cormier, Marguerite, E-13-14, 107, 349, 431, 547-548

Cormier, Marguerite, S1-51

Cormier, Marguerite, S2-776

Cormier, Marie, E-85, 135, 406, 435, 437, 518, 523, 529, 546-547

Cormier, Marie, S1-213-214

Cormier, Marie Angelique, E-85

Cormier, Marie Anne, E-349

Cormier, Marie Joseph, E-363

Cormier, Marie La Blanche, E-381

Cormier, Marie Madeleine, E-85

Cormier, Marie-Madeleine, S1-76

Cormier, Marie-Madeleine, S2-653

Cormier, Michel, E-546

Cormier, Nicolas, E-85

Cormier, Paul, E-547

Cormier, Pierre, E-85-86, 408, 518, 524, 546-548

Cormier, Pierre, S1-213

Cormier, Rosalie, E-10-11, 47, 85

Cormier, Rose, E-85

Cormier, Rose Marguerite, E-85

Cormier, Simon, E-86

Cormier, Thomas, E-86, 456, 473

Corne, Caume, N-252

Corne, Mathurine, N-252

Cornet, Marie, E-64, 173

Cornevin, Francois, E-291

Cornibert, Philippe, E-60

Cornier, Marie Anne, E-86, 147-148

Cornoualle, Mathurin, S3-896

Cornu, Catherine, E-47, 262

Cornu, Charles Julien, E-367

Cornu de Nailly, Etienne, E-86

Cornu de Nailly, Michel Jean Francois, E-86

Cornu de Nailly, Pierre Etienne, E-86

Cornuaud, Catherine, E-322

Coronel, Francoise, S1-49

Corporal, Magdeleine, E-38

Corporon, Anne, E-38, 86, 329, 418

Corporon, Anne Magdalen, E-86, 113

Corporon, Baptiste, E-86

Corporon, Cecile, F-69

Corporon, Cecile, N-27

Corporon, Cecile, S1-90

Corporon, Jean, E-86

Corporon, Jean, N-43, 242

Corporon, Jean Charles, N-242

Corporon, Jean Marie Victor, N-43, 242

Corporon, Jehan, E-456

Corporon, Magdelaine, E-38, 86

Corporon, Marguerite, S2-590

Corporon, Marguerite Joseph, E-298

Corporon, Marie, E-80, 405

Corporon, Marie Blanche, E-86

Corporon, Martin, E-524

Corporon, Pierre, E-86, 433

Corrales, Bernarde, F-33

Corrige, Philippon, S3-1096
Cortise, Marianne Josephe, C-2
Cosmard, Francois, S1-214
Cosnard, Hilaire-Francois, S2-444
Cosnard, Marguerite, S2-444
Cosnard, Marie, E-623
Cossa, Marguerite, E-110, 346
Cosset, Anne, S1-216
Cosset, Barthelemy, E-86-87, 145
Cosset, Berthelemy, S1-214-216
Cosset, Francoise, E-86
Cosset, Francoise, S1-215
Cosset, Guillaume, E-86
Cosset, Guillaume, S1-215
Cosset, Jean, E-1, 17
Cosset, Jean Robert, E-87
Cosset, Jean-Robert, S1-215-216
Cosset, Louise-Genevieve, S1-216
Cosset, Marguerite, E-87
Cosset, Marie-Francoise, S1-216
Cosset, Marie-Madeleine, S1-214
Cosset, Pierre, S1-214, 216
Cosset, Rene, E-38, 100, 122
Cosset, Rose, S1-215
Cossin, Antoine, E-387
Cosson, Pierre-Charles, S2-743
Costa, Joseph, F-41
Coste, Adelle Louise, E-87
Coste, Alexandre Francois, E-87
Coste, Anastasie, E-631, 638
Coste, Anastasie, S1-217-218
Coste, Anastasie Melanie, E-87, 642
Coste, Anne, S1-217-219
Coste, Antoine Marie Xavier, E-87
Coste, Barbe, E-37, 87-89, 189, 438, 631-632, 638-639, 641
Coste, Barbe, S1-217-218
Coste, Benjamin, E-366, 631-632, 638, 642
Coste, Benony Leon, E-87
Coste, Cecile, E-631
Coste, Cecile, S1-218-219
Coste, Charles-Amand, S1-217
Coste, Desire Edmond, E-87

Coste, Etienne, E-46, 87-89, 179, 437-438, 631-632, 638, 641-641
Coste, Etienne, S1-217-219
Coste, Francois, E-57-58, 87, 361, 434, 524, 631, 638, 641
Coste, Francois, S1-216-219, 229
Coste, Francois, S3-1097
Coste, Francois Alexandre, E-89, 641
Coste, Francoise Plante, E-370
Coste, Jan, S3-1097
Coste, Jean, E-1, 55, 87-89, 179, 434, 436-438, 631-632, 641-642
Coste, Jean, S1-216-219
Coste, Jean, S2-471
Coste, Jean Jr., E-642
Coste, Jean Sr., E-638
Coste, Joseph, E-56, 58, 87-88, 631, 638, 641
Coste, Joseph Etienne, E-88
Coste, Josephe, E-631, 642
Coste, Laurent, E-290
Coste, Laurent, S1-217
Coste, Louis Emmanuel, E-88
Coste, Madeleine, E-89, 351, 438, 632, 639
Coste, Magdeleine Charlotte, E-642
Coste, Marguerite, C-36
Coste, Marguerite, F-23, 25
Coste, Marguerite, N-59, 64
Coste, Marie, E-35, 88, 631, 638
Coste, Marie Arsene, E-88
Coste, Marie Francoise, E-89
Coste, Marie Louise, E-89
Coste, Marie Magdeleine, E-641
Coste, Marie-Madeleine, S1-218
Coste, Paul Edouard, E-89
Coste, Pelagie, E-632, 639, 642
Coste, Pierre, E-632, 638, 642
Coste, Pierre, S1-216, 218-219
Coste, Pierre, S3-1097
Coste, Rosalie, S1-216
Coste, Simon, E-87, 632, 638, 642
Coste, Theodore Magloire, E-89
Coste, widow, E-1
Costet, Francoise, E-58

Costuas, Francoise, S1-67
Cotard, Guillaume, S3-1108
Cotillon, Jean, E-83, 89
Cotillon, Joseph, E-83, 89
Cotinet, Marie Jeanne, E-588, 596
Cottard, Pierre, E-515
Cottard, Robert, E-473
Couagne, Jean Baptiste, E-89, 107
Coude, Ma., S3-1147
Coudect, Marguerite, C-92, 102
Coudron, Francois, S3-854
Coudron, Mathurin, S3-854
Coueffe, Marguerite, E-304, 332
Couiard, Marie, S3-903
Couillard, Guillaume, S1-86
Couillard, Guillaume, S3-896
Couillard, Marie, S1-86
Couillard, Marie, S3-896
Couillard, Pierre, E-87-89, 181, 361, 364-365, 435
Couillaud, Marie, E-385
Couindeau, Pierre, E-354
Coullon, Jean, E-89, 386
Coullon, Mr., E-183
Coullon, Suzanne, E-89, 386
Coulombie, Guillemette, E-259
Coulon, Clercy Henry Francois, E-183
Coulon, Raymond, E-66
Coulonge, Marie, E-403
Coumallon, Madelaine, E-370
Coumau, Anne, E-14
Coumo, Marie, E-357
Counts, Jean Nicolas, E-413
Coupard, George, E-255
Coupard, George, S2-513
Coupe, Therese, S1-370
Coupeau, -----, N-246
Coupeau, Jean, E-97
Coupeaux, Joseph, S1-244
Coupeaux, Olivier, S1-30
Coupeaux, Rose, S1-154
Coupex, Marie Magdalen, E-275
Coupiau, Marie, S1-333
Coupiau Desaleur, Marguerite Renee, E-109
Coupiaux, Anne, E-624
Coupio, Marie-Josephe, S2-650
Couppe, Jacquemine, S1-271

Couquilles, Charles Nicolas, E-46

Courage, Brice, E-89, 337

Courage, Francois, E-89, 337

Courage, Jean, E-89

Courdan, Jean Baptiste Joseph, E-89, 316, 317

Courdoan, Joseph, E-89

Couriacault, Marie, E-89, 96

Couriacault, Nicolas, E-89

Courisan, Jean, E-90, 182

Courisan, Pierre, E-90, 182

Cournoyer, Elizabeth, S1-323

Courounat, Mr, E-386

Courpon, Savinien de, E-456

Courpron, Mathieu, E-18, 90

Courrand, Pierre, E-168

Courraud, Marie, E-17, 90

Coursin, Catherine, E-353, 403

Coursin, Jean Baptiste, E-357, 406

Coursin, Pierre, E-340, 403, 406

Courtenay, Esther, E-565

Courtenay, Esther, S2-456

Courthiau, Marianne, E-150, 267

Courtin, Charlotte Louise, F-33

Courtin, Francoise, F-33, 41

Courtin, Jacques Marie, F-33

Courtin, Louis, E-289, 556

Courtin, Louis, F-33

Courtin, Marie, E-556

Courtin, Mathurine, E-426

Courtin, Mathurine Olive, E-556

Courtin, Mathurine Olive, F-33

Courtney, Esther, F-3

Courtois, Guillaume, E-623, 625

Courtois, Julie, E-623

Courtois, Julienne, E-623

Courtois, Pierre Marie, E-623

Courtois, Sophie, E-623

Courtoit, Francois, E-270

Cousin, Charlotte, E-90, 156

Cousin, Hypolite, N-249

Cousin, Jacquelin, E-585

Cousin, Jaqueline, E-586, 592

Cousin, Jean, C-37

Cousin, Jean, E-90

Cousin, Jean, F-71, 107

Cousin, Jean, N-58

Cousin, Jean, S1-219

Cousin, Jean-Francois, S1-219

Cousin, Julien, E-585, 592

Cousin, Louis-Mathurin-Jean, S1-219

Cousin, Marie Blanche, C-37

Cousin, Marie Blanche, E-116, 118

Cousin, Marie Blanche, F-71, 107

Cousin, Marie Blanche, N-58

Cousin, Pierre, E-90, 585-586, 592

Cousin, Yves, S1-219

Couson, Charles, E-585, 595

Cousseau, Marie, E-36

Cousset, Bartholome, E-90, 375

Cousset, Pierre, E-90, 375

Coussin, Julien, E-586

Coussot, Suzanne, E-137, 190-191

Coutaneau, Adrien, E-344

Coutant, Francois, E-17

Coutant, Jean, E-90

Coutant, Jean Louis, E-90

Coutant, Louis, E-90

Coutant, Marie Jeanne, E-90

Coutant, S. F., E-258

Coute, Marie Anne, E-85

Couteau, Marguerite, E-90, 156

Couteiller, Marguerite Marie, E-51

Coutir, Francoise, S1-55

Coutour, Jean, N-203

Coutrain, Jacques, E-404

Couture, Marianne, E-113, 194

Couturier, Mr., E-51

Couvard, Silvine, C-14, 93

Couvenance, Jacques, S1-219-220

Couvenance, Jean-Louis, S1-220

Couvenance, Louis-Martin, S1-220

Couvenance, Marie Jeanne, E-644

Couvenance, Marie-Renee, S1-220

Couvenance, Narie-Jeanne, S1-220

Couvenance, Olive-Blanche, S1-220

Couvillier, Francois, E-599

Couzine, Jean, N-232

Covais dit Ledreux, George, E-379

Covais dit Ledreux, Joseph, E-379

Covais dit Ledreux, Marie Olive, E-379

Covois dit Ledreux, Joseph, E-90, 379

Covois dit Ledreux, Marie Magdelaine, E-90, 379

Cozeaux, Jean, E-391

Credo, Elisabeth, E-154

Cremois, Magdeleine, E-72, 90

Cren, Francois, E-420

Creon, Jeanne, E-73, 131

Crepeau, Francois, E-90, 329

Crepeau, Jean, E-90

Crepeau, Pierre, E-90

Crepelle, Guillaume, E-152

Crepon, Antoine, E-585, 595

Crepon, Antoine Martin, E-585, 596

Cres, Paul, E-302, 347

Crespeau, Jean, E-72

Crespeau, Louise Marie, E-90, 196

Crespeau, Pierre, E-90, 196

Creste, Francois, S3-861

Cretan, Jean-Francois, S2-506

Crete, Francois, S1-220

Crete, Francois, S2-614

Crete, Francois, S3-861

Crete, Francoise-Elizabeth, S1-221

Crete, Jean, S1-220

Crete, Jean, S3-861

Crete, Yves, N-232

Cretin, Claude, E-369

Creunier, Marie, E-91, 357

Creunier, Mathieu, E-91, 357

Creviliers, Christophe, E-585, 591

Crezonet, Francois, E-175, 349

Crigoue, Azeline, E-350

Crochet, Charlotte, S1-222

Crochet, Francois, C-28

Crochet, Francois, S1-223

Crochet, Francois-Louis, S1-222

Crochet, Francoise, F-63, 71

Crochet, Francoise, S1-222
Crochet, Francoise-Pelagie, S1-223
Crochet, Guillaume, C-28
Crochet, Guillaume, F-71
Crochet, Guillaume, S1-221-222
Crochet, Guillaume, S3-824
Crochet, Jacquemine-Julienne, S1-221
Crochet, Jean, C-28
Crochet, Jean, F-65, 71
Crochet, Jean, S1-223
Crochet, Jean-Francois, S1-221
Crochet, Jean-Guillaume, S1-222
Crochet, Jean-Joseph, S1-222
Crochet, Jean-Marin, C-28
Crochet, Jeanne, C-28
Crochet, Jeanne, S1-222-223
Crochet, Joseph, S1-221
Crochet, Julien, C-28
Crochet, Julien, F-71
Crochet, Julien, S1-223
Crochet, Louis, S1-221
Crochet, Marguerite, F-63, 71
Crochet, Marguerite-Perinne, S1-223
Crochet, Pelagie, C-28
Crochet, Pelagie, S1-223
Crochet, Yves, C-8, 26, 28, 86
Crochet, Yves, F-63, 71
Crochet, Yves, S1-52-53, 221-223
Crochet, Yves, S2-437, 582
Crochet, Yves-Jean, S1-223
Crochet, Yves-Joseph, S1-222
Crocsinais, Joseph, S3-967
Croizol, Francoise, S2-505
Cron, Henry, C-81
Cronier, Jeanne, E-91, 370
Cros, Pierre Jean, E-45, 145
Cruchon, Jean Rene, E-91
Cruchon, Marguerite, E-91, 295
Cruchon, Marie, E-283, 438
Cruchon, Marie Louise, E-91, 389
Cruchon Latour, Jean Rene, E-295, 389
Crugeau, Rene, E-280
Crugeon, Jean, E-280
Cruh, -----, S3-1066

Cruier, Louis, E-295
Crujon, Francois, E-403
Cruon, Charles, E-22
Cudenet, Anne, E-616
Cudenet, Antoine, E-623
Cudenet, Auguste, E-623
Cudenet, Benjamin Marie, E-623
Cudenet, Francois Rene Isaac, E-623
Cudenet, Jean Baptiste, E-623
Cudenet, Louis Auguste, E-623
Cudenet, Marie Adelaide Jeanne, E-623
Cudenet, Pierre, E-623
Cudenet, Veronique, E-623
Cuilleau, Jacque, S3-1074
Cuisinier, Antoine, E-41, 91
Cuisinier, Jean Baptiste, E-34, 41, 91, 302
Cuisinier, Pierre, E-29, 91, 143, 146
Culant, -----, S3-985
Culliard, Jacques, E-91
Culliard, Louis, E-91
Cuq, Georges, E-91
Cussonnelle, Claude, E-385
Cytier, Jean, E-409

D

D'Acarette, Marie, E-40, 266
D'Aigle, Marie Rose, E-93
d'Aigle, Jean, E-177
D'Aigre, Marie Magdaleine, E-162, 164, 166-167
D'Ailleboust, Charles Joseph, E-102, 109, 392
D'Aillebout, Marice Charlotte, E-109
D'Ambreville, Jean Baptiste Henry, E-282
D'Amon, Isabelle, E-16
D'Angeac, Andre, S2-626
d'Anjou, Anne, E-70, 391
d'Annette, Jeanne, E-134
d'Apremont, Charles Francois Delalande, E-97
d'Apremont, Pierre Francois, E-97

d'Aprendestique, Marianne, E-511
d'Aprendestique, Martin, E-473
D'Arme, Cecile-Francoise, S1-257
D'Arme, Francois-Gabriel, S1-257
D'Arme, Nicolas, S1-256-257
D'Arme, Philippe-Nicolas, S1-256-257
D'Arme, Servanne-Julienne, S1-257
D'Arme, Simon-Francois, S1-257
D'Aspre, Emmanuel, N-148
D'Aunis, Mathurin, F-45
D'Entremont, Abraham, E-604
D'Entremont, Cecile, C-64, 115
D'Entremont, Charles, E-603
D'Entremont, Firmin, E-603
D'Entremont, Jacque Mieu, S3-1099
D'Entremont, Jacques, E-604
D'Entremont, Joseph, E-604
D'Entremont, Magdelaine, E-603
D'Entremont, Marguerite, E-603
D'Entremont, Marie, E-603-604
D'Entremont, Pierre, E-603
D'Entremont, Simon, E-603
d'Entremont, Abraham, E-106
d'Entremont, Anne, E-106, 181
d'Entremont, Anne, E-334
d'Entremont, Augustin, E-273
d'Entremont, Augustin, E-30
d'Entremont, Cecile, E-273
d'Entremont, Cecile, E-431
d'Entremont, Cecile, N-107
d'Entremont, Charles, E-334
d'Entremont, Charles, E-89, 106-107
d'Entremont, Etienne, E-334
d'Entremont, Jacques, E-106, 186
d'Entremont, Jean, E-106
d'Entremont, Jeanne Mius, E-390
d'Entremont, Jeanne Mius, E-61, 66, 127-128
d'Entremont, Joseph, E-106-107
d'Entremont, Joseph, N-107

INDEX SOURCES   C=Chatellerault;   E=Acadians in Exile;   F=Acadian Families;   N=Nantes;   S=St-Malo

d'Entremont,Joseph David, E-106
d'Entremont,Joseph Demius Ecuyer Sieur, E-106, 271
d'Entremont,Madelaine, E-106, 127, 162-163, 167, 266
d'Entremont,Magdalen de Mius, E-41
d'Entremont,Marguerite, E-106
d'Entremont,Marguerite Mius, E-323
d'Entremont,Marie, E-149, 323
d'Entremont,Marie, E-81, 127-128, 144-145, 267, 271
d'Entremont,Marie Jeanne Charlotte, E-106
d'Entremont,Marie Josephe, E-89, 107, 271, 273
d'Entremont,Marie Josephe, N-107
d'Entremont,Melle Demius, E-274
d'Entremont,Mius, E-132
d'Entremont,Pierre, E-145
d'Entremont,Pierre, E-378
d'Entremont,Pierre Marin, E-107
d'Entremont,Simon, E-106-107
d'Entremont,Simon, E-329, 334
D'Entremont(Lendremont), Filhipe Mieux Cenier, E-456
d'Entremont- See also Mius
d'Estimauville,Jean Baptiste Philippe, E-11 109
d'Estimauville,Philippe, E-11, 109
D'Harmes,Henriette Magdelaine, E-112
D'Harmes,Philippe Nicolas, E-112
Dabadie, Louis, E-266
Dabouville, Felicite Theotiste, E-92
Dabouville, Jean Baptiste, E-92
Dabouville, Jean Baptiste Henry, E-92
Dabouville, Joseph, E-92
Dabouville, Marguerite Elizabeth, E-92
Dabouville, Marie Madeleine, E-92

Dabouville, Pierre, E-92
Dabouville, Pierre Alexandre, E-92
Dabouville, Rosalie, E-92
Daccarette, Catherine, E-92, 268
Daccarette, Marie, E-92, 106
Daccarette, Marie Jeanne, E-92, 105
Daccarette, Michel, E-92, 105, 264, 268, 300
Daccarrette, Marie, E-51, 300, 328
Dachut, Michel Jean Joseph, E-92
Dadu, Pierre, E-92, 270
Dagnaud, Jean, E-92
Dagnaud, Louis Joseph, E-92
Dagorne, Marguerite, S1-373
Dagorne, Marguerite, S3-951
Dagueneau, Marie, E-112, 332
Daguere, Marie Anne, E-81
Daguerre, Jean, E-92-93, 153
Daguerre, Joannis, S2-442
Daguerre, Julie, E-92
Daguerre, Margin, S1-220
Daguerre, Marie, E-93, 179, 313
Daguerre, Marie, S2-442-443
Daguerre, Michel, E-93
Daguerre, Pelagie, E-93
Daguerre, Sophie, E-93
Daguet, Anne Francoise, E-93
Daguet, boy, E-93
Daguet, Marie Elizabeth, E-93
Daguet, Rene, E-93, 376
Daguet, Rene, S2-688
Daigle, -----, S1-243, 272
Daigle, -----, S2-620
Daigle, Abraham, E-94, -96
Daigle, Abraham, F-35
Daigle, Adelaide, F-35
Daigle, Alain, E-93
Daigle, Alexander, S2-614
Daigle, Alexandre, E-93-94, 274, 324
Daigle, Alexandre, N-43
Daigle, Alexandre, S1-231-232, 340
Daigle, Alexis, F-23
Daigle, Alexis, N-182
Daigle, Alexis, S1-235
Daigle, Alexis Maturin, E-93

Daigle, Alexis-Maturin, S1-231-232
Daigle, Angelique, E-283, 569
Daigle, Angelique, S2-569-570
Daigle, Anne, C-77-78
Daigle, Anne, E-93, 108, 307, 350, 366, 412, 419, 433-434, 436, 438, 634, 643
Daigle, Anne, F-55, 61, 63, 87
Daigle, Anne, N-46, 131-132
Daigle, Anne, S1-39, 136, 142-144, 236, 241, 251, 331, 352
Daigle, Anne, S2-621, 623, 668, 670, 716-718
Daigle, Anne, S3-847
Daigle, Anne Appoline, E-93
Daigle, Anne Francoise, E-93
Daigle, Anne Genevieve, E-558
Daigle, Anne Genevieve, F-31
Daigle, Anne Genevieve, N-49
Daigle, Anne Josephe, F-87
Daigle, Anne Marie, E-93
Daigle, Anne Marie Catherine, E-113
Daigle, Anne-Genevieve, S1-251
Daigle, Anne-Josephe, S1-141-240
Daigle, Anne-Marie, S1-241, 243
Daigle, Auguste, E-96
Daigle, Bernard, E-524
Daigle, Bernard, F-27
Daigle, Bernard, N-43, 47
Daigle, Bernard, S1-234-235, 238, 252
Daigle, Bernard, S2-569
Daigle, Brigide, S1-245
Daigle, Brigitte, C-91, 114
Daigle, Casimir, S3-865, 868
Daigle, Casimir-Theodore, S1-249
Daigle, Catherine, C-5
Daigle, Catherine, E-417
Daigle, Catherine, F-51
Daigle, Catherine, N-159, 227
Daigle, Catherine, S1-239-240
Daigle, Catherine, S2-753, 755
Daigle, Cecile, E-93
Daigle, Charles, C-157

188

INDEX SOURCES C=Chatellerault; E=Acadians in Exile; F=Acadian Families; N=Nantes; S=St-Malo

Daigle, Charles, C-27, 48, 132-133
Daigle, Charles, E-93, 96, 298, 305, 608, 610, 613
Daigle, Charles, F-11, 27, 95
Daigle, Charles, N-44, 191, 197, 200, 233
Daigle, Charles, S1-30, 90, 121, 231-234, 236, 239-240, 247-249, 253, 305, 344, 388, 393
Daigle, Charles, S2-554, 753
Daigle, Charles, S3-880, 906, 987
Daigle, Charles Augustin, E-557
Daigle, Charles Daniel, N-43
Daigle, Charles Lazare, E-93
Daigle, Charles Lazare, N-46
Daigle, Charles-Marc, S1-235
Daigle, Charles-Marie, S1-232
Daigle, Claire, C-50
Daigle, Claire, E-181, 187
Daigle, Claire, S2-451
Daigle, Claire, S3-994, 1017
Daigle, Constance, E-93
Daigle, Edouard, E-93, 558
Daigle, Edouard, F-31
Daigle, Edouard, N-48
Daigle, Elizabeth, F-31
Daigle, Elizabeth, N-49
Daigle, Elizabeth, S1-232, 240
Daigle, Emelie Adelaide, F-37
Daigle, Emilie Adelaide, N-45
Daigle, Etienne, F-27
Daigle, Etienne, N-44
Daigle, Eulalie, E-94
Daigle, Eulalie, F-31
Daigle, Eulalie, N-47
Daigle, Eustache, F-21, 27
Daigle, Eustache, N-43-44, 89, 191, 234
Daigle, Eustache, S1-234-235, 315-317
Daigle, Eustache, S3-1058
Daigle, Fabien, N-44
Daigle, Fanny, E-4-5
Daigle, Felicite, F-97
Daigle, Felicite, S1-239, 240
Daigle, Felicite, S2-667, 669-670, 754
Daigle, Felicite, S3-866-867
Daigle, Firmin, E-94

Daigle, Firmin, N-46
Daigle, Firmin, S1-247
Daigle, Flore, C-7
Daigle, Francois, C-2, 6, 18, 23, 42, 49, 104-106
Daigle, Francois, E-94-96, 196, 556
Daigle, Francois, F-31, 35, 37
Daigle, Francois, N-44, 47-48
Daigle, Francois, S1-114, 235-236, 240, 245, 344, 387, 391
Daigle, Francois, S3-828, 865, 906-907
Daigle, Francois Alexandre, E-94
Daigle, Francois Alexandre, F-37
Daigle, Francois Alexandre, N-44-45
Daigle, Francois Joseph, N-45
Daigle, Francois Josephe, F-37
Daigle, Francois-Joseph, S1-249
Daigle, Francois-Marin, S1-236
Daigle, Francoise, C-18, 48
Daigle, Francoise, E-94, 380, 382-384, 414, 556-558, 573, 580, 635
Daigle, Francoise, F-31
Daigle, Francoise, S1-114, 121, 236, 238, 342-343, 383, 388
Daigle, Francoise, S3-906
Daigle, Francoise-Appoline, S1-249
Daigle, Francoise-Jeanne, S1-237
Daigle, Francoise-Modeste, S1-241
Daigle, Genevieve, E-631
Daigle, Genevieve, S1-247
Daigle, Genevieve-Jeanne, S1-251
Daigle, Genevieve-Marie, S1-249
Daigle, Genevieve-Simone, S1-237
Daigle, Genevieve-Sophie, S1-237
Daigle, Gertrude, S1-234
Daigle, Gregoire, S1-236-237, 248

Daigle, Gregoire, S2-492, 506, 510, 554, 662, 717, 732
Daigle, Gregoire, S3-966, 982, 987, 1065
Daigle, Helene, C-47, 49
Daigle, Helene, S1-388, 392
Daigle, Helene-Catherine, S1-236, 339, 344
Daigle, Helenne Catherine, S3-907
Daigle, Honore, E-94, 96, 556-558, 580
Daigle, Honore, F-31
Daigle, Honore, N-47
Daigle, Isaac Joseph, N-44
Daigle, Isabelle Luce, E-94
Daigle, Isabelle-Luce, S1-231
Daigle, Isidore, S2-522
Daigle, Isidore, S3-844
Daigle, Jean, C-5, 28-29, 44
Daigle, Jean, E-93-96
Daigle, Jean, F-19, 27, 39, 81, 87, 89
Daigle, Jean, N-34, 44-46, 101, 190, 196
Daigle, Jean, S1-38-39, 88, 136, 141-143, 161, 203, 238-240, 242, 250, 252-253, 283, 352, 359
Daigle, Jean, S2-523, 555, 621, 668-669, 738, 754
Daigle, Jean, S3-832, 834, 839-840, 847, 869, 972-973, 1058
Daigle, Jean Augustin, N-46
Daigle, Jean Baptiste, C-29
Daigle, Jean Baptiste, E-94, 96, 263, 415, 417
Daigle, Jean Baptiste, F-31, 39, 45, 55
Daigle, Jean Baptiste, N-45-47, 121, 196
Daigle, Jean Baptiste Alexandre, E-94
Daigle, Jean Charles, E-93, 95, 556-558, 580
Daigle, Jean Charles Alexandre, E-94
Daigle, Jean Francois, E-94, 556
Daigle, Jean Louis, C-28-29
Daigle, Jean Louis, F-39
Daigle, Jean Louis, N-45

Daigle, Jean Pierre, C-29
Daigle, Jean Pierre, E-94, 556
Daigle, Jean Pierre, N-48
Daigle, Jean Pierre Toussaint, N-47
Daigle, Jean Rene, F-39
Daigle, Jean Rene, N-47
Daigle, Jean-Baptiste, S1-234, 243-244, 247
Daigle, Jean-Baptiste, S2-729, 754
Daigle, Jean-Baptiste Amans, S1-252
Daigle, Jean-Baptiste-Alexandre, S1-231-232
Daigle, Jean-Charles, S1-249
Daigle, Jean-Charles-Alexandre, S1-231
Daigle, Jean-Joseph, S1-235, 237, 242
Daigle, Jean-Pierre, S1-241, 247
Daigle, Jeanne, C-29
Daigle, Jeanne, E-427
Daigle, Jeanne, F-35
Daigle, Jeanne-Madeleine, S1-241
Daigle, Joseph, C-140
Daigle, Joseph, C-15, 38
Daigle, Joseph, E-94-95, 556, 580
Daigle, Joseph, F-39, 55
Daigle, Joseph, N-46, 72
Daigle, Joseph, S1-102-103, 144, 232, 243-245, 247-248, 253, 325
Daigle, Joseph, S2-553, 612, 779
Daigle, Joseph, S3-883, 1024
Daigle, Joseph Gregoire, N-44
Daigle, Joseph Michel, E-94
Daigle, Joseph Michel, F-31
Daigle, Joseph Michel, N-48
Daigle, Joseph Pierre, E-96
Daigle, Joseph-Charles, S1-251
Daigle, Joseph-Marc, S1-244
Daigle, Joseph-Marie, S1-243
Daigle, Joseph-Silvain, S1-244
Daigle, Judith, S1-238
Daigle, Julie, E-161
Daigle, Leandre, E-94
Daigle, Louis, F-35

Daigle, Louis Francois, E-94
Daigle, Louis Joseph, E-94
Daigle, Louise, F-35
Daigle, Luc Julien Pascal, E-95
Daigle, Luc Pascal, E-95
Daigle, Luce, F-25
Daigle, Madelaine, E-95, 279, 356
Daigle, Madeleine, N-82
Daigle, Madeleine, S1-238, 240, 243-244
Daigle, Madeleine, S2-440
Daigle, Madeleine-Francoise, S1-241
Daigle, Madeleine-Marguerite, S1-234
Daigle, Magdelaine, C-149
Daigle, Marguerite, C-140-141
Daigle, Marguerite, C-29, 38, 69
Daigle, Marguerite, E-94-95, 140, 280, 381, 383, 414, 599
Daigle, Marguerite, F-23, 25, 59, 69, 81, 97
Daigle, Marguerite, N-17, 27, 33, 47, 59, 64-65, 86, 109-110, 191, 197, 210, 224, 251
Daigle, Marguerite, S1-103, 114, 120-121, 132-133, 142, 154, 203, 233, 235-236, 239-240, 243-246, 248, 251, 268, 305, 359
Daigle, Marguerite, S2-533, 667, 669, 694, 706
Daigle, Marguerite Louise, N-46
Daigle, Marguerite-Anastasie, S1-237
Daigle, Marguerite-Cecile, S1-233
Daigle, Marguerite-Felicite, S1-231
Daigle, Marguerite-Jeanne, S1-251
Daigle, Margueritte, S3-839, 860, 877, 892
Daigle, Marie, C-158
Daigle, Marie, C-5, 34, 91-92, 105-106, 114
Daigle, Marie, E-635
Daigle, Marie, F-19, 21, 25, 31, 81, 89, 95

Daigle, Marie, N-9, 20-22, 25, 44, 47, 73, 89, 234
Daigle, Marie, S1-38, 45, 88, 161, 232-233, 236, 239241, 245, 248, 279
Daigle, Marie, S2-525, 554, 667, 670, 717, 732, 754
Daigle, Marie, S3-840, 883
Daigle, Marie Angelique, E-282
Daigle, Marie Catherine, E-95
Daigle, Marie Francoise, E-95
Daigle, Marie Genevieve, E-95
Daigle, Marie Jeanne, E-95
Daigle, Marie Jeanne, F-35
Daigle, Marie Jeanne Jacquelin, E-95
Daigle, Marie Joseph, C-15
Daigle, Marie Josephe, N-34
Daigle, Marie Josephe Marguerite, E-95, 557, 608, 613
Daigle, Marie Josephine, E-610
Daigle, Marie Judith, C-158
Daigle, Marie Judith, N-46
Daigle, Marie Louise, E-95
Daigle, Marie Madeleine, N-49
Daigle, Marie Magdelaine, F-31
Daigle, Marie Magdeleine, C-32
Daigle, Marie Magdeleine, E-95, 163, 279, 562
Daigle, Marie Marguerite, E-95, 558
Daigle, Marie Marguerite, F-31
Daigle, Marie Marguerite, N-49
Daigle, Marie Osithe, F-95
Daigle, Marie Ozitte, S3-879
Daigle, Marie Reine, C-158
Daigle, Marie Reine, E-96
Daigle, Marie Rosalie, E-417
Daigle, Marie Rose, C-39, 49, 77
Daigle, Marie Rose, E-96, 263, 280
Daigle, Marie Rose, N-34, 48, 68, 190
Daigle, Marie Rose, S3-894, 898, 1104
Daigle, Marie Therese, E-96
Daigle, Marie Thereze, C-6, 106
Daigle, Marie-Anne, S1-251
Daigle, Marie-Blanche, S1-249
Daigle, Marie-Francoise, S1-251

INDEX SOURCES   C=Chatellerault; E=Acadians in Exile; F=Acadian Families; N=Nantes; S=St-Malo

Daigle, Marie-Jeanne, S1-241
Daigle, Marie-Josephe, S1-102
Daigle, Marie-Louise, S1-248
Daigle, Marie-Madeleine, S1-233
Daigle, Marie-Madeleine, S2-452,, 472
Daigle, Marie-Marguerite, S1-234
Daigle, Marie-Osithe, S1-247
Daigle, Marie-Ozite, S1-153
Daigle, Marie-Rosalie, S2-753
Daigle, Marie-Rose, S1-153, 161, 235, 238, 247-248, 316, 393
Daigle, Marie-Rose, S2-622, 694
Daigle, Marin, E-635
Daigle, Marin, S1-236, 245-246, 383, 388
Daigle, Marin, S3-828, 906-907
Daigle, Martin, S1-162
Daigle, Mathurin, E-557
Daigle, Mathurin, N-240
Daigle, Michel, E-96, 356, 557
Daigle, Michel-Gregoire, S1-248
Daigle, Miniac, S1-153, 247-248
Daigle, Minias, E-89, 93, 95-96, 324, 557
Daigle, Olive-Victoire, S1-237
Daigle, Olivier, C-39
Daigle, Olivier, E-33, 93-96, 162, 167, 412, 415, 456, 556-558, 580, 622
Daigle, Olivier, F-31, 95
Daigle, Olivier, N-47-48, 212, 251
Daigle, Olivier, S1-136, 153, 232, 236, 246, 248, 250, 316
Daigle, Olivier, S2-533, 694, 717
Daigle, Olivier, S3-864-865, 877, 879, 892, 894, 982, 1005, 1034
Daigle, Olivier-Raphael, S1-248, 250
Daigle, Osite, F-17
Daigle, Osithe, S1-248

Daigle, Paul, E-93-96, 281, 288, 322, 556-558, 580
Daigle, Paul, F-33
Daigle, Paul, N-112
Daigle, Paul, S1-22, 69, 93, 142, 239-242, 247-248, 250, 252-253
Daigle, Paul, S2-555, 667, 754
Daigle, Paul, S3-832, 869
Daigle, Paul Marie, N-45
Daigle, Paul Olivier, E-96, 557
Daigle, Paul-Olivier, S1-252
Daigle, Pelagie, E-96
Daigle, Pelagie, F-31
Daigle, Pelagie, N-47
Daigle, Pierre, C-141
Daigle, Pierre, C-28-29, 40
Daigle, Pierre, E-94, 96, 138, 190, 280, 415, 556
Daigle, Pierre, F-39
Daigle, Pierre, N-45, 47-48, 68, 111, 190, 212, 251
Daigle, Pierre, S1-6, 232, 234-235, 242, 248, 252
Daigle, Pierre, S2-554
Daigle, Pierre, S3-880, 898, 1058
Daigle, Pierre Joseph, E-96
Daigle, Pierre-Edouard, S1-249
Daigle, Rene-Jean, S1-250
Daigle, Romain, C-48
Daigle, Romain, E-635
Daigle, Romain, S1-245
Daigle, Rosalie, E-47, 286, 356
Daigle, Rose, N-112
Daigle, Rose, S1-239-240, 242, 248, 253
Daigle, Rose, S2-555
Daigle, Rose-Marie, S1-305
Daigle, Simon, F-31
Daigle, Simon, N-47
Daigle, Simon, S1-253
Daigle, Simon Francois, E-96
Daigle, Simon Paul, E-94
Daigle, Simon Pierre, E-93-96, 556-558, 580
Daigle, Simon Pierre, F-31
Daigle, Simon Pierre, N-48, 105, 251-252
Daigle, Symon, E-94

Daigle, Theotiste, C-40, 48, 92, 105, 110-111
Daigle, Theotiste, S1-121, 235, 387, 389
Daigle, Ursule, S1-88, 99, 239-241
Daigle, Ursule, S3-834
Daigle, Ustache, N-234
Daigle, Victoire-Marie, S1-234
Daigle, Victor, E-94, 557
Daigle, Victor, F-31
Daigle, Victor, N-47
Daigle, Vincent Auguste, E-96
Daigle , Helene Catherine, C-42-43
Daignars, Marie, E-180
Dailbon, Pierre, E-176
Dailbon, Pierre, S1-320
Dailleboust, Charles Josephe, E-31, 97, 125, 392
Dailleboust, Pierre, E-97
Dailli, Andre, E-415
Dailli, Andre Joseph, E-97, 415
Daingle, Jacques, S3-1029
Daingue, Genevieve, E-1
Dalby, Jacques, S1-231
Dalencon, Paul, E-156
Dalon, Jeanne Michelle, E-181
Daloux, Francois, E-97, 168
Daloux, Jean Francois, E-97, 168
Daly, Alice, C-vii-viii
Dameue, Marie, F-53
Dameue, Marie, N-82, 183
Damon, Louis, E-97, 349
Damour, Jean Francois, N-49
Damour, Joseph, N-49, 147, 187
Damour, Louis, N-49
Damour, Marie Rose, F-75
Damour, Marie Rose, N-49, 147
Damour, Rose, N-187
Damours, Mathieu, E-473
Damours, Rene, E-473
Dampierre, Francoise, E-83, 89
Damsin, Joseph, E-103
Dandepax, Marie Magdelaine Adelaide, E-97
Dandoneau, Andre, E-73, 97, 168
Dandoneau, Francois, E-73, 97
Dandoneau, Pierre, E-97

Dange, Genevieve, E-639

Dangeac, Catherine Francoise, E-97, 143

Dangeac, Gabriel, E-97, 143, 295

Dangeac, Marguerite, E-104, 127, 303

Dangerac, Mr., S1-224

Daniau, Louise, E-127

Daniau, Magdelaine, E-127

Daniaud, Etienne, E-97

Danieau, Elisabeth, E-100

Daniel, Laurent, E-159

Daniel, Marie Jeanne, E-384

Danigrand, Agnes, E-332

Danjan, Marie Jeanne, E-64, 97

Danjou, Marie, E-292, 307

Danjou, Marie Anne, E-390, 441

Danquet, T., S3-919, 951

Danten, Louis, S3-904

Dantin, Agathe, S1-255

Dantin, Anne, F-73

Dantin, Anne, N-50

Dantin, Anne, S1-254

Dantin, Barthelemy, S1-253-256

Dantin, Florian-Gilles, S1-256

Dantin, Florien, C-29

Dantin, Florien, N-50

Dantin, Gabriel, S1-254-255

Dantin, Jean, S1-254

Dantin, Jeanne, C-29

Dantin, Jeanne, F-73

Dantin, Jeanne, N-50

Dantin, Jeanne, S1-254-255

Dantin, Joseph, S1-254-255

Dantin, Judith, N-49

Dantin, Julie, F-73

Dantin, Julie, N-50

Dantin, Louis, C-29, 51, 84

Dantin, Louis, F-73

Dantin, Louis, N-49-50, 55, 210, 222, 229

Dantin, Louis, S1-8, 253-256, 268

Dantin, Marguerite, S1-254

Dantin, Marie, C-29

Dantin, Marie, F-73

Dantin, Marie, N-50

Dantin, Marie Anne, C-29

Dantin, Michel, S1-254

Dantin, Perinne, N-49

Daotel, Marie, E-145

Daraspe, Francois, E-98

Daraspe, Jeanne Susanne, E-98

Daraspe, Pierre, E-98

Darbenne, Francois, E-585

Darbois, Ursule, E-578

Darce, Jeanne, E-64-65

Dardenne, Francois, E-594

Dardet, Bonaventure, S1-256

Dardet, Louis-Auguste, S1-256, 311

Dardet, Mr., E-127

Dardy, Anne, E-98, 402

Dardy, Francois, E-98, 402

Darembourg, Anne, E-98

Darembourg, Jacque, E-98

Darembourg, Jean, E-193

Darembourg, Jean, E-98

Darembourg, Jean, S2-648

Darembourg, Jean Baptiste, E-98, 193

Darembourg, Jean Baptiste, F-47

Darembourg, Jean Baptiste, N-67

Darembourg, Jean Pierre, E-98

Darembourg, Madeleine, S2-783

Darembourg, Marie, S2-650

Darembourg, Marie Jeanne, F-47

Darembourg, Marie Jeanne, N-67

Darembourg, Marie Joseph, E-98, 275, 429

Darembourg, Marie Josephe, E-275

Darembourg, Marie-Jeanne, S2-648

Darembourg, Pierre, E-81, 98, 275

Darnois, Jean, E-98, 280

Darnois, Marie Josephe, E-98

Daroguy, widow, E-1

Darois, Anne Francoise, E-99

Darois, Elisabeth, C-30

Darois, Elizabeth, F-53

Darois, Elizabeth, N-50, 169

Darois, Etienne, C-30

Darois, Etienne, E-99

Darois, Etienne, F-53

Darois, Etienne, N-50, 169

Darois, Isabelle, E-426

Darois, Jacques Etienne, N-50

Darois, Jerome, E-524

Darois, joseph Etienne, N-50

Darois, Marie, F-53

Darois, Marie, N-50

Darois, Marie, S2-746

Darois, Marie Anne Louise, E-99

Darois, Marie Elizabeth, N-50

Darois, Marie Magdelaine, E-99

Darois, Marie-Josephe, S1-178, 334

Darois, Rose, C-30

Darois, Simon Francoise, E-99

Darois, Susanne, E-99

Darois, Susanne, F-53

Darois, Suzanne, N-50

Darois, Ursule, E-317, 422, 426-427

Daroquy, Jeanne, E-365, 632, 643

Daroy, Madelene, E-357

Darque, Delle, E-155

Darque, Elisabeth, E-155

Darras, Antoine, E-98

Darras, Francois, E-98

Darrasse, Pierre, E-314, 419

Darrigrand, Eglentine, E-98

Darrigrand, Jean, E-98

Darrigrand, Jean Baptiste, E-53, 98-99, 417

Darrigrand, Jean Baptiste Achille, E-99

Darrigrand, Jeanne Emely, E-99

Darrigrand, Jeanne Marie Palmire, E-99

Darrigrand, Marie Lily, E-99

Darrochy, Bernard, E-99

Darrochy, Jeanne, E-99, 361-363

Darroquil, Jeanne, S2-520

Darseneau, Abraham, E-548

Darseneau, Augustin, E-548

Darseneau, Claude, E-548

Darseneau, Francois, E-548

Darseneau, Jacques, E-548

Darty, Pelagie, S1-264

Darvois, Marguerite, E-571

Darzilante, Anne, E-23, 82

Dastaric, Joannis, E-112, 158

Dau, Noel, S1-339

Daubenigue, Germain Guy, E-99

Daubenigue, Marie Rose Desire, E-99, 291

Daude, Anne Catherine, E-99, 172

Daude, Jean Claude, E-99

Daude, Jeanne Baptiste, E-99, 126

Dauly, Jeanne, S1-223

Daunas, Jean, E-99, 140

Dauphin, Francois, S3-1088

Dauphin, Francoise, S2-545

Dauphine, Paul, E-368

Dauple, Pierre, S3-1061

Dausant, Marguerite, C-79

Dausche, Anne, E-83, 298

Dautant, Francois, S3-963, 994, 1017, 1069, 1071

Dauterive, Marie, E-97

Dautoville, Jean, S1-279

Dautoville, Jean, S3-1084

Dautoville, Jean Louis, S3-1084

Dautoville, Jeanne, S1-279

Dautoville, Jeanne, S3-1084

Dautoville, Perinne, S1-279

Dautriche, Mr., E-375

Dauvert, Marie, E-283

Daviaud, -----, E-5-6

Daviaud, Louise, E-393, 431

David, -----, S3-939

David, Aimable Modeste, E-292

David, Allain, S2-489

David, Bastien, E-179, 313

David, Benoit, E-99

David, Daniel, E-100, 141

David, Gabriel, E-100

David, Genevieve, E-100, 169

David, Genevieve Elizabeth, E-354

David, Jan, S3-929

David, Jean, E-100

David, Jeanne, E-100

David, Joseph, E-99, 603

David, Louis, E-100

David, Magdelaine, E-100

David, Marie, E-40, 100, 115-118, 332, 431

David, Marie, S1-257

David, Marie, S2-512

David, Marie Madeleine, E-52, 337

David, Michel, E-100, 141

David, Vincent, S3-1074

Davoine, Pierre, E-391

Davoir, Jacques, F-63, 85

Davou, Mathieu, E-100, 267, 347

Davy, Marguerite, E-354

Dayneau, Elisabeth Eleonore, E-160

de Bat, Marie, E-80, 264

De Bazaniere, Marie Susanne, E-309

De Beaupre, Michel, E-524

De Beaupre, Pierre, E-524

de Belisle, Anne, E-278, 388

De Belle Isle, Marie Joseph, E-390

De Bellefontaine, Anastasie, F-67, 107

De Bersac, Vincent, E-330

De Bon, Louise, S1-197

De Bou, Louise, E-77

De Brecy, Laurence, S2-542

de Castera, Sauveur, E-268

De Catalougne, Elizabeth, E-36

de Chatto Giron, Marie , E-389

De Chavigny, Elisabeth, E-66, 77

de Cugnac Dubourdet, Louise, E-36

De Dreneuf, Padot, S3-1066

De Faillieres, Pages, E-428

De Falaise, Margueritte, E-89

De Forest, Michel, E-456

De Ganne, Marguerite Elizabeth, E-36

De Ganne, Michel, E-36

De Gorney, Fabienne, E-420

De Gravier, Philipe Bertain, S1-332

De Grossette, M.C., E-343

De Guery, Suzanne, E-114

De Gui, M. Marcenay, E-585, 591

De Haret, Jeanne, E-326

de Hay, Charles, E-264

De L'Esperance, Baron, S1-356

De L'Esperance, Baron, S1-356

De L'Esperence, Charles Gabriel Sebastien, E-104, 388

De La Begasse, Angelique-Francoise-Raoul, S1-352

De La Belliere-Bourgeois, Marguerite, S1-319

De La Boue, Francois, E-509

De La Boue, Louis, E-509

De La Boue, Noel, E-473

De La Boue, Pierre, E-509

De La Boue, Rene, E-509

De La Chabosiere, -----, S3-1128

De La Chabossiere, Thomas, S3-1128

De La Chelle, Huet, E-283

De La Croix, Anne, C-31

De La Croix, Francois, C-32

De La Croix, Jerome, C-30-32, 76, 90, 129, 136

De La Croix, Jerome Francois, C-31

De La Croix, Marianne, C-31

De La Croix, Rose, C-31, 90, 129

De La Faye, Jeanne, C-30-31, 90, 129, 136

De La Foresterie, Angelique, F-37

De La Foresterie, Jean, F-37, 49

De La Foresterie, Jeanne, F-49

De La Foresterie, Marie Rosalie, F-49

DE La Forestrie, Jeanne, C-57-58

De La Forestrie, Angelique, N-52, 117, 181

De La Forestrie, Angelique-Madeleine-Marie, S1-260

De La Forestrie, Anne, S1-261

De La Forestrie, Jean, C-57, 151

De La Forestrie, Jean, N-7, 51-52, 93, 117, 181, 200, 243

De La Forestrie, Jean, S1-79, 259-262

De La Forestrie, Jean Marie Michel, N-51-52

De La Forestrie, Jean Michel, N-51

De La Forestrie, Jean-Charles-Joseph, S1-262

De La Forestrie, Jean-Joseph, S1-262

De La Forestrie, Jean-Marie-Michel, S1-261

De La Forestrie, Jeanne, N-92-93

De La Forestrie, Jeanne, S1-260-262

De La Forestrie, Jeanne-Charlotte, S1-262

De La Forestrie, Joseph, N-51

De La Forestrie, Joseph, S1-259, 261-262, 284, 320

De La Forestrie, Marie Adelaide, N-52

De La Forestrie, Marie Madeleine, N-51

De La Forestrie, Marie Rosalie, C-58

De La Forestrie, Marie Rosalie, N-7, 51-52, 243

De La Forestrie, Marie-Madeleine, S1-261

De La Forestrie, Marie-Rosalie, S1-260-261

De La Forestrie, Marie-Rose, S1-261

De La Forestrie, Paul Michel, N-51

De La Forestrie, Reyne-Laurence, S1-260

De la Forestrie, Marguerite, S1-260

De La Foreterie, Jean, E-35

De La Fortemoison, Marie Anne Charlotte, E-343

De La Garde, Gartau, F-63

De La Garde, Leonard, F-63

De La Garde, Leonor, F-85

De La Haye, Denis, E-157

De La Haye, Jean Baptiste, N-205

De La Houssaye, Anne, E-69

De La Houssaye, Henry Jean, C-32, 149

De La Houssaye, Pierre Jean, C-32, 149-150

De La Huassaye, Anne, S2-680

De La Martinerie, Angelique Francoise, E-186

De La Masiere, Jean Baptiste, F-67

De La Masiere, Jean Francois, F-67

De La Masiere, Louise Celeste, F-67

De La Masiere, Rose Jeanne, F-67

De La Maziere, Jean Baptiste, N-52-53

De La Maziere, Jean Francois, C-11, 32-33, 86

De La Maziere, Jean Francois, N-52-53, 178, 211

De La Maziere, Louise Cecile, N-52

De La Maziere, Louise Celeste, N-53

De La Maziere, Marguerite, C-32-33

De La Maziere, Marguerite, N-52-53

De La Maziere, Marie, N-53

De La Maziere, Rose, N-53

De La Maziere, Rose Jeanne, N-52

De La Morvonnais, Jacques-Jean-Michel, S1-38

De La Poterie, Caroline, E-322

De La Roche, Jean, S3-916

De La Rue, Anne Marie, S3-1093

De La Rue, Jeanne, S1-77

De La Rue, Marie-Anne, S2-608

De La Touche, Bernard Texier, C-112

De La Touche, Pierre Alexis Texier, C-112

De la Touche, Michel-Jean, S1-251

De La Touche De Bonabry, Vincent, S2-668

De La Tour, Jeanne, E-392

De La Tour, Joane St. Estienne, E-301, 392

De La Tour, Marguerite de St Etienne, E-329

De la Tour, Jeanne, E-71

De la Vallee, Thomas, E-585, 592

De La Valliere, Barne Le Neuf, S2-777

De LaBorde, Charles Francois, E-102

De LaBorde, Louis Mazer, E-102

De LaChelle, Alexandre, E-102

De LaChelle, Huet, E-102

De LaCroix, Jean, E-102

De LaCroix, Marie Joseph, E-102

De Laforestrie, Jean, S2-468-469

De Laforestrie, Jean, S3-899, 901, 1004, 1057

De Laforestrie, Jeanne, S2-468

De Laforestrie, Jeanne, S3-899

De Laforestrie, Joseph, S3-901, 915

De LaForeterie, Jean, E-102

De LaForeterie, Joseph, E-102

De LaMestre, Joseph Espiau, E-3, 103

De LaMestre, Noble Homme Jean Francois Espiau, E-103

De LaMotte, Rose Opportune, E-88

De Lanne, Della Saube, E-12

De LaPierre, Joseph, E-103

De LaPierre, Marie, E-103

De Launay, -----, S1-198

De Launay, Jean, E-13

De Launay, Jeanne, E-13, 104

De Laune, Jean, E-1, 74

De Launy, Mr., E-78

De Laurier, Renaud, E-524

De Lavergne, Marie Suzanne, E-405

De Lavergne, Paul Joseph Guillaume, E-405

De Lepeau, Julien, S1-262

De Lepeau, Pierre, S1-262, 319

De Line, Jan, S3-1004

De Line, Perinne Marguerite Adelaide, S3-1004

De Line, Pierre, S3-1004

De Loyal, Miquel, E-102

De Loyat, Michel Migue, E-65

De Lyc, Pierre, S1-353

de Malvilain, Isabelle, E-137

de Malvilain, Jean Nicolas, E-137

De Mathe, Francois, S1-264

De Mathe, Jean-Servanne, S1-264

De Mathe, Marie, S1-3

De Mathe, Marie, S3-968

De Mochaise, Catherine, E-71-72

De Moitemon, Nicolas Maximilien Joseph, E-71

De Montalembert de Cers, Jean, E-330

De Montalembert de Cers, Pierre, E-330

de Nailly, Etienne Cornu, E-12

De Neuvilly, Louis Noel Adam, E-344

De Neuvilly, Rene Francois Adam, E-344

De Nohier, Louis, E-40

De Paucrair, Eudes, S3-1066

De Pensens, Mr., S1-280

De Peruse, Decars, C-132

De Ponbomcoup, Charles, E-524

de Pontbriau, Francois, E-34, 107

de Pontbriau, George, E-34

de Pontbriau, Jean, E-34

de Pontbriau, Jeanne, E-34, 107

de Rangot, Marie, E-97

de Ravenelle, Pierre, E-97

De Rue Village named after Alexandre Girouard, E-215

De Serres, Dame, S1-386

de St-Boars, Theodore, E-10

De St-Vilme, Mrs., E-119

De St. Vilme, Mrs., S1-280

De Surcelin, Isabeau, E-77

De Testant, Antoine, E-586, 591

De Touche, Claude, E-13

De Touche, Claude Francois Pagnaud, E-13

De Tourbide, Catherine, S1-264

De Tourbide, Helene, S1-264

De Tourbide, Jeanne, S1-265

De Tourbide, Jeanne-Francoise, S1-264

De Tourbide, Marie, S1-264

De Tourbide, Marie-Anne, S1-265

De Tourbide, Martin, S1-264

De Tourbide, Pierre, S1-264-265

De Trouy de Verjuziere, Andre, E-110

De Trouy de Verjuziere, Jean Charles, E-110

De Vauselle, Guillaume, C-69

De Villejoin, Gabriel Rousseau, S2-777

Deban, Jean Baptiste, E-158, 432

Debaunay, Nicolas Pierre, E-164

DeBazaniere, Marie Susanne, E-308

DeBellair, Antoine, E-442

Debellair, Pierre, E-143

DeBellefontaine, Michel, E-100

DeBersac, Pierre, E-100

DeBersac, Vincent, E-100

Debert, Jean, E-524

Debest, Joseph, E-100

Debest, Michel, E-100-108

Debien, Jean, C-30, 76

Debien, Jean, E-635

Debien, Silvin, C-30

Debien, Silvin (Sr.), C-152

Debient, Jean, C-152

Debins, Louis, E-100

Debins, Pierre, E-100, 301

DeBled, Charles, E-100, 380

DeBled, Joseph Marie, E-100, 380

Debois, Cecile-Jeanne, S1-19

Debon, Bertrand, E-100

Debon, Charles, E-78, 100-101

Debon, Charles, S1-196, 258-259

Debon, Denis, S1-258

Debon, Francoise, S1-259

Debon, Gillette, S1-258-259

Debon, Ignace Stanislas, E-100

Debon, Jacques, E-100, 304

Debon, Jacques, S1-194, 258-259

Debon, Jacques, S2-596

Debon, Jeanne, S1-258-259

Debon, Louise, E-78, 101

Debon, Louise, S1-196, 258

Debon, Marie, E-387, 430

Debon, Pierre, S1-82, 258-259

Debosque, Pierre, E-264

Debou, Jacques, E-623

Debou, Marie Jeanne, E-623

Debou, Marie Jeanne Jacqueline, E-623

Deboux de Villemort, Marie Sophie, C-53

Debreuy, Nicolas-Bruno, S1-351

Debroise, Andre, E-54, 101

Debroise, Magdelaine, E-54, 101

Debrosse, Jeanne, E-54

Debry, P., S3-870

Decaens, Pierre, E-103

Decamp, Cesar, E-623

Decamp, Jean Louis, E-88, 119

Decan, Jean Francois, S3-1073

Decan, Jean Pierre, S3-1073

Decan, Jean-Francois, S1-259

Decan, Jean-Pierre, S1-259, 338

Decan, Michel, S3-1073

DeCarbarret, Marie, E-342, 391, 416

DeCastera, Sauveur, E-254

DeCatalougne, Elisabeth, E-102

Dechapare, Jacques Martain, E-101

Dechapare, Jean, E-101

Dechapare, Marie Anne, E-101

Dechapare, Martin, E-101

DeChatto Giron, Marie, E-389

Dechef, Marianne, E-101

Deckapare, Martain, E-316

Decoigne, Louise, E-258

DeCorbie, Francoise, E-103, 157

Decouagne, Jean Baptiste, E-101, 308

Decouagne, Michel, E-101, 308

Decour, Catherine, C-27

Decour, Catherine, S1-222

DeCourte, Silveire, E-369

Decourte, Mathieu, E-280

Decouvenance, Marie Jeanne, E-193, 299

Decoux, Charles Gabriel Jean, E-101, 404

Decoux, Honore, E-101, 326

Decoux, Jacques-Louis-Marie, S1-358

Decoux, Jean, E-101, 326

Decoux, Louis, E-101
Decoux, Marie Philippe, E-113, 194
Decoux, Pierre, E-101
DeCoylor, Marie, E-174
DeCresnes, Andre, E-181, 314, 601
Decrevisse, Caluding, E-601
Decroutte, Jeanne, S1-330
Decroutte, Jeanne, S3-1099
DeCugnac Dubourdet, Louise, E-102
DeFalaise, Sieur, E-101
Defalaise, Marguerite, E-101, 308
DeFallere, Pages, E-371
Defaut, Michel, E-123
Defonds, Jean, E-101, 264
Deforest, Anne Rosalie, S3-1032
Deforest, Gabriel, E-503
Deforest, Ignace, S3-1083, 1088, 1099
Deforest, Jacque, S3-1032, 1083, 1088
Deforest, Jean Baptiste, E-503
Deforest, Magdelainne, S3-888
Deforest, Marguerite, S3-1080
Deforest, Marie, E-503
Deforest, Michel, E-473, 503
Deforest, Pierre, E-503
Deforest, Rene, E-503
Defrenche, Marie, E-153
Defriche, Jeanne, S1-81
Degalbaril, Jeannis, E-101, 391
Degalbaril, Marie, E-101, 391
Degan, Claude, E-123
Degan, Marguerite, E-64-65
DeGanne, Anne, E-101
DeGanne, Louis Francois, E-101
DeGanne, Marguerite Elizabeth, E-102
DeGanne, Michel, E-102
Deganne, Louis Francois, E-392
Deganne de Falaise, Anne, E-392
Degast, Joseph, C-38, 80
Degast, Rosalie, E-65
Degastannialde, Marie, E-112, 158

Degaune, Anne Angelique, E-300, 392
Degautin, Anne, E-127, 304
Degillot, Miss, S3-915
DeGlain, Mathieu, E-102, 319
DeGlain, Pierre, E-102, 319
Degoulin Doyen, Francois Marie, E-104
DeGourville, Josephe Marie, E-432
DeGourville, Michel Dupont du Vivier, E-432
Degoutin, Francois Marc, E-102, 356
Degoutin, Jean Charlotte, E-102
Degoutin, Jeanne, E-102
Degoutin, Louise, E-102, 395
Degoutin, Mathieu, E-102, 395
Degoutin, Messire Francois, E-102
Degre, Jean Baptiste, E-130
Degre, Marguerite, E-130
Degree, Alexandre, E-151
Deguere, Marie, S3-1023
DeGuery, Suzanne, E-430
Deguise, Catherine, E-46
DeHaret, Jeanne, E-278
Dehaule, Francois, E-63
Dehitrabide, Anne, E-624
DeHory, Anne, E-187
Dehouliere, Jean, C-118
Delaborde, Charles Francois, E-432
Delabouchere, Pierre, N-242
DeLaBoulardrie, Charlotte, E-388
DeLaChasse, Charles, E-258
DeLaChasse, Miss, E-258
DeLaChasse, Mr., E-258
DelaColombiene, Pierre Antoine Hecorne, E-197
DeLaCroix, Gille Girad dit, E-268
DeLaCroix, Jean, E-111
DeLaCroix, Marie, E-111
DeLaCroix, Marie Josephe, E-111
Delacroix, Jean Charles, E-146
Delacroix, Marie, E-181
Delacroix, Michel, E-15

delaCroix, Jerome, C-135, 137, 152
DelaForest, Pierre, E-267
DelaForetrie, Marie Madeleine, E-368
Delafoy, Jeanne, E-102, 142
Delafoy, Pierre, E-142
Delage, Marie, E-102
Delahay, Denis, E-103, 157
Delahay, Michel, E-103, 157
Delahoussaye, Anne, E-370
Delaisse, Jeanne, E-404
Delalande, Andre Nicolas, E-103, 315
Delalande, Michel, E-103, 315
Delalande, Sylvain, E-299
Delamare, Elisabeth, E-87
DeLaMartinerie, Angelique Francoise, E-190
delaMaziere, Jean Francois, C-115-116
Delamestre, Joseph Espiau, E-440
DelaPlace, J.A., E-386
Delaplace, Jeanne Angelique, E-12
Delaporte, Joseph, C-52
Delaprimerois, Sieur Moreau, S3-1050
Delarambour, Genevieve, E-103
Delarambour, Pierre, E-103
Delareguy, Gratienne, E-112
Delarue, Francois Philippe, E-103, 158
Delarue, Gabriel, E-103, 158
Delasee, Marie, E-65, 69
Delatouche, Malo, S3-829
DeLaTour, Charlotte Saint Etienne, E-173
DeLaTour, Marie, E-264
Delatour, Jourjon, E-91
DeLaune, Jacques, E-121
DeLaune, Jean, E-271
Delaune, Augustin, N-53
Delaune, Christophe, E-103, 104, 170
Delaune, Christophe, F-67, 107
Delaune, Christophe, S1-374
Delaune, Christopher, C-33, 99
Delaune, Christopher, N-53-54
Delaune, Eustache, E-104

Delaune, Eve Emily, S3-975
Delaune, Jean, C-33, 99
Delaune, Jean, E-104
Delaune, Jean, F-67, 107
Delaune, Jean, N-54
Delaune, Jean, S1-4
Delaune, Jean Baptiste, C-33
Delaune, Jean Baptiste, F-67, 107
Delaune, Jean Baptiste, N-53
Delaune, Jean Jacques, E-104
Delaune, Joseph, E-104
Delaune, Louis Auguste, F-67, 107
Delaune, Louis Auguste, N-53-54
Delaune, Marie Celeste, F-67, 107
Delaune, Marie Celeste, N-53-54
Delaune, Marie Elisabeth, E-104
Delaune, Marie Francoise, E-104
Delaune, Marie Henriette, E-104
Delaune, Marie Joseph, E-104
Delaune, Marie Marguerite, E-104
Delaune, Michel, E-104
Delaune, Michel, N-53
Delaune, Michel, S3-857, 859
Delaune, Mr., E-189
Delaune, Nicolas, E-104
Delaune, Nicolas Pierre, E-104
Delaune, Pierre, E-104
Delaune, Pierre, F-67, 107
Delaune, Pierre, N-54
Delaune, Pierre Basile, N-54
Delaune, Polycarpe, E-104
Delaune, Simonne, S1-344
Delaune, Susanne Marie, E-104
Delaune, Yves, S3-975
Delauneau, Jeanne, E-155
DeLaunne, Christophe, E-274
Delaurier named after Nicholas Babineau surnamed Delaurier, E-209
Delavertu, Olive Georgine, E-183
Delaville, Francoise Jacqueline Bonnaventure, E-439

Delavilleblanche, Michel, S3-856, 858
Delepeaux, Julien, S3-1028
Delepeaux, Pierre, S3-1007, 1011, 1028
Delgres, Francois, E-432
Delhomme, Marguerite, E-373, 376
Delien, Mademoiselle, S2-655
Deligne, Pierre, E-427
Deline, Jean, S1-263
Deline, Marie Madeleine, E-558
Deline, Marie-Madeleine, S1-263
Deline, Perinne-Marguerite-Adelaide, S1-263
Deline, Perrine Marguerite, E-558
Deline, Pierre, E-558, 580
Deline, Pierre, S1-80, 263
Deline, Pierre, S2-705
Delisle, Francoise, E-107, 153
Delmas, Francois, E-103, 419
Delmas, Marie Therese, E-103, 419
Delmas, Pierre, E-103, 419
Deloche, Mr., E-392
Deloigne, Mr., E-258
Delon, Jeanne, E-140
Delord, Anne, E-103, 419
Delord, Jean, E-100, 364
Delormo, Marie, F-63
Delort, Guillaume, E-66, 104-105, 108, 300
Delort, Louis, E-105, 300
Delort, Marie Charlotte, E-105, 108
Delostre, Pierre, E-105, 193
Delot, -----, S3-1095
Delot, Guillemette, S1-2
Delouche, Francois, E-293
Delouin, Marie, E-63, 105
Deloumeau, Jean, E-265
Delousarger, Elisabeth, E-343, 384
DeLoyal, Michel, E-131, 432
DeLoyal, Revier, E-432
Delphere, Antoine, E-78
Delphin, Francois, E-105
Delphin, Francois Louis, E-105
Delphin, Louis, E-105, 182

Delphin, Louis Francois, E-105
Delpierre, Jacques, E-105
Delpierre, Joseph, E-36, 105
Delpierre, Marie Catherine, E-441
Deluges, Charles Francois, E-414
DeLyc, Pierre, E-152
Demalirlan, widow, S3-1092
Demanan, Pierre Joseph, E-73
Demar, Philippe Joseph, E-115
Demars, Nicolas, E-156
Demasson, Jacques, E-17, 105
Demaziere, Paul, E-174
Demeric, Charles, E-105
Demestre, Marie, S2-515
Demeure, Jeanne, S1-1
Demeure, Jeanne, S3-1074
Demeurs, Balthazar, E-105, 178
Demeurs, Jean Baptiste, E-105, 178
DeMonchy, Thomas Jean, E-383
deMondion, Jean Baptiste, C-127
Demontie, Anne Francoise, N-253
Demontie, Cecile, N-253
Demontie, Francoise Madeleine, N-253
Demontie, Joseph Claude, N-253
Demontie, Joseph Rene Marie, N-253
Demontie, Louis, N-253
Demontie, Louis Jean Marie, N-253
Demony, Anne Marie, E-105
Demony, Michel, E-105
Demoulin, Mare, E-119
Demoulin, Marie, E-256
Denesle, Michel, E-127
DeNesmond, Jean Michel Toussaint, E-105
DeNesmond, Pierre, E-105
Denier, Marie Anne, E-100
Deniget, Mr., E-390
Denion, Julien, N-67, 152, 192
Deniot, Anne, E-409
Denis, Charles, E-92, 105
Denis, Louise, E-97
Denis, Pierre, E-106

Denis, Will, E-213

Denis de Bonnaventure, Charles, E-92, 105

Denis de Frousac, Richard, E-473

Denizard, Anne Marie, E-308, 363

Dennollain, Jean Pierre, E-256

Denoailles, Jean, E-74, 106

Denoailles, Jean Baptiste, E-74

Denoel, Marguerite, E-30

Denohic, Jean Baptiste, E-106, 328

Denohic, Louis, E-106, 266, 328

Denoix, Elois, E-283

Denollain, Jean Pierre, E-105

Denot, Marie, E-638

Denot, Pierre Francois, E-34, 428

Denovai, Marie, S2-582

Denozier, Marie, E-100

DePensens, Mr., E-119

Depontbriand, Quemper, S3-934

Depred, Magdelaine Dion, E-15, 150

Depuget, Charle Francois, E-162

DePuigibeaut, Marguerite Barbe, E-387

Dequel, Marie, S2-781

Dequel, Marie, S3-923

Dequillat, boy, E-107

Dequillat, Jean, E-107, 135

Dequillat, Jean Raymond, E-107, 153

DeRavena, Durson, E-128

DeRavenel, Pierre Jacques, E-376

DeRavenel, Suzanne, E-376

Derayer, Mr., E-308

Derayer, Pierre, E-107

Dere, Jean, E-69, 259, 352

Derein, Gabriel, E-25, 313

DeRenoille, Marie Angelique, E-128, 376

Derien, Jean, S1-264

Derien, Jean, S3-971, 990

Derien, Malo, S3-971

Derivi, Marie, S1-310

DeRnagot, Marie, E-143

Deroche, Jean, E-107

Deroche, Joseph, E-107

Deroche, Julien, E-107

Deroche, Louis, E-13, 107-108

Deroche, Marguerite Rosalie, E-107

Deroche, Marie Anne, E-108

Deroche, Marie Joseph, E-108

Deroche, Nicolas, E-145

Deroger, Josephe, E-122

Derosse, Marie Louise, E-7

Derron, Pierre Auguste, E-108

Derron, Theotiste, E-108

Dervieux, Etienne, E-72

Des Broizes, Marie, S1-57

Des Croutes, Charlotte, C-70

Des Croutes, Charlotte, N-126

Des Croutes, Charlotte, S3-1006, 1038

Des Croutes, Jeanne Cecile, C-70

Des Croutes, Jeanne Cecile, S3-1088

Des Croutes, Pierre, C-70

Des Croutes, Pierre, S3-1006, 1088

Des Guertz, Marie, S2-532

Des Landes, Louis, S3-1011

des Longchamps, Francoise Catherine Lair, E-12

Desaleuo, Francoise, E-428

Desaleur, Denys, E-108

Desaleur, Francoise, E-35

Desaleur, Marguerite Renee Coupiau, E-108

Desaleur, Marie Josephe, E-352

Desaleur, Pierre, E-9

Desaluer?, Francoise, E-35

Desaugier, Mr., E-371

Desaugiers, Marc Antoine, E-10

Desaulnais, Delatouche, S3-860, 868

Desavay, Marie Francoise, S3-993

Desbeau, Anne, E-9

Desbois, Louise Charlotte, E-35, 156

Desbois, Susanne, E-99

Desbous, Marie, E-126, 139, 387

Deschamp, Francois, S1-222

Deschamps, child, E-108

Deschamps, Euphrosine, E-93

Deschamps, M., E-358

Deschamps, Madeleine, E-100, 108

Deschamps, Marguerite, E-586, 593

Deschamps, Marie Jeanne Francoise, E-408

Deschamps, Olivier, E-108

Deschamps, Philippe, E-108

Deschamps, Pierre, E-327, 440

Deschepare, Martin, E-23

Descouteaux, Therese, C-53

Descouteaux, Therese, E-12

Descouteaux, Therese, F-35

Descroutes, Charlotte, F-7

Descroutes, Charlotte, S2-584, 586

Descroutes, Jeanne-Cecile, S1-324

Descroutes, Jeanne-Cecile, S2-587

Descroutes, Pierre, S1-324

Descroutes, Pierre, S2-586

Desforest, Etienne, E-108, 256

Desforets, Birgitte, E-190

Desforets, Victor, E-331

Desforges, Jacques, E-34

Desfroux, Francois, E-108

Desfroux, Jean, E-108, 256

Desgobe, Marie Madeleine, E-108

Desgobe, Nicolas, E-108

Desgranges, Michel Dominique, E-158

Desgraviers, Philipe Bertain, E-43

Desgre, Paul, E-416

Desgrouas, Francois, E-278

Desguentz, Lafrenlais, S3-884

Desguest, -----, S3-899

Desguest, J., S3-901, 903

Desguets, Marie, S1-329

Desguets, Pierre, Sr., S1-329

Deshaleur, Pierre, E-631, 639

Deshaleur, Rosalie, E-639

Deshay, Robert Jean, E-194

Deshayes, Marie, E-103, 158

Deshays, Guillaume, E-108, 389

Deshays, Jean Ambroise, E-108, 389

Desire, Jean, E-379, 413

Desjardins, Antoine, E-353
Deslandes, Francois, E-4-5
Deslandes, Francois Loyer, E-4-5
Deslandes, Jean, E-22, 294
Deslandes, Julie Ester, E-5
Deslandes, Julie Ester Loyer, E-4
Deslandes, Julien, S1-363
Deslandes, Jullien, S3-1011
Deslandes, Marie, S1-363
Deslandes, Marie, S3-1011
Deslandes, Nicolas, E-5
Deslandes, Nicolas Loyer, E-4
Deslandes, Simon Loyer, E-4-5
Deslandes, Victoire, E-5
Deslandes, Victoire Loyer, E-4
Desmanaud, Pierre Joseph, E-172
Desmarest, Agathe Vincent, E-21, 319
Desmarest, Agethe, E-21, 411
Desmarest, Claude Joseph Leroy, E-308-309
Desmarest, Mr., E-349
Desmaret, Mr., E-175
Desmars, Rene, S3-1150
Desmorandiere, Pauh, N-246
Desnortaine, Jean, E-586, 591
Desnortaine, Jean Pierre, E-591
Desor, Sophie, E-10
Despiet, Pierre, E-105, 108
Despiet, Pierre Paul, E-105, 108
Despoue, Apolline, E-108
Despoue, Charle Francois, E-108
Despoue, David, E-108-109, 132, 366, 378
Despoue, Francois, E-109
Despoue, Joseph, E-108
Despoue, Marie Madeleine, E-109
Despres, Marie Anne, E-31, 109
Despres, Pierre, E-31, 109
Desprez, Charles Luc, E-263
Desprez, Etienne Romain, E-263
Desprez, Mathurin, S2-642
Desquin, Pierre, E-12, 109
Desroaches, Jean, S2-441
DesRoches, Jeanne, E-109, 145
DesRoches, Olivier, E-109, 145

Desroches, Antoinette, E-40
Desroches, Etienne, S2-783
Desroches, Francoise, S1-337
Desroches, Guillaume, E-355
Desroches, Jean, E-158, 179
Desroches, Jeanne, S1-333-334
Desroches, Louise, E-442
Desroches, Louise, S2-783-784
Desroches, Marguerite, E-19-20, 355
Desroches, Olivier, S1-333
Desroches, Perrine, E-128, 132
Desroziers, Marie, E-21, 353
Dessagnes, Dugas, E-418
Dessaudrays Lossieux, Rene, E-308-309
Destienne de Montluc de la Riviere, Henriette Catherine, E-109
Destienne de Montluc de la Riviere, Jean Baptiste, E-109
Desvaches, Antoine, E-108-109
Desvages, Jean Baptiste, E-59, 109
Desvages, Thomas, E-59, 109
DesVaux, Joseph, E-181
Desvaux, Anne, C-50
Desvaux, Anne, E-177, 187
Desvaux, Jacquemine, S1-221
Desvaux, Julien, S1-93
Desvaux, Marie, C-107
Desvaux, Mathurin, S3-862
Desveau, Jacques, C-41
Desveau, Jacques, E-368
Desveau, Jacques, S2-687
DesVeaux, Pierre, E-118
Desveaux, Francois, S1-363
Detailles, Elizabeth, E-125
Detas, Mr., S3-1089
Detcheberry, Isabelle, E-263
Detchepare, Cecile, E-110
Detchepare, Martin, E-110
Detchepare, Pierre, E-110
Detcheverry, Cecile, E-302
Detcheverry, Estevennie, E-35, 278
Detcheverry, Francois, E-154, 302
Detcheverry, Jean-Louis, S1-264

Detcheverry, Pierre, E-154, 266, 302-303
Detchevery, Cecile, S1-218
Detheverry, Louise, E-174
Detheverry, Pierre, E-174
Deuret, Arnaud, S3-1055
Devages, Jean Baptiste, E-180
Devaix, Genevieve, E-110
Devalle, Alexandre, E-72
Devau, Joseph, E-266
Devau, Marie Josephe, E-112
Devaucene, George Thomas, E-110, 346
Devaucene, Thomas, E-110, 346
Devaud, Joseph, E-17, 183
Devaut, Cecile, S3-1068
DeVaux, Pierre, E-150
Devaux, Agathe, E-110
Devaux, Ange, E-110
Devaux, Anne, E-104, 110, 178, 258
Devaux, Anonime, E-110
Devaux, Antoine, E-110
Devaux, Augustin, E-551
Devaux, Cecile, E-551
Devaux, Cecile, S2-480, 490, 495, 504
Devaux, Genevieve, E-411
Devaux, Jacques, E-24, 102, 110-112, 157, 169, 176, 178-179, 267, 270, 551
Devaux, Jacques, S1-261, 320, 371
Devaux, Jean, C-113
Devaux, Jean, E-111, 112, 177, 551
Devaux, Jean Jacques, E-111
Devaux, Jean Pierre, E-111
Devaux, Jeanne, S1-356
Devaux, Joseph, E-110-111, 440
Devaux, Joseph, S1-265
Devaux, Louis, E-111
Devaux, Louise Felicite, E-111
Devaux, Marguerite, E-111, 340
Devaux, Marie, C-94
Devaux, Marie, E-53-54, 98-99, 111, 176-179, 417
Devaux, Marie, F-3, 81
Devaux, Marie, N-154
Devaux, Marie, S2-731-732, 734

Devaux, Marie, S3-966
Devaux, Marie Jenne, E-111
Devaux, Marie Josephe, E-111-112
Devaux, Mathurine, S2-536
Devaux, Michel, E-110, 176, 367, 524
Devaux, Michel, S1-321
Devaux, Paul, E-61, 110-112, 368
Devaux, Pierre, C-41, 94
Devaux, Pierre, E-110-112, 176, 178, 411, 551, 586, 595
Devaux, Pierre, S1-340
Devaux, Pierre, S2-731
Devaux, Rosalie Susanne, E-112
Devaux, Susanne Rosalie, E-112
Devaux, Vincent, E-54, 61, 111
Devers, Jacques, E-112
Devers, Jacques Raimond, E-14, 112
DeVerteuil, Jacques Alexis, E-160
DeVerteuil, Leonard, E-160
Devetre, Marie, E-326, 337
Devey, Marie Jeanne, E-305, 412
Deviaux, Jacques, E-104
Devieu, Louise, E-600
Deville, Jeanne, E-79, 132
Devoisin, Marguerite, E-414, 438
Devon, Claudine, E-309, 353
Dezaleur, widow, E-1
Dezguets, Jean-Joseph, S1-87
Dhangou, Pierre, E-97
Dhiarce, Jeanne, E-137, 278, 388
Dhibarboure, Francois, S1-76
Dhiriberry, Jeanne, E-179, 313
Diant, J., E-83
Diant, Joseph, E-148
Diarce, Victoire, E-586, 595
Diard, Jacques, E-112
Diard, Jacques Francois, E-292, 332
Diard, Louis, E-112, 126, 332
Diard, Marie, E-112, 332
Diard, Marie Anne, E-332
Diard, Mr., E-291
Diaron, Angelique, S3-973

Diart, Anne, E-339, 370
Dibarboure, Anne Susanne, E-112
Dibarboure, Antoine, E-112
Dibarboure, Francois, E-112, 315, 325
Dibarboure, Francois, S1-358
Dibarboure, Laurent, E-112, 158
Dichon, Pierre, E-280
Dicoise, Marie, E-586, 593
Didier, Marie, S2-594
Didier, Marie, S3-962, 992
Didier, Marie Barbe, S3-990, 1029
Didier, Marie-Barbe, S2-595
Didion, Antoine, E-112, 304
Didion, Jean, E-112, 304
Didou, Francois, E-113, 194
Didou, Pierre, E-113, 194
Dieneau, Catherine, E-17, 105
Dienn, Jeanne-Barbe, S2-543
Dierce, George, E-113
Dierce, Louis, E-113
Digan, Jean Pierre, E-123
Dille, Marie Modeste Flore, E-193, 194
Dimanche, Claudine, E-326
Dimon, Marie, E-78
Dingle, Genevieve, E-9, 99, 642
Dingle, Jacques, S2-438, 647
Dingle, Jacques, S3-962, 992, 1029-1030
Dingle, Madeleine, S2-438, 440, 647, 768
Dingle, Magdelaine, C-52
Dingue, Magdeleine, S3-1030
Dion, Anne, E-599
Dion, Basile, E-599
Dion, Jean, E-113, 311
Dion, Marguerite, E-599
Dion, Rosalie, E-113, 311
Dion, Rose, E-600
Dionet, Andre, E-309
Diot, Jean, N-176
Dirube, Catherine, E-135, 174
Dischant, Marie, E-189
Dithochefort, Jean, E-132
Diutas, Thomase, S3-1089
Dixmier, Jacques, E-86, 113
Djarce, George, E-113
Dohier, Mathurine, S3-984

Doice, -----, S3-1048
Doiron, Abraham, E-481
Doiron, Adelaide, C-79
Doiron, Alexaindre, S1-275
Doiron, Alexandre, C-34
Doiron, Alexandre, F-5
Doiron, Alexandre, N-54-55, 189
Doiron, Alexandre, S1-265-266, 276
Doiron, Alexandre, S2-448, 454
Doiron, Alexandre, S3-826, 980
Doiron, Alexis, C-34
Doiron, Alexis, E-96, 113-114, 559
Doiron, Alexis, S1-266-268, 271, 273
Doiron, Alexis, S2-706
Doiron, Alexis, S3-891, 939, 944, 947
Doiron, Alexis Gregoire, C-34
Doiron, Alexis Gregoire, E-2
Doiron, Alexis Gregoire, N-49, 55
Doiron, Alexis-Gregoire, S1-8, 255, 266, 268-269, 272
Doiron, Amable Ursule, N-57
Doiron, Anastasie, E-99
Doiron, Angelique, C-39
Doiron, Angelique, E-96
Doiron, Angelique, F-47, 95
Doiron, Angelique, N-18, 22, 225
Doiron, Angelique, S1-85-86, 99, 105, 153, 246, 248, 316
Doiron, Angelique, S2-533, 694, 737, 742, 747
Doiron, Angelique, S3-848, 879, 894, 896
Doiron, Anne, C-80
Doiron, Anne, E-113, 548, 559
Doiron, Anne, F-35, 49
Doiron, Anne, S1-157, 275-276
Doiron, Anne, S2-635-636
Doiron, Anne, S3-1130
Doiron, Anne Dorothee, F-33
Doiron, Anne Dorothee, N-57, 92, 250
Doiron, Anne Hippolite, C-61
Doiron, Anne-Dorothee, S1-271
Doiron, Barthelemy, E-113

Doiron, Basile-Francois, S1-274
Doiron, Benjamin, N-56
Doiron, Benony, S1-269
Doiron, Catherine, E-113
Doiron, Charles, E-481, 524
Doiron, Charles, S1-113, 269-270, 275-276
Doiron, Charles, S2-438
Doiron, Charles, S3-826
Doiron, Charles-Adrien, S1-266
Doiron, Dorate, S1-271
Doiron, Elizabeth, S1-269, 276
Doiron, Emelie, E-113
Doiron, Emelie, F-35
Doiron, Eulalie Elizabeth, N-56
Doiron, Francois-Xavier, S1-267-268
Doiron, Francoise, C-34
Doiron, Francoise, F-73
Doiron, Francoise, N-50, 55
Doiron, Francoise, S1-276
Doiron, Francoise Jos., E-2
Doiron, Francoise-Joseph, S1-268
Doiron, Genevieve, F-7
Doiron, Gervaise, S1-271-272
Doiron, Gregoire, C-34
Doiron, Gregoire, E-559
Doiron, Gregoire, N-55, 229
Doiron, Gregoire, S1-136, 149, 267-268, 274, 294
Doiron, Gregoire, S3-947
Doiron, Gregoire Michel, E-2
Doiron, Gregoire-Michel, S1-268
Doiron, Guillaume-Rene, S1-272
Doiron, Helene, F-11
Doiron, Henriette Catherine, E-113
Doiron, Ignace, S1-269
Doiron, Isaac, F-5
Doiron, Isaac, N-55
Doiron, Isaac-Alexandre, S1-266
Doiron, Jacche, S2-636
Doiron, Jacques, C-34
Doiron, Jacques, F-21
Doiron, Jacques, N-56
Doiron, Jacques, S1-40, 169, 265, 270-271, 275-276

Doiron, Jacques, S3-935, 1134
Doiron, Jacques Francois, C-35
Doiron, Jacques-Francois, S1-270
Doiron, Jan Baptiste, S3-831
Doiron, Jean, E-113-114, 473, 481, 524, 559
Doiron, Jean, F-21, 33
Doiron, Jean, N-55-57, 92, 186, 201, 250
Doiron, Jean, S1-271-272
Doiron, Jean, S3-942-944
Doiron, Jean Baptiste, C-35, 61, 142, 153
Doiron, Jean Baptiste, E-113, 114, 548, 559
Doiron, Jean Baptiste, F-5, 35, 109
Doiron, Jean Baptiste, N-55-57, 207, 218
Doiron, Jean Baptiste Cesar, C-35
Doiron, Jean Baptiste Cesar, N-57
Doiron, Jean Charles, F-35
Doiron, Jean Charles, N-57
Doiron, Jean Louis, N-57
Doiron, Jean Pierre, N-55
Doiron, Jean-Baptiste, S1-271-272
Doiron, Jean-Baptiste, S2-758
Doiron, Jean-Charles, S1-267-268, 273
Doiron, Jean-Jacques, S1-270
Doiron, Jeanne, E-481
Doiron, Jeanne, S2-455, 644
Doiron, Jeanne Elizabeth, E-637, 644
Doiron, Josaphat, S1-267-268, 271, 273-274, 309
Doiron, Joseph, E-113, 548, 559
Doiron, Joseph, F-5, 21
Doiron, Joseph, N-54, 56
Doiron, Joseph, S1-119, 125, 268, 273
Doiron, Joseph, S2-612
Doiron, Joseph, S3-944, 1078
Doiron, Joseph Simon, C-35
Doiron, Joseph Simon, N-56
Doiron, Joseph-Gregoire, S1-274

Doiron, Joseph-Marie, S1-267
Doiron, Josephat, C-87
Doiron, Josephat, S2-587, 607, 706
Doiron, Josephat, S3-891, 942-943, 945, 947
Doiron, Josette, E-42, 126
Doiron, Louis, E-524
Doiron, Louis, N-56
Doiron, Louis, S1-266, 271
Doiron, Louis Toussaint, F-35
Doiron, Louis Toussaint, N-57
Doiron, Madeleine, C-84, 89
Doiron, Madeleine, E-261, 559
Doiron, Madeleine, F-5, 43, 101
Doiron, Madeleine, N-55, 91, 93, 144, 151
Doiron, Madeleine, S1-3, 275-276
Doiron, Madeleine, S2-469, 673, 715
Doiron, Madeleine-Josephe, S1-113
Doiron, Madeleine-Ursule, S1-265
Doiron, Magdeleine, S3-1111, 1129, 1135-1136
Doiron, Maire, C-51
Doiron, Marguerite, C-49, 83
Doiron, Marguerite, E-115, 117-118, 548
Doiron, Marguerite, F-67, 73, 77, 87
Doiron, Marguerite, N-57, 142-143
Doiron, Marguerite, S1-162, 272, 276, 387, 391
Doiron, Marguerite, S2-659, 663-664, 671-673
Doiron, Marguerite Joseph, N-250
Doiron, Marguerite Josephe, E-124
Doiron, Marguerite Josephe, F-33, 35
Doiron, Marguerite-Josephe, S1-272
Doiron, Margueritte, S3-1115
Doiron, Margueritte, S3-912, 925
Doiron, Marie, C-79-80

Doiron, Marie, E-16, 43, 113-114, 118, 261, 327-328, 413, 439, 644

Doiron, Marie, F-5, 35, 39, 73

Doiron, Marie, N-10, 50, 55, 57, 109, 207, 219

Doiron, Marie, S1-52, 97, 266

Doiron, Marie, S2-431, 438-440, 526

Doiron, Marie, S3-833, 881, 937, 943

Doiron, Marie Appolitte, C-35

Doiron, Marie Blanche, C-79-80, 142-143

Doiron, Marie Blanche, N-134

Doiron, Marie Genevieve, E-114

Doiron, Marie Honorine Hypolite, C-34

Doiron, Marie Honorine Hypolite, N-57

Doiron, Marie Honorine Hypolithe, E-114

Doiron, Marie Hypolithe Honore, F-35

Doiron, Marie Hypolithye Honore, E-114

Doiron, Marie Jacquelin Florentine, E-114

Doiron, Marie Josephe, C-39, 62

Doiron, Marie Josephe, E-12, 113-114, 124, 420, 440, 559

Doiron, Marie Josephe, F-3, 11, 13

Doiron, Marie Josephe, N-62, 102

Doiron, Marie Madeleine, C-56

Doiron, Marie Madeleine, E-114, 292, 342

Doiron, Marie Pelagie, C-61

Doiron, Marie Pelagie, E-114

Doiron, Marie Pelagie, N-101-102

Doiron, Marie Rose, E-559

Doiron, Marie Rose, F-5

Doiron, Marie Rose, N-55

Doiron, Marie Victoire, E-2

Doiron, Marie-Anne, S1-275

Doiron, Marie-Blanche, S1-267

Doiron, Marie-Genevieve, S1-274

Doiron, Marie-Jacquelin-Florentine, S1-274

Doiron, Marie-Josephe, S1-114, 202, 300

Doiron, Marie-Josephe, S2-525, 612

Doiron, Marie-Madeleine, S1-117, 267-268

Doiron, Marie-Madeleine, S2-456-457, 462, 605, 639

Doiron, Marie-Marthe, S1-275-276

Doiron, Marie-Pelagie, F-35

Doiron, Marie-Rose, S1-265, 268, 275-276

Doiron, Marie-Victoire, S1-269

Doiron, Marin, C-34

Doiron, Marin, N-54

Doiron, Mathurin, F-5

Doiron, Mathurin, N-55

Doiron, Mathurin-Luc, S1-266

Doiron, Michel, E-114, 548

Doiron, Modeste, S1-271

Doiron, Noel, E-481, 524

Doiron, Olivier, S1-269

Doiron, Paul, C-74, 79, 153

Doiron, Paul, E-114, 548

Doiron, Paul, F-39

Doiron, Paul, N-134

Doiron, Paul, S1-275-276

Doiron, Pelagie, C-151

Doiron, Philippes, E-481

Doiron, Pierre, C-34

Doiron, Pierre, E-481, 524, 548, 559, 644

Doiron, Pierre, N-55-56

Doiron, Pierre, S1-269, 272-273

Doiron, Pierre, S2-636

Doiron, Pierre, S3-944

Doiron, Pierre-Josaphat, S1-273

Doiron, Rosalie, E-48, 114

Doiron, Rose, C-74, 84, 151

Doiron, Rose, E-47

Doiron, Rose, F-35, 37

Doiron, Rose, N-44, 57

Doiron, Rose, S1-151, 276

Doiron, Rose, S2-481

Doiron, Rose Lucile, C-35

Doiron, Rose Lucile, N-57

Doiron, Rose-Germaine, S1-273

Doiron, Sebastienne, E-114

Doiron, Severin, C-146

Doiron, Severin, C-88

Doiron, Severin, E-113-114

Doiron, Severin, S1-274

Doiron, Simon, S1-271-272

Doiron, Simon-Gregoire, S1-269

Doiron, Simon-Joseph, S1-270

Doiron, Suzanne, E-114, 174, 326

Doiron, Theodore, S1-267-268

Doiron, Thomas, C-34, 80

Doiron, Thomas, F-5, 21, 49

Doiron, Thomas, N-54, 56

Doiron, Thomas, S1-265, 270, 275-276

Doiron, Thomas, S2-636

Doiron, Thomas, S3-826, 1130

Doiron, Ursule, C-34

Doiron, Ursule, F-21, 35

Doiron, Ursule, N-56

Doiron, Ursule-Olive, S1-270

Doiron, Victoire, C-34

Doiron, Victoire, E-114

Doiron, Victoire, N-55

Doive, Alexandre, S2-624

Dolbert, Helene, S2-525

Dolet, Marguerite, E-69, 258

Domet, Thomas, S1-254

Domideau, Marie, E-300, 311

Domilly, Jean, E-114

Dominge, Marie, E-77, 264

Dominique, Pierre, E-298

Dommaud, Marguerite, E-295

Donaille, Francoise, E-371

Donaine, Marie Joseph, E-123

Donat, Jeanne Therese, S1-122

Dondoneau, Andre, E-385

Donnadieu de Pellissier Chevalier Dugres, Louis Joseph, E-114, 430

Donnadieu de Pellissier Chevalier Dugres, Marc Antoine, E-114, 430

Dono, Hippolyte Antoinette, E-192

Dople, Pierre, S3-1061

Doquin, Marie, E-257

Dore, Rose, C-155

Dorin, Louis, C-7, 106

Dorin, Rene, C-13

Dornat, Jean, E-51, 114
Dornat, Louise, E-51, 114
Dorotee, Anne, E-309
Dorothee, negro, E-114
Dorsier, Jean, E-586, 597
Dos, M., C-vii
Dosset, -----, E-6
Dotel, Anne, E-313, 386
Dottelonde, Francoise Elisabeth, E-146
Doty, Jean, E-114, 115, 319
Doty, Marie, E-115
Doty, Marie Louise, E-115
Douague, Jean Berin, E-115, 412
Douaigrain, Marguerite Josephe, E-123
Douaran, Marie Magdelainne, S3-876
Douat, Anne, E-21
Doucet, -----, E-5-6
Doucet, Adelaide, C-128, 158
Doucet, Adelaide Veronique, C-2, 36
Doucet, Adelaide Veronique, E-115
Doucet, Aegustin, C-36, 91, 121-123
Doucet, Alexis, E-494
Doucet, Ange, F-71, 107
Doucet, Anne, C-26
Doucet, Anne, E-21, 78-79, 83, 110, 115, 119, 170, 178, 345, 474, 547
Doucet, Anne, F-79
Doucet, Anne, S1-198-200, 281, 373
Doucet, Anne, S3-961, 1050
Doucet, Anne Helene, E-599
Doucet, Anselme, E-116, 118-119
Doucet, Antoine, E-115
Doucet, Antoine Jean, E-115
Doucet, Armand, E-599
Doucet, Aubin, E-300
Doucet, Auguste-Pierre, S1-279
Doucet, Augustin, F-71
Doucet, Augustin, S1-276-279
Doucet, Augustin, S2-680, 723
Doucet, Augustin, S3-942-943, 1012, 1031, 1050, 1059, 1084

Doucet, Augustin Jean, E-115
Doucet, Augustin Sylvestre, C-36
Doucet, Augustin-Silvestre, S1-277
Doucet, Augustine, C-35
Doucet, Belony, E-116
Doucet, Bernard, E-494
Doucet, Catherine, E-115
Doucet, Catherine Therese, E-115
Doucet, Cecile, E-115, 327, 637, 644
Doucet, Charles, E-115-116, 118, 280, 473, 524
Doucet, Charles, F-67
Doucet, Charles Isaie, E-599
Doucet, Claire, E-259, 378
Doucet, Claire, S2-515
Doucet, Claire Eisabeth, E-115
Doucet, Clairette, E-115
Doucet, Claude, E-487, 494
Doucet, Claude, S1-198
Doucet, Clause, E-348
Doucet, Eleonore, F-71, 107
Doucet, Eleonore Honorine, C-37
Doucet, Eleonore Honorine, N-58
Doucet, Elizabeth, E-115, 132, 144, 325
Doucet, Emilie, E-116
Doucet, Emmanuel Victoire, E-116
Doucet, Emmanuelle Victoire, C-36, 60, 123
Doucet, Etienne, E-116, 386, 395
Doucet, Euphrosine, N-58
Doucet, Felicite, E-116, 598, 637
Doucet, Francois, E-115-118, 524, 547
Doucet, Francois, F-71
Doucet, Francois, N-81
Doucet, Francois, S1-278
Doucet, Francois, S2-437
Doucet, Francois, S3-1065
Doucet, Francois-Adrien, S1-278
Doucet, Francoise, C-52-53

Doucet, Francoise, E-51
Doucet, Francoise, F-63, 79
Doucet, Francoise, N-81-82
Doucet, Francoise, S1-236
Doucet, Francoise, S2-437-438, 440, 554
Doucet, Francoise, S3-987, 1065
Doucet, Francoise Louise, E-116
Doucet, Genevieve, C-128
Doucet, Genevieve, E-116
Doucet, Germain, E-118, 456, 473
Doucet, girl, E-115
Doucet, Gracieuse, E-632, 639, 642
Doucet, Honorine Eleonor, E-116
Doucet, Jacques, C-42
Doucet, Jacques, E-115-118, 494
Doucet, Jacques Charles, E-116
Doucet, Jacques Marc, E-116
Doucet, Jean, C-35
Doucet, Jean, E-55, 68, 115-116, 118, 159, 334, 355, 504, 524-525, 637
Doucet, Jean, S1-215, 276, 278
Doucet, Jean, S2-749
Doucet, Jean Baptiste, F-71, 107
Doucet, Jean Baptiste, N-58
Doucet, Jean Baptiste Joseph, E-140
Doucet, Jean Baptiste Michel, C-37
Doucet, Jean Baptiste Michel, F-71
Doucet, Jean Baptiste Michel, N-58
Doucet, Jean Marie, E-618
Doucet, Jean Pierre Marie, E-116
Doucet, Jean Simon, E-6
Doucet, Jean Simon fils, E-3-4
Doucet, Jean-Baptiste, S1-277
Doucet, Jeanne, E-40, 307, 494, 504, 618
Doucet, Jeanne, N-109
Doucet, Jeanne Gabrielle, E-116
Doucet, Joachim, S1-276, 278
Doucet, Joseph, C-2, 10, 36, 60, 92, 118-119, 123-124, 128

Doucet, Joseph, E-1, 37-38, 56, 57, 115-119, 632, 642
Doucet, Joseph, F-71, 107
Doucet, Joseph, S1-276, 278
Doucet, Joseph Basile, E-559
Doucet, Joseph Benjamin Francois, E-116
Doucet, Joseph Prospert, E-117, 639, 642
Doucet, Joseph Sr., E-639
Doucet, Joseph-Basile, S1-279
Doucet, Josephine, E-632, 639, 642
Doucet, Justice, S1-276
Doucet, Laurent, E-494, 525
Doucet, Louis, E-118, 334, 504, 525, 548
Doucet, Louise, E-632, 639, 642
Doucet, Luc Edouard, E-117
Doucet, Madeleine, S1-238
Doucet, Madeleinette, E-47
Doucet, Magdalen Genevieve Emelie, E-117
Doucet, Magdelaine, E-44, 117, 322, 342, 504, 524, 547-548
Doucet, Magdelaine, F-71, 107
Doucet, Marguerite, C-61, 90
Doucet, Marguerite, E-19, 23, 61, 82, 117, 132, 196, 328, 335, 340, 350, 370, 473, 504, 547-548, 637
Doucet, Marguerite, F-71, 107
Doucet, Marguerite, S2-515
Doucet, Marguerite Benony, C-37
Doucet, Marguerite Eleonore, E-117
Doucet, Marguerite Madeleine, C-35
Doucet, Marguerite Madeleine, N-58
Doucet, Marie, C-2, 16, 36, 84, 91, 121-122, 128
Doucet, Marie, E-68, 83, 112, 117, 126, 178, 188, 334, 350, 368, 428, 494, 548, 618
Doucet, Marie, F-33, 77
Doucet, Marie, N-146, 201
Doucet, Marie, S1-277-278
Doucet, Marie Anne, E-117

Doucet, Marie Anne Pelagie, E-117, 118
Doucet, Marie Antoinette, E-118
Doucet, Marie Blanche, E-118
Doucet, Marie Felicite, E-118
Doucet, Marie Josephe, C-57, 124
Doucet, Marie Judith, E-456
Doucet, Marie Madeleine, E-341
Doucet, Marie Magdalen Susanne, E-118
Doucet, Marie Marguerite, E-118
Doucet, Marie Marguerite, F-107
Doucet, Marie Marthe, F-71
Doucet, Marie Perrine, E-4, 6, 118
Doucet, Marie Renee Adelaide, E-118
Doucet, Marie Rose, E-118
Doucet, Marie Sophie, E-118
Doucet, Mathieu, E-504, 525
Doucet, Michel, C-36-37
Doucet, Michel, E-24, 115-118, 357, 547
Doucet, Michel, F-71, 107
Doucet, Michel, N-58
Doucet, Modeste, E-639
Doucet, Mr., E-334
Doucet, Olive Eugenie, E-118
Doucet, Pelagie, E-599
Doucet, Perrine Adelaide, E-618
Doucet, Pierre, E-116-118, 259, 286, 337, 456, 473, 494, 504, 547-548, 559, 618
Doucet, Pierre, S1-277-279
Doucet, Pierre, S3-881, 999, 1016, 1084
Doucet, Pierre Marin, E-118
Doucet, Pierre-Michel, S1-279
Doucet, Reine, E-639
Doucet, Remi, E-117
Doucet, Rene, E-525
Doucet, Renee, E-632, 642
Doucet, Renee-Catherine, S1-277
Doucet, Rose, E-314
Doucet, Rose, S1-277
Doucet, Simon, E-115-116, 118, 286

Doucet, Stanislas, E-119
Doucet, Toussaints, E-504
Doucet, Victoire, C-54, 71
Doucet, Victoire, E-119
Doucet, Zoe, E-119
Doucet, Zoe Joseph, E-119
Doucet , Jacque, C-127
Doucet, Mathieu - Village named after Mathieu Doucet, E-210
Douchelin, Pierre Francois, E-178
Doucin, Jean, E-441
Doucin, Pierre, S3-999
Doudin, Reine, S1-195
Doueroen, Marie Joseph, S3-967
Douesron, Marie, S3-942
Douesseron, Angelique, S3-877
Douet, Anne, S3-1151
Douet, Francoise Rose, E-51, 119, 319
Douguet, Denys, E-102
Douillet, Jean, E-158
Douillet, Marie, E-119, 159
Doussain, Marie, E-101, 391, 416
Doussain, Marie Magdelaine, E-119, 256
Douteau, Jean, E-119, 356
Douteau, Pierre, E-119, 356
Douve, Modeste, S1-128
Douvelle, Marie Francoise, E-120
Douville, Anne, E-79, 104, 109, 120, 132-133, 141, 169
Douville, Anne, S1-180, 199, 280-281, 332, 375
Douville, Francois, E-93, 102, 119-120, 176, 259, 411
Douville, Francois, S1-77, 180, 279, 281-282, 320
Douville, Francois, S2-516, 729
Douville, Francois, S3-964
Douville, Francoise, E-32, 119, 141, 264, 282, 411
Douville, Francoise, S1-280-282
Douville, Francoise, S2-731
Douville, Jacque, S3-964
Douville, Jacques, E-54, 119-121, 263, 411
Douville, Jacques, N-195

Douville, Jacques, S1-280-282, 284
Douville, Jacques, S2-517
Douville, Jean, E-55, 104, 119, 378
Douville, Jean Francois, E-119
Douville, Jean-Francois, S1-280
Douville, Jeanne-Marie, S1-282
Douville, Joseph, E-42
Douville, Julien Francois, E-119
Douville, Julien-Francois, S1-280
Douville, Louis, E-119
Douville, Louis Gabriel, E-119
Douville, Louis-Gabriel, S1-281
Douville, Louise, E-28, 61, 170, 263, 411
Douville, Louise, S1-77, 281-282, 375
Douville, Louise, S2-730
Douville, Louise , S3-964, 978
Douville, Louise Gabriel, E-119
Douville, Louise-Gabriel, S1-281
Douville, Louise-Gabrielle, S1-77
Douville, Louise-Jeanne, S1-282
Douville, Marguerite, S1-281
Douville, Marianne Louise, E-79
Douville, Marianne-Louise, S1-201
Douville, Marie, E-119
Douville, Marie, S1-280
Douville, Marie Francoise, E-42, 98, 104, 120, 311, 315, 373, 411
Douville, Marie Francoise, S3-975
Douville, Marie Judith, E-120
Douville, Marie Roge, S3-964
Douville, Marie-Francoise, S1-280, 282, 332
Douville, Marie-Francoise, S2-729-731
Douville, Marie-Judith, S1-282
Douville, Mathieu, E-120, 160
Douville, Mr., E-43, 123, 311, 432
Douville, Philippe, S1-281-282
Douville, Philippe, S3-978

Douville, Philippe Charle, E-120
Douville, Philippe-Charle, S1-281
Douville, Philippe-Charles, S1-35
Douville, Pierre, E-120
Douville, Pierre, S1-281
Doux, Andre, E-120, 384
Doux, Pierre, E-120, 384
Douxeis, Marguerite, E-120, 293
Douxeis, Michel, E-120
Doye, Jacquelin, E-120, 150
Doye, Jean, E-120, 150, 150
Doyer, Jacqueline, S1-337
Doyer, Jacquemine, S1-259, 338
Doyer, Jacquemine, S2-620
Doyer, Jacquemine, S3-981
Doyer, Jan, S3-981
Doyer, Jean, S1-337
Doyer, Jean, S2-620
Doyer, Mathurine, S2-515, 784-785
Doyon, Catherine, S2-607
Doziote, Marie, C-166
Dragon, Marie Jeanne, C-36
Draonet, Rene, E-143, 157
Drapeau, Anne, F-85
Drapeau, Louis, E-381
Draunet, Rene, E-21
Drean, Jeanne, E-55, 300
Dreouaux, Guillaume, S3-980
Driant, Ernest, E-439
Drillot, Gaspard, E-120
Drillot, Jacob Henri, E-120
Drillot, Jean Gaspard, E-120
Drillot, Marie Susanne, E-120
Drivant, Antoine, E-120, 303
Drivant, Joseph, E-120, 303
Dro, Anne, E-327
Droguet, Pierre, S2-733
Droit, Louis, E-120, 442
Droit, Marie Jeanne, E-120, 338
Droit, Pierre, E-120, 338
Dronhet, -----, E-35
Dronhet, Mr., E-144
Droual, Charles, E-420
Droual, Jean Marie, E-422
Droual, Laurant, E-425
Droual, Marie Jeanne, E-422, 425, 428

Drouet, Catherine, E-343
Drouet, Louis, E-120, 153
Drouet, Renee, E-43, 347
Drouillet, Mr., E-313
Drouineau, Catherine, E-121, 140, 265
Drouineau, Crespin, E-140
Drouineau, Francois, E-121, 140
Drouineau, Pierre, E-121, 140
Droune, Anne, E-595
Dry, Perinne, S2-430
Du Clos, Dominique, E-65
Du Clos, Marie, E-65
Du Clos, Mr., E-70
Du Dreneuf, Padot, S3-1066
Du Liscoet, Quemper, S3-934
Du Martin, Marie, E-68
Du Mesnil, Francois Robert, E-42
Du Mesnil, Francois-Robert, S1-97
Du Mesnil, Marie Marguerite, E-42
Du Mesnil, Marie-Marguerite, S1-97
Du Mesnil, Marie-Marguerite, S2-512
Du Portail, Jeanne-Marie-Therese, S1-196
Du Puy, Anne, S3-1112
Du Rocher, Francois, E-87
Du Routois, Julien, S1-181, 317
Du Routois, Jullien, S3-1066
Du Ruteton, Julien, S3-1050
Du Savey, Marie-Francoise, S2-719
Du Vivie, Jean Baptiste, E-79
Duand, Marie Joseph, E-421
Duaron, Jean Charles, E-559
Duaron, Josephe, S3-1031
DuBaie, Jean, E-386
Dubay, Marie Catherine, E-121
Dubay, Marie Louise, E-121, 363
Dubignon, Julien, S1-166
Duboc, Madeleine, S1-86
Duboc, Madeleine, S2-514
Duboc, Magdelaine, S3-915
Duboc, Marie-Madeleine, S2-695
Duboc, Pierre, S2-514

INDEX SOURCES C=Chatellerault; E=Acadians in Exile; F=Acadian Families; N=Nantes; S=St-Malo

Duboc, Pierre, S3-915
Duboe, Pierre, E-121
Duboe, Pierre Jacques, E-121
Dubogne, Anne Marie, E-78
Dubogue, Pierre, E-255
Dubois, Alexis Bertrand, E-121, 269
Dubois, Alexis Guillaume, E-121
Dubois, Catherine, E-318
Dubois, Francois, E-121, 161
Dubois, Francois, F-75
Dubois, Isabelle, C-85, 120
Dubois, Jacques, E-339
Dubois, Jacques, F-69
Dubois, Jacques, N-27, 191, 107, 231
Dubois, Jacques Olivier, E-121
Dubois, Jean, E-121-122, 350
Dubois, Jeanne Blanche, E-121
Dubois, Jeanne Marie, E-376
Dubois, Joseph, C-64
Dubois, Joseph, E-121, 148
Dubois, Joseph, S1-242, 283
Dubois, Joseph, S2-561, 622
Dubois, Joseph, S3-1058, 1064, 1080
Dubois, Joseph Ange, C-28
Dubois, Joseph Ange, F-39
Dubois, Joseph Ange, N-45
Dubois, Joseph Ange, S1-242
Dubois, Joseph Endre, E-264
Dubois, Joseph Francois, E-115
Dubois, Louis, C-67
Dubois, Louis, E-119, 121, 159
Dubois, Louis Marie, C-29
Dubois, Louis-Marie, S1-283
Dubois, Louis-Marie, S2-622
Dubois, Louise Charlotte, E-586, 595
Dubois, Louise Marie, E-121
Dubois, Madeleine, S1-283
Dubois, Magdelaine, E-51, 121, 161
Dubois, Marguerite, S2-622
Dubois, Marguerite Ange, C-28-29
Dubois, Marguerite Ange, F-39
Dubois, Marguerite Ange, N-45
Dubois, Marguerite Ange, S1-242, 353

Dubois, Marguerite Ange, S3-1058
Dubois, Marguerite-Ange, S1-283
Dubois, Marie, E-51, 121, 140, 149, 160, 169
Dubois, Marie Anne, E-35
Dubois, Marie Blanche, C-67
Dubois, Marie Blanche, E-121
Dubois, Marie-Blanche, S1-283
Dubois, Marie-Jeanne, S1-209
Dubois, Nicole, E-279
Dubois, Olivier, E-98, 121
Dubois, Olivier, F-63
Dubois, Olivier, N-156, 180
Dubois, Olivier, S2-734
Dubois, Pierre, C-99
Dubois, Pierre, E-121-122, 149
Dubois, Pierre, N-231
Dubois, Pierre, S1-43
Dubonville, Pierre, E-122
Duboquet, Jacques, E-122, 441
Duboquet, Marguerite, E-122, 441
Dubord, Francoise, E-122, 370
Dubord, Joseph, E-122, 370
Duborg, Jacques, E-586, 595
Duborg, Marie, E-586, 595
Dubos, Anne Magon, S3-934
Dubos, Pierre, E-90
Duboscq, Joseph, S1-284
Duboscq, Madeleine, S1-261-262, 284
Duboscq, Marie, S1-284-285
Duboscq, Pierre, S1-261, 283-285
Duboscq, Pierre-Jacques, S1-284
Dubosq, Claude, E-405
Dubosq, Pierre, S2-513
Dubouchaud, Francoise, C-86
Dubourdien, Gabriel, E-122
Dubourdien, Marie Josephe, E-122
Dubourdieu, Francoise, S1-337
Dubourdieu, Jean, S1-337
Dubourg, ----- , S3-1089
Dubourg, Etienne, S3-1089
Dubourg, Flore, S3-1089
Dubourg, Mr., S3-1089
Dubourg, Mrs., S3-1089

Dubreucq, Antoine Florent Joseph, E-122, 196
Dubreucq, Antoine Joseph, E-122, 196
Dubroqua, Jeanne, E-172, 267
Dubuisson, Etienne, E-122
Dubuisson, Jacques, E-189
Dubuisson, Jean Baptiste, E-122, 181, 384
Dubuisson, Joseph, E-122
Dubuisson, Louis Etienne, E-122
Dubuisson, Marguerite, E-79
Dubuisson, Simon, E-122, 196
Dubuisson, Simon Joseph, E-122
Ducas, Cler, S3-870
Ducas, Pierre, E-438
Ducas, Rose, E-65
Duchaigne, Jeanne, E-387
Duchambon, Lange, E-178
Duchamps, Pierre Bouard, E-379
DuChanin, Augustin Victor, E-360
DuCharme, Marie, E-122
Duchasseau de la Renerie, Anne, E-127, 266
Duchemin, Julien, S1-285
Duchemin, Marguerite, E-69, 370
Duchemin, Marguerite, S2-680
Duchene, Jacques F., E-586, 596
Duchene, Jan, S3-1093
Duchene, Jean, E-387
Duchene, Jeanne, E-122, 387
Duchene, Marc, E-122, 387
Duchene, Marie, N-230
Duchenot, Jacques-Chenee, S2-699
Ducheron, Marie Magdeleine, E-81, 138, 261
Duchesne, Anne, S1-1
Ducles, Marie, S1-195
Duclin, Joseph, E-370
Duclos, Anne, E-126
Duclos, Anne, S1-307
Duclos, Anne, S2-438
Duclos, Jacque, E-98, 141
Duclos, Jacques, S1-332
Duclos, Louis, S1-195

Duclos, Marie, E-146, 342
Duclos, Mr., E-70, 98, 104, 132, 176, 341, 431
Duclos, Mr., S1-320
Duclos, Olivier, S3-1147
Duclos, Perinne-Guerier, S1-146
DuCorbier, Francoise, E-103
Ducos, Marie, E-12
Ducostau, Francois Denis, E-122
Ducour, Jacques, E-319
Ducrocq, Francois, E-424
Ducrocq, Marie Jeanne, E-92
DuCron, Barbe, E-122
DuCron, Pierre, E-122
Ducuys De Salvega, Antoinette, E-313
Dudognon, Jean, E-139
Dudognon, Louise Esther, E-122, 139
Dudognon, Pierre, E-139
Dudouit, Francois, S2-478
Dudouit, Francois, S3-1018
Dudouit, Francoise, S2-478, 526
Dudouit, Francoise, S3-1018
Dudouit, Joseph, S2-478
Dudouit, Joseph, S3-1018
Dudouit, Michel, S3-1018
Duelion, Mathieu, E-264
Dueron, Angelique, S3-892
Dufau, Gabriel, E-283
Dufau, Magdelaine, E-313
Dufaut, Gille, E-78, 123
Dufaut, Gille Michel, E-123
Dufaut, Jean, E-123
Dufaut, Louis, E-123
Dufaut, Marie Marguerite, E-635
Dufaut, Michel, E-78
Dufeu, Jean Baptiste Antoine, E-276
Duffau, Gilles, S1-285
Duffau, Marguerite, E-98, 402
Dufraine, Marguerite, E-123
Dufraine, Rene, E-123, 378
Dufresne, Joseph, S2-567
Dufresne, Pierre, S3-1084
Dugan, Jean Baptiste, E-123
Dugan, Jean Pierre, E-123
Dugast, Abraham, E-456, 473, 525

Dugast, Abraham, S1-76, 171, 226
Dugast, Abraham, S2-558, 619
Dugast, Adelaide, S1-300
Dugast, Agnes, C-11
Dugast, Agnes, S1-63, 304-305
Dugast, Agnes, S2-753
Dugast, Agnes, S3-888, 1120
Dugast, Agnesse, E-483
Dugast, Alexandre, E-177
Dugast, Alexandre, S2-435
Dugast, Alexis, C-57
Dugast, Alexis, F-43
Dugast, Alexis, N-91
Dugast, Alexis, S1-285-288, 298, 307
Dugast, Alexis, S2-462-463, 482, 629
Dugast, Alexis, S3-1103, 1136, 1138
Dugast, Amand, S1-158, 287, 290-291
Dugast, Amant, S2-532
Dugast, Ambroise, C-37-38, 131
Dugast, Ambroise, F-23
Dugast, Ambroise, N-58-59
Dugast, Ambroise, S1-287-288
Dugast, Ambroise, S2-463, 656
Dugast, Ambroise, S3-1142-1143
Dugast, Anastasie, F-43, 107
Dugast, Anastasie, N-62
Dugast, Anastasie, S1-293, 299
Dugast, Anastasie-Marguerte, S1-300
Dugast, Angelique, E-628
Dugast, Angelique, S1-34, 172, 217, 224-225, 227, 297
Dugast, Angelique, S2-567, 740
Dugast, Angelique, S3-1090
Dugast, Anne, C-37, 58, 64, 71, 141
Dugast, Anne, E-58, 123, 181, 384, 429, 456, 475, 483
Dugast, Anne, F-7, 25, 43, 81, 107
Dugast, Anne, N-61-63, 65, 93-94, 224
Dugast, Anne, S1-72, 111-112, 167, 171-172, 243, 289, 291, 293, 296-299, 303, 305, 307

Dugast, Anne, S2-469, 483, 567, 630, 671, 678
Dugast, Anne, S3-940, 1135-1136
Dugast, Anne Joseph , C-56-57, 89
Dugast, Anne Josephe, F-43
Dugast, Anne Josephe, N-91-92
Dugast, Anne Marguerite, N-61
Dugast, Anne Marie, C-37
Dugast, Anne Marie, F-23
Dugast, Anne Marie, N-59, 65
Dugast, Anne Osite, F-25
Dugast, Anne Osite, N-64-65, 86-87
Dugast, Anne Perinne, F-43
Dugast, Anne Perrine, N-64
Dugast, Anne-Josephe, S1-286-287, 306
Dugast, Anne-Josephe, S2-462
Dugast, Anne-Marie, S1-305
Dugast, Antoine, S1-288-289, 294
Dugast, Antoine, S3-950, 1045
Dugast, Bernard, F-85
Dugast, Blaise, N-59
Dugast, boy, S1-286
Dugast, Cecile, C-38
Dugast, Cecile, N-62
Dugast, Cecile-Anne, S1-299
Dugast, Cecille, F-43
Dugast, Celeste, F-23
Dugast, Celeste, N-59
Dugast, Chalres, N-59-61, 210, 223, 225
Dugast, Charles, C-140-141, 37-38
Dugast, Charles, E-123-124
Dugast, Charles, F-5, 23, 29, 49, 81
Dugast, Charles, S1-111, 231, 235, 287-291, 293, 342
Dugast, Charles, S2-467, 518, 532, 701
Dugast, Charles, S3-940, 948, 950, 1045, 1128
Dugast, Charlotte-Amelie, S1-300
Dugast, Claire, F-87, 93
Dugast, Claire, S1-15, 19, 28, 69, 75, 172

Dugast, Claire, S2-458-459, 476
Dugast, Claire, S3-872-874, 922
Dugast, Claude, C-37
Dugast, Claude, E-123-124, 150, 285, 302, 403, 473, 525
Dugast, Claude, F-23, 25, 37
Dugast, Claude, N-19, 59-60, 63-64, 215
Dugast, Claude, S1-287, 290, 303, 305
Dugast, Claude, S2-671
Dugast, Claude, S3-1003
Dugast, Claude Bernard, E-123
Dugast, Constant Ambroise, N-58
Dugast, Elisabeth, S3-933
Dugast, Elizabeth, C-38, 64, 82-83, 159
Dugast, Elizabeth, F-27, 43
Dugast, Elizabeth, N-62, 106, 140-141, 254
Dugast, Elizabeth, S1-105, 302-305
Dugast, Elizabeth, S2-483, 531-533, 589-590, 656
Dugast, Elizabeth-Eulalie, S1-299
Dugast, Emilie, S1-300
Dugast, Etienne, N-61
Dugast, Eulalie, C-58
Dugast, Eulalie, E-283
Dugast, Eulalie, N-94-95
Dugast, Eulalie, S1-301
Dugast, Eulalie, S2-482-483
Dugast, Eulalie Celeste, C-38
Dugast, Eulalie Celeste, N-62
Dugast, Felicite-Marguerite, S1-291
Dugast, Francois, C-38
Dugast, Francois, E-123, 525
Dugast, Francois, F-43
Dugast, Francois, N-62
Dugast, Francois-Basile-Etienne, S1-299
Dugast, Francoise, E-483
Dugast, Francoise, N-74, 136
Dugast, Francoise, S1-34-35, 171, 224, 227, 287, 293, 296, 298, 376
Dugast, Francoise, S2-480, 600, 629, 740

Dugast, Francoise, S3-916, 1106, 1110
Dugast, Gregoire, S1-286
Dugast, Isabelle, C-83
Dugast, Isabelle, F-25, 45
Dugast, Isabelle, S1-65, 362
Dugast, Isabelle, S2-461, 657-658
Dugast, Izabelle, S3-1116
Dugast, Jacques, E-123-124
Dugast, Jean, E-123-124
Dugast, Jean, F-53
Dugast, Jean, N-101, 206
Dugast, Jean, S1-296, 304-305, 371
Dugast, Jean, S3-940, 1045, 1121
Dugast, Jean Baptiste, C-26, 35, 39, 71, 143
Dugast, Jean Baptiste, E-123-124
Dugast, Jean Baptiste, F-7, 11, 35
Dugast, Jean Baptiste, N-24, 59-62, 98, 214, 217, 223
Dugast, Jean Baptiste, S3-961, 1031, 1050, 1081, 1105, 1121-1122
Dugast, Jean Charles, C-38
Dugast, Jean Charles, E-124
Dugast, Jean Charles, F-23
Dugast, Jean Charles, N-59-60
Dugast, Jean Gregoire, N-61
Dugast, Jean Louis, E-124
Dugast, Jean Marie, N-62
Dugast, Jean Marie Alexis, E-124
Dugast, Jean Marie Alexis, F-35
Dugast, Jean Pierre, C-38
Dugast, Jean Pierre, E-124
Dugast, Jean Pierre, F-35, 41, 43
Dugast, Jean Pierre, N-62
Dugast, Jean-Baptiste, S1-171, 201, 289, 291-295, 300
Dugast, Jean-Baptiste, S2-596
Dugast, Jean-Charles, S1-290-291
Dugast, Jean-Gregoire, S1-294
Dugast, Jean-Pierre, S1-306
Dugast, Jean-Pierre-Marin, S1-301

Dugast, Jeanne, C-67, 81
Dugast, Jeanne, E-322, 346, 353, 483
Dugast, Jeanne, S1-202, 364
Dugast, Jeanne, S2-533, 553, 558-559, 561, 698
Dugast, Jeanne, S3-1015, 1080
Dugast, Josaphat, S1-286
Dugast, Joseph, E-123-124, 483, 525
Dugast, Joseph, F-23, 43, 49
Dugast, Joseph, N-60-62, 64, 93, 178, 197, 224-225
Dugast, Joseph, S1-34-35, 224, 226, 286-290, 296-300, 306-307
Dugast, Joseph, S2-469, 480, 500, 543, 674
Dugast, Joseph, S3-852, 1103, 1109, 1135-1136, 1138, 1141, 1143
Dugast, Joseph Simon, C-38
Dugast, Joseph Simon, N-59
Dugast, Joseph-Augustin, S1-300
Dugast, Joseph-Firmin, S1-295
Dugast, Joseph-Simon, S1-291
Dugast, Josephe, S1-293
Dugast, Liduvine, E-124
Dugast, Lisette, S1-172
Dugast, Louis Ambroise, F-23
Dugast, Louis Ambroise, N-59
Dugast, Louis Joseph, E-124
Dugast, Madeleine, S1-112, 147, 158, 218, 302
Dugast, Madeleine, S2-519
Dugast, Magdelaine, E-363, 472
Dugast, Magdeleine, F-27
Dugast, Magdeleine, S3-948, 1097
Dugast, Marguerite, C-38
Dugast, Marguerite, E-19, 82, 124, 175, 190, 290, 315, 323, 325, 349, 408, 483
Dugast, Marguerite, F-23, 25, 37, 43, 73, 109
Dugast, Marguerite, N-19-20, 31, 35, 37, 60, 62, 210, 215, 224
Dugast, Marguerite, S2-472, 613, 619-620, 657, 694, 741

Dugast, Marguerite, S1-35, 64-65, 154, 161, 163, 168, 170-171, 224, 226, 227, 235, 289, 291, 296-298, 300, 302-303

Dugast, Marguerite Blanche, N-33, 65

Dugast, Marguerite Euphrosine, N-61

Dugast, Marguerite Joseph, S3-1050, 1112

Dugast, Marguerite Josephe, C-11-12, 26

Dugast, Marguerite Josephe, N-14, 58

Dugast, Marguerite-Blanche, S1-305

Dugast, Marguerite-Josephe, S1-64, 146-147, 200-201, 287, 292, 304-305

Dugast, Margueritte, S3-905, 921, 961

Dugast, Marie, C-38, 45, 58-59, 71, 158

Dugast, Marie, E-88, 129, 362, 434, 437, 439, 457, 475, 483, 633, 643

Dugast, Marie, F-7, 25, 27, 43, 55, 99

Dugast, Marie, N-6, 61-62, 65, 70-71, 96, 160, 216-217

Dugast, Marie, S1-20, 35, 147, 163-164, 224, 226, 292-293, 295, 297-298, 301-303, 305, 361

Dugast, Marie, S2-460, 463, 482, 487, 488, 496, 596, 599, 618, 757

Dugast, Marie, S3-935, 1081, 1108, 1114, 1123, 1141

Dugast, Marie Francoise, N-62

Dugast, Marie Joseph, S3-940, 950

Dugast, Marie Josephe, C-38

Dugast, Marie Josephe, E-124, 616

Dugast, Marie Josephe, F-23

Dugast, Marie Josephe, N-60

Dugast, Marie Louise, N-62

Dugast, Marie Madeleine, C-26, 56

Dugast, Marie Madeleine, N-90, 100

Dugast, Marie Magdelaine, F-5, 25

Dugast, Marie Marguerite Pelagie, E-124

Dugast, Marie Osite, N-63, 66, 209

Dugast, Marie Rose, C-39

Dugast, Marie Rose, F-43

Dugast, Marie Rose, N-98, 130

Dugast, Marie Victoire, N-65

Dugast, Marie-Anne-Julienne, S1-295

Dugast, Marie-Jeanne, S1-294

Dugast, Marie-Jeanne, S2-711

Dugast, Marie-Josephe, S1-289-291, 294-295, 305

Dugast, Marie-Josephe, S2-706

Dugast, Marie-Madeleine, S1-289, 307

Dugast, Marie-Madeleine, S2-460-461, 518

Dugast, Marie-Osithe, S1-303

Dugast, Marie-Rose, S1-286, 306

Dugast, Marie-Victoire, S1-305

Dugast, Marin, C-39

Dugast, Marin, F-11

Dugast, Marin, N-62, 223

Dugast, Marin, S1-113, 202, 292-293, 300-301

Dugast, Marin, S2-432

Dugast, Marin, S3-961, 1031, 1081

Dugast, Mathurin, N-60

Dugast, Mathurin, S1-292-293

Dugast, Michel, F-55

Dugast, Michel, N-160, 216

Dugast, Michel, S2-757

Dugast, Mr., S3-1072

Dugast, Olivier, S1-292-293

Dugast, Olivier Marie, N-61

Dugast, Olivier-Marc, S1-301

Dugast, Osite, S1-305

Dugast, Ozitte, S1-304-305

Dugast, Paul, C-45, 56, 58, 82

Dugast, Paul, F-25, 27

Dugast, Paul, N-3, 63, 66, 70, 90, 94, 209, 215, 223

Dugast, Paul, S1-7, 74, 301-303, 361-362

Dugast, Paul, S2-460, 482, 656

Dugast, Paul, S3-871, 874, 933, 935, 961

Dugast, Paul Joseph, F-59

Dugast, Perpetue, C-57, 156-157

Dugast, Perpetue, N-24

Dugast, Perpetue, S1-286, 290, 292-293, 295, 301

Dugast, Pierre, C-11-12, 16, 38-39, 83

Dugast, Pierre, E-124, 624

Dugast, Pierre, F-11, 25, 35, 43, 45

Dugast, Pierre, N-14, 33, 36, 62-65, 86, 141, 178, 210, 215, 224

Dugast, Pierre, S1-63-65, 156, 170, 286-287, 289, 291, 294, 298, 303-307, 380, 388

Dugast, Pierre, S2-467, 469, 532, 550, 630, 657, 678, 695

Dugast, Pierre, S3-916, 1003, 1045, 1105-1106, 1110-1112, 1114, 1116-1117, 1120, 1138

Dugast, Pierre Anthoine, S3-940, 948

Dugast, Pierre Olivier, F-23

Dugast, Pierre Olivier, N-60

Dugast, Pierre-Cyrille, S1-295

Dugast, Pierre-Ignace, S1-289

Dugast, Pierre-Olivier, S1-291

Dugast, Prosper, S1-304-305

Dugast, Remy, S1-304-305

Dugast, Rene Olivier, C-38

Dugast, Rene Olivier, N-59

Dugast, Rose, F-43

Dugast, Rose, N-64

Dugast, Simon, C-141

Dugast, Simon, N-63, 209, 223

Dugast, Simon, S1-302-303, 362

Dugast, Simon, S2-461

Dugast, Simon, S3-872

Dugast, Theodore, E-124

Dugast, Victoire, S1-289, 294

Dugast, Victoire, S2-519

Dugast, Victoire, S3-950

Dugast, Victoire Ange, C-38

Dugast, Victoire-Ange, S1-291

Dugast, Victoire-Marie, S1-294

Dugast, Victor-Osite, S1-305

Dugast, Zacharie, S1-112
Dugat, Simon, F-25, 29
Dugat, Victoire, F-101
Dugoutt, Pierre, S3-976
Duguay, Pierre, E-28, 93, 110, 176, 274, 377, 393, 428
Duguay, Pierre, S1-320
Duguay, Pierre, S2-723
Dugue, Francois, E-125, 390
Dugue, Helene, S1-148
Dugue, Jacques, E-125, 390
Dugue, Joseph, E-125
Dugue, Marie, E-125, 280, 322
Dugue, Pierre, E-104, 135
Duguesnel, Jacques, E-288
Duguy, Elisabeth, E-22, 349
DuHaget, Charles, E-125, 392
DuHaget, Robert, E-125, 392
Duhal, Laurence, S2-535
Duhal, Laurence, S3-849
DuHalle, Marie Anne, E-101
Duhamble, Veronique, E-34
Duhamel, Anne, S3-955
Duhier, Andre, E-415
Duhon, Anne, E-331, 560
Duhon, Augustin, F-63, 79
Duhon, Augustin, N-66, 217
Duhon, Augustin Marie, E-125
Duhon, Azunte, E-421
Duhon, Cyprien, E-125, 163, 331, 560
Duhon, Cyprien-Pierre, S1-310
Duhon, Elisabeth, E-15-16, 421, 554
Duhon, Elizabeth, F-83
Duhon, Elizabeth, N-2-3
Duhon, Euphrosine, C-69, 71, 130
Duhon, Euphrosine, E-440
Duhon, Euphrosine, F-57
Duhon, Francois Marie, E-125
Duhon, Francoise, S1-274, 309-310
Duhon, Honore, E-125-126, 422, 554, 560
Duhon, Honore, F-63, 79
Duhon, Honore, N-65-66, 218
Duhon, Honore Jacques Marie Louis, E-125
Duhon, Isabelle, E-331
Duhon, Jacques, F-79

Duhon, Jacques, N-66
Duhon, Jean Baptiste, E-560
Duhon, Jean Baptiste, F-41
Duhon, Jean Baptiste, N-3, 65, 165, 169
Duhon, Jean Charles, E-125
Duhon, Jean Charles, F-79
Duhon, Jean Charles, N-66
Duhon, Jean Pierre, E-125
Duhon, Jean-Baptiste, S1-309
Duhon, Jean-Charles, S1-310
Duhon, Joseph, E-125
Duhon, Joseph, F-111
Duhon, Louis Desire, N-66
Duhon, Magdalen, E-422
Duhon, Marguerite, E-423-425, 577
Duhon, Marguerite, F-51
Duhon, Marguerite, N-169-170
Duhon, Marguerite, S1-12, 106, 268, 273, 309-310
Duhon, Marguerite, S2-467
Duhon, Margueritte, S3-891
Duhon, Marie, E-125, 314, 420, 426, 560, 575
Duhon, Marie, N-165
Duhon, Marie, S1-12, 86, 274, 309-310
Duhon, Marie, S2-678
Duhon, Marie Blanche, E-428
Duhon, Marie Elizabeth, E-125
Duhon, Marie Francoise, E-126
Duhon, Marie Josephe, E-424
Duhon, Marie Magdalen, E-420, 425-426
Duhon, Marie Magdalen, F-51
Duhon, Philippe Marie, E-126
Duhon, Pierre, S1-15, 106, 273-274, 309-310
Duhon, Pierre, S2-606
Duhon, Pierre, S3-891, 1010
Duhon, Pierre-Jean, S1-310
Duhon, Robert Francois, N-65
DuJaut, Michel, E-132
Dujour, Marie, E-126
Dujour, Marie Anne, E-112, 332
Dula, Jean, E-72, 138
Dulaurent, Michel-Pierre, S1-312
Dulin, David Jean Francois, E-147, 386

Dumaine, Jean, E-292
Dumaine, Pierre, E-126, 408
Dumaine, Sebastien, E-126, 408
Dumas, Henri, E-326
Dumas, Jean, E-126, 389
Dumas, Jean Baptiste, E-99, 126
Dumas, Louis, E-126
Dumas, Pierre, E-99, 117, 126
Dumay, Roze, E-176
Dumenil, Marguerite, E-262
Dumenil, Marie Francoise, E-11, 109
DuMesnil, Francois Robert, E-126
DuMesnil, Marie Marguerite, E-126
Dumesnil, Michel Denis Francois de Salles Gouillou, E-158
Dumeynieu, Anne, E-128, 389
Dumon, Marie, C-52
Dumoncel, Victoire, E-345
Dumond, Vincent, S3-932
Dumonsel, Jacques, E-126
Dumont, -----, S3-920
Dumont, Anne, E-126, 291
Dumont, Anne, F-63
Dumont, Anne, S1-307-308
Dumont, Anne, S2-438-440
Dumont, Anne, S3-937, 1030
Dumont, Christophe, E-126, 157
Dumont, Christophe Alexis, E-29, 126, 157
Dumont, Gilles, E-624
Dumont, Helene, C-70, 96
Dumont, Helene, F-7
Dumont, Helene, N-126-127
Dumont, Helene, S1-308
Dumont, Helene, S2-436, 440, 586-587
Dumont, Helene, S3-1038
Dumont, Jean Baptiste, E-126
Dumont, Jean-Baptiste, S1-307
Dumont, Jeanne, S1-264
Dumont, Jeanne Francoise, E-624
Dumont, Joseph, C-70
Dumont, Joseph, E-70, 126-127, 146, 432
Dumont, Joseph, F-7
Dumont, Joseph, S1-307-308

Dumont, Joseph, S2-435, 438, 586

Dumont, Joseph, S3-937-938, 1038

Dumont, Joseph, N-81, 126

Dumont, Marie, E-126

Dumont, Marie, N-80

Dumont, Marie, S1-308

Dumont, Marie, S2-435, 586

Dumont, Marie, S3-937-938

Dumont, Marie Joseph, E-126

Dumont, Marie Madeleine, E-127

Dumont, Marie-Josephe, S1-308

Dumont, Marie-Madeleine, S1-308

Dumont, Mr., E-157

Dumont, Pierre, N-65

Dumont, Pierre, S1-308

Dumont, Servanne, N-65

Dumont, Servanne, S1-264, 309

Dumont, Suzanne, E-127

Dumont, Suzanne, S1-308

Dumont, Vincent, S2-503

Dumouard, Jeanne, E-120

Dumoulain, Mathurin, E-299

Dumoulain, Mathurine, E-262

Dumoulin, Michelle, E-105

Dumoulin, Mr., E-117

Dumovard, Jeanne, E-303

Dunas, Jean, E-140, 352

Duperret, Mr., E-302

Duperron, -----, S3-975

Dupeux, Philippe, E-127

Dupeux, Pierre, E-66, 127

Dupin, Gabriel, E-105, 256

Dupleix, Claude, E-26, 127

Dupleix, Silvain, E-26, 127

Duplessis, Adelaide Anastasie, E-127

Duplessis, Anastasie, E-295

Duplessis, Anastasie, S1-52, 351

Duplessis, Anastasie, S2-581-582

Duplessis, Anastasie-Adelaide, S1-256, 311

Duplessis, Claude, S3-1039

Duplessis, Claude Antoine, C-44

Duplessis, Claude Antoine, F-19

Duplessis, Claude Antoine, N-69

Duplessis, Claude Antoine, S3-969

Duplessis, Claude-Antoine, S1-256, 310-311, 351-352

Duplessis, Denis Charles, E-174

Duplessis, Denis Charles, E-258

Duplessis, Francois-Marin, S1-311

Duplessis, Marie, E-295

Duplessis, Marie, F-19

Duplessis, Marie, N-69-70

Duplessis, Marie, S1-353

Duplessis, Marie, S2-581, 584

Duplessis, Marie, S2-621

Duplessis, Marie Louise, C-44

Duplessis, Marie-Louise, S1-311, 351

Duplex, Jean, C-93

Dupoey, Jean Baptiste, E-385

Dupon Du Chambon, Jeanne, E-387

Duponceau, Etienne, E-127

Duponceau, Jean Michel, E-127

Dupont, Adelaide, S1-312

Dupont, Anne, E-19, 109, 145

Dupont, Anne Claire, E-303

Dupont, Anne Henriette, E-411

Dupont, Anne-Claire, S2-626

Dupont, Anne-Henriette, S2-729

Dupont, Antoine, E-110

Dupont, Elizabeth, S1-312

Dupont, Emee Charlotte, E-127

Dupont, Emelie, S1-312

Dupont, Felicite, E-353

Dupont, Francois, E-109, 127-128, 132

Dupont, Francois-Pierre, S1-312

Dupont, Francoise, S1-312

Dupont, Genevieve, S1-312

Dupont, Jacques, S2-504

Dupont, Jean, E-16

Dupont, Jean, S1-206, 208, 311-312

Dupont, Jean, S3-953-954, 981

Dupont, Jean Baptiste, E-127

Dupont, Jean Baptiste Ange, E-390

Dupont, Jeanne, E-61, 127

Dupont, Jeanne, S1-312

Dupont, Jeanne-Marie, S1-194

Dupont, Joseph, E-127, 178, 290

Dupont, Louis, E-61, 127, 390

Dupont, Marie, S1-312

Dupont, Michel, E-303, 456

Dupont, Mr., E-128

Dupont, Nicolas, E-128, 376

Dupont, Nicolas Maurice, E-128, 376

Dupont, Perrine, E-128, 132

Dupont, Pierre, S1-312

Dupont, Pierre-Jean, S1-312

Dupont de Duchambon, Jean Baptiste Ange, E-127

Dupont de Renom, Michel, E-127

Dupont De Zenon, Anne-Claire, S1-356

Dupont DeRenon, Anne Claire, E-104, 127, 388

Dupont DeRenon, Charles Leopold, E-104

Dupont Duchambon de Dumaine, Louis, E-66, 127-128

Dupont Duchambon de Dumaine, Mathieu, E-65, 128

Dupont Duvivier, Mr., E-149

Dupont Ecuyer Chevalier du Viviere Devannes, Francois, E-127, 266

Dupont Gourville, Dupont Duvivier, E-128

Dupont Gourville, Michel, E-128, 149

Dupont Seigneur Duvivier, Jean, E-127, 266

Duponte, Rene, E-307

Duportail, Jeanne Thereze, E-78, 101

Dupray, Marie Anne, E-402

Dupre, Marguerite, E-598

Dupre, Philippe, E-161

Dupres, Catherine, S2-722

Dupuch, Jean, E-126, 128, 389

Dupuch, Pierre, E-128, 389

Dupuget, Anne Marie, E-139

Dupuis, Amand Charles, E-128

Dupuis, Amand-Perre, S1-315

Dupuis, Ambroise, C-22

Dupuis, Ambroise, F-89, 91

Dupuis, Ambroise, S1-6, 145, 209, 313-315

INDEX SOURCES   C=Chatellerault; E=Acadians in Exile;   F=Acadian Families;   N=Nantes; S=St-Malo

Dupuis, Ambroise, S3-875-876, 885, 895, 921-922, 1102
Dupuis, Angelique, E-134, 404
Dupuis, Anne, C-11-12, 155, 166
Dupuis, Anne, E-53-54, 111, 163, 359
Dupuis, Anne, F-79, 81
Dupuis, Anne, N-14
Dupuis, Anne, S1-62-66, 70, 313, 365
Dupuis, Anne, S3-823, 827, 888, 1120
Dupuis, Anne Marie, C-4, 68
Dupuis, Anne Marie, F-13, 89
Dupuis, Anne Marthe, E-182, 188, 280, 284, 305, 390, 413, 608, 610-611, 613-614
Dupuis, Anne-Marie, S1-5, 10, 25
Dupuis, Anne-Marie, S2-571
Dupuis, Antoine, E-41, 128-130, 525
Dupuis, Augustin, S1-313
Dupuis, boy, S1-314
Dupuis, Cecile, F-23
Dupuis, Cecile, N-114-115
Dupuis, Cecile, S2-562-563, 567, 569, 733
Dupuis, Cecile, S3-1025
Dupuis, Charles, C-38
Dupuis, Charles, E-128-129, 370
Dupuis, Charles, F-27
Dupuis, Charles, N-4, 44, 66, 209, 221
Dupuis, Charles, S1-234, 315-317
Dupuis, Charles, S2-563, 707
Dupuis, Charles, S3-894, 898
Dupuis, Delle Jerome, E-182
Dupuis, Dupuy, E-129
Dupuis, Elizabeth, C-40
Dupuis, Elizabeth, N-5, 67
Dupuis, Elizabeth, S1-71, 313-314
Dupuis, Elizabeth Marie Therese, E-128
Dupuis, Ephigenie, E-128
Dupuis, Etienne, E-128-129
Dupuis, Etienne, F-27, 29

Dupuis, Etienne, N-63, 66, 209, 221
Dupuis, Etienne, S1-243, 315-316
Dupuis, Etienne, S3-898
Dupuis, Euphrosine, E-129, 186, 189
Dupuis, Fabien, E-129
Dupuis, Felix, E-129
Dupuis, Firmes, E-129
Dupuis, Francois, E-129
Dupuis, Francois Soline, E-129
Dupuis, Francoise, E-96, 395
Dupuis, Francoise-Genevieve, S1-313
Dupuis, Frosine, E-129, 187, 439
Dupuis, Germain, E-128-130, 283, 332, 608, 610, 613
Dupuis, Hiacinte, E-160
Dupuis, Hiacinte Anne, E-160, 268
Dupuis, Isabelle, F-17, 25
Dupuis, Isabelle, S1-145
Dupuis, Jacques Guillaume, E-129
Dupuis, Jean, E-40, 129, 380, 480, 525
Dupuis, Jean Baptiste, E-128-129, 165
Dupuis, Jean Marie, E-196
Dupuis, Jean Marie Germain, E-129, 608, 610, 613
Dupuis, Jean-Baptiste, S1-313-314
Dupuis, Jean-Charles, S1-315
Dupuis, Jean-Simon-Raphael, S1-314
Dupuis, Joseph, C-39-40, 141
Dupuis, Joseph, E-129
Dupuis, Joseph, F-17, 25
Dupuis, Joseph, N-66-67, 209, 221, 234
Dupuis, Joseph, S1-103, 154, 243, 247, 316-317
Dupuis, Joseph, S2-532, 563
Dupuis, Joseph, S3-894, 897-898
Dupuis, Laurent-Charles, S1-315
Dupuis, Louise, E-264

Dupuis, Madeleine, E-129
Dupuis, Madeleine, N-44, 89, 234
Dupuis, Madeleine, S1-103, 234-235, 315, 317
Dupuis, Madeleine, S2-550, 563, 707
Dupuis, Magdelaine, F-21, 27
Dupuis, Magdelaine, S3-875
Dupuis, Marguerite, C-158
Dupuis, Marguerite, E-43, 129, 560
Dupuis, Marguerite, F-27, 49, 91, 95
Dupuis, Marguerite, N-4, 7, 221, 243
Dupuis, Marguerite, S1-30-31, 33, 145, 195, 234-235, 244, 313-317
Dupuis, Marguerite, S2-553, 569
Dupuis, Marguerite-Marie, S1-315
Dupuis, Margueritte, S3-1152
Dupuis, Marie, C-22, 89
Dupuis, Marie, E-149, 153, 283, 286, 322, 395, 480, 554, 560, 565
Dupuis, Marie, F-89
Dupuis, Marie, N-7, 31, 66
Dupuis, Marie, S1-145-146, 211, 313
Dupuis, Marie, S3-895, 1020
Dupuis, Marie Anne, E-129
Dupuis, Marie Elisabeth Therese, E-608, 610, 613
Dupuis, Marie Francoise, E-160
Dupuis, Marie Josephe, E-129, 273, 280, 284, 415, 561, 569, 608, 613
Dupuis, Marie Josephe, N-86
Dupuis, Marie Josephe Esther, E-129, 608, 613
Dupuis, Marie Josephine, E-610
Dupuis, Marie Josephine Esther, E-610
Dupuis, Marie Madeleine, N-66
Dupuis, Marie Marguerite, E-130, 608, 610, 613
Dupuis, Marie Theotiste, E-608, 610, 613

Dupuis, Marie-Anne-Claire, S1-315

Dupuis, Marie-Josephe, S2-449-450, 562, 565

Dupuis, Martin, E-480

Dupuis, Martin, N-114

Dupuis, Martin, S1-10, 30, 70

Dupuis, Mary, E-114

Dupuis, Michel, E-129, 473

Dupuis, Michelle, E-129

Dupuis, Mr., E-186

Dupuis, Paul, E-130

Dupuis, Pierre, E-130, 172, 480

Dupuis, Pierre-Ambroise, S1-314

Dupuis, Pierre-Joseph, S1-316

Dupuis, Sieurs, C-149

Dupuis, Silvain Victor, E-18, 180

Dupuis, Simon, E-129-130, 287

Dupuis, Theotiste Marie, E-130

Durand, Anne, E-344

Durand, Baptiste, E-130

Durand, Barthelemy, E-131

Durand, Bertrand, S1-222

Durand, Catherine, E-153, 293

Durand, Charles Amable, E-130-131

Durand, Daniel, E-130

Durand, Daniel Simon, E-130

Durand, Elisabeth, E-18, 130, 180, 266, 370

Durand, Etienne, E-130

Durand, Francois, E-21, 130-131, 172

Durand, Francoise, E-68, 97, 130, 354

Durand, Francoise, F-55

Durand, Francoise, N-160, 216

Durand, Francoise, S1-60-61

Durand, Francoise, S2-757

Durand, Henriette, E-329

Durand, Jacques, E-73, 131, 386

Durand, Jean, E-36, 130-131, 135, 195, 259, 352

Durand, Jean Baptiste, E-130-131

Durand, Jeanne, E-68, 131, 379, 387, 393

Durand, Jeanne Therese, E-130-131

Durand, Joseph, S3-825

Durand, Julienne, C-28

Durand, Julienne, F-71

Durand, Julienne, S1-221-222

Durand, Julienne, S3-824

Durand, Laurent, E-130, 194

Durand, Leonard, E-131

Durand, Louise, E-127, 131, 155, 344

Durand, Louise, S1-221

Durand, Louise Francoise, E-66, 131

Durand, Magdeleine, E-130, 131, 137, 255, 314, 378

Durand, Marguerite, E-131, 294, 353

Durand, Marie, E-51, 60, 72, 149, 344, 378, 386

Durand, Marie Anne, E-131

Durand, Marie Marguerite, E-131

Durand, Marie Rosalie, E-131

Durand, Marie Suzanne, E-131

Durand, Martin, E-131

Durand, Mathieu, E-320

Durand, Michel, S1-317

Durand, Nicolas, S1-317

Durand, Pierre, E-17, 30, 68, 90, 130-131, 317

Durand, Pierre Joseph, E-131

Durand, Rene, E-442

Durand, Renee, E-120

Durand, Sebastien, E-130, 266

Durand, Suzanne, E-73, 131, 386

Durant, Francois, S2-585

Durantois, Francoise, E-624

Duranton, Francois, E-126

Durel, Anne, E-356

Durel, Anne Marie, E-131, 355

Durel, Charles, E-79, 131-132

Durel, Charlotte Anne, E-132

Durel, Judith, E-94, 132, 371

Durel, Judith, N-196

Durel, Julianne, E-276

Durel, Marguerite, E-132, 379, 413

Durel, Marianne, F-63

Durel, Marie, E-293

Durel, Marie Elizabet, E-132

Durel, Marie Jeanne, E-379

Durel, Marie Judith, F-81

Durel, Marie Judith, N-45-46

Durel, Pierre, E-79, 132

Durelle, Marie Judique, E-93

Dureste, Bechec, E-4

Duret, Arnaud, S2-782

Duret, Arnaut, S3-923

Durget, Etiennette, E-255

Durier, Anne Elizabeth, E-132

Durier, Francois, E-132

Durier, Guillaume, E-132

Durier, J.J., E-132, 144

Durier, Jean, E-44, 115, 132, 159

Durier, Jeanne, E-132

Durier, Marianne Elizabeth, E-132

Durier, Michel, E-132

Durier, Rene, E-132

Durieux, Pierre Joseph, E-409

Duroche, Francois, S2-513

Durocher, Francois, E-132, 255, 291

Durocher, Joseph, E-132

Duronlois, Julie, E-618

Duronlois, Lucie, E-618

Durouca, Martin, E-128, 132

Durouca, Pierre, E-128, 132

Dusale, Jean Laurent, E-18, 180

Duslautes, Sebois, S3-1115

Dusseau, Suzanne, E-30-31, 268

Dusseaut, Marguerite, E-121, 161

Dutailler, -----, S3-832

Dutailles, Sebois, S3-851

Dutel, Angelique, S2-591

Duthe, Cerise, E-344

Duthe, Jean Francois Cerise, E-86

Dutour, Antoinette, E-405

Dutraque, Jean Baptiste, E-132, 267

Dutrieu, Etienne, E-133

Dutrieu, Jean, E-66, 133, 438

Dutrieu, Jean Joseph, E-133

Dutrieu, Marie Agathe, E-133

Dutrieu, Marie Martine, E-133

Duuinier, Jean Baptiste, E-103

Duval, Anne, C-82, 95

Duval, Anne, E-133, 355

Duval, Anne, F-71

Duval, Anne, S1-263, 319
Duval, Anne, S2-546
Duval, Anne, S3-1028
Duval, Anne Marie, E-371
Duval, Charles, C-82
Duval, Charles, E-133, 355
Duval, Charles, F-71
Duval, Claude, S1-318
Duval, Francois, S1-318
Duval, Francoise-Jeanne-Marie, S1-318
Duval, Guillaume, S3-1028
Duval, Jacques, C-36
Duval, Jacques, E-115
Duval, Jean Baltazard, E-358
Duval, Jean Pierre, E-133
Duval, Jeanne, S2-719
Duval, Jeanne-Francoise, S1-318
Duval, Judith, E-355
Duval, Julien, S1-318
Duval, Laurent, S1-260
Duval, Louis, S1-318
Duval, Louise Charlotte, E-133
Duval, Marguerite, E-133
Duval, Marie Elisabeth, E-17, 159
Duval, Marie Madeleine, E-142, 148
Duval, Marie-Josephe, S2-611
Duval, Mr., E-195
Duval, Pierre, E-133
Duval, Samson, S1-263, 319
Duval, Samson, S3-986, 1028
Duval, Sanson, S2-592
Duval, Thomas, S1-318
Duvault, Jean, C-40, 48
Duvault, Pierre, C-40, 113
Duver, Christophe, E-25, 265
Duver, Martial, E-265
Duverger, Anne Angelique, E-418, 428
DuVerges, Catherine, E-102, 319
Duvergier, B., E-375
Duvergier, Elisabeth, E-375
Duvergue, Louis, E-132
Duvier, -----, S3-968
Duvier, Janne, S3-968
Duvier, Jeanne, S1-3
Duvier, Panivace, S1-3

Duvier, Panivace, S3-968
Duvignac, Jan, S3-995
Duvignac, Jean, S2-545
Duvivier, Claude, E-366, 419
Duvivier, Claude, S1-331
Duvivier, Henriette, S1-321
Duvivier, Jacques, E-586, 596
Duvivier, Jacques, S1-320-321
Duvivier, Jacques, S3-1009
Duvivier, Jean, E-133
Duvivier, Jean, S1-321
Duvivier, Jean Baptiste Abel, E-133, 267
Duvivier, Jean-Baptiste, S1-198, 321
Duvivier, Jean-Baptiste-Abel, S1-261
Duvivier, Jean-Baptiste-Habel, S1-319
Duvivier, Jean-Hector, S1-320
Duvivier, Louis, S1-320
Duvivier, Marianne, E-20, 345
Duvivier, Marie, E-267, 335
Duvivier, Marie, S1-261, 321
Duvivier, Marie, S3-915
Duvivier, Marie Anne, C-9
Duvivier, Marie-Anne, S1-320
Duvivier, Marie-Henriette, S1-321
Duvivier, Marie-Madeleine, S1-320
Duvivier, Melle, E-586, 596
Duvivier, Michel, S1-321
Duvivier, Mr., E-386
Duvivier, Mrs., E-403
Duvivier, Pierre, S1-320-321
Duvivier, Theotiste, E-335
Duvivier, Theotiste, S1-320-321
Duvu, Jacque, S3-1009
Duzel, Marie Judith, C-158
Dyon, Jean Baptiste, E-265

E

Eassagnolles, Blaise, E-134
Eassagnolles, Nicolas, E-134
Ecuyer, Jean Delongais, E-134
Edeline, Pierre, S1-81
Edoux, Catherine, E-123
Eiffel, Gustave, E-39
Elicalde, Catherine, E-17, 153

Elie, Charles-Francois, S1-321
Elie, Francois, S1-321
Elie, Francois, S3-991
Elie, Francoise, E-134, 389
Elie, Magdeleine, E-134
Elie, Thomas, S1-321
Elie, Thomas, S3-991
Elier, Pierre, E-326
Eliot, Amand Victor, E-365
Eliot, Victor, E-15, 180
Ellie, Madelene, E-456
Eloy, Damien, N-241
Emeraud, Anne, N-77, 186
Enaisy, Marguerite, E-104, 169
Enegre, Angelique, E-64, 134
Eneo, Pierre, N-198
Enet, Jacque, E-134
Eningre, Francois, E-134
Enjeau, Marie Jeanne, E-134, 394
Eon, Guillaume, S2-691
Eon, J. deLaGlenne, S3-837
Eon, Pierre Jean (Rev.), F-105
Epagnon, Marguerite, E-373
Epergo, Louis, S1-248
Erard, Catherine, E-181, 314
Erault, Marie, S2-777
Erault, Marie, S3-929
Eriassy, Brigitte, E-176
Eriassy, Brigitte, S1-320
Erie, Marguerite, S2-579
Ermange, Marie Jeanne, E-134, 379
Ermange, Pierre, E-134, 379
Ernault, Marie, N-133, 184
Errage, Madeleine, E-26
Escoules, Marie, E-134, 404
Escuyer, Marie, E-134, 377
Eslin, Marguerite, E-138
Esnard, Francois, E-134
Esnard, Jacques, E-385
Esnard, Jean, E-43, 143
Esnard, Jean Charles, E-134
Esnard, Marie, E-107, 135, 153
Espenard, Jean Baptiste, S3-952
Espiau de Le Mestre, Jean Francois, C-71
Essagnolles, Blaise, E-404
Essagnolles, Nicolas, E-404
Estelle, Modeste LeBlanc, E-610

Estere, Marie, E-347
Estevin, Alexandre, E-174, 265
Estier, Marie, E-135
Estournel, Marie Anne, E-197
Etcheverry, Antoine, E-135
Etcheverry, Cecile, E-135
Etcheverry, Francois, E-135
Etcheverry, Genevieve, E-135
Etcheverry, Isabelle, E-135
Etcheverry, Jean Baptiste, E-135
Etcheverry, Jean Pierre, E-135
Etcheverry, Joseph, E-135
Etcheverry, Louise, E-135
Etcheverry, Louise Francoise
  Marie, E-135
Etcheverry, Marguerite, E-135
Etcheverry, Marguerite Gene-
  vieve, E-135
Etcheverry, Marie Melanie, E-
  135
Etcheverry, Martin, E-135
Etcheverry, Pierre, E-135
Etertes, Fs., S3-856
Etesse, -----, S3-958
Etesse, Thomas, S3-957
Etienne, D., S3-835
Etienne, Jean, E-338
Etier, Marie, E-280, 318
Etier, Pierre, E-11, 27, 29, 65,
  68, 77, 100, 125, 135, 140-142,
  280, 300, 337, 373, 377, 385,
  391, 393, 430
Etoille, Belle, S3-1073
Etoille, Charles Belle, S3-1073
Euse, Jacques, C-150
Evain, Joseph, E-53
Evain, Marguerite, E-108
Evegnier, George, E-32
Eveillard, Catherine, E-27
Even, Nicolas Mathurin, S3-829
Evrard, Alexandre, E-136
Evrard, Jean, E-136
Extra, Eleonore, E-138, 266
Eymar, Louise, E-136, 382
Eymard, Charles, E-136
Eymard, Claude, E-136, 382
Eymard, Jean Baptiste Julien, E-
  136
Eymard, Jeanne Marie Felicite,
  E-136
Eymard, Joseph Marius, E-136

Eymard, Julien, E-136, 382
Eymard, Louis Joseph Julien, E-
  136
Eymard, Louise Adelaide Julienne, E-136

F

Fabre, Jacques, E-586, 591
Fabre, Marguerite, N-67, 152,
  192
Fabre, Roch, N-67, 152, 192
Fabreau, Jean, E-119
Fabry, Andre, E-385
Facau, Jeanne Francoise, E-388
Facquet, Jean, E-137
Faillafais, Jean, E-137
Faillafais, Suzanne, E-137
Faillofais, Adelaide, E-191
Faillofais, Joseph, E-191
Faillofais, Mr., E-191
Faillofais, Suzanne, E-190, 191
Faillofais, Suzanne Francoise,
  E-183, 191
Faillofaix, Jean, E-190
Falaise, Margueritte de, E-107
Falavel, Elizabeth, E-266
Faligaud, Louis, E-137, 319,
  408
Famcerneau, Anne, E-93
Fanereaux, Anne, E-41
Faquet, Jacques, E-137, 149
Faquet, Suzane, E-28
Farais, Magdelaine, S3-993
Faraneau, Marguerite, E-143,
  153
Fardel, Anne, E-498
Fardel, Bernard, E-498
Fardel, Jean, E-474, 498
Fardel, Louis, E-498
Fardel, Marie, E-498
Fardel, Olivier, E-498
Fardel, Pierre, E-498
Fardet, Angelique, S1-322
Fardet, Francois, S1-322
Fardet, Marie, S1-322
Fardet, Marie-Anne, S1-322
Fardet, Pierre, S1-322
Fardy, Carlos, F-85
Farine, Jean, F-97
Fasneau, Francoise, N-185

Fatre, Catherine, E-440
Faucher, Catherine, E-413, 417
Faucheux, Guillaume, E-137,
  314
Faucheux, Henry, S2-690
Faucheux, Louise Angelique, E-
  16, 137
Faucheux, Marie Louise Ange-
  lique, E-80, 137
Faucheux, Mathurin, E-80, 137,
  314
Faucoeur, Therese, E-121, 140
Faucon, Elisabeth, E-72, 137
Fauconnier, Rene, E-15, 321
Fauillet, Claude, E-314
Faulcon, Claudine, C-105
Faulcon, Fabien, C-40
Faulcon, Marguerite, C-40
Faulcon, Pierre, C-40, 105
Faulcon, Simon (Father), C-107
Fauquet, Jean, E-137
Fauquet, Magdeleine Marguer-
  ite, E-137
Fauquet, Marie, E-137
Fauquet, Marie Magdeleine, E-
  137
Fauquet, Mr., E-189
Fauquet, succession of, E-356
Faur, Marguerite, E-38, 86
Faure, Bernard, E-159
Faure, Jean, E-61
Faure, Pierre, E-61
Faureau, Anne, E-341
Faures, Madeleine, E-114
Faures, Marguerite, E-354
Faurest, Marie, E-364
Faurne, Antoine, E-358
Fautoux, Georges, E-137, 278
Fautoux, Leon, E-137, 278
Fauvel, Marie Blanche, E-144
Fauze, Pierre, E-350
Faveraux, Anne, S1-255
Favereau, Jean, E-431
Faverole, Pierre, S3-1066
Faverolle, -----, S3-1066
Faverot, Marie Anne, E-14, 350
Favier, Jean, C-vii
Favre, Guillaume, E-123, 137
Favre, Jacques, C-106
Favre, Jean, E-11, 137, 141, 393
Favre, Renee, C-13, 103

Favreau, Mr., E-302
Fayet, Angelique, E-73
Fechant, Marie Rose, E-138
Feillet, Joachim, S1-58
Felgere, Anne Marie, E-138
Felgere, Marie Anastasie, E-138
Felgere, Marie Anne, E-138
Felgere, Pierre, E-138, 273
Fely, Marie, E-138, 389
Fenelon, Francois, E-138, 384
Feniou, Jean, E-90, 156
Fequant, Jeanne, S1-84-85
Fequant, Jeanne, S2-515
Ferand, Gerand, E-166
Feraud, Anne Eulalie, E-138
Feraud, Joseph, E-138, 288
Feraud, Joseph Marin, E-138
Feraud, Thomas, E-138
Feraud, Yves Claude, E-138
Ferdinand, Louis Antoine, N-99, 249
Fere, Jean, S2-485
Fereroll, Antoine, E-358
Feriac, Guillaumette, E-353, 381
Ferie, Francois, E-138, 266
Fermall, Aimee, E-299
Fermane, Claude Eti, E-586, 597
Fermane, Elisabeth, E-586, 597
Fernandez, Marie, C-166
Ferouin, Nicolas, E-138, 441
Ferrand, Charles, E-389
Ferrand, Francois, E-15, 22
Ferrand, Jean, E-121
Ferre, Renee, C-81
Ferrec, Nicole, E-110, 411
Ferret, Benoit, E-138, 261
Ferret, Denis, S1-322
Ferret, Jean Marie, E-4, 6
Ferret, Jean-Baptiste, S1-323
Ferret, Louis, E-4, 6, 586, 591
Ferret, Louis, S1-322-323
Ferret, Louis, S3-953-954
Ferret, Louise-Francoise, S1-323
Ferret, Marguerite, E-173
Ferret, Marie Charlotte, E-138
Ferret, Marie Jeanne, E-4, 6
Ferret, Marie Magdeleine, E-81, 138
Ferret, Marie-Julien, S1-323
Ferret, Perine Louise, E-6

Ferret, Perinne, S1-323
Ferret, Perrine, E-586, 591
Ferriere, Francois, E-97
Ferroc, Barbe Anne, E-279, 284
Ferrouer, Francois, E-408
Ferry, Francois, E-138
Ferry, Jean Francois, E-138, 415
Ferte, Jeanne, S1-364
Ferte, Marie Francoise, E-20, 138
Feru, Magdeleine, E-338
Fessie, Marie, S2-548
Feste, Marie Anne, S3-976
Feste, Marie-Anne, S2-751
Fetiveau, Charles, E-83, 140
Feuche, Marie, E-81, 405
Feuillier, Baudy de , C-133
Feuilloley, Charles, E-363
Feurge, Jean, C-102, 104, 122, 135
Fevre, Anne, E-139, 284
Fevrier, Flavier, S1-6
Fevrier, Gabriel, E-13, 369
Fevrier, Marie, E-616
Fieffe, Charles, E-103
Fievre, Charles, E-379
Fillaut, Marie, E-256, 406
Filleau, Jeanne, E-27, 139
Fillemin, Anne, E-128, 376
Fillet, -----, S3-923
Filleul, Francoise, S2-685
Fillioux, Jean, E-332
Fillon, Antoinette, E-332, 346
Fillon, Jacques, E-326
Fillon, Jean, E-326
Fillon, Marie, E-125, 139, 325
Fillonneau, Jacques, E-45
Filloux, Marie, E-256, 406
Fiquet, Claude Antoine, E-624
Fiquet, Julie, E-624
Fissadane, Jean-Baptiste, S2-580
Fitel, Jean, E-44
Fittaud, Marie, E-169, 172
Fix, Anne Perrine, E-139
Fizel, Anne, E-139, 387
Fizel, Barbe Louise, E-139
Fizel, Jean Francois, E-139
Fizel, Jean Louis, E-139
Fizel, Julien, E-139, 387

Fizel, Marie Jeanne Marguerite, E-139
Fizel, Marie Madeleine Marguerite, E-139
Fizel, Nicolas, E-139
Fizel, Nicolas Francois, E-139
Flabron, Pierre, E-161
Flamand, Luxe, E-26
Flamerie De Marquisant, Antoine, E-139
Flamerie de Marquisant, Pierre Francois, E-139
Flamond, Marguerite, E-173
Flatron, Pierre, E-139
Flaud, Charlotte, S1-107, 177
Flaud, Charlotte, S2-735
Flaud, Charlotte, S3-849
Flaud, Charlotte-Laurence, S2-535
Flaud, Jean, S1-177
Flaud, Julien, S2-535
Flaud, Julien, S3-849
Flaud, Malo, S1-130
Flaute, Etienne, S3-1019
Flaverie de Marquisant, Pierre Francoise, E-187
Fleau, Pierre, S3-1150
Fleche, Marie-Jeanne, S1-231
Fleuranceau, Jeanne, E-131
Fleuri, Georges, S3-1089
Fleuri, Guillaume, S2-610
Fleuri, Guillaume, S3-1089
Fleuri, Marie, S2-610
Fleuri, Marie, S3-1089
Fleuri, Olive, S1-59
Fleuri, Olive, S3-1089
Fleuri, Paul Jean, S3-968
Fleurisson, Pierre, E-22
Fleury, Elisabeth, E-33
Fleury, Jeanne, E-300
Fleury, Olive, E-618
Fleury, Thomas-Claude, S2-438
Fleury, Vincent, S1-323
Follet, Charles, E-77, 139
Follet, Jean, E-77, 139
Fonberteau, Antoine, E-358
Fondemont, Jean, E-36
Fonrobert, Gabriel, E-86
Fonrobin, Gabriel, E-12
Fontaignier, Henry, E-65, 140

Fontaignier, Raymond, E-65, 140

Fontaillon, Jacques Benoit, E-45, 145

Fontaine, Anglebert Joseph, E-12

Fontaine, Jeanne Marie, E-344

Fontaine, Marie Jeanne, E-139, 344, 405

Fontaine, Pierre, E-140, 381

Fontaine, Pierre Jean, E-140

Fontarine, Pascal, E-95

Fontarive, Etienne, E-289

Fonteau, Marie Francoise, E-96

Fontenelle, Etienne, E-29

Fontenelle, Mr., E-128

Fontenier, -----, S3-1048

Foque, Jeanne Marie, E-188, 376

Fore, Marguerite, E-140

Forest, Alexandre, E-552

Forest, Amand-Olivier, S1-329

Forest, Anastase, E-140

Forest, Anne, F-91

Forest, Anne, S1-24, 273, 325

Forest, Anne, S2-577

Forest, Anne, S3-944

Forest, Anne Perrine, F-91

Forest, Anne-Marie, S1-327

Forest, Anne-Perinne, S1-329, 331

Forest, Anne-Rosalie, S1-324

Forest, Anne-Rosalie, S2-576

Forest, Benjamin, N-68

Forest, Benjamin, S1-325-326

Forest, Brigitte, E-554

Forest, Brigitte, S1-58-59

Forest, Brigitte, S3-923

Forest, Elizabeth, N-68

Forest, Elizabeth, S1-43

Forest, Elizabeth, S1-43

Forest, Elizabeth, S3-1101

Forest, Elizabeth Marie, S1-325

Forest, Elizabeth-Marie, S1-325

Forest, Etienne, E-618

Forest, Etienne, F-91

Forest, Etienne, S1-326-327, 347

Forest, Etienne Gilles, F-91

Forest, Etienne-Gilles, S1-330-331

Forest, Francois, E-618

Forest, Francois, S1-330

Forest, Francois-Jean, S1-327

Forest, Francoise, E-618

Forest, Gabrielle, S2-602

Forest, Germain, E-140

Forest, Ignace, E-618

Forest, Ignace, S1-324-325

Forest, Ignace, S3-1099

Forest, Jacques, C-11

Forest, Jacques, E-552

Forest, Jacques, F-81, 91

Forest, Jacques, N-68

Forest, Jacques, S1-14, 43, 63-64, 244, 324, 325-329, 382

Forest, Jacques, S2-576, 600

Forest, Jacques, S3-888, 1004, 1024, 1099-1101

Forest, Jean, E-525, 552, 618

Forest, Jean, F-91

Forest, Jean, S1-326, 331

Forest, Jean-Baptiste, S1-327

Forest, Jean-Baptiste-Francois, S1-328

Forest, Jean-Jacques, S1-330

Forest, Jean-Joachim, S1-327

Forest, Jeanne, E-618

Forest, Jeanne Isabelle, F-91

Forest, Jeanne-Elizabeth, S1-330

Forest, Jeanne-Isabelle, S1-331

Forest, Joseph, E-140, 552

Forest, Joseph, S1-64

Forest, Joseph Victor, F-91

Forest, Joseph-Victor, S1-328, 331

Forest, Josephe, S1-327

Forest, Judith, E-360

Forest, Julien, E-122

Forest, Louise Francoise, E-618

Forest, Madeleine, C-11

Forest, Madeleine, E-113-114, 580

Forest, Madeleine, N-13-14

Forest, Madeleine, S1-63-64, 77, 79-80, 324-325, 329

Forest, Madeleine, S2-704, 719

Forest, Madeleine-Josephe, S1-259, 263

Forest, Magdelaine, F-81

Forest, Magdeleine, S3-964, 978

Forest, Magdeleine Joseph, E-102, 267

Forest, Magdeleine Josephe, S3-1004

Forest, Marguerite, C-67

Forest, Marguerite, F-31

Forest, Marguerite, N-48, 68, 105, 212, 231

Forest, Marguerite, S2-561

Forest, Marguerite-Genevieve, S1-326

Forest, Marguerite-Theodose, S1-326-327

Forest, Margueritte, E-552

Forest, Marie, E-171, 624

Forest, Marie, F-91

Forest, Marie, N-68

Forest, Marie, S1-14, 63, 325-326, 329

Forest, Marie, S2-528, 576

Forest, Marie , S3-1100

Forest, Marie Adelaide, F-91

Forest, Marie Lucie, E-618

Forest, Marie-Adelaide, S1-330-331

Forest, Marie-Josephe, S1-327

Forest, Michel, E-525

Forest, Michel, S1-58, 324

Forest, Olivier Leblanc, S1-326-327

Forest, Paul, E-140

Forest, Pierre, E-95, 525

Forest, Pierre, F-39, 91

Forest, Pierre, N-68

Forest, Pierre, S1-14, 63, 324, 327-328, 330, 377

Forest, Pierre, S2-465, 576, 708

Forest, Pierre, S3-923, 966, 1013, 1101

Forest, Pierre-Guillaume, S1-329

Forest, Pierre-joseph, S1-327

Forest, Pierre-Nicolas, S1-325

Forest, Rene, E-525

Forest, Servanne Julienne, F-91

Forest, Servanne-Julienne, S1-330-331

Forest, Victor, E-624

Forest, Victor, F-91

Forest, Victor, S1-46, 324, 328-331

Forest, Victor, S2-708
Forest, Victor, S3-926, 1099
Forest, Rene - Village named
    after Rene Forest, E-214
Foresterie, Joseph, E-368
Forestier, Anne, E-140, 413
Forestier, Jaques, E-20
Forestier, Pierre, E-146
Foretier, Jean, E-26
Forget, Jacques, E-316
Forget, Marie, C-158
Forinet, Elizabeth, E-586, 595
Forquet, Charle, E-110
Forrestier, Pierre, E-348
Forsyth, Hewitt L. (Mrs.), C-vii-
    viii
Forterie, Joseph, E-79
Fortin, Guillaume, S3-914
Fortin, Lambert, E-90
Fossaume, Charles, E-411
Fouace, Marie, S1-17
Fouasse, Nobleman Pierre, S1-
    357
Foubert, Charles, E-59, 140,
    326, 404
Foubert, Francois, E-140, 404
Foubert, Pierre, E-140
Foucaud, Charles, E-121, 140,
    265
Foucaud, Elisabeth, E-149, 153
Foucaud, Francois, E-140
Foucaud, Jacques, E-140
Foucaud, Jean, E-51, 140
Foucaud, Marie, E-99, 140, 352
Foucaud, Mr., E-258
Foucaud, Pierre, E-83, 140
Foucaux, Jeanne, E-476
Fouchard, Marie Josephe, E-140
Fouche, Francoise, S2-668
Foucher, Andre, E-159, 316
Foucher, Antoine, E-275
Foucher, Catherine, E-264
Foucher, Marie, E-122, 146, 264
Foucher, Marie Anne, E-140,
    177
Foucher, Marie Perette, E-140
Fouchet, Louis, C-viii
Foucheux, Mathurin, E-405
Fouere, Jeanne, E-289
Fougeraud, Andre, N-68, 190
Fougeraud, Jean, N-48, 68, 190

Fougerey, P., S3-968
Fouginet, Etienne, F-29
Fouquet, -----, S1-280
Fouquet, Anne, E-32, 141, 367
Fouquet, Anne, S1-332
Fouquet, Aubin, E-306
Fouquet, Aubin, S2-598
Fouquet, Charle, S3-973
Fouquet, Charles, E-141, 367
Fouquet, Charles, S1-331-332
Fouquet, Charles, S2-737
Fouquet, Charlotte, F-65
Fouquet, Elizabeth, S1-332
Fouquet, Francoise, S1-332
Fouquet, Jan, S3-964, 972-973
Fouquet, Jean, E-26, 141, 194,
    404
Fouquet, Jean, F-65, 81
Fouquet, Jean Aubin, E-141,
    293
Fouquet, Jean Martin, E-141
Fouquet, Jean-Aubin, S1-331-
    332
Fouquet, Jean-Aubin, S2-580
Fouquet, Jean-Baptiste, S1-331
Fouquet, Jean-Martin, S1-332
Fouquet, Jeanne Magdelaine, F-
    81
Fouquet, Louis, E-55, 79, 108,
    141, 263
Fouquet, Louis, S1-201, 331-
    332
Fouquet, Marie, E-12, 23, 143,
    178, 263
Fouquet, Marie, S1-241, 332
Fouquet, Marie, S2-664, 737-
    739, 742
Fouquet, Marie, S3-973
Fouquet, Marie Charlotte, F-81
Fouquet, Marie Judith, E-141
Fouquet, Marie-Francoise, S1-
    332
Fouquet, Marie-Judith, S1-332
Fouquet, Martin, S1-332
Fouquet, Mr., E-119
Fouquet, Pierre, E-96
Fouquet, Pierre, S1-241
Fouquet, Simon, S1-332
Fournie, Marie, E-292
Fournier, Genevieve, E-192
Fournier, Jacques, E-141, 327

Fournier, Josephe, E-40
Fournier, Marie Anne, E-258
Fournier, Marie Louise, E-258
Fournier, Pierre, E-586, 594
Fournier, Thomas, E-28, 180
Fouron, Anastasie, E-100, 141
Fouron, Jean, E-141, 280
Fourquin, Jean Baptiste, E-385
Fourre, Marie, E-372
Fourtin, Louis, E-382
Fourtoune, Catherine, S1-353
Fourtoune, Catherinne, S3-1005
Foyer, Francois, S1-230
Foyer, Francois, S3-1079
Foyer, Perinne, S2-485
Foyer, Perinne Heleine, S3-1079
Foyer, Perinne-Heleine, S1-230
Fradin, Daniel, E-141
Fradin, Marguerite Petronille, C-
    61
Fradin, Marie, E-270, 346
Fragneau, Jean, E-172
Fragneau, Marie Anne, E-19,
    172
Fragneau, Pierre, E-78, 157, 376
Fraiche, Jacques, E-141
Fraiche, Joseph, E-141
Fraiche, Marie Jeanne, E-141
Fraigneau, Francois, E-142, 256
Fraigneau, Jean, E-142, 149
Framery, Jean Baptiste, E-142,
    148
Framery, Jean Joseph, E-148
Framery, Jean Josephe, E-142
Francheteau, Catherine, E-70,
    391
Francois, Charle, E-132
Francois, Jacques, E-149
Francois, Jean, E-102, 142
Francois, Louis, E-115
Francois, Marie, E-77
Francois, Michel Jean, E-12
Francois, Mr., E-128
Francois, Poirier, E-142
Francois Joseph, indian, E-142
Frapie, Francois, C-51
Frapie, Francois, E-177
Frapie, Francois, S2-431
Frederic, Jean, E-1
Fregnico, Marie, E-142
Frelot, Jean, E-142, 349

Fremin, Armand Michel, N-68
Fremin, Armand Philippe, N-68
Frenchet, Nicolas, E-315
Frenel, Marie, S1-37
Frere, Marie, E-376
Fressier, Marie, E-624
Fretel, Francois, E-142
Fretel, Francoise, E-142
Fretel, Julien, E-142
Fricourt, Joseph, E-142-143
Fricourt, Marie Rose, E-143
Fricourt, Pierre, E-142-143
Frievahoud, Jean, N-183
Frignaud, Jeannette, E-584, 596
Frigot, Marie, S1-55
Friou, Francois, F-29
Friou, Henri, E-291
Friquant, Louis, E-143
Fromantin, Elie, E-38, 143, 153
Fromantin, Jean, E-143, 153
Froment, Madeleine, E-126, 157
Fromentau, Louis, E-143
Fromentau, Louis Benjamin , E-97, 143
Fromentau, Louis de la Boucherie, E-97
Frotin, Jan, S3-980
Fumet, Jeanne Francoise, E-179, 295
Furet, Angelique, S1-260
Furet, Felicisoime, S2-499
Furet, Jeanne, S2-498
Furget, Jean, C-122
Furget, Leonard, C-122
Furne, Andre, E-143
Furne, Anne, E-143
Furne, Antoine, E-143
Furne, Elizabeth, E-143
Furne, Joseph, E-143
Furne, Pierre, E-143

G

Gabaneau, Jean, E-144, 332
Gabaneau dit Belair, Mathieu, E-144, 332
Gabauda dit Tousac, Jean, E-419
Gabet, Magdelaine, E-144, 381
Gabiau, Gabriele, S3-1150
Gaboil, Jeanne, S1-204

Gaboret, J.J., E-144
Gaboret, Rene, E-144
Gaborieau, Charles, E-332
Gaborieau, Marie, E-102, 142
Gaborit, Marie, E-99, 140
Gaborit, Pierre, E-78
Gabriel, Guillaume, S1-221
Gachinat, Jeanne, E-144, 194
Gachot, Mr., E-52
Gadion, Marie, E-144
Gadiou, Francois, E-35, 144
Gadiou, Rene, E-144
Gadouin, Bertrand, E-21, 131
Gaffe, Anne, E-144
Gaffe, Jean Baptiste, E-144
Gaget, Francois, E-264
Gagnou, Henriette, E-144, 375
Gaignerie, Susanne, E-93
Gaillard, Jacques, E-15, 34, 69, 70, 72, 77, 97, 138, 156, 158, 256, 259, 264, 346, 370, 386
Gaillard, Jeanne, E-91, 357
Gaillard, Marie, E-144, 316
Gaillard, Philippe, S2-595
Gaillard, Philippe, S3-992
Gaillon-Dumesnil, Michel Denis Francois de Salles, E-146
Gainault, Pierre, E-26, 405
Gainerie, Susanne, E-23
Gainne, Marie Magdelaine, E-368, 377
Gairal, Rose, E-122
Galais, Rene, S3-825
Galande, Jean-Baptiste, S2-546
Galant, Marie, E-376
Galerne, Charles Victor, E-604
Galerne, Etienne David, E-603
Galerne, Honore Magloire, E-603
Galerne, Jean Baptiste, E-15, 45, 603-604
Galerne, Marie, E-45
Galerne, Marie Magdelaine, E-603
Galerne, Pierre, E-604
Galet, Anne, E-12
Galet, Francoise, E-86-87
Galet, Guillaume, E-86, 371
Galherme, Charles Victor, E-144
Galherme, Jean, E-192

Galherme, Jean Baptiste, E-144-145
Galherme, Marie, E-145
Galherme, Pierre, E-145
Galien, Bon, E-624
Galien, Bon, F-103
Galien, Francois, E-624
Galien, Francois, F-103
Galien, Francois Julien, E-624
Galien, Francois Julien, F-103
Galien, Julien Francois, F-103
Galien, Louis, E-586, 597
Galien, Marie Francoise, E-624
Galien, Marie Jeanne, F-103
Galin, Louise, E-584
Galisson, Elisabeth, S3-1006
Galisson, Elizabeth, C-70
Galisson, Elizabeth, S2-586
Gallaid, Marie Catherine, E-180, 343
Gallais, Anne, E-275, 346
Gallais, Anne, S1-2
Gallais, Anne, S2-645
Gallais, Charles, E-320
Gallais, Francois, S1-333
Gallais, Francoise, S1-214-216
Gallais, Guillaume, E-78, 346
Gallais, Guillaume, S1-2, 214-215, 333
Gallais, Jean, E-320, 346
Gallais, Jean, S2-645
Galland, Henriette, E-145
Galland, Jean, E-145
Galland, Marie Marguerite, E-145
Galland, Paul, E-291
Galland, Pierre, E-145
Gallet, Anne, E-145
Gallet, Caroline, E-644
Gallet, Charles, E-145-146
Gallet, Francois, E-145
Gallet, Francois, S2-645
Gallet, Francoise, E-145-146
Gallet, Francoise, S2-645
Gallet, Guillaume, E-145-146
Gallet, Guillaume, S2-644-645
Gallet, Jean, E-145
Gallet, Jean Baptiste, E-146
Gallet, Jean Baptiste Francois, E-146
Gallet, Jeanne Jacquette, E-190

Gallet, Louis, E-146
Gallet, Marie, E-146
Gallet, Marie Anne, E-637, 644
Gallet, Marie Louise, E-644
Gallet, Marie Victoire, E-146
Gallet, Pierre, E-146
Gallet, Sophie Virginie, E-146
Gallet, Suzanne, E-38, 395
Galletier, Etienne, F-85
Gallien, Angelique, E-97, 349
Gallien, Francois, E-617
Gallien, Guillaume, E-145, 276, 381
Gallien, Jeanne, E-53, 98
Gallo, Jacques, E-8
Gallon, Pierre, E-29
Galois, Anne, S3-932
Galoudec, Anne, E-145
Galoux, Jeanne, E-327
Galuduy, Marie Magdeleine, E-152
Gandobert, Francois, E-65
Gannat, Jean, E-133
Ganot, Charles, E-109, 145
Ganot, Louis, E-109, 145
Gaquignole, Marie Anne, E-64, 149
Garanger, Jean, E-65
Garat, Jeanne, E-81, 138
Garau, Jeanne, E-53
Garault, Dominique, E-474
Garault, Marie, E-503
Garbelet, Marie, E-81
Garcia, Joseph Louis, F-41
Garcia, Juan, F-41
Garcin, Annie, E-146
Garcin, Honore, E-146, 276
Garcin, Jacques, E-146
Garcin, Marie Anne, E-146
Garconnet, Michel, E-385, 387, 389
Gard, Claude, E-357
Gard, Etienne, E-357
Gardet, Madeleine, S1-213
Gardet, Madeleine, S2-777
Gardien, Ange, E-624
Gardien, Angelique, E-624
Gardien, Etienne Francois, S3-1048
Gardien, Etienne-Francois, S1-333

Gardien, Jeanne, E-624, 618
Gardien, Julien, S1-182, 333
Gardien, Jullien, S3-1048
Gardien, Veuve, S3-1048
Garel, Cecile, C-158
Garelle, Geneveive, E-271
Garet, Guillaume, E-146
Garet, Jean, S3-944
Garnier, -----, N-69
Garnier, Anne, E-264
Garnier, Antoine, N-226
Garnier, Elisa, E-364
Garnier, Francois, E-18
Garnier, Francois, S1-327
Garnier, Francoise, E-197
Garnier, Jaques, E-264
Garnier, Jean, E-45, 146, 264
Garnier, Jean, F-49
Garnier, Jean, N-15-153, 226
Garnier, Jean, S2-532
Garnier, Jeanne, E-51, 410
Garnier, Jeanne Marie, F-49
Garnier, Jeanne Marie, N-153
Garnier, Marie, E-91, 146, 264
Garnier, Marie, N-177
Garnier, Marie Francoise, F-49
Garnier, Marie Francoise, N-153
Garnier, Michel, E-264
Garnier, Perinne, S2-584
Garnier, Pierre, E-146, 348, 394
Garnier, Thomas, E-80, 264
Garriet, Francoise, S2-689
Garriet, Francoise, S3-1069
Garsant, Marie, E-27, 153
Gaspard, Charles, E-146
Gaspard, Francois, E-146
Gaspard, Marie Felicite, E-146
Gasquet, Marguerite, E-100
Gasseau, Elisabeth, E-120, 150
Gasseau, Louis, S1-333-334
Gasseau, Marie-Perinne, S1-333
Gasset, Elizabeth, S1-337
Gatier, Magdalaine Certier, E-128
Gatignolle, Marie, E-64
Gatinant, Francoise, S2-511
Gaubon, Marguerite, E-156
Gaucelain, Anne Perrine, E-147, 291
Gaud, Marie Sophie, E-147
Gaud, Mathieu, E-147

Gaudet, Abraham, E-498, 525
Gaudet, Anastasie Desire, E-637
Gaudet, Anastasie Dorat, E-147
Gaudet, Anne, E-458, 549
Gaudet, Anne, S1-335-337
Gaudet, Anne-Josephe, S1-334
Gaudet, Antoine, E-486, 503
Gaudet, Augustin, E-525
Gaudet, Augustin, S1-335
Gaudet, Bazile, C-116
Gaudet, Bernard, E-214, 498, 525
Gaudet, Bonnaventure, E-599
Gaudet, Catherine, E-1, 55, 58, 117, 186, 438, 632, 639, 642
Gaudet, Catherine, S1-76-77
Gaudet, Cecile, E-552
Gaudet, Charles, E-147-148
Gaudet, Claude, E-498, 525, 552
Gaudet, Denis, E-457, 486
Gaudet, Dominique, E-121, 147-148, 195, 276, 306, 386
Gaudet, Dorat, E-148
Gaudet, Dorothee, E-121
Gaudet, Elisabeth, E-599
Gaudet, Elisabeth Flore Dorothee, E-147, 385
Gaudet, Fele, E-148
Gaudet, Felix, E-86, 147
Gaudet, Francois, E-147, 599
Gaudet, Francois dit Premaire, E-147
Gaudet, Francois Louis, F-71, 107
Gaudet, Francoise, E-457, 475, 495, 497
Gaudet, Francoise, S1-113
Gaudet, Genevieve, S1-336-337
Gaudet, Germain, E-142, 148, 157, 486, 599
Gaudet, Giraud, E-498
Gaudet, Guillaume, E-486
Gaudet, Jacques, E-147
Gaudet, Jean, E-147, 474, 495, 497, 525
Gaudet, Jean, S1-335
Gaudet, Jean Baptiste, E-358
Gaudet, Jean Baptiste Edouard, E-147
Gaudet, Jean Charles, E-147, 195, 276, 306

Gaudet, Jean Julien, E-624
Gaudet, Jean-Baptiste, S1-178, 334
Gaudet, Jean-Baptiste, S2-746
Gaudet, Jeanne, E-497-498, 522, 599
Gaudet, Jeanne, S1-297
Gaudet, Jehan, E-457
Gaudet, Joseph, E-147, 148, 599
Gaudet, Joseph, S1-218, 335-337
Gaudet, Joseph Anne, E-148, 599
Gaudet, Joseph Ignace, F-99
Gaudet, Joseph-Ignace, S1-334-335
Gaudet, Joseph-Ignace, S2-642, 765
Gaudet, Louis, C-41
Gaudet, Louis, F-71, 107
Gaudet, Louis Firmin, E-148
Gaudet, Madeleine, S1-335
Gaudet, Magdalen Genevieve, E-148
Gaudet, Magdelaine, E-498, 526, 552
Gaudet, Magdelaine, F-71, 107
Gaudet, Marguerite, E-43, 148, 552
Gaudet, Marguerite, F-71, 107
Gaudet, Marguerite, S1-334
Gaudet, Margueritte, C-41, 44, 64, 115-116
Gaudet, Marie, C-41, 50-51
Gaudet, Marie, E-61, 93, 96, 112, 142, 148, 177-178, 412, 456, 457, 472, 474, 497-498, 528, 549, 553, 599, 617
Gaudet, Marie, F-5
Gaudet, Marie, S1-8, 10, 218, 336-337, 340
Gaudet, Marie, S2-431, 480
Gaudet, Marie Adelaide, E-148, 195
Gaudet, Marie Anne, E-148
Gaudet, Marie Elisabeth, E-148
Gaudet, Marie Josephe, E-552, 624
Gaudet, Marie Victoire, E-148, 276
Gaudet, Marie-Anne, S1-335

Gaudet, Marie-Blanche, S1-178, 334-335
Gaudet, Marie-Madeleine, S1-334
Gaudet, Marie-Modeste, S1-76
Gaudet, Marie-Rose, S2-746-747
Gaudet, Michel, E-503
Gaudet, Modeste, C-41
Gaudet, Paschalin, E-553
Gaudet, Paul, E-549
Gaudet, Paul, S1-76, 335-337
Gaudet, Paul-Marie, S1-334
Gaudet, Pierre, C-41, 116, 151
Gaudet, Pierre, E-147-148, 474, 486, 498, 525, 549, 552
Gaudet, Pierre, S1-76, 336-337
Gaudet, Prosper, E-148-149
Gaudet, Rosalie, E-57, 435
Gaudet, Rosalie, S1-336-337
Gaudet, Rose, S1-172
Gaudet, Theodoz, E-149
Gaudet Village - named for Denis Gaudet, E-214
Gaudichon, Pierre, E-333
Gaudillon, Marie, E-307, 401
Gaudin, Anne, E-102, 149, 317, 319-320, 489, 500
Gaudin, Antoine, E-320
Gaudin, Gabriel, E-489
Gaudin, Guillaume, E-500
Gaudin, Jean, E-119
Gaudin, Jean Baptiste, E-17
Gaudin, Jeanne, E-33, 149
Gaudin, Joseph, E-149, 153
Gaudin, Laurens, E-474
Gaudin, Louise, E-149
Gaudin, Marguerite, S2-623
Gaudin, Marie, E-318-319, 500
Gaudin, Marie Magdelaine, E-474
Gaudin, Pierre, E-17, 149, 153-154, 336, 489, 500
Gaudin, Sebastien, E-586, 591
Gaudric, Elisabeth, E-53
Gaudrot, Helenne, S3-858
Gaudu, Francoise, S2-448
Gaudu, Guillaume, S2-475
Gaugeau, Pierre, E-121, 149, 159
Gaumain, Jan, S3-1023

Gaumain, Malo, S3-1082
Gauman, Jean, S3-1023
Gaume, Marie, E-409
Gaurand, Anne, E-64, 149
Gaussin, Pierre, E-36, 61, 131, 143, 152, 370, 404, 413
Gaustie, Marie, S3-1053
Gauthier, Alexandre, E-149, 318
Gauthier, Antoine, E-150
Gauthier, Catherine, E-81, 149, 624
Gauthier, Catherine, S1-204-205, 228, 337, 367
Gauthier, Catherine, S2-723
Gauthier, Catherinne, S3-1053
Gauthier, Charles, E-120
Gauthier, Francoise, E-84
Gauthier, Guillaume, S1-228
Gauthier, Guillaume, S3-1053
Gauthier, Jacquemine, E-618, 621, 623
Gauthier, Jacquemine, S1-337
Gauthier, Jacquemine-Charlotte Francoise, S1-259
Gauthier, Jacquemine-Charlotte Francoise, S3-1073
Gauthier, Jean, E-149, 318, 332
Gauthier, Jean Baptiste, E-81, 149
Gauthier, Jean-Baptiste, S1-204, 337
Gauthier, Joseph, E-149
Gauthier, Madeleine Elizabeth, E-149, 407
Gauthier, Marguerite, E-292
Gauthier, Marie, E-137, 149, 254, 441
Gauthier, Marie, S2-769
Gauthier, Marie Anne, E-21, 52, 149
Gauthier, Marie Charlotte, E-66, 104, 105, 108
Gauthier, Marie Josephe, E-128, 149, 160, 432
Gauthier, Marie Louise, S3-1007
Gauthier, Martine, E-457
Gauthier, Michael, S1-337
Gauthier, Michel, E-120, 150
Gauthier, Mr., E-128

Gauthier, Nicolas, E-128, 149-150, 267

Gauthier, Philippe-Francois, S2-723

Gauthier, Pierre, E-22, 137, 149-150, 267, 379

Gauthier, Renee-Marie-Louise, S1-362

Gauthier, Rose Catherine, E-150

Gauthier, Sebastien, N-219

Gauthier, Simon, E-120, 150

Gauthier, Simon, S1-259, 337-338

Gauthier, Simon, S2-620

Gauthier, Simon, S3-1073

Gauthier, Simon, S3-981

Gauthier, Therese, E-15, 150

Gautron, Marie, E-129

Gautrot, Adelaide, C-44

Gautrot, Adelaide, F-19

Gautrot, Adelaide, N-69-70

Gautrot, Agnes, C-34

Gautrot, Agnes, F-19

Gautrot, Agnes, S1-345-346

Gautrot, Agnes, S2-448

Gautrot, Alexandre, C-42

Gautrot, Alexandre, F-45

Gautrot, Alexandre, S1-338-339, 344

Gautrot, Alexandre, S3-870, 872, 905, 907

Gautrot, Alexis, C-xiv, 41-42, 44, 50-51, 96, 147, 151

Gautrot, Alexis, E-93, 150-152, 178

Gautrot, Alexis, N-69

Gautrot, Alexis, S1-340, 231

Gautrot, Alexis, S2-429, 440

Gautrot, Alexis, S3-1030, 1043

Gautrot, Anastasie Marguerite Marie, E-150

Gautrot, Angelique, F-79, 107

Gautrot, Anne, S2-680

Gautrot, Anne Angelique, N-69

Gautrot, Anne Marie, E-150

Gautrot, Anne-Angelique, S1-347

Gautrot, Aspasie, F-57

Gautrot, Benonnie, S1-343

Gautrot, Catherine, F-93

Gautrot, Catherine, S1-117, 343

Gautrot, Catherine, S2-674, 699, 744

Gautrot, Catherine, S3-1033, 1070, 1078

Gautrot, Catherine-Josephe, S2-693, 701-702

Gautrot, Cecile, C-6, 17, 87, 135

Gautrot, Cecile, F-69

Gautrot, Cecile, S1-108, 347, 351

Gautrot, Cecile, S2-585, 597

Gautrot, Cecile, S3-998, 1039

Gautrot, Charles, C-41, 43

Gautrot, Charles, E-23, 33, 150-152, 287, 298, 306, 331, 420-421, 474, 525, 561

Gautrot, Charles, F-45, 57, 109

Gautrot, Charles, N-119

Gautrot, Charles, S1-340-341, 344

Gautrot, Charles, S2-615

Gautrot, Charles, S3-1118, 1126

Gautrot, Claire, S1-253

Gautrot, Claude, E-474, 525

Gautrot, Claude, N-69

Gautrot, Claude, S1-146, 238

Gautrot, Claude, S2-693

Gautrot, Claude, S3-1010

Gautrot, Etienne, F-45

Gautrot, Etienne, S1-338

Gautrot, Francois, C-43, 110-111, 125-126

Gautrot, Francois, E-457, 474, 480, 525

Gautrot, Francois, F-45

Gautrot, Francois, S1-115, 236, 290, 342

Gautrot, Francois, S2-606

Gautrot, Francois, S3-878, 907, 1128

Gautrot, Francois Marie, E-150

Gautrot, Francois Marie, F-109

Gautrot, Francois-Andre, S1-352

Gautrot, Francois-Hilaire, S1-338-339, 344

Gautrot, Francois-Xavier, S1-342

Gautrot, Francoise, F-55, 57

Gautrot, Francoise, N-169, 246

Gautrot, Francoise, S1-189, 202

Gautrot, Francoise, S3-1040

Gautrot, Gervais, E-150, 302

Gautrot, Guillaume, N-187

Gautrot, Helen, S2-757

Gautrot, Helene, C-75

Gautrot, Helene, F-55

Gautrot, Helene, N-69, 97, 131, 160, 213, 216

Gautrot, Helene, S1-179, 347-348

Gautrot, Helene, S2-621, 760

Gautrot, Helene, S3-837

Gautrot, Helenne, E-585, 591

Gautrot, Henriette-Jacquette, S1-352

Gautrot, Henry Francois, F-45

Gautrot, Henry-Francois, S1-338

Gautrot, Honore, E-151

Gautrot, Honore, F-17

Gautrot, Honore, N-233

Gautrot, Honore, S1-336, 339, 344-346, 350

Gautrot, Honore, S2-447

Gautrot, Honore, S3-878, 1137

Gautrot, Jacques, C-42

Gautrot, Jean, C-7

Gautrot, Jean, F-17, 45, 73

Gautrot, Jean, N-10

Gautrot, Jean, S1-48, 346

Gautrot, Jean, S3-1000

Gautrot, Jean Baptiste, C-42

Gautrot, Jean Baptiste, E-151

Gautrot, Jean Baptiste, F-57

Gautrot, Jean Baptiste, N-69

Gautrot, Jean Baptiste, S3-1010, 1061

Gautrot, Jean Baptiste Simon, E-151

Gautrot, Jean Charles, E-152, 561

Gautrot, Jean Charles Joseph, E-151

Gautrot, Jean Louis Laurent, E-151

Gautrot, Jean Louis Laurent, F-57

Gautrot, Jean Marie, E-151

Gautrot, Jean Marie, F-57

Gautrot, Jean Pierre, C-44

Gautrot, Jean Pierre, E-151

Gautrot, Jean-Alain, S1-339
Gautrot, Jean-Baptiste, S1-49, 342, 346-347
Gautrot, Jean-Baptiste, S2-588
Gautrot, Jean-Charles, S1-341, 345
Gautrot, Jean-Francois, S1-350
Gautrot, Jean-Pierre, S1-352-353
Gautrot, Jeanne, E-526
Gautrot, Joseph, C-43-44, 135
Gautrot, Joseph, E-151
Gautrot, Joseph, F-45, 69
Gautrot, Joseph, N-17, 69
Gautrot, Joseph, S1-152, 328, 346-347
Gautrot, Joseph, S2-462, 575, 656
Gautrot, Joseph, S3-921, 1110, 1126
Gautrot, Joseph Benoist, E-151
Gautrot, Joseph Benoit, F-27
Gautrot, Joseph-Antoine, S1-348
Gautrot, Joseph-Marie, S1-352
Gautrot, Joseph-Marin, S1-349-350
Gautrot, Joseph-Mathurin, S1-339
Gautrot, Joseph-Simon, S1-345-346
Gautrot, Julienne, S1-338-339
Gautrot, Louis, E-151
Gautrot, Louis, N-69
Gautrot, Louis Marie, C-42
Gautrot, Louis Marie, C-xiv
Gautrot, Louis Marie, E-151
Gautrot, Louis-Marie, S1-340
Gautrot, Louis-Modeste, S1-353
Gautrot, Madeleine, C-28, 42
Gautrot, Madeleine, F-39, 55, 57, 61, 63, 83
Gautrot, Madeleine, N-45, 47-48, 68-69, 111-112, 190
Gautrot, Madeleine, S1-18, 48-49, 232, 242, 338
Gautrot, Madeleine, S2-554-555, 754, 766
Gautrot, Madeleine-Rosalie, S1-340
Gautrot, Magdalen, E-151, 274

Gautrot, Magdalen Rosalie, E-151
Gautrot, Magdeleinne, S3-836, 1058
Gautrot, Marguerite, C-24, 28, 42
Gautrot, Marguerite, E-151, 182, 188, 282, 285, 288, 425, 456-458, 473-474, 476, 487, 636
Gautrot, Marguerite, F-19, 39, 47, 61
Gautrot, Marguerite, N-35, 39, 71, 119, 120, 182, 208
Gautrot, Marguerite, S1-167, 253, 340, 348, 365
Gautrot, Marguerite, S2-478, 544, 563, 593, 622
Gautrot, Marguerite, S3-889, 1018
Gautrot, Marguerite Adelaide, C-44
Gautrot, Marguerite Rosalie, F-45
Gautrot, Marguerite-Genevieve, S1-345
Gautrot, Marie, C-27, 42
Gautrot, Marie, E-20, 151, 456, 458, 473, 476, 487, 636
Gautrot, Marie, F-17, 69, 83
Gautrot, Marie, N-17-18, 69, 105
Gautrot, Marie, S1-32, 344
Gautrot, Marie, S2-636, 638
Gautrot, Marie, S3-1000
Gautrot, Marie Angelique, C-44
Gautrot, Marie Anne, E-355, 393
Gautrot, Marie Eleonore, N-69
Gautrot, Marie Genevieve, F-7
Gautrot, Marie Genevieve, N-69
Gautrot, Marie Joseph, E-152
Gautrot, Marie Josephe Pelagie, E-152
Gautrot, Marie Madeleine, C-7-8
Gautrot, Marie Madeleine, N-10, 45, 47-48, 68-69, 111-112, 190
Gautrot, Marie Madeleine Marguerite, E-151

Gautrot, Marie Magdalen, E-151-152, 274, 389
Gautrot, Marie Magdalen, F-45
Gautrot, Marie Magdalen Pelagie, E-152
Gautrot, Marie Marguerite Pelagie, E-152
Gautrot, Marie Rose, E-636
Gautrot, Marie-Angelique, S1-352
Gautrot, Marie-Anne, S1-343, 348-350
Gautrot, Marie-Anne-Renee, S1-347
Gautrot, Marie-Francoise, S1-348, 350
Gautrot, Marie-Genevieve, S1-346
Gautrot, Marie-Josephe, S1-100, 156-157, 339, 348
Gautrot, Marie-Madeleine, S1-48, 252, 342, 346
Gautrot, Marie-Madeleine-Marguerite, S1-340
Gautrot, Marie-Marguerite-Pelagie, S1-340
Gautrot, Marie-Rose, S1-342
Gautrot, Marin, C-101
Gautrot, Marin, F-17
Gautrot, Marin, S1-140, 154, 338-339, 344-346, 349-351
Gautrot, Marin, S2-448, 550
Gautrot, Marin, S3-1137
Gautrot, Mathurin, S1-351
Gautrot, Michel, S1-351
Gautrot, Nicolas, E-152
Gautrot, Nicolas, S1-351
Gautrot, Pelagie, F-7
Gautrot, Pelagie, N-69
Gautrot, Pelagie-Marie, S1-347
Gautrot, Pierre, C-44
Gautrot, Pierre, E-151
Gautrot, Pierre, F-19, 45, 57, 61, 109
Gautrot, Pierre, N-47, 69-70, 111, 182, 198
Gautrot, Pierre, S1-104, 252, 311, 336, 339, 341, 344, 351, 353
Gautrot, Pierre, S3-969, 989, 1046, 1058, 1068

Gautrot, Pierre, S2-582, 710
Gautrot, Pierre Isidore, E-152
Gautrot, Pierre-Gregoire, S1-338
Gautrot, Pierre-Joseph, S1-345
Gautrot, Pierre-Olivier, S1-349
Gautrot, Reine Anastasie, C-44
Gautrot, Reine Anastasie, N-69
Gautrot, Reine-Anastasie, S1-352
Gautrot, Renee, E-457
Gautrot, Romain, S1-343
Gautrot, Rosalie, F-109
Gautrot, Rosalie Charlotte, E-152
Gautrot, Rosalie-Anne, S1-344
Gautrot, Rose, F-45, 49
Gautrot, Rose, S1-76, 336-337
Gautrot, Rose-Marie, S1-343
Gautrot, Rose-Sebastienne, S1-349
Gautrot, Sebastienne, C-43
Gautrot, Simonne-Marie-Rose, S1-344
Gautrot, Sulia-Charles, S1-349
Gautrot, Victoire, F-45
Gautrot, Victoire-Andree, S1-339
Gautrot, Victoire-Josephe, S1-339
Gautrot , Louis, C-44
Gautrut, Marie Magdalen, E-272
Gautter, Jacquemine, E-618
Gauut, Francoise, E-394
Gauven, Jean-Marie, S1-367
Gauvereau, Jean Louis, E-280
Gauvin, Aubin, E-1
Gaveau, Marie Anne, E-174, 258
Gavery, Francoise, S1-46
Gayou Previle, Jean, E-22, 152, 174, 358
Gayou Preville, Jeanne Ange-lique, E-152, 173-174
Gayral, Raymonde, E-105, 178
Geau, Francois, E-51
Geau, Francoise, E-410
Gecans, Francois, E-34, 152
Gedee, Julienne, S1-194
Geffard, Jean, E-77, 152, 270
Geffard, Julienne, E-298

Geffard, Pierre, E-156
Geffros, Marie, S1-357
Geffroy, Francois-Louis, S1-57
Geffroy, Jean, S3-983
Geffroy, Jean Louis, S3-1079
Geffroy, Pierre, S3-983, 991, 1019
Gehanne, Thomas, S1-59
Gelin, Jesle Jean, S3-914
Gelinet, Therese, E-44, 152
Gelle, Nicolas, E-17, 105, 152, 256
Gelos, Catherine, E-152, 336
Gelos, Joannin, E-152
Gemier, Jeanne, N-49-50, 55, 229
Genard, Michel, E-107
Genas, Marguerite, E-161, 413
Genat, Genevieve, E-90 156
Gendee, Suzanne, E-77, 257
Gendre, Abraham, E-152, 561
Gendre, Abraham, S1-353
Gendre, Abraham, S2-711
Gendre, Abraham, S3-1005
Gendre, Anne Claire, E-561
Gendre, Eleonore Claire, E-152
Gendre, Eleonore-Claire, S1-353
Gendre, Guillaume, S1-353
Gendre, Guillaume, S3-1005
Gendre, Marie, E-196, 257
Gendron, Alexis, E-404
Gene, Guillaume, E-152
Gene, Gustin, E-152
Gene dit Bellion, Anne, E-278
Geneio, Marie Joseph, E-6
Genemmine, Jeanne, C-62
Genest, Francoise, E-11
Genet, Augustain, E-268, 292
Genevieve, Lamasse, E-595
Gennevais, Louis, E-153
Gennevais, Marie Anne, E-120, 153
Genou, Francois Bonaventure, E-256
Genoux, Georgine, E-56
Gentet, Louise, E-90, 196
Gentil, Anne Marie, C-41, 51-52
Gentil, Anne Marie, E-177
Gentil, Anne Marie, F-79
Gentil, Anne Marie, N-69

Gentil, Anne Marie, S3-1012, 1030, 1043, 1065
Gentil, Anne-Marie, S1-340
Gentil, Anne-Marie, S2-428, 437, 439, 723
Gentil, Celeste Victoire, E-361
Gentil, Charles, S1-353-354
Gentil, Desiree, E-365
Gentil, Elie, S2-434
Gentil, Etienne Francois, E-361
Gentil, Francois, S1-354
Gentil, Josephine Desiree, E-361
Gentil, Marianne-Anne-Marie, S2-428
Gentil, Marie, E-176, 179, 370
Gentil, Marie, N-78, 81
Gentil, Marie, S1-354
Gentil, Marie, S2-435
Gentil, Marie, S3-938
Gentil, Marie Anne, F-75
Gentil, Marie Anne, N-79-80
Gentil, Marie-Anne, S2-429, 432, 434-435, 437-438
Gentil, Marie-Francoise, S1-354
Gentil, Pierre, S1-353-354
Gentils, Anne Marie, E-178
Gentry, Jean, E-431
Gentry, Marie, E-143, 153
Geoffroy, Anne, E-153
Geoffroy, Jean, E-72, 153
Geoffroy, Marie, E-35, 72, 153, 157, 174
Geonas, Marie, E-30, 153
George, Marie Anne, E-16, 188
George, Pierre, E-77, 152
Georges, Michel, E-416
Georget, Francois, E-153, 416
Georget, Michel, E-153, 416
Gerard, Francois, E-154
Gerard, Jacques, E-131
Gerard, Marguerite, E-115
Gerard, Marianne, E-116-118
Gerard, Marie, S3-1150
Gerard, Servanne, S1-205
Geraud, Simon David, E-258
Gerault, Jeanne, E-385
Gerbault, Etienne, E-153, 391
Gerbault, Jacques, E-153, 391
Gerbert, Nicolas, E-27, 152
Gerby, Eugene, S2-585
Gergeron, Marie Anne, E-28

Geriaud, Marie, E-271
Gerine, Huguette, E-473
Gerlaut, Pierre, E-265
Germain, Guillaume, S3-1078
Germain, Marie Andree, S3-995
Germain, Marie Jeanne, E-586, 593
Germain, Mr., E-126
Germon, Magdelaine, E-475
Germonneau, Francois, E-107, 153
Germonneau, Marianne, E-107, 153
Gernad, Jacques Daniel, E-153
Gernad, Pierre, E-153
Gernand, Joseph Michel, E-162
Geroneau, Antoine, E-153, 338
Geroneau, Francoise, E-338
Geroneau, Marie, E-153, 338
Geroneau, Pierre, E-338
Gerouard, Elisabeth, E-29
Gerouard, Marie Josephe, E-29
Gerouerd, Marguerite, S3-1129
Gervais, Desiree, E-636
Gervais, Georges, E-636
Gervais, Louis, E-636
Gervais, Thomas, E-636
Gervauet, Jean, E-153
Gervauet, Marie, E-153
Gervay, Marie, E-130
Gerveau, Jacques, E-153
Gerveau, Pierre, E-153
Gervier, Jean, E-38, 357
Gervy, Jeanne, S1-2
Gerzel, Denis, S3-968
Gesan, Cecile, F-69
Geslain, Jean, S1-354
Geslin, Jean, S3-913-914
Gesmier, Augustin, S1-255
Gesmier, Gilles, S1-255
Gesmier, Gilles, S3-904
Gesmier, Gillette, S1-256
Gesmier, Jeanne, C-29
Gesmier, Jeanne, S1-255-256
Gesmier, Jeanne, S3-904
Gesmir, Gilles, C-29
Gesre, Huget, E-116
Gesu, Sieur, E-86
Geurtavais, Gaspar, S3-876
Gezecal, Francoise, S2-478

Ghyselle, Marie Dominique, E-144, 316
Giboire, Margueritte, E-326
Gibon, Louise (Miss), C-152
Gibon, Marie Louise, E-324
Gicquel, Jean, S2-583
Gicquel, Jeanne, F-7
Gicquel, Jeanne-Perinne, S2-583
Gide, Jean, E-197
Giess, Marie Elisabeth, E-571
Giffard, Anne, E-17, 149, 153
Giffard, Anne Virginie, E-153-154
Giffard, Elisabeth Jeanne, E-154
Giffard, Jean, E-93, 153-154, 290, 394, 437
Giffard, Jean Baptiste, E-149, 153-154, 290, 294
Giffard, Louis, E-154
Giffard, Marie Josephe Henriette, E-291-292
Giffard, Marie Rose, E-154
Giffard, Pierre, E-154, 290
Gifflot, Francois, S3-938
Gigault, Louise, C-6, 134
Gigaux de Grampre, Mr., E-258
Gigaux de Grandpre, Ambroise Ignace, E-154
Gigaux de Grandpre, Charles Alexis Antoine Hilaire, E-154
Gilbert, Anne, E-385, 440
Gilbert, Ebenezer, E-154
Gilbert, Francoise, E-624, 626
Gilbert, Francoise, S1-355
Gilbert, Francoise, S3-1087
Gilbert, Guillemette, S1-166
Gilbert, Jean, E-190
Gilbert, Jeanne, E-121
Gilbert, Laurence, S1-354-355
Gilbert, Louis, E-618, 624
Gilbert, Louis, S1-354-355
Gilbert, Louis, S2-593
Gilbert, Louis, S3-957-958, 1086-1087
Gilbert, Louise, S1-355
Gilbert, Marie, S1-354-355
Gilbert, Marie Francoise, S3-957-958
Gilbert, Marie Jeanne, E-618
Gilbert, Marie-Francoise, S2-593

Gilbert, Mathieu, E-332, 618
Gilbert, Mathieu, S1-354-355
Gilbert, Mathieu-Ange, S1-122, 355
Gilbert, Mathieux Ange, S3-1086-1087
Gilbert, Perinne, S2-723
Gilbert, Perinne, S3-1008
Gilbert, Pierre, E-154-155, 157, 348
Gilbert, Scholastique Hebert, E-610
Gilberton, Marie, C-43
Gilibert, Francoise, E-293
Gillaudeau, Jeanne, E-355
Gille, Noncia, E-28, 357
Gilles, Antoine-Julien, S1-356
Gilles, child, S1-356
Gilles, Jean, S1-355-356
Gilles, Jean-Blaise, S1-356
Gilles, Jeanne, S1-355-356
Gilles, Marguerite, E-33, 372
Gilles, Suzanne, E-73
Gilles, Suzanne-Marguerite, S1-356
Gillet, Rene, E-179, 295
Gillot, Angelique, E-14
Gillot, Francois, E-376
Gillot, Nicolas-Sebastien, S1-50
Gills, Marie Francoise Angelique, E-193
Gimon, Jeanne, E-20, 346
Gimon, Marie, E-36, 63
Ginet, Jean, E-73
Giome, Renee, S1-272
Giot, Francoise, S2-545
Giot, Francoise, S3-995
Giquel, Jean, S3-1077
Giquel, Jeanne Perinne, S3-1077
Giquet, Jeanne, C-70
Girard, Bertrand, E-155
Girard, Catherine, E-115
Girard, Francoise, E-385
Girard, Francoise-Renee, S1-357
Girard, Innocent Francois, E-155
Girard, Jacques, E-91, 155, 376
Girard, Jean, E-155, 281, 348, 385, 586, 593
Girard, Jean, S1-356-357

Girard, Jean Baptiste Prudent, E-155

Girard, Jean Francois, E-155, 326, 348, 376

Girard, Jeanne, E-155, 281

Girard, Joseph, E-155

Girard, Louis, E-155, 348, 412

Girard, Louise, E-314

Girard, Madelaine, E-82, 586, 591

Girard, Margueritc, C-18

Girard, Marguerite, S1-110

Girard, Marie, E-315, 377, 586, 593

Girard, Marie Anne Rose, E-155

Girard, Marie Elizabeth, E-53, 155

Girard, Marie Jeanne, E-155, 157

Girard, Marie-Francoise-Per-inne, S1-357

Girard, Marie-Renee-Perinne, S1-356

Girard, Mathieu, E-155

Girard, Pierre, E-45, 155, 315, 586, 593

Girard, Pierre, S1-356

Girard, Pierre, S2-444

Girard, Pierre-Mathurin, S1-356-357

Girard, Rene, E-155

Girard, Sophie, E-155

Girard, Sophie Aimee, E-281

Girard, Thomas, S1-357

Girardeau, Jeanne, E-55, 308

Girardeau, Pierre, E-20

Girardin, Angelique, S1-358-359

Girardin, Catherine, S1-359

Girardin, child, S1-359

Girardin, Francois, E-315

Girardin, Francois, S1-358-359

Girardin, Genevieve, E-59, 155

Girardin, Genevieve, S1-173, 358-359

Girardin, Jacques, E-59, 155

Girardin, Jean, S1-357, 359

Girardin, Jean-Baptiste, S1-358-359

Girardin, Jeanne, S1-358-359

Girardin, Joseph, S1-358-359

Girardin, Louis, E-156

Girardin, Marie, E-155, 315

Girardin, Marie-Catherine, S1-358

Girardin, Pierre, E-90, 156, 295

Girardin, Pierre, S1-357-359

Giraud, Henry, E-586, 597

Giraud, Jean, E-34-35, 307, 404

Giraud, Jeanne, E-357, 385

Giraud, Magdelaine, E-51, 114

Giraud, Marguerite, E-34

Giraud, Marguerite Francoise, E-340, 418

Giraud, Marie, E-338

Giraud, Mr., E-292

Giraud, Pierre, E-29, 155, 157

Giraud, Raymond, E-155

Giraud, Rene, S1-359

Giraud, Savinien, E-291

Giraud, Suzanne, E-259, 337

Giraude, Francoise, E-132, 152

Giraudeau, Francois, E-339

Giraudeau, Pierre, E-34, 90, 156, 350

Giraudet, Jeanne, E-31, 97

Giraudo, Luce, E-169, 325, 402

Girault, Jeanne, E-417

Giroire, Agnes, E-514

Giroire, Alexandre, E-383, 489, 525

Giroire, Amand, S1-203, 240, 359-360

Giroire, Amand, S3-839, 860

Giroire, Angelique Jean Joseph, E-156

Giroire, Anne, C-34, 41, 44, 80, 151

Giroire, Anne, E-37, 83

Giroire, Anne, F-5, 21, 27, 49

Giroire, Anne, S1-76, 265, 270, 275-276

Giroire, Anne, S2-636, 698

Giroire, Anne, S3-826, 1130

Giroire, Anne Esther, E-360

Giroire, Anne Marie, E-363

Giroire, Anne-Josephe, S1-362

Giroire, Antoine, E-26

Giroire, Charles, C-43

Giroire, Charles, E-156, 525

Giroire, Charles, F-75

Giroire, Charles, S1-360

Giroire, Charles, S3-980, 974

Giroire, Charles-Jean, S1-359

Giroire, Charlotte, E-475

Giroire, Claude, E-215, 489, 525

Giroire, David, S1-361

Giroire, Dominique, E-60

Giroire, Dominique, N-70, 146, 201

Giroire, Dominque, C-44-46, 100

Giroire, Elenne, F-79

Giroire, Elisabeth, E-156

Giroire, Esther, E-360

Giroire, Eudoxe, S1-65

Giroire, Eudoxie, S1-362

Giroire, Eudoxile, S1-360-361

Giroire, Eudoze, F-81

Giroire, Felicite, E-21, 156

Giroire, Francois, C-45

Giroire, Francois, E-156, 457, 474, 489, 525, 552, 599

Giroire, Francois, F-27

Giroire, Francois, N-71

Giroire, Genevieve, F-89

Giroire, Genevieve, S1-87-88

Giroire, Genevieve-Charlotte-Marguerite, S1-360

Giroire, Germain, E-474, 514, 525, 553

Giroire, Guillaume, E-156, 489, 525

Giroire, Guillaume, S2-698

Giroire, Helen Judith, C-12

Giroire, Helene Judith, N-15

Giroire, Helene Judith, S3-827

Giroire, Helene-Judith, S1-65, 360-361

Giroire, Honore, C-12, 44

Giroire, Honore, F-27, 79, 81

Giroire, Honore, N-70

Giroire, Honore, S1-65, 360-361

Giroire, Honore, S3-827-828, 935

Giroire, Isabelle, E-599

Giroire, Jacob, E-457

Giroire, Jacques, E-35, 156-157, 350, 383, 474, 489, 525

Giroire, Jacques, F-75

Giroire, Jacques, S1-359-360

Giroire, Jacques, S3-839, 980

Giroire, Jean, C-45

Giroire, Jean, E-156, 157, 489, 599

Giroire, Jean, N-71

Giroire, Jean Baptiste, E-156

Giroire, Jean Baptiste, F-27

Giroire, Jean Dominique, N-70

Giroire, Jean-Baptiste, S1-362

Giroire, Jean-Yves, S1-359

Giroire, Jeanne, C-45

Giroire, Jeanne, E-37, 156

Giroire, Jeanne, F-27

Giroire, Jeanne, N-71

Giroire, Jeanne-Eleonore, S1-362

Giroire, Joseph, E-156, 157, 196, 364

Giroire, Joseph, S1-361

Giroire, Joseph Magloire, N-70

Giroire, Joseph Mathieu, E-157

Giroire, Joseph-Magloire, S1-362

Giroire, Josephe, E-126, 157

Giroire, Louis, E-33, 126, 157, 599

Giroire, Louis Isaac, E-383

Giroire, Maddelaine, E-317, 473, 456

Giroire, Marguerite, C-19, 80, 84-85, 96, 100, 158-159

Giroire, Marguerite, E-21, 103, 157, 337, 360, 363, 490, 525, 552

Giroire, Marguerite, F-43

Giroire, Marguerite, N-5, 26, 144, 247

Giroire, Marguerite, S1-94-95, 106, 115-116

Giroire, Marguerite, S2-628, 673

Giroire, Marguerite Sophie, E-157

Giroire, Margueritte, S3-854, 863, 1127

Giroire, Marie, C-45

Giroire, Marie, E-71, 157, 356, 456, 472, 490, 599

Giroire, Marie, N-71

Giroire, Marie, S1-50, 52, 102

Giroire, Marie, S2-526, 767

Giroire, Marie, S3-833

Giroire, Marie Agnes Adelaide, N-70

Giroire, Marie J., E-155

Giroire, Marie Joseph, E-357, 358, 380, 382-383

Giroire, Marie Josephe, E-157

Giroire, Marie Josephete, E-148

Giroire, Marie Josephine, E-599

Giroire, Marie Magdelaine, E-553

Giroire, Marie Modeste, C-166

Giroire, Marie Modeste, E-31

Giroire, Marie Paul, F-27

Giroire, Marie Paul, N-71

Giroire, Marie Rose, F-81

Giroire, Marie Theotiste, C-65, 115-116, 160

Giroire, Marie Theotiste, N-107

Giroire, Marie-Anne, S1-361

Giroire, Marie-Paule, S1-362

Giroire, Marie-Rose, S1-361

Giroire, Michel, C-116

Giroire, Michel, E-552

Giroire, Micheleles, C-116

Giroire, Michel Jean, S1-360

Giroire, Mr., E-269

Giroire, Paul, S1-361

Giroire, Pierre, C-44, 65, 100, 115

Giroire, Pierre, E-156, 157, 489, 525

Giroire, Pierre, F-27

Giroire, Pierre, N-71

Giroire, Pierre, S1-52

Giroire, Pierre, S2-526

Giroire, Pierre, S3-833

Giroire, Prosper, C-56

Giroire, Prosper, F-27

Giroire, Prosper, N-70

Giroire, Prosper, S1-159, 302, 361-362

Giroire, Prosper, S3-827, 874, 935-936

Giroire, Prosper Honore, C-45

Giroire, Prosper-Honore, S1-360-361

Giroire, Raymond, E-157

Giroire, Rose, S1-66

Giroire, Theotiste, C-100

Giroire, Theotiste, E-272, 380

Giroire, Vernoique, C-5, 14, 17, 38

Giroire, Veronique, F-9, 19, 43, 77

Giroire, Veronique, N-38, 202

Giroire, Veronique, S1-38-39, 98, 110, 233, 298

Giroire, Veronique, S2-544

Giroire, Veronique, S3-835, 840, 843, 845, 851-852, 1047

Giroiseau, Marie, E-138, 389

Giron, Joseph, E-66

Girot, Francoise, E-61

Girou, Marie, E-141

Girouard Village named after Jacques Girouard, E-215

Girouen, Augustin, E-157, 174

Girouen, Francois, E-157

Girouet, Marie Joseph, E-157

Giroy, Elisabeth, E-59

Glain, Louise, E-594, 617-618

Glain, Marie Louise, E-157

Glain, Mathieu, E-157

Glamar, Josette, E-158

Glamov, Yves, E-158, 300

Glen, Louise, S3-1060

Glen, Marie Louise, S3-914

Glen, Mathieu, S3-914, 1060

Glernot, Ursule, S2-759

Glibert, Marie Joseph, E-122

Glienn, Jean Vincens, S3-836

Glin, Louise, S1-37

Glin, Marie-Louise, S1-42

Glin, Mathieu, S1-37, 42

Gloro, Perrine Therese, E-158, 179

Goarde, Lorin, E-171

Gobert, Guillaume, C-100

Gobert, Guillaume, N-177

Gobert, Marie, C-158

Gobert, Marie Gabriele, E-122, 196

Gobin, Cecile, E-285-287

God, Francois, E-386

Godard, Anne-Monique, S1-58

Godard, Calvin, E-158

Godbout, Antoine, S1-362-363

Godbout, Francois, S1-363

Godbout, Jean, S1-362

Godeau, Marie Josephe, E-173, 349

Godeau, Pierre, E-121
Godebou, Antoine, S3-1007
Godebou, Jan, S3-1007
Godeffroy, Charles Louis, E-158, 432
Godeffroy, Louis, E-158, 432
Godefroy, Marie, E-363
Godefroy, Victoire, E-361
Godelay, Marie Claire, E-98
Godet, Charle, N-187
Godet, Dominique, S1-283
Godet, Joseph, S1-367
Godet, Joseph, S3-1097
Godet, Joseph Ygnace, S3-1075
Godet, Joseph-Ignace, S1-295
Godet, Louis, C-151
Godet, Marguerite, C-10, 99-100, 159
Godet, Marie, C-158
Godet, Marie, S3-942, 1097
Godet, Marie Rose, S3-955
Godet, Pierre, N-187
Godet, Prudence, N-228
Godet, Rene, N-228
Godette, Marguerite, E-42
Godichon, Jacques, E-158, 293
Godin, Francois, S1-363
Godin, Francois, S3-1011
Godin, Jean, S1-363
Godin, Jean, S3-1011
Godin, Marie-Francoise, S1-363
Godion, Pierre, S1-385
Godron, Louis, S3-1150
Godron, Perinne, S1-333
Godron, Perinne, S3-1048
Goeneau, Marie, E-337
Goeslle, Therese, E-283
Goeuneau, Marie, E-118
Goghuelin, Marie, S3-957, 1086
Gogue, Nicolas, E-168
Goguelin, Marie, S1-354-355
Goguelin, Marie, S2-593
Goguelir, Marie, E-624
Gohier, Mathurine, S1-85
Gohier, widow, S1-190
Goineau, Marie Magdelaine, E-118
Golbarette, Francois, E-112, 158
Golbarette, Jeanne, E-112, 158
Gomerien, Louis, E-618
Gomerin, Louis, S1-364

Gomerin, Michel, S1-364
Gomes, Manuel, N-186
Gomez, Silverio, F-65
Gomez, Silvestre, F-65, 81
Gond, Claude, E-357
Gondouin, Jeanne, S1-172
Gonillon, Catherine, E-26, 92, 127, 300
Gonlevin, Henry, E-22, 349
Gonnot, Susanne, E-59, 109
Gontier, Alexandre Francois, E-158
Gontier, boy, E-158
Gontier, Eleonore, E-158
Gontier, Francois de Salles Alexandre, E-158
Gontier, Joseph Eleonore, E-158
Gontier, Marie Anne Agnes, E-158
Gorand, Jeanne, E-64
Gorand, Marie Anne, E-64
Gorand, veuve, E-64
Gordiau, Benjamin, S2-598
Gorge, Jan, S3-942-943
Gorin, Marie Rose, E-599
Gornee, Dorothee Constanse, N-248
Goron, Jeanne, S2-649
Gorujar, Hugette, E-33, 96
Gosselin, Catherine, E-158, 179
Gosselin, Catherine, S2-441
Gosselin, Robert, E-158, 179
Gosset, Anne Catherine Francoise, E-103, 158
Gosset, Jean, E-103, 158
Gosset, Jean Victor, E-103
Gosset, Julienne, E-403, 441
Gosset, Louise Anne, E-325
Gosset, Pierre, E-103, 303
Gouas, Thomas, S1-150
Goubert, Francois Guillaume, E-644-645
Goubert, Francois Philippe, E-158, 304
Goubert, Jean, E-17, 159
Goubert, Joseph Guillaume Jas., E-644
Goubert, Joseph Stanislas, E-17, 159
Goubert, Louis, E-644
Goubert, Nicolas, E-159

Goubert, Nicolas Francois, E-158, 304
Goudable, Antoine, E-417
Goudelin, Catherine, E-618
Goudelin, Francois, E-618, 624
Goudelin, Francois, S1-204, 257
Goudelin, Francois, S3-1023
Goudelin, Jean, E-624
Goudelin, Jeanne, E-619, 624-625
Goudelin, Josephine Marie, E-624
Goudelin, Marie, E-619, 624
Goudelin, Sainte, E-619
Goudlain, Francois, S1-34
Goudric, Elisabeth, E-417
Gouellot, Jean, S3-1113
Goueslard, Clarie, E-159
Goueslard, Leonard Louis, E-159, 303
Gouffrau dit Delage, Jean, E-38, 159
Goufrau dit Delage, Louis, E-38, 159
Goufraud, Jeanne, E-15
Gougeon, Antoine, E-457
Gougnaud, Louis, E-34
Gouillian, Jeanne, E-92, 268
Gouillon, Catherine, E-92, 105
Gouin, Anne, S1-214
Gouin, Jeanne, S1-259
Gouin, Jeanne, S3-1073
Gouin, Julien, S3-913
Gouin dit La Forme, Jean, E-97
Gouineau, Etienne, E-21, 138, 159, 377, 413
Gouineau, Louis, E-406
Goujonne, Huguette, E-472
Goulard, Jean, E-152
Goulard, Pierre, E-102, 119, 159
Goulfaud, Jean, E-159, 316
Goulfaut, Michel, E-159
Gouliasse, George, E-159, 329
Gouliasse, Jean, E-159, 329
Gouliasse, Marie Catherine, E-159
Goulmot, Louise, E-369, 409
Goumain, Malo, S3-1023
Goumard, Michel, E-393
Goumin, Marguerite, E-254
Goupil, Jeanne, E-314-315, 341

Goupil, Marguerite Yvonne, E-305

Goupy, Jean, E-304, 389

Goupy, Jeanne, E-159

Gourdeaux, Charles, E-474

Gourdel, Marianne, E-258

Gourdet, Marie, E-35, 156

Gourdet, Marie Anne, E-258

Gourdon, Angelique, E-159

Gourdon, Anne, E-159

Gourdon, Antoine, E-159-160, 169, 194

Gourdon, Francois, E-159

Gourdon, George Olivier, E-159

Gourdon, Jean, E-267

Gourdon, Jean Baptiste, E-160, 169

Gourdon, Louis, E-160

Gourdon, Louis Benomy, E-160

Gourdon, Marie, E-159-160, 259, 316

Gourdon, Marie Angelique, E-160

Gourdon, Marie Josephe, E-160, 194

Gourdon, Marie Marguerite, E-160

Gourdon, Mathieu, E-160, 267

Gourdon La Chapelle, Louis, E-279

Goureau, Honore, E-160

Goureau, Pierre, E-160

Gourey, Anne, E-331

Gourgat, Marie, E-306, 346

Gourville, Josephe Marie, E-160

Gourville, Michel, E-116, 160

Gousaume, Jean, E-160, 413

Gousaume, Pierre, E-160, 413

Gousman, Jean, C-9, 44, 46

Gousman, Jean, F-67

Gousman, Jean, N-71, 181

Gousman, Jean Thomas, F-67

Gousman, Jean Thomas, N-71

Gousman, Joseph Antoine, C-46

Gousman, Ludivine, C-45

Gousman, Rosalie Charlotte, C-46

Gousman, Rosalie Charlotte, F-67

Goussey, Louis, E-152

Goutille, Jacques, E-526

Goutro, Marguerite, E-156

Gouverneur, Jean, E-280

Gouye, Anne, E-155, 281

Gouyon, Pierre, S3-1066

Gouyon, Renee, S1-277

Grabeuil, Suzanne, E-92, 101, 270

Graffard, Guillaume, S3-1108, 1113

Graffard, Jan, S3-1108

Gramond, Marie, E-64, 349

Granard, Nicolais, E-420

Grandchamp, Guillaume, E-160

Grandchamp, Jean Francois, E-160, 282

Grandge, Marie, E-82

Grandhayes, Guillemine, E-180, 348

Grandier, G., E-195

Grandin, Angelique, E-110, 160, 265, 328

Grandin, Demoiselle, E-266

Grandin, Francois, E-161, 265

Grandin, Jean Baptiste, E-160, 268

Grandin, Marie, E-160, 268

Grandin, Nicolas, E-161, 265, 413

Grandjeaud, Andre, E-121, 161

Grandjeaud, Francois, E-121, 161

Grandmidon, Grosmidon, E-161

Grandmidon, Jean Louis, E-161

Grangean, Marie, E-416

Grangeau, Francois, E-161

Grangeau, Marie Magdalen, E-161

Granger, Aime, E-420

Granger, Amand, E-95, 161-162, 164-166, 561

Granger, Anasthasie Prudence, E-161

Granger, Anne, C-13, 156, 159

Granger, Anne, E-38, 41-44, 125, 161, 164, 283, 314, 324, 420-423, 425-426, 496, 567, 575-576

Granger, Anne, F-33, 45, 79

Granger, Anne, N-2, 72, 162, 165-166, 252

Granger, Anne, S1-80-81, 147, 158, 367-368

Granger, Anne, S2-461, 614, 700

Granger, Anne, S3-936

Granger, Anne Francoise, E-426

Granger, Anne Leonore, N-20, 72, 253

Granger, Anne Marie, E-7, 161, 562

Granger, Anne-Marie, S1-364

Granger, Annette, E-425

Granger, Anonime, E-161

Granger, Armand, E-161, 164, 561

Granger, Augustin, E-415

Granger, Augustin Albert, E-167

Granger, Augustin Vital, E-563

Granger, Augustin Vital Bede, E-161, 324

Granger, boy, E-161

Granger, Catherine, S2-613

Granger, Cecile, C-4, 63

Granger, Cecile, F-13, 17

Granger, Cecile, N-8, 104, 147

Granger, Cecile, S1-25

Granger, Cecile, S2-527, 700-703

Granger, Cecile, S3-1020

Granger, Charles, C-4, 77

Granger, Charles, E-161-163, 165-167, 562

Granger, Charles, F-39

Granger, Charles, N-72

Granger, Charles, S1-26, 103, 232, 364-365, 368-369

Granger, Charles, S2-528, 534, 544, 559, 622, 701-702

Granger, Charles, S3-1015

Granger, Charles Benjamin, E-161

Granger, Charles Benoist, N-71, 112, 182

Granger, Charles Francois Louis, E-162

Granger, Charles Marie, E-162

Granger, Charles Simon, N-72

Granger, Charles-Benoist, S1-365

Granger, Claire, S1-365, 368-369

Granger, Claude, E-164, 166, 496, 526, 580-581

Granger, Claude, N-73

Granger, Constance, E-162

Granger, Elisabeth, E-94, 128, 161-162, 165, 427, 563

Granger, Elisabeth Genevieve Walburge, E-564

Granger, Elisabeth Josephine, E-7, 162

Granger, Elizabeth, N-43

Granger, Elizabeth, S1-147, 167, 231-232

Granger, Elizabeth-Luce, S1-365

Granger, Euphrosine Sophie, E-603

Granger, Felix, E-162

Granger, Francois, E-166-167, 580

Granger, Francois, F-33

Granger, Francois, N-122, 165

Granger, Francois Rene, E-608-610, 612-613, 615

Granger, Francois Xavier, E-162

Granger, Francoise, E-96, 162, 293, 324, 567, 580

Granger, Francoise, F-31

Granger, Francoise, N-47-48, 212

Granger, Francoise, S1-176, 221

Granger, Francoise, S2-613-615, 617, 674, 748

Granger, Francoise, S3-856, 859, 861-862

Granger, Francoise Eulalie, F-99

Granger, Francoise Josephe, E-285, 295

Granger, Francoise-Eulalie, S1-367-368

Granger, girl, E-161

Granger, Ignace, F-99

Granger, Ignace, S1-367-368

Granger, Isaac Aimable, E-162, 603

Granger, Isabelle, E-93-94, 162

Granger, Jacques, E-162, 283, 496, 526

Granger, Jacques Etienne, E-162

Granger, Jacquette, E-162

Granger, Jean, C-13

Granger, Jean, E-7, 33, 74, 95, 106, 161-167, 181, 271, 322, 377, 414, 425, 562, 603

Granger, Jean, N-20, 72, 135, 184, 203, 253

Granger, Jean Baptiste, E-161-167, 283, 422, 562-563, 580

Granger, Jean Baptiste, N-73, 162

Granger, Jean Charles, E-163-164, 167, 604

Granger, Jean fils Laurent, E-1

Granger, Jean Francois, E-163

Granger, Jean Jacques, E-567

Granger, Jean Joseph, E-163, 563

Granger, Jean Joseph, N-73

Granger, Jean Jr., E-603

Granger, Jean Marie, E-163

Granger, Jean Marie, F-41

Granger, Jean Marie, N-73

Granger, Jean Marie Louis, E-163

Granger, Jean Michel, E-293

Granger, Jean Rene, N-73

Granger, Jean Simeon, E-163

Granger, Jean Simon, E-163

Granger, Jean Siriacq, E-163

Granger, Jean Sirias, E-603

Granger, Jean-Baptiste, S1-367

Granger, Jean-Baptiste-Marie, S1-366

Granger, Jeanne, F-99

Granger, Jeanne, S1-368

Granger, Jeanne Gervaise, E-411

Granger, Jeanne-Marie, S1-367

Granger, Joseph, C-5, 139, 159

Granger, Joseph, E-161, 163-166, 293, 562-563, 581

Granger, Joseph, E-359

Granger, Joseph, F-25, 99

Granger, Joseph, N-8-9, 31, 71, 182

Granger, Joseph, S1-36, 146-147, 166, 179, 225, 230, 347, 365-368

Granger, Joseph, S2-440, 452, 544, 613, 615

Granger, Joseph, S3-921, 999, 1076, 1085

Granger, Joseph Augustin, E-164

Granger, Joseph David, E-164

Granger, Joseph Francoise, E-384

Granger, Joseph Jean, E-164

Granger, Joseph Simon, E-162, 164-165, 563

Granger, Joseph-Constans, S1-366

Granger, Joseph-Constant, S1-368

Granger, Josephe Francoise, E-41, 167

Granger, Julien-Joseph, S1-367

Granger, Laurent, E-162, 164-166, 287, 457, 474, 526, 564

Granger, Laurent, N-72

Granger, Laurent, S1-365-366, 368-369

Granger, Laurent, S2-524

Granger, Lejeune Amant, E-161

Granger, Lejeune Pierre, E-162

Granger, Louis, E-1, 74, 164

Granger, Louis, N-72, 199

Granger, Louis Jean Marie, E-164

Granger, Louis Marie, E-7

Granger, Louis Mathurin, N-73

Granger, Louis Nicolas, E-164

Granger, Luc, E-164, 561

Granger, Luce, C-5, 163

Granger, Luce, N-9

Granger, Luce, S1-368-369

Granger, Madeleine, S1-368

Granger, Magdalen Luce, E-164

Granger, Magdelaine, E-164, 327, 362, 364-365, 581, 610, 608, 613

Granger, Magdeleine, C-86

Granger, Marguarite, C-13, 15, 37-38, 140, 161

Granger, Marguerite, E-1, 74, 84, 93, 104, 124, 128, 162, 164, 177, 283, 305, 415-416, 496, 574

Granger, Marguerite, N-59, 72, 135, 185, 203

Granger, Marguerite, S1-28, 102, 231, 244-245, 253, 290-291

Granger, Marguerite, S2-700-701

Granger, Marguerite Susanne, E-164

Granger, Margueritte, S3-883, 1024

Granger, Marie, C-13, 159

Granger, Marie, E-1, 33, 74, 121, 130, 164-165, 177, 349, 360, 363, 380-384, 413-416, 496, 572

Granger, Marie, N-16-17, 36, 63, 172, 253

Granger, Marie, S1-170, 283, 303, 367-368

Granger, Marie, S2-779, 783

Granger, Marie, S3-1072

Granger, Marie Anne, E-41, 44, 164-165

Granger, Marie Apoline Felicite, E-603

Granger, Marie Blanche, E-165

Granger, Marie Brigitte, E-293, 563

Granger, Marie Elisabeth, E-165

Granger, Marie Francoise, E-7, 161, 163, 165, 173, 420, 562

Granger, Marie Francoise, N-73

Granger, Marie Genevieve, E-165

Granger, Marie Jeanne, E-165, 423, 428

Granger, Marie Jn., N-203

Granger, Marie Joseph, E-315, 577

Granger, Marie Josephe, E-128-129, 163, 165-167, 293, 414, 421, 424-425, 427-428, 563

Granger, Marie Josephe, F-31

Granger, Marie Josephe, N-170

Granger, Marie Madeleine, E-40, 162, 165-166, 298, 381, 383, 386, 425-426, 562

Granger, Marie Madeleine, N-31-33, 210

Granger, Marie Magdeleine, S3-921

Granger, Marie Magdelene, F-25

Granger, Marie Marguerite, E-128-130, 166, 562, 574, 608-610, 613, 615

Granger, Marie Marthe, E-610, 612

Granger, Marie Modeste, E-166, 564

Granger, Marie Thereze, E-159

Granger, Marie-Josephe, S2-697-698

Granger, Marie-Madeleine, S1-146-147, 179-180, 291, 364, 369

Granger, Marie-Madeleine, S2-460, 528, 613, 617

Granger, Mathias, E-166

Granger, Mathurin, E-161, 164-167, 564

Granger, Mathurin, N-73

Granger, Mathurin Laurent, E-166

Granger, Michel, E-166, 386

Granger, Mr., E-163-164, 365, 373

Granger, Paul, E-356

Granger, Paul Marie, E-166

Granger, Paul Marie, N-73

Granger, Pelagie, E-167

Granger, Pelagie Felicite, E-167

Granger, Pierre, E-95, 162-167, 287, 381, 417, 496, 526, 563-564, 581

Granger, Pierre, N-147

Granger, Pierre, S2-700-701

Granger, Pierre Amand, E-165, 563

Granger, Pierre Clair, E-604

Granger, Pierre Clair Aimable, E-167

Granger, Pierre Marie, E-167

Granger, Pierre Marie, F-99

Granger, Pierre Mathurin, E-167, 562

Granger, Pierre Michel, E-167

Granger, Pierre-Marie, S1-368

Granger, Polinne Marie Felicite, E-167

Granger, Rene, E-496, 526

Granger, Rene Marie, E-167

Granger, Rosalie, E-167

Granger, Simon, E-161-164, 167, 380

Granger, Simon Francois, E-165, 562

Granger, Simon Joseph, E-166

Granger, Sophie Ephrosine, E-167

Granger, Therese, E-166

Granieo, -----, E-6

Granier, -----, E-5

Granjen, Marie, S3-1003

Grapard, Bernard, E-167

Grapard, Jean, E-167

Grapard, Jean Baptiste, E-167

Grassard, Guillaume, S2-482

Grasset, Pierre, E-153

Gratien, Francoise, S2-765

Gratien, Francoise, S3-923

Gratien, Marie, S2-781-782

Gratien, Marie, S3-923

Gratien, Yves, S2-781

Gratien, Yves, S3-923

Graveau, Guillaume, E-359

Gravier, Marguerite, E-130

Graville de Fontaines, Jacques, E-428

Gravois, Angelique-Marguerite, S1-369

Gravois, Joseph, S1-155, 369

Gravot, Etienne-Jean, S1-370

Gravot, Jacques-Francois, S1-370

Gravot, Joseph, S1-370

Gravot, Joseph, S3-1117

Gravot, Olive-Angelique, S1-370

Gravot, Therese-Gillette, S1-370

Gravot, Thomasse-Julienne, S1-370

Gravouil, Andre Jean, E-168

Gravouil, Jean, E-34, 168, 355

Gravouil, Marie, E-168

Gravouil, Pierre, E-168

Grbour, Mathurin, E-109

Grebaud, Marguerite, E-153

Grelard, Marie, E-60, 386

Greleau, Jeanne, E-123

Grellet, Francois, E-97, 168

Grellet, Jeanne, E-97, 168

Grelu, Jean, C-136

Grenard, Jean, E-168

Grenard, Marie, E-168, 404
Grenard, Marie Jeanne, E-12, 168
Grenard, Nicolas, E-168, 349, 404, 420
Grenard, Nicolas Gabriel, E-168
Grenier, Joseph, N-250
Grenier, Marie Anne, E-64, 308
Grenier, Marie Josephe, E-4-5
Grenon, Charles, N-182
Grenon, Francois, N-182
Grenot, Jean, E-168
Grenot, Marguerite, E-168
Gresil, Francois, E-356
Gressant, Francois, E-168, 290
Gressant, Joseph, E-168, 290
Gressin, Gervaise, E-586, 591
Gressin, Louis, E-586, 591
Greunais, Francoise, S1-205
Grieu, Jeanne, S2-546
Grieux, Sieur Louis, S3-1060
Grillon, Louis, E-292
Grimard, Catherine, E-142, 256
Grimard, Jean, E-84, 168
Grimard, Pierre, E-168, 376
Grimau, Francois, E-169, 325, 402
Grimau, Magdeleine, E-169, 325, 401-402
Grimaud, Louis, E-40
Grioire, Anne, N-54, 56, 71
Grion, Francois, S3-861
Grisard, Jean, E-65
Griseau, Jacques, E-335
Griseau, Marie, E-169, 335
Grisel, Jean Nicolas, E-334
Grison, Rene, S3-849
Grivel, Jean Pierre, E-103, 315
Grizard, Catherine, E-169, 358
Groassin, Marie, E-25
Grollier, Francois, E-100, 169
Gromen, Suzanne, E-303, 316
Gron, Etienne, E-355
Grornet, Jean Pierre, S3-1143
Gros, Antoinette, E-121, 140
Gros, Armand, E-169, 172
Gros, Joseph, E-169, 172
Grosin, Michel, E-169, 301
Grossard, Francois, E-160, 169
Grossard, Marie, E-160, 169
Grosse, Renee, E-80, 405

Grosset, Michel, S3-956
Grossia, Suzanne, E-38, 159
Grossin, Anne, E-169
Grossin, Anne, S1-37-38, 375-376
Grossin, Anne, S3-1009, 1060
Grossin, Baptiste Louis, E-169
Grossin, Baptiste-Louis, S1-371
Grossin, Brigitte, S1-149-150, 294, 372
Grossin, Brigitte, S2-482, 603
Grossin, Cecile, E-169-170, 594
Grossin, Cecile, S1-374-376
Grossin, Francoise, S1-372
Grossin, Henriette, E-169, 617, 624
Grossin, Henriette, F-103
Grossin, Henriette, S1-184, 294, 372
Grossin, Henriette, S2-461
Grossin, Jacques, E-63, 169-170, 586, 594
Grossin, Jacques, S1-371-372, 374-376
Grossin, Jean, E-170
Grossin, Jean, S1-371
Grossin, Jeanne-Francoise-Nicolle, S1-373
Grossin, Joseph, S1-373
Grossin, Louis, E-170, 594
Grossin, Louis, S1-370, 372, 375-376
Grossin, Louise, E-373
Grossin, Louise, N-99-100, 214
Grossin, Louise, S2-519
Grossin, Louise, S3-948
Grossin, Madeleine, S1-374, 376
Grossin, Madeleine, S2-687
Grossin, Magdeleine, E-170, 586, 593
Grossin, Marguerite, E-586, 594
Grossin, Marguerite, S1-375-376
Grossin, Marie, E-586, 592
Grossin, Marie, N-61
Grossin, Marie, S1-24, 201, 277, 294, 371-372
Grossin, Marie, S2-429, 519, 747
Grossin, Marie, S3-1045

Grossin, Marie Louise, E-170, 374
Grossin, Marie-Louise, S1-371-372, 375-376
Grossin, Marie-Louise, S2-518
Grossin, Marie-Madeleine, S1-372
Grossin, Michel, E-79, 104, 169-170, 373-374, 617, 624
Grossin, Michel, N-61, 100
Grossin, Michel, S1-199, 294, 371-374, 376
Grossin, Michel, S2-449, 518
Grossin, Michel, S3-918-919, 951, 959-960, 1001, 1009, 1045
Grossin, Michel-Pierre, S1-374
Grossin, Modeste, S1-372
Grossin, Pierre, E-63, 169-170
Grossin, Pierre, S1-37, 83, 370, 374-376
Grossin, Pierre, S2-687
Grossin, Pierre, S3-919, 951, 1009
Grossin, Pierre-Michel, S1-373
Grossin, Robert, E-170
Grossin, Robert, S1-372
Grossin, Rose, S1-375-376
Grossine, Marie, E-25
Grousard, Jean, E-169
Grousard, Jean Bernard, E-169
Grout, Marie Marguerite, E-25, 56
Grout, Pierre Nicolas, E-25
Groutelle, Marie Anne, E-31, 109
Grovillet, Pierre, S2-525
Groyeau, Catherine, E-172, 408
Gruaud, wife of, N-228
Gruenais, Anne, S2-536
Gruenais, Jean, S2-535
Gruenais, Jeanne, S2-535
Gruenais, Julienne, S2-536
Gruenais, Madeleine, S2-536
Gruet, Marguerite, E-126, 408
Guadeloupe - Cities whose registers were registered, E-399
Guaisy, Magdelaine, E-170
Guay, Louis, E-409
Guedon, Archanje, N-230

INDEX SOURCES   C=Chatellerault;   E=Acadians in Exile;   F=Acadian Families;   N=Nantes;   S=St-Malo

Guedon, Francois, E-305
Guedon, Jeanne, E-171
Guedon, Mathurin, E-171
Guedry, Anne Laurence, F-37
Guedry, Anne Laurence, N-74
Guedry, Anne Rosalie Marguerite, C-46
Guedry, Anne-Dorothee, S1-378
Guedry, Anne-Josephe, S1-380
Guedry, Antoine, N-74
Guedry, Antoine, S1-376, 378
Guedry, Antoine, S2-600
Guedry, Augustin, N-113
Guedry, Augustin, S1-160, 379-380
Guedry, Augustin, S2-560, 625
Guedry, Augustin, S3-989
Guedry, Charles, C-46, 58
Guedry, Charles, F-47
Guedry, Charles, N-22, 74, 179, 225
Guedry, Charles, S1-105, 168, 376-378, 380
Guedry, Charles, S2-599
Guedry, Charles, S3-989, 1106, 1110
Guedry, child, F-47
Guedry, Claude, C-46-47
Guedry, Claude, F-33, 39, 95
Guedry, Claude, S1-378-381
Guedry, Claude, S2-570, 671, 761
Guedry, Claude, S3-900, 902, 1113
Guedry, Francois, F-9, 41, 95
Guedry, Francois, N-75
Guedry, Francois, S2-468
Guedry, Francois-Xavier, S1-379
Guedry, Francoise, C-7, 70-71, 144
Guedry, Francoise, F-7
Guedry, Francoise, N-10, 69, 125-127
Guedry, Francoise, S1-47, 346
Guedry, Francoise, S2-583, 586-589, 767
Guedry, Francoise, S3-1006, 1010, 1038, 1077
Guedry, Henriette, F-47
Guedry, Jacques, F-37

Guedry, Jacques, N-74, 252
Guedry, Jacques-Servais, S1-377
Guedry, Jean, C-44
Guedry, Jean, F-37
Guedry, Jean, N-74, 179, 193-194, 218, 225, 235, 248
Guedry, Jean, S1-379
Guedry, Jean, S2-631
Guedry, Jean, S3-902
Guedry, Jean Baptiste, C-46
Guedry, Jean Baptiste, F-9, 41
Guedry, Jean Baptiste, N-74-75
Guedry, Jean Charles, N-76
Guedry, Jean Pierre, F-39
Guedry, Jean Pierre, N-76
Guedry, Jean-Baptiste, S1-378, 380
Guedry, Jean-Baptiste, S2-551
Guedry, Jean-Pierre, S1-377
Guedry, Jeanne, S1-160
Guedry, Joseph, C-15, 46-47
Guedry, Joseph, F-33, 37
Guedry, Joseph, N-74-75
Guedry, Joseph, S1-377-378, 380-381
Guedry, Joseph Firmin, F-39
Guedry, Joseph Firmin, N-76
Guedry, Judith, C-37
Guedry, Judith, F-71, 107
Guedry, Judith, N-58
Guedry, Laurence-Anne, S1-377
Guedry, Louise Genevieve, N-75
Guedry, Malo, F-95
Guedry, Malo-Benonie, S1-379
Guedry, Marguerite, C-47
Guedry, Marguerite, E-173
Guedry, Marguerite, E-53, 69, 302, 566, 586-587, 591-592
Guedry, Marguerite, F-9, 33, 41, 47
Guedry, Marguerite, N-37, 74-75, 179
Guedry, Marguerite, S1-376-378
Guedry, Marguerite Felicite, F-9, 41
Guedry, Marguerite Felicite, N-75
Guedry, Marguerite Victoire, N-22-23, 74, 225

Guedry, Marguerite-Victoire, S1-105
Guedry, Marie, E-173
Guedry, Marie, E-64, 70, 587, 592
Guedry, Marie, F-33, 95
Guedry, Marie, N-75
Guedry, Marie, S1-170, 380
Guedry, Marie, S3-1049
Guedry, Marie Anne, C-46
Guedry, Marie Anne, N-75
Guedry, Marie Jeanne, C-46
Guedry, Marie Jeanne, N-75
Guedry, Marie Joseph, S3-989
Guedry, Marie Josephe, N-113
Guedry, Marie Rose, F-39
Guedry, Marie Rose, N-76
Guedry, Marie-Cecile, S1-379
Guedry, Marie-Josephe, S2-560, 625-626
Guedry, Olivier, F-95
Guedry, Pierre, C-47
Guedry, Pierre, E-173
Guedry, Pierre, F-9, 37, 39, 41, 95
Guedry, Pierre, N-74-76, 225
Guedry, Pierre, S1-376, 378, 380-381
Guedry, Pierre, S2-551
Guedry, Pierre, S3-900
Guedry, Pierre David, F-47
Guedry, Pierre Jean Marie, N-75
Guedry, Pierre Joseph, F-39
Guedry, Pierre Joseph, N-76
Guedry, Pierre-Claude, S1-380
Guedry, Pierre-Jean, S1-377
Guedry, Pierre-Olivier, S1-379
Guedry, Reine Elizabeth, F-33
Guedry, Reine Elizabeth, N-75
Guedry, Sulia-Charles, S1-379
Guedry, Suliac, F-95
Guedry, Theodore, N-74
Guedry, Theodore-Felix, S1-377
Guedson, Pierre, E-19, 64
Guegan, Marie-Louise, S2-743
Guegon, Marie, E-94
Guegon, Marie Renee, E-373
Gueguan, Julien, E-420
Guellec, Michelle, E-425
Guello, Jean, S2-556
Guenain, Marie, E-587

Guenain, Marie Je, E-592
Guenard, Augustin, N-76, 103, 211
Guenard, Charles, N-76, 211
Guenard, Marie Jeanne, E-169
Guenewer, Francois, E-171, 187
Guenewer, Jean, E-171, 187
Guenewer, Jean Marie, E-171
Guenewer, Marie Elisabeth, E-171
Guenewer, Sophie, E-171
Guenin, Yves, E-25
Guenot, Cecile, C-158
Guerain, Agathe, E-118
Guerard, Anne, E-171, 353
Guerard, Francoise, E-619
Guerard, Jean, E-171
Guerard, Jean Baptiste, E-171, 353
Guerard, Marguerite, E-160, 171, 267
Gueras, Francoise, S1-204
Gueras, Guillaume, S1-17
Gueret, Claude, E-99, 172, 303
Gueret, Francois, S3-911
Gueret, Genevieve, N-197
Gueret, Pierre, E-172, 439
Guereux, Rene, N-77, 186
Guereux, Sebastien, N-186
Guerin, Alexis, S1-382
Guerin, Ambroise, S1-384
Guerin, Anastasie, S1-382-383
Guerin, Anne, E-474
Guerin, Anne-Josephe, S1-382-383
Guerin, Antoine, E-172
Guerin, Brigide, F-13
Guerin, Brigide, S1-383
Guerin, Brigitte, N-77
Guerin, Charles, S1-326, 381-382
Guerin, Charles, S3-1083
Guerin, Dominique, F-13
Guerin, Dominique, N-77, 156, 220, 239
Guerin, Dominique, S1-121, 245, 382-383, 388, 392
Guerin, Dominique, S3-870
Guerin, Elizabeth, N-77
Guerin, Francois, E-27, 457
Guerin, Francoise, F-13, 101

Guerin, Francoise, N-77-78, 156-157, 239
Guerin, Francoise, S1-73, 383
Guerin, Francoise, S2-486, 540, 736-737, 747, 751
Guerin, Francoise, S3-934, 977, 1026, 1035-1037
Guerin, Francoise Elizabeth, F-13
Guerin, Gabriel, C-2, 47, 49, 79, 126
Guerin, Gabriel, E-636
Guerin, Gertrude, S1-384
Guerin, Henriette, S1-111-112, 389
Guerin, Henriette, S3-908, 940
Guerin, Honore, E-172
Guerin, Isabelle, F-13
Guerin, Isabelle, S1-126, 383
Guerin, Jacques, C-47, 126
Guerin, Jan Baptiste, S3-976
Guerin, Jean, E-172
Guerin, Jean, S3-1138
Guerin, Jean Pierre, C-20
Guerin, Jean Pierre, F-47
Guerin, Jean Pierre, S3-1135-1136, 1138
Guerin, Jean-Baptiste, S1-384
Guerin, Jean-Pierre, S1-157, 384-385
Guerin, Jeanne, E-172, 256, 333, 413
Guerin, Jerome, E-526
Guerin, Jerome, F-47
Guerin, Jerome, N-77, 239
Guerin, Jerome, S1-124, 158, 381, 384-385
Guerin, Joseph, F-13
Guerin, Joseph, N-77, 142, 220, 239
Guerin, Joseph, S1-124, 382-385
Guerin, Louis, E-172
Guerin, Louis, S1-384-385
Guerin, Louis Olive, E-172
Guerin, Marguerite, E-172, 408
Guerin, Marguerite, S1-50, 61, 112, 382-383
Guerin, Marguerite, S2-507, 739, 746, 750-751
Guerin, Margueritte, S3-974

Guerin, Marguerite-Josephe, S1-382
Guerin, Marie, E-81, 172, 264, 270, 316, 354, 413, 425, 472
Guerin, Marie, S1-245, 383
Guerin, Marie, S3-828, 955
Guerin, Marie Agathe, E-172, 174, 298
Guerin, Marie Josephine, N-78
Guerin, Marie-Madeleine, S1-384
Guerin, Marin, S1-382
Guerin, Martin, S1-382
Guerin, Mathurin, E-286
Guerin, Pierre, C-126
Guerin, Pierre, E-172, 413
Guerin, Pierre, S1-384-385
Guerin, Simon, E-44
Guerin, Tarsile, S2-600
Guerin, Tarsille, S1-326, 330, 382
Guerin, Tarsille, S2-507, 756
Guerin, Tharzile, S3-1083
Guerin, Xavier, S1-384
Guerlauais, Jean, S2-466
Guerlavais, Ge., S3-901
Guerlova, Mathurin, S2-765
Guernard, Jean, E-169, 172, 601
Guernard, Marie Jeanne, E-172
Guerroet, Francoise, S1-220
Guerry, Jacques, E-72, 153
Guerry, Jean, E-316
Guertier, Marie Suzanne, E-159, 304
Guertin, Marie, E-29, 172
Guesdon, Pierre, E-19, 172, 262, 355
Gugo, Basile, E-172
Gugo, Marguerite Julienne, E-172
Gugon, Louise Joseph, E-419
Guguen, Gugonne, S1-172
Guguen, Gugonne, S3-872
Guguiaux, Jean, S1-195
Gui-Louvel, Claude, S1-183
Guibert, Jean, E-339
Guibert, Pierre, E-80, 264
Guibon, Marie Louise, C-30, 109

Guibon, Marie Louise, E-274, 323-325
Guichard, Francois, E-55, 309
Guichard, G.F., S3-889
Guichard, Jean, E-625
Guichard, Joseph, E-14, 425, 625
Guichard, Marie, E-120, 442
Guichard, Mathurine, E-71, 345
Guichard, Modeste, E-10
Guichard, Mr., E-55, 433
Guichard, Pierre, E-309
Guichon, Jean, E-173
Guichon, Jerome, E-173, 315
Guichon, Pierre, E-173, 349
Guiffard, Francois, S1-385
Guignard, Françoise, E-353, 381
Guignet, Marie Anne, E-65, 174
Guignette, Marguerite, E-393
Guigueneau, Jean, E-173, 404
Guigueneau, Jeanne, E-173, 404
Guilbeau, Charles, C-75
Guilbeau, Charles, E-502, 526
Guilbeau, Charlotte, E-173
Guilbeau, Elizabeth, E-173
Guilbeau, Elizabeth, N-147
Guilbeau, Francois, E-173
Guilbeau, Hugues, E-502
Guilbeau, Isabelle, E-502
Guilbeau, Isabelle, S2-700
Guilbeau, Jean, E-270
Guilbeau, Jeanne, E-473, 502
Guilbeau, Joseph, E-173
Guilbeau, Joseph, S1-35
Guilbeau, Louis, E-370
Guilbeau, Marguerite, E-137, 149, 472, 502
Guilbeau, Marguerite, S1-70
Guilbeau, Marie, E-173, 271, 502
Guilbeau, Marie Anne, E-122
Guilbeau, Marie Jeanne, E-173
Guilbeau, Marie Louise, C-75-76
Guilbeau, Marie Therese, E-276
Guilbeau, Pierre, E-17, 173, 388, 457, 474
Guilbeau, Pierre Francois, E-173
Guilbeau, Rene, E-173
Guilbert, Jane, S3-955
Guilbert, Jean, S1-371

Guilbert, Jean, S2-747
Guilbert, Jeanne, S2-747
Guilbert, Jeanne Francoise, S3-955
Guilbert, Jeanne-Francoise, S2-746
Guilbert, Robert, S2-746-747
Guilbert, Robert, S3-955
Guilbon, Charles, E-173
Guilbon, Marie Louise, E-173, 324
Guilbot, Jeanne, E-317
Guilienne, Suzanne, E-587, 592
Guillain, Francois, E-173
Guillard, Jean, S1-385
Guillard, Jean, S3-990
Guillard De La Vacherie, Messiere, C-75
Guillaud de La Vacherie, George, C-91
Guillaume, Aime-Pierre, S1-386
Guillaume, Andre, S1-386
Guillaume, Anne, E-275
Guillaume, Charlotte, S1-386-387
Guillaume, Francoise, S1-387
Guillaume, Genevieve, S1-386
Guillaume, J., E-344
Guillaume, Julien, E-173, 430
Guillaume, Julien, S1-386-387
Guillaume, Julienne-Eleonore, S1-386
Guillaume, Marie, S1-386
Guillaume, Marie-Jeanne, S1-387
Guillaume, Perinne, S1-386
Guillaume, Pierre, E-474
Guillaume, Pierre, S1-386
Guillaume dit La Roche, Julien, S2-772
Guillebaud, Jeanne, S2-558
Guillem, Raymonde, E-405
Guillemas, Pierre, E-173
Guillemas, Simon Pierre, E-173
Guillemaut, Louis, S3-960
Guilleme, Perrine Jeanne, N-185
Guillemelton, Jacques, E-332
Guillement, Marie Anne, E-419
Guillemeteau, Marie, E-74, 106
Guillemin, Jacquemine, S2-737

Guillemot, Pierre, E-95, 382-383
Guillerme, Marie Josephe, E-47
Guillet, Francois, E-152, 173
Guillet, Joseph Mathieu, E-152, 173
Guillet, Marguerite, E-369
Guillet, Marie, E-275
Guilleton, Jean, E-391
Guilleton, Jean dit La Roche, E-174
Guilleton, Louise, E-174, 391
Guilleton dit La Roche, Jean, E-29
Guillier, Marie, E-72, 90
Guillimin, Genevieve, E-174, 258
Guillolet, Francoise, E-393, 409
Guillon, Francois, E-265
Guillon, Jacques, E-55, 265
Guillon, Jean, E-91, 168, 172, 183, 309, 338, 353
Guillon, Marie, E-108, 256
Guillon, Mathieu, E-69
Guilloneau, Jean, E-390
Guillonnet, Francois, E-386
Guillonnet, Francoise, E-60, 386
Guillot, Alexis, C-48
Guillot, Alexis, S1-391-392
Guillot, Ambroise, C-2, 40, 48-49, 92, 102, 104-106, 110-111, 114, 125
Guillot, Ambroise, S1-90, 114, 235, 245, 387, 389, 392
Guillot, Ambroise, S3-828, 905, 907-908
Guillot, Anne, C-40, 47, 126
Guillot, Anne Gertrude, C-110
Guillot, Anne Gertrude, E-636
Guillot, Anne-Gertrude, S1-388-389
Guillot, Anne-Marguerite, S1-393
Guillot, Antoine, C-23
Guillot, Antoine, E-166
Guillot, Charles, C-113
Guillot, Charles, S1-111-112, 388
Guillot, Charles, S3-908
Guillot, Charles Olivier, C-47, 49

Guillot, Charles Olivier, F-49
Guillot, Charles-Olivier, S1-162, 389-392
Guillot, Dominique, C-48-49, 92
Guillot, Dominique, E-636
Guillot, Dominique, S1-388
Guillot, Elizabeth, S1-390-391
Guillot, Elizabeth-Madeleine, S1-389
Guillot, Euphrosine, S1-391
Guillot, Fabien, F-73
Guillot, Fabien, S1-388
Guillot, Fabien-Amateur, S1-388
Guillot, Francois, E-73
Guillot, Francoise, F-13
Guillot, Francoise-Gertrude, S1-392
Guillot, Genevieve, C-48, 92
Guillot, Genevieve Anne, E-636
Guillot, Genevieve-Anne, S1-388
Guillot, Gertrude, S1-387
Guillot, Isabelle, F-49
Guillot, Isabelle Julie, C-50
Guillot, Isabelle-Julie, S1-392
Guillot, Isidore-Francois, S1-389
Guillot, Jean, C-2, 47, 104
Guillot, Jean, E-69, 259, 352, 385
Guillot, Jean, S1-152
Guillot, Jean Baptiste, C-92
Guillot, Jean Baptiste, E-636
Guillot, Jean Baptiste, F-49
Guillot, Jean Baptiste, S3-908
Guillot, Jean Charles, C-40, 48-50, 81, 125-126
Guillot, Jean Michel, F-49
Guillot, Jean-Baptiste, S1-388-391
Guillot, Jean-Baptiste, S2-621
Guillot, Jean-Charles, S1-391, 393
Guillot, Jean-Michel, S1-389
Guillot, Jeanne, C-48
Guillot, Marguerite, C-42, 92
Guillot, Marguerite, E-636
Guillot, Marguerite, S1-91, 115, 246, 344, 388

Guillot, Marguerite Blanche, C-40, 105
Guillot, Marguerite-Blanche, S1-387, 389
Guillot, Marie, C-92, 126
Guillot, Marie, E-309, 340
Guillot, Marie, F-73
Guillot, Marie, S1-90, 114, 163, 388
Guillot, Marie Anne, E-69, 174
Guillot, Marie Gertrude, C-92
Guillot, Marie Joseph, C-2, 50, 104, 122
Guillot, Marie Rose, C-47-49
Guillot, Marie-Josephe, S1-91, 162, 344, 389-391, 393
Guillot, Marie-Rose, S1-392
Guillot, Paul, C-48, 81, 111, 114, 126
Guillot, Paul, E-636
Guillot, Paul, S1-388
Guillot, Pierre, C-48
Guillot, Pierre, S1-392
Guillot, Rene, C-45, 48-50, 104-105, 109-111, 117, 125-126
Guillot, Rene, F-73
Guillot, Rene, S1-121, 162, 235, 387, 391-393
Guillot, Rene, S2-639
Guillot, Rene, S3-908
Guillot, Rene Francois, C-49
Guillot, Rene-Francois, S1-392
Guillot, Simon, F-73
Guillot, Simon Francois, F-49
Guillot, Simon-Francois, S1-389
Guillot, Thomas, S1-390
Guillottin, L. , C-122
Guillou, Jean, S3-1053
Guillou, Jeanne, S2-601
Guilmet, Marie, C-93
Guilson, Bertrand, E-135, 174
Guilson, Jean, E-135, 174
Guimard, Simon, E-11, 174
Guimine, Judith, E-54
Guimine, Madeleine, E-54
Guimine, Marie, E-55
Guimon, -----, S3-846
Guinard, Louis, E-157
Guinaud, Catherine, E-157, 174
Guinaud, Jean, E-157, 174, 326
Guindet, Marie, E-174, 326

Guion, Andree, E-456, 472
Guion, Josephe, E-419
Guion, Louise, E-473
Guion, Marguerite, E-349, 473
Guiot, Fabien, C-74
Guiot, Rene, S3-1104
Guirin, Marie Agathe, E-174
Guirnard, Jean, E-61
Guirnard, Jeanne, E-17
Guironfleh, Pierre, E-174, 343
Guisard, Jean, E-65, 174
Guisard, Joseph, E-174
Guisler, Jean George, E-298
Guitard, Pierre, E-114, 326
Guiton, Magdelaine, E-33, 149
Guitteny, Cecile, S3-1150
Gulcher, Charles, E-368
Gulherme, Jean Baptiste, E-94
Gurel, Judith, E-94
Guret, Francois, S1-357
Gusepel, Francoise, S2-600
Gutierres, Maria, F-65
Guy, Marie, E-80, 405
Guymar, Perrine, N-39, 230
Guyment, Pierre, E-316
Guynet, Mr., E-316
Guyomet, Rene, S1-55
Guyomet, Renee, S1-55-56
Guyon, Baptiste, E-175
Guyon, Jean Baptiste, E-174-175, 265
Guyon, Joseph, E-175
Guyon, Josephe, E-175
Guyon, Marguerite, E-175
Guyon, Michel, E-175
Guyon Des Prez, Anne, E-24, 442

H

Habel, Jacque, E-176
Habel, Jean Baptiste, E-176, 301
Habel, Jean Hector, E-176
Habel, Jean-Baptiste, S1-319
Habel, Marie Anne, E-176
Habel, Marie Madeleinne, E-176
Habel, Michel, E-176
Habel, Pierre, E-176
Habel, Theotiste, E-176
Habel Du Vivier, Jean-Baptiste, S2-591

Habet, Jean Baptiste, E-63, 335
Hache, -----, S2-431
Hache, Ambroise, S2-439
Hache, Anastasie, E-176
Hache, Ange Frederic, N-81
Hache, Ann-Marie, C-9, 42
Hache, Anne, C-26, 34, 51, 86
Hache, Anne, E-78-79, 110,
  176, 546, 619, 628
Hache, Anne, F-71
Hache, Anne, N-80
Hache, Anne, S1-185,, 200-201,
  276
Hache, Anne, S2-430, 432, 680-
  681, 723-724
Hache, Anne, S3-1008
Hache, Anne Marie, E-176
Hache, Anne Marie, S3-1059,
  1071
Hache, Anne-Henriette, S2-430
Hache, Anne-Marie, S1-54, 340
Hache, Anne-Marie, S2-429,
  434-435
Hache, Antoine, C-53
Hache, Antoine, E-176
Hache, Antoine, N-78
Hache, Antoine, S2-428-429,
  433-434
Hache, Antoine, S3-937-938,
  1012, 1030, 1043
Hache, Antoine-Francois, S2-
  428
Hache, Baptiste, E-177
Hache, Barbe Michelle, N-81
Hache, Basile, N-80
Hache, Bonne, N-79
Hache, Bonne Marie Magdalen,
  E-176
Hache, Boone, C-50
Hache, Charles, C-51
Hache, Charles, E-176-179, 187,
  546
Hache, Charles, N-78-79
Hache, Charles, S2-430
Hache, Charles Julien, S2-428
Hache, Elisabeth, F-9
Hache, Elizabeth Marie, N-81
Hache, Eloy Paul, E-177
Hache, Eloy Paul, N-80
Hache, Eloy-Paul, S2-434-435
Hache, Flore Adelaide, N-79

Hache, Francois, C-52
Hache, Francois, E-179, 546
Hache, Francois, N-81
Hache, Francois Basile, N-80
Hache, Francois Isaac, E-177
Hache, Francois Joseph, E-177
Hache, Francois Nicolas, E-59
Hache, Francois-Basile, S2-435
Hache, Francois-Joseph, S2-435
Hache, Francois-Mathurin, S2-
  436
Hache, Francoise, E-177-178
Hache, Francoise Madeleine, N-
  82
Hache, Frederic, C-50
Hache, Frederic, F-69
Hache, Frederic, N-79
Hache, Genevieve, E-79, 110-
  111, 140, 177, 555
Hache, Genevieve, S1-200
Hache, Genevieve, S2-430-431
Hache, George, C-51
Hache, George, E-177
Hache, George, N-79
Hache, George, S3-1043
Hache, Georges, S2-429-430,
  433-434, 436
Hache, Guillaume, N-82
Hache, Guillaume-Servan, S2-
  439
Hache, Heleine, E-177
Hache, Heleine, S2-434
Hache, Helene, C-52
Hache, Helene, F-9
Hache, Helene, N-81
Hache, Helene, S2-436
Hache, Henriette, E-283
Hache, Henriette, E-79, 555
Hache, Henriette Marie, C-50
Hache, Henriette Marie, N-79
Hache, Isaac, C-50
Hache, Isaac, N-79
Hache, Isaac, S2-434-435
Hache, Jacques, C-50-51, 62,
  138
Hache, Jacques, E-177, 179,
  295, 546
Hache, Jacques, F-5
Hache, Jacques, N-79-80
Hache, Jacques, S1-113, 115,
  300

Hache, Jacques, S2-428, 430-
  432, 436, 440
Hache, Jacques, S3-911, 937-
  938, 941-943, 967
Hache, Jacques Denis, E-177
Hache, Jacques-Augustin, S2-
  431
Hache, Jean, C-51
Hache, Jean, E-16, 176-177, 429
Hache, Jean, N-82
Hache, Jean, S3-1030
Hache, Jean Adrien, N-79
Hache, Jean Baptiste, C-9, 51-52
Hache, Jean Baptiste, E-98, 133,
  176-179, 546
Hache, Jean Baptiste, F-75, 79
Hache, Jean Baptiste, N-69, 78-
  81
Hache, Jean Baptiste, S3-938,
  1012, 1030, 1043, 1059, 1065,
  1071
Hache, Jean Baptiste Charles, C-
  50
Hache, Jean Baptiste Charles,
  N-79
Hache, Jean Charles, E-177
Hache, Jean Charles, F-69
Hache, Jean Francois, N-80, 82
Hache, Jean Joseph, E-177
Hache, Jean Louis, C-51-52
Hache, Jean Louis, N-81
Hache, Jean Marie, N-78, 80
Hache, Jean-Baptiste, S1-54
Hache, Jean-Baptiste, S2-428-
  429, 432-435, 437-438
Hache, Jean-Francois, S2-437
Hache, Jean-Louis, S2-436
Hache, Joseph, C-41, 50-52
Hache, Joseph, E-82, 105, 112,
  176-179, 318, 411, 546
Hache, Joseph, F-5, 79
Hache, Joseph, N-80-82
Hache, Joseph, S1-308, 340
Hache, Joseph, S2-431, 433-
  436, 439
Hache, Joseph, S3-938, 942,
  1012, 1059, 1065
Hache, Joseph Marie, C-52
Hache, Joseph-Francois, S2-440
Hache, Joseph-Hiacinthe, S2-
  439

Hache, Joseph-Hyacinthe, S2-436

Hache, Josette, C-52

Hache, Josette, N-81

Hache, Louis, C-42, 51-53

Hache, Louis, E-78, 178

Hache, Louis, F-79

Hache, Louis, N-80-82

Hache, Louis, S1-198, 340

Hache, Louis, S2-431, 433-434, 437-440

Hache, Louis, S3-937, 1008, 1012, 1065, 1075

Hache, Louise, C-55

Hache, Louise, E-24, 178, 430

Hache, Louise, S2-430, 453, 672, 773

Hache, Louise Genevieve, E-178

Hache, Louise Marguerite, C-xiv

Hache, Madeleine, C-50

Hache, Madeleine, N-79

Hache, Madeleine-Apoline, S2-436

Hache, Madeleine-Francoise, S2-440

Hache, Magdelaine, E-546

Hache, Magdelaine Apolline, F-75

Hache, Marguerite, C-50-51, 159

Hache, Marguerite, E-17, 112, 133, 146, 151, 546

Hache, Marguerite, F-5

Hache, Marguerite, N-78, 80

Hache, Marguerite, S2-428, 437

Hache, Marguerite Henriette, C-51

Hache, Marguerite Henriette, N-79

Hache, Marguerite Henry, C-51

Hache, Marguerite Louis, C-41-42

Hache, Marguerite Louise, E-150-152, 176, 178

Hache, Marguerite Louise, N-69

Hache, Marguerite-Guillemette, S2-429

Hache, Marguerite-Louise, S1-340

Hache, Marguerite-Louise, S2-433-434, 436, 439

Hache, Marguerite-Marie, S2-432

Hache, Marguerite-Yvonne, S2-437

Hache, Marie, C-159

Hache, Marie, E-19, 112, 177-178, 376, 546, 555, 585, 593

Hache, Marie, F-7, 5, 63, 75, 79, 83

Hache, Marie, N-78, 80, 82, 146

Hache, Marie, S2-430-431, 675, 687-688

Hache, Marie, S3-1001

Hache, Marie Angelique, E-105, 178

Hache, Marie Anne, E-79

Hache, Marie Anne , S3-917-918

Hache, Marie Bonne, F-69

Hache, Marie Henriette, C-50

Hache, Marie Henriette, N-79

Hache, Marie Joseph, S3-942-943

Hache, Marie Josephe, C-52

Hache, Marie Josephe, E-159, 176, 178

Hache, Marie Josephe, F-9

Hache, Marie Madeleine, E-133, 178

Hache, Marie Modeste, E-179

Hache, Marie Osite, E-179

Hache, Marie Renee, N-79

Hache, Marie Rose, C-50

Hache, Marie Rose, N-79

Hache, Marie-Anne, S1-184-185, 199-200

Hache, Marie-Anne, S2-440

Hache, Marie-Jeanne, S2-428, 432

Hache, Marie-Joseph, S2-436

Hache, Marie-Josephe, S1-97, 321

Hache, Marie-Josephe, S2-433-434, 437

Hache, Marie-Louise, S1-340

Hache, Marie-Modeste, S2-431

Hache, Marie-Rose, S2-429

Hache, Marie-Servanne, S2-428

Hache, Marin-Baptiste, S2-432

Hache, Marin-Jean, S2-432

Hache, Michel, E-179, 526, 546

Hache, Michel, S2-432-434, 439, 680

Hache, Michel Jr., E-526

Hache, Nicolas Laurent, E-179, 295

Hache, Osite, C-53

Hache, Osite, N-82

Hache, Osithe-Francoise-Thomasee, S2-438

Hache, Paul, C-9

Hache, Paul, N-80

Hache, Paul, S2-435

Hache, Pauline, C-52

Hache, Pauline, N-81

Hache, Perinne-Francoise, S2-429

Hache, Perrine, N-79

Hache, Perrinne, C-51, 159

Hache, Pierre, C-51-53

Hache, Pierre, E-43, 78, 111, 140, 176-179, 546, 555

Hache, Pierre, F-63, 79

Hache, Pierre, N-80, 82

Hache, Pierre, S1-97, 184, 199, 272, 307

Hache, Pierre, S2-430-431, 433, 435, 438-439440, 647, 676, 723

Hache, Pierre, S3-917, 937-938, 943, 1008, 1030, 1038, 1043, 1065

Hache, Pierre Charles, C-52

Hache, Pierre Paul, C-98

Hache, Pierre Paul, S3-1059

Hache, Pierre-Jean, S2-432

Hache, Pierre-Paul, S1-54

Hache, Pierre-Paul, S2-429, 432, 434-436, 440

Hainement, Jean, F-85

Haiti, E-395-397

Hallais, Francois, S2-508

Hallais, Francois, S3-1095

Hallais, Marie, S3-1095

Hallais, Marie Janne Francoise, S3-1095

Hallais, Marie-Jeanne-Francoise, S2-508

Halley, Jeanne, E-96, 107, 355

Halley, Marguerite Catherine Adelaide, E-281, 369

Hallier, Marie Josephe, F-109

Hambourg, Francois, C-53

Hambourg, Louis Joseph, C-54

Hamel, Catherine, E-31, 317

Hamel, Jacques, E-140, 177

Hamelin, Jean Francois, E-158, 179

Hamelin, Jean Francois, S2-441

Hamelin, Nicolas, E-158, 179

Hamelin, Nicolas, S2-441, 684

Hamet, Etienne, S2-441-442

Hamet, Francois, S2-441

Hamet, Isabelle, S2-441

Hamet, Pierre, S2-441

Hamon, Anne-Madeleine, S2-442

Hamon, Cecile, S2-443

Hamon, Francois, S2-442

Hamon, Francoise, E-179, 313

Hamon, Igance, C-21, 53

Hamon, Ignace, S1-98, 130, 152

Hamon, Ignace, S2-442-443

Hamon, Ignace, S3-853, 855, 1141, 1151

Hamon, Jacques, E-179

Hamon, Jean, C-53

Hamon, Jean, E-52, 179, 313

Hamon, Jean, S2-442-443

Hamon, Jean, S3-830, 832, 853, 1023

Hamon, Jean-Baptiste, S2-442

Hamon, Jean-Francois, S2-442

Hamon, Joseph, S2-443

Hamon, Julien, S2-443-444

Hamon, Marie Modeste, C-53

Hamon, Marie-Gervaise, S2-443

Hamon, Mathurin, S2-443-444, 579

Hamon, Mathurin, S3-1023

Hamon, Olivier, S2-442

Hamon, Paul, E-424

Hamon, Victoire, E-179

Hamond, Anne Madeleine, N-83

Hamond, Catherine Francoise, N-83

Hamond, Guillaume, N-82, 183

Hamond, Ignace, N-83

Hamond, Jean Etienne, N-83

Hamond, Joseph, N-82, 183

Hamond, Marie Modeste, N-83

Hamont, Anne Magdelaine, F-77

Hamont, Guillaume, F-53

Hamont, Ignace, F-77

Hamont, Jean, F-77

Hamont, Joseph, F-53

Hamont, Marie Modeste, F-77

Hamorshaud, Catherine, E-357

Hanibar, Jean, S1-77

Hannet, Rene, E-585, 595

Hanouet, Antoine Marie Xavier, E-179

Hanouet, Catherine Adelaide, E-87-88, 179

Hanouet, Charles Stanislas, E-89

Hanouet, Nicolas Florentin, E-88

Hanouette, Catherine, E-641

Hanry, Amant, S3-1010

Hanry, Francoise, E-179

Hanry, Hustache, E-180

Hantonne, Pierre, E-439

Hapdey, Marie, E-46, 188

Haquin, Guillaume, S2-778

Harambourg, Francois, E-627

Harambourg, Francoise, E-625

Harambourg, Jean, E-625-626

Harambourg, Jeanne, E-625

Harambourg, Marie, E-625

Harbourg, Francois, F-35

Harbourg, Francois, N-207

Harbourg, Francois Henry, F-35

Harbourg, Frederic Edouard, F-35

Harbourg, Jean Louis Firmin, F-35

Harbourg, Louis Nicolas, C-53

Harcart, Suzanne, E-303

Harcoue, Pierre, E-194

Hardy, Francois, S1-202

Hardy, Francois, S2-444

Hardy, Hilaire, S2-444

Hardy, Jean, N-211

Hardy, Louis, E-18, 180

Hardy, Louise Therese, E-18, 180

Hardy, Marie Anne, E-51, 319

Hardy, Marie Jeanne, E-60, 109

Harel, Charles, S2-444

Harel, Guillemete, S2-594

Harel, Guillemete, S3-962

Harel, Louis, S2-444

Harel, Louis-Julien, S2-444

Harel, Olive, S2-595

Harel, Pierre, S3-962, 990

Harel, Y., S3-962

Harel, Yve, S3-962

Haret, Olive, S3-990

Harixague, Francois, E-180

Harixague, Pierre, E-14, 180, 258

Haron, Pierre, N-192

Harotte, Claude, S2-648

Harotte, Marie, S2-648

Harroquille, Jeanne, E-362

Harseman, Pierre, S3-1111

Harsemant, Marguerite, E-625

Harsicot, Francois, E-28, 180

Hart, Marie, E-21

Hauchecorne, Charles Antoine Gregoire, E-180, 343

Hauchecorne, Emma Euphrosine, E-180

Hauchecorne, Eugenie Desiree, E-180

Hauchecorne, Nicolas, E-15, 25

Hauchecorne, Nicolas Emmanuel, E-180, 343

Hauchecorne, Nicolas Robert, E-59, 180

Hauchecorne, Pierre Nicolas, E-180

Haudenie, Marie, N-252

Hauguel, Pierre, E-116

Hauin, Pierre Felix, E-195

Haumont, Etienne, S3-1011

Hauteville, Francois, E-180, 348

Hauteville, Marianne, E-180, 348

Hautiere, Jacques, S3-861

Hautiere, Jeanne, E-25, 265

Hautiere, Louis, E-265

Hautremer, Francois, S2-444-445

Hauville, Pierre Augustin, E-110

Havard, Jean, N-83, 228

Havard, Jean Francois, N-23, 83, 228

Havard, Jean Marie, N-83

Havard, Louis, E-157

Haymonet, Louise, E-256, 382

INDEX SOURCES C=Chatellerault; E=Acadians in Exile; F=Acadian Families; N=Nantes; S=St-Malo

Hazurier, Francois, S2-649
Heberd, Anne, C-117
Heberd, Jean Baptiste, C-117, 119
Heberd, Jean Pierre, C-124
Heberd, Pierre, C-124
Hebert, Adelaide, E-181
Hebert, Agnes, E-568
Hebert, Agnes, S1-309
Hebert, Aible, E-182
Hebert, Aimable, E-182, 184, 186, 188-189
Hebert, Alain-Mathurin, S2-465
Hebert, Alexandre, E-214, 526
Hebert, Alexis, E-176, 181, 183-184, 187-190, 384
Hebert, Alexis, S2-469
Hebert, Alexis Medard, N-90
Hebert, Alexis Thomas, F-43
Hebert, Alexis Thomas, N-92
Hebert, Alexis Toussaint, C-57
Hebert, Alexis Toussaint, N-91-92
Hebert, Alexis-Pierre, S2-447
Hebert, Alexis-Toussaint, S2-462
Hebert, Alonse, E-402
Hebert, Alphonse Honore, E-181
Hebert, Amable, E-2, 564
Hebert, Amable, F-3
Hebert, Amable, N-84
Hebert, Amand, E-181
Hebert, Ambroise, C-54, 65, 133
Hebert, Ambroise, E-184, 188-189, 191, 329
Hebert, Ambroise, F-21, 43, 73, 79, 107
Hebert, Ambroise, N-84-85, 89, 94, 136, 175, 233-234
Hebert, Ambroise, S1-16, 29, 266
Hebert, Ambroise, S2-445-448, 466, 474, 612, 629, 762
Hebert, Ambroise, S3-826, 884
Hebert, Ambroise Mathurin, C-57
Hebert, Ambroise Mathurin, F-43
Hebert, Ambroise Mathurin, N-92

Hebert, Ambroise-Alexandre-Baptiste, S2-448
Hebert, Ambroise-Mathurin, S2-463
Hebert, Anastasie, E-87-88, 437, 631, E-641
Hebert, Anastasie, S1-217-218
Hebert, Anastasie, S2-468
Hebert, Andre, F-3
Hebert, Andre, N-84
Hebert, Angelique, E-111, 179, 181
Hebert, Angelique, S2-607, 695
Hebert, Anne, C-18, 24-25, 54, 56, 68, 74, 89-90
Hebert, Anne, E-2, 113, 181, 185, 285, 287, 289, 311, 314, 325, 375, 417, 438, 587, 594-595, 601, 610, 630, 636
Hebert, Anne, F-3, 17, 25, 27, 35, 43, 87
Hebert, Anne, N-87, 90, 116, 151
Hebert, Anne, S1-3, 15-19, 65, 69, 72, 100, 114, 272
Hebert, Anne, S2-457-459, 462-463, 469, 475, 532, 606, 714-716
Hebert, Anne, S3-906, 1111
Hebert, Anne Marguerite, F-33, 49
Hebert, Anne Marguerite, N-92-93
Hebert, Anne Marie, E-105, 143, 181, 358
Hebert, Anne Marie Augustine, N-91
Hebert, Anne Marie Basile Etiennette, E-182
Hebert, Anne Osite, C-88-89
Hebert, Anne Osite, F-47
Hebert, Anne Osite, N-150
Hebert, Anne Ozite, S1-23
Hebert, Anne Perpetue, E-84, 90, 182
Hebert, Anne Symphore, N-16
Hebert, Anne Victoire, N-87
Hebert, Anne-Josephe, S1-328-330
Hebert, Anne-Josephe, S2-476-477

Hebert, Anne-Madeleine, S2-466
Hebert, Anne-Marie, S1-29, 296
Hebert, Anne-Marie, S2-461, 469, 471
Hebert, Anne-Marie-Julienne, S2-474
Hebert, Anne-Osite, S2-712-713
Hebert, Anne-Perinne, S2-477
Hebert, Anne-Simone, S2-460
Hebert, Anne-Simphorose, S1-71
Hebert, Anselme, E-182, 601
Hebert, Antoine, E-82, 181, 214, 457, 474, 510, 526
Hebert, Astasie, E-179
Hebert, Athanase, S2-450-451
Hebert, Auguste Louis, E-182
Hebert, Augustin, E-526
Hebert, Augustin, S2-565
Hebert, Barnabe Placide, E-190
Hebert, Basile, S2-445-446
Hebert, Bazile, E-182, 188, 608, 610-611, 613-614
Hebert, Benony, S2-449
Hebert, Brigide, F-3
Hebert, Brigitte, E-2
Hebert, Brigitte Josephe, E-182, 565
Hebert, Catherine, E-45, 145, 475-476
Hebert, Catherine-Josephe, S1-117-120
Hebert, Catherine-Josephe, S2-456
Hebert, Cecile, E-63, 130, 170, 176, 266, 526
Hebert, Cecile, F-63, 73
Hebert, Cecile, N-88
Hebert, Cecile, S1-83, 184, 319, 371, 374
Hebert, Cecile, S2-449, 471-472, 512, 566, 591
Hebert, Cecile, S3-917, 919, 956, 1001, 1082
Hebert, Celeste Pelagie, E-182
Hebert, Charles, C-11, 20, 50, 54-55, 57-58, 68, 101, 139
Hebert, Charles, E-181-184, 186-191, 272, 283, 429, 433, 565

Hebert, Charles, F-15, 25, 49
Hebert, Charles, N-65, 86-87, 92-93, 224, 236, 239
Hebert, Charles, S1-91, 266, 345, 371
Hebert, Charles, S2-449-453, 461, 468, 471-473, 539, 613, 617, 633, 672, 773
Hebert, Charles, S3-899, 905, 939, 944-945, 956, 994, 1017, 1051, 1082, 1139-1140
Hebert, Charles Jean, E-360, 366
Hebert, Charles Lazare, N-88
Hebert, Charles-Adrien, S2-467
Hebert, Charles-Jean, S2-471
Hebert, Charlotte, E-632
Hebert, child, F-21
Hebert, child, S2-455
Hebert, Claire, E-182, 193-194
Hebert, Claude, E-182
Hebert, Cologique, E-587, 593
Hebert, Constance, E-168, 290
Hebert, David, E-2
Hebert, Derial, S2-455
Hebert, Didier, E-115
Hebert, Dominique, E-182-183, 276, 432
Hebert, Donald J. (Rev.), C-viii
Hebert, Elisabeth, E-105, 182, 587, 594, 601, 619
Hebert, Elisabeth, S3-936, 1013
Hebert, Elisabeth Apoline, E-182
Hebert, Elizabeth, F-45, 73
Hebert, Elizabeth, N-84, 90, 94
Hebert, Elizabeth, S1-22, 24, 90, 101, 158, 329-330
Hebert, Elizabeth, S2-458-459, 475-476, 526, 709
Hebert, Elizabeth Jeanne, N-93
Hebert, Emanuel, E-474, 526
Hebert, Emilie, E-610
Hebert, Etienne, C-54-55
Hebert, Etienne, E-181, 183, 185, 188, 280, 384, 457, 474, 511, 526
Hebert, Etienne, F-27, 63, 73
Hebert, Etienne, N-31, 87, 90, 188, 233
Hebert, Etienne, S2-470

Hebert, Felicite, C-55
Hebert, Felicite, E-601
Hebert, Felicite, F-15, 111
Hebert, Felicite, N-2, 91
Hebert, Felicite-Jeanne, S2-462
Hebert, Felix, E-15, 181, 183, 187, 190
Hebert, Felix, S1-218
Hebert, Felix-Augustin, S2-467
Hebert, Ferdinand, E-17, 183, 281
Hebert, Firmain, N-90
Hebert, Firmain Joseph, C-57
Hebert, Firmin, E-183, 587, 594
Hebert, Firmin, S2-452
Hebert, Francois, C-34
Hebert, Francois, E-183, 185, 601, 625, 631
Hebert, Francois, F-5, 27, 87, 95
Hebert, Francois, N-88-90, 114, 189, 205, 224
Hebert, Francois, S1-265
Hebert, Francois, S2-454-455, 466, 469-472
Hebert, Francois, S3-826, 828, 882
Hebert, Francois Benjamin, E-137, 183, 190-191
Hebert, Francois Dominique, E-183
Hebert, Francois Louis, E-370
Hebert, Francois Louise, C-56
Hebert, Francois Serge, E-183
Hebert, Francois Yves, E-183, 185-186
Hebert, Francois-Etienne, S2-477
Hebert, Francois-Luce, S2-462
Hebert, Francois-Xavier, S1-126
Hebert, Francois-Xavier, S2-454-455
Hebert, Francoise, C-3-4
Hebert, Francoise, E-183
Hebert, Francoise, F-15, 99
Hebert, Francoise, N-91
Hebert, Francoise, S1-9, 71-72, 245-246, 348, 377
Hebert, Francoise, S2-445-446, 454-455, 458-459, 478, 484-485, 494, 624
Hebert, Francoise, S3-828, 1102

Hebert, Francoise Jacquette, E-183
Hebert, Francoise Lucie, E-183
Hebert, Francoise Magdelaine Sophie, E-183
Hebert, Francoise-Anne, S2-468
Hebert, Francoise-Pelagie, S2-465
Hebert, Francoise-Perinne, S2-478
Hebert, Gabriel, F-73
Hebert, Gabriel, N-88
Hebert, Gabriel-Simon, S2-471
Hebert, Genevieve, E-2, 631, 639
Hebert, Genevieve, F-3
Hebert, Genevieve, N-69, 84
Hebert, Genevieve, S1-346
Hebert, Genevieve, S3-1010
Hebert, Genevieve-Marie, S2-463
Hebert, George, E-183, 608, 610, 613
Hebert, Gertrude, F-79, 107
Hebert, Gertrude, N-85
Hebert, Gertrude-Anne, S2-448
Hebert, Gilles, E-186, 190
Hebert, girl, E-181
Hebert, girl, S2-464
Hebert, Gracieuse, E-180, 631, 639, 642
Hebert, Guillaume, E-189, 486, 526
Hebert, Guillaume, F-73
Hebert, Guillaume, N-86, 88
Hebert, Guillaume, S2-449-450
Hebert, Guillaume Benoist, C-55
Hebert, Guillaume Benoist, N-88
Hebert, Guillemette Louise, E-183
Hebert, Harle, S3-945
Hebert, Heleine, C-54
Hebert, Heleine, S3-873
Hebert, Helene, E-184
Hebert, Helene, F-93
Hebert, Helene, S1-16, 28
Hebert, Helene, S2-459, 477
Hebert, Isaac, N-44, 84-85, 89, 224, 233-234, 236

Hebert, Isaac, F-21
Hebert, Isaac, S2-446, 455
Hebert, Isaac-Joseph, S2-447
Hebert, Isabelle, F-3, 19, 27, 43, 93
Hebert, Isabelle, S1-149, 153
Hebert, Isabelle, S2-454-455
Hebert, Isabelle, S3-947
Hebert, Isabelle-Jeanne, S2-461
Hebert, Isidore, E-184
Hebert, J.B., S3-879
Hebert, Jacques, E-52, 184, 188-189, 486, 491, 526, 550
Hebert, Jacques, F-53, 103
Hebert, Jacques, S1-100, 125, 134
Hebert, Jacques, S2-449, 463, 616
Hebert, Jacques, S3-956, 1022
Hebert, Jacques Amand, E-184
Hebert, Jean, C-54-56, 61, 68, 84, 89
Hebert, Jean, E-1, 37, 59, 181-190, 278, 336, 474, 486, 491, 526, 550, 565, 577, 601, 632, 639, 642
Hebert, Jean, F-3, 15, 33, 35, 43, 71, 73, 87, 93, 101, 107
Hebert, Jean, N-86-88, 91, 93, 116, 144, 151, 164, 233
Hebert, Jean, S1-3, 15, 19, 28, 69, 71, 266, 330
Hebert, Jean, S2-445, 455-460, 462, 464, 469-472, 476, 662, 673, 715
Hebert, Jean, S3-872-874, 884, 922, 1013, 1062, 1111, 1119, 1129, 1132, 1135-1136
Hebert, Jean Baptiste, C-1, 4, 18, 20, 45, 55-57, 74, 149
Hebert, Jean Baptiste, E-46, 52, 113, 182, 184-189, 390, 422, 577, 587, 594, 608, 610, 614
Hebert, Jean Baptiste, F-15, 25, 27, 33, 35, 43, 87
Hebert, Jean Baptiste, N-90-92, 200, 236
Hebert, Jean Baptiste, S3-871, 935, 1062, 1106, 1111, 1116, 1118, 1120, 1122, 1126, 1130, 1133, 1136-1137

Hebert, Jean Baptiste Alexis, E-184
Hebert, Jean Baptiste Isidor, E-184, 390
Hebert, Jean Baptiste Michel, E-185, 338
Hebert, Jean Charles, E-185
Hebert, Jean Charles, F-33
Hebert, Jean Charles Louis, E-185
Hebert, Jean Clement, E-184
Hebert, Jean Francois, E-185, 187, 190
Hebert, Jean Joseph, C-55
Hebert, Jean Joseph, F-43
Hebert, Jean Joseph, N-92
Hebert, Jean Louis, C-54
Hebert, Jean Louis, N-85, 88
Hebert, Jean Louis Etienne, E-185
Hebert, Jean Pelagie, E-610
Hebert, Jean Pierre, C-1, 6, 57
Hebert, Jean Pierre, E-185
Hebert, Jean Pierre, F-33, 73, 97
Hebert, Jean Pierre, N-57, 85, 92, 250
Hebert, Jean Pierre, S3-1062
Hebert, Jean Pierre Alphonse, E-185
Hebert, Jean Prosper, E-185
Hebert, Jean-Baptiste, S1-9, 118, 140, 146, 183, 286, 291, 302-303, 329, 362
Hebert, Jean-Baptiste, S2-447, 452, 456-463, 472, 474-475, 478, 560, 574, 624, 673, 715
Hebert, Jean-Baptiste-Marie, S2-474
Hebert, Jean-Charles, S2-475
Hebert, Jean-Chrisostome, S2-473
Hebert, Jean-Joseph, S2-463
Hebert, Jean-Joseph-Laurant-Francois, S2-466
Hebert, Jean-Marguerite, S2-447-448
Hebert, Jean-Olivier-Marie, S2-462
Hebert, Jean-Pierre, S1-29
Hebert, Jean-Pierre, S2-446, 449, 475-476, 612

Hebert, Jeanne, C-62
Hebert, Jeanne, E-491
Hebert, Jeanne, N-115
Hebert, Jeanne, S1-154-155, 160, 369
Hebert, Jeanne, S2-449, 524, 558, 565, 699, 734
Hebert, Jeanne, S3-1070, 1117, 1124-1125
Hebert, Jeanne Eulalie, N-87
Hebert, Jeanne Francoise, E-185
Hebert, Jeanne Pelagie, E-608, 614
Hebert, Joseph, C-8, 55, 57-58, 62-63, 130-131
Hebert, Joseph, E-181, 184-188, 287, 305, 414-415, 423, 429, 491, 526, 550, 568, 577, 599, 601, 630, 632
Hebert, Joseph, F-27, 49, 53, 85, 87, 95, 97, 99, 109
Hebert, Joseph, N-87, 90, 92-93, 102, 178, 190, 203, 213
Hebert, Joseph, S1-3, 15, 51, 113, 116, 123, 260, 296, 328, 350
Hebert, Joseph, S2-448-450, 453-455, 458-459, 463-464, 466, 468-469, 470, 473, 478, 484, 525, 618, 688, 709, 712, 716
Hebert, Joseph, S3-882, 893, 899, 926, 946, 956, 967, 1002, 1013, 1022, 1119, 1128-1130, 1134-1135, 1138, 1140-1141
Hebert, Joseph Alexis, E-186
Hebert, Joseph David, E-186
Hebert, Joseph Hippolite, E-186
Hebert, Joseph Ignace, F-43
Hebert, Joseph Ignace, N-93-94
Hebert, Joseph Nicolas, F-51
Hebert, Joseph Olivier, E-187, 423
Hebert, Joseph-Ignace, S2-457-458, 469-470
Hebert, Joseph-Madeleine, S2-467
Hebert, Joseph-Marie, S2-468
Hebert, Joseph-Nicolas, S2-472
Hebert, Joseph-Servan, S2-461
Hebert, Joseph-Yves, S2-477

Hebert, Josephe, E-186
Hebert, Josephe, S1-118, 349
Hebert, Josephe, S3-1078
Hebert, Judith, E-129, 186
Hebert, Julien-Joseph, S2-466
Hebert, Julienne, F-87
Hebert, Julienne-Madeleine, S2-468
Hebert, Julienne-Perinee, S2-475
Hebert, la Vieille, E-181
Hebert, Leonard Francois, E-186
Hebert, Louis, E-186, 188-189
Hebert, Louis, F-73
Hebert, Louis, N-88
Hebert, Louis, S2-470
Hebert, Louis Alphonse Augustin, E-186
Hebert, Louis Ambroise, N-93
Hebert, Louis David, E-186
Hebert, Louis Gabriel, C-55
Hebert, Louis Gabriel, N-88
Hebert, Louis Jean, E-186
Hebert, Louis Jean, F-49
Hebert, Louis Jean, N-93
Hebert, Louis Marc, E-187
Hebert, Louis Marie, N-93
Hebert, Louis-Joseph, S2-469
Hebert, Louise, E-58, 187, 429, 436, 633
Hebert, Louise Felicite, E-187
Hebert, Luce, E-436
Hebert, Lucie, E-55, 57-59, 631
Hebert, Madeleine, N-22, 28, 32, 74, 90, 225
Hebert, Madeleine, S1-19, 28, 105, 123, 129, 157, 168, 217, 376-378
Hebert, Madeleine, S2-473, 510, 605, 758
Hebert, Madeleine, S3-831, 876, 890, 905, 1106-1107, 1119
Hebert, Madeleine Josephe, N-51
Hebert, Madeleine Modeste, N-164
Hebert, Madeleine Pelagie, E-575
Hebert, Magdalen Modeste, E-166, 189, 421, 423, 425-427

Hebert, Magdelaine, F-39, 47, 49, 47, 53
Hebert, Magdeleine, C-19, 38, 56
Hebert, Magdeleine, E-1, 46, 85, 87, 187, 322, 422, 575, 600, 632-633, 642
Hebert, Magloire, E-182, 187, 406
Hebert, Magloire, S1-217
Hebert, Manuel, E-18, 181, 186-187, 189
Hebert, Marguerite, C-20, 42, 46, 58, 84
Hebert, Marguerite, E-28, 52, 151, 187, 475, 486, 550, 577, 587, 593, 608, 611, 614
Hebert, Marguerite, F-15, 25, 33, 39, 45, 55, 75
Hebert, Marguerite, N-28-29, 87, 91, 146, 163, 172, 236
Hebert, Marguerite, S1-9, 107, 121, 123, 133, 149, 338-339, 344, 349, 368, 381
Hebert, Marguerite, S2-455, 458, 550, 565, 631, 656, 765, 777, 779-783
Hebert, Marguerite, S3-907, 923, 929-930, 945, 1044, 1055, 1119, 1134
Hebert, Marguerite Adelaide, N-88
Hebert, Marguerite Elisabeth, E-187
Hebert, Marguerite Josephe, N-5, 29
Hebert, Marguerite Louise, N-87
Hebert, Marguerite Sophie, N-87
Hebert, Marguerite-Anastasie, S2-467
Hebert, Marguerite-Blanche, S2-457
Hebert, Marguerite-Genevieve, S2-465
Hebert, Marguerite-Josephe, S1-126, 328
Hebert, Marguerite-Josephe, S2-635, 658
Hebert, Marguerite-Tarsille, S2-457-458

Hebert, Marianne, C-31
Hebert, Marie, C-38, 50-51, 61-62, 74, 86, 89
Hebert, Marie, E-2, 18, 68, 139, 150, 171, 176-180, 184-185, 187, 190, 270, 276, 288-289, 293-294, 302, 306, 329, 331, 422, 429, 434-438, 456, 511, 550, 568, 587-588, 594-595, 599, 601, 608-609, 611, 614, 633, 636
Hebert, Marie, F-3, 15, 25, 27, 43, 47, 49, 53, 69, 71, 85, 87, 95, 101, 103, 107, 109
Hebert, Marie, N-78-79, 84, 90-91, 93, 137
Hebert, Marie, S1-3-4, 20, 29, 118, 124, 166, 232, 298-299, 339, 348, 350, 356, 379
Hebert, Marie, S2-447, 451, 455, 457-458, 464, 466, 468-469, 471-474, 477-478, 480, 486, 490-492, 500, 506, 539, 543, 597, 630, 632-633, 660, 662, 666, 708
Hebert, Marie, S2-710, 715, 755
Hebert, Marie, S3-852, 920, 928, 977, 1109-1110, 1126, 1135
Hebert, Marie Anastasie, E-181, 184, 187
Hebert, Marie Angele, E-608, 614
Hebert, Marie Angele Nicole, E-188
Hebert, Marie Angelique, E-611
Hebert, Marie Anne, E-64
Hebert, Marie Anne Catherine, E-188
Hebert, Marie Barbe, E-188, 608, 611, 614
Hebert, Marie Cecile Rose, E-188
Hebert, Marie Claire, E-188
Hebert, Marie Elisabeth, E-108, 188, 389
Hebert, Marie Francoise, E-188
Hebert, Marie Genevieve, E-188
Hebert, Marie Henriette, E-188
Hebert, Marie Jeanne, E-384
Hebert, Marie Jeanne, N-84, 92

Hebert, Marie Josephe, C-22, 43, 72

Hebert, Marie Josephe, E-150, 188, 376

Hebert, Marie Josephe, F-45, 89, 97

Hebert, Marie Josephe, S3-895, 974, 979, 999, 1051, 1053, 1072, 1076, 1079

Hebert, Marie Julie, E-188

Hebert, Marie Louise, C-55

Hebert, Marie Louise, N-87

Hebert, Marie Madeleine, E-46, 181, 184, 188-189, 329, 418

Hebert, Marie Madeleine, N-85, 88, 136

Hebert, Marie Magdelaine, F-73

Hebert, Marie Marguerite, C-32, 149-150

Hebert, Marie Marguerite, E-52, 189, 300, 337, 439, 636

Hebert, Marie Marguerite Julie, C-55

Hebert, Marie Marguerite Julie, N-88-89

Hebert, Marie Modeste, E-189, 285-287, 564

Hebert, Marie Natalie, E-183, 190

Hebert, Marie Rose, C-55

Hebert, Marie Rose, E-384

Hebert, Marie Rose, N-88, 93

Hebert, Marie Therese, E-189

Hebert, Marie Victoire, E-189

Hebert, Marie Yvette, F-15

Hebert, Marie-Claire, S2-452

Hebert, Marie-Felicite, S2-448

Hebert, Marie-Gertrude-Josephe, S2-462

Hebert, Marie-Henriette, S2-452

Hebert, Marie-Jeanne, S2-447-448, 452

Hebert, Marie-Joseph, S1-20

Hebert, Marie-Josephe, S1-17, 18, 20, 132, 134-135, 144, 191, 225-226, 228, 230, 266, 347, 366

Hebert, Marie-Josephe, S2-450, 453, 459, 465, 473, 476, 488, 539, 563, 710, 783

Hebert, Marie-Madeleine, S1-75

Hebert, Marie-Madeleine, S2-445-446, 458, 460, 464, 467, 471, 629, 631

Hebert, Marie-Marguerite, S2-472

Hebert, Marie-Rose, S2-450

Hebert, Marin, S2-454-455

Hebert, Martine, E-472

Hebert, Mathurin, F-87

Hebert, Mathurin, S2-470, 478, 707

Hebert, Mathurin-Pierre-Francois, S2-477

Hebert, Mathurine-Marguerite, S2-474

Hebert, Michel, E-181-183, 188-189, 281, 526

Hebert, Michel, N-164

Hebert, Michel, S2-455, 469-470, 478

Hebert, Michel, S3-1018

Hebert, Michelle-Marie, S2-455, 469-470

Hebert, Mr., E-128, 382, 402

Hebert, N., E-181

Hebert, Nicolas, E-178

Hebert, Nicolas Adolphe, E-189

Hebert, Olivier, E-188, 190, 285, 587, 593

Hebert, Olivier, F-43

Hebert, Olivier, N-94

Hebert, Olivier, S2-454-455, 472

Hebert, Olivier-Constant-Mathias, S2-470

Hebert, Osite, N-150

Hebert, Osite, S2-469

Hebert, Otile, E-261

Hebert, Pascal, F-95

Hebert, Paschal, E-189, 587, 594

Hebert, Paul, E-182, 186-189, 379, 594

Hebert, Paul, S1-76

Hebert, Paul, S2-470-472, 626

Hebert, Paul Pierre, N-84

Hebert, Pauline Rose, E-189

Hebert, Pelagie, E-608, 611, 614

Hebert, Pelagie, S2-446

Hebert, Perpetue, E-599

Hebert, Pierre, C-32, 43, 56-57, 149

Hebert, Pierre, E-19, 90, 137, 181-185, 187-191, 194, 314, 376, 424, 491, 526, 550, 582, 587, 595, 601, 636

Hebert, Pierre, F-15, 27, 33, 35, 43, 47, 87

Hebert, Pierre, N-90-92, 94, 139, 188, 200, 250

Hebert, Pierre, S1-19, 23, 347

Hebert, Pierre, S2-451, 456, 458-461, 472-479, 495, 526, 646, 666

Hebert, Pierre, S3-872, 873-874, 905, 922, 951, 967, 1018, 1133

Hebert, Pierre Alexandre, E-190

Hebert, Pierre Benony, E-190

Hebert, Pierre Charles Joseph, E-190

Hebert, Pierre Jean, F-97

Hebert, Pierre Joseph, F-19, 35

Hebert, Pierre Joseph, N-94, 140

Hebert, Pierre Mrs., E-189

Hebert, Pierre Nicolas, E-189

Hebert, Pierre Prosper, E-190, 642

Hebert, Pierre-Francois, S2-478

Hebert, Pierre-Jean, S2-465, 477

Hebert, Pierre-Joseph, S2-469, 473

Hebert, Pierre-Michel, S2-461

Hebert, Prosper Francois, N-90

Hebert, Reine Eulalie, N-89

Hebert, Remi, F-21

Hebert, Remi, N-89

Hebert, Remig, N-89

Hebert, Remy, S2-446

Hebert, Rene, E-526

Hebert, Rene, S2-456

Hebert, Rene Jean, E-190

Hebert, Rosalie, C-84

Hebert, Rosalie, E-184, 190-191, 276, 299, 326, 637

Hebert, Rosalie, F-43

Hebert, Rosalie, N-144-145

Hebert, Rosalie, S1-4, 118, 124

Hebert, Rosalie, S2-458, 463, 471, 624, 673, 715

Hebert, Rose, E-4, 6, 190, 281

Hebert, Rose, S2-457-458

Hebert, Rose, S3-1129
Hebert, Rose Jeanne, N-91
Hebert, Rose Modeste, E-601
Hebert, Scholastique, E-608, 611, 614
Hebert, Sieur Gilles, E-186, 190
Hebert, Simon, E-185, 191
Hebert, Simon, F-43
Hebert, Simon, N-91-92
Hebert, Sophie, F-53
Hebert, Sophie, N-85
Hebert, Sophie-Marie, S2-464
Hebert, Susanne, E-183, 191, 292, 637, 644
Hebert, Suzanne Adelaide, E-191
Hebert, Suzanne Francoise, E-191
Hebert, Suzanne Reine Elisabeth, E-191
Hebert, Tarsile, E-191
Hebert, Tarsile, S1-246, 265
Hebert, Tarsille, N-89, 114, 189
Hebert, Tarsille, S2-454-455
Hebert, Tersile, S2-447
Hebert, Theodore, S2-451
Hebert, Theotiste, S2-452
Hebert, Theotiste Marie, E-565
Hebert, Therese, F-5
Hebert, Therese Anne, F-97
Hebert, Therese Suzanne, E-191
Hebert, Therese-Anne, S2-465
Hebert, Timothee, S2-446
Hebert, Toussaint, E-191
Hebert, Ursule, C-34, 98
Hebert, Ursule, E-439-440
Hebert, Ursule, F-5, 63, 69, 103
Hebert, Ursule, N-54-55
Hebert, Ursule, S1-125-126, 148, 265, 270, 273
Hebert, Ursule, S2-447-448, 454-455, 481, 616
Hebert, Ursule, S3-826, 939, 944, 949
Hebert, Victoire, F-87, 95
Hebert, Victoire, S1-16, 19, 28, 172, 339, 344, 389
Hebert, Victoire, S2-459, 468, 474, 477
Hebert, Victoire, S3-872

Hebert, Victoire-Genevieve, S2-467
Hebert, Victoire-Luce, S2-474
Hebert, Victor-Francois, S2-448
Hebert, Yvonne, E-191
Hecquart, Elizabeth, S2-479, 686
Hecquart, Isabelle, S2-479
Hecquart, Nicolas, S2-479, 685-686
Hedde, Charles Jacques, E-7
Hedde, Charlotte, E-7
Heden, Catherine, E-124
Hedoux, Catherine, E-124
Heiaudeau, Louise, E-320
Hellouin, Catherine, S1-205
Hellouin, Francois, S1-85
Hellouin, Francois, S2-743
Hellyes, Mr., E-136
Heloin, Catherine, S3-1042
Heloin, Francois, S3-986
Heloy, Francois, S1-56
Helquen, Catherine, E-626
Helry, Barthelemy, C-21
Hely, Jean, S2-479
Hemery, Marguerite, E-191
Henegre, Angelique, E-77, 335-336
Henengre, Angelique, S1-358
Henengre, Francois, E-9
Henengre, Francoise, E-9, 192
Henengre, Joseph, E-9, 192
Henengre, Marie, E-9
Hennerit, Anne, E-15, 321
Henon, Jeanne, S2-692
Henry, Adelaide Victoire, E-192
Henry, Adelaide-Marie, S2-505
Henry, Agathe, S2-506
Henry, Aimable Sophie, E-192
Henry, Alain, E-625
Henry, Alexis, C-58
Henry, Alexis, N-95, 178, 220, 225, 238, 248
Henry, Alexis, S2-482-483, 488
Henry, Allain-Pierre, S2-489
Henry, Amable, E-192
Henry, Amable Sophie, N-96
Henry, Amand, E-193, 299
Henry, Amand, N-97
Henry, Amand, S1-183, 220
Henry, Amant, S2-480, 490, 505

Henry, Amant, S3-1068
Henry, Amateur-Francois, S2-484-485
Henry, Ambroise, S2-498
Henry, Anastasie, C-38
Henry, Anastasie, F-43
Henry, Anastasie, S1-298-299
Henry, Anastasie, S2-493, 500
Henry, Anastasie Blanche, E-192
Henry, Anastazie, S3-1109
Henry, Angelique, F-99
Henry, Angelique, S2-502, 752
Henry, Angelique-Francoise, S2-507
Henry, Anne, F-101
Henry, Anne, S2-448, 491, 541, 662-663, 756
Henry, Anne, S3-1138
Henry, Anne Caroline, E-644
Henry, Anne Dorothee, C-159
Henry, Anne Dorothee, N-95
Henry, Anne Elisabeth Zoe Juliette, E-192
Henry, Anne Francoise, F-3
Henry, Anne Francoise, N-96, 97
Henry, Anne Joseph, F-101
Henry, Anne Josephe, N-64
Henry, Anne Josephe, S3-934
Henry, Anne Zoe Caroline, E-361, 434, 637
Henry, Anne-Helene, S2-483
Henry, Anne-Josephe, S1-138, 306-307
Henry, Anne-Josephe, S2-501-502, 752
Henry, Anne-Louise, S2-499
Henry, Anne-Marguerite, S2-481
Henry, Anne-Marguerite-Josephe, S2-488
Henry, Anne-Marie, S2-480
Henry, Anne-Theotiste, S2-498
Henry, Antoine, E-182, 193-194
Henry, Antoine, S1-296
Henry, Antoine, S2-480, 500
Henry, Athanase, S2-497-498
Henry, Augustin, E-192
Henry, B., S3-933

Henry, Barthelemy, S1-125, 132, 299

Henry, Barthelemy, S2-481-482, 499-500

Henry, Barthelemy-Charles, S2-481

Henry, Bartholome, F-87, 93

Henry, Basil, E-192

Henry, Basile, C-58, 141

Henry, Basile, S1-20, 299, 302

Henry, Bazile, N-94-95, 185, 209, 212, 220-222, 226, 229, 238

Henry, Bazile, S2-482-483, 487-488, 497, 631

Henry, Bazile, S3-900, 902, 1114, 1135-1136, 1141, 1143

Henry, Bazile Marie, C-159

Henry, Benjamin Louis, E-192

Henry, Berenice Adele, E-192

Henry, Berthelemy, S3-949

Henry, Bone Modeste, E-192

Henry, boy, S2-483

Henry, Catherine, E-35, 171, 267, 278, 353, 373, 376

Henry, Cecile, C-59

Henry, Cecile, F-55, 57

Henry, Cecile, N-95

Henry, Cecile, S1-186-189

Henry, Cecile, S2-482, 583

Henry, Cecile, S3-963, 1040

Henry, Cecile Marie, C-58

Henry, Cecile Marie, N-95

Henry, Cecile-Marie, S2-483

Henry, Cecille, E-66, 298

Henry, Charles, C-58-59, 83

Henry, Charles, E-28, 113, 192-194, 355

Henry, Charles, F-31, 99, 101

Henry, Charles, N-95, 149, 207, 250

Henry, Charles, S1-50

Henry, Charles, S2-483-487, 491-492, 494, 501-503, 506, 736, 752, 756

Henry, Charles, S3-920, 924, 927, 934, 977, 1085

Henry, Charles-Guillaume, S2-484

Henry, Charles-Isaac, S2-503

Henry, Cirille Francois, F-41

Henry, Cirille Francois, N-97-98

Henry, Cyrille-Francois, S2-505

Henry, Daniel-Jean, S2-503

Henry, Edme, E-192

Henry, Elisabeth, C-159

Henry, Elizabeth, E-192

Henry, Elizabeth, F-7, 17

Henry, Elizabeth, N-6-7, 34

Henry, Elizabeth, S1-20, 138, 165, 299

Henry, Elizabeth, S2-482, 487-488, 496, 500, 599, 630

Henry, Elizabeth, S3-971, 1141

Henry, Elizabeth Jeanne, C-58

Henry, Elizabeth Jeanne, N-95

Henry, Elizabeth-Jeanne, S2-483

Henry, Elizabeth-Modeste, S2-663

Henry, Emilie, E-617

Henry, Emilie-Augustine, S2-489

Henry, Firmain, S2-498

Henry, Francois, C-58-59

Henry, Francois, F-3, 7, 93, 99

Henry, Francois, N-6, 96

Henry, Francois, S1-20, 61, 163, 237

Henry, Francois, S2-482, 486-488, 491, 496, 503, 507, 557, 599

Henry, Francois, S3-974, 1108, 1114, 1123, 1141

Henry, Francois Ambroise, E-192

Henry, Francois Michel, N-97

Henry, Francois Nicolas, C-58

Henry, Francois Nicolas, N-95

Henry, Francois Xavier, S3-946

Henry, Francois-Barthelemy, S2-481

Henry, Francois-David, S2-488

Henry, Francois-Guillaume, S2-504

Henry, Francois-Joseph, S2-503

Henry, Francois-Marie, S2-502

Henry, Francois-Michel, S2-505

Henry, Francois-Nicolas, S2-483

Henry, Francois-Pierre, S2-503

Henry, Francois-Xavier, S1-135

Henry, Francois-Xavier, S2-484, 488-489, 492

Henry, Francoise, F-99

Henry, Francoise, S1-49, 183, 237, 318

Henry, Francoise, S2-491, 502, 506, 600, 642, 662, 666-667

Henry, Francoise Victoire, F-99

Henry, Francoise-Madeleine, S2-499

Henry, Francoise-Victoire, S2-485

Henry, Genevieve Alexandrine, E-192, 409

Henry, Germain, E-58

Henry, Germain, S2-480, 489-490, 495, 504

Henry, Germain, S3-1068

Henry, Gregoire-Francois, S2-506

Henry, Hippolyte Jean Louis, E-192

Henry, Isabelle, F-97

Henry, Isabelle, S1-307

Henry, Isabelle, S2-495-496, 498

Henry, Isabelle-Modeste, S2-494

Henry, J., N-197, 210

Henry, Jacques, F-93

Henry, Jacques Aimable, E-192

Henry, Jacques-Francois, S2-481

Henry, Jan Baptiste, S3-924

Henry, Jan Baptiste Olivier, S3-922

Henry, Je. Jo., N-178

Henry, Jean, C-160

Henry, Jean, E-499

Henry, Jean, F-97, 99, 101, 103

Henry, Jean, N-238

Henry, Jean, S1-73, 128, 236-237

Henry, Jean, S2-437, 483-484, 486, 488, 490-495, 500, 502, 504, 506, 658, 662, 666, 755-756

Henry, Jean, S3-920, 946, 977, 987, 1065, 1075

Henry, Jean Baptiste, E-31, 47, 192-194, 334

Henry, Jean Baptiste, F-31, 101
Henry, Jean Baptiste, N-96, 108, 135, 171, 185
Henry, Jean Baptiste Tranquille, E-193-194
Henry, Jean Bazile, C-160
Henry, Jean Charles, E-193
Henry, Jean Charles, N-96
Henry, Jean Felix, N-97
Henry, Jean Joseph, C-58
Henry, Jean Joseph, N-95
Henry, Jean Laurent, F-3
Henry, Jean Laurent, N-97
Henry, Jean-Baptiste, S2-490, 493, 495, 541, 665
Henry, Jean-Baptiste-Olivier, S2-476, 495-496, 665
Henry, Jean-Baptiste-Theodore, S2-486
Henry, Jean-Charlotte, S2-498
Henry, Jean-Felix, S2-504
Henry, Jean-Joseph, S2-482
Henry, Jean-Laurent, S1-21
Henry, Jean-Laurent, S2-496
Henry, Jean-Pierre, S2-488
Henry, Jean-Vincent, S2-503
Henry, Jeanne, E-89, 193, 354-355, 474
Henry, Jeanne, S1-143
Henry, Jeanne, S2-500
Henry, Jeanne Francoise, F-101
Henry, Jeanne-Francoise, S2-486
Henry, Joseph, C-51, 58-59
Henry, Joseph, E-193
Henry, Joseph, F-3, 31, 35
Henry, Joseph, N-95-97, 179, 207, 214, 216
Henry, Joseph, S1-163, 307
Henry, Joseph, S2-482, 485, 487-488, 490, 496
Henry, Joseph, S3-1151, 1123
Henry, Joseph Agapit, N-95
Henry, Joseph Alexandre, N-96
Henry, Joseph Guillaume, E-193
Henry, Joseph Philippe, N-97, 131, 213
Henry, Joseph Plilipe, F-55
Henry, Joseph-Amateur, S2-507
Henry, Joseph-Jean, S2-484
Henry, Joseph-Joachin, S2-503

Henry, Joseph-Philippe, S2-505, 621
Henry, Joseph-Sulia, S2-497
Henry, Joseph-Yves, S2-489
Henry, Julienne, S2-428
Henry, Laurent, S2-492
Henry, Louis Pierre Daniel, E-193
Henry, Louise Adele, E-193
Henry, Madeleine, N-67
Henry, Madeleine, S1-143, 183
Henry, Madeleine, S2-490-491, 496, 755-756
Henry, Madeleine Appoline, N-97
Henry, Madeleine-Josephe, S2-498
Henry, Madeleine-Marie-Francoise, S2-498
Henry, Madeleine-Suzanne, S2-507
Henry, Magdelaine, F-47, 103
Henry, Magdelaine Appoline, F-3
Henry, Magdeleine, E-98, 193-194, 354
Henry, Marguerite, C-37
Henry, Marguerite, E-625
Henry, Marguerite, F-23, 87, 99
Henry, Marguerite, S1-17, 19, 73, 182, 184, 249, 287-288, 326, 381-382
Henry, Marguerite, S2-477, 482, 485-487, 493-494, 496, 505-506, 542, 599, 603, 658, 756
Henry, Marguerite, S3-1083, 1114, 1143
Henry, Marguerite Josephe, S3-987
Henry, Marguerite Pelagie, F-103
Henry, Marguerite Rose, F-97
Henry, Marguerite Sophie, N-97
Henry, Marguerite Toussainte, F-99
Henry, Marguerite-Angelique, S2-486
Henry, Marguerite-Francoise, S2-489
Henry, Marguerite-Josephe, S1-236

Henry, Marguerite-Josephe, S2-492-493, 495-497, 506
Henry, Marguerite-Pelagie, S1-128, 137-138
Henry, Marguerite-Pelagie, S2-501-502
Henry, Marguerite-Rose, S2-495
Henry, Marguerite-Sophie, S2-505
Henry, Marguerite-Toussainte, S2-485
Henry, Marie, C-53, 58
Henry, Marie, E-12, 94, 193, 194, 354, 499, 619
Henry, Marie, F-35, 93, 97
Henry, Marie, N-95
Henry, Marie, S1-66, 69, 73, 117, 144, 183, 237, 318, 367, 377
Henry, Marie, S2-484-485, 492-496, 526, 756
Henry, Marie, S3-823, 846, 1075
Henry, Marie Angelique, E-105, 193
Henry, Marie Anne Rosalie, E-193
Henry, Marie Catherine, E-138, 261
Henry, Marie Catherine Desiree, E-637
Henry, Marie Jeanne Adelaide, E-193
Henry, Marie Josephe, F-3, 101
Henry, Marie Josephe, N-97
Henry, Marie Josephe, S3-832
Henry, Marie Josephine, N-96
Henry, Marie Madeleine, N-94-95
Henry, Marie Magdalen, E-193
Henry, Marie Magdelaine, F-31
Henry, Marie Magdeleine, C-59
Henry, Marie Margueritte Madeleine, E-192
Henry, Marie Rose, C-59
Henry, Marie Rose, N-95
Henry, Marie Sophie, N-97
Henry, Marie-Anne, S2-499
Henry, Marie-Helene, S2-501
Henry, Marie-Jeanne, S2-482

Henry, Marie-Jeanne-Made-leine, S2-494

Henry, Marie-Josephe, S1-21-22, 250

Henry, Marie-Josephe, S2-486, 491, 497, 500, 758

Henry, Marie-Madeleine, S1-41-42

Henry, Marie-Madeleine, S2-484, 496

Henry, Marie-Magloire, S2-507

Henry, Marie-Rose, S2-493-494

Henry, Martin, E-499, 526

Henry, Martin, S2-497

Henry, Maximilien, F-97

Henry, Maximilien, S2-489, 494-495

Henry, Maximilien, S3-934

Henry, Michel Amand Alexan-dre, E-192-193, 299, 431

Henry, Nicolas, E-192

Henry, Nicolas Francois, E-193

Henry, Nicolas Jean Marie, E-192

Henry, Olivier-Paul, S2-499

Henry, Osithe, S2-438

Henry, Ozite, S1-73

Henry, Ozite, S2-493, 496

Henry, Paul, E-193-194, 275

Henry, Paul, S1-69, 135-136, 139, 142, 251

Henry, Paul, S2-483, 497-500, 523, 760

Henry, Paul, S3-829

Henry, Pelagie, S2-502

Henry, Perinne, S2-485

Henry, Perinne-Jeanne, S2-485

Henry, Pierre, C-38, 95

Henry, Pierre, E-105, 192-193

Henry, Pierre, F-3, 15, 41, 55, 97, 99, 101, 103

Henry, Pierre, N-95-98, 191, 194, 207, 213, 216

Henry, Pierre, S1-128, 137, 187, 298

Henry, Pierre, S2-480-481, 485, 490, 492, 498-502, 504-506, 657-658, 752

Henry, Pierre, S3-920, 924, 926, 933-934, 946, 949, 987-988, 1068, 1109, 1113

Henry, Pierre Charles, C-59

Henry, Pierre Charles, E-194

Henry, Pierre Charles, N-95

Henry, Pierre David, E-194

Henry, Pierre David, N-96

Henry, Pierre fils, S3-934

Henry, Pierre Francois, C-59

Henry, Pierre Francois, E-194

Henry, Pierre Marin, N-97

Henry, Pierre Similien, N-96

Henry, Pierre-Charles, S2-486

Henry, Pierre-Isaac, S2-504

Henry, Pierre-Laurent, S2-504

Henry, Pierre-Marin, S2-504

Henry, Remy-Charles, S2-484

Henry, Robert, E-474, 526

Henry, Rosalie, S2-490, 663

Henry, Rose, C-82

Henry, Rose, E-16, 113, 355-356, 430

Henry, Rose, F-71

Henry, Rose, S2-772-773

Henry, Rose Adelaide, N-96

Henry, Rose Anastasie, F-31

Henry, Rose-Eulalie, S2-480

Henry, Simon, S1-61, 168

Henry, Simon, S2-491, 506

Henry, Simon, S3-920, 946, 977, 987

Henry, Simon-Jean, S1-270

Henry, Simon-Jean, S2-506-507

Henry, Thomas, E-354

Henry, Timothe, S2-500

Henry, Ursule, F-31

Henry, Ursule, N-96

Henry, Victoire, S2-487

Henry, Victoire Adelaide, E-194

Henry, Victoire Alexandrine, E-193

Henry, Vincent, E-354

Henry, Yvonne, E-625

Henry, Yvonne-Germenne, S2-489

Henry, Zoe, E-438

Hequet, Toussaint, S3-1053

Heraud, Elisabeth, E-89, 386

Heraudais, Jean, S3-916

Heraut, Mr., E-128

Heraux, Jacque, S3-951

Heraux, Jean, S3-951

Herbat, Marie Therese, E-323

Herbert, Catherine, E-113, 194

Herbert, Joseph, E-113, 194

Herbert, Julien, S2-507

Herbert, Jullien, S3-965

Herbert, Laurent, S3-1048

Herbert, Olivier, S2-507

Herbert, Olivier, S3-965

Herbert, Scholastique, E-314

Heri, Jean, N-240

Heriot, Jeanne, N-152, 192

Heriotte, Anne, E-194, 274, 358

Heroux, Francois, S2-685

Herpe, Francoise, E-619

Herpe, Francoise, S1-364

Herpe, Louis, S1-364

Herpin, Charles, S1-322

Herpin, Charles, S2-507-508

Herpin, Charles, S3-1095

Herpin, Charles Marie, E-625

Herpin, Desiree Anne, E-619

Herpin, Elizabeth, E-22, 150, 194

Herpin, Elizabeth, S2-652-653

Herpin, Frederic Auguste, E-619

Herpin, Isabelle, S3-1096

Herpin, Jacques, E-194

Herpin, Jean, E-73, 142, 144, 159, 194, 526, 625

Herpin, Jean, S2-508

Herpin, Jean Marie, E-625

Herpin, Jeanne Francoise, E-619

Herpin, Jeanne Julienne, E-625

Herpin, Jeanne Marie, E-619

Herpin, Julien, E-619

Herpin, Julien, S2-508

Herpin, Julien, S3-1095

Herpin, Julien Marie, E-625

Herpin, Julienne, E-623, 625

Herpin, Louise, E-625

Herpin, Marie, E-194, 391, 619, 625, 627

Herpin, Marie, S2-508, 719-721

Herpin, Marie, S3-997, 1096

Herpin, Marie Anne, E-194

Herpin, Marie Joseph, S3-1091

Herpin, Marie Magdelaine, E-194

Herpin, Marie-Josephe, S2-720

Herpin, Noel, S2-507

Herpin, Pierre, E-160, 194

Herpin, Rene, E-160, 194

Herpin, Rene, S2-653
Herpin, Sebastien, S2-508
Herrue, Pierre, S3-833
Hersent, Pierre Nicolas Misael, E-434
Hertart, Catherine, S1-178
Hertevent, Sieur, E-147
Herve, Charlotte, S2-691
Herve, Claude, E-195, 406, 587, 595
Herve, Claude, S2-508-509
Herve, Francois, E-34, 159
Herve, Francoise-Guillemette, S2-478
Herve, Jacques, E-195
Herve, Jean, S1-261
Herve, Julien, S1-259
Herve, Jullien, S3-901
Herve, Marie, F-103
Herve, Marie, N-10, 219
Herve, Michelle, N-51-52
Herve, Michelle, S1-259, 261
Herve, Michelle, S3-901
Herve, Perrine, F-23
Herve, Perrine, N-138, 167, 240
Hervel, Jaquette, E-282, 284
Hervi, Laurence, S2-478
Hervi, Laurence, S3-1018
Hervi, Marie, S1-354
Hervois, Marie, C-158
Hervouet, Jacques, N-98, 130, 217
Hervouet, Pierre, N-98, 217
Hervy, Anne, S2-598
Hervy, Guillaume, E-195
Hervy, Jean, E-195, 391
Hery, Jacques, E-195
Hesberd, Anne, S3-870
Hesberd, Jean, S3-870
Hesbert, Marie, E-137, 149
Heslouin, Catherine, S2-509, 643
Heslouin, Catherine, S3-1042
Heslouin, Francois, S2-509, 643
Heslouin, Francois, S3-986, 1023-1024, 1042
Heslouin, Marie-Gabrielle, S2-509
Hesry, Marie, S1-86
Hesry, Marie, S3-896
Hetaud, Catherine, E-275

Heto, Anne, E-274
Heubert, Andre, E-195
Heubert, Angelique, E-110
Heubert, Anne, E-195
Heubert, Anselme, E-195
Heubert, Pierre, E-195
Heubert, Pierre Anne, E-195
Heure, Francoise, S3-837
Heure, Guillaume, S3-837
Heurteur, Louis, S1-263
Heurtevant, Louis Michel, E-370
Heurtevent, Andre, E-148, 195
Heurtevent, Jacques, E-148, 195
Heurtevent, Marie Anne, E-189
Heurtevent, Michel Alexis, E-189
Heuze, Anne Marie, F-5
Heuze, Cecile-Marguerite, S2-510
Heuze, Charles, C-60
Heuze, Charles, F-5
Heuze, Charles, N-99, 206, 214
Heuze, Charles, S2-511
Heuze, Gilles Francois, C-59
Heuze, Gilles-Francois, S2-510
Heuze, Gregoire, F-5
Heuze, Gregoire, N-99
Heuze, Ignace, C-59-60
Heuze, Ignace, F-5
Heuze, Ignace, N-98-99, 214, 249
Heuze, Ignace, S1-117, 309
Heuze, Ignace, S2-509-511, 601-603, 691, 718, 743
Heuze, Ignace, S3-1007
Heuze, Jacques, C-60
Heuze, Jacques, N-98-99, 249
Heuze, Jacques, S1-309, 377
Heuze, Jacques, S2-509-511
Heuze, Jean, C-60
Heuze, Jean, N-99
Heuze, Jean Baptiste, F-5
Heuze, Jean Baptiste, N-99
Heuze, Jean-Baptiste, S2-510
Heuze, Jeanne, N-65
Heuze, Jeanne, S1-308
Heuze, Joseph Francois, C-60
Heuze, Joseph-Francois, S2-511
Heuze, Manuel Julie, N-99
Heuze, Marie, S1-370

Heuze, Marie Anne, C-60
Heuze, Marie Anne, N-99
Heuze, Marie Rose, N-99
Heuze, Marie-Anne, S2-510
Heuze, Mathurin-Charles, S2-510
Heuze, Pierre, C-60
Heuze, Pierre, F-5
Heuze, Pierre, N-99
Heuze, Pierre Ignace, N-98-99, 100, 214
Heuze, Pierre-Ignace, S2-510
Heuze, Renee, S1-135
Heuze, Robert, S2-511
Hiart, Guillaume, S3-849
Hiart, Marie, S2-536
Hibraud, Elizabeth, E-379
Hide, Joseph Augustin, E-276
Hilaire, Alexis, S1-83
Hilaire, Alexis, S2-512
Hilaire, Jean, S2-512
Hilaire, Sr., E-10
Himay, Andree, S2-595
Himly, Jean, E-42
Hinel, Jean, S3-852
Hinet, Thomas, S3-837, 839
Hingault, -----, S3-929
Hiriart, Bertrand, E-195, 290, 335, 438
Hiriart, Guillaume, E-438
Hiriart, Jean, E-195, 388
Hiriart, Jean (Sr.), E-195
Hiriart, Jean Joseph, E-195
Hiriart, Jeanne Angelique, E-195
Hiriart, Marie, E-195
Hiron, Jeanne, S2-619
Hispan, Bernard, E-91, 196
Hispan, Jean Baptiste, E-90, 196
Hiver, Francoise, E-120, 150
Hocuois, Marie Magdalen, E-324
Hode, Michel, S2-623
Hodgson, J.B., E-10
Hoffman, Marie, E-156-157
Hofman, Marie Eve, E-156
Hoguigne, Mathurin, S3-928
Hoguigue, Mathurin, S2-783
Hoguigue, Michel, S2-777
Hoguigue, Michel, S3-929
Hoguigue, Rene, S2-777

Hoguigue, Renee, S3-929
Hoison, Marguerite, C-74
Holerin, Catherine Selvenn, E-261
Holey, Marie Catherine, E-96
Holley, Jeanne, E-94-95, 196
Holley, Jeanne, F-35, 37
Holley, Thomas, E-196
Holley, Thomas, F-35
Holpe, Eve, E-590, 592
Homel, Jean, E-371
Honore, Joseph Louis, E-644
Honouet, Catherine Adelaide, E-89
Hosmin, Marie, E-156, 196
Hosmin, Stephin, E-196
Hospital, Francois, E-66
Hospital, Jean, E-632
Hostclin, Guillaume Francois, E-327
Houardon, Thomas Calegan, F-59
Houart, Barthelemy, E-196
Houart, Jean, E-196
Houart, Jean Paul Rene, E-196
Houart, Marie, E-196
Houchrouah, Pierre Marie, E-416
Houel, Catherine, E-293
Houillard, Marie, E-145, 320
Houin, Jean Marie, E-196
Houin, Marie Catherine, E-415
Houin, Marie Jeanne, E-285
Houin, Marie Josephe, E-196, 282-285
Houitte, Jean, S2-603
Hourde, Pierre, S2-520
Hourdequin, Jean Francois, E-122, 196
Hourdequin, Marie Jeanne, E-122, 196
Hourtioux, Jacques, E-196, 257
Hourtioux, Jean, E-196, 257
Houry, Charles, E-196
Houry, Marie Collette, E-196
Houssais, Pierre, N-217
Houze, Jean, S2-494
Houze, Nicole, S1-49
Huachecorne, Nicolas Emma-nuel, E-59
Huar, Mathieux, S3-970

Huar, Pierre, S3-970, 994, 1054
Huard, Charles Eugenie, E-196
Huard, Jacques, S3-1101
Huard, Jean, E-196
Huard, Jean Philippe, E-196
Huard, Marie Anne, E-197
Huard, Noel, E-62, 197
Huard, Philippe, E-62, 196-197
Huard, Pierre Antoine, E-197
Huault, Louise, S2-692
Hubel, Theretiste, S1-262
Huber, Madelon, E-601
Hubert, Josephe, E-144
Hubert, Pierre, S3-1082
Hubon, Julien, N-192
Huchez, Marie, E-114
Hudin, Marie, S2-765
Huem, Margueritte, E-112, 304
Huere, Francoise, S2-757-758
Huere, Guillaume, S2-757
Huere, Jacques, S2-757-758
Huere, Jeanne, S2-757
Hueret, Marie Catherine, E-172
Huert, Francoise, N-160, 216
Huet, Bernard, S3-866
Huet, Francois, S2-504
Huet, Guillaume, S2-615, 685
Huet, Guillaume, S3-1019
Huet, Jan, S3-1106, 1117, 1119
Huet, Jean, S1-12, 349
Huet, Jean, S3-1102, 1104-1105, 1107, 1109, 1111, 1114-1117, 1120, 1122
Huet, Louis, S3-829
Huet, Louise, S1-44
Huetaud, Louis, S3-860
Hugon, Jacques, E-197
Hugon, Marie Madeleine, E-72, 197, 348
Huguen, Jean, S1-93
Huguet, Francois, E-97
Huguet, Francois, S2-587
Huguet, Francoise, E-97, 168
Huguet, Joseph, S2-563
Huiet, Pierre, S3-911
Hulin, Jean, E-197, 442
Hulin, Julien, E-197
Hurit, Francois, S3-849
Hurtaud, Rene, E-140
Hurtaud, Renee, E-404
Hurtin, Claude, E-197

Hurtin, Jean, E-197
Huvelin, Pierre, N-219
Huzaud, Genevieve, C-155
Hyacinthe, Josseline, N-34
Hyacinthe, Josseline, S1-166
Hyacinthe, Josseline, S3-971
Hyline, Barbe, S2-771
Hyriart, Dominique, E-112
Hyriart, Gratienne, E-158

I

Ibat, Jeanne Marie, E-57
Icard, Francois, E-254
Icard, Honore, E-254
Iger, Jacques, E-254, 441
Iger, Louis, E-254, 441
Ijetou, Jeanne Francois, E-270, 327
Illiaquer, Marie Anne, E-164, 167
Illiaquer, Marie Jeanne, E-163
Imbert, Antoinette, E-29, 254
Imbert, Bertrand, E-254, 268
Imbert, Jean, E-29, 254
Imbert, Pierre, E-254, 268
Imbourg, Louis, E-254
Imbourg, Marguerite, E-254, 419
Ino, Marguerite, F-57
Isler, Chretian, E-159

J

Jaard, Guy, E-1, 22
Jacaud, Anne, E-26, 27, 127, 255
Jacaud, Hipolyte, E-17
Jacaud, Jeanne Francois, E-388
Jacaud, Thomas, E-255
Jachaud, Catherine, C-91, 121
Jacob, Francois, E-255
Jacob, Francoise, E-388
Jacob, Louise Amelie, E-255
Jacob, Pierre, E-93
Jacquelin, Antoine, E-84
Jacquelin, Henry, E-84
Jacquement, Marie, S2-691
Jacquement, Marie, S3-970
Jacquemin, Anne, S1-38, 201, 203

Jacquemin, Anne, S2-440
Jacquemin, Anne, S3-860, 938
Jacquemin, Antoine, E-33, 255
Jacquemin, Henry, E-255
Jacquemin, Jacques, E-33, 255
Jacquemine, Anne, C-36
Jacqueminne, Anne, S1-277
Jacques, Anne, F-65, 85
Jacques, Jean, E-19
Jacques, Jean, F-85
Jacques, Joseph, F-85
Jacques, Marie, F-85
Jacques, Pierre Joseph, F-85
Jacques, Victoire, F-85
Jacquet, Andre Joseph, E-255, 403
Jacquet, Andre-Joseph, S2-513-514
Jacquet, Antoine, S2-512-514, 649
Jacquet, George Noel, E-255
Jacquet, George-Noel, S2-513
Jacquet, Jacques, E-255
Jacquet, Jacques, S2-513-514
Jacquet, Jeanne, S2-514
Jacquet, Joseph, E-121, 255
Jacquet, Joseph, S1-284-285
Jacquet, Joseph, S2-512, 514
Jacquet, Marie, S1-285
Jacquet, Marie Francoise, E-121, 255, 356
Jacquet, Marie Joseph, E-255
Jacquet, Marie-Francoise, S1-284
Jacquet, Marie-Francoise, S2-513-514
Jacquet, Marie-Josephe, S2-514
Jacquet, Pierre, E-255
Jacquet, Pierre, S2-512, 514
Jacquet, Simon, E-255
Jacquet, Simon, S2-513
Jacquet, Therese, S2-513-514
Jacquette, Joseph, E-34, 152
Jacquier, Marie, E-622
Jafreteau, Marguerite, E-131
Jagoux, Anne, S1-288
Jagoux, Anne, S3-950
Jagueneau, Jean, E-33, 168
Jagueneau, Jeanne Francoise, E-388
Jagueneau, Magdeleine, E-337

Jagueneau, Marianne, E-337
Jagueneau, Marthe, E-36, 430
Jahan, Francois, S2-512
Jala, Laurent, S3-1150
Jallory, Gilles, S1-204
Jambar, Francois, S3-1009
Jambar, Jan Baptiste, S3-1009
Jambart, Appolinne, E-619
Jambart, Pierre, E-625
Jambon, Marie, E-139, 284
Jame, Elizabeth, E-255
Jame, Etienne, E-130, 255, 293, 379
James, Louis Laurent, E-108
Jamet, Bernard, S3-913-914
Jamet, Marie, C-164
Jamet, Marie, E-134, 377
Jamin, Mathurin, E-134, 394
Jamont, Madeleine, E-82
Jananeau, Clement, E-131
Jandron, Louise, E-32, 339
Janeau, Jeanne, E-319
Jannot, Etienne, E-255
Jannot, Francois, E-255, 276
Janpierre, Jean, E-256, 406
Janpierre, Marie, E-256, 406
Janpierre, Pierre, E-406
Jaouanec, Bernard, E-256
Jaouanec, Marie Jeanne, E-256
Jaquelain, Marie Jeanne, E-326, 436
Jaques, Jean, E-172, 256, 325
Jaquest, Joseph, E-44, 103
Jaquet, Joseph, S3-914
Jaquien, Antoine, E-587, 595
Jaquien, Jacques, E-587, 595
Jaquien, Jeanne, E-587, 595
Jaquien, Marie, E-587, 595
Jariau, Marie Catherine, E-100, 380
Jarouselle, Susanne, E-473
Jarraud, Andre, E-108
Jarraud, Jeanne, E-108, 256, 294
Jarreau, Magdelaine, E-294
Jasmin, Anne, S2-604
Jaubert, Antoine, E-295
Jaud, Jeanne, E-256, 333
Jaud, Pierre, E-256, 333
Jaudeau, Marianne, E-142, 256
Jaudeau, Pierre, E-142, 256
Jaudee, -----, N-198

Jaudon, Jacques, E-77
Jaume, Francois, E-293
Jaume, Marie, E-293
Jaunet, Jeanne Gabrielle, N-68
Jaunon, Angelique, C-61
Jaunon, Jean, C-60, 123
Jaunon, Louis Joseph, C-36, 54, 60, 123
Jaunon, Louise, C-123
Jaunon, Marguerite Radegonde, C-61
Jaunon, Marianne, C-60
Jaury, Louis Toussaint, E-405
Jayeux, Nicolas, E-354
Jeaillard, David, E-256
Jeaillard, Jacques Henri, E-256
Jean, Elisabeth, E-133
Jean, Francoise, E-95
Jean, Jacques, E-99, 140
Jean, Maistre, E-526
Jean, Marie, S2-652
Jean, Marie Anne, E-303, 327, 393
Jean, Pierre, E-78, 269, 376
Jeanbar, Francois, S1-278
Jeanneau, Marie, E-12, 270
Jeaunais, Louise, C-165
Jelusseau, Marie, E-286, 419
Jeunne, Jgs. Mullote, S3-985
Jezecal, Francois, S3-986
Jezegable, Marie Therese, S3-957
Jezegable, Marie-Therese, S2-593
Joan, Pierre, E-474
Joanne, Anne, C-27
Joanne, Anne, F-79
Joanne, Anne, S1-201
Joanne, Anne, S2-646
Joanne, Anne Perinne, C-26
Joanne, Anne Perinne, S3-1050
Joanne, Anne-Perinne, S1-201
Joanne, Jacquas, C-27
Joanne, Jacque, S3-1050
Joanne, Jacques, F-79
Joanne, Jacques, S1-201
Joanneau, Jean, E-44
Jobert, Andre, S1-84
Jobert, Andre, S2-515
Jobert, Elizabeth, S2-515
Jobert, Mr., E-128

Joffriau, Jacques, E-457
Joffroy, Jacques, E-119, 256
Joffroy, Jean, E-119, 256
Jogui, Jean Francois, E-284
Johnson, Bille - named after
  William Johnson, E-209
Joius, Marie, S2-772
Jolivet, Hyacinthe, E-131
Jolivet, Jeanne, E-77, 152
Jolivet, Marie Anne, E-108, 256
Jollet, Jean Hilaire, E-105, 256,
  382
Jollivet, Hiacynthe, E-161
Jollivette, Etienne Hiacinthe, E-
  440
Jolly, Antoine, E-256-257
Jolly, Antoine Martin, E-256
Jolly, Catherine, E-256-257
Jolly, Charles, S2-428
Jolly, Claude, E-257
Jolly, Elizabeth, E-257
Jolly, Estienne Sebastien, E-257
Jolly, Francois, E-256, 257
Jolly, Francoise, E-318, 431
Jolly, Francoise Gabriel, E-431
Jolly, Gabriel, E-77, 257, 258
Jolly, Gabrielle, E-68, 322
Jolly, Jacques Francois, E-257
Jolly, Jean, E-257, 414
Jolly, Jean Michel, E-257
Jolly, Jeanne, E-144, 257
Jolly, Joseph, E-257
Jolly, Julie Felicite, E-257
Jolly, Laurent, E-196, 257
Jolly, Louise, E-305
Jolly, Louise Catherine, E-257
Jolly, Louise Francoise, E-257
Jolly, Marguerite, E-69
Jolly, Marie, E-408, 619, 625
Jolly, Marie, S1-193-194
Jolly, Marie Anne, E-257
Jolly, Marie Francoise, E-196,
  257
Jolly, Marie Gabrielle, E-257
Jolly, Marie Rose, E-257
Jolly, Mathieu, E-256
Jolly, Perpetue, C-162
Jolly, Pierre, E-77, 257, 320
Jolly, Sebastien, E-69, 258
Jolly, Simon Gabriel, E-258
Jolly, Suzanne, E-68-69, 258

Jolly, Toussaint, S3-1088
Jonchere, Catherine, E-84, 168
Jonhulaud, Jon, S3-863
Jonome, Marie, E-587, 592
Jonon, Louis Jgspeh, C-123
Jorg, Marguerite Brind, S1-255
Joriny, Pierre, E-121
Joseph, girl, E-258
Joseph, indian, E-142
Joseph, Magdeleine, E-35
Joseph, Marguerite, S2-563
Jossant, Jacques, E-123
Jossant, Jean, E-131, 430
Jossaume, Charles, E-38, 293,
  315, 342
Josseau, Jean Baptiste, E-258
Josseau, Jean Marie, E-258
Jossel, Louise, E-259
Josselin, Mathurin, S2-477
Josset, Helene, E-14, 180, 258
Josset, Louise, E-259
Josset, Louise Anne, E-258-259
Josset, Mathurin, E-258
Joua, Michelle, S2-685
Jouanea, Jeanne, E-318
Jouanne, Louis, S1-49
Jouanne, Marie Anne, E-95
Jouanne, Perinne, S1-197
Jouanneau, Marie, E-325, 432
Jouanneau, Nicolas, E-27, 139
Jouannet, Anne Leprince, E-611
Joubert, Antoinette, E-21
Joubert, Genevieve, E-300
Joubert, Jeanne, E-97, 121, 168
Joucan, Jeanne, S2-645
Joucan, Jeanne, S3-1054
Joucan, Mathurin, S2-645
Joucan, Mathurin, S3-1054
Jouequet, Marie Susanne, E-193
Joufert, Pierre, E-100, 169
Jouger, Marie, S2-610
Jouger, Marie, S3-1089
Jouglas, -----, E-19, 22
Jouis, Marie, E-430
Jouquen Des Moulins, Jean-
  Baptiste, S2-691
Jourdain, Charles, E-12, 270
Jourdain, F., S3-984
Jourdain, Francois, S2-515, 784
Jourdain, Francois, S3-984
Jourdain, Jean Baptiste, E-258

Jourdain, Louis, E-258
Jourdain, Louis, S3-1083
Jourdain, Louis Perpetue, E-258
Jourdain, Victoire, E-258, 365
Jourdan, Delle, E-364
Jourdan, Jacque, S3-980
Jourdan, Madelaine, E-120, 338
Jourjon, Antoine Mathieu, E-
  174, 258
Jourjon, Guillimin, E-258, 340
Jourjon, Suzanne, E-258
Joussant, Jacques, E-78
Joussant, Jean, E-13
Joussaume, Charles, S2-730
Jousseame, Jeanne, E-359, 378
Jousseaume, Anne Modeste, E-
  258
Jousseaume, Anne-Modeste, S2-
  516
Jousseaume, Charles, E-79, 141,
  255, 258-259, 264
Jousseaume, Charles, S1-200
Jousseaume, Charles, S2-514-
  516
Jousseaume, Charlotte, E-259
Jousseaume, Charlotte, S2-516
Jousseaume, Jean, E-259
Jousseaume, Louis Claire, E-259
Jousseaume, Louise, S2-516
Jousseaume, Louise-Claire, S2-
  515
Jousseaume, Marie Anne, E-36,
  259
Jousseaume, Susanne, E-259
Jousseaume, Susanne, S2-516
Joussiaume, Charles, E-282
Joussuance, Marguerite, E-83,
  140
Joussume, Jean, E-330
Jouve de Senchon, Marie
  Catherine, E-109
Joyeux, Francois, E-259, 294
Joyeux, Jean, E-259, 294
Ju, Marie, S1-322
Jude, Mathurine, E-98, 402
Jude, Vincente, C-23, 137
Judice, Louis, F-65
Juguier, Andre, E-259
Juguier, Jean Francois, E-259,
  415
Juhel, Marie-Louise, S2-603

Juhel, Maudet, E-413
Juillet, Jean, E-160
Julemil, Mr., E-419
Julian, Marie Anne, N-2, 252
Julien, Constance, S1-24
Julien, Genevieve, E-259, 345
Julien, Jean, E-172, 259
Julien, Jean Guillaume, E-258-259
Julien, Louis, E-69, 259, 337, 406, 409
Julien, Pierre, E-270, 346
Julien, Pierre Roch, E-259
Juliene, Genevieve, E-296
Juliet, Jean Baptiste, E-259
Juliet, Julien, E-259
Julot, Marianne, E-130
Junguerre, Nicolas, S2-669
Juon, Jean, E-260
Juon, Marguerite, E-260, 425
Jusaud, Mr., E-375
Justice, Augustin, C-35
Jutand, Jean, E-84
Juteau, Francois, E-256
Juxtaux, Renee, S1-203
Jyasson, Jacques, E-43
Jyasson, Marguerite, E-43
Jyasson, Marie Madeleine, E-43

K

Karguainou, Jean, S2-601
Kerchetuit, Marie Gertrude, E-347
Kerdonis, Anne, E-261, 427-428
Kergenou, Jean, S1-209
Kergue, Francois Joseph, E-261
Kergue, Jacques Francois, E-261
Kerhoen, Anne, E-141
Kerhoen, Anne, S1-331
Kifre, Pierre, E-117
Kimine, Anne, F-5
Kimine, Anne, N-100
Kimine, Anne, S2-505, 516-518, 580-581, 597, 627
Kimine, Anne-Louise, S2-518
Kimine, Daniel, S2-516
Kimine, Francoise, S1-193, 215
Kimine, Francoise, S2-517
Kimine, Genevieve, S2-518
Kimine, Jacques, F-5

Kimine, Jacques, N-100
Kimine, Jacques, S1-193, 282
Kimine, Jacques, S2-516-518, 580, 626
Kimine, Jean, S2-517
Kimine, Judith, S1-282
Kimine, Judith, S2-517, 598
Kimine, Madeleine, S1-282, 374
Kimine, Madeleine, S2-626-627
Kimine, Marguerite, F-65, 81
Kimine, Marguerite, S2-517, 580
Kimine, Marie, F-5
Kimine, Marie, N-100
Kimine, Marie, S2-516
Kimine, Marie Perrine, N-99-100, 214
Kimine, Marie-Josephe, S2-518
Kimine, Marie-Madeleine, S2-517
Kimine, Pierre, F-5
Kimine, Pierre, N-99-100, 214
Kimine, Pierre, S1-201, 289, 371
Kimine, Pierre, S2-517-519, 598, 603, 627, 646
Kimine, Pierre-Louis, S2-518
Kimine, Victoire Francoise, F-5
Kimine, Victoire Francoise, N-100
Kimine, Victoire-Francoise, S2-519
King, Wellems, E-66, 261
King, Welloby, E-66, 261
Kirvan, Marie Francoise Dominique, E-383
Klain, Antoine, E-159, 180
Knabhause, Jean Guillaume, E-261
Knabhause, Joseph, E-261
Koe, Andre, E-138, 261
Koe, Domas, E-138, 261
Kuntz, Andre, E-261
Kuntz, Marie Antoinette Eugenie, E-261
Kuntz, Noel, E-114, 261
Kyrie, Marie Joseph, E-148, 276

L

L'Allemand, Marie Louise, E-587, 592
L'Allemande, Paul, E-587, 593
L'Anglois, Jacque, E-117
L'Anglois, Marie, E-275
L'Ars, Francoise, E-318, 382
L'Ecolier, Jean, E-59
L'Ege, Michel, E-45
L'Eguyer, Louis, E-295, 344
L'Esperance, Baron, S2-626
L'Esperance, Charles, E-303
L'Esperance, Charles de Sivert Baron, E-127
L'Esperance, Charles Gabriel Sebastien de Sivert Baron de, E-127, 303
L'Esperance, Marie, S2-725
L'Espinage, Marie Anne, E-52
L'Estibaudois, Francoise Marguerite, E-282
L'Hebert, Paul, S3-897
L'Hebert, Pierre, S3-897
L'Hermite, Charles, E-440
L'Hermite, Marguerite, E-18, 424
L'Hermite, Marie-Josephe, S1-358
L'Honstabet, Jeanne, E-169, 402
L'Hoste De Beaulieu, Achille-Leonor, S1-362
L'Hotellier, Jeanne, S1-354
L'Hotellier, Louis, S1-354
L'Hotellier, Louis, S2-596-597
L'Hurier, Guillaume Antoine, E-147, 306
L'Hurier, Marie Rose, E-147, 306
La Beauve, Antoine, S3-969
La Beauve, Euphrosine, S3-969, 1000, 1068
La Beauve, Marguerite, S3-1046
La Bore, Louis, S2-519
La Bore, Rene, S2-519
La Caille, Marie Barbe, S3-993
La Caille, Marie-Barbe, S2-719
La Chuere, Francois, S1-319
La Chuere, Francois, S2-592
La Chuere, Francois, S3-986

La Chuere, Jacquemine, S2-592
La Chuere, Jacquemine, S3-986
La Chuere, Jacquette, S1-263, 319
La Chuere, Jacquette, S3-1028
La Commere, -----, S3-1096
La Doyee, Marie-Catherine, S2-721
La Faille, Michel, S2-521
La Fargue, Genevieve, S1-1
La Fond, Antoine, S2-521
La Fond, Guillemette, S2-521
La Fond, Pierre, S2-521
La Fond, Savas, S2-521
La Fond, Sebastia, S2-521
La Frainne, Chre. George, S1-280
La Gaijnerie, Suzanne, S1-280
La Legros, -----, S3-960
La Montagne, Francois, S2-520
La Motte, Alexandre, S2-769
La Mouline, Gabriel, S2-472
La Perriere, Alexis, E-504
La Perriere, Jacques, E-474
La Perriere, Magdelaine, E-504
La Perriere, Nicolas, E-504
La Perriere, Pierre, E-504
La Pierre, Marie, F-39
La Roche, Aime-Pierre, S1-387
La Roche, Andre, S1-387
La Roche, Charlotte, S1-387
La Roche, Genevieve, S1-387
La Roche, Guillaume, S1-387
La Roche, Julie, S1-387
La Roche, Julien, S1-387
La Roche, Julien Guillaume, S1-386-387
La Roche, Julienne-Eleonore, S1-386, 387
La Roche, Marie, S1-386
La Roche, Marie-Jeanne, S1-387
La Roche, Perinne, S1-387
La Roche, Pierre, S1-387
La Roque, Anne-Marie, S2-546
La Roque, Francoise-Jeanne, S2-546
La Roque, Jean, S2-436, 545-547, 594
La Roque, Jean-Marin, S2-546
La Roque, Jeanne-Marie, S2-546

La Roque, Jeanne-Reine, S2-546
La Roque, Julienne-Josephe, S2-545
La Rosette Village, E-215
La Sauvagere, Pierre, E-35
La Sonde, Charles, N-10, 109
La Sonde, Genevieve, N-10, 109
La Sonde, Jean Baptiste, N-10, 109, 171, 219, 222
La Sonde, Judith, C-160
La Sonde, Julie, N-10, 109, 171, 222
La Sonde, Marc, S1-254
La Sonde, Marguerite, F-73
La Sonde, Marguerite, N-49, 229
La Sonde, Marguerite, S1-253-255
La Treille, Louise, E-326
La Vaquere, Andre, S2-548
La Vaquere, Jean, S2-548
La Vaquere, Julien-Francois, S2-548
La Vaquere, Marin-Francois, S2-548
La Ville, Sieur, S1-386
Labadie, Catherine, E-262
Labadie, Francois, E-262
Labadie, Jeanne, E-264, 415
Labadie, Marguerite, E-11, 262
Labadie, Marie Alain, E-128
Labardier, Francois, E-262
Labardier, Francoise, E-318
Labardier, Jean, E-262
Labarre, Elizabeth, E-525
Labarre, Guillaume, E-262
Labarre, Joseph, E-19, 262
Labarre, Marie, E-514
Labarre, Guillaume, E-19
Labat, Jean, E-474
Labauve, Anne, E-262, 428-429
Labauve, Anne, E-47
Labauve, Antoine, E-262, 295
Labauve, Antoine, F-11
Labauve, Antoine, S2-581, 683, 775
Labauve, Augustine, N-101
Labauve, Euphrosine, C-7
Labauve, Euphrosine, N-10
Labauve, Euphrosine, S1-48, 220

Labauve, Euphrosine, S2-683
Labauve, Francois, E-526, 553
Labauve, Francoise, E-305
Labauve, Honore, E-262
Labauve, Jean, C-23, 137
Labauve, Jean, E-262
Labauve, Jean, F-53
Labauve, Jean, N-100, 206
Labauve, Jeanne Eulalie, N-101
Labauve, Madeleine-Josephe, S2-775
Labauve, Magdalen Augustine, E-262
Labauve, Marguerite, C-8
Labauve, Marguerite, E-262, 282, 295
Labauve, Marguerite, F-9, 11, 43
Labauve, Marguerite, N-11, 64, 123-124, 178, 198
Labauve, Marguerite, S1-52
Labauve, Marguerite, S2-581-582
Labauve, Marie, C-23, 137
Labauve, Marie, E-262
Labauve, Marie, N-101
Labauve, Marie Aimee Francoise, E-262
Labauve, Marie Madeleine, N-101
Labauve, Pierre, C-137
Labauve, Pierre, E-61, 262
Labauve, Pierre, F-53
Labauve, Pierre Marie, N-101, 204, 206
Labauve, Rene, E-47, 262, 299
Labauve, Ursule, E-108
Labauve, Ursule, E-262, 299
Labauve, Victoire Reine, N-101
Labbe, Anne Josephine, E-262, 630
Labbe, Charlotte, E-262
Labbe, Francois, S1-37
Labbe, Guillaume-Michel, S2-543
Labbe dit Merceau, Joseph, E-262, 630, 632
Labeau, Marie, E-183, 281
Label, Jeanne, E-141
Lablanche, Marie, E-272
Laborde, Adelaide Flore, E-263

Laborde, Bastien, S2-519
Laborde, Bernard, E-263
Laborde, Catherine, E-152
Laborde, Charles, E-263
Laborde, Charles Francois, E-79, 263, 315, 393, 411, 432
Laborde, Charles-Francois, S1-199
Laborde, Charles-Francois, S2-722, 730
Laborde, Euphrosine, E-263
Laborde, Felicite Caroline, E-637
Laborde, Francois, E-263
Laborde, Guillaume, E-192, 263-264, 280
Laborde, Guillaume, E-96
Laborde, Jean, E-263-264, 371
Laborde, Jean Baptiste, E-263-264
Laborde, Jeannit, E-263
Laborde, Julie Eleonore, E-263, 637
Laborde, Lesieur, E-29, 266
Laborde, Lesieur, S2-627
Laborde, Louise, E-263
Laborde, Louise Caroline Felicite, E-263
Laborde, Marguerite, E-264
Laborde, Marguerite, E-92
Laborde, Mr., E-114
Laborde, Pierre, E-264
Laborde, Rose Sophie, E-264
Laborgne, Alexandre, E-264
Laborgne, Anne, E-101, 264
Laborie, Mr., E-258
LaBorne, Guillaume, E-96
Labossai, Jacques, E-373
Labossai, Jean Baptiste, E-373
Labotte, Jehan, E-457
Laboureau, Jacques, E-51
Labove, Euphrosine, S2-480
Labranche, Jean, E-77, 264
Labranche, Pierre, E-77, 264
LaBuine, Marguerite, E-371
Lacase, Joseph, E-264, 415
Lacase, Raymond, E-264, 415
Lacaye, Anne, E-264
Lacaye, Francois, E-265
Lacaye, Jean, E-264
Lacaye, Jean Baptiste, E-80, 264

Lacaye, Jean Louis, E-264
Lacaye, Louis, E-80, 146, 264-265
Lacaze, Joseph, E-414
LaChapelle, Pierre, E-154
Lachapelle, Antoine, E-265
Lachapelle, Gillotte, E-174, 265
Lachapelle, Louis Gourdon, E-265
Lachapelle, Thomas, E-265
Lachaume, Anne, E-175, 419
Lachaume, Joseph, E-45, 259, 265, 294, 380-381, 402
Lachaume, Marie Catherine, E-161, 265, 413
Lachaume, Sieur Joseph, E-100
Lachaumer, Joseph, E-597, 587
Lachausse, Joseph, S1-122
LaChivre, Nicolas Louis, E-87
Lachou, Julien, E-432
LaClair, Raphael, E-378, 429
Lacombe, Anne, E-265
Lacombe, Anne, S2-520
Lacombe, Anne-Marie, S2-520
Lacombe, Catherine, E-320, 326
Lacombe, Daniel, S2-519
Lacombe, Jean Baptiste, E-124, 265
Lacombe, Louis, S2-520
Lacombe, Louis-Daniel, S1-75
Lacombe, Louis-Daniel, S2-519-520
Lacombe, Marie, S2-520
Lacombe, Nanon, S2-520
Lacombe, Pierre-Charles, S2-520
Lacombe, Rene, E-265
Lacondre, Jan, S3-911
Lacoque, Elisabeth, C-165
Lacour, Jeanne, E-265
Lacour, Michel, E-121, 265
Lacour, Pierre, E-121, 265
Lacquet, Andre Joseph, E-423
Lacroix, Alexandre, S2-546
Lacroix, Anne, E-636
Lacroix, Anne Francoise Milly, E-265
Lacroix, Catherine Milly, E-13
Lacroix, Francois, E-25, 265
Lacroix, Francois Mathieu, E-265

Lacroix, Jacques, S2-520
Lacroix, Jean, E-25, 40, 106, 130, 265-266, 292, 342, 636
Lacroix, Jean Daniel, E-138, 266
Lacroix, Jean Jacques, E-23
Lacroix, Jean Jaque, E-266
Lacroix, Jeanne, E-259
Lacroix, Jerome, E-636
Lacroix, Marguerite Milly, E-38, 51
Lacroix, Marie, E-117, 404
Lacroix, Marie Anne, E-636
Lacroix, Marie Catherine, E-138, 266
Lacroix, Marie Joseph, E-111
Lacroix, Marie Joseph, E-266
Lacroix, Marie Milly, E-40, 106, 266
Lacroix, Marie Rose, E-266
Lacroix, Michel, E-265-266
Lacroix, Mr., E-265
Lacroix, Nicolas, E-130
Lacroix, Nicolas, E-266
Lacroix, Rene, E-266, 342
Lacroix, Susanne Francoise, E-266
Ladou, Jacques, E-264
Ladou, Thomas, E-45, 264-265
Ladoyer, Jacquemine, S3-1073
Ladret, Marthe, E-114, 319
Lafague, Magdeleine, S3-1097
Lafargue, Anne, E-266, 351
Lafargue, Anne, S1-219
Lafargue, Genevieve, E-135, 266, 302
Lafargue, Jean, E-98-99
Lafargue, Jeanne, E-438
Lafargue, Jeannette, E-267
Lafargue, Madeleine, S1-216-218
Lafargue, Marie, E-403
Lafargue, Marie Anne, E-404
Lafergue, Anne, E-26, 281, 436
Lafevre, Thomas, E-91
Lafitte, Andre, E-267
Lafitte, Anne Madelaine, E-127, 266
Lafitte, Bernard, E-266, 267, 411

Lafitte, Claude Bernard, E-266, 352

Lafitte, Jean, E-127, 132, 266-267

Lafitte, Jeanne Bernardine, E-132,267

Lafitte, Messire, E-106

Lafitte, Michel, E-266-267, 411

Lafitte, Pierre, E-587, 595

LaFontaine Gaillard, Jeanne Marguerite, E-121

Laforest, Jean Baptiste, E-267

Laforest, Jeanne, E-150

Laforest, Jeanne de, E-267

Laforest, Marc Antoine, E-150, 267

Laforest, Marie Anne, E-267

Laforest, Rose Francoise Virginie, E-267

Laforetrie, Jean, E-267

Laforetrie, Jean Baptiste, E-267

Laforetrie, Jeanne, E-267

Laforetrie, Joseph, E-267

Laforetrie, Joseph, E-386

Laforetrie, Marguerite, E-267

Laforetrie, Marie Anne, E-267

Laforetrie, Marie Madeleine, E-267

Laforetrie, Marie Rosalie, E-267

LaFourcade, Jean, E-172

LaFourcade, Jerome, E-172

Lafourcade, Jean, E-267

Lafourcade, Jerome, E-267

Lafresnay, Marie, E-298

LaGaijnerie, Susanne, E-119

Lagaraine, Jean, E-368

Lagarainne, Marie Josephe, E-44, 316

Lagaranne, Jean Baptiste, C-61, 151

LaGarelle, Cecile, E-271-272, 274

Lagarelle, Cecile, F-63, 69

Lagarenne, Anne, E-268

Lagarenne, Cecile, C-63

Lagarenne, Cecile, E-268

Lagarenne, Cecile, N-76, 103-104, 211

Lagarenne, Charle, E-268

Lagarenne, Claire, E-268

Lagarenne, Genevieve, E-2, 74, 268

Lagarenne, Genevieve, N-37, 179, 187

Lagarenne, Jean, E-55, 268, 367

Lagarenne, Jean, N-37, 76, 179, 201, 211

Lagarenne, Jean Baptiste, C-63

Lagarenne, Jean Baptiste, E-268

Lagarenne, Jean Baptiste, F-35

Lagarenne, Jean Baptiste, N-103, 179

Lagarenne, Jean Charles Satis, E-181, 384

Lagarenne, Joseph, E-268

Lagarenne, Lange, E-268

Lagarenne, Louis, E-268, 332, 367

Lagarenne, Marie Jeanne, E-181

Lagarenne, Marie Josephe, E-32, 44, 70, 268, 332, 368

Lagarenne, Marie Rose, E-181

Lagarenne, Marie-Josephe, S1-198

Lagarenne, Marie-Josephe Chenet, S1-190

Lagarenne, Michel, E-384

Lagarenne, Mr., E-74

Lagarenne, widow, E-2

Lagargille, Charles, E-276

Lagarine, Marie Joseph, E-145

Lagasse, Anne, E-517

Lagasse, Gabriel, E-517

Lagasse, Jeanne, E-517

Lagasse, Marguerite, E-474, 517

Lagasse, Marie, E-513

Lagasse, Pierre, E-517

Lagatu, Marie, E-9

Lage dit LaTulipe, Alexandre, E-160, 268

Lage dit LaTulipe, Etienne, E-160, 268

Lagilbert, Marie Goguelin, S3-958, 1087

Lagneu, Francois, E-625

Lagoannere, Blaise, E-268

Lagoannere, Jean Pierre, E-268

Lagon, Francoise, E-319

Lagrange, Anne Henriette, E-30, 268

Lagrange, Jean Martin, E-30, 254, 268

Lagrange, Louise, E-254, 268

Lagroix, Jacques, E-269, 332

Lagroix, Louis, E-269, 332

Lagroux, Marguerite, E-121, 269

Laguerre, Magdalen, E-60

Lahaye, Madeleine, C-72

Lahaye, Madeleine, F-21

Lahaye, Madeleine, F-21

Lahaye, Madeleine, S2-595

Lahaye, Marie, E-103, 158

Lahaye, Perine, S1-185

Lahaye, Pierre, C-98

Lahaye, Pierre, E-269, 426

Lahaye, Therese Marguerite, C-98

Lahaye, Therese Marguerite, E-269, 426

LaHoussaye Cysen, M. Samuel, E-13, 343

Laidet, Francois, E-348

Laidet, Marie Magdeleine, E-356

Laigle, Marie Therese, E-196, 257

Lailleuaut, Laurent, S3-1102

Laine, Jean, E-377

Lair des Longchamps, Francoise Catherine, E-86

Laisne, Claude, S2-684

Laisne, Claude, S3-1019

Laisne, Jeanne, S2-684, 687

Laisne, Jeanne, S3-1019

Laisne, Laurence, S2-591

Laisne, Laurence, S3-931

Laisse, -----, E-1

Lajeune, Catherine, E-262, 295

Lajeune, Catherine, S3-969

Lajeune, Marguerite, E-29

Lajeune, Marguerite, E-29

Lajon, Rene, C-61

Lalandam, Magdalen, E-282

Lalande, Anne, E-190, 637

Lalande, Emelie, F-35

Lalande, Emelie, N-102

Lalande, Emilie, C-61

Lalande, Eulalie, C-61

Lalande, Eulalie, N-102
Lalande, Euphrosie, F-53
Lalande, Euphrosine, N-82, 183
Lalande, Jean Baptiste, E-269
Lalande, Jean Edouard, F-35
Lalande, Jean Edouard, N-102
Lalande, Joseph, C-61, 143
Lalande, Joseph, E-193, 269
Lalande, Joseph, F-35
Lalande, Joseph, N-101-102
Lalande, Joseph Edouard, N-101
Lalande, Madeleine, C-97
Lalande, Madeleine, N-152,
  167, 193
Lalande, Marguerite, E-637, 644
Lalande, Marie, N-73
Lalande, Pierre, E-269, 280
Lalande, Sylvin, E-269
Lalee, Francoise, E-276, 440
Laliberte, Marie, E-269
Lalloue, Amand, E-457
Lalung, Julien, E-172-173
Lamaestre, Joseph, N-230
Lamaistre, Francois Louis, E-3
Lamanquet, Gillette, S1-258
Lamare, Jacques, E-393
Lamare, Jacques Bedvineau, E-
  269
Lamare, Jean Bedvineau, E-269,
  393
Lamare, Louis, E-269
Lamare, Marguerite, E-269
Lamarque, Bernardine, E-359
Lamarque, Marguerite, E-418
LaMartinerie, Angelique, E-186,
  190
Lamasse, Francoise, E-587, 595
Lamasse, Genevieve, E-587
Lamasse, Suzanne, E-587, 595
Lamau, Mr., E-358
Lambelot, Huguette, E-456
Lambert, Anne, E-587, 592
Lambert, Anne, S1-361
Lambert, Anne, S2-510
Lambert, Francois, S2-521-522
Lambert, Jean, E-263
Lambert, Marie Elisabeth, E-71
Lambert, Pierre, N-213
Lambert, Radegonde, E-456,
  472
Lambert, Rene, S2-521

Lambert, Sr., S2-759
Lambert, Toinette, E-122, 370
Lamberteche, Jean Baptiste, E-
  64-65, 269
Lamberteiche, Jeanne, E-269
Lamberteiche, Marie, E-269
Lambrouin, Marguerite, E-111
Lamestre, Marie, C-165
Lamontagne, Alexandre, E-526
Lamontagne, Jacques, E-527
Lamontagne Village named after
  Julien L'Orsurnamed La
  Montagne, E-210
Lamorue, Madeleine, E-304
Lamothe, Alexandre, C-44
Lamothe, Alexandre, S1-353
Lamothe, Charles, E-587, 597
Lamouline, Charles, S1-217
Lamouline, Charles Philippon,
  S3-1096
Lamouline, Francoise Philippon,
  S3-1096
Lamouline, Gabriel Claude, S3-
  1096
Lamouline, Gabriel Phillippon,
  S3-996, 1095-1096
Lamoureaux, Jean Louis, C-62
Lamoureaux, Louis , C-61-62
Lamoureux, Adelaide, F-71, 107
Lamoureux, Elisabeth, E-270
Lamoureux, Francois, E-587,
  595
Lamoureux, Hilaire, E-270, 327
Lamoureux, Jean, E-12, 418
Lamoureux, Jean Baptiste, E-31,
  74, 270, 341, 368, 604
Lamoureux, Jean dit Rochefort,
  E-270
Lamoureux, Jean Heli, E-270
Lamoureux, Jean Louis, F-71,
  107
Lamoureux, Louis, E-270
Lamoureux, Louis, F-71, 107
Lamoureux, Louis dit Rochefort,
  E-270
Lamoureux, Magdeleine, E-269,
  332
Lamoureux, Marie Anne, E-132,
  267
Lamoureux, Marie Jeanne, E-22,
  150

Lamoureux, Marie Judith, E-270
Lamoureux, Martin, E-270
Lamoureux dit Rochefort, Louis,
  E-187
Lamude, Marie Therese, E-191
Lamusse, Jean, S1-354
Lamusse, Jeanne, S2-596-597
Lamy, Francoise, E-69
Lamy, Marie, E-13, 92, 270, 402
Lanbiere, Mathieu, E-90
Lance, Barbe Jeanne, E-644
Lanchois, Marguerite, E-600
Lanclos, Marie, E-28
Lanco, Jeanne Theresse, E-14
Lancon, Anne, E-164
Landais, Jeanne, E-34
Landal, Francois, S3-1132
Landelle, Guillemette, E-617
Landieu, Jean, E-600
Landieu, Pierre, E-600
Landois, Jeanne, E-307
Landon, Jacques, E-138, 389
Landrais, Jean, S2-738
Landre, Jean, E-113
Landreau, Jean, E-318
Landreau, Marie, E-270, 346
Landreau, Pierre, E-316, 339
Landrin, Anonime, E-270
Landrin, Benjamin, E-164
Landrin, Francois, E-270, 356
Landrin, Joseph, E-270
Landrin, Magdelen, E-164
Landrin, Marguerite Genevieve,
  E-30
Landrin, Marie, E-270
Landrin, Marie Marguerite, E-
  270
Landrin, Rene, E-271
Landry, Abraham, E-173, 271,
  482, 527
Landry, Abraham, S1-176
Landry, Abraham, S2-526, 535
Landry, Abraham, S3-833, 849
Landry, Abraham Isaac, E-271
Landry, Abraham Isaac, N-107
Landry, Adelaide, E-271, 605
Landry, Agnes, C-160
Landry, Agnes Julie, N-107
Landry, Aimable, F-61
Landry, Aimable Etienne, E-271
Landry, Alexis, S1-9

Landry, Alexis-Charles, S2-527

Landry, Amable, E-145

Landry, Amable Etienne, N-107

Landry, Anastasie, E-19, 343

Landry, Ange, C-59, 62

Landry, Angelique, S2-567, 620

Landry, Anna, F-99

Landry, Anne, E-41-42, 106-107, 162, 167, 271, 283, 285, 367, 482, 565, 603-604

Landry, Anne, F-25, 33, 69, 101

Landry, Anne, N-106, 165

Landry, Anne, S1-33, 367, 368

Landry, Anne, S2-728-729

Landry, Anne Adelaide, E-271

Landry, Anne Adelaide, F-61

Landry, Anne Adelaide, N-107

Landry, Anne Apoline, C-63

Landry, Anne Appoline, N-103-104

Landry, Anne Bonne Marie, C-63

Landry, Anne Bonne Marie, N-104

Landry, Anne Marie, E-271, 287, 604

Landry, Anne Marie, F-31

Landry, Anne Marie Magdalen, E-271

Landry, Anne Marie Victoire, N-104

Landry, Anne Modeste, E-347, 352

Landry, Anne Susanne, F-17

Landry, Anne Suzanne, N-108

Landry, Anne-Marguerite, S2-528

Landry, Anne-Marie-Jeanne, S2-543

Landry, Anne-Yvonne, S2-536

Landry, Annette, E-282

Landry, Anselm, E-16, 271-272

Landry, Anselme, F-7

Landry, Anselme, N-25, 102, 197, 202

Landry, Anselme, S1-39, 70, 92, 116, 137

Landry, Anselme, S2-481, 522, 524, 529, 566, 766

Landry, Anselme, S3-844, 941

Landry, Antoine, C-64

Landry, Antoine, E-474, 482, 527

Landry, Antoine, F-25

Landry, Antoine, S1-37

Landry, Antoine, S2-510, 524, 531, 542

Landry, Antoinette, E-456, 472

Landry, Armand, S2-535

Landry, Baptiste, E-527

Landry, Bastien, C-63

Landry, Bastien, N-103

Landry, Benjamin, C-10

Landry, Benjamin, E-273

Landry, Benjamin, F-75

Landry, Benjamin, N-153, 177

Landry, Benjamin, S2-524

Landry, Blanche-Charlotte, S2-522

Landry, Bonne Louise, C-66

Landry, Bonne Louise, N-107

Landry, Bonne Marie, F-69

Landry, Bonne Marie Adelaide, E-271

Landry, Bonne Marie Louise, E-271

Landry, Bonnie Louise Marie, F-61

Landry, Catherine, E-482

Landry, Catherine, F-5

Landry, Catherine, N-122

Landry, Catherine Reine Victoire, E-271

Landry, Cecile, C-158

Landry, Cecile, E-266, 476, 482

Landry, Cecile, S1-232-233

Landry, Cecille, S3-880

Landry, Charle Mathurin, E-271

Landry, Charles, C-62-63, 81

Landry, Charles, E-60, 271-273, 282, 527

Landry, Charles, F-3, 21

Landry, Charles, N-102-103, 139, 175

Landry, Charles, S1-40, 52, 113

Landry, Charles, S2-431, 524-527, 534, 536, 642, 679, 732

Landry, Charles, S3-833, 967, 1027, 1034, 1047, 1080

Landry, Charles-Joseph, S2-536

Landry, Charles-Marie, S2-523, 527

Landry, Charles-Pierre-Alain, S2-525

Landry, Charlotte Blanche, N-102

Landry, Claire, F-15

Landry, Claire, S1-206-207

Landry, Claude, E-474, 482, 527

Landry, Claude, N-105-106

Landry, Claude, S1-207, 238

Landry, Claude, S2-530

Landry, Clet, S2-531

Landry, Elisabeth, S3-1047

Landry, Elizabeth, C-40

Landry, Elizabeth, N-106

Landry, Elizabeth, S1-39-40, 99, 104

Landry, Elizabeth, S2-538, 710, 729

Landry, Elizabeth-Augustine, S2-532

Landry, Etienne, C-64

Landry, Etienne, S1-45

Landry, Etienne, S2-526, 529-530

Landry, Eufrosie, S2-530

Landry, Euphrosine, S2-527

Landry, Euphrosine-Josephe, S2-526

Landry, Eustache, N-106

Landry, Eustache, S2-528, 530-531

Landry, Firmain, S2-533

Landry, Firmin, C-63

Landry, Firmin, E-272

Landry, Firmin, F-3

Landry, Firmin, N-103, 206

Landry, Firmin, S2-432

Landry, Firmin Gregoire, E-272

Landry, Firmin-Gregoire, S2-529-530

Landry, Firmin-Pancrace, S2-525

Landry, Francois, C-63, 93, 115

Landry, Francois, E-271-273, 527

Landry, Francois, F-3, 69

Landry, Francois, N-103, 175, 177, 254

Landry, Francois, S3-868-869

Landry, Francois Marie, N-103

Landry, Francois-Jean-Theo-dore, S2-537

Landry, Francois-Marie, S2-523

Landry, Francois-Mathurin, S2-536

Landry, Francoise, E-272

Landry, Francoise, S1-29, 208, 212, 314

Landry, Francoise, S2-538, 713, 717, 729, 742, 749

Landry, Francoise, S3-885, 887, 1016, 1034

Landry, Frederic, C-63

Landry, Frederic, N-104

Landry, Gabriel, E-272

Landry, Genevieve, E-272

Landry, Genevieve, F-21

Landry, Genevieve, S2-525

Landry, Germain, C-10, 63

Landry, Germain, E-268, 271-272, 274, 482, 527

Landry, Germain, F-63, 69

Landry, Germain, N-76, 103-104, 165, 175

Landry, Gregoire, E-31, 604

Landry, Grineo, F-31

Landry, Helene, E-21, 272

Landry, Helene, F-13

Landry, Helene, N-155-157, 176, 239

Landry, Helene, S1-177

Landry, Helene, S2-530, 710, 734-735, 774

Landry, Helenne, S3-857, 1052, 1064

Landry, Hilaire, C-63

Landry, Hilaire, F-17

Landry, Hilaire, N-104

Landry, Hilaire, S1-89, 211

Landry, Hilaire, S2-527-528, 531, 541, 701, 710

Landry, Hilaire, S3-1052

Landry, Honnore, E-151, 271-272, 274

Landry, Honore, S2-522, 562

Landry, Isaac Abraham, F-61

Landry, Isabelle, E-482

Landry, Isabelle, F-25

Landry, Isabelle-Bertranne, S2-530

Landry, Isabelle-Joseph, S2-536

Landry, Jan fils, S3-851

Landry, Jean, C-63-64, 94

Landry, Jean, E-106, 271-174, 305, 411, 414, 433, 482, 527, 573, 604-605, 619

Landry, Jean, F-3

Landry, Jean, N-43, 48, 103-105, 180, 212, 231, 238

Landry, Jean, S1-91, 118, 175, 238, 328, 330

Landry, Jean, S2-522, 526, 528-531, 533, 539, 544, 559, 565, 714

Landry, Jean, S3-844, 877, 900, 921, 1033, 1049, 1052

Landry, Jean Baptiste, C-39, 63-64

Landry, Jean Baptiste, E-272

Landry, Jean Baptiste, F-17, 21, 25

Landry, Jean Baptiste, N-104-106, 108, 225, 227

Landry, Jean Baptiste, S3-898, 924, 1152

Landry, Jean Baptiste Leonor, C-65

Landry, Jean Baptiste Leonor, E-272

Landry, Jean Baptiste Leonor, F-61

Landry, Jean Baptiste Thomas, E-267

Landry, Jean Charles, F-69

Landry, Jean Charles, S1-364

Landry, Jean Charles, S3-1015

Landry, Jean Etienne, E-272

Landry, Jean Francois, E-272, 604

Landry, Jean Jacques, C-62

Landry, Jean Jacques, F-69

Landry, Jean Jacques Freder-ique, E-272

Landry, Jean Joseph, E-273

Landry, Jean Pierre, E-273

Landry, Jean Pierre, F-21

Landry, Jean Pierre, N-109

Landry, Jean Raphael, F-17, 101

Landry, Jean Raphael, N-108

Landry, Jean-Baptiste, S1-13, 92, 100, 246, 291, 316

Landry, Jean-Baptiste, S2-523, 527-528, 530-533, 540, 543-544, 667

Landry, Jean-Baptiste-Raphael, S2-542

Landry, Jean-Charles, S2-533-534, 538, 559

Landry, Jean-Frederic-Gabriel, S2-529-530

Landry, Jean-Marie, S2-523

Landry, Jean-Pierre, S2-525, 528, 537, 541-542

Landry, Jean-Raphael, S2-539

Landry, Jean-Sebastien, S2-526

Landry, Jeanne, C-68

Landry, Jeanne, E-42-43, 482

Landry, Jeanne, F-3, 61, 101

Landry, Jeanne, N-111, 116

Landry, Jeanne, S1-32

Landry, Jeanne, S2-554

Landry, Jeanne Marguerite, F-61

Landry, Jeanne Marguerite, N-107

Landry, Jeanne Marie, C-160

Landry, Jeanne-Guillemette, S2-543

Landry, Jeanne-Perinne, S2-535, 540

Landry, Joseph, C-15, 62, 64-66, 100, 116, 155, 160

Landry, Joseph, E-121, 162, 271-274, 431, 603-605

Landry, Joseph, F-17, 61, 101

Landry, Joseph, N-106-108, 187, 197-198

Landry, Joseph, S1-40, 98, 106

Landry, Joseph, S2-527, 531-538, 540, 543, 714

Landry, Joseph, S3-843, 849, 1021, 1027, 1037

Landry, Joseph Claire, N-107

Landry, Joseph-Charles, S2-522, 536

Landry, Joseph-Giroire, S2-539

Landry, Joseph-Marie, S2-543

Landry, Joseph-Paul, S2-537

Landry, Joseph-Pierre, S2-523

Landry, Julein-Joseph, S2-535

Landry, Julien Rolland, N-107

Landry, Lesnes Rene, E-457

Landry, Louis, F-3

Landry, Louis, N-103

Landry, Louis , C-63

Landry, Louis-Abel, S2-526

Landry, Louis-Pierre, S2-539

Landry, Madeleine, N-162, 171-172

Landry, Madeleine, S1-47, 92, 98, 100, 106, 125, 134, 161, 174, 176-177, 328

Landry, Madeleine, S2-617, 668, 735, 748, 778, 780

Landry, Madelleine-Olive, S2-536

Landry, Magdalen Genevieve, E-273

Landry, Magdalen Genevieve, F-61

Landry, Magdalen Helli, E-273

Landry, Magdeleine, C-66

Landry, Magdeleine, E-162, 271, 273-274, 307, 380, 422, 425, 427, 476, 573, 605

Landry, Magdeleine, S3-856, 863, 1014

Landry, Marguerite, C-10, 14, 63, 81, 94, 160, 166

Landry, Marguerite, E-30-31, 47-48, 89, 106-107, 125, 163, 273-274, 307, 416, 482, 501, 560, 604

Landry, Marguerite, F-3, 17, 19, 21, 25, 53, 59, 75, 101, 103

Landry, Marguerite, N-12, 39, 103-104, 106, 139, 147, 165, 230

Landry, Marguerite, S1-47, 98, 100, 125, 134, 161, 231, 238

Landry, Marguerite, S2-438, 449, 463, 523-525, 528, 531, 534, 541-542, 577, 616, 642, 693, 695-696, 700-701, 703, 744

Landry, Marguerite, S3-956, 1021-1022, 1027, 1030, 1041

Landry, Marguerite Genevieve, N-108

Landry, Marguerite Gertrude, E-273

Landry, Marguerite Luce, E-273

Landry, Marguerite Modeste, N-104

Landry, Marguerite-Francoise, S2-526

Landry, Marguerite-Genevieve, S2-532, 541-542

Landry, Marguerite-Gertrude, S2-529-530

Landry, Marguerite-Josephe, S2-537, 542

Landry, Marie, E-42, 47, 138, 273, 284, 456-457, 473-474, 482, 555, 564, 574

Landry, Marie, F-17, 53, 63, 79, 81, 101

Landry, Marie, N-42, 46-48, 66-67, 114-115, 122, 153, 177, 194, 196, 205

Landry, Marie, S1-10, 13, 30, 40, 70, 105, 116, 210, 316, 324

Landry, Marie, S2-445, 464, 523, 528, 531-535, 538, 565-567, 569, 618, 714, 753

Landry, Marie, S2-523, 542

Landry, Marie, S3-884, 898, 926, 1002

Landry, marie, C-39-40, 66

Landry, Marie Anne, C-64

Landry, Marie Auguste, E-273

Landry, Marie Blanche, N-121

Landry, Marie Elizabeth, E-273, 604

Landry, Marie Joseph, F-21

Landry, Marie Josephe, C-81

Landry, Marie Josephe, E-125, 272, 274, 288, 372, 413, 573, 603

Landry, Marie Louise, E-274

Landry, Marie Madeleine, N-42-43, 104-105, 238

Landry, Marie Madeleine Adelaide, E-274

Landry, Marie Magdalen Marguerite, E-274

Landry, Marie Magdelaine, F-15, 17

Landry, Marie Magdelaine Adelaide, E-274, 605

Landry, Marie Marguerite, F-17

Landry, Marie Marguerite, N-86, 88, 108

Landry, Marie Olive, F-5

Landry, Marie Olive, N-25-26, 102, 197

Landry, Marie Rose, C-63

Landry, Marie Rose, E-274

Landry, Marie Rose, N-103

Landry, Marie Theotiste, C-160

Landry, Marie Victoire, C-63

Landry, Marie Victoire, E-274

Landry, Marie Victoire, N-104

Landry, Marie-Anne, S2-540

Landry, Marie-Blanche, S2-573-574

Landry, Marie-Josephe, S1-180

Landry, Marie-Josephe, S2-525, 642

Landry, Marie-Louise, S2-529-530

Landry, Marie-Luce, S2-529

Landry, Marie-Madeleine, S1-6, 238, 314

Landry, Marie-Madeleine, S2-525, 541, 543, 642, 690

Landry, Marie-Madeleine-Adelaide, S2-539

Landry, Marie-Madeleine-Marguerite, S2-529-530

Landry, Marie-Olive, S2-522

Landry, Marie-Perinne, S2-536

Landry, Mary, E-556, 558

Landry, Michel, E-273-274, 288

Landry, Mr., E-45, 145

Landry, Olivier-Charles, S2-527

Landry, Osithe, S1-91-93, 141, 175-177

Landry, Osithe, S2-522, 748

Landry, Ozite, S2-760

Landry, Ozite, S3-830, 848, 862

Landry, Paul, C-93

Landry, Paul, E-272, 274

Landry, Paul, S1-157, 169

Landry, Paul, S2-537-538, 565, 635

Landry, Paul, S3-1130-1132, 1134-1136

Landry, Perinne-Tarsille, S2-523

Landry, Perrine, E-457

Landry, Pierre, C-72

Landry, Pierre, E-271, 274, 474, 482, 487, 527, 603-604

Landry, Pierre, F-17, 101

Landry, Pierre, N-47, 106, 108
Landry, Pierre, S1-40, 279, 366
Landry, Pierre, S2-450, 486,
  525, 527, 533-534, 536, 538-
  540, 543, 569, 573-574, 576,
  713-714, 729, 736, 745, 780
Landry, Pierre, S3-847, 851,
  881, 883, 897, 927, 942-943,
  1014-1015, 1021, 1028, 1033-
  1034, 1037, 1047, 1051, 1072,
  1082, 1119
Landry, Pierre Elie, N-104
Landry, Pierre Joseph, N-239
Landry, Pierre Louis, N-108
Landry, Pierre-Isaac, S2-532
Landry, Pierre-Joseph, S2-527
Landry, Pierre-Josephe, S2-539
Landry, Pierre-Marie, S2-543
Landry, Prosper, C-18
Landry, Prosper, F-21
Landry, Prosper, N-108-109
Landry, Prosper, S1-101
Landry, Prosper, S2-495, 531,
  540-542, 665
Landry, Prosper, S3-924-925
Landry, Reine Catherine, N-104
Landry, Rene, C-62, 65
Landry, Rene, E-106, 271-274,
  474, 482, 527, 560, 565
Landry, Rene, F-61, 101
Landry, Rene, N-105, 107, 171,
  231
Landry, Rene, S1-305
Landry, Rene, S2-524, -539,
  542-544, 557, 759, 778
Landry, Rene, S3-843, 1051,
  1069
Landry, Rolland, C-160
Landry, Rosalie, S2-663
Landry, Rosalie, S3-841
Landry, Rosalie-Marguerite, S2-
  532
Landry, Rose, F-17
Landry, Rose, N-104, 106
Landry, Rose Adelaide, N-106
Landry, Sebastien, F-3
Landry, Selme, E-274
Landry, Servanne, F-101
Landry, Servanne, S2-543
Landry, Servanne-Laurence, S2-
  542

Landry, Simon, F-21, 61
Landry, Simon, N-109, 238
Landry, Simon, S1-365
Landry, Simon, S2-531, 544,
  555, 593, 696
Landry, Simon-Joseph, S2-541
Landry, Victoire, E-274
Landry, Zacharie-Joseph, S2-
  535
Landuman, Therese, E-86
Laneau, Anne, E-274
Laneau, Francois, E-274
Laneau, Francoise, E-274
Laneau, Marie Judith, E-274
Lanes, Francoise, E-317, 378
Langau, Francoise, E-61, 275
Langau, Margueritte, E-275
Langau, Nicolas, E-275
Langau, Nicolas Francois, E-61,
  275
Lange, Marie Barbe, E-52
Lange, Mr., E-268
Langelvelt, Tobie, E-587, 592
Langeois, Jacques, E-599
Langevin, Antoine, E-275
Langevin, Jean, E-275
Langevin, Louis, E-275
Langira, Elumette, E-593
Langlade, Bernard, E-183
Langlais, Anne, E-275
Langlais, Jeanne, E-275
Langlais, Pierre, E-275
Langline, Angelique, F-103
Langline, Jean Louis, F-103
Langline, Marie Jeanne, F-103
Langlira, Elumette, E-587
Langlois, Andre, S2-544-545
Langlois, Angelique, E-303, 328
Langlois, Clotilde, E-98, 193-
  194, 275
Langlois, Francois, E-146, 275
Langlois, Francois, S2-544-545
Langlois, Francois-Marie, S2-
  544-545
Langlois, Henriette, S2-544-545
Langlois, Jacques, E-98, 110,
  275, 352
Langlois, Jean, E-275
Langlois, Jeanne, E-323
Langlois, Jeanne Francoise, E-
  275, 323-324

Langlois, Marie, E-275
Langlois, Marie, S1-1
Langlois, Marie Jeanne, E-275
Langlois, Nicolas, E-145, 275
Langlois, Noel, E-275
Langlois, P., E-319
Langlois, Rene, E-362, 407
Lango, Margueritte, E-294
Lango, Nicolas, E-294
Langrez, Jan, S3-995
Langrez, Jean, S2-545
Languille, Gabrielle, S1-85, 205,
  257
Languille, Gabrielle, S2-509,
  643
Languille, Gabrielle, S3-1042
Languille, Mathurinne, S2-640
Lanie, Louis Francois, E-275
Lanie, Thomas, E-275
Lanios, Marie Magdalen, E-405
Lannelongue, Armant, E-275,
  294
Lannelongue, Arnaud, E-275,
  380
Lannelongue, Jean Baptiste, E-
  275, 380
Lannelongue, Pierre, E-275, 294
Lanos, Pierre, S2-545
Lanos, Pierre, S3-983
Lanoue, Antoine, S1-311
Lanoue, Charles, S2-753
Lanoue, Marguerite, S2-753
Lanoue, Pierre, E-457, 527
Lanoue, Rosalie, E-361
Lanoue named after Peirr
  LaNoue, E-213
Lanouvelle, Marie, E-144, 381
Lantigny, Jean Rene, E-276, 279
Lantigny, Rene, E-276
Laoge, Marie, E-145, 276
Laparede, Jacques, E-16
Laparede, Mathurin, E-16
LaPerelle, Jean Francois de la
  Salle, E-195
LaPerrelle, Jean, E-148, 276
LaPerrelle, Jean Louis Francois
  Desales, E-148, 276, 386
Lapert, Jean Baptiste, E-281
Lapeurdie dit Barrier, Martial,
  E-276, 440
LaPierre, Marie Josephe, E-551

LaPierre, Marie Magdelaine, E-100, 276, 309

LaPierre, Marie Marguerite, E-269

LaPierre, Marie Suzanne Evee, E-276

LaPierre, Michel, E-276, 309, 551

LaPierre, Pierre, E-276

Lapierre, Anne, E-276, 303, 313, 321

Lapierre, Charles, E-587, 589, 593

Lapierre, Francois, E-146, 276, 475, 509, 527

Lapierre, Francoise, E-16, 146, 172, 276, 598

Lapierre, Jacques, E-510, 551

Lapierre, Jean Baptiste, E-183

Lapierre, Joseph, E-184, 190-191, 276, 326

Lapierre, Madeleine, C-46

Lapierre, Madeleine, E-254

Lapierre, Madeleine, S1-380

Lapierre, Madeleine, S2-551-552

Lapierre, Magdeleine, S3-897, 902

Lapierre, Marguerite, E-269

Lapierre, Marie, C-47

Lapierre, Marie, E-276, 509, 587, 589, 593

Lapierre, Marie, S1-381

Lapierre, Marie, S2-675, 677

Lapierre, Marie, S3-900

Lapillier, Por. SaCotoste, S3-1048

Lapointe, Marguerite, S1-363

Lapointe, Marguerite, S3-1011

Laporte, Nicolas, E-376

Laporte, Radegonde, E-276

Laporte, Rene, E-376

Lapree, Rosalie, C-157

Lapretrie, Jeanne, S3-899

LaPrieur, Marguerite, E-263

LaPrieur, Marie, E-264

Laquentini, Arnaud, E-156

Larche, Michel, E-513

Lard, Jean Patrouil, E-387

Lardy, Marie Jeanne, E-60

Lardy, Marie Louise, E-115

Lareu, Catherine, E-256, 276

Large, Marie Josephe, E-114, 430

Large, Mr., E-369

Larges, Marie Jeanne, E-80, 277

Larges, Pierre, E-80, 277

Larieux, Mathieu, E-45, 145

Larnac, M., E-83

Laroc, Ambroise, E-277

Laroc, Jean, E-277

Laroche, Christine, E-314

Laroche, Francois, E-277

Laroche, Francoise, E-359

Laroche, Jean, E-277, 302, 378, 408

Laroche, Jeanne Marie, E-28, 369

Laroche, Julien Guillaume, E-277

Laroche, Marie, E-277

Laroche, Marie Pierre, E-277

LaRoche Letang, Jean Baptiste, E-106

Laroche Letang, Pascal Paulin, E-106

LaRoix, Jeanne, E-376

Laromaind, Marie, E-311

Laroque, Jean, S1-49, 187

Laroque, Jean, S3-1028

Laroque, Jeanne, C-160

Laroque, Marie Joseph, C-161

Laroses, -----, S3-1096

Larouis, Francois, S3-995

Larralde, Joannis, E-35, 278

Larralde, Pierre, E-35, 278

Larretche, Michel, S1-358

Larroque, Marie, E-178

Lartigue, Dame, E-20

Lartigue, Jeanne, E-278, 326

Lartigue, Joseph, E-137, 278, 326, 388

Lartigue, Magdelaine, E-137, 278

Lartigue, Marguerite, E-278, 388

Lartigue, Mrs., E-388

Larue, Arnaud, E-66

Larue, Francoise, E-319

Larue, Jean Pias, E-66

Larue, Pierre, E-379

Lasalle, Dominique, S1-356, 358

Lasalle, Landrais, S1-136

LaSauvagere, Pierre, E-278

Lascoret, Jean, E-275, 380

Lascoret, Jean Baptiste, E-275, 278, 380

Lasonde, Marguerite, C-29

Lasonde, Margueritte, S3-904

Lasse, Jeanne, E-138, 441

Lasserre, child, E-278

Lasserre, Earlene, C-vi, ix

Lasserre, Francois, E-278-279

Lasserre, girl, E-279

Lasserre, Jean, E-279

Latour, Anne, S1-230

Latour, Anne, S3-1098

Latour, Charles, E-475

Latour, Charlotte, E-173

Latour, Jacques, E-475

Latour, Jeanne, E-473

Latour, Marie, E-279, 359

Latour, Susanne, E-279

LaTreille, Louise, E-191

Latton, Etienne, N-249

Laubaio, Bertrand, E-279

Laubaio, Jeanne, E-265, 279

Laubejoye, Jeanne, E-91, 370

Laubin, Francois, S2-579

Laugier, Louis, E-168

Laugouette, Margueritte, E-588, 591

Laumonier, Jean, E-91, 370

Launay, Charlotte, S2-613, 615

Laune, -----, E-1

Laune, Mr., E-74

Laurant, Francoise, E-369

Laurant, Madeleine, F-57

Laurant, Magdeleine, C-69, 130

Laure, Francoise, E-320

Laure, Marguerite, S1-76

Laure, Marie, S1-260

Laure, Marie Joseph, E-279

Laurend, Mathurin, S3-1147

Laurent, Catherine, E-22, 279, 412

Laurent, Etienette, E-625, 629

Laurent, Francois, E-279

Laurent, Francois, S3-853

Laurent, Francoise, E-350

Laurent, Jean, E-619, 625

Laurent, Jean, S1-1
Laurent, Jean, S3-1074
Laurent, Jeanne, E-619
Laurent, Jeanne, S1-1
Laurent, Jeanne, S3-1074
Laurent, Louis, E-619
Laurent, Madeleine, S2-452
Laurent, Magdeleine, S3-1017
Laurent, Marie, E-11
Laurent, Marie Anne, E-276, 279, 350
Laurent, Pierre, E-22, 279
Laurent, Rosalie, E-619
Laurent, Rose, E-149
Laurent, veuve, E-64
Laurenty, Pierre, F-83
Laurin, Angelique, E-319
Lauriol, Charles, E-12, 279
Lauriol, Madeleine, E-12, 279
Laurs, Marie Francoise, E-51, 319
Lauterre, H., S3-1088
Lauvealle, Joseph, E-152
Lauzet, Guillaume, E-36
Lauzet, Jean, E-36, 332
Lavache, Alexis, E-124, 152, 279
Lavache, Alexis, S1-340
Lavache, Alexis, S2-547-548
Lavache, Anne, S2-548
Lavache, Anne Marie Josephe, E-279
Lavache, Anne-Theodose, S2-547
Lavache, Charles Joseph, E-279
Lavache, Elizabeth-Blanche, S2-547, 727-728
Lavache, Firmin-Gregoire, S1-249
Lavache, Firmin-Gregoire, S2-548, 557
Lavache, Francois, E-279
Lavache, Francois, S2-547-548, 727
Lavache, Honore, E-279
Lavache, Jean Charles, E-279
Lavache, Jean-Baptiste, S1-121, 249
Lavache, Jean-Baptiste, S2-547-548

Lavache, Jean-Charles, S2-547-548
Lavache, Joseph, E-279
Lavache, Joseph, S2-547-548
Lavache, Louise Nicole, E-279
Lavache, Marguerite, E-427
Lavache, Marguerite, S2-547-548
Lavache, Marguerite Blanche, E-279, 424
Lavache, Theodose, E-279
Laval, Pierre, E-430
Lavalee, Genevieve, E-517
Lavalee, Marguerite, E-517
Lavallee, Jeanne, E-476
Lavanant, Francois, E-284
Lavanant, Francoise Charlotte, E-279, 284-285
Lavanant, Maitre Francois, E-279
LaVaquier, Andre, E-280, 440
LaVaquier, Jean, E-280
Lavarieux, Marie, E-311
Lavasseur, Catherine Cecile, E-389
Lavaud, Jean, E-284
Lave, Catherine, E-407
Laveille, Claude, S3-1094
Laveille, Jean, S3-1094
Lavenir, Grave (Mrs.), E-321
Laveque, Marie Joseph, E-412
Laveque, Maurice, E-412
Lavergne, Alphonse, E-125, 270, 280, 322
Lavergne, Anne, E-393
Lavergne, Barthelemy, E-196
Lavergne, Catherine, E-72, 137
Lavergne, Cecile, C-51
Lavergne, Cecile, E-78, 111, 140, 176-179, 188, 264, 367, 637, 644
Lavergne, Cecile, S1-97, 184, 199
Lavergne, Cecile, S2-431, 723
Lavergne, Cecile, S3-917, 943
Lavergne, Clement, E-125, 280
Lavergne, Francois, E-280
Lavergne, Francoise, E-351
Lavergne, Genevieve, E-178
Lavergne, Genevieve, S2-430
Lavergne, Jacques, C-55

Lavergne, Jacques, E-264, 280
Lavergne, Jacques, N-109, 251
Lavergne, Jean, E-264, 280
Lavergne, Jean Baptiste Alexandre, N-110
Lavergne, Marguerite, C-59
Lavergne, Marguerite, E-71, 69, 280
Lavergne, Marguerite, F-35
Lavergne, Marguerite, N-110, 166-167, 232
Lavergne, Marie, C-43, 55
Lavergne, Marie, E-183, 185, 188, 280
Lavergne, Marie, F-63
Lavergne, Marie, N-87-88, 233
Lavergne, Marie Madeleine, N-110
Lavergne, Marie Magdalen, E-280
Lavergne, Marie Magdelaine, F-31
Lavergne, Osithe, E-192
Lavergne, Ozee, E-637
Lavergne, Pierre, E-95, 280
Lavergne, Pierre, F-31, 35
Lavergne, Pierre, N-109-110, 166, 232, 251
Lavergne, Pierre Benjamin, E-280
Lavergne, Pierre Benjamin, N-110
Lavergne, Rose, E-118, 194, 263-264, 280, 637, 645
Lavergne, Victoire, F-31, 41
Lavergne, Victoire Bellarmine, N-110
Lavigeon, Marie, E-139, 325
Lavigne, Anne, E-34, 281
Lavigne, Anne, S1-335
Lavigne, Anne, S2-549
Lavigne, Barbe, S1-76
Lavigne, Barbe, S2-549
Lavigne, Charles, E-266, 281, 351
Lavigne, Charles, S1-335
Lavigne, Charlotte, S1-335
Lavigne, Charlotte, S2-471
Lavigne, Genevieve, S2-549
Lavigne, Madeleine, S2-549
Lavigne, Magdalen, E-281

Lavigne, Marguerite, E-168
Lavigne, Marguerite, S2-549
Lavigne, Marie Anne, E-333, 369
Lavigne, Nicolas, S2-549
Lavigne, Pierre, E-281, 588, 596
Lavine, Jan, S3-830
Laviolleau, Vincent, N-252
LaVoie, Rene, E-366
Lavoie, Etiennette, S1-230
Laycom, Mathieu, E-138
Le Baron, Charlotte, S2-742, 748
Le Baron, Mr., S1-355
Le Bart, Jacques, E-52
Le Biedee, Perrine, N-110, 251
Le Bigot, Claude, N-110
Le Botte, Therese, S1-97
Le Botte, Thereze, E-42
Le Bourgeois, Andre, S3-971
Le Bourgeois, Andree Francoise, S3-1082
Le Bourgeois, Andree-Francoise, S2-566
Le Bourgeois, Francois, S2-566
Le Bourgeois, Francois, S3-1082
Le Bourgeois, Michel, S1-392
Le Bret, Isabelle, S2-530
Le Breton, Charles, E-406
Le Breton, Jacques, S2-452
Le Breton, Jean, C-27
Le Brun, Madeleine, N-100-101, 206
Le Brun, Marie, N-136
Le Buffe, Jean-Baptiste, S1-280
Le Buffe, Modeste, S1-193
Le Cam, Jeanne, C-79
Le Caplain, Jeanne, S1-180-181
Le Carcelier, Elizabeth, E-66
Le Cattelier, Anne, E-45
Le Caux, Olive, E-20
Le Charpentier, Charles, S3-972, 979
Le Charpentier, Georges, S3-979
Le Charpentier, Jeanne, E-41, 299
Le Charpentier, Louis, S3-972
Le Chartier, Suzanne, S2-651
Le Chaux, Jean, E-294

Le Chevalier, Jean, E-294
Le Chevalier, Marie-Louise, S2-580
Le Chevalier, Rose Aimee, E-294
Le Chevalier Du Gouillon, Mr., S1-331
Le Claiur, Raphael, E-294
Le Cler, Guillaume, S1-230
Le Clere, Anne, E-588, 592
Le Coc, Claude, C-vii-viii
Le Codet, Francois, E-588, 591
Le Codet, Marie, E-588, 591
Le Codet, Yves, E-588, 591
Le Cointe, Marie, S2-669
Le Compte, Gille, S3-965
Le Coq, Francoise, N-123
Le Coq, Guillaume, C-69
Le Coq, Guillaume, N-123
Le Coq, Jacque, S3-1017
Le Coq, Jacques, C-69, 130
Le Coq, Jacques, S2-452
Le Coq, Jean Marie, S3-850
Le Coq, Jean Pierre, N-123
Le Coq, Marie, N-123
Le Coq, Marie Janne Louise Magdeleine, S3-1017
Le Coq, Marie-Jeanne-Louise-Madeleine, S2-452
Le Coq, Pierre, S3-1017
Le Coq, Pierre Francois, C-69, 130-131
Le Coq, Pierre Francois, N-123
Le Coq, Victoire, N-123
Le Cor, Janne Helene, S3-1094
Le Cor, Jeanne, S3-1094
Le Cor, Jullien, S3-1094
Le Cor, Yves, S3-1094
Le Corps, Jeanne-Helene, S1-197
Le Couet, Perinne, S2-583
Le Doyen, Julien-Auguste, S2-582
Le Faibre, Claude Epiphane, F-85
Le Feuvre, Madeleine, S2-691
Le Fevre, Jeanne, S1-41
Le Forestier, Etiennette, S2-724
Le Franc, Rober, S3-1093
Le Francois, Jacques, S1-193
Le Francois, Marie, S1-329

Le Galais, Julien, S2-548
Le Gentil, -----, S2-668
Le Gentil, Nobleman Hugues-Jean, S2-759
Le Gentilhomme, Jeanne, S2-684
Le Gentilhomme, Scolastique, F-35
Le Gerrie, Antoine Francois, E-26
Le Glaher, Marie Perrine, E-14
Le Goff, Martiale, E-18, 66
Le Grecque, Guilhaume, E-588, 591
Le Grecque, Julienne, E-588, 591
Le Grecque, Marguerite, E-588, 591
Le Grecque, Marie, E-588, 591
Le Guay, Jacques, S1-375
Le Gueaux, Jacques, S1-136
Le Haire, Marguerite, E-66, 329
Le Havre, E-296-297
Le Havre and the Acadians in 1758-1762, E-297
Le Jamtel, Perinne, S1-46
Le Jeune, Marie-Josephe, S2-545
Le Juge, Elizabeth, N-10
Le Launay, Eustache, E-13
Le Launay, Jean, E-13
Le Lievre, Claudine, S2-604
Le Lievre, Jeanne, S2-590-591
Le Lievre, Julien, S2-590
Le Lievre, Quentin, S2-590-591
Le Lorre, Francois Pierre, F-93
Le Louis, -----, N-198
Le Loutre, Mr., S2-446
Le Luc, Andre, E-18
Le Luren, Jean, S1-138
Le Maitre, Charles Marie, E-299
Le Maitre, Francoise Vincente, E-299
Le Maitre, Gabriel, E-299
Le Maitre, Guillaume, E-299
Le Maitre, Jean Maurice, E-299
Le Maitre, Marie Charlotte, E-299
Le Maitre, Nicolas, E-299
Le Male, Louis, E-86
Le Manquet, Anne, S1-75

Le Manquet, Gilete, E-78
Le Manquet, Marianne, S1-75
Le Marinnier, Magdelaine, E-41
Le Masson, Pierre Anne, E-77
Le Matelot, Bertrand, E-16
Le Matelot, Marie Anne, E-288
Le Matelot, Pierre, E-288
Le Maux, Marie Vincent, N-249
Le Mee, Jacques, S1-256
Le Mercier, Suzanne, S1-284
Le Mestre, Francois , C-72
Le Mestre, Jean Baptiste, C-71
Le Mestre, Joseph, C-71
Le Mestre, Pierre, C-71
Le Meteyer, Gabriel, E-52
Le Monnier, Francois, S3-931
Le Monnier, Louis, S1-319, 321
Le Nouvel, Alain, S2-592
Le Nouvel, Alain, S3-986
Le Nouvel, Anne-Francoise-
  Roberte, S2-592, 641
Le Nouvel, Anne-Francoise-
  Roberte, S3-953-954
Le Nouvel, Perinne, S1-323
Le Nouvel, Perrine, E-4
Le Nouvel, Pierre, S1-319, 323
Le Nouvel, Pierre, S2-592, 641
Le Nouvel, Pierre, S3-953, 986
Le Nouvelle, Anne, E-588
Le Nouville, Pierre, E-588
Le Nouville, Vincente, E-588
Le Page, Jean Baptiste Joseph,
  E-31
Le Page, Louis Guillaume, E-31
Le Penn, Francois, E-294
Le Petit, Charlotte, S2-535
Le Poitre, Francoise, S2-635
Le Potevin, Jeanne, S2-761
Le Prevost, Madeleine, E-299
Le Prieur, Jean, S2-596, 772
Le Prieur, Marie, S1-258, 386
Le Prieur, Marie, S2-596, 721,
  772
Le Pron, Pierre, S2-593
Le Provost, Francoise, S1-386
Le Quessy, Marie, S3-959
Le Rat, Jean, N-243
Le Rembourg, Jan, S3-983
Le Rembourg, Jan Noel, S3-983
Le Roux, Etienne, S2-593
Le Roux, Michelle, S2-643

Le Roux, Michelle, S3-985
Le Roux, Yves, S2-593
Le Roy, -----, S3-958
Le Roy, Dominique, S2-608
Le Roy, Dominique Francois,
  S3-1093
Le Roy, DuBourbonnier, S3-
  830, 832, 839
Le Roy, Eulalie, S2-594
Le Roy, Francoise Charlotte,
  S3-1093
Le Roy, Francoise-Charlotte,
  S2-608
Le Roy, Genevieve, N-49, 147,
  187
Le Roy, Guillaume, S1-190
Le Roy, Henriette, S2-594
Le Roy, Jean, S3-1093
Le Roy, Jean Michel, S3-957-
  958
Le Roy, Jean-Michel, S2-593
Le Roy, Marie-Josephe, S2-594
Le Roy, Michel Corentin, S3-
  957
Le Roy, Michel-Corentin, S2-
  593
Le Roy, Olive, S1-190
*Le Roy, Olivier, S2-544, 593
Le Roy, Pierre, C-72
Le Roy, Pierre, S2-545, 593-594
Le Roy, Prosper, S2-594
Le Roy, Rosalie, S2-594
Le Roy, Susanne, S2-594
Le Sauvage, Francoise, E-313,
  321
Le Sauvage, Thomas, E-313
Le Sec, Martin, E-588, 592
Le Sommer, Francois, F-91
Le Terrier, Jacques, S2-594
Le Terrier, Jacques, S3-962,
  990, 992, 1029
Le Terrier, Jean Baptiste, S3-
  990, 1029
Le Terrier, Jean-Baptiste, S2-
  595
Le Terrier, Jeanne, C-64
Le Terrier, Thomas, S2-594-595
Le Terrier, Thomas, S3-962,
  990, 992, 1029
Le Timbre, Ollive Marie, S3-
  1095

Le Timbre, Ollive-Marie, S2-
  508
Le Tollierec, Julien, S3-825
Le Tollierec, Louis Francois,
  S3-825
Le Tollieret, Henry Amable, N-
  128-129
Le Tollieret, Julien, C-72
Le Tollieret, Julien, S2-595
Le Tollieret, Louis, N-128-129
Le Tollieret, Louis, S2-562
Le Tollieret, Louis , C-73
Le Tollieret, Louis-Francois, S2-
  595
Le Tollieret, Marie Adelaide, C-
  72
Le Tollieret, Marie Adelaide, N-
  129
Le Tollieret, Marie Julie, N-129
Le Tollieret, Marie Sophie, N-
  128
Le Tollieret, Marie-Adelaide,
  S2-595
Le tollieret, Louis Francois, C-
  72
Le tollieret, Marie Julie, C-73
Le Tourneur, Jeanne, S1-259
Le Tourneur, Jeanne, S3-997
Le Tourneur, Jeanne-Marie, S1-
  258
Le Tourneur, Pierre, S1-258
Le Tourneur, Pierre, S2-772
Le Tourneur, Pierre, S3-978,
  981, 984, 997
Le Tuillier, Adelaide, N-129
Le Tuillier, Augustin, N-129
Le Tuillier, Augustin Bon, N-
  129
Le Tuillier, Felicite, N-129
Le Tuillier, Isidore, N-129
Le Tuillier, Jean Charles, N-129
Le Tuillier, Marie Rose, N-124,
  129, 198
Le Tuillier, Rene, N-124, 129,
  187, 198
Le Tullier, Adelaide, C-73
Le Tullier, Augustin, C-73
Le Tullier, Felicite, C-71
Le Tullier, Isidore, C-73
Le Tullier, Jean Charles, C-73
Le Tullier, Marie Rose, C-73

Le Tullier, Michel Marin, C-73
Le tullier, Rene, C-32, 73
Le Vaigneur, Francois Antoine Marie, E-404
Le Varieux, Anne, E-311
Le Varieux, Dominique, E-27, 311-312
Le Varieux, Marie, E-28, 312
Le Verdier, Anne Genevieve, E-306
Le Voyer, Guillemette, S2-596, 772
Le-----, Louis, S2-539
Leard, Catherine Victoire, E-363
Leard, Jean Guillaume, E-363
Leardiu, Thomas, S3-932
Lebalque, Marie Jeanne, E-281, 384
LeBan, Charlote, E-113
Lebasque, Francois, E-527
Lebasque, Pierre, E-475
LeBauve, Marguerite, C-8
Lebe, Catherine, E-402
LeBeau, Anne, E-323-325, 433,
Lebeau, Francoise, C-95, 112
Lebeau, Joseph, E-307
Lebeau, Marie, E-307
Lebeaujour, Catherine, E-80, 277
LeBeauve, Madeleine, E-431
Lebeauve, Euphrosine, S1-346
LeBechee, Jean Pierre, E-190, 281
LeBechee, Pierre Louis, E-281
Lebedel, Eustache, S3-1101
Lebedel, Francois, S3-1101
Lebedel, Michel, S3-1101
Lebel, Jeanne, E-367
LeBenard, Augustin, E-421
Lebert, Anne, F-49
Lebert, Anne, S1-243
Lebert, Anne, S2-550, 575
Lebert, Anne, S3-893
Lebert, Anne Josephe, F-9
Lebert, Anne Josephe, N-121
Lebert, Anne-Josephe, S1-345
Lebert, Anne-Josephe, S2-549, 551
Lebert, Charles, C-66
Lebert, Charles, F-21

Lebert, Charles, N-110, 118, 248
Lebert, Charles, S1-154
Lebert, Charles, S2-549, 551, 575
Lebert, Charles, S3-893
Lebert, Etienne, E-155
Lebert, Etienne, E-281, 369
Lebert, Etienne Denis, E-155
Lebert, Etienne Denis, E-281
Lebert, Etienne Joseph, E-155
Lebert, Etienne Joseph, E-281
Lebert, Guillaume, E-146, 159
Lebert, Jean, S2-552
Lebert, Jean Baptiste, S3-878
Lebert, Jean Charles, C-66
Lebert, Jean Charles, N-110
Lebert, Jean-Baptiste, S1-345
Lebert, Jean-Baptiste, S2-551-552
Lebert, Jean-Charles, S2-550
Lebert, Jeanne, S1-345
Lebert, Jeanne, S2-447, 550, 662
Lebert, Jeanne, S3-878
Lebert, Joachin, S2-551-552
Lebert, Joseph, N-111
Lebert, Judith, E-129
Lebert, Louis, E-183, 281
Lebert, Marguerite, C-46
Lebert, Marguerite, E-289
Lebert, Marguerite, F-9
Lebert, Marguerite, N-74-75, 111
Lebert, Marguerite, S1-12, 380
Lebert, Marguerite, S2-465, 551-552, 575
Lebert, Marguerite, S3-902
Lebert, Marguerite-Francoise, S2-550
Lebert, Marguerite-Marie, S2-552
Lebert, Marie, E-281
Lebert, Marie, F-21
Lebert, Marie, N-111
Lebert, Marie, S2-550-551, 575
Lebert, Marie Anne Aimee, E-281, 369
Lebert, Marie Jeanne, E-188
Lebert, Marie Joseph, S3-900
Lebert, Marie Josephe, C-47, 66

Lebert, Marie Josephe, F-39
Lebert, Marie Josephe, N-76
Lebert, Marie Madeleine, C-64
Lebert, Marie Madeleine, N-110, 118, 248
Lebert, Marie Modeste, E-183
Lebert, Marie Modeste, E-289
Lebert, Marie-Jeanne, S2-552
Lebert, Marie-Josephe, S1-381
Lebert, Marie-Josephe, S2-551-552
Lebert, Marie-Madeleine, S2-550
Lebert, Michel, S2-550
Lebert, Paul, C-46-47
Lebert, Paul, F-39
Lebert, Paul, N-111
Lebert, Paul, S1-380-381
Lebert, Paul, S2-551-552
Lebert, Paul, S3-900, 902
Lebert, Pierre, C-47
Lebert, Pierre, F-39
Lebert, Pierre, N-111
Lebert, Pierre, S1-12
Lebert, Pierre, S2-551-552, 575
Lebert, Pierre, S3-894, 902
Lebert, Pierre Joseph, C-66
Lebert, Pierre Joseph, N-110
Lebert, Pierre-Jean, S2-550
Lebert, Pierre-Jean-Joseph-Joachin, S2-552
Lebert, Pierre-Joseph, S2-551
Lebert, Sophie Aimee, E-155
Lebert, Sophie Aimee, E-281
LeBescon, Mr., E-289
Lebescons, Austin, E-125
Lebet, Marie, E-80, 264
LeBeuffe, Marie Francoise, E-332
LeBeuffe, Modeste, E-338
Lebien, Francois, E-281
Lebien, Jean, E-281
Lebigot, Julien, S1-67
LeBlais, Jeanne, E-185
Leblanc, -----, S3-976
Leblanc, Adelaide, F-39
Leblanc, Adelaide, N-119
Leblanc, Aelia, C-153
Leblanc, Agathe, E-93-96, 281, 423, 558, 580
Leblanc, Agnes, E-414

INDEX SOURCES C=Chatellerault; E=Acadians in Exile; F=Acadian Families; N=Nantes; S=St-Malo

Leblanc, Agnes, F-109
Leblanc, Agnes, S1-336, 341
Leblanc, Agnes, S2-563
Leblanc, Alain, E-560, 565
Leblanc, Alain, S1-31, 244, 364
Leblanc, Alain, S2-553, 559
Leblanc, Alexis, E-4, 6, 567
Leblanc, Amable Andre, F-3
Leblanc, Aman, S2-559
Leblanc, Amand, S2-558, 562, 579
Leblanc, Amant-Francois, S2-561
Leblanc, Ambroise, E-47, 282
Leblanc, Anastasie, E-84-85, 282, 298, 306, 359, 608, 611, 614
Leblanc, Andre, C-67
Leblanc, Andre, E-475, 527
Leblanc, Andre, F-55
Leblanc, Andre, N-113
Leblanc, Andre, S2-711
Leblanc, Andre-Marie, S2-556
Leblanc, Angelique-Cecile, S2-568
Leblanc, Anne, C-18, 56, 74, 117
Leblanc, Anne, E-92, 151, 187-188, 190, 271, 273, 282, 380, 424, 427, 490, 587, 593, 608, 610-611, 613-614
Leblanc, Anne, F-5, 13, 35
Leblanc, Anne, N-37, 77, 119-120, 122, 156, 161-163, 165-166, 204, 220, 232, 239
Leblanc, Anne, S1-35, 90, 115, 137, 230, 382-383, 393
Leblanc, Anne, S2-459, 572, 578, 605-606, 762-763, 765
Leblanc, Anne, S3-890, 941, 1044, 1061-1062, 1098
Leblanc, Anne Genevieve, E-282
Leblanc, Anne LePrince, E-611
Leblanc, Anne Marguerite, N-121
Leblanc, Anne Marie, N-120
Leblanc, Anne-Julie, S2-576
Leblanc, Anselme, E-196, 282-286, 319, 408, 566
Leblanc, Anselme, S1-229

Leblanc, Anselme, S2-553, 741
Leblanc, Anselme, S3-1090
Leblanc, Ansite, E-148
Leblanc, Antoine, E-283-284, 475, 492, 527
Leblanc, Antoine, N-114
Leblanc, Apoline-Eulalie, S2-571
Leblanc, Appoline Eulalie, F-13
Leblanc, Appoline Eulalie, N-117
Leblanc, Armand, S2-607
Leblanc, Augustin, E-262, 282
Leblanc, Augustin, S1-211
Leblanc, Augustin, S2-556, 586, 702-703, 744
Leblanc, Augustin, S3-1046, 1056
Leblanc, Augustin-Marie, S2-553-554
Leblanc, Baptiste, S3-941
Leblanc, Barbe, C-65
Leblanc, Barbe, F-55
Leblanc, Barbe, N-113
Leblanc, Barbe-Anne, S2-557
Leblanc, Basile, E-380, 570
Leblanc, Beloni, S2-565
Leblanc, Bernard, E-282, 527
Leblanc, Bibianne, N-161
Leblanc, Bibienne, E-282, 420, 422, 425
Leblanc, Blanche, C-64, 68
Leblanc, Blanche, E-273-274, 305-306, 423
Leblanc, Blanche, F-3, 15
Leblanc, Blanche, N-43, 105, 116, 148, 231, 238
Leblanc, Blanche, S2-464, 529-530, 558, 576, 698-699
Leblanc, Blanche Secille, E-282, 305
Leblanc, Bonaventure, S2-569
Leblanc, Brigitte, E-166, 580-581
Leblanc, Brigitte, N-73
Leblanc, Casimir, S1-237, 249
Leblanc, Casimir, S2-563
Leblanc, Casimire, S2-732
Leblanc, Casimire, S3-893, 966, 982, 1025

Leblanc, Catherine, E-103, 158, 282, 490, 524
Leblanc, Cazimir, S2-554
Leblanc, Cecile, C-60, 81
Leblanc, Cecile, E-306, 380
Leblanc, Cecile, F-21
Leblanc, Cecile, N-139
Leblanc, Cecile, S2-524-525, 642
Leblanc, Cecile, S3-1027
Leblanc, Charles, C-66-67, 147
Leblanc, Charles, E-282-288, 322, 492, 527, 557, 565-567
Leblanc, Charles, F-31, 55, 61, 63
Leblanc, Charles, N-4, 47, 72, 111-113, 116, 130, 182, 190, 241
Leblanc, Charles, S1-32, 242, 252-253
Leblanc, Charles, S2-543, 554-557, 717
Leblanc, Charles, S3-988
Leblanc, Charles Francois, N-121
Leblanc, Charles Marie, C-68
Leblanc, Charles Marie, N-116
Leblanc, Charles-Jean, S2-556
Leblanc, Christine Elizabeth, E-160, 282
Leblanc, Claire, S1-211
Leblanc, Claire, S2-568-569, 703, 710-714, 716-717, 733
Leblanc, Claire, S3-982, 1034, 1041, 1052, 1076
Leblanc, Claude, C-66-68, 88, 146
Leblanc, Claude, E-173, 282, 566
Leblanc, Claude, F-15, 39, 55
Leblanc, Claude, N-112-114, 118, 161, 178, 193, 208
Leblanc, Claude, S1-206, 364
Leblanc, Claude, S2-533, 553, 556-561, 572, 602, 625, 698, 734, 762
Leblanc, Claude, S3-988-989, 1015, 1049, 1067, 1080, 1106
Leblanc, Claude Antoine, E-288-289

Leblanc, Claude Marie, E-282, 566

Leblanc, Claude Marie, F-111

Leblanc, Claude Marie Auguste, E-283

Leblanc, Crepin, S3-1025

Leblanc, Crespin, S2-568-569

Leblanc, Daniel, E-213, 457, 475

Leblanc, Daniel, S2-565

Leblanc, Dominique, S2-563

Leblanc, Elie, C-3

Leblanc, Elie, S1-9

Leblanc, Elie, S3-1102

Leblanc, Elisabeth, E-102, 283, 421-422, 590, 593

Leblanc, Elisabeth, S3-825, 889, 927, 1051, 1090

Leblanc, Elizabeth, C-22, 24, 72-73, 96-97, 160

Leblanc, Elizabeth, F-19, 21, 39

Leblanc, Elizabeth, N-35, 39, 119-120, 128-129, 164-165, 193, 208, 241

Leblanc, Elizabeth, S1-128, 137-138, 167

Leblanc, Elizabeth, S2-450, 503, 539, 542, 553, 562, 564, 567, 578, 595, 658, 707, 764, 765

Leblanc, Elizabhette, C-136

Leblanc, Eloi, E-283

Leblanc, Etienne, C-72

Leblanc, Etienne, F-21

Leblanc, Etienne, S2-558, 561-562

Leblanc, Etienne, S3-1056, 1080

Leblanc, Etienne-Simon, S2-567

Leblanc, Eustache Gregoire, E-608, 611, 614

Leblanc, Felicite, S1-21, 27-28, 211

Leblanc, Felicite, S2-484

Leblanc, Felix, C-67, 72

Leblanc, Felix, E-284,,415

Leblanc, Felix, F-21

Leblanc, Felix, N-105, 231

Leblanc, Felix, S1-283

Leblanc, Felix, S2-558, 561-562, 575, 595

Leblanc, Felix, S3-825, 1015, 1056, 1080

Leblanc, Firmin, E-283

Leblanc, Francois, C-62, 67

Leblanc, Francois, E-283, 286-287, 491, 527, 614

Leblanc, Francois, F-37

Leblanc, Francois, N-112, 115

Leblanc, Francois, S1-26

Leblanc, Francois, S2-449, 524, 562, 565, 570, 716

Leblanc, Francois, S3-982

Leblanc, Francois Bernard, E-124

Leblanc, Francois Joseph, E-283

Leblanc, Francois Marie, E-283

Leblanc, Francois Mathurin, E-283

Leblanc, Francois-Joseph-Marc, S2-575

Leblanc, Francois-Xavier, S2-578

Leblanc, Francoise, E-165, 283, 385, 456, 562, 566, 572

Leblanc, Francoise, F-61

Leblanc, Francoise, N-120

Leblanc, Francoise, S2-555, 559, 563

Leblanc, Gabriel, E-283, 611, 614

Leblanc, Genevieve, C-88, 146-147

Leblanc, Genevieve, E-113-114, 569

Leblanc, Genevieve, F-37, 61

Leblanc, Genevieve, N-118, 120, 150

Leblanc, Genevieve, S1-274

Leblanc, Genevieve, S2-556, 572, 718, 769

Leblanc, Georges Robert, E-283

Leblanc, Gregoire, S2-561

Leblanc, Gregoire-Charles, S2-557

Leblanc, Guillaume, E-285-287

Leblanc, Heleine, E-271

Leblanc, Helene, S2-522, 560-563

Leblanc, Henri, E-283

Leblanc, Honore, E-281, 288-289, 558, 567

Leblanc, Isabelle, F-87

Leblanc, Isabelle, S2-494, 579, 607

Leblanc, Jacque Antoine Benoit, E-283

Leblanc, Jacques, E-282-283, 285, 475, 490-491, 527

Leblanc, Jacques, F-5, 23, 37, 43

Leblanc, Jacques, N-64, 114-115, 122, 178

Leblanc, Jacques, S2-562-563, 565, 567, 576, 589

Leblanc, Jacques, S3-1025

Leblanc, Jacques Hypolithe, E-283

Leblanc, Jacques Joseph, E-283

Leblanc, Jacques Philippe, E-283

Leblanc, Jacques Pierre Marie, E-283

Leblanc, Janne Francoise, E-284

Leblanc, Janne Louise, S3-976

Leblanc, Jean, E-125, 139, 282-286, 289, 425, 490-491, 527, 555, 566-570, 611, 614

Leblanc, Jean, F-5, 9, 15, 61

Leblanc, Jean, N-19, 89, 113-114, 119, 121-122, 169, 177, 189, 194

Leblanc, Jean, S1-11, 33

Leblanc, Jean, S2-559-562, 564, 566-567, 575, 577

Leblanc, Jean, S3-882, 888-890, 894, 902, 927, 930, 989, 1032, 1049, 1056

Leblanc, Jean Baptiste, C-67

Leblanc, Jean Baptiste, E-2, 282-285, 288, 381, 554, 566-568, 608, 611, 614

Leblanc, Jean Baptiste, F-17, 23, 37, 55, 67

Leblanc, Jean Baptiste, N-113, 115-117, 181

Leblanc, Jean Baptiste, S3-902, 1051, 1082

Leblanc, Jean Baptiste Guillaume, E-284

Leblanc, Jean Baptiste Simon, E-284

Leblanc, Jean Charles, C-67

Leblanc, Jean Charles, F-3

Leblanc, Jean Charles, N-113

Leblanc, Jean Claude, N-121

Leblanc, Jean dit Derico, N-120

Leblanc, Jean Francois, E-283-284, 611

Leblanc, Jean Jacques, F-23

Leblanc, Jean Jacques, N-114-116, 176

Leblanc, Jean Jacques, S3-1025, 1033, 1080

Leblanc, Jean M., E-2

Leblanc, Jean Marie, E-284

Leblanc, Jean Marie Aime, E-284

Leblanc, Jean Martin, F-37

Leblanc, Jean Martin, N-117

Leblanc, Jean Pierre, E-284

Leblanc, Jean-Baptiste, S1-23, 28, 210

Leblanc, Jean-Baptiste, S2-432, 467, 555, 559, 564-569, 573-574, 577-578, 606, 619, 745

Leblanc, Jean-Baptiste-Caliste, S2-576

Leblanc, Jean-Baptiste-Rene, S2-567

Leblanc, Jean-Cleandre, S2-575

Leblanc, Jean-Felix, S2-571

Leblanc, Jean-Jacques, S1-114

Leblanc, Jean-Jacques, S2-553, 563, 567-569, 571, 659, 733

Leblanc, Jean-Pierre, S2-563

Leblanc, Jeanne Barbe, E-285

Leblanc, Jeanne Francoise, E-285

Leblanc, Jeanne Genevieve, E-285

Leblanc, Jeanne Marie, E-114

Leblanc, Jeanne Victoire, E-285

Leblanc, Jeanne-Francoise, S2-652

Leblanc, Jeanne-Louise, S2-540, 751

Leblanc, Jeanne-Marie, S2-572

Leblanc, Joseph, C-68, 139

Leblanc, Joseph, E-2, 104, 188-190, 282-289, 306, 390, 417, 422-423, 566-570, 581, 608-609, 611, 613-614

Leblanc, Joseph, F-3, 5, 9, 37, 59

Leblanc, Joseph, N-112, 114, 116-117, 120-122, 152, 167, 182, 190, 193, 199, 212, 231, 241

Leblanc, Joseph, S1-30, 35, 378

Leblanc, Joseph, S2-555, 562-563, 565-566, 569-571, 573, 576-577, 703, 739, 753

Leblanc, Joseph, S3-1113

Leblanc, Joseph Auguste, E-285, 611, 614

Leblanc, Joseph dit Jamlo, N-116

Leblanc, Joseph Marie, E-285

Leblanc, Joseph Mathurin, E-285

Leblanc, Joseph Olivier, E-285

Leblanc, Joseph Theodore, C-68

Leblanc, Joseph-Amand, S2-577

Leblanc, Joseph-Firmin, S2-560

Leblanc, Joseph-Marie, S2-574

Leblanc, Joseph-Olivier, S2-575

Leblanc, Josephe, E-382

Leblanc, Josephine, E-363

Leblanc, Judith, E-417

Leblanc, Julie, E-285

Leblanc, Julien, E-286

Leblanc, Julien, S3-896

Leblanc, LaBlanche, E-274

Leblanc, LaBlanche, S2-561

Leblanc, Lazare, E-286

Leblanc, Louis, E-283, 406

Leblanc, Louis At., E-2

Leblanc, Louis Laurent, S3-976

Leblanc, Louis Pascal, E-286, 419

Leblanc, Louis Rene, N-113

Leblanc, Louis-Laurent, S2-751

Leblanc, Madeleine, C-54, 57, 60, 63, 94, 97

Leblanc, Madeleine, E-115-116, 118, 138, 179, 286, 288, 324, 422-423, 426, 526

Leblanc, Madeleine, N-4, 111-112, 115, 130, 141-142, 163, 199, 241, 254

Leblanc, Madeleine, S1-40, 89, 99

Leblanc, Madeleine, S2-554-555, 622, 657, 770

Leblanc, Magdalen Felicite, E-286

Leblanc, Magdalen Victoire, E-286

Leblanc, Magdalene, E-151

Leblanc, Magdelaine, F-17, 37, 41

Leblanc, Maitre Charles, E-279-280

Leblanc, Marguerite, E-2, 18, 118, 141, 151, 284, 286-289, 305, 380-383, 422-425, 490, 524, 567, 572, 576, 581, 608, 611, 614

Leblanc, Marguerite, F-3, 37, 49, 61, 63, 79, 103

Leblanc, Marguerite, N-34, 36, 48, 87, 92, 112, 119-120, 122, 152, 154, 167, 169, 193, 218

Leblanc, Marguerite, S1-23, 35, 132, 137, 145, 149-150, 164-165, 171, 224, 226, 278, 297, 298-299

Leblanc, Marguerite, S2-449-451, 453, 468, 489, 511, 543, 558, 563, 564, 569, 575, 589, 612-613, 619, 703, 731-733, 749

Leblanc, Marguerite, S3-899, 930, 956, 966, 1016, 1056, 1139

Leblanc, Marguerite Anastasie, E-286, 301, 427

Leblanc, Marguerite Blanche Ian, E-568

Leblanc, Marguerite Genevieve, E-286

Leblanc, Marguerite Modeste, E-287

Leblanc, Marguerite Monique, E-189

Leblanc, Marguerite Ozite, E-2, 36, 196, 369

Leblanc, Marguerite Victoire, E-287

Leblanc, Marguerite-Anne, S2-574

Leblanc, Marguerite-Cecile, S2-563

Leblanc, Marguerite-Genevieve, S2-555, 573-574

Leblanc, Marie, C-44, 46, 62, 64, 68, 166

Leblanc, Marie, E-2, 4, 6, 16, 18, 95, 123, 129-130, 163, 165, 273, 283, 287, 302, 306, 356, 364-365, 390, 406, 408, 421-422, 428, 490, 524, 554, 560-567, 569

Leblanc, Marie, F-3, 5, 7, 21, 25, 31, 37, 57, 61, 81

Leblanc, Marie, N-6, 46, 72, 95-96, 102, 112, 114, 116, 118, 120-121, 149, 155-156, 182, 196, 207

Leblanc, Marie, S1-20, 26-27, 79, 95, 343, 365, 368-369

Leblanc, Marie, S2-522, 525, 531, 554-555, 562, 573-574, 578, 622, 707, 734

Leblanc, Marie, S3-875, 967, 1005, 1064, 1141

Leblanc, Marie Anne, C-69

Leblanc, Marie Anne, E-79, 96, 287, 344

Leblanc, Marie Anne, N-118

Leblanc, Marie Antoinette, E-287

Leblanc, Marie Appoline, N-112

Leblanc, Marie Blanche, E-94-96, 167, 304, 557, 580

Leblanc, Marie Blanche, F-31

Leblanc, Marie Blanche, N-47

Leblanc, Marie Catherine, E-30

Leblanc, Marie Francoise, C-67

Leblanc, Marie Francoise, E-287

Leblanc, Marie Francoise, F-55

Leblanc, Marie Francoise, N-113

Leblanc, Marie Genevieve, E-2

Leblanc, Marie Genevieve, F-23

Leblanc, Marie Genevieve, N-116

Leblanc, Marie Jacquette, E-287

Leblanc, Marie Jeanne, E-287, 608, 614

Leblanc, Marie Joseph Marguerite, E-287

Leblanc, Marie Josephe, C-4

Leblanc, Marie Josephe, E-285, 287, 306, 380, 555

Leblanc, Marie Josephe, F-13, 37, 47

Leblanc, Marie Josephe, N-19, 47, 84, 117, 127, 235

Leblanc, Marie Madeleine, N-162

Leblanc, Marie Magdelaine, F-45

Leblanc, Marie Magdelaine, S3-1015

Leblanc, Marie Magdeleine, C-96

Leblanc, Marie Magdeleine, E-37, 81, 138, 151-152, 167, 262, 284, 323-325, 343, 350, 421, 425, 433, 557, 570

Leblanc, Marie Marguerite Antoinette, E-288

Leblanc, Marie Modeste, N-121

Leblanc, Marie Rose, C-67

Leblanc, Marie Rose, F-55

Leblanc, Marie Rose, N-113-114

Leblanc, Marie Susanne, E-431

Leblanc, Marie Therese, E-288

Leblanc, Marie Victoire, E-608, 611, 614

Leblanc, Marie-Anne, S2-573

Leblanc, Marie-Blanche, S2-576, 702-703

Leblanc, Marie-Claire, S1-353

Leblanc, Marie-Elizabeth, S2-573

Leblanc, Marie-Francoise, S2-557

Leblanc, Marie-Genevieve, S2-568

Leblanc, Marie-Josephe, S2-569, 571-572

Leblanc, Marie-Madeleine, S1-167, 326-327, 340, 364, 366

Leblanc, Marie-Madeleine, S2-533, 539, 559, 563, 568, 606, 618, 619, 646, 699, 769

Leblanc, Marie-Marguerite, S2-566-567

Leblanc, Marie-Rose, S2-556

Leblanc, Marin, E-288

Leblanc, Marin, S2-562, 699

Leblanc, Marine, E-18

Leblanc, Marinne, S1-33-34

Leblanc, Marthe, F-17

Leblanc, Marthe, N-108

Leblanc, Marthe, S2-538-539, 559

Leblanc, Martin, E-288

Leblanc, Mathurin, N-141, 254

Leblanc, Mathurin, S1-32

Leblanc, Mathurin, S2-657

Leblanc, Mathurine Francoise, N-120

Leblanc, Michel, C-68

Leblanc, Michel, F-13

Leblanc, Michel, N-117

Leblanc, Michel, S1-10

Leblanc, Michel, S2-571-572

Leblanc, Modeste, E-568, 608, 609, 611, 614

Leblanc, Moise, E-567, 569

Leblanc, Moise, F-37

Leblanc, Moise, S2-566

Leblanc, Moise-Jean, S2-570

Leblanc, Moyse, F-75

Leblanc, Moyse, N-52, 115, 117, 181

Leblanc, Mr., E-425

Leblanc, Nicolas, E-282-283, 285-286

Leblanc, Nommee, E-288

Leblanc, Odile, E-568

Leblanc, Olive-Michelle, S2-571

Leblanc, Olive-Victoire, S2-717

Leblanc, Olivier, C-141

Leblanc, Olivier, E-288, 383, 566

Leblanc, Olivier, F-21

Leblanc, Olivier, N-110, 118, 186, 188, 210, 248

Leblanc, Olivier, S1-167

Leblanc, Olivier, S2-467, 575, 579, 607, 708, 733

Leblanc, Olivier, S3-895, 897

Leblanc, Ollivier Marie Eusebe, E-288

Leblanc, Osite, S2-558

Leblanc, Ozite, E-147

Leblanc, Paul, C-68-69

Leblanc, Paul, E-166, 282, 288-289, 299, 322, 567

Leblanc, Paul, F-39

Leblanc, Paul, N-118-119, 204

Leblanc, Paul, S1-35, 99, 230
Leblanc, Paul, S2-572-573
Leblanc, Paul, S3-1044, 1067, 1098
Leblanc, Pierre, C-56, 67, 100
Leblanc, Pierre, E-2, 282-283, 285-289, 344, 419, 475, 490-491, 527, 555, 566-567, 569
Leblanc, Pierre, F-9, 21, 39, 47, 61, 79, 81
Leblanc, Pierre, N-39, 46, 86, 118-122, 196, 207-208, 224
Leblanc, Pierre, S1-27, 124, 132, 137, 167
Leblanc, Pierre, S2-450, 460, 540, 549, 551, 564, 566, 573-576, 578-579, 605, 607, 618, 678
Leblanc, Pierre, S3-890, 893, 927, 930, 1032, 1037, 1062
Leblanc, Pierre Antoine, E-289
Leblanc, Pierre Etienne, E-289
Leblanc, Pierre Honore, C-67
Leblanc, Pierre Honore, F-55
Leblanc, Pierre Honore, N-113
Leblanc, Pierre Marie, E-289
Leblanc, Pierre Marin, S3-1056
Leblanc, Pierre Olivier, N-118
Leblanc, Pierre Paul, E-289
Leblanc, Pierre Paul, N-121
Leblanc, Pierre-Honore, S2-556
Leblanc, Pierre-Marin, S2-561, 575-576
Leblanc, Pierre-Michel, S2-560
Leblanc, Pierre-Paul, S2-575
Leblanc, Pierre-Simon, S2-576
Leblanc, Raimond, E-93, 284, 287, 289, 415, 427, 569
Leblanc, Reine Victoire, E-289, 611
Leblanc, Rene, C-68
Leblanc, Rene, E-283, 475, 491, 527
Leblanc, Rene, F-3, 61
Leblanc, Rene, N-111, 116
Leblanc, Rene, S2-554
Leblanc, Rosalie, C-27
Leblanc, Rosalie, F-39
Leblanc, Rosalie, N-113, 119
Leblanc, Rosalie, S1-45, 249

Leblanc, Rosalie, S2-576-578, 646, 717, 765
Leblanc, Rosalie Genevieve, N-112
Leblanc, Rosalie-Josephe-Aimee, S2-566
Leblanc, Rose, F-43
Leblanc, Rose, N-64, 178
Leblanc, Scholastique, F-3
Leblanc, Silvestre, C-69
Leblanc, Simon, C-68
Leblanc, Simon, E-2, 150, 162, 164, 283-287, 289, 421, 569-570
Leblanc, Simon, F-3, 5, 17, 61, 91
Leblanc, Simon, N-114-116, 120, 122, 189, 237
Leblanc, Simon, S1-35, 138, 150, 171, 224, 227, 229, 325
Leblanc, Simon, S2-553, 555, 564-565, 567, 569-570, 576-578, 694, 740
Leblanc, Simon, S3-884-885, 887, 890-891, 927, 1032, 1083, 1090
Leblanc, Simon Anselme, S3-1098
Leblanc, Simon Augustin, E-289
Leblanc, Simon Joseph, E-358
Leblanc, Simon Louis Marie, E-289
Leblanc, Simon Paul, E-289, 568, 609, 611, 614
Leblanc, Sn., S3-1098
Leblanc, Sylvestre, N-118-119
Leblanc, Therese Francoise Julienne, E-109
Leblanc, Thomas, E-305, 416
Leblanc, Thomas, F-59
Leblanc, Ursule, C-25, 45, 100
Leblanc, Ursule, E-60, 289
Leblanc, Ursule, F-9, 33, 67
Leblanc, Ursule, N-38, 70, 146, 201-202
Leblanc, Victoire Reine, E-609, 614
Leblanc, Victoire-Felicite, S2-553
Leblanc, Victor, C-24
Leblanc, Victor, E-569

Leblanc, Victor, F-9, 19, 21
Leblanc, Victor, N-35, 118, 121, 248
Leblanc, Victor, S1-15, 79, 167
Leblanc, Victor, S2-570, 574, 577-578, 605, 707
Leblanc, Victor, S3-875, 889, 893
Leblanc, Victor Charles, N-121
Leblanc, Viviane, F-47
Leblanc, Yves, E-2, 282, 284, 286, 289
Leblanc, Yves, N-120
Leboeuf, Jean, S1-42
Lebois, J.B., S3-832
Lebon, Pierre, S1-387
Leborgne, Alexandre, E-290, 390, 475, 478
Leborgne, Anastasie, E-289
Leborgne, Anne, E-260
Leborgne, Emanuel, E-478
Leborgne, Francois, E-154, 168, 290
Leborgne, Genevieve Francoise, E-168, 290
Leborgne, Jean, E-290
Leborgne, Jeanne, E-153-154, 290, 478
Leborgne, Jeanne Virginie, E-290
Leborgne, Louis, E-56, 154
Leborgne, Louis Nicolas, E-58, 154, 290, 408
Leborgne, Marie, E-30, 31, 37, 478, 632
Leborgne, Marie Joseph, E-128, 290
Leborgne, Michel, E-58-59, 154, 168, 289-290, 403, 408
Leborgne, Pierre Laurent, E-290
Leborgne, Rosalie Perrine, E-290, 408
Leborgue, Marie Josephine Daigre, E-611
Lebornge, Marie Anne, E-641
LeBotte, Thereze, E-126
Lebourg, Marguerite, E-291
Lebourg, Suzanne, E-63, 302
Lebourgeois, Michel, C-50
Lebret, Pierre, S3-868
Lebreton, Anastasie, E-291

Lebreton, Anne, E-103, 291, 315
Lebreton, Anne Henriette, E-291
Lebreton, Charles, E-291-294
Lebreton, Charles, S2-471, 579
Lebreton, Charles-Louis-Toussaint, S2-579
Lebreton, Denis, E-291
Lebreton, Emilie Henriette, E-291-292
Lebreton, Francois, E-291-292, 341, 404
Lebreton, Francois Jean Marin, E-99, 291
Lebreton, Francois Laurent, E-147, 291
Lebreton, Francois Michel, E-292-293, 307
Lebreton, Francois Victor, E-291
Lebreton, Francois-Charles, S2-579
Lebreton, Germain Guy, E-291
Lebreton, Henry, E-291
Lebreton, Jacques, E-183, 292
Lebreton, Jean, E-65, 291-292, 356
Lebreton, Jean, S1-222
Lebreton, Jean Baptiste, E-291-292
Lebreton, Jean Baptiste Marin, E-291-292
Lebreton, Jean Francois, E-191, 292, 644
Lebreton, Jean Francois Stanislas, E-292
Lebreton, Jean Nicolas, E-291-292
Lebreton, Jeanne, S1-374
Lebreton, Joseph, E-292
Lebreton, Louis, E-138
Lebreton, Louise, E-292, 307
Lebreton, Marguerite, E-95, 103, 292, 315
Lebreton, Marguerite, S2-579
Lebreton, Marie, E-291-292
Lebreton, Marie, S1-317
Lebreton, Marie Anne, E-137, 190, 293
Lebreton, Marie Esther, E-292

Lebreton, Marie Louise, E-74, 293
Lebreton, Marie-Jeanne, S2-728
Lebreton, Pierre, E-292-294
Lebreton, Silvain, E-291-293
Lebron, Jeanne, E-121, 161
Lebrun, Anne Marie, E-158, 293
Lebrun, Charles, E-293
Lebrun, Etienne, E-293
Lebrun, Francois, E-55
Lebrun, George, E-293
Lebrun, Jean, E-33, 149
Lebrun, Jeanne, E-16, 66
Lebrun, Louis, E-293
Lebrun, Magdelaine, E-285
Lebrun, Marie, E-283, 285-286, 288, 608-609, 611
Lebrun, Marie Josephe, E-332
Lebrun, Marie Magdeleine, E-262, 307
Lebrun, Rene, E-120, 293
Lebubbe, Aubin, E-259, 293, 315
Lebuff, Charles-Francois, S2-597
Lebuffe, Aubin, S2-516
Lebuffe, Aubin, S3-919
Lebuffe, Cecile-Jean, S2-580
Lebuffe, Charles, S2-580-581
Lebuffe, Charles Francois, E-108, 263, 306, 431
Lebuffe, Charles Louis, E-293
Lebuffe, Charles-Louis, S2-580
Lebuffe, Francois Ernest Daniel, E-293
Lebuffe, Jean Baptiste, E-119, 132
Lebuffe, Jean-Marie, S2-580
Lebuffe, Louis Aubin, E-141, 293
Lebuffe, Louis Aubin, S3-919, 972-973
Lebuffe, Louis-Aubin, S1-331
Lebuffe, Louis-Aubin, S2-517, 580-581
Lebuffe, Marguerite, E-293
Lebuffe, Marguerite, S2-580
Lebuffe, Marie Francoise, E-293
Lebuffe, Marie Magdeleine, E-293

Lebuffe, Marie-Francoise, S2-580-581
Lebuffe, Modeste, E-339
Lebuffe, Modeste, S2-580-581
Lebuffe, Theodore, E-293
Lebuffe, Theodore Thomas, E-293
LeCame, Jeanne, E-374
LeCame, Jeanne Pelagie, E-293
LeCame, Julien, E-293
LeCame, Pelagie, E-293
LeCame, Pierre, E-166-167, 293
Lecan, Anne, S2-532
Lecan, Etienne, S3-879
Lecan, Jean, S1-86
LeCarcelier, Elizabeth, E-261
Lecas, Marguerite, E-32, 403
LeCattelier, Anne, E-381
LeCaux, Olive, E-151
LeCharpentier, Charle, E-98
LeChavalier du Gouillon, Mr., E-141
Leche, Marie, E-409
Lechelle, fils, Mr., E-258
LeChevalier, Jean, E-154
LeChevalier, Rose Aimee, E-154
Lechien, Allain, S3-878
Leclair, Jean Raphael, E-294
Leclair, Joseph, E-294
Leclair, Pierre, E-24, 294
Leclaire, Aaron, S3-846
Leclerc, Anne, E-73, 294
Leclerc, Catherine, E-411
Leclerc, Jean, E-294
Leclerc, Pierre, E-73, 82, 294
LeClercc, Marie, E-161
Leclercq, Louis Marie Augustine, E-183
Leclere, Guillaume, S3-1079
Lecode, Marie, E-321
Lecode, Marie Madeleine, E-336
Lecode, Sebastienne, E-183, 347
LeCoeur, Marguerite Renee, E-417-418
Lecointre, Marie Rose Susanne, E-147, 385
Lecompte, Francois, E-101
Lecompte, Jean Baptiste, E-293-294

Lecompte, Jeanne, E-281

Lecompte, Magdelaine, E-294

Lecompte, Marie Angelique Barbe, E-293-294

Lecompte, Suzanne, E-276

LeComte, George Augustin, E-147, 306

Lecomte, Magdelaine, E-22

Lecomte, Marie, N-130, 195, 199

Leconte, Anne, S3-1092

Leconte, Jean, E-32, 294, 384

Lecoq, Catherine, E-294

Lecoq, Francoise, F-57

Lecoq, Guillaume, F-57

Lecoq, Jacques, F-57

Lecoq, Jeanne, E-303, 313

Lecoq, Jeanne-Helene, S1-197

Lecoq, Marie, E-188, 190, 565

Lecoq, Marie, F-57

Lecoq, Pierre, F-57

Lecoq, Victoire, F-57

Lecoq, Yves, S1-197

Lecot, Genevieve, E-196

Lecouet, Perinne, S3-1077

Lecoufe, Gilles, S3-1087

Lecouffle, Gille, S1-122

Lecoulant, -----, S3-915

Lecoulant, Jean, S3-916

LeCouriaut, Marie, E-93

Lecourt, Jan, S3-849

Lecoutour, J., N-203

Lecouturier, Marie Marthe Victoire, E-59, 180

Lecraiq, Guillaume, E-275, 294

Lecraiq, Luc, E-275, 294

Lectaire, Marguerite, E-72, 299

Lecuier, Guillaume, S2-439

Lecuier, Thomas, S2-428

Lecuyer, Anne, E-259, 294

Lecuyer, Catherine, E-405

Lecuyer, Louis, E-259, 275, 294

Lecuyer, Madeleine, E-275, 294

Lecuyer, Marie, E-134

Lecuyer, Michel, E-294

Ledan, Marie, E-428

Leday, Louis, E-315

LeDesdet, Francois, E-417

LeDesdet, Michel Auguste, E-295, 417

Ledesdet, Francois, E-295

LeDeuc, Pierre, E-93, 342

Ledez, Marie Barbe, E-16

LeDiffan, Marie Francoise, E-380

LeDolanec, Joseph, E-285

Ledou, Catherine, E-124

Ledourdais, -----, S3-930

Ledoux, Jean Francois, E-295

Ledoux, Louise, E-295

Ledoux, Marie, E-388

Ledoux, Pierre, E-295

LeDru, Jean Jacques, E-283, 288, 382

Ledru, Anonime, E-295

Ledru, Jean Jacques, E-295

Leduc, Pierre, E-23

Leduc, Pierre, E-28, 346, 431

Lefebure, -----, S3-1008

Lefer, Jeanne, E-625

Lefeure, Marie Anne, E-456

Lefevre, Anne Francoise, E-103

Lefevre, Captain, E-10

Lefevre, Catherine, E-77, 139

Lefevre, Christophe, E-588, 596

Lefevre, Elisabeth, E-379

Lefevre, Francois, E-97, 275, 295

Lefevre, Francoise, E-92, 105, 315

Lefevre, Genevieve, E-97, 143, 295

Lefevre, Jacques, E-91, 295

Lefevre, Jean Pierre, E-284

Lefevre, Louis, E-94, 365

Lefevre, Marie, E-362, 348

Lefevre, Marie Louise Perronne, E-295

Lefevre, Mathurine, E-195

Lefevre, Pierre, E-295

Lefevre, Pierre Louis Jacques, E-295

Lefevre, Thomas, E-295

Leflou, Marie Joseph, E-313

Leflou, Marie Joseph, E-313

Leforest, Jacque, S3-1004

Leforest, Pierre, S3-1004

Lefort, Marie Francoise, E-414

Lefort, Marie Marguerite, E-298

Lefour, Mauriet, E-588, 596

LeFrainne, Chre. George, E-119

Lefranc, Genevieve, E-474

LeFrancois, Anne, E-317

LeFrancois, Marguerite Elisabeth, E-158, 304

Lefrevost, Marie, E-15, 55

Lefut dit Aubin, Louis, E-176

Lefut dit Aubin, Louis, S1-320

Legagneur, Claude Louis, F-109

LeGalle, Anne, E-179

LeGalle, Julien, E-179

Legalle, Anne, E-295

Legalle, Julien, E-295

LeGallen, Marguerite, E-423

LeGallenne, Charles Jean, E-384

LeGaloudec, Francois, E-283

Legaloudec, Jacquette, E-42

Legandre, Marie, S3-1150

Legangnoux, Joseph, S3-852

Legannieux, Guillaume, N-187

Legarainne, Marie Josephe, E-70, 79

Legardeur de Repentigny, Louis, E-109

Legay, Marie, S1-327

Lege, Michel, N-186

Legendre, Abraham, S1-249

Legendre, Abraham, S2-704, 710

Legendre, Anastasie Angelique, E-295

Legendre, Anastasie Angelique, F-11

Legendre, Anastasie-Angelique, S2-582

Legendre, Bertrand, S3-1150

Legendre, Francois, C-8

Legendre, Francois, E-262, 295

Legendre, Francois, F-9, 11

Legendre, Francois, S1-48, 52

Legendre, Francois, S2-581-582

Legendre, Francois, S3-1046, 1068, 1150

Legendre, Henriete, S3-1046

Legendre, Henriette, F-9

Legendre, Henriette, N-11

Legendre, Henriette, S1-52, 352

Legendre, Henriette, S2-581-582

Legendre, Jean Baptiste, F-11

Legendre, Jean Baptiste, N-123-124, 129, 198, 205

Legendre, Jean Francois, E-295

Legendre, Jean Francois, F-11
Legendre, Jean-Baptiste, S2-582
Legendre, Jean-Francois, S2-581
Legendre, Louis, F-11
Legendre, Louis, N-123, 198
Legendre, Louis-Joseph, S2-582
Legendre, Margueritte, C-74, 153
Legendre, Mathurin, E-262, 295
Legendre, Mathurin, F-11
Legendre, Mathurin, S2-581
Legendre, Pierre, E-104
Legendre, Rose, F-11
Legendre, Rose, N-124
Legendre, Yves, F-11
Legendre, Yves, N-123, 198
Legendre, Yves-Francois, S2-582
Legentil, H.J.,S3-835, 844
LeGentilhomme, Scolastique, E-196
Legentilhomme, Jeanne, S3-1019
Leger, Catherine, E-156, 295
Leger, Catherine, S1-357, 359
Leger, Elizabeth, E-295
Leger, Etienne, E-296
Leger, Francois, E-296, 417, 513
Leger, Francoise, C-10
Leger, Francoise, E-30
Leger, Francoise, F-75
Leger, Jacqueline, E-296
Leger, Jean, E-15, 72, 141, 156, 295-296
Leger, Jean, F-9
Leger, Jean, S1-357
Leger, Jean Louis, E-296
Leger, Joseph, E-70
Leger, Louis, F-9
Leger, Marie Francoise, E-296, 417
Leger, Michel, F-85
Legeret, Marie, E-357
Legerier, Antoine, E-36, 296
Legerrie, Antoine Francois, E-296
Legerrie, Louis Francois, E-296
Legilot, -----, S3-915
LeGloahee, Pierre Marie, E-427

LeGo, Pierre, E-164, 424
LeGoff, Francoise, E-421
LeGoff, Pierre, E-118, 166
Legoff, Louise, E-186
Legossen, Dominique, E-18
LeGouarec, Pierre Marie, E-285
Legoutte, Mathurin, S1-145
Legoux, Michelle, N-67, 152, 192
LeGranche, Pierre, E-167
LeGrand, Estienne, E-414, 426
LeGrand, Janne Pelagie, E-285
LeGrand, Jean Jacques, E-283
LeGrand, Jean Michel, E-163, 381
Legrand, -----, S3-968
Legrand, Elizabeth, S2-732
Legrand, Genevieve, E-457
Legrand, Jean, N-248
Legrand, Louis, S3-940
Legrand, Marie, E-32, 141, 291, 327
Legrand, Marie Claire, E-102
Legrand, Mr., S3-968
Legris, Jacques, E-197
Legris, Mr., E-197
Legris, Victoire, E-197
Legros, Jean, E-296
Legros, Jean Joseph, E-296
Legros, Marie, S3-959-960
LeGualt, Pierre, E-424
Leguay, Jacque, E-23, 169
Leguay, Pierre, E-369
Legue, Jean, S2-692
Legueaux, Jacques, S1-250
Legueule, Claire, E-599
Legueule, Francois, E-599
Legueule, Jean Baptiste, E-599
Legueule, Luce, E-599
Legueule, Marie, E-599
Legueux, Pierre, S1-141
Legueux, Pierre, S2-670
Lehaye, Magdelaine, S3-825
Lehaye, Therese, N-168
LeHir, Joseph, E-182
Lejeune, -----, S3-960
Lejeune, Adelaide, F-83
Lejeune, Alexis, E-298
Lejeune, Alexis, F-45, 83
Lejeune, Alexis, N-125
Lejeune, Alexis Simon, E-297

Lejeune, Amand, E-297-298, 305
Lejeune, Amand, F-45, 47, 63, 83
Lejeune, Amand, N-124-125, 127, 193, 235
Lejeune, Amant, C-136-137
Lejeune, Anastasie Jeanne, N-124
Lejeune, Anne, C-46-47
Lejeune, Anne, E-47, 262, 297, 333, 588, 595
Lejeune, Anne, F-33, 39
Lejeune, Anne, N-69, 113
Lejeune, Anne, S1-346, 378-381
Lejeune, Anne, S2-560, 584, 588, 625, 768
Lejeune, Anne, S3-900, 902, 989, 1010, 1113
Lejeune, Anne Adelaide, N-124
Lejeune, Anne-Marie, S2-585
Lejeune, Antoine, E-145
Lejeune, Barnabe, S2-588
Lejeune, Basile, E-66, 298
Lejeune, Benjamin, E-428
Lejeune, Catherine, C-44
Lejeune, Catherine, E-262, 458
Lejeune, Catherine, F-11, 19
Lejeune, Catherine, N-69
Lejeune, Catherine, S1-256, 311, 351
Lejeune, Catherine, S2-581, 683, 775
Lejeune, Cecille, E-422
Lejeune, Claire, E-433
Lejeune, Claire, S2-587
Lejeune, Claude, E-507
Lejeune, Edmee, E-457, 474
Lejeune, Elizabeth, C-44
Lejeune, Elizabeth, E-428
Lejeune, Elizabeth, F-23
Lejeune, Elizabeth, N-168
Lejeune, Elizabeth, S1-347, 353
Lejeune, Elizabeth, S2-768
Lejeune, Eloy, S2-582-583, 585
Lejeune, Eloy, S3-1039
Lejeune, Etienne, S2-589
Lejeune, Euphrosine, S2-583
Lejeune, Eusebe, F-7
Lejeune, Eustache, C-70, 144
Lejeune, Eustache, E-422

Lejeune, Eustache, F-7
Lejeune, Eustache, N-125, 235
Lejeune, Eustache, S1-188-189
Lejeune, Eustache, S2-546, 583-588, 768
Lejeune, Eustache, S3-1006, 1038-1040, 1060, 1077
Lejeune, Felicite, C-54
Lejeune, Felicite, F-79, 107
Lejeune, Felicite, N-85
Lejeune, Felicite, S1-19
Lejeune, Felicite, S2-447-448, 588
Lejeune, Francois, E-298, 305, 380
Lejeune, Francois, F-7
Lejeune, Francois, S1-109
Lejeune, Francois, S2-583, 585-586, 589-590, 697
Lejeune, Francois, S3-1039-1040
Lejeune, Francois Mathurin, N-125
Lejeune, Francois-Marie, S2-585
Lejeune, Francois-Zenon, S2-584
Lejeune, Francoise, S2-675
Lejeune, Francoise-Eugenie, S2-585
Lejeune, Genevieve, C-70
Lejeune, Genevieve, E-298
Lejeune, Genevieve, N-125
Lejeune, Genevieve-Charlotte, S2-584
Lejeune, Gilette, E-298
Lejeune, Gregoire, C-70, 144
Lejeune, Gregoire, F-7
Lejeune, Gregoire, N-126-127
Lejeune, Gregoire, S1-274, 308
Lejeune, Gregoire, S2-436, 584, 586-588, 768
Lejeune, Gregoire, S3-1006, 1010, 1038-1039
Lejeune, Gregoire Alexis, N-126
Lejeune, Gregoire-Eustache, S2-586
Lejeune, Helene, S2-588
Lejeune, Helene Sophie, N-126
Lejeune, Isabelle, S2-588, 767-768

Lejeune, Jean, C-7, 46, 70-71
Lejeune, Jean, E-298
Lejeune, Jean, F-7, 47
Lejeune, Jean, N-10, 19, 69, 124-127, 183, 193, 206, 208, 235
Lejeune, Jean, S1-47, 346
Lejeune, Jean, S2-576, 583, 586-589, 767
Lejeune, Jean, S3-1006, 1010, 1038, 1077
Lejeune, Jean Baptiste, F-7, 11
Lejeune, Jean Baptiste, N-125
Lejeune, Jean Charles, C-70-71, 144-145
Lejeune, Jean Charles, N-40, 127-128, 245
Lejeune, Jean Charles, S3-1061
Lejeune, Jean Charles Joseph, C-71
Lejeune, Jean Marie, N-126
Lejeune, Jean Michel, E-298
Lejeune, Jean-Baptiste, S1-53
Lejeune, Jean-Baptiste, S2-583-584
Lejeune, Jean-Charles, S1-347
Lejeune, Jean-Charles, S2-588
Lejeune, Jeanne Marie, N-125
Lejeune, Jeanne Olive Elizabeth, C-70
Lejeune, Jeanne-Olive-Eliza-beth, S2-587
Lejeune, Jerome, S2-588-590
Lejeune, Joseph, E-66, 83, 298
Lejeune, Joseph, F-45, 63, 83
Lejeune, Joseph, N-125
Lejeune, Joseph, S2-590
Lejeune, Joseph, S3-963
Lejeune, Joseph Jean Charles, N-128
Lejeune, Josephette, E-145, 276
Lejeune, Julien, F-7
Lejeune, Julien, N-126-127
Lejeune, Louis, E-298
Lejeune, Madeleine, N-125
Lejeune, Magdelaine, F-45
Lejeune, Magdeleine, E-298
Lejeune, Marguerite, C-7
Lejeune, Marguerite, E-29, 31, 90, 156
Lejeune, Marguerite, F-45, 83

Lejeune, Marguerite, N-10, 125, 161
Lejeune, Marguerite, S1-47-49
Lejeune, Marguerite, S2-584, 587, 762
Lejeune, Marguerite Catherine, E-298
Lejeune, Margueritte, S3-1000
Lejeune, Marie, E-83, 298
Lejeune, Marie, F-7
Lejeune, Marie, N-126-127
Lejeune, Marie, S2-589
Lejeune, Marie Anne, E-298
Lejeune, Marie Charlotte, E-298
Lejeune, Marie Joseph, C-161
Lejeune, Marie Josephe, E-303, 428
Lejeune, Marie Madeleine, N-125
Lejeune, Marie Magdelaine, F-7
Lejeune, Marie Marguerite, E-298
Lejeune, Marie Rose, E-298
Lejeune, Marie Rose, F-7, 45, 83
Lejeune, Marie Rose, N-125
Lejeune, Marie-Jeanne-Perinne-Madeleine, S2-584
Lejeune, Marie-Josephe, S1-347
Lejeune, Marie-Josephe, S2-470, 583, 585-586, 594
Lejeune, Marie-Madeleine, S2-584
Lejeune, Martin, E-475
Lejeune, Mathurin, S2-589
Lejeune, Ozite, S2-583
Lejeune, Paul, E-297-298, 333
Lejeune, Perpetue, E-277, 422
Lejeune, Pierre, E-475, 528
Lejeune, Pierre, N-127
Lejeune, Pierre, S1-311
Lejeune, Pierre, S2-625
Lejeune, Pierre Alexis, N-125
Lejeune, Pierre Martin, E-457
Lejeune, Pierre Paul, E-298
Lejeune, Robert, S3-959
Lejeune, Rosalie, F-45, 83
Lejeune, Rosalie, N-124-125
Lejeune, Rosalie, S2-589
Lejeune, Servan, N-125

Lejeune, Servan Francois, N-125

Lejeune, Servan Mathurin, F-7

Lejeune, Servan-Mathurin, S2-585

Lejeune, Theotiste, E-298

Lejeune, Theotiste, S2-590

Lejeune, Ustache, N-235

Lejeune, Zeno, F-7

Lejourne, Denis, E-298

LeJuge, Elizabeth, C-7, 56

Lejuge, Elisabeth, S3-1000, 1062

Lejuge, Elizabeth, F-33

Lejuge, Elizabeth, S1-47, 50, 55

Lejuge, Elizabeth, S2-460, 475

Lejuge, Mathurin, S1-115

Lejure, Michelle, S2-620

Lejure, Michelle, S3-981

Lekom, Claudien, E-172, 174, 298

Lekom, Mathieu, E-172, 174, 298

Lelardon, Elisabeth, S3-1023

Lelardon, Elizabeth, S2-443

LeLarge, Marie Jeanne Bona-venture, E-335

LeLarge - See also LeSarge

Lelbanc, Joseph Olivier, N-121

Lelievre, Francois, E-100, 298, 331, 347

Lelievre, Jeanne, E-625

Lelievre, Marie Anne, E-32, 73

Leloir, Marguerite, S2-429

Lelojais, Catherine, E-54, 101

Lelon, Marie, E-96

Lelong, Joseph, N-251

Lelorre, Francois-Pierre, S1-120

Leloup de l'Epine, Veronique, E-91

Leluc, Julie Marie Joseph, E-95, 425

Leluc, Marie, E-424

Leluc, Marie Catherine, E-125

Leluc, Marie Josephe, E-196, 284

Leluc, Marie Rene, E-421

Leluc, Marie Renee, E-299, 422

Leluc, Nicole Marie Louise, E-299, 421, 426

Leluc, Nicolle, E-420-421, 423, 427-428

Leluc, Perrine, E-95

Leluc, Pierre, E-299

LeLuch, Andres, E-420

Lelurron, Jean, S3-1088

Lemagre, Pelagie Lafrenes, S3-1028

Lemaire, Germain, N-180-181

Lemaire, Jeanne, S1-204

Lemaire, Philippe Francois, E-72, 299

LeMaitre, Francois, E-191, 286

Lemaitre, Marie Suzanne Modeste Angelique, E-87, 179

Lemamire, Joseph, N-180

LeManquet, Gillet, E-100, 101

LeManquet, Marie, E-126

Lemanquet, Anne, E-408, 412

Lemanquet, Anne, S1-41

Lemanquet, Bernardine, E-299, 359

Lemanquet, Gabrielle, S2-783

Lemanquet, Gillette, S1-196

Lemanquet, Marianne, S2-520

Lemanson, Marie, E-302

Lemarchand, George, E-262

Lemarchand, George, E-299

Lemarchand, Jean, E-262

Lemarchand, Jean, E-299

Lemarchand, Julien, E-306, 346

Lemarchand, Jullienne, E-195

Lemarchand, Pierre, E-299

LeMares, Marie Jeanne, E-287

Lemarie, Jacques, S2-622

Lemarinier, Marie Magdelaine, E-299

LeMarinnier, Thomas, E-41, 299

Lemarquant, Louis, S3-986

LeMarrec, Perrine, E-118

LeMarrec, Yves, E-289

LeMasson, Jean Baptiste Charles, E-194

Lemasson, Angelique Aimee, E-626

Lemasson, Augustin Felix, E-193, 299

Lemasson, Jacques Villaneuve Louis, E-299

Lemasson, Marie Magdeleine Elisabeth, E-192-193, 299

Lemasson, Pierre, E-626

Lemasson, Pierre Anne, E-299

LeMate, Jeanne, E-96

LeMatelot, Guillaume, E-284

LeMatelot, Marie Anne, E-289, 299

LeMaurens, Magdalen, E-332

Lembert, Marie, E-547

Lembert, Philippe, E-528

Lemercier, Louis Andre, E-299

Lemercier, Marie Rose Fran-coise, E-299

Lemercier, Renee, S2-560

Lemercier, Suzanne, E-121

Lemercier, Suzanne, S1-261

Lemercier, Suzanne, S3-915

Lemetayer, Thomas, E-22, 433

Lemeteyer, Gabriel, E-300

Lemeteyer, Michel Louis, E-300

Lemeur, Mathieu, E-300

Lemeur, Mathieu, E-55

Lemeur, Nicolas, E-300

Lemeur, Nicolas, E-55

Leminous, -----, S3-930

Lemoine, Antoine Philippe, C-xiii

Lemoine, Bertrand, E-300

Lemoine, Germain, S3-930

Lemoine, Gilles, E-300, 311

Lemoine, Henri, S3-1092

Lemoine, Jacques, E-440

Lemoine, Jeanne, E-81, 149, 300, 311

Lemoine, Jeanne, S1-389

Lemoine, Joseph, E-300

Lemoine, Julienne, C-50

Lemoine, Julienne, S1-392

Lemoine, Mathurin, S1-19

Lemoine, Rene, E-300

Lemoine, Suzanne Marguerite, E-300

Lemole, Louis, E-437

Lemonie, Gillette, E-22, 433

Lemonier, Marie Jeanne, E-588, 596

Lemonnier, Claude, S2-591

Lemonnier, Francois, S2-591

Lemonnier, Louis, S2-591

Lemonnier, Marie-Jeanne, S2-591

Lemonnier, Marie-Louise, S2-591

Lemordan, Isabelle, E-158, 300

Lemordant, Marie, S2-739

Lemordant, Marie, S3-952

Lemorinier, Jacques, E-433

Lemoule, Elizabeth Genevieve, E-300, 337

Lemoule, Pierre, E-300, 337

Lemoureaux, Marie Adelaide, C-62

Lemoyne, Marie Angelique Adelaide, E-267

Lencon, Louis Francois Aubin, E-300

Lencon, Nicolas, E-300

Leneau, Francois, E-440

Lenee, Marie Jeanne, C-72

Lenee, Marie-Jeanne, S2-595

Leneuder, Yves, S2-477

Leneuf, Alexandre, E-513

Leneuf, Barbe, E-105, 300

Leneuf, Barbe, E-392

Leneuf, Barbe, E-513

Leneuf, Francois, E-475

Leneuf, Jacques, E-513

Leneuf, Jean Baptiste, E-513

Leneuf, Joseph Alexandre, E-300

Leneuf, Joseph Alexandre, E-92

Leneuf, Juditte, E-513

Leneuf, Louis, E-300

Leneuf, Louis, E-392

Leneuf, Marguerite, E-340, 418

Leneuf, Marguerite, E-513

Leneuf, Marie Joseph, E-513

Leneuf, Michel, E-300

Leneuf, Michel, E-475, 513

Leneuf, Michel, E-92, 105, 392

Leneuf, Philipe, E-300

LeNeuf de la Valliere, Marguerite, E-101, 392

LeNeuf sieur de Beaubassin, Philipe, E-92

Lenfant, Antoine, E-301

Lenfant, Jean Baptiste, E-301

Lenfant, Marguerite, E-301

Lenfant, Marie Elizabet, E-301

Lengendre, Henriette, C-8

Lengepas, Jean Baptiste Michel, E-301

Lengepas, Michel, E-301, 319

LeNormand, Pierre, E-419

LeNormand, Vincent, E-96

LeNouvelle, Anne, E-595

LeNouvelle, Pierre, E-595

LeNouvelle, Vincente, E-595

Lenouvelle, Perrine, E-586, 591

Leonar, Catherinne, S3-996

Leonard, Catherine, S2-607

Leorion, Louis, S3-928

Lepage, Jean Baptiste Joseph, E-301, 385

Lepage, Louis, E-301

Lepage, Louis Guillaume, E-301, 385

Lepage, Marie Adelaide, E-301

Lepage, Marie Elisabeth Pelagie, E-301, 385

Lepage, Mathieu, E-301

Lepage, Michel Joseph, E-301, 385

Lepage, Paul Louis, E-301

Lepage-Jacquemin, Etiennette, E-33, 255

Lepape, Julien, S2-724, 765

Lepare, Martin, E-355

Lepechou, Augustain, E-44

Lepeigneul, Olivier, S1-301

Lepeltier, Thomas, S1-77

LePenn, Francois, E-275

Leperdrieux, Marie Rosalie, E-115

Leperle, Elizabeth, E-100, 301

Leperle, Jean Baptiste, E-301

Lepont, Laurent, E-287

LePort, Marie Francoise Rene, E-189

Leport, Germain, E-301

Leport, Julien, S3-1102

Leport, Laurent, E-301, 286

LePorteur, Jean Baptiste, E-166

Leporteur, Jean Baptiste, E-40

Lepreur, Joseph, E-1, 74

LePrevost, Francoise, E-173, 430

LePrevost, Madeleine, E-193, E-194

LePrevost, Simon Nicolas, E-194

Leprevost, Anne Felicite, E-147

LePrieur, Jaques, E-263

LePrieur, Marie, E-173, 262

Leprieur, Marie, S1-77

Leprieur, Marie, S3-978, 997

Leprince, Anne, E-256

Leprince, Anne, E-302, 347, 427

Leprince, Anne, E-608-609, 611, 614-615

Leprince, Anne, S2-704

Leprince, Antoine, E-123-124

Leprince, Antoine, E-14, 528

Leprince, Antoine, E-302, 421

Leprince, Antoine, F-19

Leprince, Antoine, S2-767

Leprince, Barbe, E-609, 615

Leprince, Barbe, E-611

Leprince, Charles, E-302, 347

Leprince, Cyprien, E-287, 302, 356, 390, 412

Leprince, Francois, E-26, 302

Leprince, Francois, E-528

Leprince, Francois Firmin, N-128

Leprince, Isabelle, F-59

Leprince, Jacques, E-475

Leprince, Jean Marie Joseph, E-302

Leprince, Joseph, E-53, 302

Leprince, Judith, E-150

Leprince, Judith, S2-592

Leprince, Julie, F-19

Leprince, Madeleine, E-16, 302

Leprince, Marguerite, E-150

Leprince, Marguerite, E-302, 325, 420

Leprince, Marguerite, F-59

Leprince, Marie, E-302, 421, 423

Leprince, Marie, F-19

Leprince, Marie, S2-767

Leprince, Marie Barbe, E-188

Leprince, Marie Barbe, E-285, 331, 356, 420

Leprince, Marie Ludivine, E-302, 390

Leprince, Marie Magdelaine, E-63

Leprince, Marie Magdeleine, E-331

Leprince, Marie Marguerite, E-302

Leprince, Marie Sophie, C-98

Leprince, Olivier, E-53, 302

Leprince, Olivier, N-128

Leprince, Simon, E-302

Leprince, Tranquille, E-302

Leprince, Tranquille, E-63

Leprince, Tranquille, F-59

Leprince - See also Prince

Lerat, Sieur Rene, E-190

LeRaux, Elizabeth, E-317

Leris, Jean, E-135, 302

Leris, Simon Gabriel, E-135, 302

Lermite, Florian, S1-256

Lermite, Pierre, E-426

Leron, Julienne, S2-475

Leroux, Guillaume, E-52

Leroux, Marie, E-110, 265

Leroy, Anne, E-120

Leroy, Anne, E-303, 626

Leroy, Antoine, E-303

Leroy, Catherine, E-317

Leroy, Catherine, E-61

Leroy, Charles, E-120

Leroy, Charles, E-71-72, 303

Leroy, Eulalie, E-303

Leroy, Gregoire Libiere Joseph, E-303

Leroy, Guillaume, E-303, 327

Leroy, Jacques, E-303

Leroy, Jacques, E-82

Leroy, Jacques Francois, E-103

Leroy, Jean, E-328, 626

Leroy, Jean Francois, E-295, 303, 327, 393

Leroy, Jean Michel, S1-354

Leroy, Jeanne, C-123

Leroy, Jeanne, E-51, 303, 316

Leroy, Josephe, E-411

Leroy, Justine Georgette, E-38, 51

Leroy, Louis, E-626

Leroy, Louise, E-626

Leroy, Louise, S1-122

Leroy, Marianne, C-60, 123

Leroy, Martine, E-298

Leroy, Paul, E-303

Leroy, Pierre, E-114

Leroy, Pierre, E-303

Leroy, Pierre, E-588, 596

Leroy, Quentin, E-303

Leroy, Therese, E-172

Leroy, Therese, E-303

LeSage, Angelique, E-94

Lesaichet, Francoise, S1-16, 67

LeSarge, Marie Jeanne Bonna-venture, E-336

LeSarge - See also LeLarge

LeSarn, Petronille, E-384

Lesauvage, Francois, E-303

Lesauvage, Thomas, E-303

Lescuier, Michel, E-303

Lescuier, sons, E-303

Lesene, Nicolas, E-54, 303

Leseque, Francoise Alexis, E-303, 350

Leseque, Jean Francois, E-303

Lesmesy, M., E-325

Lesongeoux, Marie, S3-923

Lespeau, Jan Baptiste, S3-1090

Lespinge, Marie Anne, E-189

Lesquels, Mr., E-368

Lesquier, Jeanne, E-304

Lesquin, Francois, E-280

Lessenne, Francois, E-112, 304, 332

Lessenne, Jean, E-304, 332

Lessenne, Marie Jeanne, E-112, 304

Lessieu, Marie Anne, E-340

Lestang, Etienne, E-22, 408

Lestard, Bignon, N-105

Lestard, Josephe, E-142

Letamps, Guillaume, S1-57

Letang, Etienne Clermont Laroche, E-74, 304

Letang, Paschal Poulin Laroche, E-74, 304

Letellier, Daniel, E-57

Letellier, Pierre, E-304

Letellier, Rosalie, E-304

LeTerrier, Jeanne, E-431

Leterrier, Jacques Joseph, E-626

Leterrier, Jeanne, F-61

Letestu, Cezar-Auguste, S2-532

Letestu, Dudemene, S3-876

Letiecq, Joseph Sebastien, E-304

Letiecq, Pierre, E-304

Letiecq, Pierre Gatien, E-304

Letimbre, Helene, S2-691

Letourneur, Barbe-Genevieve, S2-596

Letourneur, Genevieve, S1-312

Letourneur, Genevieve, S2-596

Letourneur, Jacques, E-304, 389

Letourneur, Jean, E-304, 389

Letourneur, Jeanne Marie, E-100

Letourneur, Jeanne Marie, E-304, 623

Letourneur, Jeanne-Marie, S2-596

Letourneur, Julienne, S2-596

Letourneur, Marie, E-169, 325

Letourneur, Marie-Julienne, S2-596

Letourneur, Nicolas, S2-595

Letourneur, Perinne, S1-312

Letourneur, Perinne, S2-596

Letourneur, Pierre, S1-78

Letourneur, Pierre, S2-595-596

Letourneur, Rosalie, E-58

Letrang, Suzanne, E-12

Letranye, Antoine, E-28, 304

Letranye, Catherine, E-28, 304

Letullier, Adelaide, E-2, 74

Letullier, Adelaide, F-69

Letullier, Augustin, E-2, 74

Letullier, Francois Isidore, E-2, 74

Letullier, Francoise Adeleaide, E-2, 74

Letullier, Henry Aimable, F-21

Letullier, Isidore, F-69

Letullier, Jean Charles, E-2, 74

Letullier, Jean Charles, F-69

Letullier, Julien, F-21

Letullier, Louis, F-21

Letullier, Marie Adelaide, F-21

Letullier, Marie Rose, E-2, 74

Letullier, Marie Rose, F-11

Letullier, Michel Felicite, E-2, 74

Letullier, Rene, E-2, 74

Letullier, Rene, F-11, 69

Levanier, Elisabet, E-80, 277

Levannier, Thomas, S3-964

Levant, Yvonne, S2-489

LeVarieux, Marie, E-98

Levasseur, Louis, E-304, 308

Levasseur, Marie Suzanne Rose, E-159, 304
Levasseur, Pierre Guillaume, E-159, 304
Levasson, Marie Michelle, E-28, 369
Levaux, Pierre, E-17
Levecot, Marthe, E-123
Levecque, Guillaume, E-371
Leveille, Marie Anne, E-305, 412
Leveque, Marie, E-305
Leveque, Marie, S1-2
Leveque, Marie, S3-932
Leveque, Marie Joseph, E-305
Leveque, Marthe, E-378
Leveque, Maurice, E-305
Leveque, Mr., E-62
LeVerdier, Anne Genevieve, E-147
Levergne, Cecile, S3-1008
Levesque, Elizabeth, E-121, 149
Levesque, Pierre, S3-942-943
Levesue, Marie, E-319
Levier, Catherine, E-406
Levieux, Jean, E-41, 378
Levir, Jacques, N-130
Levir, Joseph, N-98, 129, 217
Levis, Joseph, C-73
Levis, Joseph, S1-292
Levis, Joseph, S2-596
Levis, Joseph, S3-1081
Levis, Louis Nicolas Joseph, C-73
Levraud, Jean, E-71, 348
Levron, Alexis, E-305, 420
Levron, Alexis, F-59
Levron, Anastasie, E-297-298
Levron, Anastasie, F-45, 47, 63, 83
Levron, Anastasie, N-124, 127, 235
Levron, Anne, E-255, 483, 609, 611, 615
Levron, Anne Marguerite, E-305
Levron, Baptiste, E-305
Levron, Francois, E-27, 475
Levron, Francois Pierre, E-305
Levron, Genevieve, C-47
Levron, Gregoire Noel, E-615
Levron, Jacques, E-483

Levron, Jean Marie, E-305
Levron, Joseph, E-305
Levron, Joseph Marie, F-57
Levron, Madeleine, S2-780
Levron, Mae Anne, E-27
Levron, Magdelaine, E-483
Levron, Magdeleine, S3-923
Levron, Marie, E-483
Levron, Marie, F-57
Levron, Marie Francoise, E-424
Levron, Marie Josephe, E-305, 609, 615
Levron, Marie Josephe Francoise, E-305
Levron, Marie Josephine, E-611
Levron, Marie Magdalen Pelagie, E-305
Levron, Marie Marthe, E-305, 609, 612, 615
Levron, Michel, E-305
Levron, Michel, F-57, 59
Levron, Pierre, E-282, 305-306, 380, 609, 611-612, 615
Levron, Pierre Gregoire Noel, E-305, 612
Levron, Pierre Marie, E-305
Levron, Pierre Mathurin, E-306
Levron, Pierre Paul, E-306
Leyritz, Malo, S1-20
Lhaumiere, Jean Gabriel, E-69
Lherinitti, Leonnard, E-306
Lherinitti, Marie, E-306
Lhermite, Charles, E-306
Lhermite, Nicolas, E-306
Lhermite, Therese, E-166
Lhor, Francoise, E-320, 326
Lhuis, Antoine, E-409
Liard, Catherine Victoire, E-361, 365
Liard, Jacques, E-306, 346
Liard, Marie Francoise, E-46, 87-88
Liard, Pierre, E-365
Liard, Yves, E-306, 346
Libaudo, Bonaventure, E-113
Liber, Agnes, E-306
Liber, Francoise Agnes, E-306, 429
Liber, Jean Baptiste, E-343
Liber, Pierre, E-306, 343
Liberi, Francoise, S1-56

Liberi, Jean Baptiste, E-323
Liege, Louis (Mr.), C-150
Liege, Nicholas Etienne Dominique, E-269
Lieuron, Joseph, E-182
Liglen, Madeleine, E-84
Ligommier, Louise, E-299
Ligonniere, Louise, E-72
Limousin, Etienne, E-194
Lingre, Francois, E-306
Lingre, George, E-287, 306
Lingre, Jean Francois, E-306
Lingre, Marie Joseph, E-306
Linivet, Jeanne, E-389
Lintaut, Marie, S2-779
Lion, Elizabeth, S2-642
Liot, Louise, E-300
Liot, Marie Madgalen, E-184
Liot, Michel, E-52, 300
Lirois, Perrine, C-161
Lissereau, Louis, E-13
Litouat, Pierre, N-247
Littou, Leonard, E-186
Livier, Claude, E-306
Livier, Therese, E-306, 408
Livois, Ambroise-Pierre, S2-598
Livois, Francoise, C-161
Livois, Francoise-Nicole, S2-599
Livois, Jean, E-307
Livois, Jean, S2-597
Livois, Jeanne-Celeste, S2-599
Livois, Judith, E-306
Livois, Judith, S2-598
Livois, Louis Pierre, S3-919
Livois, Marie, N-16
Livois, Marie, S2-599
Livois, Marie Anne, E-306
Livois, Marie Madeleine, C-12
Livois, Marie Madeleine, E-306
Livois, Marie Madeleine, N-15
Livois, Marie Magdelaine, F-51
Livois, Marie Rose, F-27
Livois, Marie-Anne, S2-597, 599
Livois, Marie-Madeleine, S2-597-598
Livois, Marie-Rose, S2-598
Livois, P., S3-918
Livois, Perinne-Francoise, S2-598

Livois, Pierre, E-306-307, 365
Livois, Pierre, S2-597-599
Livois, Pierre, S3-918-919, 956
Livois, Pierre-Joseph-Jean, S2-598
Livois, Rene, E-307
Lizaac, Elisabeth, E-122
Lobeau, Marie Magdeleine, E-307
Lobeau, Pierre, E-307
Lociriget, Louis, E-369
Logoannere, Blaise, E-92
Logoannere, Jean Pierre, E-92
Lohier, Marie, S2-521
Loian, Michel, S1-279
Loignon, Jean, E-307, 401
Loignon, Nicolas, E-307, 401
Loiret, Rene, N-247
Loiseau, Jean, E-28, 332
Loiseleur, Jean Baptiste, C-42, 74, 153
Loizeau, Joseph, E-307
Loizeau, Mathieu, E-307
Lombard, Antoine, E-371
Lombard, Antoine Simeon, E-307
Lombard, Joseph Antoine, E-307
Lombard, Mr., E-428
Lombard, Nicolas, E-139, 344
Lombard de Sogues, Antoine, E-154
Longchamp, -----, S2-535
Longchamp, Anne Madeleine, E-307
Longchamp, Anne Theotiste, E-307
Longchamp, Francoise, E-307
Longchamp, Jean, E-307
Longchamp, Jeanne, E-307
Longchamp, Pierre, E-307
Longrasi, Louis, E-292, 307
Longrasi, Pierre, E-292, 307
Longueepee, Marguerite, E-81
Longuepee, Ambroise, S3-1114
Longuepee, Anne Joseph, S3-989
Longuepee, Cecile, S3-1007
Longuepee, Jean, S3-916
Longuepee, Jean-Pierre, S1-301
Longuepee, Louis, N-113

Longuepee, Louis, S3-914, 916, 1114
Longuepee, Marguerite, S3-911
Longuepee, Marie Josephe, N-113-114
Longuepee, Pierre, S1-43
Longuepee, Pierre, S3-916, 989, 1007, 1031
Longuepee, Pierre Louis, S3-1060
Longueppe, Joseph, N-98
Longuespe, Ambroise, S1-377
Longuespee, Ambroise, F-99
Longuespee, Ambroise, S2-487, 599-600, 602
Longuespee, Anne, F-89
Longuespee, Anne, S2-601-602
Longuespee, Anne-Josephe, S2-511, 600
Longuespee, Anne-Louise, S2-603
Longuespee, Cecile, S1-363
Longuespee, Cecile, S2-544
Longuespee, Corantine, S2-601
Longuespee, Corentine, F-89
Longuespee, Helene, F-89
Longuespee, Helene, S2-601
Longuespee, Helene-Appoline, S2-601
Longuespee, Helene-Rosalie, S2-603
Longuespee, Janvier, F-99
Longuespee, Janvier-Pierre, S2-599
Longuespee, Jean, F-89
Longuespee, Jean, S1-377
Longuespee, Jean, S2-600-602, 745
Longuespee, Jean Baptiste, F-89
Longuespee, Jean Jacques, F-89
Longuespee, Jean-Baptiste, S2-601
Longuespee, Jean-Jacques, S2-600-601
Longuespee, Jean-Louis, S2-599
Longuespee, Jean-Pierre, S2-603-604
Longuespee, Joseph, C-59
Longuespee, Joseph, F-5
Longuespee, Joseph, S2-509, 601

Longuespee, Laurentine-Urienne, S2-601
Longuespee, Louis, F-89, 99
Longuespee, Louis, S2-559-560, 599-602
Longuespee, Louis-Joseph, S2-603
Longuespee, Louis-Toussaint, S2-603
Longuespee, Marguerite, F-89
Longuespee, Marguerite, S1-356
Longuespee, Marguerite, S2-601, 761
Longuespee, Marguerite-Josephe, S2-600
Longuespee, Marguerite-Olive, S2-600
Longuespee, Marie, F-89
Longuespee, Marie, S2-601
Longuespee, Marie-Barbe, S2-603
Longuespee, Marie-Francoise-Jeanne, S2-600
Longuespee, Marie-Josephe, S2-559-561, 602
Longuespee, Olivier-Theodore, S2-603
Longuespee, Pierre, F-89
Longuespee, Pierre, S2-510, 599, 601-602, 604
Longuet, Suzanne, E-34, 157, 307
Longueville, Andree, E-621
Lonnain, Madeleine, E-44
Lonville, Mr., E-428
Lope, Francoise, S2-609
Lope, Madeleine, S1-371
Loppe, Anastasie, E-9
Loppe, Jacques, E-9
Loppe, Jean, E-9
Loppe, Louis, E-9
Loppe, Magdeleine, E-9
Loppe, Pierre, E-9
Loppinot, Charles, E-307
Loppinot, Jean, E-40
Loppinot, Jean Chrisostome, E-40, 64, 101, 307-308
Loppinot, Jeanne, E-101, 308
Loppinot, Louise Charlotte, E-64, 308

Loppinot de la Fresillier, Jean, E-80
Loppinot de la Fresillier, Louis, E-80, 405
Loquet, Louis, E-441
Loquin, Jacquemine, E-23, 342
Lor, Elisabeth, E-308
Lor, Francoise, E-27, 319
Lorain, Jeanne, E-22
Loranr, Marie Anne, E-304
Lord, Anne, F-35
Lord, Anne, N-109, 110, 166, 232
Lord, Annie, E-600
Lord, Basile, E-600
Lord, Marguerite, C-44
Lord, Marguerite, F-67
Lord, Marguerite, N-71
Lord, Marie, E-600
Lord, Pierre, E-317, 600-601
Lord, Pierre, N-109
Loreal, Charles, E-285
Loreal, Eulalie, E-94
Loreal, Jean Louis, E-95, 308, 417
Loreal, Louis, E-415
Loreal, Marie Catherine, E-79, 287
Loreal, Marie Joseph, E-308
Lorec, Marie, E-306
Lorec, Pierre, E-383
Lorec, Vincent, E-426
Lorent, Jean Francois, E-308-309
Lorent, Jeanne, E-308-309
Lorent, Marie Anne, E-308
Lorent, Pierre, E-160, 268
Lorient, E-308
Lorieux, Marie, E-336
Lorphelin, Julien, E-626
Lorrain, Anne Caroline, E-361
Lorrain, Anne Marie, E-308, 363, 365
Lorrain, Anne Marie Caroline, E-360, 364
Lorrain, Jacques, E-308, 363
Lorraine, Simon, E-55, 308
Lorre, Gilette, S1-259
Lorre, Gilette, S3-901
Lort, Alexandre, E-485
Lort, Jacques, E-485

Lort, Julien, E-475
Lort, Marie, E-485
Lort, Pierre, E-485
Lorthion, Francois, E-100, 276, 309
Lorthion, Rene, E-276, 309
Lory, Marguerite, E-63, 105
Lossieux, And., S3-930
Lossieux, Andre, S3-937
Lossieux, Rene, E-308-309
Lossoie, Francois, S3-936
Lossois, Francoise, S3-936
Lost, Alexandre, E-309
Lost, S. Pierre, E-309
Lotellier, Gens, E-309
Lotellier, Henris, E-309, 353
Lothe, Pierre, E-389
Lotman, Marguerite, E-120, 338
Lotte, Pierre, E-66
Loudreau, Louis, E-359
Louedin, Etienne, S3-869
Louet, Jacques, S2-477
Louet, Julienne, S1-162
Louis, Jean, E-309
Louis, Simon Sin, S3-880, 884
Louisain, Marie Francoise, E-309, 340
Louisain, Yvon, E-309, 340
Louisbourg and the Acadians, E-310-311
Louisbourg in Canada, E-309-310
Louise, indian, E-142
Louisse, Pierre, E-23
Louiste, Pierre, E-342
Loules, Mr., E-383
Loumeau, Jean, E-15
Loumeau, Pierre, E-140, 404
Louquet, Jean, S3-833
Lours, Marie Anne, E-169, 358
Lourteig, Jean, E-311
Lourteig, Pierre, E-311, 437
Loustalet, Jacques, E-300, 311
Loustalet, Jean, E-300, 311
Loustaneau, Pierre, E-113, 311
Loveat, Jean Louis, E-41
Lovoyer, Pierre, E-345
Loya, Francois, S2-604
Loya, Michel, S2-604
Loya, Pierre, E-311, 315
Loya, Pierre, S1-356

Loyal, Jacques, E-311
Loyal, Marie Joseph, E-311
Loyal, Marie Rose, E-28, 69, 311, 418
Loyal, Michel, E-126, 179, 311-312, 418, 430, 432
Loyal, Michel, S1-308
Loyal, Michel, S2-433, 435, 773
Loyal, Revier, E-312
Loyol, Michel, C-52
Loyset, Marie Charlotte, E-92
Lozier, Francoise, S2-608
Lozier, Francoise, S3-1093
Lubert, Cecile, E-312
Lubin, Jean Pascal, E-285
Lucas, Janne, S3-994
Lucas, Jean, E-430
Lucas, Jean, S2-604, 773
Lucas, Jeanne, S2-451-452
Lucas, Joseph, S2-452
Lucas, Joseph, S3-994
Luci, Isabelle, E-312
Lucien, Louis, E-414
Luneteau, Francois, C-97
Lunoux, Pierre, S3-994
Luquette, Charles, E-312
Luquette, Isabelle, E-312
Luzeray, Marie, E-105, 108
Lyonais, Jean, S1-389

M

Mabon, Francois, N-182
Mabraud, Marguerite, E-65
Mace, Gille, E-303, 313
Mace, Jean, E-303, 313
Mace, Laurent, E-288
Mace, Louise, C-51
Mace, Louise, S2-429
Mace, Louise, S3-1043
Mace, Marie, E-626
Mace, Marie, S1-277
Mace, Marie Josephe, E-601
Mace, Marie Louise, E-295
Mace, Michel, E-626
Mace, Pierre, S2-604
Macerolle, Marie, E-98
Machard, Antoine, E-166
Macle, Basile, F-65
Macle, Charles, F-65
Macle, Charles Daniel, F-65

Macoin, Claude, E-313
Macoin, Louis, E-313
Macquignon, Marie Barbe, E-16
Maffar, Jean Antoine, S1-44
Magdelene, indian, E-326
Magnan, Elisabeth Rose, E-313
Magnan, Pierre, E-313
Magnant, Anne, E-30, 313
Magnel, Francois, E-337, 375
Magon, Magon nee, S3-934
Magre, Marie Jeanne, E-269
Mahau, Henry, E-313
Mahau, Jean Francois, E-313, 405
Mahe, Adrienne-Anne, S2-592, 641
Mahe, Adrienne-Anne, S3-953
Mahe, Anne, S3-986
Mahe, Francois, S2-477
Mahe, Mathurine, S3-1054
Maheux, Francois, E-280, 440
Maheux, Francois, S2-548
Mahey, Mathurinne, E-346
Mahez, Mathurine, S2-644
Maigne, Jean, E-179, 313
Maigne, Pierre, E-179, 313
Maihol, Anne Joseph, E-313
Maihol, Jean, E-313
Maihol, Joseph, E-313, 338
Maillachard, Marie Susanne, E-86, 113
Maillard, Jean, E-25, 313
Maillard, M., E-278
Mailler, Elisabeth, E-149
Maillet, Adelaide, E-600
Maillet, Charles-Joseph, S2-606
Maillet, Elisabeth, E-22, 145, 318, 320
Maillet, Elizabeth, C-24
Maillet, Elizabeth, N-35
Maillet, Euphrasine, E-600
Maillet, Felix, S2-605
Maillet, Francois-Michel, S2-606
Maillet, Gregoire, C-24
Maillet, Gregoire, S1-14-15, 28, 167
Maillet, Gregoire, S2-575, 578-579, 605-607, 639
Maillet, Jacques, E-600
Maillet, Jacques, S2-605

Maillet, Jean, E-313
Maillet, Jean Joseph, E-600
Maillet, Jeanne Helene, E-600
Maillet, Joseph, E-600
Maillet, L'Ange, E-600
Maillet, Madeleine, S2-605
Maillet, Marguerite, S2-575, 579, 605-607
Maillet, Marie, E-313
Maillet, Marie-Eufrosine, S2-606
Maillet, Marie-Josephe, S2-606-607
Maillet, Michel, S2-607
Maillet, Pierre-Simon, S2-606
Mainguet, Marie, E-119, 159
Maintenon, Marie, E-12, 109
Maintenu, Michel, E-353
Mainville, Jean, E-313
Mainville, Jean Joseph, E-313
Mainville, Jean Julien, E-313
Maison, Barbe, E-74, 106
Maison, Claude, E-313, 386
Maison, Jeanne, E-313, 386
Maisonat, Judith, E-428
Maisonnat, Alexis, E-550
Maisonnat, Judith, E-550
Maisonnat, Le Sieur, E-528
Maisonnat, Louis, E-550
Maisonnat, Marianne, E-550
Maisonnat, Marin, E-550
Maissonat, Judith, S2-770
Maissonnat, Anne, E-30, 268
Maistrejean, Antoine, E-314
Maistrejean, Jacques, E-314
Maistrejean, Rosalie, E-314
Maithe, Catherine, E-32, 294, 348
Maitre, Augustin Michel Marie, E-314
Maitre, Jean Louis, E-314
Maitre, Joseph, E-314
Maitre, Louis Marie Germain, E-314
Maitre, Marie Barbe Josephe, E-314
Maitre, Michel, E-314
MaitreJean, Antoine, E-125
Maizan, Yves, S1-145
Maizonnat, Anne, E-254
Malard, Mathurin, E-314

Malard, Mathurin Claude, E-314
Maleveque, Catherine, C-2, 104
Malfait, Francoise, S1-385
Malfait, Jacques, S2-768
Malfait, Jean, S1-56
Malfait, Jean, S2-607
Malfait, Pierre, S2-607
Malfe, Jean, S3-996
Malfe, Pierre, S3-996
Maliven, Guillaume, S1-272
Mallet, Antoine, E-314
Mallet, Etienne, E-69, 174
Mallet, Francois, S2-608
Mallet, Francois, S3-1093
Mallet, Francoise Genevieve, E-619
Mallet, Guillaume Francois, E-619
Mallet, Jeanne, E-173, 314, 404
Mallet, Louis, E-619
Mallet, Louis, S2-608
Mallet, Louis, S3-1093
Mallet, Magdelaine, E-314
Mallet, Pierre, S2-608
Mallivers, Guillaume, S1-56
Maloisel, Marie Perrine, S3-981
Maloisel, Marie-Perinne, S2-620
Malvilain, Adrien, S2-608-609
Malvilain, Charles, S2-608-609
Malvilain, Isabelle, E-314
Malvilain, Jean Nicolas, E-314
Man, George, E-181, 314, 404
Man, Guillaume, E-181, 314, 404
Manberg, Antoine, E-377
Mancel, Anne, E-98, 101, 314, 419
Mancel, Charles, E-315
Mancel, Francois, N-4, 111, 130, 199
Mancel, Jean, N-5, 130, 195-196, 199
Mancel, Jeanne Susanne, E-112, 311, 315, 325
Mancel, Jeanne-Suzanne, S1-356, 358
Mancel, Louis, N-130, 195, 199
Mancel, Marie, E-120
Mancel, Marie Francoise, E-315
Mancel, Robert, E-87, 159, 314-315

Mancel, Robert, S1-215, 372

Mancel, Susane Marie, E-120

Manche - Department in France, E-315

Maney, Francoise, E-588, 596

Manffene, George, E-70

Mannegy, Francois Etienne, E-194

Mannet, Cesar, E-18

Mannys, Marguerite, E-303

Manquet, ----, E-408

Manseau, Francois, E-315

Manseau, Jean, E-155, 315, 376

Manseau, Jeanne, E-275

Mansel, George, E-159

Mansel, Robert, E-170, 259, 283

Mansel, Robert, S2-516

Manson, Anne Eulalie, E-103, 315

Manson, Marguerite, E-425

Manson, Pierre, E-103, 315

Manuel, Antoine, E-315

Marachal, Jeanne, E-57

Marandel, Jean Baptiste, E-618

Marboeuf, Marie, E-101, 326

Marcade, Jean, S3-1089

Marcadeau, Marie Magdeleine, E-345

Marcadeau, Marie-Madeleine, S2-643

Marcadet, Francois, E-626

Marcadet, Francois, S2-610

Marcadet, Jean, E-315

Marcadet, Jean, S2-609-610

Marcadet, Jean Baptiste, E-626

Marcadet, Judith, S1-82

Marcadet, Louison, S2-609

Marcadet, Lucas, S2-609

Marcadet, Marie Genevieve, E-173, 315

Marcadet, Marie-Madeleine, S2-609-610

Marcadet, Modeste, S1-59

Marcadet, Modeste, S2-609-610

Marcel, George, C-51

Marcel, George, E-110, 123, 177, 346

Marcel, George, S2-429, 433, 645

Marcel, Robert, E-371

Marchand, Anne, E-349, 416

Marchand, Antoine, E-315

Marchand, Francois, E-315

Marchand, Joseph, E-315

Marchand, Louis, E-315

Marchand, Louis Francois, E-315

Marchand, Louis Laurent, E-315

Marchand, Louise, E-29, 254

Marchand, Marie, E-34, 107, 315

Marchand, Marie Therese, E-288

Marchand, Renee, S1-171, 358

Marchand, Renote, E-57, 435

Marchant, Andre, E-82

Marchant, Marc, E-82

Marchaud, Renee, E-34, 316

Marchet, Marie Joseph, S3-953

Marchet, Marie-Josephe, S2-641

Marchouan, Jeanne, E-65, 140

Marcier, Rose, E-390, 441

Marcillat, Catherine, E-257, 316, 350, 369

Marcoucci, Germain Marie, E-144, 316

Marcoucci, Mathieu, E-316, 144

Mare, Francois, E-255

Marechal, Marie Anne, E-100

Marechal, Mr., E-161

Mares, Esther, E-184

Marestier, Antoine, S3-955

Marestier, Francois, S3-955

Maret, Anne, S1-323

Maret, Guillemette, E-70, 328

Marette, Joseph-Jean, S2-573

Margery, Cristoffe, E-475

Margorie, Aleix, E-45

Margorie, Jeanne, E-45, 316

Margorie, Pierre, E-45, 316

Margot, Francoise, E-22, 294

Margre, Marie Magdelaine, E-297, 333

Marguerie, Alexis, E-69

Margueritte, Jean, E-303, 316

Margueritte, Simon, E-303, 316

Marguet, Charlle, C-105

Maria, Marguerite, E-159

Marichal, Jeanne, E-36, 55, 58-59

Marie, Alexandre, E-316

Marie, Barbe, E-316, 354

Marie, Claude, S2-610

Marie, Francois, S2-536

Marie, Jan, S3-837

Marie, Jeanne, S1-34

Marie, Louis, S3-986, 1048

Marie, Marguerite, E-159, 316

Marie, Noel, S3-1079

Marie, Olive, S1-182, 333

Marie, Ollive, S3-1048

Marie, Perinne, S2-642, 765

Marie, Pierre, E-354

Marie, Pierre, S3-1079

Marie, Rose-Jeanne, S2-610

Marie Anne Francoise, indian, E-316

Marie Joseph, indian, E-316

Marie Louise, indian, E-316

Marillon, Andre, E-358

Marion, Jean, E-304, 389

Marison, S. P., E-588, 596

Maron, Anne, E-140, 352

Marot, Elisabeth, E-197

Maroux, Jeanne, E-319

Marque, Marie-Anne, S2-782

Marquer, Elizabeth, S2-778

Marquet, Francoise, S2-782

Marquin, Francois, S3-923

Marquis, Francois, S2-781

Marquis, Jean Baptiste, E-45

Marres, Naster, E-425

Marsa, Leonarde, E-66, 375

Marsais, Jean, E-376

Marsais, Marie, E-172, 413

Marsan, J.J., E-32

Marsanne, Blaise, E-588, 591

Marsay, Simon, E-316, 331

Martain, Marie, E-102

Martain, Pierre, E-102

Martay, Simon, E-316

Marteau, Louis, E-122

Marteau, Louise, E-139

Martial, Marie, C-2

Martin, -----, S3-915

Martin, Adelaide, E-316

Martin, Adelaide Albertine, E-158

Martin, Anastasie, E-89, 316-317, 419, 581

Martin, Andre, E-499

Martin, Andree, E-458, 475

Martin, Angelique, E-159, 160,
  169, 188, 194, 265, 318
Martin, Anne, E-317, 403
Martin, Anne Marguerite, E-97
Martin, Antoine, E-316
Martin, Antoine, S1-38
Martin, Antoine, S3-1060
Martin, Barbe, E-22, 346
Martin, Barnable, E-457, 476
Martin, Barthelemy, E-160, 317-
  318, 320, 330
Martin, Brigitte, S1-154-155,
  170-171, 295, 369
Martin, Brigitte, S3-1121, 1124-
  1125
Martin, Cecile, S2-432
Martin, Cecille, E-499
Martin, Charles, E-117, 133,
  317, 320
Martin, Charlotte, E-412
Martin, Claire, E-276, 440
Martin, Dejannie, E-268, 332
Martin, Denis, E-317
Martin, Elisabeth, E-19, 317-
  318, 355, 600
Martin, Etienne, E-320, 495,
  528
Martin, Francois, C-56, 74, 117
Martin, Francois, E-27, 51, 61,
  84, 255, 317-320, 326, 378
Martin, Francois, S1-44
Martin, Francois Joachim, C-74
Martin, Francoise, E-15, 31,
  131, 314, 317, 404, 409, 423,
  426-427, 430, 581, 600
Martin, Francoise, S2-548
Martin, Froisine Marie, E-317
Martin, Germain, E-317
Martin, infant, E-316
Martin, Isabelle, E-160, 317,
  320
Martin, Jacques, E-69, 98, 111,
  142, 259, 303, 318-319, 333,
  349, 392, 409, 499, 510
Martin, Jacques Christophe, E-
  318
Martin, Jacques Francois, E-318
Martin, Jean, E-17, 51, 53, 61,
  135, 142, 145, 149, 155, 157,
  317, 320, 322, 499, 528, 600

Martin, Jean Baptiste, E-317,
  378
Martin, Jean Silvain, E-318
Martin, Jeanne, E-34, 156, 268,
  318, 325, 367, 494
Martin, Jeanne Marguerite, E-
  318
Martin, Joseph, E-188, 318-319,
  322, 382
Martin, Louis, E-27, 317-318
Martin, Louis, S2-610
Martin, Louise, E-130, 318
Martin, Louise Robertine, E-
  318, 149, 158
Martin, Madeleine, S2-611
Martin, Magdelaine, E-108, 494,
  600
Martin, Marguerite, C-117
Martin, Marguerite, E-174, 194,
  262, 318-319, 391, 456, 472
Martin, Marguerite Jean, E-319
Martin, Marguerite Jeanne, E-
  301
Martin, Marianne, E-319
Martin, Marie, E-29, 111, 123,
  137, 145, 157, 194, 282, 287,
  298, 307, 317, 319, 325, 330-
  331, 345, 351, 359, 408, 457,
  475-476, 494, 499, 556, 600
Martin, Marie, S1-37, 42, 206
Martin, Marie, S2-560, 626-627
Martin, Marie, S3-914, 1049,
  1060
Martin, Marie Anne, C-74-75
Martin, Marie Anne, E-21, 51,
  146, 318-319
Martin, Marie Catherine, E-114-
  115, 319
Martin, Marie Francoise, E-319
Martin, Marie Jacqueline, E-319
Martin, Marie Josephe, E-158,
  319, 425
Martin, Marie Magdelaine, E-
  27, 319, 524
Martin, Marie Sophie, E-320
Martin, Marie Therese, E-626
Martin, Martin, E-317
Martin, Mathieu, E-457, 475,
  528
Martin, Michel, E-317, 319
Martin, Narie, F-15, 33

Martin, Nicolas, E-140, 320
Martin, Paul, E-319-320
Martin, Pierre, C-74, 117
Martin, Pierre, E-22, 30-31, 114,
  149, 262, 313, 316-320, 358,
  457, 475, 499, 528
Martin, Pierre Alexis, C-74
Martin, Pierre Etien, N-195
Martin, Pierre Felix, E-19
Martin, Pierre Marthe, E-320
Martin, Pierre Paul, E-320
Martin, Pierre-Paul, S2-611
Martin, Rene, E-494, 528
Martin, Rene, S1-154, 170
Martin, Renee, E-499
Martin, Rosalie, E-320, 326
Martin, Rose, E-320
Martin, Sophie Amelie, E-320
Martin, Suzanne, E-333
Martin, Theodore, S2-611
Martin, Veronique, S2-611
Martin, Victoire, E-145-146,
  320
Martineau, Anne, E-320
Martineau, Francoise, S2-519
Martineau, Marie, E-320
Martineau, Pierre, E-385
Martinet, Guillaume, E-626
Martinet, Jacques, E-317, 320,
  331
Martinet, Jean, E-626
Martinet, Jean Baptiste, E-588,
  596
Martinet, Joseph, E-317, 320
Martinet, Louis, E-320
Martinet, Marie Anne, E-320
Martinique, E-320-321
Martinique - Cities where reg-
  isters were researched, E-398
Martissan, Jean Francois, E-321
Marugat, Jeanne, E-55
Marvale, Claudine Auguste, E-
  99, 291
Mary, Jeanne, E-412
Maryin, Pierre Felix, E-320
Marzelles, Francois, E-80
Maserolle, Marie, E-103
Mason, Barbe, E-74, 304
Masqueille, Marie Catherine, E-
  174, 391
Masro----, Simon, S3-894

Mass House - Church of St-Laurent, E-213

Masse, Francoise, E-321

Masse, Gille, E-321

Masse, Jeanne, E-15, 321

Masselin, Pierre, S3-888, 896, 898

Masseloc, Francois, E-600

Masson, Francois, E-321-322, 402, 419

Masson, Henriette Sophie, E-322

Masson, Marguerite, E-440

Masson, Marianne, E-61

Masson, Pierre, E-172, 408

Massonneau, Jean, E-144, 381

Massonnier, Pierre, E-315

Masurier, Francois, S3-983

Masurier, Marie, S3-983

Matard, Jacques, E-369

Matelot, Marie Anne, E-288, 322

Matelot, Paderne, E-322

Matelot, Rose, E-289

Matha, Elizabeth, E-322

Mathe, Jeanne, E-440

Mathe, Marianne, E-440

Mathieu, Anne, E-120

Mathieu, Marie, E-280, 322

Mathieu, Pierre, E-169, 358

Mathurin, -----, S3-922

Matrat, Pierre, E-322

Matre, Francois, E-135, 302

Matte, Francoise, S2-477

Maubillon, Anne Marguerite, E-317, 378

Maucretieu, Jean Guillaume, E-281

Maudain, Joseph, E-329

Maudet, Mr., E-302

Mauduit, Louis, E-622

Maudy, Jean, E-419

Maufrais, Marie, S1-256

Mauge, Pierre, E-117, 322

Mauger, Adam, E-571

Mauger, Barthelemy, E-571

Mauger, Francois, E-571

Mauger, Marie Elisabeth, E-571

Mauger, Pierre, E-571

Maugras, Anne, E-41, 91

Maunaud, Marie, E-330

Maunie, Jean Claude, E-322

Maunie, Marie Rose, E-322

Maurau, Francois Marie, E-322

Maurau, Gabriel, E-322

Maurel, Jean Honore, E-140

Maurg, Francoise, E-125

Maurice, Jean, E-53, 63, 105

Maurice, Louis, F-85

Mauron, Jacques, E-262

Maury, Francoise, E-390

Maury, Marie Therese, E-161

Mauselle, Alexis, E-588, 594

Maussion, Annette, E-321, 419

Mauvier, Gilles, S2-611

Mauvier, Jeanne-Michelle, S2-611

Mauvier, Marie-Jeanne, S2-611

Mavby, Anne, E-19

Maxeroune, Marie, E-116

Maxiere, Francois, E-177

Maxime, P., E-33, 407

Maxsonne, Marie, E-98, 275

Mayer, Therese, E-9

Mayer, Xavier, E-267

Mayet, Elisabeth, E-322

Mayet, Etienne, E-322

Mayet, Gregoire, S3-876, 890

Mayet, Jacques, E-322

Mayet, Jacques, S3-876, 890

Mayet, Jean Joseph, E-322

Mayet, Joseph, E-322

Mayet, Louis, E-322

Mayet, Louise, E-322

Maynau, Anne, E-318, 320

Mayou, Francois, E-322, 353

Mayou, Francoise, E-322, 353

Mayrac, Marie, E-137, 278

Mazare, Francois, E-588, 596

Maze, Francois, E-147

Mazerolle, Anne, F-13

Mazerolle, Anne-Francoise, S2-612

Mazerolle, Elizabeth-Marie, S2-612

Mazerolle, Etienne, F-13

Mazerolle, Isabelle, F-13

Mazerolle, Joseph, F-13

Mazerolle, Joseph, S2-612

Mazerolle, Marie, E-352

Mazerolle, Marie, F-13

Mazerolle, Marie-Perpetue, S2-612

Mazerolle, Simon, C-24, 69

Mazerolle, Simon, F-13

Mazerolle, Simon, N-188

Mazerolle, Simon, S1-209, 211

Mazerolle, Simon, S2-612, 762, 770

Mazerolle, Simon-Pierre, S2-612

Maziere, Francois, S2-613, 688

Mazierer, Francois, E-376

Mazieres, Jean, E-322

Mazieres, Marie, E-322, 327

Mazierre, Jean Baptiste, E-322

Mazierre, Marguerite, E-162, 322

Mazurier, Francois, S2-686-687

Mazurier, Francois, S3-1019

Mazurier, Marie, E-626

Mazurier, Marie, S2-685-687

Meaux, Antoine, E-323

Meaux, Jean Pierre, E-323

Meaux, Raymond, E-323

Meaux, Sophie Olympe, E-323

Mechien, Christine, E-40, 266

Mechin, Jeanne, E-22, 328

Mechin, Marie Anne, E-17, 393

Megreau, Angelique, E-73

Megreau, Pierre, E-73

Megrelle, Angelique, E-73

Meguier, Marguerite, E-158, 179

Meguier, Marguerite, S2-441

Mehaut, Mrs., E-258

Meheust, L. (Mrs.), C-vii

Meige, Elisabeth, E-409

Meillon, Jeanne Simone, E-416

Meillon, Simone, E-391, 416

Melaize, Marie Anne, E-173

Melancon, Adelaide Marie Catherine, E-7, 323

Melancon, Amand Fidele, E-323

Melancon, Ambroise, E-7, 47, 323, 484, 528

Melancon, Ambroise, N-134

Melancon, Ambroise, S2-615

Melancon, Angelique, C-31, 97, 136

Melancon, Angelique, N-65, 167

Melancon, Anne, C-82

Melancon, Anne, E-255, 323, 346, 420, 617

Melancon, Anne, S1-149

Melancon, Anne, S2-489, 565, 619

Melancon, Anne, S3-945

Melancon, Anne Josephe, C-87

Melancon, Anne Marie, E-323, 343, 570

Melancon, Anne-Josephe, S2-616-617, 706

Melancon, Anne-Marie, S2-619

Melancon, Cecile, C-79, 161

Melancon, Cecile, E-47, 334-335, 472, 508

Melancon, Cecile, F-39, 97, 99, 103

Melancon, Cecile, N-96, 133-135, 171, 184-185, 203

Melancon, Cecile, S1-126-127, 137, 163

Melancon, Cecile, S2-502

Melancon, Cecile, S3-927

Melancon, Charles, E-323, 457, 475, 484, 528

Melancon, Charles Louis Denis, E-323

Melancon, Charles-Marie, S2-618

Melancon, Cherubain, C-76

Melancon, Claude, E-323

Melancon, Denis, E-275, 323-324

Melancon, Elisabeth, E-323, 523

Melancon, Elisabeth, S3-861

Melancon, Elizabeth, S1-220, 232

Melancon, Elizabeth, S2-614-615

Melancon, Etienne, E-324

Melancon, Etienne, S1-176, 221

Melancon, Etienne, S2-613-615, 617, 748

Melancon, Etienne, S3-856, 859, 861-862

Melancon, Francois, E-151, 325, 570

Melancon, Francois, S2-616

Melancon, Francoise, E-484, 530

Melancon, Francoise, S2-615

Melancon, Francoise-Dorothee, S2-614

Melancon, Francoise-Guille-mette, S2-615

Melancon, Genevieve, E-619, 626

Melancon, Genevieve, S2-614-615, 749

Melancon, Germain, S1-145, 148, 150, 273

Melancon, Germain, S2-489, 616-617

Melancon, Isabelle, E-483, 508

Melancon, Isabelle, S2-618, 748

Melancon, Isabelle-Pelagie, S1-291

Melancon, Jean, C-82

Melancon, Jean, E-124, 183, 271, 323, 419, 508, 528, 561, 570, 604

Melancon, Jean, F-109

Melancon, Jean, N-72

Melancon, Jean, S1-341

Melancon, Jean, S2-613, 615-616, 619

Melancon, Jean, S3-1118

Melancon, Jean Baptiste, E-7, 125, 323-325, 433, 570

Melancon, Jean Charles, E-323

Melancon, Jean Joseph, E-7

Melancon, Jean Louis, E-324

Melancon, Jean-Baptiste, S2-619

Melancon, Jeanne, F-47, 49

Melancon, Jeanne, N-32, 138

Melancon, Jeanne, S1-157

Melancon, Jeanne, S2-638-639

Melancon, Jeanne, S3-1107

Melancon, Jerome Marie, C-76

Melancon, Joseph, E-8, 37, 95, 124, 324, 570

Melancon, Joseph, F-103

Melancon, Joseph, S1-106, 125, 147, 149, 176, 290

Melancon, Joseph, S2-564, 613-740, 748

Melancon, Joseph, S3-856, 945

Melancon, Joseph Michel, E-7

Melancon, Joseph-Marie, S2-617

Melancon, La Blanche, S2-615

Melancon, Louis Charles Denis, E-324

Melancon, Louis Francois Marie, E-324

Melancon, Louis Michel, E-324

Melancon, Louise, C-129

Melancon, Louise Rosalie, E-81

Melancon, Madeleine, N-20, 72, 105, 135, 203, 231, 253

Melancon, Madeleine, S1-341

Melancon, Madeleine, S2-522, 533, 565, 615-616

Melancon, Magdeleine, C-13

Melancon, Magdeleine, E-1, 41, 74, 150-151, 162, 165, 484, 509, 561

Melancon, Magdeleine, S3-844, 877, 1118

Melancon, Marguerite, C-161

Melancon, Marguerite, E-8, 96, 108, 150-151, 283-284, 302, 420-421, 427, 508, 570

Melancon, Marguerite, F-57, 59

Melancon, Marguerite, S1-176

Melancon, Marguerite, S2-564, 618-619, 739

Melancon, Marguerite, S3-952

Melancon, Marguerite Fran-coise, E-324, 619

Melancon, Marguerite-Fran-coise, S2-614-615

Melancon, Marie, E-89, 95-96, 113, 324, 484, 508, 557, 619

Melancon, Marie, S1-147, 158, 176

Melancon, Marie, S2-440, 461, 524, 566, 614-619, 748-749

Melancon, Marie, S3-859, 862

Melancon, Marie Cecile, C-79

Melancon, Marie Francoise, E-324

Melancon, Marie Josephe, E-8, 116, 118-119, 124, 324

Melancon, Marie Josephe, S1-290

Melancon, Marie Josephe Lucie, E-324

Melancon, Marie Louise, C-30-31, 76, 92, 129, 152

Melancon, Marie Louise, E-324

Melancon, Marie Magdelaine, F-109

Melancon, Marie Magdeleine, E-8, 152, 162, 314, 324, 350, 570

Melancon, Marie Marguerite, E-324, 416

Melancon, Marie Marthe, E-161, 167, 324, 570

Melancon, Marie Yvonne, E-324

Melancon, Marie-Josephe-Lucie, S2-614-615

Melancon, Marie-Madeleine, S2-619

Melancon, Marie-Marthe, S2-619

Melancon, Michel Joseph, E-324

Melancon, Ositte, E-53, 302

Melancon, Ozite, S2-617

Melancon, Paul, E-528

Melancon, Paul, S2-618

Melancon, Perrine, C-76

Melancon, Philippe, E-508, 528

Melancon, Philippe, S2-618

Melancon, Pierre, C-30, 75-77, 109, 152

Melancon, Pierre, E-16, 37, 81, 173, 274, 323, 325, 350, 433, 457, 475, 484, 508, 528, 557, 570

Melancon, Pierre, S2-618-619, 638-639

Melancon, Pierre Francois, E-7, 325

Melancon, Pierre Louis Francois, C-76

Melancon, Pierre Louis Francois, E-325

Melancon, Rosalie, E-152

Melancon, Rose Hyacinthe, E-325

Melancon, Rose Rosalie, E-8, 570

Melancon, Rose-Rosalie, S2-619

Melay, Rene, S1-119

Melays, -----, S3-1090

Melays, Julien, S2-619

Melays, Rene, E-132, 315, 325

Melays, Rene, S1-172

Melays, Rene, S2-567, 619-620

Mele, Janne, S3-1147

Melere, Anne, N-177

Melin, Francois, E-20

Melin, Marie, E-20, 325

Melle, Michel, E-344

Melliard, Perrine, C-161

Mellion, Madeleine, S1-257

Melococinieur, R., S3-869

Melon, Jean, E-409

Meminyac, -----, S3-846

Menage, Jean Baptiste, E-325, 432

Menanceau, Joseph, E-325

Menancon, Joseph, S3-939, 941, 949

Menancon, Pierre, S3-941

Menant, Francoise, E-272

Menard, Anne, E-89, 386

Menard, Francois, E-169, 325

Menard, Jacques, S1-3

Menard, Jean, E-38, 144, 169, 194, 325, 402

Menard, Julienne Janne Francoise, S3-1096

Menard, Julienne-Jeanne-Francoise, S2-652

Menard, Louis, F-65

Menard, Marguerite, E-122, 387

Menard, Pierre, E-326, 436

Menard, Pierre, F-65

Menard, Rene, E-169

Menard, Simon, E-97

Menasso, Joseph, S3-930

Menier, Francoise Thomase, E-325, 420

Menier, M.A., C-vii

Menniser, Jean Julien, E-325

Menniser, Mathurin Jean, E-325

Menot, Yves, S1-16

Menou, Catherine, E-350, 372

Menu, Michel, E-63

Mequet, Christope, S2-620

Mequet, Christophe, S3-981

Mequet, Nicolas, S1-85, 337

Mequet, Nicolas, S3-981, 984, 1073

Mequet, Nicolas Guillaume Michel, S3-981

Mequet, Nicolas-Guillaume-Michel, S2-620

Mequet, Simeon, S3-981

Merand, Henriette, E-325, 392

Merceau, Joseph, E-630, 632

Mercereau, Angelique, E-340, 406

Merceron, Jeanne, E-21

Merceron, Pierre, E-325, 337

Merchand, Joseph, E-14

Merchand, Louis, E-14

Mercier, Alexandre, E-516

Mercier, Anne, E-325

Mercier, Elisabeth, E-13, 69, 325, 418

Mercier, Francois, E-325

Mercier, Jean Baptiste, E-376

Mercier, Joseph, E-516

Mercier, Julien, E-139, 325

Mercier, Louis, E-190-191, 326

Mercier, Louis Andre, E-326

Mercier, Magdelaine, E-516

Mercier, Marie, E-456, 472

Mercier, Marie Francoise Cecile, E-326

Mercier, Marie Joseph, E-516

Mercier, Paul, E-114, 142, 174, 326, 370

Mercier, Pierre, E-17, 34, 191, 318, 325-326, 475

Merenand, Marie Anne, E-117

Mererer, Francois, E-272

Mergreau, Antoine, E-73, 588, 592

Merienne, Genevieve, S2-487

Meritte, Francois, E-301

Merle, Francois, C-110-111

Merle, Jean, E-326, 337

Merle, Pierre, E-22, 326, 337

Merloteau, Michel, E-320, 326

Merloteau, Pierre, E-320, 326

Merven, Jan, S3-976

Merveu, Tanguy, S3-1028

Merville, Victoire, E-387

Mervin, Guillaume, S1-159

Mervin, Guillaume, S2-620

Mervin, Jean, S2-620

Mervin, Sophie, S2-620

Meryain, Joseph, S2-662

Merzeau, Jacques, E-101, 326

Merzeau, Marie, E-101, 326

Mesilliere, Mr., E-387
Meslan, Pierre, E-139, 284
Mesle, Guillaume, S2-685
Mesle, Janne, S3-1147
Mesle, Jeanne, S1-194
Mesle, Mathurinne, S1-195
Mesle, Rene, S3-1090
Mesrolle, Marie, E-27, 98
Messeme, Emeery de, C-32
Mestre, Joseph, C-131
Metay, Pierre Andre, E-358
Metayer, Jacques, E-155
Metayer, Jean, E-328, 392
Metayer, Jeanne, E-155, 326,
  376
Metayer, Marie, E-326, 376
Metayer, Pierre, E-155, 326, 376
Meteran, Francois, N-206
Metivier, Marie Anne, E-358
Metot, Marie, F-39
Metot, Marie, N-39, 208
Metra, Anne Marguerite, F-81
Metra, Anne Marguerite, S3-
  1151
Metra, Anne-Marguerite, S2-
  621
Metra, Jacques, C-76
Metra, Jacques, F-81
Metra, Jacques, S2-621
Metra, Jacques, S3-842, 858
Metra, Jean, C-77
Metra, Jean, F-81
Metra, Jean, N-213
Metra, Jean, S1-131, 152, 390
Metra, Jean, S2-442, 621, 678
Metra, Jean, S3-837, 839, 842,
  853, 855, 858, 1151
Metra, Jean Nicolas, N-131
Metra, Joseph, F-55
Metra, Joseph, N-97, 131
Metra, Marie Modeste, C-77
Metra, Nicolas, C-77
Metra, Nicolas, F-55
Metra, Nicolas, N-97, 130-131,
  213
Metra, Nicolas, S2-621
Metra, Nicolas, S3-842, 858
Meunier, Catherine, N-111
Meunier, Catherine, S1-235
Meunier, Catherine, S2-554
Meunier, Jean, E-326

Meunier, Marie, S1-154, 170
Meunier, Nicolas, C-61
Meunier, Prosper, E-326, 376
Meyer, Francois, E-626
Meynard, Elisabeth, E-177
Meyracq, Laurens Domeinge, E-
  278, 326
Micaud, Bernard, E-588, 595
Michaud, Gabrielle, E-134, 389
Michaud, Marie, E-18, 90
Michaud, Pierre, E-357
Michaut, Francois, E-326
Michaut, Georges, E-326, 364
Michaut, Jean, E-292
Michel, Alexandre, S2-623
Michel, Anne, C-28, 67, 78
Michel, Anne, E-121
Michel, Anne, F-31, 39, 61
Michel, Anne, N-45, 48, 105,
  132, 212, 231
Michel, Anne, S1-242, 283, 330
Michel, Anne, S2-539, 561,
  716-718
Michel, Anne, S3-982, 1058,
  1080
Michel, Anne-Josephe, S2-622
Michel, Anne-Marguerite, S2-
  622, 624
Michel, Antoine, E-326
Michel, Basile, E-115, 327, 637,
  644-645
Michel, Catherine, S1-341
Michel, Catherinne, S3-1118
Michel, Cecile, C-20, 53
Michel, Cecile, F-77, 81
Michel, Cecile, N-32
Michel, Cecile, S1-130, 132,
  151-152
Michel, Cecile, S2-442, 621
Michel, Cecile, S3-842, 853
Michel, child, E-326
Michel, Elizabeth, E-439-440
Michel, Euphrosine, C-78
Michel, Euphrosone, N-132
Michel, Francois, C-77-78
Michel, Francois, E-141, 475,
  528
Michel, Francois, F-61, 63
Michel, Francois, N-131-132,
  190, 231, 241

Michel, Francois, S2-555, 621-
  623
Michel, Francois, S3-1080
Michel, Francoise, S1-136, 223
Michel, Gabriel, E-327
Michel, Gertrude, F-45
Michel, Gertrude, N-132
Michel, Gertrude, S1-196
Michel, Gertrude-Olive, S2-624
Michel, indian, E-326
Michel, Isidore, E-327
Michel, Jacques, E-327
Michel, Jean, E-78
Michel, Jean, N-132
Michel, Jean Louis, C-78
Michel, Jean-Pierre, S2-622
Michel, Jeanne, E-83, 406
Michel, Jeanne, S2-624
Michel, Jeanne-Jacquemine, S2-
  623
Michel, Joseph, C-78
Michel, Joseph, F-45
Michel, Joseph, N-132
Michel, Joseph, S2-624-625
Michel, Joseph-Francois, S2-
  624
Michel, Joseph-Marie, S2-621
Michel, Louis, C-65
Michel, Louis, F-31
Michel, Louis, N-48, 105, 212,
  231
Michel, Louis, S2-561
Michel, Louis, S3-1080
Michel, Louis Mathieu, E-327
Michel, Madeleine, S2-677, 725
Michel, Magdelaine, F-45
Michel, Magdelaine, E-327
Michel, Magdeleine, S3-855
Michel, Marguerite, C-74, 78-
  79, 153
Michel, Marguerite, E-114, 327
Michel, Marguerite, F-39
Michel, Marguerite, N-131-132,
  134
Michel, Marie, E-53, 327
Michel, Marie, F-45, 61, 63
Michel, Marie, N-132
Michel, Marie, S1-248, 250
Michel, Marie, S2-624, 713-714
Michel, Marie Anne, E-327
Michel, Marie Josephe, N-60

Michel, Marie Louise, N-132
Michel, Marie Madeleine, C-78
Michel, Marie Madeleine, N-132
Michel, Marie-Josephe, S2-456
Michel, Marie-Madeleine, S2-622, 624, 726
Michel, Mathurin, S2-623
Michel, Mr., E-53
Michel, Olivier, S2-623
Michel, Olivier-Henry, S2-623
Michel, Pierre, C-78
Michel, Pierre, E-327, 364
Michel, Pierre, F-45
Michel, Pierre, N-132
Michel, Pierre, S1-118, 349
Michel, Pierre, S2-624-625, 663
Michel, Pierre-Thomas-Marie, S2-625
Michel, Rose, E-141, 327
Michel, Rose Marguerite, C-77
Michel, Rose-Marguerite, S2-622
Michel, Suliac-Germain, S2-624
Michel, Therese, S2-623
Michel, Victoire-Euphrosine, S2-622
Michelet, Jean, E-64
Michelle, Cecile, S2-580
Michelle, Marguerite, E-113
Michelon, Catherine, E-350
Michelon, Desiree, E-99, 126
Midi, Francois, E-172, 256
Midy, Etienne, E-156
Mien, Genevieve, E-283
Mieuce, Rosalie, S3-1039
Mieusse, Claire, E-191
Mieusse, Marguerite, E-183, 281
Mignault, Alexis, E-515
Mignault, Cecile, E-515
Mignault, Jean, E-515
Mignault, Jean Aubin, E-475
Migneau, Cecile, E-529
Mignon, Pierre, E-333
Miguel, Mr., E-146, 342
Milaire, Marie Francoise, E-327
Milaire, Nicolas, E-327
Milanais, Jacques Barthelemy, E-327

Milanais, Marie Genevieve, E-327
Milcent, Marie Rose, E-309, 340
Milion, Simone, E-40
Mille, Michel, E-160
Miller, Nicolas, E-588, 596
Millet, Anne, E-304
Millet, Gabriel, E-355
Millet, Guillaume, E-327
Millet, Jean, E-313
Millet, Louis, E-322, 327
Millet, Marie, E-313
Millet, Suzanne, E-270, 327
Millient, Francois, E-68, 327
Million, Jean, E-303, 327
Million, Louis, E-327, 393
Million, Marie, E-327
Million, Marie Pelagie, E-303, 327, 393
Millon, Anne, E-11, 174
Millon, Pelagie, E-293
Millort, Pallagie, E-292, 307
Millou, Jeanne Simone, E-295
Milly, Gaspard, E-22
Milly, Jean, E-22
Milly, Margueritte Catherine, E-51
Milly, Sieur Jean, E-51
Milly de la Croix, Anne Francoise, E-110
Milly de la Croix, Michel, E-110
Milly La Croix, Gaspard, E-328
Milly La Croix, Jean, E-328
Milly La Croix, Margueritte Catherine, E-328
Milly La Croix, Marie, E-328
Milly La Croix, Michel, E-328
Milly LaCroix, Catherine, E-343
Milly-Boutin, Marguerite, E-154
Milon, Marie, E-370, 376
Milon, Rose, E-257
Milord, Nicolas, E-114, 328
Milot, Eulalie, E-40, 166
Milot, Laurent, E-40
Mimet, Jeanne, E-20
Minaud, Jean, E-328, 370, 392
Minaud, Pierre, E-328, 370, 392
Mine, Jeanne, E-23, 82
Mineaud, Francois, E-22
Minet, Elisabeth, E-275, 294
Minet, Julienne, E-336, 352

Minet, Julienne, S2-633
Mingot, Elisabeth, E-34, 318
Miniac, Allain, S2-580
Miniac, Guillaume, S2-669
Miniac, Guillaume, S3-833, 854, 860
Miniac, Pierre, S3-862, 869
Minouet, Marguerite, E-379
Minoux, Alain, S3-1150
Minoux, Francoise, S3-1150
Minoux, Perine, S3-1099
Miot, Jean Nicolas, E-70, 328
Miot, Marie, E-70, 328
Miot, Renee, E-100
Mioulee, Allain, S3-830
Mira, Cecile, E-363
Mirabeau, Ignace, E-100
Mirande, Baptiste, E-552
Mirande, Charle, E-552
Mirande, Esther Barbe, E-328
Mirande, Francoise, E-522
Mirande, George, E-328
Mirande, Georges, N-195
Mirande, Jean, E-328
Mirande, Jean Baptiste, E-29, 328
Mirande, Jean Baptiste Alexis, E-328
Mirande, Joseph, E-80, 528
Mirande, Marie, E-552
Mirande, Paul, E-552
Mirande, Pierre, E-552
Mirande, Pierre Joseph, E-328
Mirande, Therese, E-526
Mirandy, Josephe, E-80
Mirant, Genevieve, E-16, 137
Mirassou, Marthe, E-266, 411
Mirat, Marie Josephe, E-106
Mire, Henri, E-329
Mire, Jean, E-329
Mire, Jean Baptiste, E-329
Mire, Jean Louis, E-329
Mire, Marie Jeanne, E-329
Mire, Pierre, E-329
Mireau, Joseph Demiur, E-107
Mireau, Marie, E-107, 329, 334
Mirey, Pierre, E-103
Mius, Abraham, E-329, 475
Mius, Anastasie, S2-625-626
Mius, Benjamin, S2-560, 625-626

Mius, Cecile, S1-276

Mius, Charles, E-506

Mius, Claire, E-182, 187, 190-191

Mius, Firmin, S2-625

Mius, Jacques, E-475

Mius, Jean-Baptiste, S2-625

Mius, Marguerite, E-506

Mius, Marie, E-90, 329

Mius, Marie-Josephe, S2-625-626

Mius, Rosalie, S2-583, 585

Mius, Veronique, S2-625

Mius - See also d'Entremont

Mius D'Entremont, Benjamin, N-113

Mius D'Entremont, Cecile, N-107

Mius D'Entremont, Joseph, N-107

Mius D'Entremont, Magdelaine, E-479

Mius D'Entremont, Marie, E-475

Mius D'Entremont, Marie Josephe, N-107

Mius D'Entremont, Philippe, E-476, 479

Mius d'Entremont, Cecile, C-35, 65

Mius d'Entremont, Cecile, F-61, 71

Mius d'Entremont, Jacques, F-103

Mius d'Entremont, Jacques Ferdinand, F-103

Mius d'Entremont, Joseph, C-65

Mius d'Entremont, Marie Joseph, C-64

Mius d'Entremont, Marie Josephe, F-61

Miusse, Benjamin, S3-989

Moguet, Francois, E-61, 140

Moine, Gabriel, E-430

Moine, Juliene, F-109

Moine, Martine, E-17

Moineau, Louise, E-91, 357

Moineette, Marguerite, S2-512

Moinet, Julien, S3-1017

Moinette, Marguerite, E-44, 255

Moinot, Marie Anne, E-90

Moisant, Francois, E-144, 316

Moissard, Antoine, E-625

Moitie, Michel, E-439

Moitier, Renez, E-418

Molet, Jean, E-329

Mollard, Antoine, F-29

Mollay, Catherine, E-69, 370

Molle, Catherine, S2-680

Mondion, Gabriel, C-78

Mondion, Jean Baptiste de, C-1, 78, 117, 119

Mondion, Pierre Jean Baptiste, C-78

Mondion, Rene, C-79

Mondon, Ely, S3-962

Mondon, Francoise, S2-594

Mondon, Francoise, S3-962, 992

Mondon, Thomas, S2-594

Mondon, Thomas, S3-962

Monet, Antoine, E-66, 329

Monet, Francois, E-17, 61

Monet, Marie Francoise, E-571

Monet, Nicolas, E-329

Monet, Nicolas Bernard, E-329

Monezeau, Ludivine, C-11

Monge, Mr., E-369

Monge, Odile, E-344, 386

Monier, Andre, E-36

Monier, Louis, E-374

Monier dit Surgise, Andre, E-105

Monineau, Pierre, E-172, 174, 298

Moniot, Alex. Bernard, E-588, 591

Moniot, Marie, E-406

Moniquet, Jacques Alexis, E-313

Monjean, Jean Jacques, E-329, 331

Monjean, Marc Elie, E-329, 331

Monmouceau, Susanne, E-345

Monnerie, Francois, E-61, 138, 142-143, 316, 347, 392, 408

Monnerie, George, E-275, 337

Monnerie, Jean Francois, E-152, 169

Monnet, Nicolas, E-418

Monnier, Anne, E-159, 329

Monnier, Claude, E-330

Monnier, Francois, E-61

Monnier, Jean, E-134, 330, 377

Monnier, Jean Baptiste, E-330

Monnier, Jean Claude, E-54, 330

Monnier, Jeanne, E-22

Monnier, Mathieu, E-330

Monnier, Pierre, E-87, 148

Monnier, Sophie Gertrude, E-330

Monnierie, Francois, E-338

Monnot, Michel, E-330

Monory, Mr., E-160

Monpeza, Jean, E-114, 319

Mons, Cecile, S1-218

Mons, Cecile-Charlotte, S2-626

Mons, Elizabeth, E-100, 330

Mons, Francois, S2-626

Mons, Marie, S2-626

Mons, Pierre, E-330

Mons, Pierre, S2-626

Montagne, Jacques, E-359

Montaine, Anne Agathe, E-330

Montaine, Pierre, E-330

Montalembert de Cers, Jean, E-71

Montalembert de Cers, Pierre, E-71

Montamat, Francois, E-330

Montamat, Jean Francois, E-330

Montamat, Jean Pierre, E-330

Montamat, Louis, E-330

Montamat, Marie Adeleide, E-330

Montamat, Marie Louise, E-330

Montamat, Marie Victoire, E-330

Montard, Louis, E-1, 22, 259

Montard, Suzanne, E-259, 330

Montary, Jacques, E-318

Montary, Jacques, S2-517

Montary, Marguerite, E-320

Montassier, Jean, E-44, 152

Montaudi, Jacques, E-255

Montaudi, Jacques, S2-513

Montaury, Margueritte, E-160

Montaury, Marie, E-345-346

Montaury, Pierre, E-102, 111, 319

Montet, Francoise, F-109

Montet, Guillaume, E-330-331, 425, 440, 571, 580

Montet, Jean Baptiste, F-109
Montet, Jean Baptiste Guillaume, E-330
Montet, Jeanne Marie, E-331
Montet, Joseph, F-109
Montet, Joseph Adam, E-331
Montet, Marguerite, E-331
Montet, Marguerite, F-109
Montet, Marie Elizabeth, E-331
Montet, Marie Francoise, E-331
Montet, Pierre, E-571
Montet, Pierre, F-109
Montet, Pierre Paul, E-331
Montet, Pierre Paul, F-109
Montet, Pierre Vincent, E-331
Monthorie, Marguerite, E-135
Montigaud, Marie, E-325
Montmillian, Marie Genevieve, E-298, 331
Montorg, Marguerite, E-301
Montory, Anne, S2-627
Montory, Gregoire, S2-627
Montory, Jacques, E-331
Montory, Jacques, S2-626-627
Montory, Jacques-Aubin, S2-627
Montory, Jean Francois, E-331
Montory, Jean-Baptiste, S2-627
Montory, Joseph, S2-627
Montory, Louis, S2-627
Montory, Marie, E-331
Montory, Marie Joseph, E-331
Montory, Marie-Rose, S2-627
Montory, Pierre, E-331
Montory, Pierre, S2-626
Montours, Jacques, S2-603
Montreal, Louis Francois, F-41
Monvilain, Janne, S3-994
Monvilain, Jeanne, S2-452
Moquet, Louise Francoise, E-60
Moran, Gabriel, E-331
Moran, Marie Anne Barbe, E-331
Morand, Genevieve, E-137, 314
Morand, Julienne, S2-428
Morand, Pierre, S2-428
Morange, Jean, F-97
Morbihan - Department in France, E-331
Mordant, Joseph, E-329, 331
Mordant, Louise, E-329

Moreau, Andre, E-72, 137
Moreau, Anne, F-17
Moreau, Elisabeth, E-172
Moreau, Elizabeth, E-316, 331
Moreau, Etienne, E-144, 332
Moreau, Francois, C-133
Moreau, Francois Marie, E-331
Moreau, Francois Marie, F-17
Moreau, Gabriel, E-331-332
Moreau, Gabriel, F-17
Moreau, Germain Marie, E-332
Moreau, Germain Marie, F-17
Moreau, Guillaume, S3-1050
Moreau, Isay, E-331
Moreau, Jacques, C-43
Moreau, Jacques, E-137
Moreau, Jean, E-112, 332
Moreau, Jeanne, E-28, 332
Moreau, Louis, E-100, 332
Moreau, Marguerite, E-316, 331
Moreau, Marie, E-36, 144, 319, 332
Moreau, Marie Anne Barbe, E-332
Moreau, Marie Madeleine, E-127, 390
Moreau, Maximin, F-17
Moreau, Pierre, E-160
Moreau, Pierre, S3-825
Moreau, Pierre Vincent, E-332
Moreau, Pierre Vincent, F-17
Moreau, Sebastien, E-160
Moreau, Susanne, E-12
Moreau, Susanne, E-65
Moreau, Susanne, E-65, 292
Morel, Anne Marie, E-143
Morel, Elisabeth, E-84-85, 332
Morel, Fleury, E-332, 346
Morel, Jean, E-332
Morel, Jean Baptiste, E-332, 346
Morel, Jean Baptiste Louis, E-332
Morel, Jean Francois, E-145, 268, 332
Morel, Jean Henry, E-81, 149
Morel, Jean Pierre, N-184
Morel, Jean-Henry, S1-337
Morel, Joseph, N-133, 184
Morel, Louis, N-133, 135, 184
Morel, Louis Jean, N-185
Morel, Marguerite, E-308-309

Morel, Marie, E-262, 295
Morel, Marie, F-11
Morel, Marie, S2-581
Morel, Rene, E-120, 384
Morel, Vauve, C-112
Morelais, Marguerite, E-193
Morice, Mr., E-128
Moricon, Guillaume, N-247
Morie, Anne, E-458, 514
Morillon, Perrine, E-137
Morin, Antoine, E-514
Morin, Antoine, S3-1028
Morin, Catherine, E-144, 304, 332
Morin, Charles, E-514
Morin, Claude, E-269, 293, 304, 332
Morin, Constance, E-162
Morin, Gregoire, E-294
Morin, Jacques, E-514
Morin, Jacques Francois, E-514
Morin, Jean, E-514
Morin, Louis, E-514
Morin, Louise, S2-731
Morin, Magdeleine, E-269, 332
Morin, Marguerite, E-514
Morin, Marguerite, S1-122
Morin, Marie, E-473, 514
Morin, Pierre, E-325, 457, 476, 517
Morin, Reine Elisabeth, E-191
Morisset, Antoine, E-262
Morisset, Charles, E-108
Morisset, Elie, E-55
Morisset, Marie, E-19, 262
Morissonneau, Jean, E-71, 348
Morlaix, E-333
Morlaix and the Acadians, E-333
Morlan, Antoine, S2-628
Morland, Antoine, E-333, 588, 595
Morland, Francois, E-65, 297, 333, 588, 595
Morland, J.H., E-588, 595
Morland, Jean Gilles, E-297, 333
Morland, Joseph, E-333
Morrea, Esthere, E-188
Morvan, Antoine, E-333
Morvan, Jan, S3-991

Morvan, Jean, S1-321

Morvan, Jean, S3-991

Morvan, Louise Francoise, E-333

Morvan, Marie Gillette, S3-991

Morvan, Marie Louise, E-333, 418

Morvan, Marie-Gillette, S1-321

Morvan, Marin, S3-991

Morvan, Pierre, E-73, 275

Morvan, Rene, S3-991

Morvan, Yves, E-333, 418

Mosquito Cove now known as Thorne Cove, E-209

Mosser, Adam, E-571

Motorie, Anne, E-619, 603

Mouchet, Marie, S1-262

Mouchet, Marie, S3-1028

Mouchon, Jacques, E-333, 369

Mouet, Martin, E-256, 333, 404

Mougin, Jacques, E-63

Moulaisant, Marguerite, E-116

Moulaison, Anne, E-30, 107, 334, 433

Moulaison, Caesar Auguste, E-334

Moulaison, Cecile, C-161

Moulaison, Etienne, C-79

Moulaison, Etienne, E-334

Moulaison, Etienne, N-134-135

Moulaison, Felicite, C-83, 161

Moulaison, Felicite, E-47, 192-194, 334

Moulaison, Felicite, N-96, 135, 171, 185

Moulaison, Francois, C-79

Moulaison, Francois, E-334, 374

Moulaison, Francois, N-133

Moulaison, Francois Joseph, N-133

Moulaison, Gabriel, C-36

Moulaison, Gabriel, E-15, 163, 334, 359

Moulaison, Gabriel, F-77

Moulaison, Gabriel, N-134

Moulaison, Gabriel, S1-366

Moulaison, Jacques, C-142-143

Moulaison, Jacques, C-79-80

Moulaison, Jacques, E-334-335

Moulaison, Jacques, F-39, 99

Moulaison, Jacques, N-96, 133-135, 171, 184-185, 203

Moulaison, Jacques, S1-127

Moulaison, Jean Baptiste, E-334

Moulaison, Jean Louis Francois, N-133

Moulaison, Jean Pierre, N-135

Moulaison, Jeanne, E-118, 334

Moulaison, Joseph, E-334-335

Moulaison, Joseph, F-77

Moulaison, Louis Auguste, C-161

Moulaison, Ludivine, C-46, 161

Moulaison, Magdalen, E-334

Moulaison, Magdeleine, C-10

Moulaison, Marguerite, C-122-124, 128

Moulaison, Marguerite, C-2, 6, 10, 36-37, 57, 60, 85, 161

Moulaison, Marguerite, E-115-118

Moulaison, Marguerite, N-92, 250

Moulaison, Marie, E-271

Moulaison, Marie, N-135

Moulaison, Marie Anne, N-184

Moulaison, Marie Anne Francoise Therese, N-135

Moulaison, Marie Felicite, N-171

Moulaison, Marie Francoise, N-133, 184

Moulaison, Marie Josephe, C-10

Moulaison, Marie Josephe, E-31

Moulaison, Marie Josephe, E-31, 106

Moulaison, Marie Josephe, F-19

Moulaison, Marie Magdalen, E-163

Moulaison, Marie Modeste, E-47, 193

Moulaison, Marie Modeste, F-99

Moulaison, Marie Sophie, N-134

Moulaison, Marie Therese Julie, C-79

Moulaison, Marie Therese Julie, E-334

Moulaison, Marie Therese Julie, N-133

Moulaison, Marie-Modeste, S1-127-128

Moulaison, Marie-Modeste, S2-504

Moulaison, Modeste, E-47, 334

Moulaison, Pierre, C-124

Moulaison, Pierre, E-60, 334

Moulaison, Pierre, F-77

Moulaison, Pierre, N-72, 135, 185, 203

Moulaison, Rose, C-79-80

Moulaison, Rose, F-39

Moulaison, Rose, N-134

Moulaison, Sophie, F-39

Moulaison, Sophie, N-134

Moulaison, Therese Adelaide, C-79

Moulaison, Therese Adelaide, N-133

Moulaison, Victoire, C-161

Moulaison, Victoire, N-135

Moulaison, Victoire Marguerite, E-335

Mouleon, Marie Modeste, E-334

Moulin, Auguste, E-335

Moulin, Julien, S3-913-915

Moulin, Louis, E-186

Moulin, Michel, S3-916

Moulin, Nicolas, E-29, 172

Moulin, Pierre, E-335

Mouline, Charles, S3-1095

Moultin, Marie Magdelaine, E-27

Mounerie, Francois, E-30, 169, 335

Mounerie, Georges, E-107

Mounerie, Jean Francois, E-326

Mounier, Anne, E-80

Mounier, Claude, E-335

Mounier, Louis, E-63, 335

Mounier, Marie, E-40

Mounier, Marie Louise, E-335

Mouquet, -----, N-210

Mous, Francois, S2-471

Mous, Francois, S3-1097

Mousseau, Francois, E-315

Mousseau, Marie, E-142, 256

Mousseau, Pierre, E-35, 315

Mousset, Antoine, E-335

Mousset, Catherine, E-89, 337

Mousset, Michel, E-335

Moussion, Jean, E-270
Mousson, Jacques, S2-735
Mousson, Jeanne, S2-669
Moustie, Louis, E-126
Moutardier, Louis, E-363
Mouthier, Jacques, C-22
Moutier, Jean Louis Charles, E-81
Moutier, Pierre Guillaume, E-159
Mouton, Abraham, E-600
Mouton, Angelique, E-195-196, 335, 438
Mouton, Antoine, E-335
Mouton, Antoinette, E-335
Mouton, Antoinette Angelique, E-335
Mouton, Appoline, E-335
Mouton, Charles, E-600
Mouton, Denis Francois, E-335
Mouton, Emmanuel Guillaume, E-335
Mouton, Emmanuel Jean Baptiste Louis, E-335
Mouton, Francois, E-335-336
Mouton, Georges, E-600
Mouton, Guillaume, E-195
Mouton, Guillaume Royer, E-336
Mouton, Jean, E-77, 134, 289, 335-336, 528
Mouton, Jean, S1-358
Mouton, Jerome, E-55, 77, 135, 335-336
Mouton, Julien, E-336
Mouton, Louis, E-336
Mouton, Louise Catherine, E-336
Mouton, Madeleine, E-329
Mouton, Marguerite, C-54-55, 61
Mouton, Marguerite, E-181, 183, 187, 336
Mouton, Marguerite, F-71, 73, 107
Mouton, Marguerite, N-87, 233
Mouton, Marie Jeanne Catherine, E-336
Mouton, Nicolas Guillaume, E-336
Mouton, Philippe, E-18, 180

Movan, Perine, E-72
Moy, Francois, E-159
Moyne, Jean Baptiste Francois Xavier, E-191
Moynot, Marie Anne, E-90
Moyse, Anne, E-124, 283
Moyse, Anne, F-95
Moyse, Anne, S1-378-380
Moyse, Anne, S2-497, 570-571, 632
Moyse, Anne, S3-1113
Moyse, Anne-Marie, S2-632
Moyse, Basile Jean, N-136
Moyse, Bazile, C-162
Moyse, Bazile-Ignace, S2-631
Moyse, Benoni, S3-854, 902, 1027, 1135-1136
Moyse, Benonie, S1-94, 116, 379
Moyse, Benonie-Estienne, S2-630
Moyse, Benony, C-80, 162
Moyse, Benony, N-135-136, 247
Moyse, Benony, S2-628, 630-632, 671
Moyse, Cecile, N-64, 178
Moyse, Cecile, S1-116, 156, 298, 306, 379, 384, 392
Moyse, Cecile, S2-483, 510, 629-632, 661, 671
Moyse, Cecile, S3-1138
Moyse, Charles, C-162
Moyse, Charles, E-24, 329
Moyse, Charles, N-136
Moyse, Cyprien Benony, N-136
Moyse, Donatien, C-162
Moyse, Felicite, E-191
Moyse, Francois, C-157
Moyse, Francois, E-188, 528
Moyse, Francois, E-329
Moyse, Francois, N-136
Moyse, Francois, S1-285, 380
Moyse, Francois, S2-445, 628-633
Moyse, Francois, S3-1103, 1110
Moyse, Francois-Alexandre, S2-630
Moyse, Francois-Jean, S2-631
Moyse, Francoise, E-329, 370
Moyse, Francoise, S1-68

Moyse, Gertrude, S2-632
Moyse, Jean, C-19, 80, 162
Moyse, Jean, N-137
Moyse, Jean, S1-115-116, 299, 379
Moyse, Jean, S2-628, 630
Moyse, Jean, S3-823, 827, 854, 1027, 1105, 1110, 1112, 1127, 1138
Moyse, Jean Baptiste, N-26, 135, 137
Moyse, Jean Baptste, S3-929, 1103
Moyse, Jean-Baptiste, S2-628, 631-632
Moyse, Jean-Joseph, S2-630
Moyse, Jeanne, C-81, 83
Moyse, Jeanne, F-21
Moyse, Jeanne, N-78, 139, 142, 220
Moyse, Jeanne, S2-641-642, 660-661
Moyse, Jeanne, S3-912, 1027
Moyse, Joseph, C-162
Moyse, Joseph, E-124
Moyse, Joseph, F-47
Moyse, Joseph, N-137
Moyse, Joseph, S1-380
Moyse, Joseph, S2-629-630, 632-633
Moyse, Joseph, S3-1103, 1110
Moyse, Joseph Basile, C-80
Moyse, Joseph-Francois, S2-632
Moyse, Joseph-Pierre, S2-633
Moyse, Josephe, S2-632
Moyse, Louis, E-329
Moyse, Louis, F-67
Moyse, Louis, N-136, 143
Moyse, Louis, S2-671
Moyse, Madeleine, E-124
Moyse, Madeleine, N-60
Moyse, Madeleine, S1-291-293
Moyse, Madeleine, S3-1105
Moyse, Marguerite, C-162
Moyse, Marguerite, E-277
Moyse, Marguerite, S1-285-286
Moyse, Marguerite, S2-629
Moyse, Marguerite, S3-1103
Moyse, Marguerite-Jean, S2-628
Moyse, Marie, C-19, 162
Moyse, Marie, F-47, 67, 107

Moyse, Marie, N-137, 143-144
Moyse, Marie, S1-115, 379-380
Moyse, Marie, S2-671-672
Moyse, Marie, S3-1127
Moyse, Marie Josephe, N-26
Moyse, Marie Josephine, N-137
Moyse, Marie-Josephe, S2-631-633
Moyse, Nicolas, S2-671
Moyse, Perinne-Ursule, S2-630
Moyse, Perpetue, C-19, 162
Moyse, Perpetue, S2-629, 632-633
Moyse, Pierre Benony, N-136
Moyse, Simon-Bazile, S2-630
Mullot, Claude, E-336, 352
Mullot, Jacques, E-152, 336
Mullot, Robert, E-336, 352
Mulot, Claude, S2-430, 633
Mulot, Jacques, S2-633
Mulot, Marie, S2-633
Mulot, Robert, S2-633-634, 643
Mulot, Robert, S3-985
Muniac, Allain, S1-130
Muniac, Joseph, S2-635
Munios, Jaques Prosper, E-43, 336
Munios, Pierre, E-336
Murat, Cecile, E-320, 367-368
Murat, Francois, E-302
Muret, Francoise, E-321, 419
Muriat, Cecile, E-367
Muriat, Lucile, E-368
Murzeau, Pierre, E-159
Mutot, Jacques, E-588, 594
Muy, Jean Baptiste, E-336

N

Nachau, Francoise, E-626
Nadau, Cecille, E-326
Nadau, Henry, E-326
Nadau, Marie, E-325
Nadaud, Helene, E-403
Nadaud, Jean, E-325
Nadaud, Marie, E-11
Nadeau, Catherine, E-337
Nadeau, Cecille, E-337
Nadeau, Chief, E-10
Nadeau, Francois, E-140, 337
Nadeau, Francoise, E-385

Nadeau, Francoise Elizabeth, E-337
Nadeau, Henry, E-337
Nadeau, Jacques, E-337
Nadeau, Jean, E-337, 370, 376, 385
Nadeau, Jeanne, E-279, 337, 412
Nadeau, Magdeleine, E-337
Nadeau, Marianne, E-375
Nadeau, Marie, E-89, 337
Nadeau, Philippe, E-89
Nadeau, Pierre, E-89
Nadoux, Marie, E-415
Nangy, Elizabeth Genevieve, E-300, 337
Nantois, Jacques, E-528
Naples, Mr., E-403
Naquin, Ambroise, E-337
Naquin, Ambroise, F-47
Naquin, Ambroise, N-138
Naquin, Ambroise, S1-157
Naquin, Ambroise, S2-634-635
Naquin, Ambroise, S3-1104-1105, 1107, 1119
Naquin, Ambroise-Francois, S2-635
Naquin, Angelique, E-337
Naquin, Angelique, S2-637-638
Naquin, Anne, C-81
Naquin, Anne, F-49
Naquin, Anne, S1-290, 342-343
Naquin, Anne, S2-636-638
Naquin, Anne, S3-1128
Naquin, Anne Marie, N-32-33
Naquin, Anne Marie, S3-1107
Naquin, Anne-Marie, S1-157
Naquin, Anne-Marie, S2-636
Naquin, Charle, S3-1130
Naquin, Charles, C-12, 80, 133, 152
Naquin, Charles, F-49
Naquin, Charles, S1-270, 275, 343
Naquin, Charles, S2-636-639
Naquin, Elizabet, E-337
Naquin, Elizabeth, S1-157
Naquin, Elizabeth, S2-634-635, 638
Naquin, Elizabeth-Josephe, S1-130

Naquin, Franccois, S2-636-638
Naquin, Francois, C-27, 80, 132
Naquin, Francois, E-337
Naquin, Francois, F-49, 51
Naquin, Francois, S3-1130
Naquin, Isabelle, F-19
Naquin, Ives, F-49
Naquin, Jacques, F-47, 49
Naquin, Jacques, N-32, 138
Naquin, Jacques, S1-157
Naquin, Jacques, S2-638-639, 727
Naquin, Jacques, S3-1107
Naquin, Jean, F-49
Naquin, Jean, S2-605
Naquin, Jean, S3-876
Naquin, Jean-Baptiste, S2-634-635, 637-639
Naquin, Jean-Charles, S2-636
Naquin, Jeanne-Marguerite, S2-636
Naquin, Joseph, C-49
Naquin, Joseph, F-47
Naquin, Joseph, N-138
Naquin, Joseph, S1-391
Naquin, Joseph, S2-637-639
Naquin, Joseph, S3-1104
Naquin, Joseph-Jacques, S2-635
Naquin, Joseph-Suliac, S2-636
Naquin, Ludovinne, F-49
Naquin, Madeleine Helene, N-138
Naquin, Madeleine-Francoise, S2-634
Naquin, Madeleine-Helene, S2-635
Naquin, Marguerite, E-151, 337, 573
Naquin, Marguerite, S2-634, 638, 727-728
Naquin, Marguerite Ludivine, C-80
Naquin, Marguerite-Suline, S2-635
Naquin, Marianne, S2-637-639
Naquin, Marianne-Anastasie, S2-638
Naquin, Marie, C-81
Naquin, Marie, F-49
Naquin, Marie, S1-124
Naquin, Marie, S2-639, 728

Naquin, Marie-Anastasie, S2-637

Naquin, Michel, F-19

Naquin, Paul, C-81

Naquin, Paul, F-49

Naquin, Pierre, F-47

Naquin, Pierre, N-138

Naquin, Pierre, S2-634, 638-639

Naquin, Pierre-Paul, S2-635

Naquin, Rene, C-80

Naquin, Renee, F-49

Naquin, Tarsile, N-41

Naquin, Tarsile, S2-637-638

Naquin, Tarsille, C-27, 132-133

Naquin, Tarsille, F-51

Naquin, Tarsille, S2-635-636

Naquin, Tergide, S1-157

Naquin, Ursule, S2-637-638

Naquin, Yves, S2-636

Narme, Christophe, E-6

Narme, Jean Marie Antoine, E-4, 6

Narme, Jeanne Christine, E-6

Narme, Marie Jeanne Antoine Victoire, E-6-5

Narme, Marie Michel Victoire, E-5-6

Narne, Christophe, E-4-5

Narne, Marie Jeanne Christine, E-5

Naud, Jeanne, E-155, 157

Naud, Louis, E-259, 352

Naud, Marie, E-118, 259, 337, 409

Naudin, Mathieu, E-600

Naudin, Pierre, E-600

Naugue, Thomas, S2-640

Naulin, Jean, E-1

Naulin, Suzanne, E-155, 315

Naumont, Jean, E-34

Navarre, Francois, E-87-88

Navarre, Francois Gaspard, E-52

Navarre, Jacques Phiippe, E-52, 337

Navarre, Marie Therese, E-52, 337

Navaud, Francois, E-168

Navaud, Jean, E-153, 338

Navert, Joseph, E-413

Naviere, Francois, E-624, 626

Naviere, Francoise Marie, E-626

Naviere, Jeanne Antoinette, E-626

Neau, Louis, E-66, 73

Neel, Michel, E-120, 338

Neraudeau, Jean, E-142, 157, 338

Nereau, Marie, E-173, 404

Nerliau, Renee, E-100, 169

Nesles, Michel, E-137

Neuvilly, Louis Noel Adam, E-338

Neuvilly, Rene Francois Adam, E-338

Neveu, Vincent, F-63, 85

Neveu de Molmont, Jean Baptiste, E-109

Niclon, Rose, E-256

Nicod, Anne, E-372

Nicolai, Angelique, E-338

Nicolai, Anne, E-338

Nicolai, boy, E-338

Nicolai, Brigite Sophie, E-338

Nicolai, Brigitte, E-338

Nicolai, Jeanne Angelique, E-338

Nicolai, Joseph, E-338

Nicolas, Angelique, E-313

Nicolas, Anne, E-256, 333

Nicolas, Bernard, E-90, 156

Nicolas, Etienne, E-180

Nicolas, Guillaume, E-338

Nicolas, Jean, E-338

Nicolas, Jean Angelique, E-338

Nicolas, Marguerite, E-338

Nicolas, Rene, S3-904

Nicolay, Angelique, E-313

Nicole, Cecile, S1-230

Nicole, Marie, S1-230

Nicole, Marie, S3-1079

Nicole, Rose, S1-166

Nicoleure, Marie, E-152

Nicollas, Ellisabet, E-457

Niconte, Rene, S3-971

Nihil, -----, S3-1103

Ninon, Gabrielle, E-185, 338

Nioche, Denis Andre, E-338

Nioche, Eli, E-338

Niot, Marie Michelle, E-167

Niot, Mr., E-71

Niquet, Antoine Pradere, E-338

Niquet, Antoinette, E-338

Niquet, Edme Louise, E-339

Niquet, Joseph, E-338

Niquet, Joseph Foradere, E-338

Niquet, Joseph Pradere, E-339

Niquet, Pierre Cyprien, E-339

Nirode, Elisabeth, E-275

Nitre, Cecille, E-66, 298

Niurs, Claire, E-191

Nivard, Marie, E-314

Nivry, Charles, E-97

Nobiere, Marguerite-Perinne, S2-514

Nodeau, Francois, E-326

Nodin, Catherine, E-32, 339

Nodin, Louis, E-32, 339

Noel, Jean, E-339, 370

Noel, Jean, N-138

Noel, Jean Baptiste, C-163

Noel, Jean-Baptiste, S2-640

Noel, Marguerite, F-13

Noel, Marguerite, N-138

Noel, Marie, F-13

Noel, Marie, N-151

Noel, Marie Madeleine, N-138

Noel, Marie Marguerite, N-151

Noel, Marie-Madeleine, S2-640

Noel, Marie-Marguerite, S2-640

Noel, Perinne-Rosalie, S2-640

Noel, Pierre, C-163

Noel, Pierre, N-138, 151

Noel, Pierre, S2-640

Noel, Pierre, S3-998

Nogues, Charles, F-95

Nogues, Charles, S1-86

Nogues, Charles, S3-903

Nogues, Marie, F-59, 95

Nogues, Marie, S1-87

Nogues, Marie Perine, S3-903

Nogues, Marie-Perinne, S1-86

Noiret, Pierre-Alain, S2-514

Noiri, Marie, E-358

Noiril, Jean, E-358

Nolag, Marie Philippe Francoise de la Haute, E-60

Noperau, Francoise, S2-545

Noperau, Francoise, S3-995

Norau, J. Bap., S3-954

Norau, Jean-Baptiste, S3-953-954

Norau, Mathurin, S3-953

Nord - Department in France, E-339

Noreau, Jean-Baptiste, S2-592, 641

Noreau, Mathurin, S2-641

Noreau, Pierre, S2-641

Normand, Marie Cesille, E-405

Normandeau, Madeleine, E-293

Normandeau, Marguerite, E-52

Normant, Suzanne, E-269, 332

Noros, Jean Baptiste, E-588, 595

Norry, Mathurine, S2-738

Noseran, Jean, E-264

Noure, Perinne, S1-39

Nourrigeon, Louis, E-33

Nourry, Jacques, S1-88

Nourry, Jean, S1-67

Nourry, Jeanne, S1-250

Nourry, Julienne, S1-98

Noury, -----, S3-830

Noury, Jan, S3-857

Noury, Jean, S3-863

Noury, Olive, S2-774

Noury, Olive, S3-857

Noury, Yves, S2-536

Nouvi, Guillaume, S3-862

Nuirat, Cecile, C-41

Nuirat, Cecile, E-69, 83, 268, 363-364, 368, 376, 553

Nuirat, Cecile, S2-687

Nuiratte, Jean Jacques, E-528

Nuviatte, Susanne Marie, E-369

O

Offroy, Janne, S3-1014

Offroy, Jeanne, N-173

Offroy, Jeanne, S2-780

Offroy, Marie, S2-780

Oge, Julien, E-340

Oge, Marie Louise, E-340

Okin, Magdelene, S3-831

Olive, Marie, S1-43

Olive, Marie, S3-1101

Olivier, Anne, C-9

Olivier, Anne, E-177

Olivier, Anne, F-75

Olivier, Anne, N-80

Olivier, Anne, S1-54

Olivier, Anne, S2-434-436, 603

Olivier, Anne, S3-1059, 1071

Olivier, Christophe, S3-861

Olivier, Claude, S2-691

Olivier, Claude, S3-970

Olivier, Emmanuel Joseph, E-340

Olivier, Emmanuel Josephine, E-340

Olivier, Francois, S3-865

Olivier, Francoise, E-179

Olivier, Marguerite, E-371-372

Olivier, Pierre, F-75

Olivier, Pierre, N-80

Olivier, Pierre, S2-434

Olivier, Thomasee, S2-537

Ollereau, Marie, E-69, 174

Ollier, Marguerite, C-158

Ongot, Therese Angelique, E-361

Orchais, Marguerite, E-340

Oreal, Anne, S2-503

Orel, Louis, E-40

Ores, Marie Anne Francoise, E-291-292

Orge, Louis, E-340

Orger, Marie, E-406

Orger, Marie Anne, E-46

Orignot, Anne, E-181

Orillac, Marie, E-393

Orillon, Jean Baptiste, E-340

Orillon, Madeleine, E-431

Orillon, Marguerite, E-81, 340

Orillon, Perpetue, E-335

Oriolle, Jean, S2-546

Oristain, Marie, S2-626

Orly, Joseph, E-340

Orly, Louis, E-340

Orly, Louis, S1-358

Orry, Charles, N-138, 167, 240

Orry, Perrine Marguerite, N-138, 167, 240

Orset, C.F., S3-1082

Orset, Charles, S3-1082

Orset, Rosalie, S2-567

Orsonneau, Jean, E-20

Orthion, Jean, E-413

Ory, Charles, F-23

Ory, Marguerite, F-23

Ory, Marie, E-340

Ory, Ory, E-340

Ory, Perrine Marguerite, F-23

Oselet, Jean, C-81, 83

Oselet, Jean, F-21

Oselet, Jean, N-139

Oselet, Jean, S1-46

Oselet, Jean, S2-524, 641-643, 660

Oselet, Jean, S3-1027

Oselet, Jean Baptiste, C-81

Oselet, Jean Baptiste, F-59

Oselet, Jean Charles, F-21

Oselet, Jean Charles, N-139

Oselet, Jean-Charles, S2-642

Oselet, Jeanne-Olive, S2-642

Oselet, Julien, F-21, 59

Oselet, Julien, N-139

Oselet, Marie Charles, C-81

Oselet, Marie Charlotte, F-21

Oselet, Marie Charlotte, N-139

Oselet, Marie-Jeanne, S2-470, 626

Oselet, Marie-Marguerite, S2-642

Oselet, Mathurin, F-21

Oselet, Mathurin, N-139

Oselet, Mathurin-Joseph, S2-642

Oselet, Pierre-Henry, S2-642

Osserre, Andre Philippe, E-340, 418

Osserre, Emilie Felicite, E-340

Oter, Etienne, S2-771

Oter, Marie-Anne, S2-771

Oualar, Antoine, E-309, 340

Oualar, Jean, E-309, 340

Oudy, Anne, E-291-292, 341

Oudy, Cecile, E-23, 70, 102, 110-111, 265-266, 291, 341-342, 553

Oudy, Charles, E-291, 341-342

Oudy, Claude, C-61

Oudy, Claude, E-270, 341-342, 368, 553

Oudy, Etienne, E-341-342

Oudy, Henriette, E-341

Oudy, Jacques, E-22-23, 101, 266, 291, 341-342, 528

Oudy, Jacques Christophe, E-341

Oudy, Jean, E-341

Oudy, Jean Baptiste, E-101, 111, 341-342

Oudy, Jean Louis, E-341

Oudy, Joseph, E-33, 292, 341-342

Oudy, Louis, E-342

Oudy, Marguerite, E-22-23, 101, 265, 316, 342

Oudy, Marie Angelique, E-342

Oudy, Marie Anne, E-135

Oudy, Marie Charlotte, E-342

Oudy, Marie Henriette, E-342

Oudy, Marie Josephe, E-23, 101-102, 110, 341-342, 404-405

Oudy, Marie Magdelaine, E-292, 341-342, 417

Oudy, Marie-Madeleine, S2-754

Oudy, Pierre, E-103, 341-342, 356

Ouestoronest, Anne, E-457

Ouette, Christophe, E-588, 592

Ouette, Genevieve, E-588, 592

Ouette, Margueritte, E-588, 592

Oulle, Charlotte, E-41, 91

Ourtel, Guillaume, E-257

Oury, Charles, E-120

Oury, Jacques, E-95

Outremer, Francois, S3-974

Ouvrard, Jeanne, E-17, 152

Ozanne, Henry, S2-634, 643, 649

Ozanne, Henry, S3-985

Ozanne, Henry-Michel, S2-643

Ozanne, Thomas, S2-643

Ozanne, Thomas, S3-985

Ozile, Catherine, E-33, 255

P

Pacaut, Antoine, E-343, 384

Pacaut, Jean, E-343, 384

Pacet, Francoise, F-65

Pagaud, Anne, N-98, 217

Page, Colin, E-343

Pagelet, Jean-Baptiste, S2-429

Pagelet, M., S3-985

Pagelet, Pierre, S2-741

Pages, Hilaire Benjamin, E-343

Pages, Louis Francois Isaac, E-343

Pages, Marie Catherine, E-343

Paget, Pierre, E-323, 343

Pagnaud, Claude, E-343

Pagnaud, Francois, E-343

Pagnaud de Touche, Claude Francois, E-343

Pagord, Jean, C-135

Pagot, Antoinette Eleonore, E-343

Pagot, Jean, E-343

Pagot, Marie Jules, E-343

Paigis, Marie, S3-1096

Paigis, Nicolas Jean, S3-1095-1096

Paillard, Anne Antoinette, E-343

Paillard, Jean Mathieu, E-343

Paillet, Catherine, E-52, 392

Paillette, Marie Louise, E-180, 343

Paillette, Nicolas Marin, E-180, 343

Pain, Marie, E-326, 376

Pain, Mr., E-171, 353

Paing, Catherine Jeanne, E-626

Paing, Nicolas, S2-509

Paing, Nicolas, S3-1042

Paing, Nicolas-Jean, S2-643

Paing, Rene, S2-643

Pajonneau, Hyacinthe, E-64

Pala, Francois, E-343

Pala, Francois David, E-343

Palinier, Louis, E-594

Paneau, Miss, E-130

Panneau, Marie Susanne, E-174, 343

Panneau, Pierre, E-343

Panpalon, Jean Baptiste Louis Joseph, E-344

Panpalon, Louis, E-344

Panpalon, Marie Genevieve, E-344

Panpalon, Paul Georges, E-344

Papion, Jean, E-159, 329

Papon, Andre, E-344

Papon, Estienne, E-344

Papon, Jacques, E-131

Papon, Michel, E-344

Papon, Nicolas, E-344

Papon, Nicollas Adrien, E-344

Paponnet, Marie, E-344

Papuchon, Louise, E-636

Paquet, Marie Helene, E-358

Paquier, Catherine, E-128, 389

Paquier, Jean, N-248

Paradis, Jean-Baptiste-Francois, S1-171

Paradis Terrestre, E-214

Parent, Claude, E-92, 101

Parioleau, Jean, E-60, 137, 344

Paris, Anatole, E-139, 344

Paris, Andre, E-128

Paris, Andre, S1-76

Paris, Angelique, E-72, 338, 344, 392

Paris, Anne, E-274

Paris, Antoine, C-9

Paris, Antoine, E-20, 35, 71, 72, 81, 138, 287, 309, 332, 344-346, 392

Paris, Benoit, E-81

Paris, Bernard, E-287, 344

Paris, Claude Marie Joseph, E-139, 344

Paris, Francois, E-344-346

Paris, Gabriel Pierre, E-345

Paris, Gabriel-Pierre, S2-644

Paris, Genevieve, S2-610, 644

Paris, Genevieve, S3-1089

Paris, Henri Hyppolite, E-345

Paris, Hyppolite, E-345

Paris, Jean, E-119, 256, 345-346

Paris, Jean, S3-1042

Paris, Jean Baptiste, E-345

Paris, Jean Baptiste Arnauld, E-345

Paris, Jean Baptiste Pierre, E-345

Paris, Jean Francois, E-331

Paris, Jean-Baptiste, S1-336

Paris, Jeanne, E-55, 68, 117, 345, 376

Paris, Jullien, S3-911

Paris, Louis, E-345

Paris, Louis Joseph Auguste, E-259, 345

Paris, Madeleine, E-345

Paris, Marie, E-19, 71, 345, 402

Paris, Marie Anne, E-115-116, 345

Paris, Marie Genevieve, E-315, 345

Paris, Marie Gervaise, C-9, 95

Paris, Marie Gervaise, E-20, 345

Paris, Marie Gervaix, C-112

Paris, Marie Louise, E-306, 346

Paris, Marie Reine, E-332, 346
Paris, P., N-190
Paris, Pierre, E-345, 346, 439
Paris, Pierre, S1-205
Paris, Pierre, S2-643
Paris, Pierre, S3-1042
Paris, Rose, E-346
Paris, Thomas, E-306, 346
Parnel, Jan, S3-992
Parnel, Jean, S3-1029
Parnel, Olivier, S3-992
Parnel, Perinne, S2-595
Parnel, Perinne, S3-992, 1029
Parody, Catherine, E-10
Parpais, Marie Anne, E-385, 440
Parre, Eustache, E-323
Part, Brigitte, F-37, 73
Part, Brigitte, N-17, 19, 215
Part, Eustache, C-33, 64, 81-82, 99
Part, Eustache, E-346
Part, Eustache, F-67, 107
Part, Laurent, C-64, 82, 99-100
Part, Laurent, E-324
Part, Marianne, F-67
Part, Marie, E-324, 378
Part, Marie, F-107
Part, Marie Anne, C-33, 99
Part, Marie Anne, E-104, 346
Part, Marie Anne, N-54
Part, Michel, F-73
Part, Pierre, C-81
Part, Pierre, E-346
Pascal, Antoine, E-110, 346
Pascal, Charles, S2-644
Pascal, Genevieve, S2-644
Pascal, La Rose, S2-644
Pascal, Margueritte, E-110, 346
Pascaud, Mr., S1-323
Pasconal, Ursulle, E-317, 320
Pasquet, Jacques, E-354
Pasquier, Anne, E-402
Pasquier, Jean, E-139
Passier, Jean, E-22
Passier, Marie, E-22
Patain, Perrine, E-170
Patanchon, Jeanne, E-159
Patin, Marie, E-155
Patin, Perrine, E-63
Patrice, Guillaume, E-86
Patrie, Angelique, E-87, 346

Patris, Guillaume, S3-914, 1050, 1054, 1057
Patris, Louis, S3-1054
Patris, Paul, S3-1045, 1057
Patru, Michelle, S1-360
Patru, Michelle, S3-980
Patry, Angelique, S1-215-216
Patry, Angelique, S2-645
Patry, Anne, N-139-140
Patry, Anne-Perinne, S2-646
Patry, George, E-346
Patry, George, S2-645
Patry, Guillaume, E-78, 346
Patry, Guillaume, N-139
Patry, Guillaume, S1-215
Patry, Guillaume, S2-644-646
Patry, Jeanne Rosalie, N-139
Patry, Jeanne-Charlotte-Rosalie, S2-646
Patry, Louis, E-346
Patry, Louis, S2-644
Patry, Marie Modeste, N-139
Patry, Paul, C-27
Patry, Paul, N-94, 139, 200
Patry, Paul, S1-216
Patry, Paul, S2-645-646
Patry, Paul-Charles, S2-646
Paufer, Anne Francoise, N-222
Pauier, Jean, E-346
Paul, indian, E-316
Paulet, Marie Louise Genevieve, E-303
Paulin, Izabelle, E-28, 304
Paumier, Anne, E-20, 346
Pavajaud, Jean, E-270, 346
Pavajaud, Pierre, E-270, 346
Pave, Marguerite, E-80
Paye, Pierre, S1-358
Payer, Charles Joseph, E-347
Payer, Marie Magdeleine, E-347
Payere, Jean, E-347
Paynon, Marie, E-90, 182
Paysan, Jean Baptiste, E-347
Paysan, Yves, E-347
Payuereau, Gabriel, C-108
Pean, Anne, E-12, 86
Pebart, Anne Euphrosine, E-347
Pebart, Jean, E-347
Pebart, Jean Antoine, E-347
Pebart, Sophie Eulalie, E-347
Pecart, Susanne, S3-959

Pecart, Suzanne, S1-374
Pecaud, Francois, E-347
Pecaud, Francois Davie, E-347
Pecaud, Jean Charles Ermine, E-347
Pecaud, Jean Jacques, E-347
Pecaud, Louis Francois, E-347
Pecaud, Louise, E-347
Pecaud, Louise Henriette, E-347
Pecaud, Marie, E-347
Pecaud, Marie Anne, E-347
Pecaud, Marie Rose, E-347
Pecaud, Pierre, E-347
Pechelen, Joseph, S2-634
Pechen, Jeanne, S2-485
Pechot, Marie Anne, E-347
Peco, Francois, E-370
Pecot, Jaques, N-218
Pecotte, Susanne, S3-960
Pecou, Mr., E-26
Pecqueux, Nicolas, E-88
Pedesclaux, Etienne, E-180, 258
Pedron, Marie Jeanne, E-281
Pegat, Jeanne, E-302, 347
Peinaud, Antoine, E-43, 318, 347
Peinaud, Jean, E-43, 347
Peing, Nicolas Jean, S3-1042
Peing, Rene, S3-1042
Peinier, Marie Marthe, E-348, 362
Peinier, Philippe, E-348, 362
Peireau, Marie, E-146, 348
Peires, Arnaud, E-24, 348
Peires, Jean, E-24, 348
Peiroche, Gabriel, E-294
Peiroche, Magdeleine, E-294, 348
Peiroche, Michel, E-294
Peiroche, Pierre, E-294
Peiron, Jean, E-367
Pelardeau, Jean, E-333
Pelaton, Jacques, E-120
Pelaton, Jacques Henry, E-348
Pelerin, Charles, S3-1030
Pelhoux, Jeanne, S2-494
Pelisscir, Daniel, S3-983
Pellereau, Louis, E-63
Pellerin, Agathe, E-348
Pellerin, Anne, E-414, 438, 501, 516

Pellerin, Baptiste, E-529

Pellerin, Catherine, E-516

Pellerin, Charles, S2-438, 646-647

Pellerin, Estienne, E-476

Pellerin, Francois, E-458

Pellerin, Isabelle, E-516

Pellerin, Jacques, S2-647

Pellerin, Jean Baptiste, E-501

Pellerin, Jeanne, E-516

Pellerin, Madeleine, E-261, 501

Pellerin, Marc, E-348

Pellerin, Marguerite, E-130-131, 348

Pellerin, Marie, E-501, 516

Pellerin, Marie, S2-456

Pellerin, Pierre, E-501, 516

Pellerin, Pierre Philippe, E-348

Pellet, Etienne David, E-186

Pelletier, Catherine, E-28, 180

Pelletier, Marie, E-152, 173

Pelletier, Marie Louise, E-11

Pelletrot, Jeanne, E-457

Pellissier, Anne, E-138

Pellissier, Denis, E-348

Pellissier, Francois, E-348

Pellissier, Jean Baptiste, E-348

Pellissier, Louis Joseph Donnadieu de, E-430

Pellissier, Madeleine, E-348

Pellissier, Marguerite Sophie, E-348

Pellissier, Rosalie, E-348

Pellisson, Jean, E-31

Pelot, Charlotte, E-80, 391

Peltier, Marie, E-54

Peltier, Marie-Anne, S2-690

Peltier, Reine, S2-546

Peltret, Henriette, E-473

Peltret, Jeanne, E-476

Pemod, Dame Fransoisse, N-241

Penagrein, Marie, C-93

Penard, Magdeleine, E-155, 326, 348

Penaud, Francoise, E-431

Penetreau, Mr., E-371

Penhouet, J., S3-877

Penisseau, Marie, E-1, 17

Penneteau de Seanquiers, Emilie, E-154

Pennetreau de Leaugiers, Jeanne Francoise, E-154

Penotte, Louis Pierre, E-428

Pepin, Catherine, E-588, 596

Pepin, Genevieve, E-60, 348

Pepin, Gilles, E-180, 348

Pepin, Marie, E-146, 348

Pepin, Marie Therese, E-62

Pepin, Pierre, E-180, 348

Peponnot, Jacques, E-72, 348

Peppin, Charlotte Monique Francoise, E-109

Peragne, Jeanne, E-318

Peraudeau, Jean Baptiste, E-97, 349

Peraudeau, Jeanne, E-172

Peraudeau, Marie Therese, E-97, 349

Perault, Marguerite, E-307

Perault, Pierre Charles, E-10

Perce, Francoise, E-624

Perceveau, Mathurin, S2-647

Perceveau, Olivier, S2-647

Percheron, Jacques Hector, E-34

Percheron, Martin, C-25

Perchet, Antoine, E-349, 416

Perdriel, Guilleaume, S3-845

Perdriel, Yvonne, S1-146

Perel, Laurent, E-189

Perez, Antoine, S2-483

Perez, Jeanne, S2-483

Perieau, Francois, E-349

Perigor, Pierre, E-22

Perigord, Marie, E-168, 404

Perigord, Marie Elisabeth, E-168, 349, 420

Perigord, Pierre, E-349

Perin, Charlotte-Marie, S2-743

Perin, Jacques, E-349, 394

Perin, Jeanne, E-349, 394

Peringauet, Jean Jacques, E-299, 359

Pernaud, Alexis, E-4

Pernin, Jean Louis, E-159

Pero, Jean, S3-1074

Perocheau, Francoise, E-153

Perogon, Jeanne, E-319

Perogon, Marie, E-142, 349

Peron, Francois, E-14

Peron, Francois M., E-14

Perost, Denis, E-349

Perost, Jean, E-349

Perot, Jeanne, E-298

Peroucho, Bertrand, N-99, 249

Peroucho, Manuele, N-99, 249

Perouty, -----, N-192

Perov, Modeste, S2-723

Perpon, Georges, E-349

Perrain, Claude, E-173, 349

Perrain, Marie, E-173, 349

Perraudaux, Francois, E-430

Perre, Antoine, E-27, 175, 349

Perre, Jan, S3-983

Perre, Jean, E-175, 349

Perre, Jeanne, E-27, 349

Perrein, Jerome, E-152

Perrez, Francoise, S1-264-265

Perrez, Pierre, S1-264

Perrier, Charles, E-165

Perrier, Pierre, E-349

Perrin, Julien, S2-647

Perrin, Pierre, S2-647

Perriot, Pierre, E-421

Perrogon, Jeanne, E-317

Perrogon, Pierre, E-168

Perron, Antoine, E-14

Perron, Jean, E-64, 349

Perron, Modeste, S3-1008

Perronnet, Jean Marc, E-267, 306

Perronnet, Jean-March, S2-597

Perropon, Jeanne, E-320

Perroquet, Francois, E-349

Perroquet, Pierre, E-349

Perrot, Jean, E-303, 350

Perrot, Madeleine, S2-593

Perrotin Petitpre, Magdelaine, E-90

Perruquier, Merchand, E-14

Perry, Anne Therese, E-350

Perry, Jean, E-350

Perry, Pierre Leonard, E-350

Persiancaude, Jeanne, E-589, 594

Perthuit, Marie Anne, E-64, 149

Pertuis, Jean, E-70, 77

Pertus, Louis, E-350

Pertus, Marie Julie, E-350

Pertus, Mr., E-369, 386

Peruau, -----, E-6

Peruau, Nicolas Alexis, E-6

Peruchet, Marguerite Victoire, E-140

Peruse des Cars, Louis Nicolas de, C-53, 71

Perusses, Marquis de, C-135

Peselet, Marie, E-458, 476

Pesquier, Anne, E-13

Petain, Perinne, S1-374

Petavin, Louis, E-10

Petineri, Charles, E-589, 596

Petit, -----, E-8

Petit, -----, N-192

Petit, Anne Louise Thereze, E-340

Petit, Anne Marguerite, E-350

Petit, Antoine, E-256

Petit, Etienne, E-350

Petit, Francoise, E-102, 356

Petit, Jacques, E-476, 507

Petit, Jean, E-350, 366, 589, 591

Petit, Jean, S3-1150

Petit, Jean Pierre, E-350

Petit, Jullien, S3-824

Petit, Louise, E-62

Petit, Marguerite, E-34, 157

Petit, Marguerite Louise, E-8

Petit, Marie, F-67

Petit, Marie, N-143

Petit, Marie, S1-263

Petit, Marie, S2-671

Petit, Marie, S3-1004

Petit, Marie Joseph, E-350

Petit, Marie Louise, E-32

Petit, Marie-Joseph, S1-173

Petit, Marie-Louise, S1-57

Petit, Pierre, E-160, 274, 350, 366

Petit, Pierre Etienne, E-350

Petit, Pierre Zoe, E-8, 350

Petit, Simon, E-32, 140, 350, 372

Petit Boismorel, Jean, E-59

Petit Boismorel, Marie Josephe, E-59

Petit d'Arvilliers,Louise, E-197

Petitbois, Marie, E-350

Petitbois, Nicolas, E-350

Petithomme, Antoine-Julien, S1-356

Petitpas, Angelique, E-92, 350

Petitpas, Anne, E-156, 350, 479

Petitpas, Anne Pelagie, E-350

Petitpas, Barthelemy, E-351

Petitpas, Cecile, E-589, 594

Petitpas, Cecile, S1-172

Petitpas, Cecile, S2-649-650

Petitpas, Charles, E-479

Petitpas, Charles, S2-649

Petitpas, Claude, E-350-351, 458, 476, 479

Petitpas, Francois, E-14, 351

Petitpas, Francois, S2-648

Petitpas, Francoise, S2-648

Petitpas, Genevieve, S2-649-650

Petitpas, Guillaume, E-59, 85, 93, 135, 154, 168, 290, 350-352, 394, 403, 408

Petitpas, Henriette, E-479

Petitpas, Isabelle, E-472

Petitpas, Jacque, S3-983

Petitpas, Jacques, E-351, 479, 589, 594

Petitpas, Jacques, S1-172

Petitpas, Jacques, S2-512, 643, 648, 650, 686

Petitpas, Jacques-Francois, S2-649

Petitpas, Jacquette-Henriette, S2-649

Petitpas, Jean, E-29, 351

Petitpas, Jean, S2-648, 650

Petitpas, Jean Baptiste, E-175, 195, 351-352, 419, 437-438

Petitpas, Jean-Baptiste, S2-471

Petitpas, Joseph, E-266, 281, 351

Petitpas, Joseph Zephirin, E-351

Petitpas, Josephine, E-77, 154, 294, 336

Petitpas, Judith, S1-254

Petitpas, Louis, E-351

Petitpas, Louis Toussaint, E-351

Petitpas, Madeleine, E-92-93, 266, 281

Petitpas, Madeleine, S1-335

Petitpas, Marie, E-24, 329, 336, 352, 479, 589, 594

Petitpas, Marie, S2-512, 634, 643, 648-650

Petitpas, Marie, S3-985

Petitpas, Marie Anne, E-352

Petitpas, Marie-Jeanne, S2-649

Petitpas, Martin, E-479

Petitpas, Nicolas, E-14, 26, 336, 351-352

Petitpas, Nicolas, S2-634, 643, 648

Petitpas, Nicolas, S3-985

Petitpas, Paul, E-352, 479,

Petitpas, Pelagie, E-352

Petitpas, Pierre, E-352, 479

Petitpas, Pierre Francois, E-352

Petitpas, Robert, E-589, 594

Petitpas, Robert, S2-649-650

Petitpas, Rozalie Angelique, E-352

PetitPre, Magdelaine Perrotin, E-379

Petitpre, Perrotin, E-379

Petors, Yves, E-428

Petrus, Thomas, E-589, 591

Petry, Michele, F-75

Pettitot, Madeleine, N-72

Pevot, Jeanne, S2-506

Pevron, Pierre, E-298

Peyrelongue, Jeanne, E-27, 349

Peyroux, Mr., F-41

Pezant, Jean Aimable, E-352

Pezant, Jean Baptiste, E-352

Pezant, Marie Eleonore, E-352

Pezant, Pierre, E-352

Pezant, Pierre Louis, E-352

Phelipaud, Jean, E-146

Phelipoh, Guy, E-352

Phelipoh, Jeanne, E-266, 352

Phelipot, Francois, S2-650

Phelipot, Guy, S2-650

Phelipot, Jean, S2-650

Phelipot, Jeanne, S2-650

Phelipot, Louis, S2-650

Phelipot, Marie, S2-650

Phelippot, Jacques, E-318

Philbert, Charles, S3-978, 996

Philibert, Charles, S2-650-652

Philibert, Jean, S2-650-652

Philibert, Joseph, S2-651

Philibert, Marie, S2-651

Philibert, Nanette, S2-651

Philibert, Pierre, S2-651

Philibert, Suzanne-Michelle, S2-652

Philibert, Thomas, S2-651

Philipe, Rene, E-167

Philipot, Jeanne-Francoise, S1-82

Philippe, Etienne Charles, E-352

Philippe, Jean, E-38

Philippe, Jean Charles, E-140, 352

Philippe, Jean Pierre, E-18, 180

Philippe, Joseph, E-352

Philippe, Nicolas, E-140, 149, 352

Philippon, Antoine, S2-653

Philippon, Charles, S2-652-653

Philippon, Gabriel, S2-653

Philippon, Gabriel-Claude, S2-652

Philippon, Jean, S2-652

Philippon, Jean-Baptiste, S2-653

Philippon, Jeanne, S2-507-508

Philippon, Louise, S2-653

Philippon, Sebastienne, S2-653

Philippot, Basile, E-352

Phillippon, Janne, S3-1095

Phily, C.G., S3-946-948

Phily, E.G., S3-944

Phily, Sieur, S3-944

Phirhaulec, Laurent, E-409

Phlipe, Francois Marie, S3-923

Pias LaRue, Arnaud, E-353

Pias LaRue, Jean, E-353

Piau, Perinne, S1-48

Pibaud, Andre, E-82, 403

Picard, Catherine, E-589, 593

Picard, Etienne, E-322, 353

Picard, Jean, E-353

Picard, Marie Madeleine, E-353

Picaud, Pierre, E-300

Pichard, Jean, E-309

Pichard, Jean Baptiste, E-353

Pichard, Marie Magdeleinne, E-103, 176, 185, 309

Pichard, Marie-Madeleine, S1-320

Pichard, Thomas Francois, E-353, 438

Picherau, Antoine, C-104

Pichon, Louis Amand Constant, E-147

Pichon, Marie Anne, S3-1019

Pichon, Pierre, E-159

Pichot, Anne, E-626

Pichot, Anne Barbe, E-622

Pichot, Francois, E-353

Pichot, Francois, S2-653-654

Pichot, Jeanne, E-86, 143

Pichot, Madeleine, E-270

Pichot, Marianne, E-589, 594

Pichot, Marie Anne, S3-983

Pichot, Marie-Anne, S2-479, 684-687

Pichot, Marie-Madeleine, S2-653

Pichot, Michel, S2-654

Pichot, Perrine Francois, C-166

Pichot, Pierre, S2-654

Pichot, Pierre Yves, E-626

Pichot, Rene, C-167

Pichot, Rene, E-74, 293, 626

Pichot, Rene, S2-653-654

Picot, Francoise-Raphaelle-Berthedine, S1-94

Picot, Marie Victoire, E-192

Piedefer, Francois Emmanuel, E-193

Pieplu, Michel, E-431

Pierraud, Nicolas, E-337

Pierre, Agnes, S2-465

Pierre, Antoine, E-69

Pierre, Francois, E-353

Pierre, Gilles, S3-952

Pierre, indian, E-71, 353

Pierre, Jean fils, E-603

Pierre, Joseph, E-353

Pierre, Marguerite, F-93

Pierre, Nathalie, S2-567

Pierre, Pierre, E-353, 403, 406

Pierre, Simon, F-93

Pierre, Simon, S1-208

Pierre, Simon, S2-674

Pierre Gabriel, indian, E-316

Pierre Paul, -----, E-353

Pierri, Simon, E-66

Pierrond, Philippe, E-128

Pierrot, Joseph, E-172

Pierrot, Nicolas, E-123, 378

Pierson, Anne, F-83, 109

Pierson, Anne, N-20

Pierson, Antoine, E-589, 591

Piertie, Jean, S3-866

Piet, Jean, S2-675

Piete, Rene, N-232

Piette, Casimir, E-171, 353

Piette, Charles, E-171, 353

Pigeon, Dominique, S2-654

Pigeon, Jean, S2-654

Pigeon, Marie Anne, E-293-294

Pigeot, Louis, E-21, 353

Pigeot, Nicolas, E-21, 353

Pigniou, Benoist, E-27, 139

Piguel, Gilles, C-60

Piguel, Gilles, S2-511

Pihau, Joseph, S3-1147

Pilain, Jeanne, E-356

Pilay, Marie Anne, E-293

Pillard, Marie Sophie, E-146

Pilon, Jeanne, E-356

Pilon, Jeanne Elisabeth, E-356

Pilot, Marianne, E-130

Pimal, Jean, E-386

Pinard, Charles, E-90

Pinard, Guillaume, E-353, 381

Pinard, Pierre, E-97, 353, 381

Pinart, Anne, S1-194-195

Pinau, Francois, C-93

Pinceau, Louis, E-353

Pincer, Anne Marie, E-353

Pincer, Francois, E-354

Pincer, Jean, E-353-354

Pincer, Marie, E-353

Pincer, Marie Elisabeth, E-354

Pincer, Marie Francoise, E-354

Pincer, Paul, E-354

Pinchard, Jean, E-168, 420

Pineau, Anne, E-169, 335

Pineau, Francois, E-354

Pineau, Francoise, E-171

Pineau, Genevieve, E-354

Pineau, Guillaume, E-316, 354

Pineau, Jacques, E-19, 354

Pineau, Jean, E-12, 21, 34, 44, 354, 368

Pineau, Jean Daniel, E-354

Pineau, Joseph, E-355

Pineau, Louis, E-131, 354-355

Pineau, Louise, E-90, 354

Pineau, Magdeleine, E-354

Pineau, Marguerite Modeste, E-354

Pineau, Marie, E-34, 65, 168, 354-355, 403

Pineau, Marie Anne, E-355

Pineau, Marie Jeanne, E-355

Pineau, Philibert, E-12, 19, 168, 355

INDEX SOURCES C=Chatellerault; E=Acadians in Exile; F=Acadian Families; N=Nantes; S=St-Malo

Pineau, Pierre, E-77, 139
Pineau, Sebastien, E-19, 354-355
Pinet, Angelique, F-9
Pinet, Anne, E-355
Pinet, Anne Charlote, E-355
Pinet, Antoine, E-510
Pinet, Brigite, E-356, 430
Pinet, Brigitte, C-55, 101
Pinet, Brigitte, N-87
Pinet, Brigitte, S1-129
Pinet, Brigitte, S2-453, 660, 672, 679
Pinet, Brigitte, S3-1115
Pinet, Charles, C-82
Pinet, Charles, E-93, 107, 133, 355-356
Pinet, Charles, F-63, 71
Pinet, Charles, N-196
Pinet, Charles, S1-3, 252
Pinet, Charles, S2-654-655
Pinet, Francoise, E-355
Pinet, Jean, E-510
Pinet, Jean, S2-655
Pinet, Jean Baptiste, C-55
Pinet, Jean Baptiste, E-355-356, 430
Pinet, Jean-Baptiste, S2-453, 672-773
Pinet, Jeanne, E-355
Pinet, Jeanne Charlotte, E-355
Pinet, Jeannette, S2-655
Pinet, Joseph, E-135, 356
Pinet, Joseph, S1-252
Pinet, Lazare, E-355
Pinet, Louis, C-55
Pinet, Louis, E-355
Pinet, Louis, F-63, 71
Pinet, Madeleine, S1-252
Pinet, Marguerite, S1-3
Pinet, Marie, E-28, 78, 135, 195, 291, 355-356, 406, 510
Pinet, Marie, F-69
Pinet, Marie, S2-655
Pinet, Marie Brigitte, C-85
Pinet, Marie Brigitte, E-356, 430
Pinet, Marie Magdelaine, F-71
Pinet, Marie Magdelen, E-356
Pinet, Marie-Brigitte, S2-772-773
Pinet, Marie-Josephe, S1-252

Pinet, Martin Charles, C-82
Pinet, Michel, E-356
Pinet, Mr., E-264
Pinet, Noel, C-82
Pinet, Noel, E-355-356, 430, 510, 529
Pinet, Noel, F-71
Pinet, Noel, S2-772
Pinet, Paul, E-356
Pinet, Philippe, E-355-356, 476
Pinet, Pierre, E-356
Pinet, Pierre, S1-252
Pinet, Pierre Amant, E-356
Pinet, Pierrette, E-356
Pinet, Rosalie, E-356
Pingre, Charlotte, N-152, 244
Pinochet, Cecile Magdelaine, E-112
Pinochet, Cecile-Madeleine, S1-257
Pinochet, Louis, S1-257
Pinochet, Nicolas, S1-257
Pinochet, Pierre Nicolas, E-356
Pinochet, Servanne-Francoise, S1-257
Pinou, Noel, S1-282
Pinsart, Anne, S3-1147
Pinsart, Jan, S3-1147
Pinsart, Jean, S1-194-195
Pinson, Anne, E-185, 390
Pinson, Marie, E-11, 137
Pinsonneau, Jean, E-119
Pinsonneau, Marie, E-119, 356
Pion, Louise, E-44, 441
Piou, Galard, S3-1089
Piout, Mr., S3-1089
Piout, Mrs., S3-1089
Piper, Francoise, E-18
Piperon Lafosse, Angelique, E-102, 356
Piperon Lafosse, Antoine, E-102, 356
Pique, Catherine, E-315
Pireau, Francois, S2-442
Pirerate, Madeleine, S1-355
Pirion, Barbe LePrince, E-612
Piriou, Francois, E-356
Pirou, Pierre, S1-360
Pirou, Pierre, S3-980
Pises, Marguerite, S1-195
Pistre, Claude, S3-841

Pit, Marie, S3-847, 850
Pitard, Andre, E-356
Pitard, Jean, E-38, 86
Pitard, Marguerite, E-356
Pitard, Michel, E-340, 357
Pitard, Pierre Michel, E-46, 357
Pitard, Suzanne, E-357, 385
Pitre, Agnes, F-13
Pitre, Agnes, N-78, 142, 220
Pitre, Agnes, S1-380
Pitre, Agnes, S2-568, 570, 631, 659, 660-661, 671-672, 674
Pitre, Amand, C-35, 38, 82
Pitre, Amand, F-15, 23, 27
Pitre, Amand, N-145
Pitre, Amand, S1-3, 288
Pitre, Amand, S3-933, 1125, 1143
Pitre, Amant, S2-655-656
Pitre, Ambroise, C-82-83
Pitre, Ambroise, E-357
Pitre, Ambroise, F-27
Pitre, Ambroise, N-140-141, 175
Pitre, Ambroise, S1-4, 158, 302
Pitre, Ambroise, S2-655-657
Pitre, Ambroise, S3-933, 1129, 1140, 1143
Pitre, Angelique, E-115, 116, 118, 357
Pitre, Angelique, N-58
Pitre, Anne, C-43
Pitre, Anne, E-47, 52, 334, 357, 392
Pitre, Anne, F-45, 69
Pitre, Anne, N-17, 145
Pitre, Anne, S1-152-153, 347, 349
Pitre, Anne, S2-624, 656, 666, 670, 673
Pitre, Anne, S3-1126
Pitre, Anne Henriette, N-145
Pitre, Anne Joseph, E-193
Pitre, Anne-Blanche, S2-662
Pitre, Anne-Genevieve, S2-662
Pitre, Anne-Josephe, S1-126-127
Pitre, Anne-Ludivine, S2-655-656, 673
Pitre, Anselme, C-83
Pitre, Anselme, F-45

Pitre, Anselme, N-141-142, 254
Pitre, Anselme, S1-304
Pitre, Anselme, S2-502, 541, 657-658, 666
Pitre, Anselme, S3-922, 924, 1116
Pitre, Antoine, N-116
Pitre, Antoine, S1-114
Pitre, Antoine, S2-568, 659, 674, 690
Pitre, Antoine, S3-1025, 1033
Pitre, Augustin, S2-669
Pitre, Augustin-Francois, S2-668
Pitre, Bazile, S2-655-656
Pitre, Benjamin, C-83-84
Pitre, Benjamin, F-77
Pitre, Benjamin, N-68, 78, 142-143, 220
Pitre, Benjamin, S2-641, 643, 659-661
Pitre, Benjamin, S3-912-913
Pitre, Camille, E-32, 357
Pitre, Canute, S2-660
Pitre, Catherine, E-472
Pitre, Cecile, N-143
Pitre, Cecile-Olive, S2-661
Pitre, Cecille, F-77
Pitre, Charles, C-78
Pitre, Charles, E-29, 357
Pitre, Charles, F-101
Pitre, Charles, S1-349
Pitre, Charles, S2-491, 494, 501, 503, 624, 656, 658, 661, 663
Pitre, Charles, S3-920
Pitre, Charles-Paul, S2-669
Pitre, Charlotte, S2-669
Pitre, Charlotte Marie, F-97
Pitre, Charlotte-Marie, S2-667, 669
Pitre, Christine, C-53, 58
Pitre, Christine, E-192-193
Pitre, Christine, F-31, 35
Pitre, Christine, N-95, 207
Pitre, Claude, C-83
Pitre, Claude, E-357, 494, 529, 571
Pitre, Claude, F-67, 77, 87
Pitre, Claude, N-142-143
Pitre, Claude, S1-126

Pitre, Claude, S2-659, 663-665, 668, 670-674, 694, 702
Pitre, Claude, S3-912, 925, 1115
Pitre, Claude Marc, E-357
Pitre, Claude-Jean, S1-322
Pitre, Elisabeth, E-357
Pitre, Elizabeth, F-21
Pitre, Elizabeth, N-108-109, 140-141
Pitre, Elizabeth, S2-495, 541, 665-666, 696
Pitre, Elizabeth, S3-922, 924
Pitre, Elizabeth Olive, N-142
Pitre, Elizabeth-Modeste, S2-663
Pitre, Etienne, F-77
Pitre, Etienne, N-143
Pitre, Euphrosine-Francoise, S2-673
Pitre, Felicite, F-97
Pitre, Felicite, S2-668-669
Pitre, Francois, E-91, 357, 494, 529
Pitre, Francois, F-75, 97
Pitre, Francois, N-143
Pitre, Francois, S1-168
Pitre, Francois, S2-664-665, 669, 672, 674
Pitre, Francois, S3-925
Pitre, Francois Thomas, E-357
Pitre, Francois-Jean-Baptiste, S2-661
Pitre, Francoise, C-55
Pitre, Francoise, E-280
Pitre, Francoise, F-67, 107
Pitre, Francoise, N-109, 144, 251
Pitre, Francoise, S2-610, 660
Pitre, Francoise-Madeleine, S2-668
Pitre, Francoise-Olive, S2-671
Pitre, Genevieve, N-142
Pitre, Genevieve Louise, C-84
Pitre, Genevieve-Marguerite, S2-674
Pitre, George Larie, C-84
Pitre, Germain, C-43, 78, 84
Pitre, Germain, E-157, 357-358
Pitre, Germain, F-43, 45
Pitre, Germain, N-144
Pitre, Germain, S1-152, 347

Pitre, Germain, S2-624, 663, 673
Pitre, Germain, S3-1129
Pitre, Germain Jean, E-357
Pitre, Gregoire-Marie, S2-673
Pitre, Henriette, F-43
Pitre, Henriette, N-145
Pitre, Honore-Marie, S2-664
Pitre, Isabelle, F-101
Pitre, Isabelle, S2-494, 658, 662
Pitre, Isabelle Olive, F-45
Pitre, Isabelle-Olive, S2-658
Pitre, Jacques, F-97
Pitre, Jacques, S2-669
Pitre, Jacques Francois, E-28, 357
Pitre, Jacques-Francois, S2-668
Pitre, Jacquette, E-35
Pitre, Jean, C-83
Pitre, Jean, E-476, 494
Pitre, Jean, F-21, 45, 77, 87, 97
Pitre, Jean, N-103, 108, 141, 143, 175
Pitre, Jean, S1-62, 359
Pitre, Jean, S2-476, 491, 495, 541, 657, 665-667, 670, 672
Pitre, Jean, S3-866-868, 922, 924, 1116
Pitre, Jean Baptiste, E-358
Pitre, Jean Baptiste, F-15
Pitre, Jean Baptiste, N-144-145
Pitre, Jean Charles, C-83
Pitre, Jean Louis, N-140
Pitre, Jean Marie, F-27
Pitre, Jean Marie, N-140-141
Pitre, Jean Pierre, F-45
Pitre, Jean Pierre, N-142
Pitre, Jean Vincent, F-15
Pitre, Jean-Baptiste, S2-660, 667, 669, 671
Pitre, Jean-Charles, S2-662-663
Pitre, Jean-Marie, S1-142
Pitre, Jean-Marie, S2-667, 670
Pitre, Jean-Pierre, S2-657-658
Pitre, Jeanne Marguerite Pitre, E-283
Pitre, Jehan, E-458
Pitre, Joachim Charles, N-142
Pitre, Joachim-Charles, S2-658
Pitre, Joseph, E-357-358
Pitre, Joseph, F-85, 97, 101

Pitre, Joseph, S1-144
Pitre, Joseph, S2-493, 568, 659, 661, 668, 670
Pitre, Joseph, S3-866
Pitre, Joseph Francois, N-141
Pitre, Joseph Rene, N-141
Pitre, Joseph Vincent, N-145
Pitre, Joseph-Francois, S2-657
Pitre, Joseph-Pierre, S2-662-663
Pitre, Judith-Marguerite-Genevieve, S2-658
Pitre, Julie Aimee, N-144
Pitre, Louis Constant, F-67
Pitre, Louis Constant, N-144
Pitre, Louise Genevieve, N-143
Pitre, Madeleine, E-147, 357
Pitre, Madeleine, N-142-143, 145
Pitre, Madeleine Rose, N-145
Pitre, Madeleine-Modeste, S2-660
Pitre, Magdelaine, F-43, 77
Pitre, Magdelaine, S3-920
Pitre, Marc, E-494
Pitre, Marguerite, C-78
Pitre, Marguerite, E-143, 358
Pitre, Marguerite, F-23, 45, 77, 97, 101
Pitre, Marguerite, N-68, 103, 132, 140, 142-143, 175
Pitre, Marguerite, S1-64, 119-120, 322, 349
Pitre, Marguerite, S2-624-625, 657, 663, 667, 669, 673
Pitre, Marguerite Bibianne, S2-666
Pitre, Marguerite-Charlotte, S2-661
Pitre, Marguerite-Genevieve, S1-71
Pitre, Marguerite-Genevieve, S2-672
Pitre, Marguerite-Josephe, S2-663
Pitre, Marguerite-Ludivine, S2-658
Pitre, Marguerite-Marie, S2-669
Pitre, Marguerite-Tarsille, S2-656
Pitre, Margueritte Genevieve, S3-922

Pitre, Marie, C-21, 37, 84
Pitre, Marie, E-358, 476, 529
Pitre, Marie, F-27, 43, 47, 77, 87, 97
Pitre, Marie, N-140-141, 143, 145
Pitre, Marie, S1-4, 62-63, 124, 131, 135, 138-139, 141, 144, 158, 213, 288, 325, 341, 343, 349
Pitre, Marie, S2-470, 485, 488, 493-495, 503, 573, 624-625, 656, 659-660, 665-666, 673
Pitre, Marie, S3-1142-1143
Pitre, Marie Anne, E-148, 358
Pitre, Marie Anne Victoire, E-358
Pitre, Marie Christine, E-313
Pitre, Marie Francoise, F-45
Pitre, Marie Francoise, N-142
Pitre, Marie Madeleine, F-101, 103
Pitre, Marie Magdeleine, S3-876, 890, 934
Pitre, Marie Martine, N-144
Pitre, Marie Victoire, F-23
Pitre, Marie Victoire, N-58-59
Pitre, Marie Victoirre, S3-1143
Pitre, Marie-Blanche, S2-670
Pitre, Marie-Cecile, S2-671
Pitre, Marie-Charlotte, S2-664
Pitre, Marie-Francoise, S2-657
Pitre, Marie-Josephe, S2-745-746
Pitre, Marie-Ludivine, S2-671
Pitre, Marie-Madeleine, S1-137
Pitre, Marie-Madeleine, S2-501-502, 605-606, 639, 752
Pitre, Marie-Perinne, S2-669
Pitre, Marie-Rose, S2-673
Pitre, Marie-Victoire, S2-656
Pitre, Marin, S2-662
Pitre, Martin, F-109
Pitre, Martin, N-243
Pitre, Martin Benony, C-55
Pitre, Martin Benony, N-87
Pitre, Martin-Beonie, S2-672
Pitre, Mathurin, N-143
Pitre, Michel, E-358
Pitre, Michel, S2-605, 639
Pitre, Michel, S3-876

Pitre, Natalie, F-23
Pitre, Natalie, N-116
Pitre, Natalie, S3-1025
Pitre, Nathalie, S1-114
Pitre, Nathalie, S2-567-568, 659, 733
Pitre, Olive Julie, N-144
Pitre, Olivier, F-67, 107
Pitre, Olivier, N-143-144
Pitre, Olivier, S1-349
Pitre, Olivier, S2-470, 624, 661, 671-672
Pitre, Olivier, S3-1129
Pitre, Olivier-Charles, S2-664
Pitre, Paul, C-55
Pitre, Paul, N-87
Pitre, Paul, S2-453, 660, 664-665, 672, 674, 773
Pitre, Paul, S3-925, 1115, 1139
Pitre, Paul Ambroise, C-82
Pitre, Paul Ambroise, F-27
Pitre, Paul Ambroise, N-141
Pitre, Pierre, E-358, 494
Pitre, Pierre, F-43, 97
Pitre, Pierre, N-145
Pitre, Pierre, S2-662, 666, 668-669
Pitre, Pierre Andre, N-145
Pitre, Pierre Olivier, C-57, 84, 90
Pitre, Pierre Olivier, F-43
Pitre, Pierre Olivier, N-144-145
Pitre, Pierre-Olivier, S2-457, 673
Pitre, Prudente-Jeanne, S2-669
Pitre, Raphael, S2-664-665, 672-674
Pitre, Rene, N-215
Pitre, Romain, N-144
Pitre, Simon, E-143, 358
Pitre, Simon, S1-114, 117, 120
Pitre, Simon, S2-465, 568, 659, 674, 693
Pitre, Simon, S3-998, 1025, 1033, 1078
Pitre, Simon Joseph, E-358
Pitre, Susanne, S2-476-478, 495-496, 501, 665
Pitre, Suzanne, F-87
Pitre, Suzanne, S1-16
Pitre, Suzanne, S3-922

Pitre, T., S3-1116
Pitre, Te., S3-1115
Pitre, Tersile, S2-656, 667
Pitre, Tranquille, C-3
Pitre, Tranquille, F-15
Pitre, Tranquille, N-6, 140, 145, 237
Pitre, Tranquille, S1-4, 389
Pitre, Tranquille, S2-624, 655-656
Pitre, Tranquille, S3-933, 1115-1116, 1129, 1133-1134, 1140, 1143
Pitre, Ursule, F-75
Pitre, Ursule Francois, C-35
Pitre, Ursule-Francois, S1-270
Pitre, Ursule-Francoise, S2-665
Pitre, Victoire, F-67
Pitre, Victoire, N-144
Pitre, Victoire, S2-671-672
Pitre, Zozime, S2-656
Pittaluga, Nicolette, E-440
Pittalugue, Augustin Antoine, E-181, E-182, 358
Pittalugue, Manuel, E-358
Pitteau, Anne, E-77
Pivert, Jean, E-325, 337
Pivon, Jeanne, E-355
Pizan, Lazare, E-21
Place, Dominique, E-279
Plaideau, Elizabeth, E-256-257
Plaideau, Gabrielle, E-257
Plaideau, Marguerite, E-358
Plancard, Aimee, E-327, 393
Planchon, Louis, E-169, 358
Planson, Guillaume, E-358
Planson, Pierre, E-358
Plansonet dit Lepine, Pierre, E-358
Plantagenet, Henry, E-40
Plante, Jean Paul, E-358
Plante, Marie Catherine, E-358
Plante, Simon, E-358
Plaquaire, Pierre, E-316
Plasonet dit Lepine, Pierre, E-22
Plasonet dit Lepine, Thibault, E-22, 358
Pledeau, Pierre, E-122, 359, 409
Plentaud, Marie Rose, E-313
Plomcard, Anne, E-330
Ploque, Marie Madeleine, E-626

Ploton, Anastasse, E-359
Ploton, Jean, E-359
Pochet, Elisabeth Jeanne, E-626
Pochet, Jean Michel, E-626
Poerier, Marie, S3-994
Poesnel, Antoine, E-617
Poesnel, Jean Marie Joseph, E-617
Poesnel, Marie Francoise, E-617
Poesnel, Perrine Harang., E-617
Poesnel, Pierre Jean Baptiste, E-617
Poetie, Marie Claire, E-355
Poignet, Jan, S3-1146
Poignet, M., S3-1146
Poignier, Charles, E-335
Poiltier, Anne, E-146
Poinau, Francois, E-359
Poinau, Laurent, E-359, 378
Poinau, Marie, E-359
Poinot, Marguerite, E-100
Poinsa, Francois, E-299
Poinsteau, Andre, E-418
Poinsteau, Catherine, E-24, 418
Poinsteau, Jean, E-53, 418
Poinsteau, Marie, E-53, 428
Poinsu, Nicolas, S2-675
Pointe-aux-Chenes now known as Stoney Beach, E-209
Pointel, Jeanne Marguerite, E-627
Pointel, Marie, S2-763, 779
Pointel, Marie, S3-1061
Pointier, Rene, E-319, 359
Poiree, Helene, S1-38
Poirier, Abraham, S1-229
Poirier, Alain, E-366
Poirier, Alexis, E-359, 366
Poirier, Alin, E-429
Poirier, Ambroise, E-548
Poirier, Anastasie, E-359
Poirier, Ange Marie, E-359
Poirier, Ange Narcis, E-359
Poirier, Angelique, E-44, 165
Poirier, Angelique Antoinette Adelaide, E-361-362
Poirier, Anne, C-5, 139, 159
Poirier, Anne, E-17, 84, 163-164, 181, 338, 359, 381, 383, 406-407, 435, 515, 546, 548
Poirier, Anne, N-8-9

Poirier, Anne, S1-36, 218, 366
Poirier, Anne Marguerite, E-360
Poirier, Anselme, E-156, 360, 363
Poirier, Antoine, S2-676
Poirier, Antoine Edouard, E-360
Poirier, Balthasar, E-360
Poirier, Basile, E-360-363, 365
Poirier, Bernard, E-546
Poirier, Bonne Marie Francoise, E-360
Poirier, Catherine, E-360, 549
Poirier, Catherine Aimee Bernardine, E-360, 405
Poirier, Cecile, E-549
Poirier, Celeste Agathe, E-360
Poirier, Charles, E-360, 363
Poirier, Claude, E-363, 366, 515, 627
Poirier, Claude, S3-1084
Poirier, Clotilde, E-361
Poirier, Constant, E-633, 639
Poirier, Edouard Leandre, E-361
Poirier, Elisabeth, E-361
Poirier, Elise, E-632, 639
Poirier, Elise Julie, E-642
Poirier, Elizabeth, E-17
Poirier, Emelie Clemence, E-361
Poirier, Emelie Victorine, E-361
Poirier, Ernest Raoul, E-361
Poirier, Esther, E-360
Poirier, Felix Eugene Napoleon, E-361
Poirier, Francois, E-1, 360-361, 363-365, 547, 549
Poirier, Francois, S2-675
Poirier, Francois, S3-986, 1028
Poirier, Francois Alexandre, E-361-362
Poirier, Francoise, E-360-361
Poirier, Francoise-Jeanne, S2-429
Poirier, Francoise-Marie, S2-676
Poirier, Genevieve, E-37, 57, 87, 362, 435-434, 437, 632, 639, 643
Poirier, Georges, E-360
Poirier, Godel, E-362
Poirier, Guillaume, E-364, 546

Poirier, Helene, E-362

Poirier, Henriette, E-365

Poirier, Jacques, E-1, 35, 359-366, 434, 547, 632, 642

Poirier, Jacques Augustin, E-362

Poirier, Jacques Jr., E-637, 642

Poirier, Jacques pere, E-639

Poirier, Jean, E-83, 139, 187, 348, 359, 361-364, 366, 549

Poirier, Jean Baptiste, C-86

Poirier, Jean Baptiste, E-19, 164, 327, 359, 361-365, 367, 431, 515, 529, 548, 632, 639, 642

Poirier, Jean Claude, E-363

Poirier, Jean Jacques, E-363

Poirier, Jean Pierre, E-308, 360-361, 363-365

Poirier, Jeanne, E-365, 549, 632, 639

Poirier, Jeanne Melanie, E-642

Poirier, Jeanne-Francoise, S2-675

Poirier, Jehan, E-458

Poirier, Joseph, E-29, 59, 87-88, 119, 121, 186-187, 287, 360-361, 363-365, 433, 436, 546-549, 572, 632, 642

Poirier, Joseph, S2-451, 675-677

Poirier, Joseph, S3-970

Poirier, Joseph Thomas, E-363

Poirier, Louis, E-1, 56, 58, 99, 189, 359, 361-363, 365, 434, 436-437, 515, 529, 632, 639, 643

Poirier, Louis Denis, E-360, 405

Poirier, Louis Frederic Alexandre, E-363

Poirier, Louis Jacques Francois, E-364

Poirier, Louis Sr., E-639

Poirier, Louise, E-366

Poirier, Louise Appoline, E-364

Poirier, Louise Julie, E-364

Poirier, Louise Marie, E-642

Poirier, Lucie, E-37, 56, 633, 639, 643

Poirier, Madeleine, S1-215-216, 223, 228-230

Poirier, Madeleine, S2-553, 577, 676-677, 740

Poirier, Magdelaine, C-163

Poirier, Magdelaine, E-36, 141, 156, 364, 390, 549, 627

Poirier, Magdeleine, S3-1090, 1098

Poirier, Marguerite, C-25

Poirier, Marguerite, E-21, 82-83, 86, 116, 145, 327, 335-336, 364, 368, 549, 572, 639

Poirier, Marguerite, N-42, 205

Poirier, Marguerite, S1-214-215

Poirier, Marguerite, S2-676-677

Poirier, Marguerite Elisabeth, E-364

Poirier, Marie, C-62, 86-87, 163

Poirier, Marie, E-164, 183-184, 188-189, 274, 322, 326, 364, 377-378, 390, 433, 457, 476, 526, 546, 548-549, 632-633, 639

Poirier, Marie, S2-451-453, 675, 677

Poirier, Marie Adelaide, E-364

Poirier, Marie Anne, E-364

Poirier, Marie Anne Paule, E-364

Poirier, Marie Elizabeth, E-365

Poirier, Marie Etienne, E-643

Poirier, Marie Francoise, E-572

Poirier, Marie Josephe, E-29, 61, 117, 164, 365, 368, 572

Poirier, Marie Louise, E-365, 367

Poirier, Marie Louise Pelagie, E-639

Poirier, Marie Madeleine, E-301, 306-307, 365

Poirier, Marie Madeleine, N-147

Poirier, Marie Victor, E-365

Poirier, Marie-Josephe, S2-676

Poirier, Marie-Madeleine, S2-597-599

Poirier, Martin, E-365, 633

Poirier, Michel, E-258, 307, 364-365, 458, 476, 515, 529, 546, 548-549

Poirier, Michel, N-42

Poirier, Michel, S1-214

Poirier, Michel, S2-597

Poirier, Mr., E-279, 287, 365

Poirier, Nicolas, E-361

Poirier, Olivier, E-365

Poirier, Pauline Desiree, E-365

Poirier, Pelagie, E-37, 57, 182, 365, 434, 436-437, 632, 639, 643

Poirier, Perrine, S3-952

Poirier, Pierre, E-83, 348, 362-363, 365, 367, 529, 546, 548-549

Poirier, Pierre Alexis, E-572

Poirier, Pierre Constant, E-643

Poirier, Pierre Leon, E-361, 365

Poirier, Pierre Vincent, E-367

Poirier, Pierre-Alexis, S2-676

Poirier, Rene, E-362

Poirier, Rosalie, E-1, 20, 38, 303, 365-366, 418, 631, 643

Poirier, Rose, E-366

Poirier, Simon, E-182, 359, 361, 366, 632, 639, 642

Poirier, Sophie Celeste, E-366, 637, 642

Poirier, Victoire, E-366, 402

Poirier, Zelie Victoire, E-366

Poiro, Jean-Baptiste, S1-218

Poiron, Jean, E-390

Poissan, Jean Jacques, E-366

Poissan, Madeleine, E-366

Poissard, Marie Catherine, E-19

Poisson, Francois Amand, E-361

Poisson, Marie, S2-428

Poitevin, Catherine, S2-675

Poitevin, Elisabeth, E-366

Poitevin, Etienne, E-93, 108, 307, 350, 366, 412, 419

Poitevin, Etienne, S1-331

Poitevin, Francoise, S2-546

Poitevin, Genevieve, E-108-109

Poitevin, Jacques, S2-674

Poitevin, Jean, E-152, 377

Poitevin, Jeunuieve, E-366

Poitevin, Judith, E-110, 119, 371

Poitevin, Louis, E-141

Poitevin, Louis, S1-331

Poitevin, Madele, E-263

Poitevin, Madeleine, S2-722

Poitevin, Magdelaine, E-263, 371, 327, 372, 394

Poitevin, Marie, E-141, 312, 366, 419

Poitevin, Marie, S1-332

Poitevin, Marie Josephe, E-141, 350, 366

Poitevin, Marie Judith, E-141, 367

Poitevin, Marie Magdelaine, E-109

Poitevin, Marie-Josephe, S1-331

Poitevin, Marie-Judith, S1-331-332

Poitevin, Ursule, E-5-6, 307, 331, 366, 393

Poitevin, Ursule, S2-722

Poitier, Anne, C-63

Poitier, Anne, N-37, 76, 103, 179, 211

Poitier, Anne Appoline, C-85

Poitier, Anne Appoline, N-146

Poitier, Anne Pauline, F-33

Poitier, Anne Pauline, N-146

Poitier, Baptiste Olivier, F-19

Poitier, Baptiste-Olivier, S2-678

Poitier, Catherine, S2-677, 679

Poitier, Cecile, F-69

Poitier, Charles, N-188

Poitier, Charles Victor, C-84

Poitier, Charles Victor, F-33

Poitier, Charles Victor, N-146, 200

Poitier, Charlotte, F-35

Poitier, Charlotte, N-94, 139, 200

Poitier, Charlotte, S2-678

Poitier, Christopher, F-35

Poitier, Christopher, N-94, 139, 200

Poitier, Constance, F-33

Poitier, Constance, N-146

Poitier, Francois Constant, F-33

Poitier, Francois Constant, N-146

Poitier, Francoise, S2-743

Poitier, Francoise-Marie, S2-678

Poitier, Jacques Silvin, F-19

Poitier, Jean-Baptiste, S2-678

Poitier, Joseph, S2-677, 679

Poitier, Magdeleine, F-69

Poitier, Marie Constance, C-84

Poitier, Marie Constance, N-146

Poitier, Marie Henriette, F-83

Poitier, Marie Henriette, N-146, 147, 187

Poitier, Marie Madeleine, N-129, 147

Poitier, Marie Magdeleine, C-73, 86

Poitier, Olivier, F-19

Poitier, Pierre, C-84

Poitier, Pierre, F-19, 33

Poitier, Pierre, N-70, 146, 201-202, 207

Poitier, Pierre, S1-210

Poitier, Pierre, S2-677-679

Poitier, Pierre Laurent, C-84

Poitier, Pierre Laurent, F-33

Poitier, Pierre Laurent, N-146

Poitier, Pierre-Charles, S2-678

Poitier, Pierre-Paul, S2-678

Poitier, Silvain, S2-678-679

Poivre, -----, E-5-6

Pojet, Judith, S2-671

Polinier, Louis, E-589

Pollard, Nora Lee , C-vii

Pollart, Suzanne, E-269, 393

Pollet, Marie Antoinette, E-343

Pollin, Georges, E-141, 367

Pollin, Nicolas, E-141, 367

Polon, Secille, E-266, 342

Poly, Francois, E-370

Pominville, Gabriel, E-367

Pommeret, Marie, S2-536

Pommier, Genevieve, E-256

Ponce, Marie Anne, E-27, 349

Poncet, Marie, E-130, 175, 266

Pongerart, Cosme, S1-195

Pongirard, Michelle, S2-622

Ponion, Angelique, E-367

Pons, Marianne, S2-483

Pons, Marie, E-350

Pontbrian, George, E-34

Pontbrian, Jean, E-34

Pontou, Margueritte, E-589, 593

Poponnet, Marie, E-295

Poquet, Jean, C-142

Porcher, Jacques, E-155

Porcheron, child, S2-679

Porcheron, Madeleine, S2-679

Porcheron, Martin, C-14, 82, 85, 93, 101, 103, 108

Porcheron, Martin, S1-379

Porcheron, Martin, S2-672, 679, 772-773

Porcheron, Martin, S3-1115, 1140

Porcheron, Martin Charles, S3-1140

Porcheron, Martin-Charles, S2-661, 679

Pordriel, Joseph, S2-489

Porel, Victor, S3-1013

Port Louis and the Acadians in 1759, E-367

Portier, Anne, S2-670

Portier, Anne, S3-866

Portier, Francoise, E-359, 409

Portier, Jean, S2-670

Portier, Jean, S3-866

Portier, Marie, E-354

Portier, Michel, E-354

Post, Mr., E-87

Post, Nicolas, E-87

Potdevin, Jeanne, S2-611

Potdevin, Judith, S1-280

Potdevin, Marie, S2-737

Potdevin, Marie, S3-973

Potel, Jacquette, S3-954

Potel, Marie, S2-592

Potel, Marie, S3-986

Potel, Marie Francoise, E-31, 301

Potet, Marie, E-472

Potevin, Genevieve, E-108

Potevin, Judith, E-95

Poti, Marie, E-369

Potier, Angelique, E-110, 268, 270, 342, 378

Potier, Anne, E-2, 73, 74, 131, 267-268, 274, 346, 367, 377, 428, 551

Potier, Cecile, E-367

Potier, Charles, E-270, 317, 367-368

Potier, Charles Victor, E-367

Potier, Charlotte, E-367

Potier, Charlotte, S1-262

Potier, Charlotte, S2-646

Potier, Charlotte, S3-1057

Potier, Christophe, E-41, 110, 367-368, 371, 551

Potier, Christophe, S2-646

Potier, Christophe, S3-1057

Potier, Claire, C-41
Potier, Claire, E-111, 268, 368
Potier, Claire, S2-687
Potier, Gilles, E-367
Potier, Jacque, S3-981
Potier, Jacques Christophe, E-267, 366, 368-369
Potier, Jean, E-268, 270, 341, 367-368, 377, 529
Potier, Jean Baptiste, E-551
Potier, Jean Charles, E-368
Potier, Jean Jacques, E-368
Potier, Jean Louis, E-69, 267, 341, 368
Potier, Joseph, E-368
Potier, Louis, C-41
Potier, Louis, E-123, 169, 186, 268, 320, 367-369, 376-377, 551
Potier, Louis, S1-371
Potier, Louis, S2-687
Potier, Louis Jacques, E-368
Potier, Louise, E-300
Potier, Louise M., E-431
Potier, Louise M., S2-776
Potier, Marguerite, E-112, 368-369
Potier, Marianne Anne, E-317
Potier, Marie, E-110-112, 157, 179, 368, 377-378, 550
Potier, Marie Angelique, E-55, 81, 274, 341-342, 368
Potier, Marie Anne, E-368
Potier, Marie Claire, E-270, 368
Potier, Marie Dominique, E-368
Potier, Marie Henriette, C-151
Potier, Marie Henriette, C-41
Potier, Marie Henriette, E-2, 74, 368, 375-376
Potier, Marie Magdelaine, E-294, 368-369, 377-378
Potier, Marie Marguerite Elisabeth, E-31, 301
Potier, Marie-Henriette, S2-687-688
Potier, Michel, E-368
Potier, Pierre, E-112, 194, 367-368, 550
Potier, Pierre, S2-726
Potier, Pierre, S3-855
Potier, Rene Francois, E-368

Potier, Susanne Marie, E-369
Potty, Francois, E-36
Potty, Jean Baptiste, E-36, 286, 369
Potty, Marguerite, E-36, 369
Potty, Marie Anne, E-369
Pouchin, Antoine, E-281, 369
Pouchin, Antoine Pierre Saint Sire, E-281, 369
Pougeard, Martial, E-369, 409
Pouget, Jean, E-28, 369
Pouget, Jean (Jr.), C-118
Pouget, Pierre, E-329, 370
Poujet, Jacques, C-86, 98
Poujet, Jean, C-85, 96, 120
Poujet, Pierre, C-86
Poujet, Rene, C-85
Poulain, Anne, S1-221
Poulain, Dujardne, S3-1014
Poulain, Jacque, S3-1014
Poulard, Anne, E-333, 369
Poulard, Nicolas, S2-680
Poulard La Bruyere, Nicolas, E-69, 370
Poulet, Guillaume, E-458
Pouliquen, M., C-viii
Pounsteau, Marguerite, E-130
Poupart, Jean, E-139, 359
Poupart, Louis, E-20, 316, 369
Poupet, Marie Anne, E-316
Poupet, Pierre Cyprien, E-316
Poupin, Helenne, S2-630
Poupon, Guillaume Gilles, E-325, 420
Pouponnat, Bernard, E-196
Pouponnet, Jeanne, E-73
Poussin, Francois, S2-779
Poussin, Rose, S1-141
Poussin, Rose, S2-670
Poutriquet, Louis Charles, E-97
Poyant, Francois, E-259, 409
Pradeau, Joseph, E-370, 376
Pradel, Etienne, E-180
Praud, Francois, E-339, 370
Praud, Francoise, C-ix
Praud, Marie, E-339, 370
Praux, Andre, E-370
Praux, Elizabeth, E-130
Praux, Marie Louise, E-370
Preau, Jean, N-252
Precieux, Anne, C-91

Precieux, Anne, S3-1084
Precieux, Joseph, F-71
Precieux, Joseph, S1-200, 276-277
Precieux, Joseph, S2-676, 680-681
Precieux, Joseph, S3-942-943
Precieux, Joseph, C-26, 35, 86, 138
Precieux, Louis, S2-681
Precieux, Louise, C-26
Precieux, Louise, E-79
Precieux, Louise, S1-200-202
Precieux, Louise-Marguerite, S2-680-681
Precieux, Marie Anne, C-35-36, 91
Precieux, Marie Anne, F-71
Precieux, Marie Madeleine, E-275, 370
Precieux, Marie-Anne, S1-276-279
Precieux, Marie-Anne, S2-431, 680
Precieux, Pierre, S2-681
Pree Bourgeois named for Jacques Bourgeois, E-209
Pree Ronde, E-215
Pregeant, Francois, E-110
Preix, Marie, E-368
Prejean, Anselme, E-370
Prejean, Cecile, S2-683
Prejean, Charles, E-370
Prejean, Charles, S2-684
Prejean, Cyprien, S2-682
Prejean, Felicite, S2-682
Prejean, Felix, S2-681
Prejean, Francois, E-370
Prejean, Francoise, E-122, 370
Prejean, Gabriel, S2-683-684
Prejean, Genevieve, S2-682
Prejean, Honore, S2-681
Prejean, Jan Baptiste, S3-969
Prejean, Jean, E-214, 476
Prejean, Jean-Baptiste, S2-682-684
Prejean, Jeanne, S2-683
Prejean, Julien, S2-682
Prejean, Louis, S2-683
Prejean, Madeleine, S2-682
Prejean, Marguerite, S2-682

Prejean, Marie, E-495
Prejean, Marie, S2-683, 724
Prejean, Marie Louise, E-328, 370
Prejean, Marie-Anne, S2-681
Prejean, Mr., E-370
Prejean, Nicolas, E-122, 370
Prejean, Nicolas, S1-220
Prejean, Nicolas, S2-682-684, 724-725
Prejean, Nicolas, S3-969
Prejean, Paul, S2-682
Prejean, Pierre, E-328, 370
Prejean, Pierre, S2-682
Prejean, Rosalie, E-129, 343, 347, 370
Prejean, Rose, S2-683
Presant, Jeanne, S3-1092
Presant, Julienne, S3-1092
Present, Catherine Marie, S3-1091-1092
Present, Catherine-Marie, S2-721
Present, Jan, S3-1091
Present, Jean, S2-721
Present, Miss, S3-1092
Pretieuse, Louise, S3-961
Pretieux, Anne, C-121
Preves, Marie Jeanne Olivier, E-432
Prevost, Charles, E-91, 370
Prevost, Jean, E-91
Prevost, Marguerite, E-371
Prevostel, Catherine, E-77, 392
Prevot, Achille, E-371
Prevot, Marie Josephe, E-124
Prevot, Marie Therese, E-371
Prieur, Anne, E-371
Prieur, Elizabeth, E-371
Prieur, Emanuel, E-371
Prieur, Genevieve, E-371
Prieur, Guillaume, E-263, 371-372
Prieur, Isabelle, E-263, 372
Prieur, Jacques, E-371
Prieur, Jean, E-143, 371
Prieur, Jean Baptiste, E-371
Prieur, Joseph, E-301, 371
Prieur, Joseph Francois, E-371
Prieur, Marguerite, E-142-143, 371

Prieur, Marguerite Joseph, E-371
Prieur, Marie, E-143, 263, 304, 371, 430
Prieur, Marie Joseph, E-371
Prieur, Marie Modeste, E-372
Prieur, Pierre, E-371-372
Prieur, Pierre Louis, E-372
Prieur dit Dubois, Guillaume, E-371
Prieure, Isabelle, E-312, 393
Prieure, Isabelle, S2-723
Prieure, Jacque, E-371
Prieure, Pierre, E-356
Prigent, Jeanne, S1-43
Prillaud, Marie, E-22
Primal, Marie, E-140
Prin, Abraham Samuel Jean, E-99, 172
Prince, Antoine, E-150, 285, 425
Prince, Jean, E-214
Prince, Joseph, E-123, 150, 285
Prince, Marie Sophie, E-424
Prince, Olivier, E-150
Prince - See also LePrince
Printel, Louis, S3-1055
Printel, Marie, N-172
Printel, Marie, S2-779
Printel, Marie, S3-1055
Priou, Francois, S2-739
Priou, Francois, S3-952
Priou, Jean, E-24, 46, 348, 357
Priou, Marie, S1-37
Priou, Marie, S2-739
Priou, Marie, S3-952
Priou, Rose, E-617
Prioul, Jean, S3-1137
Prioul, Jeanne, S1-241
Prioux, Hiacinthe, S1-60-61
Prisieu, Anne, E-269
Proard, Marie, E-372
Pronelle, Marie, S2-758
Prongier, Joseph, S3-925
Prou, Jean, E-259
Prou, Pierre, E-63
Prou, Sebastien, E-188
Proud, Anne Catherine, E-350, 372
Proud, Louis, E-350, 372
Prouet, Sebastien, E-27

Prouff, Yves, E-99
Proust, -----, S3-958
Proust, Etienne Bonnaventure, S3-957
Provost, Jacques, E-476
Provost, Jeanne, E-296, 417
Prudereniquet, -----, S3-1087
Puahh, Pierre, E-333
Pudens, Marie Felix, E-360
Puel, Marie, S3-960
Pueri, Madeleine, E-156
Puerie, Anselme, E-372
Puerie, Guillaume, E-372
Puget, Christophe dit Vadan, E-372
Puget, Joseph, E-372
Puget dit Vadan, Christophe, E-274
Pugnant, Margueritte, E-33, 372
Pugnant, Nicolas, E-33, 372
Puigibeaut, Marguerite Barbe, E-61
Puni, Victoire, C-161
Pupulus, Marie Marguerite, E-124

Q

Quailain, Jean, E-373
Quailain, Marie, E-373
Quandolle, Haunore, E-29
Quantin, Marguerite Alexandrine, E-373
Quantin, Marie, E-373
Quantin, Paul, E-373
Quara, Catherine, E-373, 376
Quara, Jean Baptiste, E-373, 376
Quare, Angelique, E-85
Quare, Therese, E-169
Quarvain, Farlin, E-196
Quatrehommes, Lise, E-431
Quatresous, Jacques, S3-950
Quaysi, Marie, E-170
Quecy, Olivier, S1-184
Quelan, Jean, E-45, 439
Quelec, Anne, E-322
Quelle, Marie Francoise, E-165
Quellec, Francois, E-427
Quellec, Marie Josephe, E-424
Quellec, Martin, E-288
Quemar, Francoise, S2-670

Quemar, Francoise, S3-866
Quemine, Alexis, E-373
Quemine, Anne, E-23, 29, 104,
  259, 293-294, 306, 371, 373,
  377, 411
Quemine, Francoise, E-78, 86,
  355, 373
Quemine, Genevieve, E-373
Quemine, Jacques, E-170, 374
Quemine, Jean, E-95, 373
Quemine, Jean Louis, E-373
Quemine, Judith, E-120, 306
Quemine, Magdeleine, E-29, 54,
  55, 170, 371
Quemine, Marguerite, E-28, 81,
  293, 373
Quemine, Marie, E-263, 371,
  373
Quemine, Marie Joseph, E-373
Quemine, Marie Madeleine, E-
  373, 378
Quemine, Pierre, E-29, 170,
  355, 373-374
Quenet, Francois, E-600
Quenet, Francoise, E-600
Quenet, Marie, E-304, 389
Quenet, Marie Louise, E-600
Quentin, Suzanne, E-603
Querat, Joseph, E-117
Queray, Anne, E-65
Querel, Catherine, E-293, 420
Querel, Marie, E-93
Querel, Marie Jeanne, E-368
Querel, Pelagie, E-167
Querel, Pierre, E-93, 373
Querel, Pierre Marie, E-289
Querel, Yves, E-373, 414
Queret, Pierre Marie, E-116
Querray, Marie, E-276
Querre, Jacques, E-316, 354
Querrier, Marguerite, E-178
Quesney, Jeanne, S1-362
Quesniere, Anne, E-141
Quesniere, Anne, S1-332
Quessy, Anne, E-61, 141, 293,
  550
Quessy, Anne Marie, E-553
Quessy, Bonaventure, E-627
Quessy, Brigite, E-63, 292, 301,
  316, 550

Quessy, Cecile, E-63, 104, 112,
  169-170, 550, 587, 594
Quessy, Francoise, E-620, 627
Quessy, Genevieve, E-620
Quessy, Guillaume, E-516
Quessy, Jacques, E-550
Quessy, Jean, E-63, 170, 176,
  516, 526, 550
Quessy, Jean Baptiste, E-627
Quessy, Jean Sr., E-526
Quessy, Jeanne, E-169
Quessy, Joseph, E-550, 553
Quessy, Louise, E-365
Quessy, Mad., E-589, 596
Quessy, Magdelaine, E-63, 133,
  176, 276, 309, 374, 553
Quessy, Marguerite, E-103-104,
  176, 301, 627
Quessy, Marie, E-169, 374, 516,
  524, 549-550, 627
Quessy, Marie, S3-1045, 1101
Quessy, Marie Auxitte, E-627
Quessy, Marie Magdelaine, E-
  176, 267
Quessy, Michel, E-516, 526,
  550, 627
Quessy, Michel, S3-988, 1100-
  1101
Quessy, Paul, E-621, 627
Quessy, Paul, S3-994
Quessy, Pierre, E-516, 526, 627
Quessy, Pierre Michel, E-627
Quessy, Roger, E-457, 476
Quessy - See sometimes Kessis
Questi, Marie, E-368
Queyrnier, Marie, E-196
Quiau, Paul, S1-185
Quidort, Jeanne, E-12
Quiescy, Marguerite, C-99
Quievey, Paul, S3-961
Quillay, Joseph, E-22
Quimine, Francois, E-55
Quimine, Francoise, S3-972
Quimine, Jacque, S3-972
Quimine, Pierre, C-151
Quimine, Pierre, S3-948, 1045,
  1054
Quineville, Marie Catherine, E-
  86, 418
Quital, Francois, S3-996
Quivot, Jean, S1-282

Quoniam, Bon Antoine, E-374
Quoniam, Therese, E-334, 374
Qusey, Cecile, S3-1009

R

Rabas Lapichardiere, Jacques,
  E-375, 438
Rabasse, Jean, S1-48
Rabier, Angelique Heleine, C-
  32, 149
Rabot, Francois, S1-2
Rabot, Francois, S3-932
Rabot, Francoise, S1-2
Rabot, Joseph, S3-932
Rabot, Rose, S1-2
Rabot, Rose, S3-932
Rabouin, Marie, E-337, 375
Raby, Therese, E-12, 279
Rache, Charles, C-50
Racicot, Jean, E-179
Racicot, Rene, S3-1022
Racle, Hugue, E-600
Racois, Surgeon-Major, S2-613
Racquet, Jean, E-375
Racquet, Jean Mathias, E-144,
  375
Radau, Pierre, E-375
Radou, Francois Jr., E-627
Radou, Francois Sr., E-627
Radou, Marie, E-257
Radou, Mathurin, S3-1042
Radoub, -----, S2-441, 684
Radoub, Charles, S2-441, 684
Radoub, Jean-Baptiste, S2-441,
  684
Radoub, Marguerite, S2-441,
  684
Radoub, Victoire, S1-44
Radoux, Jean, E-619
Rafferaye, Guillemette, S1-182
Raffray, Gilles, S3-860
Raffy, Adelaide, E-627
Raffy, Constant, E-627
Raffy, Francois Augustin, S3-
  1095-1096
Raffy, Guillemette, S2-704
Raffy, Marie, E-627
Raffy, Rene, E-627-628
Raffy, Rene, S2-553
Raffy, Rene, S3-1098

Rafi, Guillemette-Francoise, S1-352
Rafin, Catherine, E-66, 375
Rafin, Nicolas, E-66, 375
Rageot, Mathurin, S2-591
Rageot, Mathurin, S3-931
Rageot, Pelagie, S2-591
Rageot, Pelagie, S3-931
Raget, Marie Elisabeth, E-70
Ragot, Anne, E-137
Rail, Jean Baptiste, E-375
Raileau, Henriette, E-413
Raimbaud, Claudine, C-114
Raimbeau, Magdelaine, E-32, 403
Raimon, Jean, E-178
Raimon, Marie, C-3, 127
Raimond, Francoise, F-95
Raimond, Francoise, S1-86
Raimond, Francoise, S3-903
Raizain, Francois, E-376
Raizain, Jean Baptiste, E-376
Rajot, Mathurin, S3-931
Rambauts, Marie, E-589, 592
Rambeau, Charles, E-440
Rambeaur, Elisabeth, E-90, 375
Rambeaur, Jean, E-90, 375
Rambourg, Felix, S2-479, 685
Rambourg, Francois, E-620, 627
Rambourg, Francois, S2-479, 684-687
Rambourg, Francois-Noel-Guillaume, S2-685
Rambourg, Francoise, E-627
Rambourg, Francoise-Renee, S2-685
Rambourg, Guillaume-Michel, S2-685
Rambourg, Jean, E-627
Rambourg, Jean, S2-479, 684-685, 687
Rambourg, Jean-Francois-Etienne, S2-686
Rambourg, Jean-Noel, S2-686
Rambourg, Jean-Pierre, S2-479, 686
Rambourg, Jeanne, E-80
Rambourg, Jeanne-Francoise, S2-687
Rambourg, Jerome, S1-375

Rambourg, Jerome, S2-479, 686-687
Rambourg, Marie, S1-172
Rambourg, Marie-Jeanne, S2-512, 686
Rambourg, Martin, S2-479, 686
Ramigeau, Marie, E-133
Ramirez, Francois, F-33
Ramirez, Jean, F-33
Rancurel, Jean Baptiste, E-163
Randeau, Jacques Philipe Urbin, E-290
Raoul, Francois, S3-856
Raoul, G., S3-856
Raoul, Guillaume, S3-848
Raoult, Guillaume, E-298
Rapasse, Antoine, E-322
Raquin, Jean, E-155, 256, 276
Rassicot, Anne Marguerite, F-83
Rassicot, Anne Marguerite, N-147
Rassicot, Anne-Marguerite, S2-688
Rassicot, Jean Baptiste, C-41, 151
Rassicot, Jean Baptiste, E-2, 74, 375
Rassicot, Jean Baptiste, F-83
Rassicot, Jean Baptiste, N-49, 146-147, 187
Rassicot, Jean Francois, E-375
Rassicot, Jean Francois, F-83
Rassicot, Jean Francois, N-147
Rassicot, Jean-Baptiste, S2-687-688
Rassicot, Jean-Francois, S2-688
Rassicot, Louis, N-147
Rassicot, Louis, S2-688
Rassicot, Marie, E-326, 376
Rassicot, Marie Henriette, F-83
Rassicot, Marie Henriette, N-147
Rassicot, Marie-Henriette, S2-688
Rassicot, Mr., E-74
Rassicot, Rene, E-376
Rassicot, Rene, F-83
Rassicot, Rene, N-146
Rassicot, Rene, S1-51
Rassicot, Rene, S2-463, 687-688
Rassicot, Renee, E-376

Rassicot, widow, E-2
Rastet, Charles, E-347
Ratier, Jean Baptiste, E-368, 376
Ratier, Rene, E-376
Ratte, Josephe, E-183
Ratte, Magdelaine, E-276, 309
Rauge, Genevieve, E-78, 376
Rauger, Marie, E-51, 114, 370, 376
Rault, Jean, E-78
Rault, Marthe, E-376, 394
Raux, Angelique, S2-689
Raux, Anne, E-14, 168, 287, 315, 327, 344, 376
Raux, Elie, E-376
Raux, Etienne, E-55, 345, 376
Raux, Francois, E-406
Raux, Guillaume, S3-929
Raux, Jacques, E-59, 412
Raux, Jean, E-155, 376
Raux, Julienne, S1-166, 222
Raux, Louis, E-376
Raux, Louis, S2-689
Raux, Louis-Joseph, S2-689
Raux, Marguerite, S1-223
Raux, Marie, E-44, 152
Raux, Marie Magdelaine, E-393
Raux, Michel, E-21, 52
Raux, Pierre, S2-689
Raux, Pierre Jacques, E-412
Raval, Jeanne, E-377
Ravaleux, Anne, S2-690
Ravaleux, Henry, S2-689
Ravaleux, Henry, S3-1069
Ravaleux, Jan Henry Francois, S3-1069
Ravaleux, Jean, S1-33
Ravaleux, Jean, S2-543, 689
Ravaleux, Jean-Henry, S2-642
Ravaleux, Jean-Henry-Francois, S2-689
Ravaleux, Olive, S2-690
Ravaud, Marie, E-155, 376
Ravaux, Catherine, E-155
Raveau, Pierre, C-31
Ravenel, Pierre Jacques, E-128
Ravenel, Suzanne, E-128
Raveton, Antoine, E-90
Ravilly, Etienne, C-viii
Rayer, Laurent, E-376
Rayer, Mr., E-308

Rayer, Pierre, E-376
Rayl, Jean Baptiste, E-376
Rayl, Pierre Therese, E-376
Rayne, Gabriel, E-78, 376
Rayne, Jacques, E-78, 376
Rayne, Jean, E-376
Real, Marie Magdelaine, E-71
Reault, Jacques, E-418
Rebecca, Wardon, E-314
Rebin, Jean, E-188, 376
Rebin, Michel, E-188, 376
Rebouho, Marie, E-589, 594
Rebour, Jan, S3-904
Rebour, Laurent, S3-904
Recteau, Henriette, E-172
Reculard, Baptiste, E-281
Recule, Joseph, E-358
Recule, Marie Catherine, E-358
Reculoux, Servan, S3-935
Redouze, Marie Joseph, C-132
Regaud, Jacques, E-376
Regaud, Jean, E-326, 376
Regnauidin, Mr., E-42, 126
Regnauldin, Charles-Louis, S2-512
Regnauldin, Julie, S2-512
Regnauldin, Sr., S1-97
Regnault, -----, S3-960
Regnault, Francois, E-197
Regnault, Pierre, E-620
Regnault, Ursule, E-363
Regner, Pierre, E-161, 265
Regnier, Catherine, E-315, 376
Regnier, Francois, E-376
Regnier, Marie, E-105
Reignier, Jacques, E-385
Reignier, Marie Therese, E-362
Reine, Francoise, S2-761
Reine, Francoise, S3-911
Remand, Louis, E-51
Rembourg, Francois, S3-1019
Rembourg, Jean, S3-1019
Remiguea, Marie Suzanne, E-133
Remond, Antoine, E-377
Remond, Jeanne, E-159, 377
Remond, Louis, E-377
Renard, Anne, S2-603
Renard, Jean, E-264
Renard, Pierre, E-26
Renard, Suzanne, E-259, 330

Renau, Jean, C-115-116
Renau, Marie, E-368
Renaud, A., S3-951
Renaud, Adelaide, C-158, 163
Renaud, Alexis, C-52
Renaud, Alexis, N-81
Renaud, Alexis, S2-437
Renaud, Alexis, S3-1065
Renaud, Andre, E-12, 255, 274, 377-378, 389
Renaud, Andre, S2-513-514
Renaud, Anne, E-377
Renaud, Anne, S2-648
Renaud, Anne, S2-677
Renaud, Anselme, S2-677
Renaud, Antoine, S3-959
Renaud, Augustin, S1-373
Renaud, Augustin, S3-951
Renaud, Catherine, E-359
Renaud, Charles, E-627
Renaud, Charles, S2-691
Renaud, Charles Joseph, E-51, 319
Renaud, Charles-Pierre, S1-212
Renaud, Colette, E-2, 74, 267, 377
Renaud, Collet, F-11, 69
Renaud, Collet, N-124, 129, 198
Renaud, Collette, C-32, 73
Renaud, Francois, E-36, 377, 589, 592
Renaud, Francois, S2-690
Renaud, Francoise, E-589, 593
Renaud, Francoise, S1-373
Renaud, Francoise, S3-951
Renaud, Gilles Yves, E-317, 378
Renaud, Guillaume, S2-691
Renaud, Isidore Marin, C-87
Renaud, Isidore Marin, N-147
Renaud, Jacques, E-377, 627
Renaud, Jane, S2-598
Renaud, Jean, C-62, 75, 109, 139
Renaud, Jean, C-73, 86-87
Renaud, Jean, E-2, 74, 112, 294, 364, 368, 371, 377-378
Renaud, Jean, F-69
Renaud, Jean, N-129, 147, 185, 187, 243
Renaud, Jean, S3-1077
Renaud, Jean Baptiste, E-377

Renaud, Jean Charles, E-377
Renaud, Jean-Baptiste-Julien, S2-691
Renaud, Jeanne, E-627
Renaud, Jeanne, S1-373
Renaud, Jeanne Felicite, E-36, 377
Renaud, Jeanne-Laurence, S2-692
Renaud, Joseph, C-163
Renaud, Joseph Abraham, N-147
Renaud, Juliet, S2-677
Renaud, Laurent, E-359, 378
Renaud, Louis, C-163
Renaud, Louis, E-134, 377, 378
Renaud, Louis, S2-675
Renaud, Louis Auguste, C-86-87
Renaud, Louis Auguste, N-147
Renaud, Louis-Francois-Jean, S2-692
Renaud, Madeleine Eulalie, E-317, 378
Renaud, Magdeleine, C-74, 109
Renaud, Magdeleine Joseph, E-378
Renaud, Marguerite Aimee, C-163
Renaud, Marguerite Victoire, E-378
Renaud, Marie, C-163
Renaud, Marie, E-81, 123, 153, 271, 287, 294, 338, 359, 378
Renaud, Marie, S2-443-444
Renaud, Marie, S3-1023
Renaud, Marie Anne, C-87
Renaud, Marie Anne, E-378
Renaud, Marie Anne, N-147
Renaud, Marie Francoise, E-589, 594
Renaud, Marie Josephe, C-59
Renaud, Marie Josephe, F-5
Renaud, Marie Josephe, N-98-99, 249
Renaud, Marie Madeliene, C-74
Renaud, Marie Marguerite, E-190
Renaud, Marie Rose, E-73, 377
Renaud, Marie-Josephe, S1-309

Renaud, Marie-Josephe, S2-509, 511

Renaud, Mathurin, E-93, 104, 135, 330, 341, 350, 377-378, 431

Renaud, Pierre, E-377-378, 627

Renaud, Pierre, S2-677

Renaud, Pierre, S2-690-692

Renaud, Pierre, S3-970, 979, 992, 1007, 1018

Renaud, Pierre David, C-87

Renaud, Pierre David, N-147

Renaud, Pierre-Jean-Baptiste, S2-692

Renaud, Quintin, E-18, 288

Renaud, Renault, S2-690

Renaud, Rene, S2-443

Renaud, Rene, S3-1023

Renaud, Rosalie, E-378

Renaud, Suzanne Marie, E-378

Renaud, Ursule, E-364, 572

Renaud, Ursule, S2-675-677

Renaud, Veronique, C-32-33

Renaud, Veronique, E-30, 272, 377

Renaud, Veronique, F-67

Renaud, Veronique, N-52-53

Renaud, Yves-Joseph, S2-691

Renaudet, Bastien, E-379

Renaudet, Francois, E-378-379

Renaudet, Jacques Louis, E-379

Renaudet, Jean, E-379

Renaudet, Jean Francois, E-379

Renaudet, Jeanne, E-379

Renaudet, Magdeleine, E-379

Renaudet, Marie Jeanne, E-379

Rener, Jeanne, S1-333

Reniere, Pierre, S3-875-876

Renoche, Genevieve, E-379, 405

Renon, Veronique, E-376

Renon, Veronique, S2-688

Renou, Andre, E-358

Renou, Jeanne, E-394

Renou, Pierre, E-122, 313, 386

Renoul, Mr. , S3-915

Renoux, Helene, S3-995

Renoux, Madeleine, F-91

Renoux, Madeleine, S1-328

Renoux, Magdeleine, S3-1099

Renvertet, Jean, E-305

Repoussard, Anne Elizabeth, E-187

Repuce, Anne Marie, E-189, 379

Repuce, Pierre, E-379

Repussard, Elizabeth, E-182

Repussard, Nommee Elizabeth, E-186

Resse, Servant, E-413

Reste, -----, E-6

Restier, Amelie, E-255

Reteau, Henriette, E-379, 413

Reteau, Pierre, E-413

Retre, Cathera, E-328

Reuglet, Anne Marie, E-168, 404

Reveillard, Rene, S1-189, 347

Reveillard, Rene, S3-1077

Reveillon, Serry de, C-107

Rever, Anne, S2-461

Rever, Jeanne, E-109, 145

Revers, Francoise, S1-337

Revers, Francoise, S2-620

Revers, Francoise, S3-981

Reverse, Henriette, E-134, 379

Reverse, Henry, E-134, 379

Reverse, Jacques, E-134, 379

Reverseau, Francoise, E-344

Reverseau, Marie, E-68, 130

Reveu, Marie, E-409

Reville, Amande, E-358

Revis, Marie Elisabeth, E-599

Revol, Gabriel, E-90, 379

Revol, Louis Bertrand, E-90, 379

Revol, Magdeleine Bertrand, E-379

Revol, Marie Olive, E-379

Rey, Marguerite, E-126, 389

Reynaud, Francois, S1-76

Ribou, Magdelaine, E-45, 439

Ricard, Jeanne, E-138, 266

Ricard, Marie Charlotte, E-144

Ricard, Nicolas, E-158

Ricaud, Anne, E-180, 348

Richard, -----, E-407

Richard, Agnes, E-379, 399

Richard, Alexandre, E-380, 485, 529, 547

Richard, Amand, S2-692, 698

Richard, Amand, S3-1072

Richard, Anastasie Marguerite, F-59

Richard, Angelique, F-25, 27

Richard, Angelique, N-31, 43, 47

Richard, Angelique, S1-146, 179, 234, 252

Richard, Angelique, S2-569, 637

Richard, Angelique, S3-921

Richard, Anne, E-129, 136, 275, 278, 298, 305, 380, 418, 428, 476, 481, 609, 611-612, 615

Richard, Anne, S2-585, 613, 697-698, 700

Richard, Anne, S3-1039

Richard, Anne Magdeleine, E-100, 380

Richard, Anne Suzanne, E-609, 612

Richard, Anonime, E-380

Richard, Anselme, E-380, 573

Richard, Anselme, F-31

Richard, Anselme, S2-697

Richard, Antoine, E-481

Richard, Auguste, F-31

Richard, Basile, E-380-384, 572

Richard, Basile marie, F-111

Richard, Bazile Marie, E-380

Richard, Brigitte, E-173, 182, 382, 427, 573

Richard, Catherine, E-60, 186, 380, 382-383, 427-428, 472, 578

Richard, Catherine Josephe, E-425, 427

Richard, Cecile, C-4

Richard, Cecile, F-13

Richard, Cecile, N-7-8

Richard, Cecile, S1-25

Richard, Cecile, S2-696, 701-703

Richard, Cecile, S3-1020

Richard, Cecille, E-485

Richard, Charles, E-42, 118, 128, 380, 424-425, 581

Richard, Charles, F-23, 59, 93

Richard, Charles, S1-96, 117

Richard, Charles, S2-674, 693-694, 699, 744

Richard, Charles, S3-1020, 1024, 1033, 1070, 1078

Richard, Charles Gregoire, E-380

Richard, Charles Pierre Paul, N-148

Richard, Claire, E-156

Richard, Dorothee, F-15

Richard, Dorothee, N-42, 238

Richard, Dorothee, S1-206

Richard, Dorothee, S2-560

Richard, Dorothee, S3-1049

Richard, Elisabeth, E-26-27, 322, 380, 600

Richard, Elizabeth, F-59

Richard, Elizabeth Joseph, E-380

Richard, Esther, E-615

Richard, Etienne, E-381

Richard, Felicite, E-136

Richard, Firmain-Amateur, S2-695

Richard, Francois, E-353, 381-382

Richard, Francois, F-15

Richard, Francois, S1-206

Richard, Francois, S2-560

Richard, Francois, S3-1049

Richard, Francoise, E-381

Richard, Francoise Emilie, E-381

Richard, Gabriel Pierre Joseph, E-381

Richard, Genevieve, E-15, 25, 55-58, 190, 631, 633, 641

Richard, Genevieve, F-93

Richard, Genevieve, S1-117, 119-120

Richard, Genevieve, S2-568, 674, 693, 744

Richard, Genevieve, S3-1033, 1078

Richard, Genevieve-Marguerite, S2-701

Richard, Germain, E-381-383

Richard, Gregoire, S2-699

Richard, Henry, E-381

Richard, Honore, F-97

Richard, Honore, S1-154, 246

Richard, Honore, S2-533, 664, 694-695, 702

Richard, Honore, S3-892

Richard, Jacques, E-144, 380-381

Richard, Jacques, S2-700

Richard, Jacques Anselme, E-381

Richard, Jacques Julien Marie, E-381

Richard, Janne Magdelaine, S3-1086

Richard, Jean, C-17

Richard, Jean, E-45, 100, 265, 278, 380-381, 402, 529

Richard, Jean, F-17, 69

Richard, Jean, S1-25, 47, 108, 122, 351

Richard, Jean, S2-464, 528, 558, 574, 585, 695-696, 700, 703

Richard, Jean, S3-1039, 1041, 1052

Richard, Jean Baptiste, C-6, 17, 22, 87, 134

Richard, Jean Baptiste, E-381, 572

Richard, Jean Baptiste, N-148

Richard, Jean Charles, E-381

Richard, Jean Charles, F-41, 101

Richard, Jean Jacques, N-226

Richard, Jean Marie, E-381

Richard, Jean Pierre, F-17

Richard, Jean-Baptiste, S2-695, 697, 698, 701

Richard, Jean-Joseph, S2-700

Richard, Jean-Pierre, S2-696

Richard, Jeanne, E-353, 381

Richard, Jeanne, F-65, 81

Richard, Jeanne Madeleine, S1-122, 355

Richard, Jeanne Magdelaine, E-45, 381

Richard, Joseph, E-165-166, 380-383, 547, 572, 609, 612, 615

Richard, Joseph, F-31, 57

Richard, Joseph, N-148

Richard, Joseph, S1-45, 155, 278

Richard, Joseph, S2-507, 558, 674, 692-693, 696-700, 702-703, 744

Richard, Joseph, S3-1041, 1070

Richard, Joseph Amand, S3-843, 1052

Richard, Joseph Ignace, E-286, 381-383, 572

Richard, Joseph-Amand, S2-539, 699

Richard, Joseph-Marie, S2-696

Richard, Joseph-Vincent, S2-697

Richard, Julien Marie, E-382

Richard, Julien Marie, F-31

Richard, Louis, E-382

Richard, Louis David, E-382

Richard, Louis Isaac, E-382

Richard, Louis Jean, E-382

Richard, Louise, E-338

Richard, Madeleine, N-119

Richard, Madeleine, S1-30, 32, 210

Richard, Madeleine, S2-580

Richard, Magdelaine, E-382, 472, 547

Richard, Marguerite, C-17, 87

Richard, Marguerite, E-13-14, 189-190, 256, 381-382, 384, 485, 547

Richard, Marguerite, F-59, 65, 69, 97

Richard, Marguerite, N-23-24

Richard, Marguerite, S1-108, 297

Richard, Marguerite, S2-463-464, 539, 552, 694-697, 699-701, 704, 745, 750

Richard, Marguerite Barbe, E-609, 612, 615

Richard, Marguerite Genevieve, N-148

Richard, Marguerite Rosalie, E-609

Richard, Marguerite-Genevieve, S2-703

Richard, Marguerite-Josephe, S2-693, 701, 704, 744

Richard, Marguerite-Marie, S2-694

Richard, Marie, E-2, 130, 182, 184, 186, 188-189, 316, 318, 381, 384-385, 407, 435, 437, 485, 547-548, 564, 598

Richard, Marie, F-15, 31, 59, 87

Richard, Marie, N-148
Richard, Marie, S1-109, 346
Richard, Marie, S2-543, 586, 696-698, 700-702, 759
Richard, Marie, S3-841, 843
Richard, Marie Anne, E-303, 382, 422
Richard, Marie Anne, F-3
Richard, Marie Anne, N-84, 171
Richard, Marie Anne Francoise, E-136, 382
Richard, Marie Anne Marguerite Olive, E-383
Richard, Marie Blanche, E-5-6, 116, 118, 164, 167, 559, 608-609, 612-613, 615
Richard, Marie Elizabeth, E-26, 383
Richard, Marie Elizabeth, F-57
Richard, Marie Esther, E-609, 612
Richard, Marie Felicite, F-59
Richard, Marie Genevieve, F-71
Richard, Marie Josephe, C-6, 63, 87, 134-135
Richard, Marie Josephe, E-383
Richard, Marie Josephe, F-17, 65, 71
Richard, Marie Josephe, N-9-10, 104
Richard, Marie Josephe, S2-528
Richard, Marie Marthe, E-383
Richard, Marie Reine, E-383
Richard, Marie Rosalie, E-612
Richard, Marie Roze, F-23
Richard, Marie-Anne, S2-778
Richard, Marie-Blanche, S1-278-279
Richard, Marie-Blanche, S2-663-664, 699, 702
Richard, Marie-Claire, S2-704
Richard, Marie-Esther, S2-699, 702
Richard, Marie-Josephe, S1-49
Richard, Marie-Josephe, S2-527, 697, 701, 703
Richard, Marie-Marguerite, S2-703
Richard, Marin, S2-699
Richard, Martin, E-485, 529
Richard, Martin, S2-697

Richard, Mathurin, E-38
Richard, Maurice Marc, E-383
Richard, Melein, E-383, 437
Richard, Michel, E-181, 379-380, 382-384, 399, 458, 476, 481, 486, 547
Richard, Mr., E-372
Richard, Nicolas, E-383
Richard, Paul, E-380
Richard, Paul, S2-700-702
Richard, Perrine, E-383
Richard, Pierre, C-4, 29, 63, 139
Richard, Pierre, E-157, 194, 256, 273, 380, 382-384, 476, 529, 547, 573, 580, 636
Richard, Pierre, F-13, 15, 17, 31, 87
Richard, Pierre, N-8, 84, 104, 147-148, 239, 250
Richard, Pierre, S1-25
Richard, Pierre, S2-527-528, 558, 613, 663, 693-698, 700-704, 711, 718
Richard, Pierre, S3-841, 883, 892, 956, 1020, 1022, 1041, 1056
Richard, Pierre Ange, E-383
Richard, Pierre Auguste, E-383
Richard, Pierre Etienne, E-384
Richard, Pierre Jean Francois Marie, E-384
Richard, Pierre-Joseph, S2-703
Richard, Pierre-Michel, S2-700
Richard, Rene, E-380, 384, 476, 529
Richard, Rene, S2-558, 565, 698
Richard, Rosalie, E-187, 189, 402, 615
Richard, Rose, E-122, 181, 188, 384
Richard, Rose, F-15
Richard, Rose, S2-695, 704
Richard, Simon, E-173, 573
Richard, Simon Joseph, E-384
Richard, Simon Pierre, E-428
Richard, Sophie Elizabeth Josephine, E-384
Richard, Susanne, E-128, 615
Richard, Suzanne, S2-699
Richard, Thomas, E-413
Richard, Thomas, S2-702

Richard, Yves, E-384
Richard, Zacharie, E-136, 318, 382-384
Richard dit Sapin, Jean, S1-347
Richardeau, Catherine, E-120, 295, 384
Richardeau, Pierre, E-28, 120, 357, 384
Richauh, Gilles, E-589, 596
Richemon, Henry, S2-704
Richemon, Jeanne, S2-704
Richemond, Henri, E-384
Richemond, Jeanne, E-138, 384
Richer, Andre, F-91
Richer, Andre, S1-328
Richer, Andre, S3-1099
Richer, Angelique, S3-1099
Richer, Jean Baptiste Francois, E-343, 384
Richer, Marie Jeanne, F-91
Richer, Marie Jeanne Catherine, S3-1099
Richer, Marie-Jeanne, S1-331
Richer, Marie-Jeanne-Catherine, S1-328
Richer, Rose Francoise Xavier, E-343, 384
Richet, Angelique, F-91
Richeux, Francois, S2-692
Richeux, Laurence, S2-723
Richot, Andre, E-118
Ricoeur, Francois, E-281, 384
Ricoeur, Jacques, E-281, 384-385
Ricou, Arnaud, E-159
Ricoult, Michel, E-73, 385
Ricoult, Pierre, E-73, 385
Ricq, Marie Suzanne, E-344
Rifaud, Marie Rose, E-385
Rifaud, Rose, E-129
Rigart, Anne, E-408, 412
Rigaud, Jacques, E-385, 440
Rigaud, Jean, E-385
Riguest, Jean Adam, E-589, 592
Rimbaud, Vicente, C-90, 114
Rimbault, Anne, E-489
Rimbault, Francois, E-476
Rimbault, Francoise, E-474
Rimbault, Jeanne, E-475
Rimbault, Magdelaine, E-489
Rimbault, Marie, E-473

Rimbault, Rene, E-458, 476, 489

Rimbeau, Francois, E-529

Rimbeau, Magdelaine, E-529

Rio, Perrine, E-183, 185-186

Rio, Yves, E-185

Riou, Jacques, E-623

Ripe, Etienne, E-409

Riquet, Joseph Adrien Remy, E-301, 385

Riquet, Marguerite, E-301, 385

Ritau, Therese, E-131

Rivassau, Marie, E-73, 97

Riveau, Jacques, E-169

Rivet, Estienne, E-476, 510, 529

Rivet, Etienne, S2-704

Rivet, Jan, S3-964, 1004

Rivet, Jean, S1-79, 263

Rivet, Jean, S2-704-705

Rivet, Jean Philippe, E-382, 385

Rivet, Justin, S2-705

Rivet, Marie, E-510, 565

Rivet, Marie Rose, E-273-274, 385, 425, 560, 573

Rivet, Pierre, E-385

Rivet, Rene, E-510

Rivet, Rose, E-272

Rivet, Rose, S1-263

Rivet, Rose Pelagie, E-558

Rivet, Rose-Pelagie-Julienne, S2-705

Riviere, Antoine Balthazar Joachim, E-385

Riviere, Jean, E-337, 385

Riviere, Joachim, E-86, 385

Riviere, Laurent, E-385

Riviere, Marie, E-385

Riviere, Mathieu, E-338

Riviere, Oudille, E-344, 386

Riviere, Pierre, E-357, 385

Riviere, Sieur, C-135

Riviere, Susanne, E-496

Robeau, Michelle, C-96, 118

Roberjeau, Francois, E-377

Robert, Anne, S2-503

Robert, Anne Henriette, E-291

Robert, Isaac Taurin, E-147, 195, 385

Robert, Jean, E-298, 354, 392

Robert, Louis, E-89, 386

Robert, Marguerite, E-69

Robert, Marie, E-11, 137

Robert, Marie, S1-321

Robert, Marie, S3-991

Robert, Michel, E-147, 385-386

Robert, Pierre, E-166, 386

Robichaux, Alexandre, C-87

Robichaux, Alexandre, E-497, 529

Robichaux, Alexandre, N-149

Robichaux, Alexandre, S1-23, 133-134, 150-151

Robichaux, Alexandre, S2-705, 707, 709, 713

Robichaux, Alexandre, S3-945

Robichaux, Anastasie, E-181

Robichaux, Andre, S2-712

Robichaux, Angelique, N-149

Robichaux, Angelique Rose, C-88

Robichaux, Angelique-Rosalie, S2-710

Robichaux, Anne, F-21, 43

Robichaux, Anne, N-110, 118, 151, 248

Robichaux, Anne, S2-575, 718

Robichaux, Anne, S3-893

Robichaux, Anne Josephe, C-87

Robichaux, Anne Marie, C-66

Robichaux, Anne Theodore, N-149

Robichaux, Anne Therese, N-149

Robichaux, Anne-Blanche, S1-327-328

Robichaux, Anne-Blanche, S2-708, 717

Robichaux, Anne-Josephe, S2-706

Robichaux, Anne-Marie, S1-234

Robichaux, Anne-Marie, S2-549, 551, 575, 713-714

Robichaux, Anne-Theodose, S1-249

Robichaux, Anne-Theodose, S2-706, 711-712, 714, 717

Robichaux, Anne-Theotiste, S2-716

Robichaux, Augustin, S2-707

Robichaux, Benoni, S2-712

Robichaux, Charles, E-386, 497

Robichaux, Charles, F-31

Robichaux, Charles, N-95-96, 149, 178, 207, 248

Robichaux, Charles, S1-11, 79

Robichaux, Charles, S2-550, 578, 707-708, 711-712, 716

Robichaux, Charles, S3-875, 1057

Robichaux, Elizabeth, N-151

Robichaux, Estienne, E-458, 472

Robichaux, Francois, C-88, 146

Robichaux, Francois, E-497, 529

Robichaux, Francois, N-150

Robichaux, Francois, S1-249, 327-328

Robichaux, Francois, S2-465, 558, 708-710

Robichaux, Francois, S3-865, 1013

Robichaux, Francois Joseph, E-627

Robichaux, Francois Joseph, N-150

Robichaux, Francois Xavier, C-89

Robichaux, Francois Xavier, F-47

Robichaux, Francois Xavier, N-150

Robichaux, Francois-David, S2-706

Robichaux, Francois-Joseph, S2-709

Robichaux, Francois-Xavier, S2-705-706, 713

Robichaux, Francoise, S1-249

Robichaux, Francoise, S2-710-712, 718

Robichaux, Francoise-Marguerite, S2-715

Robichaux, Genevieve, S1-327

Robichaux, Genevieve, S2-709

Robichaux, Isidore, S2-710, 712

Robichaux, Isidore, S3-1005, 1034, 1052, 1076

Robichaux, Jean, S3-1013, 1067

Robichaux, Jean Baptiste, C-89-90

Robichaux, Jean Baptiste, F-47

Robichaux, Jean Baptiste, N-150

Robichaux, Jean Baptiste, S3-1052, 1076

Robichaux, Jean Pierre, C-88, 146-147

Robichaux, Jean Pierre, F-43

Robichaux, Jean Pierre, N-150-151

Robichaux, Jean-Baptiste, S1-226

Robichaux, Jean-Baptiste, S2-710-713, 718

Robichaux, Jean-Isidore, S2-710

Robichaux, Jean-Louis, S2-718

Robichaux, Jean-Michel, S2-714

Robichaux, Jean-Pierre, S2-708-709, 715

Robichaux, Joseph, C-88-89

Robichaux, Joseph, E-42, 386

Robichaux, Joseph, F-43, 47

Robichaux, Joseph, N-150-151

Robichaux, Joseph, S1-23, 145, 148, 294, 353

Robichaux, Joseph, S2-703-704, 707, 709-713, 716-717

Robichaux, Joseph, S3-875, 949, 982, 989, 1005, 1034, 1041, 1052, 1076

Robichaux, Joseph-Francois, S2-715

Robichaux, Joseph-Gervais, S2-716

Robichaux, Joseph-Landry, S2-712

Robichaux, Joseph-Prudent, S1-95

Robichaux, Joseph-Servan, S2-717

Robichaux, Josephe, S2-717

Robichaux, Judith, S1-328

Robichaux, Judith, S2-708

Robichaux, Laurant Xavier, C-89

Robichaux, Laurent-Xavier, S2-715

Robichaux, Magdelaine, E-111, 474

Robichaux, Magdeleine Anne, C-89

Robichaux, Marguerite, C-36, 88

Robichaux, Marguerite, E-627

Robichaux, Marguerite, F-17

Robichaux, Marguerite, N-149

Robichaux, Marguerite, S1-150, 344-346, 350

Robichaux, Marguerite, S2-706, 709, 717

Robichaux, Marguerite Genevieve, E-626

Robichaux, Marguerite Pelagie, S3-1041

Robichaux, Marguerite-Francoise, S2-714

Robichaux, Marguerite-Genevieve, S2-709

Robichaux, Marguerite-Pelagie, S1-249

Robichaux, Marguerite-Pelagie, S2-703, 711-712

Robichaux, Margueritte, S3-878, 1137

Robichaux, Marie, C-89

Robichaux, Marie, E-115-117, 497

Robichaux, Marie, F-43, 47

Robichaux, Marie, N-150-151

Robichaux, Marie, S1-73

Robichaux, Marie, S2-473, 475, 706, 744, 749

Robichaux, Marie, S3-905, 1016, 1026, 1035, 1075

Robichaux, Marie Blanche, S3-864

Robichaux, Marie Josefe, S3-1005

Robichaux, Marie Josephe, E-152, 561

Robichaux, Marie-Anne, S2-716

Robichaux, Marie-Blanche, S1-248, 250

Robichaux, Marie-Blanche, S2-711

Robichaux, Marie-Josephe, S1-248, 353

Robichaux, Marie-Josephe, S2-711-712, 715

Robichaux, Marie-Madeleine, S2-707

Robichaux, Marie-Marguerite, S2-710

Robichaux, Marie-Rose, S2-717

Robichaux, Marthe-Elizabeth, S2-718

Robichaux, Mathurin, S2-708-709

Robichaux, Michel, S1-249

Robichaux, Michel, S2-538, 712-714

Robichaux, Michel, S3-982, 1034, 1041

Robichaux, Michel-Jean, S2-714

Robichaux, Pierre, C-57, 89-90

Robichaux, Pierre, E-267, 386

Robichaux, Pierre, F-43

Robichaux, Pierre, N-151

Robichaux, Pierre, S1-124, 248, 250, 261

Robichaux, Pierre, S2-457, 600, 673, 709, 711, 714-718, 733

Robichaux, Pierre, S3-982, 1026, 1034, 1049, 1076, 1111

Robichaux, Pierre Joseph, N-150

Robichaux, Pierre-Ignace, S2-718

Robichaux, Pierre-Marie, S2-714

Robichaux, Prudent, E-497, 529

Robichaux, Prudhomme, E-497

Robichaux, Reine, C-89

Robichaux, Reine Rose, N-149

Robichaux, Renee, C-89

Robichaux, Renee, F-47

Robichaux, Renee, N-150

Robichaux, Renee-Rose, S2-707

Robichaux, Rose, E-111

Robichaux, Susane, E-267, 386

Robichaux, Suzanne, S1-261

Robichaux, Theodose, S2-706

Robichaux, Therese, S2-707

Robichaux, Xavier Francois, C-89

Robillard, Anastasie, S1-294

Robillard, Marie, E-195

Robin, Catherine, E-412

Robin, Francoise, C-30, 136

Robin, Jean, E-17, 105, 313, 386

Robin, Jeanne, E-354, 368

Robin, Marie, E-386, 395

Robin, Pierre, E-60, 314, 325, 386

Robin, Pierre, S2-718

Robin, Rene, E-122, 355
Robin, Sebastienne, E-160, 194
Robin, Sebastienne, S2-653
Robino, Angelique, E-140, 177
Robion, Jacques, E-386
Robion, Jean, E-73, 131, 386-387
Robion, Jean, S1-355
Robion, Jeanne, E-386
Robion, Louis, E-387
Robion, Marguerite, S1-355-356
Roblain, Laurent, E-269
Rocbert, Etienne, E-61, 387
Rocbert, Etienne Emanuel, E-61, 387
Roce, Noel, S3-984
Roch, Jean, E-100
Rochard, Nicolas Joseph, E-79
Rochat, Francois, C-72
Rochat, Francois, S2-595
Roche, Agnesse, E-29, 357
Roche, Bernard, E-122, 387
Roche, Etienne, E-139, 387
Roche, Francoise, E-257
Roche, Gilbert, E-139, 387
Roche, Jean, E-387, 430
Roche, Pierre Bernard, E-387
Rochefort, Claude, S2-719
Rochefort, Jacques Guillaume, E-387
Rochefort, Jean, E-30, 387
Rochefort, Louis, C-17, 54, 61
Rochefort and the Acadians, E-387, 388
Rochefort-sur-Mer, E-387
Rocher, Etienne, E-139
Rocher, Louise, E-257
Rochet, Jean, S3-889
Rochet, Marie Anne, E-195, 388
Rocquain, Gabriel, E-168
Rocquet, Mr., E-375
Roderigues, Olive Antoinette, E-126
Roderigues, Pierre, E-126
Rodolphe, Jean, E-159, 298
Rodrigue, Antoine, E-10, 55, 388, 437
Rodrigue, Antoine Jean Theodore, E-360
Rodrigue, Charles Joseph, E-388
Rodrigue, Jean, E-388

Rodrigue, Jean Francois, E-388
Rodrigue, Jeanne Francoise, E-104, 388
Rodrigue, Josephine, E-435
Rodrigue, Leon, E-20, 388
Rodrigue, Marie Agathe, E-388
Rodrigue, Marie Francoise, E-388
Rodrigue, Marie Louise, E-10
Rodrigue, Michel, E-20, 340, 388
Rodrigue, Olive Antoinette, E-128, 389
Rodrigue, Pierre, E-128, 389
Rodrigues, Jean, E-278
Rodrigues, Michel, E-278
Rodrique, Antoine, E-17
Roger, Annies, E-90, 375
Roger, Catherine, E-304, 389
Roger, Catherine Cecile Elizabeth, E-389
Roger, Elizabeth, E-340
Roger, Helene, E-368
Roger, Jean Francois Augustin, E-108, 389
Roger, Jean Pierre, E-389
Roger, Joseph, F-107
Roger, Marie, E-43, 45, 102, 104, 119-121, 123, 132, 160, 255, 259, 293, 301, 306, 331, 377-378, 411
Roger, Marie, F-107
Roger, Marie, S1-77, 281-282
Roger, Marie, S2-513
Roger, Marie, S2-516, 597, 729-730
Roger, Marie, S3-964
Roger, Marie Anne, E-364
Roger, Marie Elizabeth, E-79, 93, 119, 176, 311, 432
Roger, Marie Henriette, E-108, 389
Roger, Marie Jeanne, E-377, 389
Roger, Marie-Elizabeth, S1-180, 280, 320
Roger, Marie-Elizabeth, S1-199
Roger, Mathieu, E-377, 389
Roger, Mr., E-302
Roger, Pierre, E-138, 304, 389
Rohan, Jean, E-389

Rohan, Marie Jeanne, E-427
Rohan, Nicolas, E-389
Roi, Marie Marthe, E-298
Roi, Marthe, E-298
Rolain, Francois, S2-719
Rolain, Francois, S3-993
Rolain, Jean-Baptiste, S1-80
Rolain, Jean-Baptiste, S2-719
Roland, Magdeleine, E-147
Roland sieur Duverde, Joseph, E-91
Rolant, Francois, C-90, 129
Rolant, Jean, C-31, 90, 129
Rollan, Jeanne, E-620
Rolland, Genevieve, E-20, 325
Rolland, Gregoire, E-17, 393
Rolland, Jacques Francois, E-91, 151, 185, 389-390
Rolland, Jean, E-134, 389
Rolland, Joseph, E-389
Rolland, Marie Jeanne, E-161, 265
Rolland, Pierre, E-134, 389
Rolland, Rose Caroline, E-184
Rolland, Rose Catherine, E-390
Rollaud, Augustin, E-185
Rollet, Jeanne, C-6, 106
Rollin, Jean Baptiste, S3-993, 1004-1005
Roly, Elisabeth, E-390
Roma, Jean Pierre, E-127, 390
Roma, Marie Anne, E-127, 390
Romagosa, Francisco, F-21
Romain, Antoine, E-302, 390
Romain, Francois Noel, E-390
Romain, Jean Antoine, E-390
Romain, Jean Charles, E-302, 390
Romain, Jean Marie Eustache, E-390
Romain, Joseph Amant, E-390
Romain, Pierre Marie, E-390
Romillie, Jean, E-390
Romillie, Marie Joseph, E-390
Rondeau, Francoise, E-388
Rondeau, Jacques, E-290, 390
Rondeau, Jacques Philipe, E-128, 290, 390
Rondeau, Joseph, E-388
Rondet, Marie Madeleine, E-125, 390

Rondet, Simon, E-125, 390
Rondrail, Jean, E-70
Ronval, Jean Pascal, E-390
Ronval, Michel, E-364, 390
Roper, Marie, E-104
Roquairolle, Louise, E-32, 339
Roquefort, Louis, E-185
Roquefort, Mr., E-185
Roquemont, Guillaume Jean, N-151
Roquemont, Guillaume Noel, F-13
Roquille, Jeanne, E-365
Rortaud, Marie Genevieve, E-339, 370
Rosaignol, Marguerite, E-391
Rose, Jean Michel, E-84
Rose, Marie, E-620
Rose, Noel, E-620
Rosee, Christophe Jacques, E-390, 441
Rosee, Jacques Louis, E-390, 441
Roseray, Julienne, S1-328
Rosereu, Julienne, S3-1099
Rosereux, Julienne, S1-328-330
Rosereux, Louise, S1-330
Rosey, Louis, C-118
Rossard, Mr., E-332
Rossard, Sieur, E-144
Rosse, Angelique, E-627
Rosse, Angelique, S2-720-722
Rosse, Angelique-Jeanne, S2-720
Rosse, Anne, S2-720
Rosse, Barbe Simone, S3-965
Rosse, Barbe-Simone, S2-507
Rosse, Catherine, S2-720
Rosse, Charles, E-627
Rosse, Charles, S2-720
Rosse, Charles, S3-1092
Rosse, Cristophe, S3-965
Rosse, Etienne, E-627
Rosse, Etiennette, S2-720
Rosse, Francois, E-627
Rosse, Francois Rene, S3-1092
Rosse, Francois-Marie, S2-721
Rosse, Francois-Rene, S2-720
Rosse, George, S2-507, 719
Rosse, George, S3-965

Rosse, Georges, E-101, 153, 391, 416
Rosse, Jacques, S2-720
Rosse, Jane, S3-1092
Rosse, Jean, E-101, 391, 416
Rosse, Jeanne, E-153, 391
Rosse, Jeanne, S2-608-609, 720
Rosse, Laurent, S2-719
Rosse, Marie, E-195, 391
Rosse, Marie, S2-720-722
Rosse, Marie, S3-997
Rosse, Marie-Jerome, S2-719
Rosse, Marin, S2-721
Rosse, Noel, E-391, 627
Rosse, Noel, S2-719-721
Rosse, Noel, S3-965, 984, 997, 1091-1092
Rosse, Noel Francois, E-627
Rosse, Noel Joseph, S3-1091-1092
Rosse, Noel-Joseph, S2-720
Rosse, Pierre, S2-721-722
Rosse, Rene, S2-719-722, 772
Rosse, Rene, S3-997
Rosse, Thomasse Francoise, E-628
Rossi, Guillemette, E-384
Rossignol, Jean, E-70, 391
Rossignol, Louis, E-70, 80, 348, 391
Rossignol, Magdeleine, E-391
Rossignol, Marie, E-391
Rossignol, Marie Magdelaine, E-391
Rosten, Jean, E-391, 414
Roturier, Louis, E-357, 385
Roturier, Marianne, E-280
Roty, Gilles, E-174
Roty, Gilles, E-391
Roty, Jean Gilles Joseph, E-174, 391
Rouan, Marie Rose, E-160
Rouar, Olivier, S1-352
Rouault, Charlotte, S2-645
Rouault, Charlotte, S3-1054
Rouet, Francois, E-159
Rouet, Jeanne, E-77, 391
Rouge, Marie, E-377
Rouge, Marie Jeanne, E-378
Rougeon, Jean, E-174, 265
Rougerot, Jacques, S3-1150

Rouget, Antoine, C-90
Rouget, Marguerite Joseph, C-90
Rouget, Rene, C-90
Rouhaud, Louis, E-102, 142
Rouhaut, Jean, E-77
Roui, Louis, C-111
Roui, Reancoise, C-48
Roui, Rene, C-110
Roui, Francoise, C-49, 92, 110-111
Rouil, Francois, S3-995
Rouil, Francois fils, S3-995
Rouil, Pierre, S3-995
Rouis, Pierre, C-86
Roulet, Jean Bernard, E-325, 392
Roulet, Philibert, E-325, 392
Roulin, Louis, E-10
Roulin, Marie, S2-504
Roulin, Veuve, E-10
Roullaud, Jean, E-390
Roullet, Catherine, E-350, 372
Roullier, Etienne, E-394
Roumeau, Claude, E-148
Rourde, Marguerite, C-2, 128
Rous, Elene, S3-995
Rousseau, Charles Gabriel, E-120
Rousseau, Charles-Gabriel, S1-282
Rousseau, Francois, E-52, 392
Rousseau, Francoise, E-340, 357
Rousseau, Gabriel, E-300, 392
Rousseau, Jean, E-159
Rousseau, Jeanne, E-328, 392
Rousseau, Josephe, E-71, 392
Rousseau, Margueritte, E-392
Rousseau, Marie Charlotte, E-300, 392
Rousseau, Marie Josephe, E-71, 72, 330
Rousseau, Paul, N-194
Rousseau, Pierre, E-328, 386, 392
Rousseau De Viljoin, Gabriel, E-101, 125
Rousseau de Villejoint, Marguerite, E-125
Roussel, Marie, S2-591
Roussel, Marie, S3-931

INDEX SOURCES C=Chatellerault; E=Acadians in Exile; F=Acadian Families; N=Nantes; S=St-Malo

Roussel, Marie Louise, E-295
Rousset, Jeanne, E-89
Rousset, Marie, C-155
Roussiliere, Jeanne, E-476
Roussin, Antoine, E-344, 392
Roussin, Lazare Mathieu, E-344, 392
Roussin, Mr., E-188
Rousson, Jean, E-146
Roussy, Etienne, E-138
Routel, Andre, E-140
Routey, Marie, E-139, 344
Rouvray, Jacques, S2-722
Rouvray, Jeanne-Francoise, S2-722
Rouvray, Marie, S2-722
Rouvray, Pierre, S2-722
Roux, Elisabeth, E-318, 320
Roux, Guillaume, E-256
Roux, Jean, E-355
Roux, Louis, E-156, 617
Roux, Magdeleine, E-354
Roux, Michel, E-322
Rouxeau, Jean, N-152, 244
Rouxeau, Yves Cyprien, N-30, 152, 244
Rouxel, Jean, S1-144
Rouxel, Jean, S2-447
Rouxel, Therese, S2-466
Rouy, Claudeine, E-294
Rouy, Gregoire, E-82
Roy, Alexandre, E-269, 393
Roy, Andre, E-21, 159
Roy, Anne, E-393, 409
Roy, Catherine, E-393
Roy, Charlotte, E-86
Roy, Etienne, E-393
Roy, Francois, E-130, 393
Roy, Francoise, E-17, 393
Roy, Gabriel, E-327, 393
Roy, girl, E-393
Roy, Jacques, E-141, 393, 407
Roy, Jean, E-72, 348, 393, 529
Roy, Jean Pierre, E-393
Roy, Jeanne, E-393
Roy, Joseph, E-393
Roy, Louis, E-120, 332, 393, 431
Roy, Marie, E-123
Roy, Marie, N-43, 242
Roy, Marie Anne, E-269, 393

Roy, Marie Marthe, E-83
Roy, Michel, E-393
Roy, Nicolas, E-327, 393
Roy, Noel, E-21, 319
Roy, Olivier, S2-622
Roy, Pierre, E-159, 393, 409
Roy, Therese, E-99, 172
Royer, -----, E-5-6
Royer, Anne, S2-723
Royer, Francois, E-159, 377, 394
Royer, Francoise, E-318
Royer, Laurent, E-373
Royer, Marie, S2-775
Royer, Nicolas, S1-257
Royer, Pierre, E-339, 373, 393
Royer, Pierre, S2-723
Royer, Rene, E-393
Royer, Rene, S2-722
Royer, Therese, E-192
Royer, Vincent, E-394
Roze, Jacques Christophe, E-134, 394
Rozet, Marie, S3-963
Ruard, Francois, E-394
Ruard, Louis, E-394
Ruard, Pierre, E-349, 394
Ruaud, Marie, E-439
Ruault De La Mote, Jeanne, S2-692
Ruaux, Francois, E-28, 392
Ruaux, Louis, E-102, 142
Ruaux, Pierre, E-28, 337, 436
Rucet, Pierre, S3-860
Rudoux, Marie-Josephe, S1-202
Rudouze, Marie Joseph, C-27
Rudouze, Marie Josephe, F-51
Ruel, Anne-Julienne, S2-724
Ruel, Charlotte, S1-204
Ruel, Charlotte-Catherine-Francoise, S2-723
Ruel, Geffray-Jean, S1-277
Ruel, Geffroy, S3-1008
Ruel, Geffroy-jean, S2-723-724
Ruel, Guy, S2-723
Ruel, Guy, S3-1008
Ruel, Helene-Jeanne, S2-723
Ruel, Laurence-Modeste, S2-723
Ruel, Marie-Jeanne, S2-723
Ruel, Perinne, S2-723

Ruelland, Claire, E-394
Ruelland, Louise Angelique, E-394
Ruelland, Pierre, E-394
Ruelle, Anne, E-628
Ruelle, Catherine, E-628
Ruelle, Charlotte, E-81, 149
Ruelle, Charlotte, S1-337
Ruelle, Geffroy Jean, E-628
Ruelle, Gofroy Jan, S3-1038
Ruelle, Jeanne, E-628
Ruelle, Marie, E-628
Ruelle, Perrine, E-628
Ruet, Catherine, E-119, 356
Rulland, Honore, E-133
Rulland, Marie, E-66, 133
Ruoualt, Julienne, S2-691
Rusin, Pierre Louis Potevin, C-164
Rusin, Pierre Rene Potevin, C-164
Rusin, Potevin, C-163
Rusod, Marguerite, F-65
Rustin, Jean, E-376, 394
Rustin, Pierre, E-376, 394

S

Sabatier, Joseph, E-178
Sable, Marie, E-313
Sabot, Augustin, E-395
Sabot, boy, E-395
Sabot, Catherine, E-412
Sabot, Francoise, S1-3
Sabot, Francoise, S3-968
Sabot, Guillemette, S2-521
Sabot, Jean, E-395
Sabot, Jean Martin, E-395
Sabotier, Francois De Paule, E-102, 395
Sabotier, Joseph, E-102, 395
Sabourin, Charles, E-386, 395
Sabourin, Jean, E-376
Sabourin, Suzanne, E-38, 395
Saillard, Nicolas, E-10
Saint Clair, Emmanuel Joseph, E-188
Saint De La Chabossiere, Nobleman Joseph Thomas, S2-636
Saint Estienne, Anne, E-89, 475

Saint Estienne de, Marguerite, E-475

Saint Etienne, Marie, E-475

Saint Leger, Jean, S2-600

Saint Louis , Joseph, S3-881

Saint Louis , Mazerolle, S2-612

Saint Louis , Simon, S3-881

Saint Lurins, Marie Toinette, E-125

Saint Marc, Margueritte, E-264

Saint Marc, Pierre, S3-954

Saint marc, Pierre, S2-724

Saint Martin, widow, E-195

Saint Thelan, Alexis, S3-1055

Saint-Jouan, Regis de, C-vii

Saint-Louis, Marie, E-98

Saint-Melen, Jeanne, S1-306

Saint-Michel, Catherine, E-70

Saintglain, Francois, E-401

Saintglain, Marie, E-401

Saintglan, Francois, E-307

Saintglan, Marguerite, E-307

Saintglan, Marie, E-307

Saintin, Gabriel, E-29

Saintjean, Elisabeth, E-144, 375

Sainton, Alexandre, C-91

Sainton, Helaire, C-130

Sainton, Jean, C-90, 114

Sainton, Pierre, C-90, 114

Salaberry, Marie, E-135, 174

Salant, Anne, E-617

Salant, Jacques, E-617

Salant, Jacques Andre, E-617

Salant, Julien, E-628

Salarun, Marguerite, E-94

Salauvin, Jean, E-169, 402

Salauvin, Jean Mathieu, E-401

Salauvin, Mathieu, E-169, 401-402

Salavan, Marguerite, E-163

Sale, Marie, E-458, 476

Salier, Laurent, E-304

Sallabery, Jeanne Genevieve, E-128, 132

Salle, Charles Pierre, E-147

Salle, Jacques, E-276

Salle, Marie Louise Victoire, E-4, 6

Salmon, Charles, S2-724

Salmon, Elisabeth, E-153, 338

Salmon, Francois, E-172, 303

Salmon, Francois, S2-724

Salmon, Louis, S3-1077

Salmon, Mathurin, S1-195

Salmon, Mathurin, S3-1147

Salmon, Michelle, S1-176

Salveux, Anne Babin, E-620

Salvi, Pierre, E-425

Samet, Elizabeth, E-66, 261

Samie, Anne, C-91, 121-122

Samie, Georges Urbain Louis, C-91

Samie, Jean Pierre, C-91

Samie, Marie Louise, C-91

Samie, Pierre, C-91, 121

Samin, Elisabeth, E-188, 376

Samot, Jean, E-325

Samson, Anne, S1-122

Samson, Anne, S2-683-684, 724-725

Samson, Anne, S3-969

Samson, Anne Magdelaine, E-100, 265, 402

Samson, Charles, S2-683, 724

Samson, Fabien, S2-725

Samson, Fabien, S3-969

Samson, Jacques, E-152

Samson, Jean, S2-725

Samson, Jeanne, S2-654-655

Samson, Madeleine, E-275

Samson, Michel, S2-725

Samson, Remy, E-601

Samson, Thomas, S3-1053

Samsun, Jean, E-422

San, Genevieve, E-408

Sance, Marie Francoise, E-322

Sanglar, Jean, E-98, 402

Sanglar, Pierre, E-98, 402

Saniel, Marie, E-419

Sans, Jacques, E-402

Sans, Marie Francoise, E-321, 402

Sansfourche, Antoine, E-402

Sansfourche, Jean Baptiste, E-402

Sansom, Madeleine, S1-261

Sansom, Magdelaine, E-102

Sanson, Anne Magdeleine, E-45, 275, 278, 380-381

Sanson, Guionne, S3-923

Sanson, Jacques, E-131

Sanson, Magdelaine, E-259, 294

Sansovoine, Barthelemy, E-13, 402

Sansovoine, Elisabeth, E-13, 402

Santier, Maturine, E-441

Santier, Maurice, E-441

Sapin, Anne, S1-48, 108

Sapin, Jean, S3-998

Sapin, Jean Baptiste, C-87

Sapin, Marguerite, S3-998

Sapin, Marie, S1-108

Sarcellie, Isabelle, S1-190

Sarcellier, Isabau, E-66, 131

Sarot, Louise, S2-579

Sarot, Marguerite, S2-579

Sarycochard, Marie, E-256

Sasamy, Bertolo, E-366, 402

Sasany, Joseph, E-402

Satis, Jean Charles, E-402

Satis, Marie Rose, E-402

Satis, Pierre Louis, E-402

Saube de Lanne, Delle, E-279

Saubert, Louis, S3-929

Saudrais, Joseph, S3-854

Saudrais, La Salle, S3-849

Saunier, Agnes, C-137

Saunier, Agnes, C-23

Saunier, Agnes, E-262

Saunier, Anne, E-402, 589, 595

Saunier, Anne, F-53

Saunier, Anne, N-100, 206

Saunier, Charles, E-68, 402, 589, 592

Saunier, Charles, F-53

Saunier, Charles, N-82, 183

Saunier, Denis, E-403

Saunier, Elisabeth, E-90, 182

Saunier, Etienne, E-402, 589, 592

Saunier, Francoise, E-402, 589, 592

Saunier, Hilaire, E-403

Saunier, Isabelle, E-58

Saunier, Jean Augustin, E-402

Saunier, Jean Baptiste, E-402

Saunier, Jean Pierre, E-402

Saunier, Jerome, E-402-403, 423

Saunier, Joseph, E-589, 592

Saunier, Louis, E-529

Saunier, Louise, E-43-44, 347, 354
Saunier, Louise, F-73
Saunier, Louise, N-17, 108
Saunier, Louise, S1-101-102
Saunier, Louise, S2-541
Saunier, Marcel, E-529
Saunier, Marguerite, C-97
Saunier, Marguerite, E-23, 58, 101, 110, 291, 341-342, 403, 589, 595, 644-645, 589, 594
Saunier, Marguerite, F-53
Saunier, Marguerite, N-82, 183
Saunier, Marie, E-97, 349, 353, 403, 589, 592, 637
Saunier, Marie, F-51
Saunier, Marie, N-33-34
Saunier, Marie Catherine, E-353, 403
Saunier, Marie Isabelle, E-403
Saunier, Marie Joseph, F-91, 93
Saunier, Marie Magdeleine, E-299
Saunier, Marie Marguerite, C-23
Saunier, Marie-Josephe, S1-11-12, 14
Saunier, Marie-Josephe, S2-467
Saunier, Pierre, E-45, 82, 373, 402-403, 421, 423, 589, 592, 594
Saunier, Pierre Marie, E-403
Saureau, Anne, E-371
Saurin, Francois, E-403
Saurin, Helene, E-403
Sautier, Julienne, E-32, 403
Sautier, Mathurine, E-387, 403, 430
Sautier, Maurice, E-403
Sautier, Pierre, E-32
Sauvage, Celeste, S1-87
Sauvage, Elizabeth, S1-256
Sauvage, Francois, E-32, 403
Sauvage, Francois, S3-901
Sauvage, Francoise, S1-357
Sauvage, Guillaume, E-403
Sauvage, Hyacinthe, S3-889
Sauvage, Jacque, S3-878
Sauvage, Jan Pierre, S3-1095-1096
Sauvage, Jean Louis, E-124
Sauvage, Jean-Pierre, S2-652

Sauvage, Jeanne, E-403
Sauvage, Julienne, S2-652
Sauvage, Julienne, S3-1096
Sauvage, Mathurin, S3-903
Sauvage, Perrine, E-32, 403
Sauvages, Angelique, E-403
Sauvaget, Marie Francoise, N-43, 242
Sauvaguse, Jeanne, E-403
Sauvion, Gabriel, C-48, 55, 92, 110-111
Sauvion, Jean, C-92, 110
Sauvion, Jeanne, C-47, 92
Sauvion, Marie, C-92
Sauvion, Marie Anne, C-92
Savant, Jean, E-168, 404
Savant, Pierre, E-168, 404
Savari, Magdeleine, E-137
Savariau, Francoise Euphrosine Rosalie, E-101, 404
Savarre, Marie Elisabeth, E-5-6
Savary, Agnes, S2-726
Savary, Andre, S2-725-726
Savary, Anne, F-19
Savary, Anne, S1-98, 130-131
Savary, Anne, S2-678
Savary, Anne, S3-855
Savary, Anne-Madeleine, S2-677, 726
Savary, Bernard, S2-677, 725-726
Savary, Bernard, S3-855
Savary, Charles, S2-726-727, 761
Savary, Charles, S3-911
Savary, Etienne, C-167
Savary, Francois, E-141
Savary, Isaac, S2-726
Savary, Jean-Baptiste, S2-726
Savary, Jean-Charles, S2-726-727
Savary, Louis, E-141, 404
Savary, Louis, S2-726
Savary, Magdelaine, E-141, 404
Savary, Marie, E-140, 404
Savary, Marie Anne, E-59, 180, 343
Savary, Rose, S2-726
Savary, Therese, S1-219
Savary, Thomas, C-167
Savary, Thomas, N-67, 152, 192

Savat, Marie Joseph, E-404
Savat, Martin, E-404
Savatier, Rene, N-184
Savoye, Andree, E-476
Savoye, Anne, E-172, 599
Savoye, Catherine, E-475
Savoye, Charles, E-314, 404
Savoye, Divine, E-314, 404
Savoye, Felicite, E-186, 404
Savoye, Francois, E-456, 458, 500
Savoye, Francoise, E-473
Savoye, Germain, E-476, 500, 529
Savoye, Jeanne, E-476
Savoye, Joseph, E-404
Savoye, Marguerite, S2-682
Savoye, Margueritte, S3-969
Savoye, Marie, E-78, 79, 123, 132, 346, 474
Savoye, Marie, S1-198
Savoye, Marie, S2-516, 644
Savoye, Marie Josephe, E-13, 35, 404
Scalsen, Anne, N-194
Scaudel, Nicolas, E-303
Schet, Marie Louise, E-17, 159
Schlindevin, Marguerite, E-172, 174, 298
Schneider, Nicolas, N-226
Scollot, Marie Catherine, E-89
Scott, Jean, N-152, 167, 193
Seaux, Angelique, E-350-352
Seaux, Catherine, E-403
Seaux, Etienne, E-403-404
Seaux, Francoise, E-14
Seaux, Genevieve, E-58-59, 154, 168, 289-290, 403
Seaux, Louis, E-134, 404
Seaux, Marguerite, E-37, 56, 58-59, 110, 180, 404
Seaux, Marie, E-14, 21, 24, 353, 442
Seaux, Marie Jeanne, E-134, 404
Sebia, Anne, S1-56
Sebia, Anne, S2-607
Sebia, Anne, S3-996
Sebino, Jean-Baptiste Sr., S2-577
Sebois, J.B., S3-1115

Secal, Marianne, S3-1092

Segoillat, Emilien, E-337, 573

Segoillat, Francois Dominique, E-151, 574

Segoillot, Dominique, S2-727-728

Segoillot, Emilian, S3-1107, 1116, 1118-1119, 1122-1123, 1128

Segoillot, Emilien, S2-547, 727-728

Segoillot, Francois-Dominique, S2-727-728

Segoillot, Marguerite, F-27

Segoillot, Marie, S2-727

Segoillot, Marie Francoise, E-574

Segoillot, Marie-Francoise, S2-728

Segoillot, Suliac-Bertran-Marie, S2-728

Segoliat, Emilien, E-188

Segue, Francois, C-93

Segue, Guillaume, C-24, 92-93, 102-103

Segue, Jean, C-92-93, 102

Segue, Marie, C-93

Segue, Martin, C-93

Segue, Pierre, C-93

Seguin, Antoine, E-314, 404

Seguin, Jean, E-173, 404

Seguin, Pierre, E-314, 404

Seguineau, Pierre, E-35

Seigne, Pierre, E-107

Seigneur, Angelique, E-81, 405

Seigneur, Francoise, E-405

Seigneur, Jean, E-20, 71, 81, 345, 405

Seigneur, Marie Josephe, E-80, 405

Seillon, Francois, E-405

Seillon, Jean Francois, E-405, 421

Seime, Marie, E-53, 428

Selhay Detcheverry, Jeanne Marie, E-278, 380

Sellers, Pierre, E-82

Sement, Pierre, E-58, 87, 89, 181, 361, 364, 366, 434-435

Semer, Anne Francoise, F-69

Semer, Anne-Francoise, S2-729

Semer, Francoise, F-67

Semer, Germain, N-191

Semer, Gregoire, F-67

Semer, Joseph, F-69

Semer, Joseph, N-205, 212, 246

Semer, Joseph, S2-728-729

Semer, Joseph, S3-1034, 1058, 1064

Semer, Marie, F-69

Semer, Marie Marguerite, F-67

Semer, Marie-Marguerite, S2-729

Semer, Marine, S2-729

Semer, Michel, S2-728-729

Semestre, Joseph, C-118

Semet, Marie, E-53, 428

Semet, Susanne, E-108, 389

Semeure, Basile Romain, E-405

Semeure, girl, E-405

Semeure, Mr., E-379

Semeure, Semeure, E-405

Semidon, Guillemette-Pelagie, S2-504, 705

Semidon, Sylvain, E-628

Senat, Francois Marie, E-405

Senat, Jean, E-405

Senat, Jeanne, E-405

Senat, Paul Marie, E-405

Senck, Jean, E-405

Senck, Pierre George, E-405

Senecal, Charles Francois, E-191, 327

Separe, Marie Anne, E-341, 405

Separe, Marie Modeste, E-405

Separe, Martin, E-405

Seran, Felicite, E-599

Sereau, Leonard, E-265

Serrier, Etienne, E-45, 302

Servant, Jean, E-154

Servant, Simonne, E-377, 389

Sesecal, Marie, S3-1092

Sesecal, Marie Anne, S3-1091-1092

Sesecal, Nicolas, S3-1018

Seutir, Henry, S3-1088

Sevestre, Hy., S3-903

Sevestre, Jean Francois Louis, E-360, 405

Sevestre, Pierre, E-360, 405

Sevin, Marie, F-53

Sevin, Marie, N-101, 206

Sevrin, Marie Francoise, E-405

Sevrin, Pierre Louis, E-405

Seyne, Guillaume, E-636

Sezegal, Marie-Anne, S2-721

Sibilau, Marie Anne, E-388

Sicard, Suzanne, E-26, 405

Siccaud, Francois, E-91

Sicot, Jean, E-83, 406

Sie, Marguerite, E-123

Sigala, Jean, E-109

Sigalant, Jean, E-161

Sigouital, Aemilien, S3-1107

Sigue, Pierre, C-102

Sigut, Marie, E-316, 323

Silvain, Anne, S1-83

Silvain, Anne, S3-919

Simeot, M. Louis, E-406

Simeot, Marguerite, E-406

Simeot, Marie Louise, E-406

Simeot, Mathieu, E-406

Simero, Anne, E-330

Simon, Catherine, E-195, 406

Simon, Charles, E-256, 259, 406

Simon, Francoise Anne, E-93

Simon, Jacques, E-29

Simon, Jean, E-66, 259, 340, 357, 406

Simon, Jean Baptiste, F-85

Simon, Jean Baptiste, N-230

Simon, Jeanne, E-108-109, 384

Simon, Louis, E-42

Simon, Madeleine, S2-433, 634, 643, 648

Simon, Magdeleine, E-14, 26-28, 179, 336, 351-352, 406

Simon, Magdeleine, S3-985

Simon, Marguerite, E-370

Simon, Marguerite Rose, E-15

Simon, Marie, E-42, 70, 98, 104, 126-127, 132, 141, 176, 263, 292, 312, 342, 371, 406, 431-432

Simon, Marie, S1-307-308, 320, 331

Simon, Marie Anne, E-144, 340

Simon, Marie Magdeleine, E-28

Simon, Martial, E-315

Simon, Mathurine, S1-22

Simon, Philippe, E-406

Simon, Pierre, E-28, 195, 406

Simonet, Claude, E-182

Simonet, Jean, E-98, 402
Simonet, Marguerite, E-326
Singlan, Marie Catherine, E-406
Siqut, Marie, E-369
Sire, Adelaide, E-627-628
Sire, Adelaide, S1-35, 217, 224-225
Sire, Adelaide, S2-741
Sire, Amand, E-407-408
Sire, Amand, S1-224-225, 227, 315
Sire, Amand, S2-578
Sire, Ambroise, E-406
Sire, Anastasie, E-620
Sire, Anastasie, S1-35, 216-217, 224-225, 229
Sire, Anastasie, S2-740
Sire, Anne, E-11, 182, 279, 406, 549, 551
Sire, Anne, S1-191, 192, 217, 225-226, 347
Sire, Anne, S2-753
Sire, Anne, S3-979
Sire, Barbe, E-406
Sire, Charles, S1-224, 229
Sire, Charles, S2-740
Sire, Fabien, S1-218, 226-227
Sire, Fabien, S3-1098
Sire, Felicite, S1-226
Sire, Felicite, S2-710, 783
Sire, Felicite, S3-1076
Sire, Francois, E-44, 406-407
Sire, Francoise, E-33, 407, 551, 617
Sire, Francoise, S1-225-226
Sire, Francoise, S2-504
Sire, Genevieve, E-407
Sire, Genevieve, S2-623
Sire, girl, E-406
Sire, Guillaume, E-514, 530
Sire, Guillaume, S1-228
Sire, Jacques, E-628
Sire, Jacques, S1-217, 223-225, 227-228, 297
Sire, Jacques, S3-1090, 1098
Sire, Jan, S3-979
Sire, Jean, E-290, 406-408, 437, 514, 530, 548, 551
Sire, Jean, S1-35, 191, 224-228, 230, 297, 300, 366
Sire, Jean, S2-710, 741, 783

Sire, Jean, S3-918, 1053
Sire, Jean, S3-999, 1072, 1076
Sire, Jean Baptiste, E-407
Sire, Jean Francois, E-407
Sire, Jean Jacques, E-549
Sire, Jean Yve, E-407
Sire, Jean-Baptiste, S1-224
Sire, Jean-Baptiste-Marin, S1-224-225
Sire, Josef, S3-1053
Sire, Joseph, E-149, 407, 429, 437
Sire, Joseph, S1-224-228, 366
Sire, Joseph, S3-999
Sire, Josephe, E-407
Sire, Julie, E-407
Sire, Laurent, S1-224, 229
Sire, Laurent, S2-578, 740
Sire, Laurent, S3-1098
Sire, Louis, E-530
Sire, Louis, N-60
Sire, Louis, S2-456
Sire, Louise, E-407, 435-436
Sire, Magdeleine, E-195, 351, 407, 436, 438
Sire, Marguerite, E-57, 123-124, 319, 363, 363, 407, 429, 434, 436, 549, 551, 627
Sire, Marguerite, F-37
Sire, Marguerite, N-19, 60, 215
Sire, Marguerite, S1-184-185, 227
Sire, Margueritte, S3-917
Sire, Marie, E-393, 407, 549, 551, 628
Sire, Marie, S1-191, 225-227, 366-369
Sire, Marie, S2-433-434, 653, 740, 742
Sire, Marie, S3-1085, 1117
Sire, Marie, S3-999
Sire, Marie Marguerite, E-124
Sire, Marie Victoire, E-407
Sire, Marie-Francoise, S1-224
Sire, Marie-Jeanne, S1-230
Sire, Marie-Josephe, S1-227-228
Sire, Marie-Perinne, S1-230
Sire, Michel, E-548, 551
Sire, Michel, S2-623
Sire, Modeste, E-86

Sire, Modeste, S1-225-226
Sire, Paul, E-407
Sire, Perinne-Cecile, S1-230
Sire, Perrine, E-620
Sire, Pierre, E-287, 306, 406-408, 458, 514, 530, 548-549
Sire, Pierre, S1-216, 223-226, 228-230
Sire, Pierre, S2-553, 577, 711, 740-741
Sire, Pierre, S3-1079
Sire, Pierre, S3-1085, 1090, 1098
Sire, Pierre Paul, E-551
Sire, Rosalie, E-284, 408
Sire, Rosalie, S1-224, 229
Sire, Rosalie, S2-472, 577-578, 740
Sire, Rose, E-181, 184, 187, 408, 433
Sire, Rose, S1-229
Sire, Simon, E-408
Sire, Theotiste, S1-192, 225-226
Sire, Theotiste, S2-452, 783
Sire, Theotiste, S3-1072
Sire, Veronique, S2-456-458
Sire, Victoire, S1-217-218, 227, 229
Sire, Victoire, S2-553, 577, 740
Sire, Victoire, S3-1090
Sire, Vincent, E-407-408
Sire, Xavier, E-290, 336, 408
Sire, Xavier, S1-227
Siver, Henriette, E-101
Smet, Elizabeth, S1-190
Soga, Sabine, N-99, 249
Soleau, Francois, E-84, 168
Soleau, Jean, E-172, 408
Soleau, Pierre, E-172, 408
Solle, Anne Marie, E-408
Solle, Anne Marie Joseph, E-277
Solle, Francoise, E-408
Solle, Jean, E-408
Solle, Jean, S2-520
Solle, Jean Baptiste, E-408
Solle, M., E-408
Solle, Marguerite Desiree, E-408
Solle, Marie Adelaide, E-408
Solle, Marie Francoise, E-408

Solle, Marie Louise, E-408
Solle, Nicolas, E-409
Solle, Pierre, E-409
Solle, Pierre Eloy, E-408
Solle, Simone, S1-75
Solle, Simone, S2-520
Sollee, Jean, S1-75
Sollet, Jean, E-126, 412
Sollet, Marie Francoise, E-412
Sollet, Marie Louise, E-126
Sollier, Jacques, E-361
Sonis, Antoine, E-128
Sonis, Jean Baptiste, E-128
Sony, Jeanne, E-288
Soquet, Jean, E-359, 409
Soquet, Therese, E-359, 409
Sorel, Etienne, S1-358
Soret, Etienne, S2-520
Sorin, Catherine Rose, E-369, 409
Sorin, Francois, E-369, 409
Sorin, Radegonde, E-369
Sornl, Jacob, E-409
Sornl, Louis Laurent, E-409
Sorot, Joseph, S1-37
Sot, Marguerite, E-1, 633, 643
Soubadu, Jean, E-589, 597
Soubier, succession of, E-356
Soubileau, Marie Anne, E-17
Soucaire, Jean, E-53, 109
Souchard, Jean, S1-2
Souche, Marguerite, E-379
Souchier, Antoine, E-409
Souchier, Felix, E-409
Souchier, Jean, E-409
Souchier, Marin, E-409
Souchier, Pierre Felix, E-409
Soude, Renotte, E-117
Soujolly, Marianne, E-106, 328
Soulard, Mathurin, E-393, 409
Soule, Jeanne Jeremie, E-311
Soulet, Jean, E-25, 409
Soulet, Marie, E-259, 409
Soulet, Pierre, E-265
Soullard, Louis, E-168
Souquet, Francoise, S1-363
Souquet, Jean, S3-862
Souquet, Marie, S1-363
Sourine, Etienette, E-302, 390
Sournier, Marie Joseph, S3-1100
Soy, George, N-183

Soyon, Magdeleine, E-347
Spiger, -----, N-69
Spiger, Antoine, N-152, 226
Spiger, Christian, F-49
Spiger, Christian, N-152-153, 155, 226
Spiger, Jeanne Marie, N-153
Spiger, Marie Francoise, N-153
Spinadel, Jean, E-325
St-Aubin, Alexandre, E-363, 405
St-Aubin, Francois Robert Laurent (Rev.), E-334
St-Aubin, Mr., E-361
St-Castin, Marie Joseph, E-290, 390
St-Domingue, E-395
St-Domingue - Cities where registers were researched, E-398
St-Domingue Research, E-397-398
St-Jean, Antoine, E-379
St-Jean, Antoine, E-399
St-Jean, Jean, E-379
St-Jean, Jean, E-399
St-Laurins, Marie Toinette, E-392
St-Martin, Mr., E-388
St-Michel, Catherine, E-328
St-Pierre-et-Miquelon, E-399-400
St-Pierre-et-Miquelon and the Acadians in 1763, E-400
Staipe, Marie, E-196
Staquet, Pierre Joseph, E-158
Stavan, Jean, E-27
Ste-Lucie, E-401
Ste-Lucie - Cities whose registers were researched, E-399
Stebens, boy, F-9
Stebens, Louis, F-9
Stebens, Louis, N-153
Stebens, Louis William, N-9, 153
Stebens, Marie, F-9
Stebens, Marie, N-153
Stebens, Stanislas, F-9
Stebens, Stanislas, N-153, 177, 194
Stebens, William, N-177, 194

Stenx, Mr., E-369
Sterine, Marianne, E-134
Stiven, Guillaume, N-183
Stopul, Anne, N-171, 185
Stourbe, Guillemette, E-183
Stricq, Catherine, E-424
Stricq, Marie Catherine, E-123
Suaux, Perine, E-589, 596
Subot, Francois, E-10
Sudois, Jeanne, E-409, 441
Sudois, Paul, E-409
Suec, Jean, E-409
Suec, Jean Baptiste, E-192, 409
Suehard, Gabrielle, N-68, 190
Sugois, Jeanne, E-409
Suire, Jean, E-73
Suire, Pierre, E-101
Suplet, Gabriel, E-51, 410
Surcelin, Isabeau de, E-66
Sureau, Francois, E-169, 335
Sureau, Pierre, E-410
Surgere, Mr., E-369
Susanne, Louis, E-185
Suydam, Thomas G. , C-viii

T

Tabor, Jean, E-411
Tabor, Marie Julie Bernard, E-411
Tabot, Louis, E-367
Tachet, Pierre, E-314
Tademan, Marie, E-422
Taerot, Marie, C-158
Tafaud, Jean Marie Francois, E-93
Taforet, Henri, S3-952
Taforet, Joseph, S3-952
Taforet, Pierre, S3-1084
Tailbot, Louis, E-79
Talaberi, -----, E-20
Talard, Elizabeth, E-267
Talbot, -----, S3-975
Talbot, Charles, E-411
Talbot, Charles, S2-730-731
Talbot, Charles Louis, E-367, 411
Talbot, Charles Louis, S3-993
Talbot, Charles-Louis, S2-730-731
Talbot, Francois, E-411

INDEX SOURCES C=Chatellerault; E=Acadians in Exile; F=Acadian Families; N=Nantes; S=St-Malo

Talbot, Francois, S2-730-731
Talbot, Francoise, S2-731
Talbot, Jean, S2-731
Talbot, Jean-Francois, S2-730-731
Talbot, Joseph, S2-730-731
Talbot, Louis, E-102, 110, 119-120, 127, 141, 259, 295, 311, 378, 411
Talbot, Louis, S1-199, 280-281, 308, 332
Talbot, Louis, S2-516, 518, 581-582, 729, 731
Talbot, Louis, S3-975, 993
Talbot, Louis-Charles, S2-729-731
Talbot, Marie Henriette, E-411
Talbot, Marie-Henriette, S2-729-730
Talbot, Marie-Louise, S2-730-731
Talbot, Nicolas, E-411
Talbot, Nicolas, S2-729
Talbot, Nicolas, S3-975
Talbot, Sieur, E-411
Talebot, Louis, E-432
Tallard, Claude, E-266, 411
Tallard, Elizabeth, E-266, 411
Tallard, Marie, E-36, 259, 588, 591
Talon, Josephe, S1-37
Talon, Josephe, S3-1060
Talon, Pierre Louis, E-21, 411
Talva, Mathieu, E-10
Talvart, Jacques, S3-1053
Talvas, Jean, E-110, 411
Talvas, Marie Madeleine, E-411
Talvas, Martin, E-411
Talvas, Yves, E-110, 411
Tande, Jacques Marie, E-411
Tande, Jean Jacques, E-411
Tande, Marie Guenole, E-411
Tanguy, Francoise, E-186
Tannier, Bertrand, E-412
Tannier, Mathurin, E-93, 412
Tanqueray, Jeanne, E-375, 438
Tanquerel, Charle, E-268
Tardieu, Guillaume Michel, E-408, 412
Tardieu, Leonard, E-408, 412
Tardivet, Anne, S2-557, 763

Tardivet, Anne, S3-1061
Tardivet, Charles, N-172
Tardivet, Charles, S2-779
Tardivet, Charles, S3-1055
Tardivet, Eugenie Marie, N-172
Tardivet, Eugenie Marie, S3-1055
Tardivet, Eugenie-Marie, S2-779
Tardivet, Michel, S2-763
Tardivet, Michel, S3-1061
Tardix, Jean, E-338
Tardw, Jeanne, E-591
Tardy, Louis, E-332
Tardy, Marie, E-174, 326
Tardy, Michelle, E-159
Tardy, Mr., E-369
Targe, Pierre, E-325
Tarier, Marie, E-306
Tarsille, Marguerite, S2-671
Tauqueret, Jeanne, E-172, 303
Tautain, Gille, E-123
Taveau, Philippe Thomas, E-178
Tavernier, Jean, E-305
Tavernier, Jean Charron, E-412
Tavernier, Nicolas, E-305, 412
Tavernier, Pierre, E-279, 412
Tayon, Jeanne Catherine, E-115, 412
Tayon, Rene, E-412
Tehen, Laurence, S2-729
Tehen, Laurence, S3-975
Teizan, Catherine, E-439
Tellier, Charlotte, E-412
Tellier, Jacques, E-412
Tellier, Jean Baptiste, E-412
Templais, Andre, C-107
Templais, Marguerite, C-107-108
Temple, Andre, C-24, 93-94
Temple, Andre, F-3, 81
Temple, Andre, N-202
Temple, Andre, S1-164
Temple, Andre, S2-525, 568, 731-734
Temple, Andre, S3-966
Temple, Andre Joseph, N-154
Temple, Bruno, S2-732
Temple, Charles, F-3
Temple, Charles, N-154

Temple, Charles-Casimir, S2-732
Temple, Dominique-Pierre, S2-733
Temple, Elizabeth, C-60
Temple, Elizabeth, N-154
Temple, Elizabeth, S2-511
Temple, Elizabeth-Marguerite, S2-732
Temple, Francois, E-265
Temple, Francois Joseph, C-94
Temple, Francois Joseph, N-154
Temple, Francois Marie, N-154
Temple, Hyacinthe, N-154
Temple, Hyacinthe Francois-Joseph, S2-733
Temple, Isabelle, C-94
Temple, Isabelle, F-3
Temple, Jacques, F-3
Temple, Jacques, N-154
Temple, Jacques-Olivier, S2-732
Temple, Jean, C-68
Temple, Jean, E-326, 338
Temple, Jean, F-3
Temple, Jean, N-154, 206
Temple, Jean-Andre-Gregoire-Marie, S2-732
Temple, Marguerite, C-24, 94
Temple, Marguerite, F-81
Temple, Marguerite, N-36-37
Temple, Marguerite, S2-732-734
Temple, Marie Madeleine, N-155
Temple, Marie Magdelaine, F-3
Temple, Marie-Madeleine, S2-733
Temple, Modeste, S2-732
Temple, Olivier, F-3
Temple, Olivier, N-154
Temple, Ollivier-Marcellin, S2-733
Temple, Pierre Dominique, N-154
Temple, Rene, S2-732
Temple, Servan, N-154
Temple, Servan-Francois, S2-733
Temple, Servant, F-3

Tenailleau, Gabrielle, E-257, 412

Tenailleau, Marguerite, E-28, 369

Tenieres, Mathurin, E-412

Ternant, Antoine, N-247

Ternant, Jeanne Augustine, N-247

Ternel, Elisabeth, E-391

Teronneau, Suzanne, E-155, 376

Terrade, Jean, E-353

Terrasson, Pierre, E-20, 346

Terray, Joseph Marie (Abbe), C-xiii

Terrien, Jean, E-59, 157, 412

Terrien, Louis, E-412

Terrien, Marie, E-59, 412

Terrien, Michel, S1-46

Terrien, Pierre Jacques, E-412

Terrier, Andre, E-628

Terrier, Anne, E-84

Terrier, Francois, E-628

Terrier, Francois-Guillaume, S2-661

Terrier, Francoise, E-628

Terrier, Jacquemin, E-628

Terrier, Jacques, E-628

Terrier, Jean Baptiste, E-628

Terrier, Jeanne Aimee, E-628

Terrier, Joseph, S3-970

Terrier, Julie, E-628

Terrier, Marguerite, E-30, 36, 153, 377

Terrier, Marie, E-628

Terrier, Perrine, E-628

Terrine, Jean, E-412

Terriot, Anastasie, E-296, 333, 417-418

Terriot, Angelique, F-101

Terriot, Anne, E-15, 42, 44, 269, 330, 413-414, 423, 426, 479, 485

Terriot, Anne, F-7, 17, 19, 91, 99

Terriot, Anne Gertrude, E-43-44, 555-556, 558

Terrot, Marie, E-93

Tesier, Marguerite, S1-75

Teslaud, Laurent, E-385

Tesse, Etienne, E-412

Tesse, Jean, E-412-413

Tesse, Jean Baptiste, E-413

Tesse, Marie, E-413

Tesse, Pierre, E-172, 379, 413

Tessereau, Francois, E-161, 413

Tessereau, Francoise, E-161, 413

Tessier, Francois, E-160, 335, 413

Tessier, Jean, E-123

Tessier, Louis, E-140, 413

Tessier, Marie, E-34, 160, 355, 413

Tessier, Marie, S1-204

Tessier, Marie Anne, E-149, 318

Tessier, Martial, E-52, 392

Tessier, Mathieu, E-392

Tessier, Michel, E-413

Tessier, Pierre, E-140, 280, 322, 413

Tesson, Barbe, E-153

Tesson, Barbe, S2-507

Tesson, Barbe, S3-965

Testard, Francois, E-413

Testard, Francoise, E-139, 387

Testard, Jean, E-164

Testard, Jean Baptiste, E-165, 413

Testard, Marie, S1-3, 252

Testard, Pierre, C-161

Testu, Genevieve, E-59, 155, 350

Tetu, Genevieve, S1-173

Tevenolle, Francoise, E-320

Texier, Ancelme Bernard, C-95

Texier, Bernard, C-95

Texier, Francoise Reine, C-95

Texier, Jean, E-413, 417

Texier, Marguerite, E-34, 316

Texier, Marie Anne, C-95

Texier, Pierre Alexis, C-75, 95

Thalon, Joseph, S3-1009

Thebaud, Pierre, E-142

Theisse, Marie Catherine, E-413

Thenon, Elie, E-295

Thenon, Magdeleine, E-295

Therahan, Ollivier, S3-1010

Theriette, Marie Jeanne, E-16

Theriot, -----, S3-1098

Theriot, Adelaide, S2-741-742

Theriot, Anastasie, C-5, 17, 139

Theriot, Anastasie, N-8, 153

Theriot, Anastasie, S1-36-37

Theriot, Anne, C-16, 56, 62, 71, 98, 144, 148

Theriot, Anne, N-108, 171

Theriot, Anne, S1-14, 30, 40, 137, 314-315, 366-368

Theriot, Anne, S2-438, 460, 524, 534, 538, 540, 574, 713, 736-737, 746, 750, 767, 778

Theriot, Anne, S3-885, 927, 1034, 1037, 1047, 1085

Theriot, Anne Anastasie, N-194

Theriot, Anne Marie, E-574

Theriot, Anne Marie, N-158

Theriot, Anne Marthe Divine, E-413

Theriot, Anne-Angelique, S2-752

Theriot, Anne-Jeanne, S2-738

Theriot, Annette, E-42

Theriot, Anselme, S2-750-751

Theriot, Anselme-Jean, S2-741

Theriot, Auguste-Jean, S2-744

Theriot, Augustin, C-94

Theriot, Baptiste, E-415

Theriot, Baptiste, S3-1016

Theriot, Blanche, E-282

Theriot, Bonaventure, C-79

Theriot, Bonaventure, E-458, 476

Theriot, Bonaventure, N-134

Theriot, Bricet, S2-751

Theriot, Catherine, E-173, 457, 474, 486

Theriot, Catherine, S1-309

Theriot, Catherine, S2-615

Theriot, Cecile, E-42, 414

Theriot, Cecile, S1-95-96

Theriot, Chalres, N-153, 155, 159, 226-227

Theriot, Charle, S3-973

Theriot, Charles, C-114

Theriot, Charles, E-415

Theriot, Charles, F-49, 51, 111

Theriot, Charles, S1-5, 29, 208, 212, 314

Theriot, Charles, S2-737, 742, 747, 749, 758

Theriot, Charles, S3-848, 885, 887, 1016

Theriot, Charles Francois, E-414

Theriot, Charles Gregoire, E-561

Theriot, Charles-Joseph, S2-749

Theriot, Charles-Pierre, S2-738

Theriot, Cirile, S3-976-977, 1026, 1036-1037

Theriot, Cirille, S2-505, 736-737, 756

Theriot, Claude, E-16, 166, 264, 415, 458, 476, 479, 530

Theriot, Claude, S1-51, 245

Theriot, Claude, S3-828

Theriot, Cyprien, C-94

Theriot, Cyprien, E-416

Theriot, Cyrille, S1-237, 295

Theriot, Elisabeth, E-5-6, 44, 161, 182, 271-274, 373, 414, 421, 426, 480, 563, 573, 609, 612, 615

Theriot, Elisabeth, S3-1012

Theriot, Elizabeth, C-28, 86, 94

Theriot, Elizabeth, F-5, 59, 61, 71

Theriot, Elizabeth, N-11, 81, 104, 120, 122, 163

Theriot, Elizabeth, S1-52, 222

Theriot, Elizabeth, S2-437, 736-737

Theriot, Estienne Baptiste, E-414

Theriot, Etienne, C-147

Theriot, Etienne, E-414

Theriot, Etienne, F-13

Theriot, Etienne, N-27, 155-157, 176, 180, 191, 239, 254

Theriot, Etienne, S1-95

Theriot, Etienne, S2-734-735, 744, 774

Theriot, Etienne, S3-857, 972-973, 1051, 1064

Theriot, Euphrosine, S1-290

Theriot, Fabien, S2-751

Theriot, Francois, F-101

Theriot, Francois, S1-73

Theriot, Francois, S2-486, 540, 736-737, 751

Theriot, Francois, S3-934, 976-977, 1026, 1035, 1037

Theriot, Francois Joseph, E-414

Theriot, Francois Robert, E-413, 439

Theriot, Francois-Pierre, S2-743

Theriot, Francoise, E-25, 95, 162, 380, 420, 436

Theriot, Francoise, F-59

Theriot, Francoise, S1-27, 50, 61, 132

Theriot, Francoise, S2-486, 505, 535, 564, 576, 605, 735, 738, 741, 751, 774

Theriot, Francoise, S3-857, 890, 930, 974, 1032

Theriot, Francoise Elizabeth, N-156-157

Theriot, Francoise Euphemie, E-5-6

Theriot, Francoise Josephe, C-58

Theriot, Francoise Josephe, E-28, 192-193

Theriot, Francoise-Jeanne, S2-738

Theriot, Francoise-Perinne, S2-743

Theriot, Gabriel Leonard, E-414

Theriot, Genevieve, E-55, 433

Theriot, Genevieve, F-91

Theriot, Genevieve, S1-30, 61, 106, 119, 184, 208, 237

Theriot, Genevieve, S2-745, 751

Theriot, Genevieve-Catherine, S2-744

Theriot, Germain, E-458, 476, 486, 530

Theriot, Germain, E-97, 153, 349, 412, 414-416, 438

Theriot, Gertrude, S1-73

Theriot, Gertrude, S2-736-737

Theriot, Gertrude, S3-1026, 1035-1036, 1075

Theriot, Grabelle, E-95

Theriot, Honore, S1-241, 332

Theriot, Honore, S2-737-739, 742, 748, 754

Theriot, Honore, S3-973

Theriot, Honore-Charles, S2-748

Theriot, Hufroisine, S3-1128

Theriot, Isaac, S2-739

Theriot, Isaac, S3-952, 955, 969

Theriot, Isabelle, C-8, 52

Theriot, Isabelle, E-33, 94, 161, 163, 166, 273, 383, 427

Theriot, Isabelle, F-61

Theriot, Isabelle, S1-52

Theriot, Isabelle, S2-749

Theriot, Isabelle, S3-1046, 1063

Theriot, Isabelle-Ozite, S2-746

Theriot, Isidore, E-44, 414-416

Theriot, Jacques, E-413

Theriot, Jacques, E-530

Theriot, Jacques, F-13

Theriot, Jacques, N-77, 155-157, 176, 180, 239

Theriot, Jacques, S2-734-735, 744, 749

Theriot, Jacques, S3-1016, 1064

Theriot, Jacques Julien, N-158

Theriot, Jean, C-67

Theriot, Jean, E-42, 391, 414-416, 479, 530, 555-556, 558, 564, 574

Theriot, Jean, F-13

Theriot, Jean, N-48, 73, 158

Theriot, Jean, S1-32

Theriot, Jean, S2-561, 615, 738, 742

Theriot, Jean, S3-858, 1070

Theriot, Jean Baptiste, E-162, 164, 273, 413-416, 574, 608-610, 612-613, 615

Theriot, Jean Baptiste, F-105

Theriot, Jean Baptiste, S1-5, 13, 167, 208, 228, 241, 262, 314, 329

Theriot, Jean Baptiste, S3-885, 889, 892, 895, 1016, 1032, 1090

Theriot, Jean Charles, F-13

Theriot, Jean Charles, N-158

Theriot, Jean Jacque, S3-1033, 1064

Theriot, Jean Jacques, F-91

Theriot, Jean Louis, E-414

Theriot, Jean Toussaint, N-158

Theriot, Jean-Baptiste, S2-737, 739-740, 742, 750-751

Theriot, Jean-Charles, S2-735, 743-744

Theriot, Jean-Jacques, S2-540, 693, 700, 733, 744-745

Theriot, Jeanne, C-67

Theriot, Jeanne, E-16, 476, 479
Theriot, Jeanne, F-15, 91
Theriot, Jeanne, N-6, 86, 145, 237
Theriot, Jeanne, S1-12-13
Theriot, Jeanne, S2-450, 558, 561
Theriot, Jeanne-Francoise, S2-747
Theriot, Jeanne-Marie, S2-745
Theriot, Josepfat, S3-947
Theriot, Joseph, E-94, 192-193, 414, 416,
Theriot, Joseph, F-15, 109
Theriot, Joseph, N-155, 157-158, 227-228
Theriot, Joseph, S1-61, 93, 174-175, 177, 196, 238, 241
Theriot, Joseph, S2-522, 526, 536, 614, 734-735, 737-739, 742-743, 745-750, 774
Theriot, Joseph, S3-839, 848-849, 859, 886, 892, 947, 952, 955-956, 974, 1028
Theriot, Joseph Marie, E-414
Theriot, Joseph Olivier, N-157
Theriot, Joseph-Jean, S2-748
Theriot, Joseph-Jean-Marie, S2-742
Theriot, Joseph-Marie, S2-745
Theriot, Josephe, E-96
Theriot, Josephe, S2-747
Theriot, Josephe, S3-956
Theriot, Josephine, S1-245
Theriot, Laurent-Guillaume, S2-740
Theriot, Louis, S2-740-742
Theriot, Louis Alexandre, N-155
Theriot, Louis-Alexandre, S2-743
Theriot, Luc, E-412
Theriot, Madeleine, C-9
Theriot, Madeleine, E-35, 92, 96, 122, 161-163, 170, 288, 362, 373, 414, 479, 638
Theriot, Madeleine, S2-463, 484, 488, 492-493, 502, 553, 559, 562, 571, 575, 688, 736-737, 744, 749
Theriot, Madeleine, S1-51, 54, 278, 368, 372

Theriot, Madeleine, N-212
Theriot, Madeleine-Josephe, S1-78
Theriot, Madeleine-Louise, S2-741
Theriot, Madeleine-Marie, S2-738, 742
Theriot, Magdelaine, F-31, 53, 55, 75, 97, 99
Theriot, Magdeleine, S3-946, 1022, 1056, 1059, 1071
Theriot, Marguerite, E-96, 151, 161-162, 164-166, 414-416, 425, 438, 474, 485, 561
Theriot, Marguerite, F-21, 45, 87, 91, 97, 99, 101
Theriot, Marguerite, N-8, 103, 108, 141, 175
Theriot, Marguerite, S1-13-14, 30, 32-33, 36, 62, 366
Theriot, Marguerite, S2-476, 495, 534, 541, 657, 665-666, 689, 737, 739, 750-751
Theriot, Marguerite, S3-922, 924, 999, 1069, 1116
Theriot, Marguerite Josephe, S3-977
Theriot, Marguerite-Josephe, S2-486, 736-737, 744
Theriot, Marguerite-Perinne, S2-745
Theriot, Margueritte, C-5, 83
Theriot, Marie, C-19
Theriot, Marie, E-94-96, 161-167, 264, 287-289, 415, 426, 474-475, 479, 555-556, 558, 564, 569
Theriot, Marie, F-25, 89, 91, 101
Theriot, Marie, N-31
Theriot, Marie, S1-5, 13, 28, 38, 50, 142, 146, 208, 210, 212, 251
Theriot, Marie, S2-486, 539-540, 553, 557-578, 693, 734, 736-738, 740-742, 745, 752, 755
Theriot, Marie, S3-887, 921, 1051
Theriot, Marie Anastasie, E-574

Theriot, Marie Anne, E-415, 609, 612, 615
Theriot, Marie Augustine, E-415
Theriot, Marie Blanche, E-7, 161-167, 287, 289, 382, 414, 561-562, 612, 615, 609
Theriot, Marie Catherine, E-414-415
Theriot, Marie Elisabeth, E-95, 126, 283, 415
Theriot, Marie Genevieve, E-161, 163, 165-166, 564
Theriot, Marie Genevieve, F-95
Theriot, Marie Genevieve, N-73
Theriot, Marie Jeanne, E-415
Theriot, Marie Joseph, F-81
Theriot, Marie Josephe, C-12, 45, 67, 72
Theriot, Marie Josephe, E-25-26, 94-95, 97, 138, 165-167, 284, 289, 313, 352, 415, 555-556, 558, 563, 580
Theriot, Marie Josephe, E-93
Theriot, Marie Josephe, F-21, 27, 79
Theriot, Marie Josephe, N-70
Theriot, Marie Josephe, S3-825, 827, 935, 1056, 1080
Theriot, Marie Madeleine, E-34, 93-95, 162, 166, 259, 415-416, 425, 555-556, 558, 561, 563, 580
Theriot, Marie Madeleine, N-48, 155, 159-160, 227
Theriot, Marie Madeleine, S1-62
Theriot, Marie Magdelaine, F-51, 55
Theriot, Marie Magdeleine, S3-963, 1016
Theriot, Marie Marguerite, E-416, 574, 609, 612, 615
Theriot, Marie Modeste, E-416
Theriot, Marie Rose, N-158
Theriot, Marie Simone, E-416
Theriot, Marie Theodore, E-416
Theriot, Marie Therese, E-153, 416
Theriot, Marie Yvonne, E-416
Theriot, Marie-Charlotte, S2-742

Theriot, Marie-Genevieve, S1-29

Theriot, Marie-Genevieve, S2-532

Theriot, Marie-Josephe, S1-53-54, 65, 240, 242, 360-362

Theriot, Marie-Josephe, S2-561-562, 575, 595, 744

Theriot, Marie-Madeleine, S1-61, 187, 212-213

Theriot, Marie-Madeleine, S2-743, 749-751

Theriot, Marie-Modeste, S2-747, 752

Theriot, Marie-Rose, S2-746

Theriot, Marine Elizabeth, E-166

Theriot, Mathurin-Marie, S2-738

Theriot, Mathurine, S2-739

Theriot, Modeste, S2-737

Theriot, Mrs., N-228

Theriot, Natalie-Marie, S2-749

Theriot, Olivier, F-13, 29

Theriot, Olivier, N-8, 156-158, 176, 180, 236-237, 239

Theriot, Olivier, S1-212

Theriot, Olivier, S2-527, 536, 734-735, 744, 749-750

Theriot, Olivier, S3-856-857, 1016, 1064

Theriot, Olivier Marie, F-13

Theriot, Olivier Marie, N-157-158

Theriot, Osite Perpetue, N-153, 155, 226

Theriot, Ozite Perpetue, F-49

Theriot, Paul, E-416, 573

Theriot, Perinne-Mathurine, S2-739

Theriot, Perpetue, S2-736-737, 743

Theriot, Philippe, E-476

Theriot, Pierre, C-30, 94-95

Theriot, Pierre, E-130, 414-416, 479, 486, 530, 561, 569

Theriot, Pierre, F-53

Theriot, Pierre, N-156, 159, 226

Theriot, Pierre, S1-50, 61

Theriot, Pierre, S3-955, 974, 976-977, 1026, 1036-1037

Theriot, Pierre, S2-486, 540, 718, 735-737, 739, 741-742, 746, 750-751

Theriot, Pierre Marie, E-416

Theriot, Pierre Victor, E-609, 612, 615

Theriot, Pierre-Jacques, S2-737

Theriot, Pierre-Paul, S2-745-746

Theriot, Rosalie, F-89, 91

Theriot, Rosalie, S1-5-6, 208, 314

Theriot, Rosalie-Pauline, S2-745

Theriot, Similien, N-158

Theriot, Simon, E-414

Theriot, Simon, S2-742

Theriot, Simon-Pierre, S2-740

Theriot, Tecle, C-18, 91, 114

Theriot, Tecle, S1-115, 121, 245-246

Theriot, Tecle, S3-828

Theriot, Thecle, E-636

Theriot, Theodore, F-101

Theriot, Theodore, S1-73, 147, 183, 368, 377

Theriot, Theodore, S2-486, 603, 717, 736-737, 751-752

Theriot, Theodore, S2-501

Theriot, Theodore, S3-934, 976-977, 1026, 1036-1037

Theriot, Theodose, S1-50

Theriot, Therese, E-167

Theriot, Victoire, E-349, 416

Theriot, Victoire, S2-740, 742

Theriot, Victor, E-416

Theriot, Xavier, S2-741

Thermy, Pierre, E-307

Thesson, Barbe, E-391, 416

Thesson, Elie, E-391

Thesson, Elie dit La Flourie, E-40

Thesson, Jeanne, E-40, 416

Thesson De La Flourie, Magdeleine, E-416

Thesson dit LaFloury, Elie, E-416

Theule, Jean, E-316, 369

Thezin, Joseph Eymard, E-411

Thiac, Jean, E-53, 417

Thiac, Jean Baptiste, E-417

Thiac, Marie Aglae, E-417

Thiac, Marie Clemence, E-417

Thiac, Martin, E-53, 417

Thiard, Marie, E-420-421

Thiard, Marie, F-47

Thibaud, Alexis (Jr.), E-589, 591

Thibaud, Felix, E-197

Thibaud, Jacques, E-338

Thibaud, Jean, E-139

Thibaud, Jean Marie, E-163

Thibaud, Marie, E-375

Thibaud, Marie Jeanne, E-45, 316

Thibodeaux, Agathe, S1-39, 87, 97, 108

Thibodeaux, Agathe, S2-565

Thibodeaux, Agathe, S3-835

Thibodeaux, Alexandre, N-56

Thibodeaux, Alexandre, S1-266, 271

Thibodeaux, Alexis, E-417

Thibodeaux, Alexis, S1-123

Thibodeaux, Alexis, S2-752

Thibodeaux, Anastasie, S2-755

Thibodeaux, Angelique, E-589, 593

Thibodeaux, Anne, C-14, 21

Thibodeaux, Anne, E-162-163, 302, 308, 383, 417, 559, 581

Thibodeaux, Anne, F-33

Thibodeaux, Anne, N-30, 56, 92, 152, 244, 252

Thibodeaux, Anne, S1-88, 98, 131, 271-272

Thibodeaux, Anne, S2-501-503, 755

Thibodeaux, Anne, S3-834, 850, 920, 1021

Thibodeaux, Anne Marie, C-68

Thibodeaux, Anne Marie, E-82, 422, 472, 476, 502

Thibodeaux, Anne Marie, F-39, 53, 77, 109

Thibodeaux, Anne Marie, N-42, 118, 205

Thibodeaux, Anne Marie, S3-1067

Thibodeaux, Anne-Marie, S1-107

Thibodeaux, Anne-Marie, S2-572

Thibodeaux, Antoine, C-14, 21

Thibodeaux, Antoine, E-418, 502, 530

Thibodeaux, Antoine, F-51

Thibodeaux, Antoine, N-30, 152, 244

Thibodeaux, Antoine, S1-97, 131

Thibodeaux, Antoine, S2-753

Thibodeaux, Antoine, S3-838, 850

Thibodeaux, Bazile, S2-752

Thibodeaux, Benjamin, S2-753

Thibodeaux, Blaise, C-5

Thibodeaux, Blaise, E-417

Thibodeaux, Blaise, F-51

Thibodeaux, Blaise, N-159, 205, 227

Thibodeaux, Blaise, S1-38, 98

Thibodeaux, Blaise, S2-668, 753, 755

Thibodeaux, Bonaventure, E-16, 113

Thibodeaux, Catherine, E-413, 417, 502

Thibodeaux, Catherine, N-105-106

Thibodeaux, Catherine, S1-238

Thibodeaux, Catherine, S2-530

Thibodeaux, Charles, F-103

Thibodeaux, Charles, S2-491, 501, 662, 755-756

Thibodeaux, Charles, S3-920

Thibodeaux, Charles Isaac, E-417

Thibodeaux, Charles-Isaac, S2-753

Thibodeaux, Charlotte Elizabeth, E-6

Thibodeaux, Cicille, E-502

Thibodeaux, Claude, E-502, 530

Thibodeaux, David, E-113

Thibodeaux, David, S2-753

Thibodeaux, Elizabeth, E-280, 282, 284, 286, 566, 581

Thibodeaux, Elizabeth, F-31, 55

Thibodeaux, Elizabeth, N-27-28, 47, 159

Thibodeaux, Elizabeth, S1-123

Thibodeaux, Elizabeth, S2-707, 752

Thibodeaux, Elizabeth-Jeanne, S2-755, 759

Thibodeaux, Elizabeth-Marie, S2-760

Thibodeaux, Eloi, E-296, 417, 589, 597, 602

Thibodeaux, Emilie, S1-133-134

Thibodeaux, Firmin, F-51

Thibodeaux, Firmin, N-155, 159-160, 227

Thibodeaux, Firmin, S1-39

Thibodeaux, Firmin, S2-753, 757

Thibodeaux, Firmin Blais, F-51

Thibodeaux, Firmin Blaise, N-159-160

Thibodeaux, Firmin-Charles, S2-754

Thibodeaux, Francois, E-296, 333, 417-418, 574

Thibodeaux, Francois, F-51

Thibodeaux, Francois, N-159

Thibodeaux, Francois, S2-755

Thibodeaux, Francois Eloi, E-417, 574

Thibodeaux, Francois-Belony, S2-754

Thibodeaux, Francois-Jean, S2-755

Thibodeaux, Francoise-Jeanne, S2-757

Thibodeaux, Frederic Eloi, F-75

Thibodeaux, Germain, E-417

Thibodeaux, Helene, C-14, 77

Thibodeaux, Helene, F-103

Thibodeaux, Helene, S2-755-756

Thibodeaux, Isabelle, F-51

Thibodeaux, Isabelle, S1-150

Thibodeaux, Jacques, F-55

Thibodeaux, Jacques, N-160

Thibodeaux, Jacques-Joseph-Nicolas, S2-757

Thibodeaux, Jean, E-502, 530

Thibodeaux, Jean, F-55, 75

Thibodeaux, Jean, N-28, 160, 213, 216

Thibodeaux, Jean, S2-757-758

Thibodeaux, Jean, S3-837

Thibodeaux, Jean Baptiste, E-417

Thibodeaux, Jean-Baptiste, S2-754, 760

Thibodeaux, Jean-Baptiste-Pierre, S2-759

Thibodeaux, Jeanne, E-102, 356, 395, 417, 502

Thibodeaux, Jeanne, N-159-160

Thibodeaux, Jeanne Antoinette, N-159

Thibodeaux, Jeanne Tarsile, F-103

Thibodeaux, Jeanne-Antoinette, S2-754

Thibodeaux, Jeanne-Nicole-Damase, S2-757

Thibodeaux, Jeanne-Tarsille, S2-756

Thibodeaux, Joseph, E-114, 151, 288, 322, 417, 574

Thibodeaux, Joseph, F-51, 75

Thibodeaux, Joseph, N-159

Thibodeaux, Joseph, S2-752, 756-758, 760

Thibodeaux, Joseph, S3-831

Thibodeaux, Joseph-Marie, S2-755

Thibodeaux, Josephe, E-189

Thibodeaux, Josephe, S2-758

Thibodeaux, Julienne, E-287

Thibodeaux, Madeleine, S2-743, 754, 758

Thibodeaux, Magdeleine, E-5-6, 156, 417

Thibodeaux, Marguerite, C-14, 34

Thibodeaux, Marguerite, E-6, 574

Thibodeaux, Marguerite, F-73, 75, 103

Thibodeaux, Marguerite, N-18, 41

Thibodeaux, Marguerite, S1-97, 132, 266-268, 273

Thibodeaux, Marguerite, S2-753, 766

Thibodeaux, Marguerite, S3-838, 891, 947

Thibodeaux, Marguerite Josephe, E-5, 95

Thibodeaux, Marguerite-Josephe, S2-756

Thibodeaux, Marianne, E-589, 591

Thibodeaux, Marie, C-21, 77

Thibodeaux, Marie, E-162-167, 287, 365, 375-376, 386, 417, 474-475, 502, 564, 574

Thibodeaux, Marie, F-55, 75

Thibodeaux, Marie, N-97, 127, 130, 160, 213

Thibodeaux, Marie, S1-132, 311

Thibodeaux, Marie, S2-621, 707, 753

Thibodeaux, Marie, S3-851, 858

Thibodeaux, Marie Elisabeth, E-417

Thibodeaux, Marie Josephe, F-73

Thibodeaux, Marie Josephe, N-77, 88, 186, 188

Thibodeaux, Marie Madeleine, E-14

Thibodeaux, Marie Victoire, F-103

Thibodeaux, Marie-Catherine, S1-207

Thibodeaux, Marie-Jacquemine, S2-758

Thibodeaux, Marie-Josephe, S2-757

Thibodeaux, Marie-Marguerite, S2-754

Thibodeaux, Marie-Victoire, S2-756

Thibodeaux, Martin Joseph, E-333, 418

Thibodeaux, Michel, E-502, 530

Thibodeaux, Michel, S2-753

Thibodeaux, Michel Marie, E-6

Thibodeaux, Olive-Felicite, S2-754

Thibodeaux, Olivier, C-115

Thibodeaux, Olivier, F-75

Thibodeaux, Olivier, N-160

Thibodeaux, Olivier, S1-22

Thibodeaux, Olivier, S2-664, 758-760

Thibodeaux, Olivier, S3-831, 871

Thibodeaux, Ozite, S2-760

Thibodeaux, Philippe, F-103

Thibodeaux, Philippe, S2-501, 755

Thibodeaux, Philippe, S3-920

Thibodeaux, Pierre, C-77

Thibodeaux, Pierre, E-417-418, 476, 502, 530

Thibodeaux, Pierre, F-55

Thibodeaux, Pierre, N-97, 131, 160, 213, 216

Thibodeaux, Pierre, S2-621, 757, 760

Thibodeaux, Pierre, S3-837, 858

Thibodeaux, Pierre Charles, F-103

Thibodeaux, Pierre-Charles, S2-756

Thibodeaux, Pierre-Jean-Bap-tiste, S2-759

Thibodeaux, Rene, C-115-116

Thibodeaux, Rene, N-160, 227

Thibodeaux, Rene-Marie, S2-759

Thibodeaux, Rose, S2-760

Thibodeaux, Scholastique, E-390, 441

Thibodeaux, Simon, E-311, 418

Thibodeaux, Theotiste, S2-497-498

Thibodeaux, Thomas, S2-759

Thibodeaux Village named after Pierre Thibodeau, E-215

Thiborier, Charles Felix, E-340

Thiborier, L., E-340

Thiborier, Louise Felicite, E-340

Thierry, Charlotte, E-71, 392

Thiery, Joseph, N-251

Thifaine, Marie Anne, E-263

Thilorier, Andre Basile, E-340

Thilorier, Charles Felix, E-418

Thilorier, Felicite, E-258

Thilorier, Louise, E-340

Thilorier, Louise Felicite, E-340, 418

Thio, Madeleine, E-265

Thiollet, Bernard, E-418

Thiollet, Jean, E-365, 418

Thiollet, Jean Baptiste, E-418

Thiollet, Jean Bernard, E-418

Thomas, Andre, E-13, 161

Thomas, Augustin, E-21, 418

Thomas, Benjamin, E-418

Thomas, Claude, E-418

Thomas, Felicite, E-295, 344

Thomas, Francois Joseph, E-357

Thomas, Guillaume, S3-1128

Thomas, Jean, E-13, 369, 423, 601

Thomas, Joseph, E-418

Thomas, Joseph, N-34

Thomas, Joseph, S1-166

Thomas, Joseph, S3-971

Thomas, Julienne, E-301

Thomas, Magdelaine Jacqueline, E-13

Thomas, Marianne, E-601

Thomas, Marie Andre, E-424

Thomas, Marie Francoise, E-422-424

Thomas, Marie Genevieve, E-164

Thomas, Marie Jeanne, E-299, 422

Thomas, Marie Marguerite, E-13, 418

Thomas, Perinne, S1-165, 167

Thomas, Perrine, E-628

Thomas, Perrine, N-34-35

Thomas, Perrine, S3-971

Thomas, Rose, E-306

Thomasse, Guillaume, E-418

Thomasse, Pierre, E-188, 418

Thomassin, Elisabeth, E-92

Thomazeau, M., E-27, 319

Thomin, Perrine, E-45

Thoret, Anne, S1-214

Thoreu, Anne, S2-444

Thourat, Marie Catherine, E-266, 411

Thubert, Jean, E-86, 418

Thuiller, Pierre, E-590, 592

Thural, Emmanuel Bernard, E-148

Tibierge, Marie Anne, E-27, 255

Tienloup, Anne Francoise, E-418, 428

Tienloup, Pierre Entre, E-418, 428

Tiennoir, Rose, S1-86

Tiercelin, Jacques, E-69, 325

Tiernay, Andre, E-575

Tiernay, Daniel, E-575

Tiernay, Jean, E-575

Tierney, Isabelle Marguerite, E-609, 615
Tierney, Isabelle Marie, E-612
Tierney, Pelagie Hebert, E-612
Tillard, Francois, E-530
Tillard, Marie, C-67
Tillard, Marie, F-55
Tillard, Marie, N-112
Tillard, Marie, S2-504, 556
Tillard, Marie Rose, E-122
Tillarde, Marie, S2-763
Tillarde, Marie, S3-988
Tille, Marguerite, E-103
Tilleu, Charles, E-90
Timine, Judith, E-373
Timme, Marguerite, E-55
Tinet, Dominique, E-325, 392
Tiphaige, Pierre, E-195
Tirelle, Francois, E-321, 419
Tirelle, Nanette, E-321, 419
Tiron, Jean Jacques, E-362, 407
Tirou, Magdelaine, C-163
Titeay, Madelain, E-419
Titot, Magdeleine, C-82
Titot, Marie Magdalen, E-323
Tochet, Pierre, E-404
Toinon, Francoise, S2-691-692
Tolbot, Louis, E-373
Tollieret, Marie Julie, C-72
Tompigny, Jeanne, E-31, 109
Tompique, Catherine, E-617
Tonguet, Charles, E-366, 419
Tonin, Philippe, E-259, 330
Torel, Marie, S2-516
Torris, Peter, E-10
Torsun, Catherine, E-36, 369
Tostivint, Rene, C-ix
Totain, Gille, E-358
Totin, Jean, S3-980
Touanon, Francoise, S2-676
Touasnon, Francoise, S3-970
Toubathe, Jeanne, E-66, 353
Touchie, Simone, E-160, 413
Touffreau, Jean, E-419
Touffreau, Louis, E-419
Tougeon, Jean, E-378
Toul, George, E-590, 592
Touliure, Marie, E-131, 317
Toulon, Isabel, S2-654
Toulon, Isabelle, S2-653
Toulon, Pierre, E-419

Toulon, Pierre Auguste, E-419
Toulouse, Jeanne, E-280
Toulouse, Jeanne, S2-548
Toupeau, Marie Elisabeth, E-103, 419
Touraine, Jean, E-254, 419
Tourangeau, Francois, E-476, 530
Tourangeau, Jeanne, E-488
Tourault, Jacquemine, C-73
Tourault, Jacquemine, S2-596
Tourault, Jacquemine, S3-1081
Tourjon, Marie, E-286, 419
Tournay, Charles Louis, E-419
Tournay, Charles Philippe, E-175, 419
Tournay, Jean Baptiste, E-175, 419
Tournay, Nicolas Louis, E-419
Tournier, Jean, E-419
Tournier, Jean Pierre, E-45, 419
Toursac, Pierre, E-420
Toussaint, Marie Magdelaine, E-119
Toussaint, Nicolas, E-43
Toussaint, Pierre, E-303, 316, 530
Toussaq, Jeanne, E-35, 278
Toussay, Marie, S1-181, 317
Touzalin, Charles, C-96, 118
Touze, Marie, S3-1066
Toyon, Jeanne Catherine, E-20
Trahan, -----, E-4, 6
Trahan, Agatha, E-168, 420
Trahan, Agnes, N-22-23, 83, 225, 228
Trahan, Agnes, S1-105-106
Trahan, Agnes, S2-770
Trahan, Alexandre, C-96
Trahan, Alexandre, E-282, 495, 530, 590, 596
Trahan, Alexandre, N-161
Trahan, Alexandre, S2-456, 762, 764, 768
Trahan, Alexandre-Jean-Baptiste, S2-769
Trahan, Alexis, E-151, 325, 420, 426
Trahan, Alexis, F-41
Trahan, Alexix Romain, C-96
Trahan, Andres, E-420

Trahan, Anne, C-34, 67, 97, 164
Trahan, Anne, E-3, 125-126, 305, 420, 560, 576, 581, 590, 593
Trahan, Anne, F-23, 51, 59, 63, 79, 95
Trahan, Anne, N-37, 162, 165, 168, 170, 204
Trahan, Anne, S1-14, 15, 100, 174, 309
Trahan, Anne, S2-467, 578, 605, 763-765
Trahan, Anne, S3-882, 886
Trahan, Anne Barbe Josephe, E-420
Trahan, Anne Genevieve, N-65-66
Trahan, Anne Julie, E-420, 575
Trahan, Anne Julie, F-79
Trahan, Anne Julie, N-162
Trahan, Anne Marguerite, N-40, 245
Trahan, Anne Marie, C-71
Trahan, Anne Marie Francoise, E-420
Trahan, Anne Olive, N-163
Trahan, Anne Pelagie, E-150, 152, 420
Trahan, Anne-Marie, S2-768
Trahan, Anne-Modeste, S2-766
Trahan, Annette, N-168
Trahan, Anselme, F-23
Trahan, Anselme, N-166
Trahan, Anselme-Marie, S2-766
Trahan, Antoine Joseph, C-71
Trahan, Antoine Joseph, F-19
Trahan, Antoine-Joseph, S2-767
Trahan, Antoinette, F-35
Trahan, Antoinette, N-167
Trahan, Athanase, E-423
Trahan, Augustin, C-67, 98
Trahan, Augustin, E-150, 282, 420, 422, 424-425
Trahan, Augustin, F-47, 51
Trahan, Augustin, N-161, 165, 208
Trahan, Augustine Pelagie, E-420
Trahan, Augustine Pelagie, F-59
Trahan, Baptiste, S2-763
Trahan, Barbe, F-57

Trahan, Barbe, N-163
Trahan, Barbe Joseph, N-163
Trahan, Benjamin, E-422
Trahan, Catherine, E-420
Trahan, Catherine, F-51
Trahan, Catherine, N-165
Trahan, Cecile, C-2, 136
Trahan, Cecile, E-125, 581
Trahan, Cecile, S2-768
Trahan, Cecile Pauline, E-420-421
Trahan, Cecile Pelagie, C-30-32
Trahan, Charles, E-420-421
Trahan, Charles, F-59, 97
Trahan, Charles, S2-584, 726, 760-761, 764
Trahan, Charles, S3-911
Trahan, Charles Marie, E-421
Trahan, Charles Marie, N-164
Trahan, Chrisosthome, E-125, 420, 423, 425-426, 575
Trahan, Chrisosthome, F-79
Trahan, Christopher, N-162
Trahan, Claude, C-67
Trahan, Claude, E-420-421, 424
Trahan, Claude, F-13, 35, 47, 55
Trahan, Claude, N-37, 112, 161-163, 166, 204, 232
Trahan, Claude, S2-445, 504, 556, 612, 762-763, 765
Trahan, Claude, S3-881, 884, 988, 1044, 1061
Trahan, Dorothee, E-82, 403
Trahan, Elizabeth, C-94-95, 160
Trahan, Elizabeth, E-94. 402, 405, 414-416, 421, 556, 580
Trahan, Elizabeth, N-158
Trahan, Elizabeth Adelaide, C-97
Trahan, Elizabeth Apolline, E-421
Trahan, Elizabeth Josephe, E-421
Trahan, Elizabeth Marguerite, E-421
Trahan, Estienne, S3-911
Trahan, Etienne, S2-761
Trahan, Etienne Augustine, N-170
Trahan, Eustache, E-128, 151, 287, 325, 420-421

Trahan, Eustache, F-57
Trahan, Felicite, F-51, 53
Trahan, Felicite, N-164-165
Trahan, Felix, N-161
Trahan, Fiacre, S2-763
Trahan, Firmin, C-164
Trahan, Firmin, E-421
Trahan, Firmin, N-204
Trahan, Firmin, S2-762-763, 765
Trahan, Firmin, S3-1061
Trahan, Francois, C-31, 97, 136
Trahan, Francois, E-582
Trahan, Francois, F-57
Trahan, Francois, N-65, 164, 167
Trahan, Francois Marie, E-421
Trahan, Francois Marie, F-33
Trahan, Francois Marie, N-166
Trahan, Francoise, E-2, 63, 181, 286-289, 302, 427, 569, 582, 587, 594
Trahan, Francoise, F-61, 95
Trahan, Francoise, N-120
Trahan, Francoise, S2-467, 612, 679
Trahan, Francoise Barbe, E-421
Trahan, Francoise Marie Barbara, F-45
Trahan, Frederic, C-164
Trahan, Frederic, N-163
Trahan, Genevieve, E-356, 577
Trahan, Genevieve, F-51
Trahan, Genevieve, n-170
Trahan, Gregoire, F-23
Trahan, Gregoire, N-168
Trahan, Gregoire Olivier, C-8
Trahan, Gregoire-Olivier, S2-768
Trahan, Guillaume, E-473, 481, 530
Trahan, Helene, E-421
Trahan, Honore Joseph, E-421, 424
Trahan, Isabelle, C-97
Trahan, Isabelle, E-94-95, 415, 590, 596
Trahan, Isidore, C-69, 96
Trahan, Isidore, E-422-423, 426
Trahan, Isidore, F-41
Trahan, Isidore, N-162-163, 232

Trahan, Isidore, S2-573
Trahan, Isidore, S3-1062, 1067
Trahan, Jacques, E-422
Trahan, Jacques, S2-769-770
Trahan, Jacques Augustin, N-161
Trahan, Jean, E-151, 294, 305, 325, 420-423, 481, 495, 530, 590, 596
Trahan, Jean, F-9, 53
Trahan, Jean, N-22, 189
Trahan, Jean, S1-99, 102, 105
Trahan, Jean, S2-764, 767, 770
Trahan, Jean Andre, E-422
Trahan, Jean Baptiste, C-96-97, 145, 148
Trahan, Jean Baptiste, E-188, 302, 403, 420-422, 424-427, 575, 577, 590, 593
Trahan, Jean Baptiste, F-31, 41, 57
Trahan, Jean Baptiste, N-163-165, 170, 252
Trahan, Jean Baptiste, S3-1044, 1061
Trahan, Jean Charles, E-299, 421-422, 424, 427, 481, 578, 590, 593
Trahan, Jean Chrisosthome, E-422
Trahan, Jean Chrisosthome, F-79
Trahan, Jean Christopher, N-162
Trahan, Jean Francois, E-422
Trahan, Jean Jean-Marie, E-422
Trahan, Jean Joseph Marie, E-422
Trahan, Jean Marie, C-97
Trahan, Jean Marie, E-422, 576
Trahan, Jean Marie, F-51, 57, 69
Trahan, Jean Marie , N-165, 218
Trahan, Jean Marie Barnabe, E-422
Trahan, Jean Marie Luc, E-422
Trahan, Jean Michel, E-422, 575
Trahan, Jean Paul, F-83
Trahan, Jean Paul, N-163
Trahan, Jean Pierre, E-420
Trahan, Jean-Baptiste, S2-556, 762, 764-766, 769, 781

Trahan, Jean-Baptiste-Marie, S1-49

Trahan, Jean-Chalres, S2-764-765

Trahan, Jean-Joseph, S2-514

Trahan, Jean-Paul, S2-765

Trahan, Jean-Pierre, S2-765

Trahan, Jeanne, E-422, 456, 472-473, 481

Trahan, Jeanne Felicite, E-423

Trahan, Jeanne Marie, E-423

Trahan, Jerome, S2-768

Trahan, Joachim, E-420-421, 423-424, 426, 428, 575

Trahan, Joachim, F-51

Trahan, Joachim, N-39, 165, 230

Trahan, Joseph, C-16, 18, 71, 94, 97-98, 144, 147-148

Trahan, Joseph, E-124, 150, 162-163, 166, 269, 286, 325, 403, 414, 420-427, 576-578, 637

Trahan, Joseph, F-5, 7, 19, 23, 31, 33, 35, 51, 59, 61, 79

Trahan, Joseph, N-2, 110, 120, 122, 162-163, 165-167, 170, 232, 240, 252, 254

Trahan, Joseph, S1-98, 110

Trahan, Joseph, S2-761-767, 769

Trahan, Joseph Marie, E-423

Trahan, Joseph Olivier, E-423

Trahan, Joseph Remi, F-35

Trahan, Joseph Rene, N-167

Trahan, Joseph Rose, E-423

Trahan, Joseph Simon, E-423, 578

Trahan, Joseph-Olivier, S2-769

Trahan, Julie, F-33

Trahan, Julie, N-166

Trahan, Laurent, C-97

Trahan, Laurent, E-2, 576

Trahan, Laurent, S1-30

Trahan, Laurent, S2-761

Trahan, Louis, C-136

Trahan, Louis, E-422-425, 428, 576

Trahan, Louis, N-193

Trahan, Louis Athanase, C-97

Trahan, Louis Athanase, F-37

Trahan, Louis Athanase, N-36, 152, 167, 218

Trahan, Louise, S2-761

Trahan, Louise Renee, N-169

Trahan, Louise Renne, F-55

Trahan, Luc, E-423

Trahan, Luce, E-423

Trahan, Lucie, S1-102

Trahan, Madeleine, C-30

Trahan, Madeleine, N-44, 50

Trahan, Madeleine, S1-11, 234

Trahan, Madeleine, S2-514, 764, 767, 769

Trahan, Magdelaine, E-99, 402-403, 423, 426, 481, 568, 576-577, 590, 596

Trahan, Magdelaine, F-27, 41, 53, 57, 95

Trahan, Marain, E-427

Trahan, Marguerite, C-55, 68, 71, 97, 144-145, 164

Trahan, Marguerite, E-2, 124, 188, 192, 298, 305, 331, 420-427, 576

Trahan, Marguerite, F-3, 13, 23, 33, 41, 51, 55, 57, 59, 79, 97

Trahan, Marguerite, N-97, 98, 116, 127-128, 162, 164, 166, 170, 213

Trahan, Marguerite, S1-27, 99

Trahan, Marguerite, S2-456, 459, 504-505, 612, 760-763, 767, 769

Trahan, Marguerite, S3-881, 1062

Trahan, Marguerite Basile, E-424

Trahan, Marguerite Catherine, E-424

Trahan, Marguerite Jeanne, N-164

Trahan, Marguerite-Aimee, S2-766

Trahan, Marie, C-164

Trahan, Marie, E-29, 185, 281, 283, 285-289, 322, 331-332, 424, 481, 570, 590, 593, 595

Trahan, Marie, F-5, 17, 23, 37, 41, 55, 77, 97

Trahan, Marie, N-2, 4, 66, 122, 166, 209, 221, 240

Trahan, Marie, S1-13, 161, 315, 317

Trahan, Marie, S2-760-761, 764-765

Trahan, Marie, S3-894

Trahan, Marie Anne, E-125, 424, 426

Trahan, Marie Anne, F-33

Trahan, Marie Anne, N-163, 166

Trahan, Marie Anne Josephe, E-424

Trahan, Marie Augustine, E-424

Trahan, Marie Bl., E-2

Trahan, Marie Blanche, C-97

Trahan, Marie Blanche, E-424, 576

Trahan, Marie Blanche, F-37

Trahan, Marie Blanche, N-36, 39, 165, 167, 218, 230

Trahan, Marie Cecile, E-636

Trahan, Marie Elisabeth, E-577

Trahan, Marie Felicite, E-424

Trahan, Marie Francoise, E-424, 590, 596

Trahan, Marie Francoise, F-51

Trahan, Marie Francoise, N-170

Trahan, Marie Helene, E-424

Trahan, Marie Jeanne, E-380, 424

Trahan, Marie Jeanne Agathe, E-425

Trahan, Marie Josephe, E-305, 420, 422-428

Trahan, Marie Josephe, F-59

Trahan, Marie Josephe, N-162

Trahan, Marie Josephe Lucie, E-324

Trahan, Marie Julie, E-425

Trahan, Marie Louise, E-425

Trahan, Marie Louise, F-53

Trahan, Marie Louise, N-164

Trahan, Marie Madeleine, C-39

Trahan, Marie Madeleine, N-2, 162, 166, 169-170, 252

Trahan, Marie Magdaleine, E-425

Trahan, Marie Magdeleine, F-79

Trahan, Marie Marguerite, E-425

Trahan, Marie Marguerite, F-31

INDEX SOURCES C=Chatellerault; E=Acadians in Exile; F=Acadian Families; N=Nantes; S=St-Malo

Trahan, Marie Marguerite, N-170
Trahan, Marie Marthe, E-426
Trahan, Marie Modeste, C-16, 98, 148
Trahan, Marie Modeste, E-124, 426
Trahan, Marie Modeste, F-7, 47
Trahan, Marie Modeste, N-21-22, 161, 164, 168
Trahan, Marie Perrotte, E-426
Trahan, Marie Renee, F-31
Trahan, Marie Renee, N-170
Trahan, Marie Sophie, N-164
Trahan, Marie Victoire, E-426
Trahan, Marie Victoire, F-51
Trahan, Marie Vincent, F-51
Trahan, Marie Vincente, E-426
Trahan, Marie-Anne-Josephe, S2-763
Trahan, Marie-Anne-Julienne, S2-765
Trahan, Marie-Jeanne, S2-769
Trahan, Marie-Jeanne-Josephe, S2-763
Trahan, Marie-Josephe, S2-761
Trahan, Marie-Josephe-Lucie, S1-176
Trahan, Marie-Josephe-Lucie, S2-614
Trahan, Marie-Madeleine, S1-316
Trahan, Marie-Madeleine, S2-766, 768
Trahan, Marin, E-260, 421-426, 590, 592,
Trahan, Marin, F-45, 57
Trahan, Marthe, F-79
Trahan, Marthe, N-162
Trahan, Mathurin, C-98, 145, 148
Trahan, Mathurin, E-18, 124, 269, 299, 420-422, 423, 426-428, 578
Trahan, Mathurin, F-23
Trahan, Mathurin, N-139, 164, 166-168, 240
Trahan, Mathurin, S2-766-767
Trahan, Mathurin-Pierre, S2-765
Trahan, Michel, E-422
Trahan, Michel, F-53

Trahan, Nicole, E-426
Trahan, Olivier, C-70, 145, 150
Trahan, Olivier, E-428
Trahan, Olivier, F-23
Trahan, Olivier, N-168, 213
Trahan, Olivier, S1-346
Trahan, Olivier, S2-587-588, 767-769
Trahan, Olivier, S3-1000, 1006, 1038-1039, 1063, 1077
Trahan, Paul, E-152, 285, 414, 420, 422-428, 571, 582, 590, 596
Trahan, Paul, F-41, 59
Trahan, Paul, N-204
Trahan, Paul Alexis, E-426
Trahan, Paul Isidore, E-426
Trahan, Paul Joseph, E-426
Trahan, Paul Raimond, E-427
Trahan, Paul Raymond, F-31
Trahan, Paul Raymond, N-170
Trahan, Paul-Isidore, S2-769-770
Trahan, Pauline, F-51
Trahan, Pauline, N-170
Trahan, Pelagie, E-150-152, 427
Trahan, Pelagie, F-57
Trahan, Philippe, E-582
Trahan, Pierre, C-68
Trahan, Pierre, E-279, 421-425, 427, 441, 575, 577
Trahan, Pierre, F-51, 53, 55, 59
Trahan, Pierre, N-116, 161, 164-165, 169-170, 246
Trahan, Pierre Baptiste, F-59
Trahan, Pierre Francois, E-427
Trahan, Pierre Gregoire, E-427
Trahan, Pierre Gregoire, F-59
Trahan, Pierre Marie, E-427
Trahan, Pierre Raymond, E-578
Trahan, Pierre Rene Augustin, E-427
Trahan, Pierre Simon, E-125, 421, 424-425, 427, 577-578
Trahan, Pierre Simon, F-31
Trahan, Pierre Simon, N-170
Trahan, Pierre-Isidore, S2-768, 770
Trahan, Pierre-Jacques, S2-763
Trahan, Raphael, E-578

Trahan, Reine Marie Joseph, E-427
Trahan, Reine Sophie, N-162
Trahan, Remon, N-252
Trahan, Rene, E-125, 150, 273, 282, 420-421, 424-427, 578
Trahan, Rene, F-57, 59, 79
Trahan, Rene Jacques, N-162
Trahan, Renne, N-162
Trahan, Romain, E-261, 424, 426-428, 578
Trahan, Rosalie, C-67
Trahan, Rosalie, E-590, 593
Trahan, Rosalie, F-41, 55
Trahan, Rosalie, N-112-113, 163
Trahan, Rosalie, S2-505, 556-557, 764-765
Trahan, Rosalie, S3-988
Trahan, Rosalie Bibianne, N-161
Trahan, Rose, C-8
Trahan, Rose, F-39, 61
Trahan, Rose, N-11
Trahan, Rose, S1-53, 189
Trahan, Rose, S3-1063
Trahan, Rose Michelle, N-168
Trahan, Rose Victoire, E-427
Trahan, Silvestre, E-317, 422-423, 426-428
Trahan, Simon, C-31
Trahan, Simon, E-44, 380, 383, 422, 424-428, 576-578
Trahan, Simon, F-41
Trahan, Simon, S2-770
Trahan, Simon Laurent, E-428
Trahan, Simon Marie, E-428
Trahan, Simon Nicolas, E-428
Trahan, Simon Pierre, E-428
Trahan, Simon-Augustin, S2-770
Trahan, Sophie Therese, N-168
Trahan, Susanne Joan, E-481
Trahan, Sylvestre, E-578, 581
Trahan, Symon, E-425
Trahan, Therese, E-428
Trahan, Therese, S2-768
Trahan, Therese Sophie, C-98
Trahan, Therese Sophie, N-168
Trahan, Thomas, E-590, 596
Trahan, Ursule, E-428

Trahan, Yves Marie, E-428
Train, Pierre, E-441
Tramzelle-Dubail, Jacques, S2-464
Tranchand, Antoine, C-6
Tranchand, Francoise, C-93
Tranchand, Rene, C-14
Tranchard, Jeanne, E-259, 294
Tranchaut, Charles, C-113
Transon, Marie Magdalen, E-166, 386
Travers, Andre, E-26
Tredis, Etienne, E-428
Tredis, Jacques, E-428
Treguy, Catherine, S2-770-771
Treguy, Denise, E-34, 428
Treguy, Etienne, S2-770-771
Treguy, Francoise, S2-771
Treguy, Guillaume, S2-771
Treguy, Jacques, S2-770-771
Treguy, Jean, E-428
Treguy, Jeanne, S2-770-771
Treguy, Jeanne Francoise, E-638
Treguy, Joseph, S2-771
Treguy, Louise, S2-771
Treguy, Madeleine, S1-322
Treguy, Marie Jeanne, E-638
Treguy, Pierre, E-428
Treguy, Pierre, S1-186
Treguy, Pierre, S2-770
Treguy, Rene, E-428
Treguy, Rene, S2-770
Treillis, Catherine, E-628
Treillis, Francoise, E-628
Treillis, Jacques, E-622
Treillis, Jeanne, E-628
Treillis, Joseph, E-628
Treillis, Louise, E-629
Trepot, Renee, S1-357
Tresgrosse, Charlotte Louise, E-629
Tresgrosse, Francois Charles, E-629
Tresgrosse, Francoise, E-629
Tresgrosse, Jean Baptiste Serve, E-629
Tresgrosse, Joseph, E-629
Tresgrosse, Louis, E-629
Tresgrosse, Louis Charles, E-629
Tresgrosse, Marie Jeanne, E-629

Tresorier, Catherine, E-418
Tresorier, Jacques, E-53, 141, 327
Tresorier, Jean, E-24, 53, 418, 428
Tresorier, Jeanne, E-53, 428
Tressin, Judith, C-160
Trevaille, Marie Sophie, E-428
Trevaille, Yves, E-428
Trezelle, Jean, E-35
Trezin, Alexandre, N-226, 229, 244
Trezin, Alexandre Andre, N-109, 170, 222
Trezin, Andre, N-170, 222
Triaud, Catherine, E-153
Trichon, Elisabeth, E-589, 594
Tricorbe, Louis, E-135, 318, 404
Tricosse, Michelle, E-314, 404
Triel, Ananie, E-64, 173
Trilly, Jean, E-439
Tripon, Jean, E-142
Tritan, Louise, E-426
Trochu, Margueritte, E-590, 592
Tronchon, Charles, E-418, 428
Tronchon, Nicolas, E-418, 428
Tronchon, Pierre Andre, E-428
Trotin, Francois, S2-595
Trotin, Francois, S3-1029
Trotin, Francoise Ollive, S3-1029
Trotin, Francoise-Olive, S2-595
Trouchard, -----, S3-1109
Trouchard, Bertrand Marie , S3-1109
Troucher, Bertran-Marie, S2-728
Troude, Cecile J., S3-960
Troude, Cecile Julienne, S3-959
Troude, Cecile-Julienne, S1-374
Troude, Pierre, S1-374
Troude, Pierre, S3-959
Troude, Victor, E-178
Trouy de Verjuziere, Andre, E-265
Trouy de Verjuziere, Jean Charles, E-265
Trujon, Marianne, E-53
Tual, Yves, S3-1054
Tudal, Anne, E-428
Tudal, Joseph, E-428-429

Tudal, Marie Joseph, E-429
Tudal, Marie Madeleine, E-429
Tudeau, Louise, E-377
Tueux, Charles, E-429
Tueux, Charles Antoine, E-306, 429
Tuffaud, Francois, E-168
Tullee, Jean Charles, N-198
Turand, Francois, E-357
Turbe, Marie Magdelaine, E-27
Tureaud, Jacques, E-256
Turgon, Charles, E-169, 185
Turgon, Charles, S1-374
Turgot, Felicite, E-58, 641
Turgot, Jacques, E-187, 429
Turgot, Julie, E-55, 633, 639, 643
Turgot, Louis, E-1, 58, 187, 429, 436, 633, 639, 643
Turgot, Louis Sr., E-639
Turgot, Louise, E-639
Turgot, Louise Felicite, E-633
Turgot, Marie Julie, E-429, 434-436
Turgot, Marie Louise Felicite, E-58, 429
Turin, Marie, E-32, 403
Turin, Mathieu, S1-364
Turnie, Jean Pierre, E-314
Turnier, Jean Francois, E-429
Turnier, Marie Josephe, E-429
Turnier, Maryte Blanche Antoinette, E-429
Turnier, Pierre, E-429
Turnier, twins, E-429
Turpin, Agathe, C-88, 146
Turpin, Agathe, N-150
Turpin, Agathe, S1-327-328
Turpin, Agathe, S2-708-709
Turpin, Agathe, S3-1013
Turpin, Marguerite, E-82
Turpin, Marguerite, S1-206, 208, 311
Turquaud, Francois, E-16

U

Uguen, Jacques, S2-481
Uret, Jean, E-66, 69
Urineau, Marie Madeleine, E-377

V

Vache, Jean Francois, E-590, 596
Vachon, Jacques, C-113, 125
Vachon, Jean, C-113
Vacquerie, Marie Magdeleine, E-178
Vailard, Genevieve, E-54, 101
Vaivre, Jeanne, S3-858
Valanchon, Marguerite, E-122, 441
Valeronne, Renault de, C-114
Valery, Ambroise, S2-771
Valery, Antoine-Jacques, S2-771
Valery, Francois, S2-771
Valery, Francois-Honore-Etienne, S2-771
Valery, Jean-Baptiste, S2-771
Valery, Joseph, S2-771
Valet, Andre, E-430
Valet, Etienne Francois, E-430
Valet, Felicite, C-161
Valet, Francois, E-430
Valet, Francoise, E-131
Valet, Francoise, E-317
Valet, Georges, E-36
Valet, Georges, E-430
Valet, Guillaume, E-173
Valet, Guillaume, E-430
Valet, Guillaume, S1-77, 386
Valet, Guillaume, S2-596
Valet, Guillaume, S2-721, 772
Valet, Guillaume, S3-997
Valet, Guillaumette, E-277
Valet, Guillemette, S1-386-387
Valet, Guillemette, S2-772
Valet, Guillomette, E-173
Valet, Guillomette, E-430
Valet, Henry, N-171, 185
Valet, Jacques, E-590, 593
Valet, Jeanne, E-430
Valet, Joseph, N-244
Valet, Louis, C-55, 85
Valet, Louis, E-356, 430
Valet, Louis, N-87
Valet, Louis, S2-453, 672, 679, 772-773
Valet, Louis, S3-1115

Valet, Louis Felix, E-114
Valet, Louis Felix, E-430
Valet, Louise, C-165
Valet, Louise, C-82
Valet, Louise, S2-773
Valet, Louise Marguerite, E-114
Valet, Louise Marguerite, E-430
Valet, Marguerite, S2-679, 773
Valet, Marguerite Louise, E-430
Valet, Marguerite Louise, N-87
Valet, Marguerite-Louise, S2-453, 661, 672-773
Valet, Margueritte, S3-1115
Valet, Marie, E-387
Valet, Marie, E-430
Valet, Marie, S2-679, 721-722, 772-773
Valet, Marie, S3-997, 1096
Valet, Marie Claudine, F-39
Valet, Marie Claudine, N-47
Valet, Marie Felicite, N-171
Valet, Marie Marguerite, E-430
Valet, Marie Therese, E-381
Valet, Marie-Marguerite, S2-773
Valet, Marie-Perinne, S1-77-78
Valet, Marie-Perinne, S2-772
Valet, Michel, E-387
Valet, Michel, E-430
Valet, Michel, S2-772
Valet, Michel, S3-997
Valet, Michel Jean, E-364
Valet, Nicolas, N-96, 135, 171, 185, 203, 216
Valet, Perinne, S1-77-78
Valet, Perinne, S2-649
Valet, Pierre, E-412
Valet, Rene, E-430
Valet, Rene, S2-772
Valet, Rosalie, E-430
Valet, Rosalie, S2-679, 773
Valet, Rose, S2-773
Valin, Aimee Victoire, E-15
Valin, Louis, E-152
Valleau, Elizabeth, E-77, 257
Vallois, Marguerite, E-121
Vallois, Marguerite, N-27, 156, 180, 191
Vallois, Marguerite, S2-734
Valo, Marguerite, F-63, 69
Valoir, Dominique, S2-774

Valoir, Dominique, S3-857
Valoir, Francois, S2-774
Valoir, Jacques, S2-735, 774
Valoir, Jacques, S3-857, 859
Valoir, Julien, S2-774
Valoir, Julien-Jean, S2-774
Valoir, Marie-Francoise, S2-774
Valoir, Therese, S2-774
Valoir, Therese-Marie, S2-774
Valois, Charles Jean, E-431
Valois, Francois, E-116
Valois, Jacques Hippolyte, E-431
Valois, Noel Francois, E-431
Valois, Thomas Huret, E-431
Valon, Marguerite, E-20
Valot, Margueritte Louise, S3-1139, 1140
Vam Berchem, Theodore, N-187
Vandebroue, Marie Catherine, E-281, 384-385
Vaneau, Marie, E-45, 316
Vanere, Suzanne, E-393
Vanier, Suzanne, E-332, 431
Vaoet, Marguerite Louise, C-54-55
Varaillon, Marguerite, E-36, 332
Varangue, Abraham Issac, C-66
Varangue, Amable Etienne, C-66
Varangue, Anne Adelaide, C-66
Varangue, Antoine, C-65
Varangue, Antoine, E-431
Varangue, Jeanne Madeleine, C-66
Varangue, Jeanne Madeleine, N-107
Varangue, Jeanne Marguerite, C-66
Varangue, Jeanne Marie, E-272
Varangue, Jeanne Marie Magdalen, E-271, 273, 431
Varangue, Jeanne Marie Magdeleine, C-65
Vareine, Marie Madeleine, E-431
Vareine, Pierre, E-431
Varenguer, Anne, E-271
Varenne, Anastasie, S2-775
Varenne, Jacques, S2-775
Varenne, Jean-Pierre, S2-775

Varenne, Madeleine-Josephe, S2-775

Varenne, Marguerite, S1-366

Varenne, Marguerite-Angelique, S2-775

Varenne, Marie, S2-546

Varenne, Marie Anne Therese, E-158, 432

Varenne, Marie-Madeleine, S2-775

Varenne, Michel, S2-775

Varenne, Pierre, S2-775

Varnier, Michel Louis Amand, E-364

Varongue, Antoine, F-61

Varongue, Jeanne, F-61

Varongues, Jeanne Marie Magdalen, E-271, 273

Varonquer, Jeanne, E-271

Vary, Cecile, E-420

Vaslet, Guillaume, S3-978

Vaslet, Marie, E-40, 100

Vaslet, Marie Perrine, S3-978

Vastel, Charles, E-116

Vatel, Marie Charlotte, E-22

Vaudal, Michel, S2-776

Vaudeste, Elizabeth, C-69

Vaudrille, Marie Anne, E-54, 431

Vaugours, Philippe, S3-984

Vaultier, Francois, S1-145

Vaume, Jacques Francois, E-431

Vaume, Jean, E-431

Vaume, Pierre Marie, E-431

Vaume, Pierre Martin, E-431

Vaury, Francois, E-369

Vausseleau, Leon, E-357

Veco, Angelique, E-22-23, 47, 346, 431

Veco, Angelique, S2-645

Veco, Anne, E-83, 361, 363-364, 366, 431

Veco, Cecile, C-33, 99

Veco, Cecile, E-108, 341

Veco, Cecile, F-67, 107

Veco, Francois, C-52

Veco, Francois, E-13, 78, 177, 265, 431-432

Veco, Francois, S1-198

Veco, Francois, S2-433, 435, 776-777

Veco, Genevieve, S2-776

Veco, Jacques, E-23, 44, 126, 176, 184

Veco, Jacques, E-286, 372

Veco, Jacques, S1-307, 320

Veco, Jacques, S2-438

Veco, Jean Baptiste, E-47, 126-127, 363-364, 431, 530

Veco, Jean-Baptiste, S1-307-308

Veco, Jean-Baptiste, S2-776

Veco, Jean-Charles, S2-776

Veco, Joseph, E-431

Veco, Madelaine, C-52, 70

Veco, Madeleine, F-7

Veco, Madeleine, N-126

Veco, Madeleine, S1-374

Veco, Madeleine, S2-433, 435, 586

Veco, Magdeleine, E-70, 126-127, 169, 177-178, 266, 432

Veco, Magdeleine, S3-1038

Veco, Marie, C-52

Veco, Marie, E-108, 126, 367, 431-432

Veco, Marie, S1-308

Veco, Marie, S2-435, 438, 776

Veco, Marie Joseph, E-126, 178, 341, 432

Veco, Marie Magdelaine, E-126-127, 432

Veco, Marie-Josephe, S1-308

Veco, Marie-Madeleine, S1-307

Veco, Marie-Madeleine, S2-435

Veco, Michel, S2-776

Veco, Pierre, E-78, 355, 361, 432

Veco, Rosalie, E-103, 358, 366, 432

Vedeau, Jeanne, E-73, 294

Veidel, Jean, E-28, 376

Veillard, Jean, S1-52

Veillet, Jean, E-359

Veio, Francois, E-90

Veiselin, Catherine, E-283

Veleste, Sophie, E-338

Veluet, Jacques, C-86, 120

Veluet, Marie, C-6, 85-86, 120

Veluet, Rene, C-85, 120

Venvre, Jeanne, S3-842

Verdeau, Francois, E-354

Verdier, Jean, E-259

Verdier, M., E-181

Verdier, Marie, E-590, 594

Verdon, Marie, E-325, 432

Verenne, Marie Anne Therese, E-158

Veret, Jean, E-24, 418

Verge, Antoine-Joseph-Christophe, S2-761

Verger, Pierre, E-80

Verguret, Jean-Noel, S1-222

Verieux, Jacques, S1-308

Vernichon, Andre, E-108

Vernon, Catherine, E-328, 370, 392

Verpillion, Elisabeth, E-329, 331

Verret, Marie Charlotte, E-261

Verrier, -----, S2-777

Verrier, Claude, S1-213

Verrier, Claude, S2-777

Verrier, Jean, E-24, 418

Verrier, Pierre, S1-213

Verrier, Pierre, S2-777

Verrier, widow, S1-213

Verriere, Marie, E-369, 409

Verrieux, Angelique, E-432

Verrieux, Anne, E-102, 120

Verrieux, Anne, S1-281

Verrieux, Anne Charlotte, E-432

Verrieux, Anne Dominique, E-263

Verrieux, Dominique, E-263, 432

Verrieux, Jacques, E-126, 178, 311, 341, 432

Verrieux, Marie, E-263, 311

Verrieux, Marie Francoise, E-432

Verrieux, Marie Joseph, E-432

Verron, Marguerite, E-44

Verteuil, Jacques Alexis, E-432

Verteuil, Leonard, E-432

Vescau, Marie, S3-937

Vesin, Jean, E-476

Vesion, Francoise, E-590, 593

Vesquau, Magdeleinne, S3-938

Vessin de Champagne, Madeleine, C-32

Veteau, Rene, E-318

Veuvre, Jeanne, C-77

Veuvre, Jeanne, F-81

Veuvre, Jeanne, S2-621

Vevein, Marie, E-116

Vevoy, Louis, E-625

Vevre, Francoise, E-256-257

Veyrier de Poliche, Claude, E-432

Viard, Francois Philippe, E-432

Viard, Marie Marguerite, E-182, 432

Viaud, Blain, E-432

Viaud, Catherine, F-77

Viaud, Jeanne, E-375, 386

Viaud, Marie, E-69

Viaud, Rose, E-432

Viaud, Yve, N-236

Vibert, Philippe, S2-505

Vicel, Marin-Francois, S2-548

Vico, Francois, S3-942-943

Vidal, Anne, E-144, 332

Vidal, Jean, E-28

Vidal, Marie Michelle, E-323-325, 433

Vidau, Anne, E-110

Vide, Jean Baptiste, E-22, 77, 391, 433

Videt, Marie, F-83

Vidot, Pierre, E-22, 433

Vieireu, Marie, E-103

Viere, Elisabeth, E-30, 313

Vigeo, Anne, E-603, 605

Vigeo, Anne Theodiste, E-604

Vigeo, Francois, E-603

Vigeo, Helene Francoise, E-604

Viger, Aime, E-145

Viger, Anne Theotiste, E-271-271

Viger, Francois, E-107, 334

Viger, Francoise, E-271

Vigier, Anne, E-271

Vigier, Anne Theotiste, E-183, 433

Vigier, Francois, E-433

Vigier, Helaine Francoise, E-183

Vigier, Isidore, E-433

Vigier, Jean Charles Guillaume, E-433

Vigier, Marie Josephe, E-433

Vigier, Stanislas, E-433

Vigne, Jean Antoine, E-329

Vigne, Marguerite, E-350, 366

Vigne, Pierre, E-27, 136

Vigneau, Adrien, E-57-58, 89, 361, 433

Vigneau, Alexandre, E-637

Vigneau, Alexandre Charles, E-433

Vigneau, Alexandre Joseph, E-433

Vigneau, Amand, E-41, 435, 438

Vigneau, Anastasie, E-131, 352

Vigneau, Angelique, E-407

Vigneau, Anne, E-78-79, 85, 433-434, 639

Vigneau, Anne, S1-219

Vigneau, Anne, S3-1097

Vigneau, Anne (or Nanette), S1-218

Vigneau, Appoline Aimable, E-434

Vigneau, Arnaud, E-434

Vigneau, Basile, E-43, 434

Vigneau, Benjamin, E-438, 633, 640, 643

Vigneau, boy, E-433

Vigneau, Caroline Artemise, E-434

Vigneau, Catherine, E-457

Vigneau, Charles, E-88, 362, 434-435, 437, 633, 643

Vigneau, Charles Alexandre, E-435

Vigneau, Charles Elie, E-434

Vigneau, Cyprien Magloire, E-434

Vigneau, Edouard, E-633, 640, 643

Vigneau, Emelie, E-56-57, 361, 434, 633, 639-640, 643

Vigneau, Ester, E-181, 183, 187, 190

Vigneau, Esther, S1-218

Vigneau, Etienne, E-56, 89, 382, 407, 435-437, 633, 643

Vigneau, Felix Orete Emma-nuel, E-435

Vigneau, Francois, E-435-437

Vigneau, Francois Jules, E-435

Vigneau, Francois Marie, E-12, 435

Vigneau, Francoise, C-9

Vigneau, Genevieve Marie, E-435

Vigneau, Gratia, E-435

Vigneau, Gratien, E-9

Vigneau, Hamans, E-435

Vigneau, Helene Sophie, E-643

Vigneau, Isidore, E-435

Vigneau, Jacques, E-433, 435

Vigneau, Jean, E-1, 254, 433-435, 437, 441, 633, 643

Vigneau, Jean, S1-219, 227

Vigneau, Jean Baptiste, E-25, 429, 433-436, 633

Vigneau, Jean Edouard, E-436

Vigneau, Jean Louis, E-436

Vigneau, Jean Sr., E-640

Vigneau, Jean-Baptiste, S1-218

Vigneau, Jeanne, E-326, 436

Vigneau, Joseph, E-9, 25, 195, 433, 435-437, 633, 640, 643

Vigneau, Joseph Jr., E-637

Vigneau, Julie, E-434, 633, 640

Vigneau, Laurent Desire, E-436, 643

Vigneau, Louis, E-1, 37, 87, 434, 436, 633, 640, 643

Vigneau, Luce, E-435

Vigneau, Luce Julie, E-436

Vigneau, Lucie, E-633, 640

Vigneau, Magdeleine, E-394, 436

Vigneau, Marguerite, E-14, 135, 315, 359, 407, 437, 630, 633

Vigneau, Marguerite, S1-299

Vigneau, Marianne, E-254, 441

Vigneau, Marie, E-17, 84, 149, 153-154, 290, 294, 351-352, 383, 437, 633, 640

Vigneau, Marie, S2-740

Vigneau, Marie Aimable Gennevieve, E-437

Vigneau, Marie Modeste, E-435

Vigneau, Marie Rose, E-87-89, 311, 437, 642

Vigneau, Melesme, E-382, 437

Vigneau, Modeste, E-84-85, 87, 360, 434, 437

Vigneau, Modeste, S1-229

Vigneau, Nicolas, E-1, 57, 87-89, 407, 429, 434, 436-438, 633
Vigneau, Nicolas Leandre, E-640
Vigneau, Nicolas Sr., E-640
Vigneau, Nicole Leandre, E-437
Vigneau, Pelagie, E-633, 640
Vigneau, Perinne, E-19, 345
Vigneau, Pierre, E-1, 85, 88-89, 122, 182, 351, 362, 433-438, 441, 633, 643
Vigneau, Pierre, S1-35
Vigneau, Pierre, S2-740
Vigneau, Pierre Jr., E-1, 634, 639, 643
Vigneau, Pierre Rock, E-362, 437
Vigneau, Pierre Sr., E-640
Vigneau, Rosalie, E-84-85, 183-184, 186, 195, 351-352, 437-438
Vigneau, Rose Eleonore, E-437
Vigneau, Simon, E-438
Vigneau, Sophie, E-56-57, 59, 438, 633-634, 639-641
Vigneau, Sophie Barbe, E-438
Vigneau, Suzanne Marie, E-438
Vigneau, Xavier, E-438
Vigneau, Zoe Anatole Aglae, E-438, 639, 643
Vigneron, Francois, E-414, 438
Vigneron, Jean, E-414, 438
Vignon, Emelie, E-438
Vignon, Joseph, E-119
Vignon, Louis, E-438
Vignon, Marie, E-58, 438
Vignon, Pierre, E-438
Vignon, Sophie, E-117
Vilain, Julien, E-625
Vilalon, Marie-Anne, S1-76
Vilalong, Cecile, S2-471, 520
Vilalong, Marc, S2-470
Vilalong, Marguerite, S2-471
Vilalong, Marie, S2-470
Vilalong, Marie-Anne, S2-472
Vilbert, Nicolas, E-359
Vildieu, Jean Baptiste, E-375, 438
Vildieu, Magdeleine, E-375, 438
Viledieu, Francois, E-590, 595

Viledieu, Marguerite, E-590, 595
Villain, Etiennette, E-629
Villaine, Roch, E-17, 34, 44, 71, 121, 159, 265, 270, 335, 348, 357, 386, 404
Villalon, Marie, E-66, 133, 438
Villalong, Cecile, S2-626
Villalong, Marc, S2-626
Villalong, Marguerite, S2-626
Villanon, Marie Jeanne, E-353, 438
Villanon, Toussaint, E-438
Villar, Francoise, E-27, 320
Villars, Charles, S2-649
Villedieu, Jean, E-439
Villedieu, Jeanice Francoise, E-438
Villedieu, Louis, E-439
Villedieu, Pierre, E-438
Villedon, Catherine, E-257
Villefayeaux, Andre, E-29, 174
Villejoin, Gabriel Rousseau de, S2-777
Villejoin, Louis-Melchior, S2-777
Villeneuve, Jean, E-439
Villeneuve, Jean Paul, E-590, 597
Villeneuve, Therese, E-439
Villiaud, Joseph, E-391
Villier, Josephe, E-331
Vincent, Agathe, S2-781-782
Vincent, Agnes, E-42
Vincent, Agnes, S1-95
Vincent, Agnes, S2-597
Vincent, Alexis, E-629
Vincent, Alexis, S2-777-778, 781-782
Vincent, Alexis, S3-929, 1055
Vincent, Alexis Louis, N-173
Vincent, Alexis-Louis, S2-780
Vincent, Anne, S1-91, 383
Vincent, Anne Blanche, C-98
Vincent, Anne Blanche, E-439-440
Vincent, Anne Blanche, F-69
Vincent, Anne Marie, F-11
Vincent, Anne-Genevieve, S2-781-782
Vincent, Anne-Marie, S1-233

Vincent, Anne-Marie, S2-547-548, 727
Vincent, Antoine, N-171-173
Vincent, Antoine, S2-778, 780
Vincent, Antoine, S3-1014
Vincent, Baptiste, S2-781
Vincent, Blanche, F-63
Vincent, Bonne, E-127
Vincent, Charles, C-69, 71, 130
Vincent, Charles, E-439-440
Vincent, Charles, F-57
Vincent, Claire, C-11
Vincent, Claire, F-81, 91
Vincent, Claire, S1-63, 324-328
Vincent, Claire, S2-576
Vincent, Claire, S3-888, 1032, 1083, 1088, 1099
Vincent, Clement, E-530
Vincent, Clement, S2-780
Vincent, Clement, S3-923
Vincent, Clotilde, E-439
Vincent, Dominique Antoine Rosalie, E-439
Vincent, Elisabet, S3-920
Vincent, Elizabeth, C-69, 130-131, 165
Vincent, Elizabeth, E-52, 172, 439, 582
Vincent, Elizabeth, F-103
Vincent, Elizabeth, N-123
Vincent, Elizabeth, S2-501, 755
Vincent, Felicite-Jeanne, S2-783
Vincent, Firmin, N-172
Vincent, Firmin, S2-642, 779, 781-782
Vincent, Firmin, S3-1055
Vincent, Firmin-Francois, S2-779
Vincent, Flore Adelaide, F-69
Vincent, Francois, E-439-440
Vincent, Francois, S2-781-782
Vincent, Francoise, C-165
Vincent, Francoise Bernadine, N-173
Vincent, Francoise Isabelle, E-3
Vincent, Frimin, C-165
Vincent, Gabriel, E-129, 439
Vincent, Genevieve, E-413, 439
Vincent, Germain, C-148
Vincent, Germain, N-172
Vincent, Germain, S2-779, 783

Vincent, Germain, S3-980, 988, 1003, 1072

Vincent, Guillaume-Julien-Alexis, S2-778

Vincent, Guillin, E-439

Vincent, Huguette, E-472

Vincent, Isabelle, E-289

Vincent, Isabelle, F-57

Vincent, Jacques, E-439

Vincent, Janvier, S2-782

Vincent, Jean, C-98, 165

Vincent, Jean, E-3, 52, 439-440, 582

Vincent, Jean, F-63, 69

Vincent, Jean, N-172, 176, 236

Vincent, Jean, S2-778, 780

Vincent, Jean, S3-1014, 1020, 1027

Vincent, Jean Baptiste, E-439-440

Vincent, Jean Baptiste, N-172

Vincent, Jean Baptiste Bernard, E-439

Vincent, Jean Baptiste Henry, E-439

Vincent, Jean Firmin, N-172

Vincent, Jean Jr., E-620

Vincent, Jean Louis, C-98

Vincent, Jean Pierre, N-173

Vincent, Jean-Baptiste, S2-779

Vincent, Jeanne, E-45, 60, 68-69, 348, 373, 439, 620

Vincent, Jeanne, N-172

Vincent, Jeanne Marguerite, F-69

Vincent, Jeanne Margueritte, C-98

Vincent, Jeanne-Charlotte-Jacquemene, S2-780

Vincent, Joseph, C-165

Vincent, Joseph, E-439-440, 580, 620, 629

Vincent, Joseph, N-163, 172

Vincent, Joseph, S2-765, 777-783

Vincent, Joseph, S3-923, 928-929, 1044, 1055

Vincent, Joseph Jr., E-620

Vincent, Joseph-Arnault, S2-782

Vincent, Julienne, S3-995

Vincent, Louis, E-354

Vincent, Louis Michel, E-439

Vincent, Louise, E-68, 130-131

Vincent, Madeleine, E-329, 560, 577

Vincent, Madeleine, N-3, 65, 165, 169, 246

Vincent, Madeleine, S2-628

Vincent, Madeleine Luce, E-440

Vincent, Marguerite, C-4, 164

Vincent, Marguerite, E-402, 420, 423-424

Vincent, Marguerite, F-13

Vincent, Marguerite, N-4, 7-8, 157, 163, 176, 236

Vincent, Marguerite, S1-25-26

Vincent, Marguerite, S2-545, 765, 781-782

Vincent, Marguerite, S3-995, 1020, 1044

Vincent, Marianne, E-498

Vincent, Marie, C-69, 98, 165

Vincent, Marie, E-3, 103, 279, 331, 440, 571, 580, 582

Vincent, Marie, N-172

Vincent, Marie, S2-548, 782

Vincent, Marie Blanche, C-98

Vincent, Marie Blanche, F-69

Vincent, Marie Charlotte Julienne, E-127

Vincent, Marie Elizabeth, C-71

Vincent, Marie Elizabeth, E-424

Vincent, Marie Eugenie, N-172

Vincent, Marie Francoise, C-165

Vincent, Marie Francoise, N-172

Vincent, Marie Gratien, E-629

Vincent, Marie Josephe, E-330

Vincent, Marie Madeleine, F-37

Vincent, Marie Madeleine, N-36, 63, 218

Vincent, Marie Magdelaine, C-16, 148

Vincent, Marie Magdeleine, F-7, 37

Vincent, Marie Magdeleine, S3-1003

Vincent, Marie Victoire, E-440

Vincent, Marie-Josseline, S2-779

Vincent, Marie-Madeleine, S1-64, 85, 170, 303

Vincent, Michel, E-476, 530

Vincent, Michel, N-171

Vincent, Michel, S1-324

Vincent, Michel, S2-778

Vincent, Nicolas Guillaume, E-127

Vincent, Pelagie, E-306, 440, 582

Vincent, Perine-Charlotte, S2-778

Vincent, Perinne Jeanne, N-173

Vincent, Perinne-Jeanne, S2-780

Vincent, Pierre, C-165

Vincent, Pierre, E-193, 215, 331, 458, 477, 530, 580, 582, 620

Vincent, Pierre, F-41

Vincent, Pierre, N-36, 63, 172

Vincent, Pierre, S1-170, 303

Vincent, Pierre, S2-779, 783

Vincent, Pierre, S3-1003, 1072

Vincent, Pierre Joseph, E-279

Vincent, Pierre-Julien, S2-778

Vincent, Renee Perrine, E-629

Vincent, Rosalie, E-51-52, 439-440

Vincent, Rose Adelaide, C-98

Vincent, Simon, S1-192, 225, 237

Vincent, Simon, S2-452, 779, 783

Vincent, Simon, S3-999, 1003, 1006, 1032, 1072

Vincent, Theodore, S3-1085

Vincent, Thomas, E-477

Vincent, Yves Charles, E-629

Vincent, Yves-Charles, S2-782

Vineau, Madeleine, E-370

Vinelli, Antoine, E-440

Vinelli, Barthelemy, E-440

Vinelli, Catherine, E-440

Vinelli, Jean Baptiste, E-440

Vinelli, Marie Anne, E-440

Vinelli, Marie Rose, E-440

Vinelli, Nicolas, E-440

Vinelly, Antoine, E-113-114

Vinet, Jeanne, E-122, 387

Vinet, Louise, E-276, 440

Vinet, Marie, E-135

Vinet, Mathurin, E-385, 440

Vinet, Pierre, E-276, 337, 440

Vinet, Renee, E-385, 440
Vinsonneau, Jean, E-36, 63
Vintra, Marie Anne Victoire, E-361
Vionnet, Magdelaine, E-29
Viot, Helene, E-280, 440
Viot, Helenne, S2-548
Virot, Marianne, E-337, 375
Viset, Helenne, S2-548
Visez, Gilette Anne, S3-955
Visez, Gilette-Anne, S2-746
Visse, Antoine, E-409, 441
Visse, Laurent, E-441
Vitet, Catherine, E-44, 441
Vitet, Etienne, E-44, 441
Vitet, Jacques, E-44
Vitet, Marie Anne, E-292
Vivion, Jean Francois, E-317
Vocelle, Jacques, E-441
Vocelle, Julie, E-441
Vocelle, Rosalie, E-441
Voeline, Lucie Marie, E-74
Vognaux, Jean, E-438
Voillet, Jeanne, C-7
Voisin, Felicite, E-629
Voisin, Jacques, E-386
Voisin, Joseph, E-617, 629
Voisin, Rene Clement, E-629
Volant, Rene, E-385
Volet, Michel, E-403, 441
Volle, Francois, E-386
Volleau, Jeanne, E-138, 441
Volleau, Pierre, E-138, 441
Vorier, Euphrosine, E-390, 441
Vorier, Joseph, E-390, 441
Voyer, Julien, E-530
Vrastine, Marie Mad., E-590, 596
Vrieu, Marie, E-418
Vrillon, Pierre, E-359

W

Walton, Rebecca, E-181, 314
Watron, George, E-181
Weibert, Marie, N-153, 177
Werling, Marie Anne, E-258
Willaumez, Jean Baptiste, E-423
Willaumez, Pelagie, E-427
Wyczynski, Michel, C-viii

X-Y

Yont, Charlote, E-197, 442
Yvel, Jeanne, S2-483
Yves, Louise, E-408
Yvon, -----, E-6
Yvon, Charles, E-120, 442, 590, 592
Yvon, Charles, S2-515, 783-785
Yvon, Charles, S3-984
Yvon, Charles-Francois, S2-784
Yvon, Charlotte, E-197, 442
Yvon, Charlotte, S2-784
Yvon, Elisabeth, E-590, 592
Yvon, Etienne, S2-784
Yvon, Francois, S2-784
Yvon, Francoise, S2-785
Yvon, Guillaume, S2-783-784
Yvon, Jacques, E-36
Yvon, Jean, S2-784
Yvon, Jeanne, S2-785
Yvon, Julienne, S2-784
Yvon, Louis, S2-784
Yvon, Louise, E-120, 153, 442
Yvon, Louise, S2-784
Yvon, Marie, S2-785
Yvon, Pierre, S2-784
Yvon, Suzanne, N-40, 245
Yvon, Victoire, S2-785

Z

Zemar, Gaspar, E-24, 442
Zemar, Marie Anne, E-24, 442
Zerby, Servane, S2-585
Zeringue, Lionel (Mrs.), C-vi, ix, xi
Zezecal, Nicolas, S2-478

CPSIA information can be obtained
at www.ICGtesting.com
Printed in the USA
BVHW061320300120
570956BV00017B/1034

9 781598 048933